HISTORICAL DICTIONARIES
OF WAR, REVOLUTION, AND CIVIL UNREST
Edited by John Woronoff

1. *Afghan Wars, Revolutions, and Insurgencies,* by Ludwig W. Adamec. 1996
2. *United States–Mexican War,* by Edward H. Moseley and Paul C. Clark, Jr. 1997.
3. *World War I,* by Ian V. Hogg. 1998.
4. *United States Navy,* by James M. Morris and Patricia M. Kearns. 1998.
5. *United States Marine Corps,* by Harry A. Gailey. 1998.
6. *Wars of the French Revolution,* by Steven T. Ross. 1998.
7. *American Revolution,* by Terry M. Mays. 1998.
8. *The Spanish-American War,* by Brad K. Berner. 1998.
9. *The Persian Gulf War,* by Clayton R. Newell. 1998.

The Spanish-American War

A Historical Dictionary

Brad K. Berner

Historical Dictionaries of War,
Revolution, and Civil Unrest, No. 8

The Scarecrow Press, Inc.
Lanham, Md., & London
1998

SCARECROW PRESS, INC.

Published in the United States of America
by Scarecrow Press, Inc.
4720 Boston Way
Lanham, Maryland 20706

4 Pleydell Gardens, Folkestone
Kent CT20 2DN, England

British Library Cataloguing in Publication Information Available

Library of Congress Cataloging-in-Publication Data

Berner, Brad K., 1952–
     The Spanish-American War : a historical dictionary / Brad K.
Berner.
        p.   cm. — (Historical dictionaries of war, revolution, and
civil unrest; no. 8)
     Includes bibliographical references and index.
     ISBN 0-8108-3490-1 (cloth : alk. paper)
     1. Spanish-American War, 1898—Dictionaries.   I. Title.
II. Series.
E715.B47   1998
973.8'9'03—dc21   98-21102
                                                               CIP

∞ ™ The paper used in this publication meets the minimum
requirements of American National Standard for Information
Sciences—Permanence of Paper for Printed Library Materials,
ANSI Z39.48-1984. Manufactured in the United States of
America.

Dedicated to my parents

Frances L. Berner
and
Harry W. Berner

Contents

Editor's Foreword

For all too many Americans, and not only those in the United States, the Spanish-American War is a forgotten war. When remembered, it seems terribly remote, hopelessly quaint and old-fashioned and often enough, of questionable relevance to the present day. Yet this war was one of the key turning points in world history. It marked the coming of age of the United States as a world power, with a military strong enough to defeat a European foe and with its own budding colonial empire, which stretched from Puerto Rico in the Atlantic to Hawaii and Guam in the Pacific and the Philippines in Asia. The Spaniards could not forget the war so easily, with their military roundly defeated, the last colonial possessions lost, and the country reduced to a minor status even in Europe. But this war affected us all in other ways, because it introduced greater deadliness in combat, with steel-clad ships, torpedoes, rapid-firing guns and heavier artillery, and armed forces who realized that efficiency was more important than chivalry.

Let us hope that its centennial will increase our knowledge—and understanding—of the Spanish-American War. Despite the military innovations, the human element has not changed that much, and war is not that different. Moreover, colonies are now a thing of the past and it takes more than military muscle and political clout to dominate the world. A good look at this *Historical Dictionary of the Spanish-American War* can teach us a lot, not only about how war is fought but also about how it is caused. This teaching is done through use of a handy introduction and chronology and a very comprehensive dictionary section. The range of entries is truly impressive, including persons, military units, battles, and weapons as well as political, economic, and social aspects. Most noteworthy is that Spain, Cuba, the Philippines, and Puerto Rico are amply covered along with the United States. Further information can be found in references listed in the bibliography.

This volume was written by someone with an evident passion for the period. Brad K. Berner studied both North American and Latin American history and the results show in his balanced coverage of this war. He has spent over a decade teaching history at the secondary and college levels, which may explain why the contents are not only informative but easy to follow. Only a person with a strong and abiding interest in the subject could have dug deep enough to find the extraordinary assortment of facts and, no less helpful, anecdotes and local color that are presented in this volume.

Jon Woronoff
Series Editor

Acknowledgments

With the approaching centennial of the Spanish-American War, it is important to remember that this brief, highly popular, and frequently forgotten war was a watershed for Cuba, the Philippines, Puerto Rico, Spain, and the United States as they entered the twentieth century. In focusing on the war, this writer included only those items from the pre-war and postwar periods directly pertinent to the war itself.

I am grateful to my parents, Frances and Harry Berner, and to my wife, Flora, for their encouragement. I hope this volume assists layman, student, and scholar alike in gaining a better understanding of this little but important war.

Acronyms and Abbreviations

Adjt.	Adjutant
Adm.	Admiral
AFL	American Federation of Labor
AP	Associated Press
aw.	above-water
b.	barbette
Brig.	Brigadier
C.	Colt
Capt.	Captain
Cc.	coal capacity—in tons
cm.	centimeter
Col.	Colonel
com.	commissioned
Com.	Commodore
Comdr.	Commander
comp.	complement—approximate number of officers and enlisted
Cpl.	Corporal
ct.	conning tower
d.	deck
DAR	Daughters of the American Revolution
dis.	displacement—in tons
Ens.	Ensign
G.	Gatling
Gen.	General
Gov.	Governor
H.	Hotchkiss
hp.	horsepower
Inf.	Infantry
La.	launched
Lt.	Lieutenant
Lt. Col.	Lieutenant Colonel
M.	Maxim
Maj.	Major
Maj. Gen.	Major General

mg.	machine gun
mgs.	machine guns
MID	Military Information Division
mm.	millimeter
N.	Nordenfelt
ONI	Office of Naval Intelligence
pdr.	pounder
Pvt.	Private
R.C.S.	Revenue Cutter Service
rev.	revolver
s.	side
Sgt.	Sergeant
sl.	slope
sp.	speed—in knots
SPN	Spanish Navy
sub.	submerged
t.	turret
tt.	torpedo tubes
USMC	United States Marine Corps
USN	United States Navy
USV	United States Volunteers

Chronology

1892
January   Jose Martí founds Cuban Revolutionary Party.
2 July   Andres Bonifacio founds Katipunan in the Philippines.

1893
January   Hawaiian government of Queen Liliuokalani is
     overthrown.

1894
January   Emilio Aguinaldo joins Katipunan.

1895
25 February   Cuban Revolt begins.
22 December   Puerto Rican section of the Cuban Revolutionary Party
     was founded in New York City.

1896
February   Valeriano Weyler becomes captain general in Cuba and
     begins reconcentration policy.
August   Philippine Revolt begins.

1897
12 February   "Does Our Flag Shield Women?" *New York Journal*
     publicizes *Olivette* incident.
10 May   Andres Bonifacio executed in internal power struggle.
4 October   Práxedes M. Sagasta becomes prime minister of Spain
     for the fourth time.
10 October   "Evangelina Cisneros Rescued by the Journal" *New
     York Journal* publicizes Evangelina Cisneros
     Incident.
25 November   Spain publishes autonomy decrees for Cuba and Puerto
     Rico.
14 December   Pact of Biak-Na-Bató temporarily halts Philippine
     Revolt.

1898

1 January	Autonomous government begins functioning in Cuba.
12 January	Autonomy Riots break out in Havana, Cuba.
15 January	Autonomous government begins functioning in Puerto Rico.
25 January	*Maine* arrives at Havana, Cuba.
9 February	De Lôme letter published in the *New York Journal*.
15 February	*Maine* blows up in harbor of Havana, Cuba.
9 March	Fifty Million Dollar Bill becomes law.
17 March	U.S. report on the *Maine* finds external cause.
22 March	Spain's report on *Maine* finds internal cause.
27 March	McKinley's ultimatum to Spain; Muñocistas win parliamentary elections in Puerto Rico.
30 March	Spain revokes reconcentration in Cuba and offers to submit *Maine* to arbitration.
6 April	Great Powers Note was written.
11 April	McKinley's "War Message" sent to Congress.
19 April	Joint Resolution providing for intervention in Cuba passes U.S. Congress.
21 April	President McKinley orders blockade of the northern Cuban coast.
22 April	First shot of the war fired by the USS *Nashville* across the bow of the *Buenaventura* off Key West, Florida.
23 April	Spain declares war; McKinley issues call for 125,000 volunteers; Spanish military decides to send Adm. Cervera's squadron to the West Indies.
25 April	United States declares war.
1 May	Battle of Manila Bay; Lt. Andrew S. Rowan meets with Cuban insurgent General Calixto García at Bayamo, Cuba.
2 May	President McKinley authorizes army expedition to Manila, Philippines.
4 May	Gov. General Basilio Augustín creates Consultative Assembly of notables and militia in Philippines.
11 May	Naval engagements at Cárdenas Bay and Cienfuegos, Cuba.
12 May	U.S. squadron bombards San Juan, Puerto Rico.
19 May	Adm. Cervera's squadron arrives at Santiago, Cuba; Emilio Aguinaldo lands at Cavite, Philippines.
25 May	First expedition of the Eighth Corps leaves San Francisco for the Philippines.
26 May	Secretary of the Navy John D. Long orders Adm. Dewey not to have "political alliances" with Filipino insurgents.

28 May	Consultative Assembly convenes in Manila, Philippines.
29 May	Adm. Cervera's squadron blockaded by U.S. Navy at Santiago, Cuba.
3 June	*Merrimac* fails to block Santiago harbor entrance.
10 June	First Marine Battalion lands at Guantánamo, Cuba.
12 June	Filipino insurgent assembly declares Philippine independence.
20 June	Aserraderos Conference takes place.
21 June	U.S. flag hoisted over Guam.
22 June	U.S. Fifth Corps begins landing at Daiquirí, Cuba; Escario's column leaves Manzanillo, Cuba, for Santiago; naval engagement off San Juan, Puerto Rico.
24 June	Battle of Las Guásimas, Cuba.
1 July	Battles of San Juan Hill and El Caney, Cuba; 337 day siege of Baler, Philippines begins; First expedition of the Eighth Corps lands at Cavite, Philippines.
2 July	Escario's column reaches Santiago, Cuba.
3 July	Naval Battle of Santiago, Cuba.
7 July	United States annexes Hawaii.
8 July	Adm. Cámara's squadron ordered to return to Spain.
10 July	Adm. Dewey threatens war with Germany at Manila Bay, Philippines.
17 July	Santiago, Cuba, capitulates; autonomous Puerto Rican legislature convenes and Luis Muñoz Rivera proclaims "We are Spaniards and wrapped in the Spanish flag we will die."
18 July	Naval engagement at Manzanillo, Cuba; Almodóvar del Río, Spain's minister of state, begins Spain's quest for negotiations.
21 July	Naval engagement at Nipe Bay, Cuba.
25 July	Guantánamo, Cuba capitulates; U.S. forces land at Guánica, Puerto Rico; Puerto Rican autonomous legislature disbands.
1 August	Ca. 4,200 sick American soldiers at Santiago, Cuba.
3 August	Round Robin Letter signed.
9 August	Battle of Coamo, Puerto Rico.
12 August	Manzanillo, Cuba, bombarded by U.S. navy; Armistice Protocol signed in Washington, officially ending hostilities.
13 August	Battle of Manila, Philippines.
14 August	Capitulation of Manila Agreement signed.
26 September	Dodge Commission appointed to investigate the conduct of the War Department.

1 October	Negotiations of the Treaty of Paris between Spain and the United States begin in Paris, France.
18 October	Formal transfer of Puerto Rico to the United States.
10 December	Treaty of Paris signed.

1899

1 January	Cuba formally transferred to the United States.
17 January	United States claims Wake Island.
4 February	Philippine Insurrection begins.
6 February	Treaty of Paris ratified by U.S. Senate.
19 March	Treaty of Paris signed by Spain's Queen Regent.
11 April	Exchange of peace treaties at Washington, D.C., officially ends the war.
2 June	337-day siege of Baler, Philippines, ends.

Introduction

The date was 15 February 1898, and it was a quiet night as Capt. Charles Sigsbee sat writing a letter in his captain's room aboard the *Maine* in the harbor of Havana, Cuba. Suddenly, at 9:40 p.m. an explosion convulsed the ship. The *Maine* was destroyed, 266 officers and sailors were killed, and even though an official United States investigation did not directly blame Spain, the American public, much of its press, and many politicians demanded revenge. Two months later the United States went to war against Spain crying "Remember the Maine, to Hell with Spain!"

The Spanish-American War was America's most popular and most quickly forgotten war. It was a "splendid little war": for in a little over three months, from 21 April to 13 August, U.S. military forces decisively defeated Spain and took control of Cuba, Guam, the Philippines, and Puerto Rico. Significantly, its costs were low: $250 million in direct costs and only 379 combat fatalities. A flurry of films and literary and historical works extolled the victory. Within a few years, however, it passed from the nation's historical memory, becoming, if remembered at all, a quaint war in a quaint time. For Spain, the overwhelming defeat became known as "the disaster." Most of its overseas empire had been lost, its commanders returned home to be court-martialed, and generals, newspapers, and politicians quickly blamed each other for the defeat.

At the end of a century of world wars, the Spanish-American War is somewhat familiar. Disease proved more deadly than bullets, causing 90 percent of U.S. fatalities and eventually killing 20,000 Spanish soldiers after they had returned home. Ineptitude in planning and execution plagued both sides, and the U.S. Army and Navy engaged in constant wrangling over strategy and tactics. A popular press in both countries urged their nations on to war and U.S. filmmakers provided a few legitimate, and a host of spurious, films to meet an insatiable public demand. Yet, it remains a highly unfamiliar war. The Spanish-American War was fought in an age of empire when many assumed that the last of the great destructive wars of humankind had passed, and it was considered healthy for a nation and a generation to be bloodied a bit in a limited test of arms. Moreover, for the United States, humanitarianism and expansionism united in justifying going to war. In the eyes of many who fought, it was a war fought with honor against an honorable foe at a

1

time when flags were kissed and swords tendered in surrender, and when the fighting ceased, Spanish and U.S. soldiers openly fraternized.

Background to War

In the late 1890s the United States was coming out of an economic depression, and vibrant Populist and reform movements challenged the status quo. A significant number of political and military leaders such as Theodore Roosevelt, Henry Cabot Lodge, and Alfred Thayer Mahan were advocating an expansionist foreign policy, and a new "steel" navy had been built to project American power. With the inauguration of William McKinley as president, the Republican Party controlled the White House and both houses of Congress. In contrast, Spain had experienced two decades of internal peace through the *turno pacífico*, an alternating power arrangement between the Conservative and Liberal Parties. Nevertheless, the Spanish government of the Queen Regent María Cristina and the Conservative ministry of Antonio Cánovas were confronted by colonial demands for autonomy and popular revolts for independence in Cuba and the Philippines. In response, Spain sent more than 200,000 soldiers overseas in a futile effort to retain its colonial empire.

Three years after the establishment of the Cuban Revolutionary Party by José Martí in 1892, the Cuban revolt began in February 1895 under the leadership of Martí and Maj. Gen. Máximo Gómez. Adopting a "scorched-earth" policy and guerrilla tactics intent on exhausting Spain's economic and military capability to retain control of Cuba, the insurgent movement quickly spread throughout the island even though Martí was killed early on in the war. Insurgent general Antonio Maceo carried the war into western Cuba and Calixto García, who commanded the insurgent forces in eastern Cuba, drove the Spanish into defensive positions. In response, Spain sent over 200,000 soldiers to the island. Under the direction of Governor-General Valeriano Weyler, many civilians were forced to move, or reconcentrate, into Spanish-controlled positions, and a defensive *trocha* system of trenches was built which extended across the island in an effort to isolate the insurgents. The American "yellow press," epitomized by William R. Hearst's *New York Journal* and Joseph Pulitzer's *New York World*, quickly took up the insurgent cause, demonized Weyler, excoriated Spain for its reconcentration policy, and propagandized events such as the *Olivette* incident of February 1897 and the cause of Evangelina Cisneros. In violation of U.S. neutrality laws, filibustering expeditions from the United States attempted to supply the insurgents with arms and ammunition. Although the U.S. administration of Grover Cleveland initially declared its neutrality, preferring the retention of Spanish control to an insurgent republic, Spain's refusal of an offer of U.S. arbitration and its continuing inability to suppress a revolt that was damaging U.S. economic investments in Cuba brought forth from Cleveland a warning of possible future direct U.S. involvement in his state of the union message on 7 December 1896.

In the Philippines, Spain's authority was initially challenged by a reformist movement led by José Rizal; however, it was soon surpassed by the Katipunan, a clandestine armed independence movement founded by Andres Bonifacio in 1892. Led by the Katipunan, the armed revolt began in August 1896; however, under the command of Lt. General Camilo Polavieja, Spain put the revolutionaries on the defensive through effective military campaigns, wholesale summary executions, which included Rizal, and relocation of large numbers of civilians into Spanish-controlled areas. Furthermore, the revolt was hampered by disunity as Bonifacio was executed by his fellow revolutionaries and Emilio Aguinaldo assumed command of the revolt. Eventually what proved to be a temporary lull in the fighting was negotiated through the Pact of Biak-Na-Bató in December 1897, with Aguinaldo and a group of his closest associates going into exile.

Alone among its major colonies, Puerto Rico—the "ever-faithful isle"—was peaceful. Although a strong autonomist movement led by Luis Muñoz Rivera achieved a fusion with the Spanish Liberal Party, a small independence movement led by the exiled Ramón Emeterio Betances proved incapable of organizing any armed resistance. However, Puerto Rican independence activists in New York City affiliated themselves with the Cuban Revolutionary Party in an attempt to link the struggles in both colonies.

By 1897, the mounting casualties and expense of putting down the revolts were seriously damaging an already financially strained Spain. Upon the ascension to power of the Liberal ministry of Práxedes Mateo Sagasta on 4 October 1897, the Spanish government tried a new approach. Autonomy was granted to Cuba and Puerto Rico, and the unpopular Weyler was removed from command in Cuba. However, Spain proved incapable of defeating the Cuban insurgents, and although autonomy prospered in Puerto Rico, it failed to take root in Cuba as the insurgents rejected any such compromise and continued their war of independence.

Upon the ascension to power in the United States of the Republican administration of President William McKinley, both Spain and America were led by men who believed they could forestall war between their countries through diplomacy despite the exhortations of the Spanish military press and of American "jingoes" such as Theodore Roosevelt and Henry Cabot Lodge. Events soon overwhelmed diplomacy with the publication of the De Lôme letter on 9 February 1898 and the *Maine* disaster on 15 February. Despite the efforts of McKinley and Speaker of the House Thomas B. Reed, Congress was swept up into a war fever. By the end of March, the McKinley administration issued an ultimatum to Spain that included Cuban independence, a demand, which if met, would have meant the end of the Spanish government. Feeble attempts at mediation by the Great Powers and the Vatican and a last minute Spanish concession of suspending hostilities in Cuba proved ineffectual. Finally, on 19 April 1898, the U.S. Congress authorized the use of force by McKinley to resolve the Cuban situation. Consequently, McKinley quickly ordered a partial blockade of the Cuban coast and issued a call for 125,000 volunteers. Responding to these U.S. actions, Spain declared war on 23 April, and two days later, on 25 April, the United States declared war, making the declaration retroactive to 21 April to legally cover its actions from that date forward.

A "Splendid Little War"

On 27 July 1898, weeks before the end of the war, John Hay, U.S. ambassador to Great Britain, wrote to Theodore Roosevelt calling the war a "splendid little war." For Hay, an ardent expansionist, a war that had commenced in an idealistic fervor to free Cuba from its oppressive Spanish colonial overlord but soon turned into a war of empire justified the American cause. Few in the United States initially disagreed.

Upon the outbreak of war an overwhelming majority of the press and public in both countries patriotically supported their respective countries' war efforts. Among the few in open opposition in Spain were the small Spanish Socialist Workers Party, Republican politician Francesc Pi i Margall, and writer José Martínez y Ruiz "Azorín". Secretly, Admiral Pascual Cervera y Topete, Spain's most illustrious sailor, warned the government of certain defeat. In the United States, few were openly opposed to the war and even antiwar critics such as John Mitchell, the black American editor of the *Richmond Planet*, social reformer Jane Addams, industrial magnate Andrew Carnegie, Booker T. Washington, and Democratic presidential candidate William Jennings Bryan patriotically supported a war to liberate Cuba.

However, a war to liberate Cuba soon developed its own dynamic and became a war of empire as Commodore George Dewey's Asiatic Squadron left Mirs Bay, China, on 27 April, steamed into Manila Bay in the Philippines, and annihilated the Spanish squadron under the command of Admiral Patricio Montojo on 1 May. Within days McKinley ordered the formation of an army expeditionary force, which became known as the Eighth Corps, to go to the Philippines. As Dewey's naval force blockaded Manila, the Eighth Corps, embarking from San Francisco, began to arrive at the end of June and throughout July. It was confronted by a three-cornered political situation in which Filipino insurgents under the leadership of Emilio Aguinaldo, Spanish, and U.S. forces faced off against each other.

As American volunteers and regular forces moved into camps such as Camp Alger near Washington, D.C., Camp Thomas in Georgia, and camps at Tampa, Florida, and San Francisco, California, in April and May, the U.S. Army, which had numbered only 25,000 men before the war, skyrocketed to 290,000 men, overwhelming the government's capacity to effectively organize and supply its units. Moreover, ill-disciplined volunteers and a lack of sufficient medical facilities and personnel soon promoted the spread of diseases, particularly typhoid, in the stateside camps.

While the Fifth Corps, under the command of Maj. Gen. William R. Shafter, was being formed at Tampa, Florida, to invade Cuba, U.S. naval forces, under the command of Rear Admiral William T. Sampson, fought major naval engagements at Cárdenas and Cienfuegos, Cuba, on 11 May and extended their blockade around Cuba and Puerto Rico. However, they failed to stop the arrival at Santiago, Cuba, on 19 May of a Spanish relief squadron under the command of Adm. Pascual Cervera. Consequently, Santiago became the focus of U.S. military efforts in Cuba. By the end of May Santiago was blockaded, and the Fifth Corps, after embarking from Tampa, began landing east of Santiago at Daiquirí, Cuba, on 22 June.

Shafter's plans of organizing and reinforcing his forces before moving on Santiago were quickly rent asunder as American forces, under the command of Maj. Gen. Joseph Wheeler, moved inland and engaged Spanish forces at the battle of Las Guásimas on 24 June. Believing reports of the approach of a large Spanish relief column and fearing the effects of disease the longer his forces remained in Cuba, Shafter quickly ordered an attack on Santiago's defenses; accordingly, on 1 July, U.S. forces, outnumbering the Spanish defenders by 16 to one, attacked and took the Spanish positions at El Caney, Kettle Hill, and San Juan Hill, at a cost of nearly 1,500 total casualties, twice the number of Spanish casualties. Two days later, on 3 July, Adm. Cervera's squadron attempted to escape and was annihilated by U.S. naval forces under the immediate command of Commodore Winfield S. Schley. Fortunately for the disease-ravaged Fifth Corps, Santiago capitulated on 17 July.

Although Spain's army wanted to continue the war, Sagasta's government quickly moved toward a negotiated settlement. In mid-July censorship was decreed and parliament was suspended, and on 18 July France was asked to act as an intermediary in starting negotiations. France accepted, and Jules Cambon, France's ambassador to Washington, attempted during the end of July and early August to negotiate an armistice. Nevertheless, the American military juggernaut continued as U.S. forces, under the command of Maj. Gen. Nelson A. Miles, the commanding general of the U.S. Army, landed on the southern Puerto Rican coast at Guánica on 25 July. In a 19-day campaign, Miles's forces, while sustaining 43 total casualties, overran half of the island and were only stopped by the signing of the Armistice Protocol on 12 August. Officially the shooting had stopped, but the news had not reached the Philippines when on 13 August the Eighth Corps, in a prearranged battle, took Manila, and on 14 August Spain's Governor-General Fermín Jáudenes y Álvarez officially capitulated.

In compliance with the Armistice Protocol, evacuation commissions were formed and supervised the repatriation of Spanish forces from the conquered islands, with the United States paying for the repatriation of captured Spanish forces. To maintain order in the islands, American military governments were established, and peace commissions were appointed by the Spanish and U.S. governments to negotiate a final peace treaty at Paris, France. Led by Eugenio Montero Ríos and William R. Day, respectively, the Spanish and American Peace Commissions began their negotiations on 1 October; however, the U.S. commission dictated most of the contents of the Treaty of Paris, which was signed on 10 December.

The treaty's ratification proved problematic. Because a war to liberate Cuba had turned into a war of empire, the Anti-Imperialist League was formed in November 1898. Composed of members such as Jane Addams, Andrew Carnegie, Grover Cleveland, Samuel Gompers, and Carl Schurz, the league worked assiduously to oppose a treaty that it saw as a violation of traditional American principles. A vigorous debate ensued in the U.S. Senate. George F. Hoar, Republican senator from Massachusetts, led the opposition. Those in favor of ratification included Henry Cabot Lodge, Republican senator from Massachusetts, and William Jennings Bryan, who believed that ratifying the treaty would quickly result in the granting of independence to the Philippines. Two days after war broke out between American and Aguinaldo's Filipino nationalist forces on 4 February 1899, the treaty was ratified by the U.S. Senate by one vote on 6 February. The vote in Spain's parliament, the Cortes, was too narrow for ratification; therefore, the Queen Regent María Cristina invoked her constitutional powers and signed the treaty on 19 March. With the exchange of ratifications in Washington, D.C., on 11 April, the war was officially over.

The Aftermath of War

The Spanish-American War was an old and a new war. An old empire, Spain's, had fallen, sparking a period of intense self-criticism, which gave impetus to a regenerationist movement and a literary movement later known as the Generation of '98. A newly born global power, the United States, had been bolstered in its combination of idealism and self-interest and was on its way to becoming the world's policeman in immediately confronting the war's sad sequel as it fought a bloody and divisive three-year war against Aguinaldo's Filipino nationalist forces.

Counterpoised to archaic weapons of war such as black powder, monitors and rams, and the soon-to-be-outmoded dynamite guns were mobile repair ships, modern rapid-fire guns, torpedoes, smokeless powder, and steel warships. Analyzing the military aspects of the war, German Rear Admiral Max Plüddemann, who had been an observer with the U.S. Navy, pointed out in his *Comments of Rear-Admiral Plüddemann, German Navy, on the Main Features of the War with Spain* (1898) that no developments during the war would lead to a radical change of views on the conduct of naval warfare. The battleship's supremacy was evident, torpedoes were ineffective overall, Spanish mines frequently failed to operate, and American claims of damage inflicted by its naval bombardments were exaggerated. Even though rapid-fire guns were used by both the Spanish and American Navies, the accuracy of U.S. naval gunfire, which was less than 2 percent, was much better than that of the Spain's, which was miserable. Plüddemann's short-sighted viewpoint, like that of most of his contemporary observers, was soon outmoded and proved wrong. He had failed to understand that the incipient technologies used during the war would soon be improved and profoundly change naval warfare when used in World War I.

Old heroes were broken and new heroes made. Theodore Roosevelt, who had commanded the Rough Riders during the 1 July battles at Santiago, Cuba, was catapulted onto the national stage, and Lt. John J. Pershing, later to command U.S. forces in World War I, was awarded the Silver Star for commanding his Tenth U.S. Cavalry troops during the battles of 1 July at Santiago, Cuba. Spanish Adm. Pascual Cervera was lionized by the U.S. press and public, only to return home in ignominy until he cleared his name by publishing the government's orders that had sent his squadron to its doom. Maj. Gen. Nelson Miles and his supporters were effectively destroyed in the "Embalmed Beef" scandal. The controversy between Admirals William T. Sampson and Winfield S. Schley proved divisive for the U.S. Navy, and the War Department's management of the war effort was investigated by the Dodge Commission.

Viewpoints

Opinions on the war have been as varied as their authors and times. For a brief period immediately following the war, American writers extolled the victorious U.S. effort and proclaimed that the nation's Civil War scars had finally been healed. As historical attention, buffeted by World War I and the Depression, fell into the doldrums, a critical, indifferent, and even vilifying attitude emerged. U.S. imperialism and a weak McKinley controlled by financial interests were excoriated, both the "yellow press" and a small cabal of political insiders were blamed for causing the war, and a societal "psychic crisis" of the 1890s posited to explain the popular support for the war. Recent scholarship, however, has rehabilitated McKinley as a decisive leader attuned to the nation's mood and depicted him as America's first modern president. The "yellow press," rather than causing the war, has been seen as riding a wave of popular opinion, and the projection of power by the U.S. into the Pacific Ocean area eventually would bring it into confrontation with an expanding Japanese Empire.

Because present-day readers are removed by a century of profound change from the Spanish-American War and by a deep ignorance concerning the war, it is crucial to listen to the war's participants in understanding the conflict. In his humorous and poignant memoir of the war *The Little War of Private Post* (1960), Charles J. Post, an artist-soldier who served as a private in Company E of the Seventy-First New York Infantry during the fighting at Santiago, Cuba, summed up the viewpoint of a "little man" in a "little war" writing, "for those who are in war and battles and on the fighting line, there is no triviality in shaking dice with death. It makes no difference whether a man gets his along with twenty thousand others, or falls while on outpost duty all by himself. He is a hundred per cent casualty to himself. For him there is no lesser percentage. What more could there be to give?" Summing up the war's results in his memoir *Always the Young Stranger* (1952), the poet Carl Sandburg, who had served with the Sixth Illinois Infantry in Puerto Rico, wrote, "It was a small war edging toward immense consequences." Many of those consequences are still present today.

Note to Reader: Bold type in entries indicates a cross-reference. Ship specifications appear throughout the book in the following format (for abbreviations, see p. xiii):

La. 1887, dis. 3,042, hp. 4,400, sp. 17
Armament: 6–6.4″, 8–6pdr. H., 6–3pdr. H. rev., 5–14″ tt.
Cc. 500, comp. 370

The Dictionary

—A—

ABRIL Y OSTALO, MARIANO (1861–1935). A Puerto Rican journalist and poet who warned of encroaching U.S. influence and supported **autonomy** before the war. Writing in *La Correspondencia de Puerto Rico* and *La Democracia* upon the outbreak of war, he supported Spain, claiming that Puerto Ricans would defend themselves to the death in shedding their blood in defense of Spain. He praised the heroic combat off **San Juan**, **Puerto Rico**, of the Spanish ships *Terror* and *Isabella II* against the *St. Paul* on 22 June 1898. In the postwar period, Abril opposed U.S. annexation while serving as editor of *La Democracia*, was a legislator in the government, and in 1931 became the official historian of Puerto Rico.

ACOSTA Y EYERMANN, EMILIO DE (d. 1898). Captain, second in command of the Spanish cruiser *Reina Mercedes*, which was stationed at **Santiago**, **Cuba**. He was reportedly kind to captured U.S. sailors after the *Merrimac* failed to block the Santiago harbor entrance on 3 June 1898. During the U.S. bombardment of 6 June, Acosta was mortally wounded when a shell cut off his right leg and hand; nevertheless, he continued directing his men in extinguishing the fires on the *Reina Mercedes*.

ADJUTANT GENERAL'S DEPARTMENT, U.S. ARMY. Directed by Brig. Gen. **Henry C. Corbin**, it was the most important of the bureaus in the **War Department**, responsible for administering the **U.S. Army's** affairs. Composed of six officers, 105 permanent clerks, and 195 temporary clerks, the department was the bureau of orders and records of the army. It maintained the records of the War Department, issued all orders and regulations from Secretary of War **Russell A. Alger** and Maj. Gen. **Nelson A. Miles**, kept personnel records, ran the **Military Information Division**, supervised recruiting and **National Guard** officers, transmitted correspondence between army units, and was responsible for the mobilization of all militia, regulars and **volunteers**.

9

ADRIA. Danish steamer with an anomalous status. Chartered by the **U.S. Army Signal Corps**, it served under Danish colors with a Danish crew. Fitted with cable gear of the Mexican Telegraph Company, it arrived off **Santiago, Cuba**, on 1 June 1898. When the men on board refused to go near enough to shore to effectively grapple **cables**, the *Texas* and *Oregon* were placed between the ship and the Spanish shore batteries; nevertheless, it failed to cut any live cables. During the 6 June U.S. naval bombardment of Spanish positions at Santiago, several shells passed over the ship, and its crew refused to continue, claiming their work was illegal because the ship was a neutral ship and that their government would not protect them in cutting international cables.

ADULA. British steamer of the Atlas Line. Chartered by U.S. Consul Louis A. Dent, at Kingston, Jamaica, it evacuated 323 neutrals and four Americans from **Cienfuegos, Cuba**, on 10 May 1898. On 23 May, it was stopped by U.S. naval forces under the command of Com. **Winfield S. Schley** as it entered Cienfuegos. The captain reported he had seen the outline of Adm. **Pascual Cervera's Squadron** as it approached **Santiago, Cuba**, on the night of 18 May and that the squadron had left Santiago. Com. Schley concluded that Adm. Cervera's Squadron was in Cienfuegos harbor.

AGONCILLO, FELIPE (1868–1941). Filipino insurgent representative. A well-educated and wealthy lawyer, his prewar proposal of a Filipino-American alliance was rejected by the **State Department** on 15 December 1897. Hoping to secure U.S. recognition of Philippine independence, Agoncillo went to Washington after the **Armistice Protocol** of 12 August 1898. After President **William McKinley** had rejected his request to be present at the **Treaty of Paris** negotiations in a 1 October 1898 meeting, Agoncillo went to Paris, where he was rebuffed by the U.S. negotiators. As president of the newly formed Diplomatic Commission, he returned to the U.S. and worked against the ratification of the Treaty of Paris. In letters and memoranda, which the State Department ignored, Agoncillo argued that neither Spain nor the United States had any legal right to enter into an agreement with respect to the **Philippines**, because the Philippines had been an independent country before the Spanish-American War had ended.

AGUADORES, CUBA, BATTLE OF (1 JULY 1898). A fortified Spanish coastal strong point located on the western side of the San Juan River three miles east of the **Santiago, Cuba**, harbor entrance. It was shelled by U.S. naval forces in a feint to cover the landing of

U.S. forces at **Daiquirí, Cuba**, on 22 June 1898, resulting in seven Spanish wounded.

On 1 July, its 274-man garrison was bombarded again by U.S. naval forces and attacked on land by the **Thirty-Third Michigan Infantry** under the command of Brig. Gen. **Henry M. Duffield** as a diversion to the main U.S. assault on the **San Juan Heights**. Arriving three hours later than planned, Duffield's attack was neutralized by effective Spanish fire and the fact that the 700-foot railroad bridge crossing the San Juan River gorge had been blown up previously by the Spanish. After sustaining casualties of two killed and ten wounded, Duffield withdrew to **Siboney** in the early afternoon.

AGUINALDO Y FAMY, EMILIO (1869–1964). Leader of Filipino nationalist forces fighting against Spain, and president of the short-lived Philippine Republic from 1898 to 1901. Of mixed Tagalog-Chinese ancestry, Aguinaldo was born into a family that was part of the local **Cavite** elite. After joining the **Katipunan**, he rose to leadership in Cavite province and became the undisputed leader of the **Philippine Revolt** after the execution of **Andres Bonifacio** on 10 May 1897.

With the revolt stalemated by mid-1897, Aguinaldo negotiated the **Pact of Biak-Na-Bató** and went into exile, arriving in **Hong Kong** on 31 December 1897. He later wrote in *True Version of the Philippine Revolution* (1899) that, prior to and immediately following the outbreak of the Spanish-American War, he had several meetings with American officials—Lt. Comdr. Edward P. Wood of the *Petrel*, **E. Spencer Pratt**, and **Rounseville Wildman**—which led him to believe that the United States would support Philippine independence. Responding to Com. **George W. Dewey's** cable telling him to come as soon as possible, Aguinaldo returned to the **Philippines** on 19 May 1898 on the *McCulloch* and met with Dewey, who provided him with arms and ammunition.

On 24 May, Aguinaldo established a dictatorial government by proclamation, and an assembly declared Philippine independence on 12 June. On 23 June, he formed a new revolutionary government with himself at its head. However, the **McKinley administration** had no intention of recognizing his government. On 26 May Secretary of the Navy **John D. Long** cabled Dewey not to have political alliances with Aguinaldo's insurgents.

By the time the first U.S. expeditionary forces of the **Eighth Corps** arrived in late June, Aguinaldo's forces had completely surrounded **Manila**. Although Aguinaldo issued a formal declaration of Philippine independence and appealed to the world's powers for recognition of the Philippine Republic in early August, relations with the United

States rapidly deteriorated as his forces were excluded from the prearranged **Battle of Manila** on 13 August 1898 and the resulting **capitulation** of Manila. As president of the newly established republic, Aguinaldo led his forces in the **Philippine Insurrection**. After being captured by U.S. forces in March 1901, he signed an oath of allegiance to the United States.

AIBONITO, PUERTO RICO. See ASOMANTE HILLS, PUERTO RICO, SKIRMISH AT

ALBANY. (USN) British-built **protected cruiser**. Formerly the *Almirante Abreu*, it was the sister ship to the *New Orleans*. It was purchased by the **U.S. Navy** from Brazil on 16 March 1898 for $1,205,000. Not completed, it was detained in England throughout the war.

ALCÁNTARA PENINSULAR REGIMENT. Based in **Manzanillo, Cuba**, one battalion, under the command of Lt. Col. Baldomero Barbón, formed part of **Escario's Column**. Upon the column's arrival at **Santiago, Cuba**, on 3 July 1898, it was assigned to the eastern defenses of the city in the **Fort Canosa** area and then to the front lines, relieving the **Asia Regiment**. Lt. Col. Barbón represented the battalion at the 15 July 1898 council of commanders meeting that unanimously agreed that Santiago should capitulate.

ALEJANDRINO, JOSÉ (1871–1951). Filipino insurgent representative who accompanied the **Asiatic Squadron** to the **Philippines** and witnessed the naval **Battle of Manila Bay** on 1 May 1898. Having failed while in Japan in 1897 to secure financial and material support for the insurgent cause, Alejandrino, an ardent advocate of independence, endorsed working with and receiving arms from the United States as a matter of expediency because the only way to counteract U.S. intentions was to be sufficiently armed. In *The Price of Freedom: Episodes and Anecdotes of Our Struggle for Freedom* (1949) he chastised the United States for not helping an already independent Philippines, viewed its capture and retention of **Manila** on 13 August 1898 as illegal under international law, and blamed the United States for causing the **Philippine Insurrection**.

ALERTA. (SPN) A 43-ton **gunboat** commanded by Lt. Luis Pasquín. Armed with one 1.65-inch gun, it was involved in combat against U.S. ships at the battle of **Cárdenas Bay, Cuba**, on 11 May 1898.

ALFONSO XII. (SPN) Unprotected **cruiser**. A two-funneled cruiser built on a cellular system with 12 watertight compartments, it was a sister ship to the *Reina María Cristina* and *Reina Mercedes*. It served as the flagship at **Havana, Cuba**, but could not move because of totally disabled engines. Anchored close to the *Maine*, its boats helped rescue survivors of the explosion on 15 February 1898.

La. 1887, dis. 3,042, hp. 4,400, sp. 17
Armament: 6–6.4″, 8–6pdr. H., 6–3pdr. H. rev., 5–14″ tt.
Cc. 500, comp. 370

ALFONSO XII. (SPN) A 5,063-ton auxiliary **cruiser**. Formerly a steamer owned by the **Transatlantic Company**, it was used to deliver troops and supplies to **Cuba**. After leaving Spain in June 1898, it came under fire from the *Hawk* and *Castine* while trying to run the **blockade** and ran aground burning west of **Havana, Cuba**, on 5 July.

ALFONSO XIII. (SPN) A 4,831-ton auxiliary **cruiser**. Formerly the most luxurious steamer of the **Transatlantic Company**, it was commanded by Capt. José María Gorordo during the war and used to transport soldiers and supplies to **Puerto Rico**. After arriving at **San Juan, Puerto Rico**, on 5 May 1898, with soldiers and cannons, it could not continue on to **Cuba**, so it remained in Puerto Rican waters, delivering supplies to **Mayagüez** and **Ponce**.

ALFONSO XIII (1886–1941). Son of Queen Regent **María Cristina** and Alfonso XII, King of Spain. Since his father had died in 1885, his mother, the queen regent, ruled until Alfonso became king in 1902. As king he married a granddaughter of Queen Victoria of **Great Britain** and reigned until 1931 when, blamed for abrogating the constitution and the collapse of parliamentary government, he left Spain without formally abdicating. Alfonso died in exile.

ALFONSO XIII BATTALION. An 800-man permanent **Spanish Army** battalion in **Puerto Rico**. On 30 May 1898, three companies were stationed at **Ponce**, one at Adjuntas, one at **Yauco**, and one at Guayanilla. While under the command of Col. Julio Soto, the battalion vacated **Mayagüez** after an **engagement at Hormigueros** on 10 August, and during its retreat to **San Juan**, part of the battalion was involved in a **skirmish at Las Marías** on 13 August. Soto was arrested and imprisoned by Spanish authorities in Puerto Rico for not having defended Mayagüez and taken to Spain where he was absolved by the highest Spanish military court. The entire battalion left Puerto Rico for Spain on the *Gran Antilla* on 20 October 1898.

ALGER, RUSSELL ALEXANDER (1836–1907). Secretary of War (March 1897–July 1899). Prior to the war, Alger, a wealthy lumber magnate and former Republican governor of Michigan, told President **William McKinley** that not going to war would destroy the **Republican Party** and insisted that **Congress**, if necessary, would declare war without the president. During the war he was continually in conflict with Maj. Gen. **Nelson A. Miles**, complained of people pressuring for favors yet pressured McKinley for his own favored appointments, and seeing no need to reorganize the army, continually overstated its readiness.

While his son Capt. Frederick M. Alger served on the staffs of Maj. Gen. **William R. Shafter** in **Cuba** and Maj. Gen. Nelson A. Miles in **Puerto Rico**, Alger became enmeshed in controversy over the "**immunes**," privately stating that as a rule "men of color" were not to be commissioned above the rank of lieutenant. During the negotiations that ended the war, he favored taking all of the **Philippines**. He was so severely criticized for his poor administration of the **War Department** that he requested an official investigation in September 1898; therefore, McKinley appointed the **Dodge Commission**, which indirectly criticized Alger's management. He defended his administration in his *The Spanish-American War* (1901) by blaming insufficient congressional funding in part for the army's unpreparedness. Upon being ordered by McKinley to resign, he did so on 19 July 1899 and was soon appointed as a senator from Michigan, later winning election and serving until his death.

ALICANTE. Spanish hospital steamer of the **Transatlantic Company**, commanded by Capt. Antonio Genís. Sailing under the Red Cross flag, it arrived at **Martinique** on 23 April 1898. When Capt. **Fernando Villaamil** arrived on the *Furor* on 10 May, Genís informed him of the defeat at the **Battle of Manila Bay** on 1 May and about the squadron of Adm. **William T. Sampson** being off northern **Puerto Rico**. Genís then assisted Villaamil to leave at midnight by illuminating the buoys at the harbor entrance.

Remaining at Martinique throughout the war, the *Alicante* finally left on 4 August under safe conduct to convoy sick and wounded Spanish soldiers from **Santiago**, **Cuba**, to Spain. Carrying the first repatriated Spanish soldiers to arrive in Spain, it left Santiago on 8 August with 1,069 soldiers, one woman, five children, and 11 priests and monks and arrived at La Coruña, Spain, on 23 August 1898.

ALMIRANTE ABREU. **See** *ALBANY*

ALMIRANTE OQUENDO. (SPN) **Armored cruiser** commanded by Capt. **Joaquín Lazaga y Garay**. Spanish built and patterned on the British *Aurora* class, it was a sister ship to the *Vizcaya* and *Infanta*

María Teresa. The *Almirante Oquendo* had an armored belt that extended two-thirds of its length and a protective deck that was flat over the belt and curved at the extremities, leaving a high unprotected freeboard. Its 11-inch guns were mounted fore and aft in single barbettes with lightly armored hoods, whereas its 5.5-inch guns were without any armored protection except shields.

Its bottom was fouled because the *Almirante Oquendo* had left **Cuba** on 1 April 1898, crossed the Atlantic Ocean to join Adm. **Pascual Cervera's Squadron** at Cape Verdes on 19 April, and recrossed the Atlantic with the squadron, arriving at **Santiago, Cuba**, on 19 May. Short of ammunition during the **Naval Battle of Santiago** on 3 July, the *Almirante Oquendo* was the last Spanish cruiser to leave the harbor at 10:00 a.m. and the second ship to be destroyed. The breechlock of one of its 5.5-inch Hontoria guns blew out, and the ship was hit a countable 68 times by fire from the *Indiana*, *Iowa*, *Oregon*, and *Texas*. Forced ashore burning at 10:35 a.m., it broke in two upon being beached seven miles west of the harbor entrance. Its crew was rescued by the *Harvard* and *Gloucester*.

La. 1891, dis. 6,890, hp. 13,700, sp. 20.2
Armor: s. 12–10″, d. 2–3″, b. 9″, ct. 12″
Armament: 2–11″, 10–5.5″, 2–2.7″, 8–2.2.″, 8–1.4″, 2 M. mgs., 8 tt. (2 sub.)
Cc. 1,050, comp. 484

ALMODÓVAR DEL RÍO, DUKE OF (1859–1906).

Spanish minister of state, Almodóvar, Juan Manuel Sánchez y Gutiérrez de Castro, was educated in England, and as a member of the **Cortes**, he was a prominent member of the **Liberal Party**. Although experienced in budgetary matters, he had limited foreign policy experience when he replaced **Pío Gullón y Iglesias** as minister of state on 18 May 1898.

Blaming the United States for having started the war, on 18 July 1898, Almodóvar began Spain's diplomatic quest for a negotiated settlement when he asked the government of **France** to present Spain's request for a suspension of hostilities to the United States. During the negotiations of the **Armistice Protocol** and **Treaty of Paris**, Almodóvar favored giving up another island instead of **Puerto Rico**, wanted either an arbitration or U.S. assumption of the **Cuban debt**, and believed Spain should retain the **Philippines** because the U.S. occupation of **Manila** was illegal, having occurred after the Armistice Protocol had been signed on 12 August. Having authorized **Jules Cambon**, France's ambassador to the United States, to sign the Armistice Protocol, Almodóvar was not appointed to Spain's **Peace Commission** to negotiate the Treaty of Paris because he was widely blamed for having lost the war. He later served as minister of state in the cabinets of **Práxedes M. Sagasta** and **Segismundo Moret** in 1901 and 1903 and represented Spain at the Algeciras Conference.

ALVARADO. (SPN) **Gunboat** commanded by Lt. Mauricio Aranco, a torpedo officer. A British-built sister ship to the gunboat *Sandoval*, it was used to raise torpedo **mines** at the entrance of **Santiago, Cuba**'s harbor, on the night of 2 July to allow Adm. **Pascual Cervera's Squadron** to leave the next day and fight the **Naval Battle of Santiago**. After the **capitulation** of Santiago, both the **U.S. Navy** and **U.S. Army** claimed the *Alvarado* as a **prize of war**. Eventually, Secretary of War **Russell A. Alger** ordered it turned over to the navy. It was placed under the command of Lt. **Victor Blue**, put into service, and used in the U.S. naval attack on **Manzanillo, Cuba**, on 12 August 1898. It was sold in 1912.

La. 1895, dis. 106, sp. 19
Armament: 1–2.24″, 1–1pdr. N. rev.

AMAZONAS. See *NEW ORLEANS*

AMERICAN FEDERATION OF LABOR (AFL). Founded in 1886, under the leadership of **Samuel Gompers** and the Cigar Makers' International Union, its largest affiliate, the AFL consistently supported Cuban independence and the recognition of the **belligerent rights** of the Cuban insurgents. Opposed to a war against Spain, the AFL warned of the hysteria following the *Maine* disaster of 15 February 1898. However, after war was declared, the AFL changed its policy and supported the U.S. war effort.

AMERICAN RED CROSS. Founded in 1881 under the leadership of **Clara Barton**, the Red Cross established the Central Cuban Relief Committee and distributed relief supplies to the Cuban civilian population from late 1897 until it pulled out of **Cuba** on 10 April 1898. During the Spanish-American War, the Red Cross became a vital national relief organization even though it had consistent trouble in coordinating with the **U.S. Army** Medical Corps, particularly on the issue of the presence of female **nurses** in a war zone.

The Red Cross sent field agents to military **camps** in the United States to find out what services were necessary; provided cots, clothes, food, and medical equipment; assisted in the relief of discharged and furloughed men; helped soldiers to communicate with their relatives; fed both Spanish **prisoners of war** and Cuban refugees at **Key West, Florida**; and served the military as a nursing and relief auxiliary.

Although the Red Cross conducted minor relief efforts in the **Phil-**

ippines and **Puerto Rico**, most of its wartime effort was undertaken during the **Santiago**, **Cuba campaign**. It chartered the ship *State of Texas* to bring supplies to Santiago and by 9 July had established its own hospital at **Siboney** and delivered supplies to the frontline field hospital of the First Division of the **Fifth Corps**. Female nurses assisted the sick and wounded, and the Red Cross fed refugees at **El Caney** and the civilian population of Santiago after it capitulated on 17 July.

AMPHITRITE. (USN) Double-turret **monitor** commanded by Capt. C. J. Barclay. It was a sister ship to the *Monadnock*, *Miantonomoh*, and *Terror*. During the war it frequently had to be towed by larger ships because of its small fuel capacity, slowness, engine problems, and instability in the open sea. It served on the Cuban **blockade**, bombarded **San Juan**, **Puerto Rico**, on 12 May 1898, where it received several hits, and put ashore a landing party that occupied the lighthouse at Cape San Juan, Puerto Rico (6–9 August). After the war it served as a training vessel and guard ship in New York harbor and was sold in 1920.

La. 1883, com. 1895, dis. 3,990, hp. 1,600, sp. 10.5
Armor: s. 9″, d. 1.75″, b. 11.5″, t. 7.5″, ct. 7.5″
Armament: 4–10″, 2–4″, 2–6pdr, 2–3pdr, 2–1pdr, 2–37mm.
Cc. 270, comp. 150

ANDERSON, THOMAS McARTHUR (1836–1917). Brigadier general, commanded the first expedition of the **Eighth Corps** to **Manila**, **Philippines**. Trained as a lawyer, Anderson, a Civil War veteran and career military officer, arrived at the Presidio in San Francisco, California, on 23 May 1898 and had one day to inspect his 2,500-man command. Leaving San Francisco on 25 May, his forces captured **Guam** on 21 June and arrived at Manila on 30 June. Establishing his command post at **Cavite**, he met with Adm. **George W. Dewey** and **Emilio Aguinaldo** on 1 July. When Aguinaldo questioned him about U.S. intentions, Anderson told Aguinaldo that the United States did not want colonies.

Prior to the 13 August **Battle of Manila**, Anderson, now in command of the First Division of the Eighth Corps, notified Aguinaldo not to let his insurgent forces enter the city during the upcoming battle. When some 4,000 insurgents entered the suburbs, he called upon Aguinaldo to withdraw his troops, and Aguinaldo complied. After briefly commanding U.S. forces during the **Philippine Insurrection**, he was succeeded by Maj. Gen. **Henry W. Lawton**, returned to the United States, and wrote in "Our Rule in the Philippines," *North American Review* (February 1900) that during the war, Aguinaldo had every reason to expect U.S. support for Philippine independence and that the origins of the resulting insurrection could be traced back to the U.S. refusal to let Aguinaldo's forces cooperate with U.S. forces. Anderson retired in 1900.

ANDRÉ, EDOUARD C. (1840–1911). Belgian consul at **Manila, Philippines**. After British Consul **E. H. Rawson-Walker** died of illness, André became the intermediary in the Adm. **George W. Dewey**-Gov. Gen. **Fermín Jáudenes y Álvarez** negotiations, which resulted in the prearranged **Battle of Manila** on 13 August 1898 and its resulting **Capitulation of Manila Agreement**. Believing the Filipino insurgents only represented a minority of the population, André did not favor them, and although Maj. Gen. **Wesley Merritt** was skeptical, Adm. Dewey had full confidence in André during negotiations.

ANITA. A 170-foot, 900-horsepower **yacht** that served as a *New York Journal* **press boat**. Prior to the war the *Anita* lent its name to the *Anita* **Expedition** and during the war saw service in the Caribbean. The *Anita* was one of the first boats to enter the harbor of **Santiago, Cuba**, after the city's **capitulation** on 17 July 1898. Upon docking in the city, three *Journal* employees distributed thousands of copies of the *Journal* and placarded the city with lithographs showing the wreck of the *Maine*, with the legend "Remember the Maine" at the top, and at the bottom, "Buy the Journal." Maj. Gen. **William R. Shafter** was so incensed that he had them expelled from the city and had a detail tear down the lithographs.

ANITA **EXPEDITION.** Named after the *Anita*. The *New York Journal* organized and paid for a congressional delegation that went to **Cuba** in March 1898. Called the "Congressional Cuban Commission," it included senators Hernando Money (Mississippi), John M. Thurston (Nebraska), and Jacob H. Gallinger (New Hampshire) and representatives William Alden Smith (Michigan) and Amos Cummings (New York). Thurston's wife went along and, along with other members of the delegation, wrote articles for the *Journal* depicting the terrible conditions in Cuba caused by Spanish policy. After Mrs. Thurston died on 14 March of a heart attack, the *Journal* said it had been caused by the horrors she had seen. After the commission returned to Washington, D.C., Thurston and Gallinger spoke in the Senate, with Gallinger claiming that over 600,000 Cubans had perished as a result of Spanish policy during the **Cuban Revolt**.

ANNAPOLIS. (USN) **Composite gunboat** commanded by Comdr. **John J. Hunker**. A barquentine-rigged, single-screw steamer with a clipper bow, its hull was sheathed and coppered for work in the tropics. Assigned to the North Atlantic Station, it participated in the Cuban **blockade**, convoyed the **Fifth Corps** to **Daiquirí, Cuba**, and shelled **Siboney** on 22 June 1898 to assist in the Fifth Corps's landing at Daiquirí. In company with the *Wasp* and *Leyden*, it sank the Spanish gunboat *Jorge Juan* on 21 July in **Nipe Bay**. It later escorted troops to **Guánica, Puerto Rico**, and was present when U.S. troops first landed at **Ponce**. Serving as a training ship from 1920 onward, it was transferred to the Maritime Commission in 1940 and survived until 1950 when it was scrapped.

La. 1896, com. 1897, dis. 1,010, hp. 1,000, sp. 12
Armament: 6–4", 4–6pdr., 2–1pdr.
Cc. 324, comp. 146

ANTI-IMPERIALISM. Opposition to U.S. imperialism arose during the war, as many who had supported a war to liberate Cuba, such as Susan B. Anthony and Andrew Carnegie, became vocal opponents of a war for territorial acquisition. Initially few in number, the movement came to include the greater part of the eminent figures of the literary and intellectual world—such as William Dean Howells and Mark Twain—and many prominent business leaders, politicians, and social activists. It also found strong support in the religious and black, German, and Irish-American communities. However, its leadership was basically an old guard movement in conflict with a younger generation who supported U.S. imperialism.

Many of its adherents favored economic expansion through free trade rather than political domination and based their arguments on racism and antiracism, American traditions, and antimilitarism. Focusing mainly on the **Philippines**, the movement said little about **Cuba** and nothing about **Puerto Rico**. During the Spanish-American War the anti-imperialist movement failed to develop a large following and was initially overwhelmed by the war's successful outcome, only gaining momentum with the formation of the **Anti-Imperialist League**.

ANTI-IMPERIALIST LEAGUE. Stemming from an earlier anti-imperialist group organized in Boston, Massachusetts, in June 1898, it was officially formed in November 1898 by prominent Boston professional men and reformers to oppose the **McKinley administration**'s policy to conquer and colonize the **Philippines**. The league conducted a petition and lobbying campaign to oppose the ratification of the **Treaty of Paris** by the U.S. Senate. Directly following the passage of the treaty, the league called for an end to the just-begun **Philippine Insurrection** on the basis of Philippine independence. It grew quickly and nationally, and despite the fact that 41 prominent Americans, including Charles Francis Adams, Jane Addams, Edward Atkinson, Andrew Carnegie, **Grover Cleveland**, **Samuel Gompers**, and David Starr Jordan served as vice presidents of the league, it failed to stop U.S. intervention in the Philippines.

ANTONIO LÓPEZ. (SPN) Unprotected **cruiser**. One of the larger steamers of the **Transatlantic Company**, it left Cádiz, Spain, on 16 June 1898 and carried military supplies to **Puerto Rico**. After it ran ashore six miles west of **San Juan, Puerto Rico**, on 28 June while trying to escape the U.S. cruiser *Yosemite*, Spanish forces unloaded its cargo, taking an electric light that was installed at the harbor entrance and numerous cannons, which were placed in various San Juan batteries. On 16 July the U.S. cruiser *New Orleans*, upon sighting the *Antonio López*, shot 40 projectiles at it, and it burned for days.

ARAÑA Y GOIRI, SABINO DE (1865–1903). Basque leader and founder of the **Basque Nationalist Party**. An ardent advocate of an independent Basque state, he refused to ally with the socialists, opposed Spain's policy in **Cuba**, was elected to municipal office in 1898, and was jailed after the war for having sent a telegram to **Theodore Roosevelt** congratulating him on the U.S. liberation of Cuba from Spanish rule.

ARMISTICE PROTOCOL (12 AUGUST 1898). On 18 July 1898, **Almodóvar del Río**, Spain's minister of state, telegraphed **Fernando León y Castillo**, Spain's ambassador in Paris, asking him to propose that the French government authorize **Jules Cambon**, its ambassador in Washington, D.C., to present a Spanish proposal of negotiation to the U.S. government. Owing to French officials being either ill or on vacation, the French did not consent until 21 July; accordingly, on 22 July the official Spanish note was sent to Cambon. After a missing cipher key caused a four-day delay, the coded communication was finally decoded and delivered by Cambon on 26 July to President **William McKinley**.

After three and a half days of intense debate within a cabinet divided over the issue of the **Philippines**, the **McKinley administration**, having left the issue to be the subject of future negotiations, finally responded on 30 July with its specific list of demands, from which McKinley refused to budge during the next two weeks of discussions. Finally, having agreed to hold the peace conference in Paris and to exclude any Filipino representation, a protocol, instead of a treaty, was drawn up to avoid immediate legislative interference in both countries.

On 12 August, the protocol was signed in the White House by Cambon for Spain and by Secretary of State **William R. Day**. Its basic points were: 1) Spain relinquished sovereignty over **Cuba**; 2) Spain ceded **Puerto Rico** and an island in the Ladrones, to be selected by the United States, to the United States; 3) the United States occupied and held the city, bay, and harbor of **Manila** pending the conclusion of a treaty of peace, which would determine the control, disposition, and government of the Philippines; 4) Spain agreed to almost immediately evacuate Cuba and Puerto Rico; 5) commissioners were to be appointed to negotiate a treaty of peace in Paris; and 6) hostilities were declared suspended.

Both governments quickly issued official proclamations suspending hostilities, work began on convening a peace conference in Paris to negotiate a final treaty ending the war, and **evacuation commissions** were appointed. Major unresolved issues, which were relegated to the conference in Paris, included the Philippines, the status of Spanish citizens in the ceded territories, the public debt, state property, legal cases and future trade.

ARMORED CRUISER. Slower than a **protected cruiser**, an armored cruiser had both side and deck armor, which was not as thick as the armor on a **battleship**. Using **Harveyized steel armor**, the two U.S. armored cruisers, the *New York* and the *Brooklyn*, had continuous side armor from waterline to battle deck. The side armor of Spanish armored cruisers usually only extended several feet above the waterline, leaving an eight- to ten-foot-wide unprotected strip running the length of the ship between the side armor and the barbette. Also unprotected were ammunition hoists leading to the 5.5″ guns' magazines, and the same guns were protected only by shields. Such problems proved costly in battle for four of Spain's six armored cruisers: the *Almirante Oquendo*, *Cristóbal Colón*, *Infanta María Teresa*, and *Vizcaya*. The *Emperador Carlos V* was part of Adm. **Manuel Cámara's Squadron**, and the *Princesa de Asturias* saw no action during the war.

ARMY, SPAIN. A powerful political institution in the late nineteenth century, the army normally acted in concert with civilian leaders in its duty to save Spain from dissolution and did not attempt to establish a military dictatorship. However, when the administration of **Práxedes M. Sagasta** attempted to decrease its size and make it more subordinate to civilian authorities in the late 1880s, the army blocked any such changes and retaliated by blocking proposals for Cuban reforms.

Based on a structure that included a permanent army and a reserve, the army consumed 18 percent of Spain's budget in 1895. Because most of this funding went to pay the salaries of officers, who numbered one officer for every six soldiers and one general for every 100 soldiers, the army chronically lacked funds for equipment, logistical support, and adequate field training. Furthermore, although all Spanish men past the age of 19 were obliged to serve in the army, such service could be avoided by a payment of between 1,500 and 2,000 pesetas. Consequently, most soldiers were conscripted from the lower classes.

The outbreak of the **Cuban** and **Philippine Revolts** in the mid-1890s resulted in the dispatch of over 225,000 troops overseas, so that by 1898, the army, which totaled 492,077 troops, had 152,284 in Spain and the adjacent islands, 278,457 in **Cuba**, 51,331 in the **Philippines**, and 10,005 in **Puerto Rico**. In spite of the fact that Spain's army was numerically vastly superior to the **U.S. Army** upon the eve of the Spanish-American War, it was poorly prepared, and when Spain lost control of the seas early in the war, it was unable to resupply and reinforce its overseas forces during the conflict.

ARMY, UNITED STATES. By act of **Congress** on 22 April 1898, the army of the United States was divided into two branches. One was the regular army and the other was composed of **volunteers**. Initially, the regular army consisted of 2,143 officers and 26,040 enlisted men scattered throughout military posts and garrisons from coast to coast.

Having been assigned a limited role in overseas operations, the army, which had no units larger than a regiment, had no central military staff, no institution to conduct strategic planning, and was hampered by the division of authority between Secretary of War **Russell Alger** and the **commanding general**, Maj. Gen. **Nelson A. Miles**. Moreover, there had been no training in combined Army-Navy operations and no provision for transporting troops overseas. However, it was not a decaying force. Most generals had been in the Civil War, and most junior officers were West Point graduates; moreover, its units had fought in the Indian wars on the frontier. Officer schools had been established, and breech-loading guns, **Krag-Jörgensen** bolt-action rifles, and **smokeless powder** introduced.

Without resorting to a draft, the army increased tenfold in three months through volunteers; however, because of political pressure from the **National Guard** and its political supporters, which resulted in the defeat of the **Hull Bill**, the regular army was restricted to only 65,000 men. By August 1898, it had increased to 59,600 men, selected from 102,000 applicants. Recruits were simply assigned to expanded existing units, and hundreds of regular officers were assigned to command volunteer units.

Consisting of five regiments of artillery and ten field batteries, which were scattered across the country, the artillery of the regular army was increased during mobilization to seven regiments, which were complemented by eight volunteer batteries of heavy artillery and 16 volunteer batteries of field artillery.

On 7 May the **War Department** formed the volunteer and regular armies into seven corps, and an eighth was formed on 21 June. Only the **Fifth** and **Eighth Corps** left the United States during the war. The Fifth fought in the **Santiago, Cuba, campaign**, and the Eighth, in the **Philippines**. From 1 May through 30 September 1898, the army sustained 2,910 deaths, or a little over 1 percent of the total army. Total casualties included 23 officers and 257 enlisted men killed, four officers and 61 enlisted men died from wounds, 80 officers and 2,485 enlisted men died from disease, and 113 officers and 1,464 enlisted men were wounded.

ARROYO, PUERTO RICO. Located on the southeastern Puerto Rican coast, it was peacefully occupied under threat of bombardment by U.S. naval forces on 1 August 1898. Since Spanish forces had evacuated before the arrival of the *Gloucester* and *Wasp*, a guard of 35 men from the *Gloucester*, landing in the late morning, was openly received on the beach by a large number of people. Lt. **Richard Wainwright** conferred with the captain of the port and Mayor José María Padilla, who delivered the town without a gesture of protest. Surrender terms included the continuation of political authorities and priests in their positions, launches in the harbor were to be used by U.S. forces, and all property and documents of the Spanish government were to be surrendered. The U.S. flag was raised at 11:28 a.m., and a guard from the *Gloucester* was left in charge until the landing of the main U.S. force of 5,000 under the command of Maj. Gen. **John R. Brooke** began on 3 August. These events were covered by **Carlton T. Chapman** in "How the Stars and Stripes Came to Arroyo," *Harper's Weekly* (3 September 1898). Subsequently, a brief skirmish with 40 mounted Spanish **guerrillas** under the command of Capt. Salvador Acha occurred on the outskirts of town.

ASERRADEROS CONFERENCE (20 JUNE 1898). Atop a high hill 18 miles west of the **Santiago, Cuba**, harbor entrance, a one-hour strategy meeting between U.S. and Cuban insurgent commanders took place at Aserraderos in the hut of Cuba insurgent General **Jesús Rabí**. After coming ashore on four small boats, the official U.S. party rode on muleback to confer with Cuban Maj. Gen. **Calixto García**. Among the leaders present at the meeting were García, Rabí, and Brig. Gen. Demetrio Castillo y Duany, representing the insurgents, and Adm. **William T. Sampson** and Maj. Gen. **William R. Shafter**, representing the U.S. forces. Observers included Capt. **Arthur H. Lee** of the British Army, Capt. Count von Goetzen of the German Army, and correspondents **Frederic S. Remington** of the *New York Journal*, **Caspar Whitney** of *Harper's Weekly*, and **Stephen Bonsal** and **Richard H. Davis** of the *New York Herald*.

Shafter accepted García's recommendation to land U.S. forces first at **Daiquirí** and then **Siboney**, and García promised to concentrate about 1,000 troops under Gen. Castillo to assist in the landings while another force of 500 under the command of Gen. Rabí would make a demonstration at **Cabañas** to mislead the Spanish. Furthermore, it was agreed that Sampson's naval forces, in addition to shelling the landing sites, would add to the deception by bombarding Cabañas, the *Morro*, and forts located at Siboney and **Aguadores**. After the U.S. forces had disembarked, Sampson would transfer García's troops from Aserraderos by sea to Daiquirí and to Siboney.

ASIA REGIMENT. By the end of June, there were eight companies totaling 1,096 men stationed west of **Santiago, Cuba**, in positions at Punta Cabrera, Monte Real, and Cobre to repulse any landing by U.S. forces at **Cabañas**. During the battles of 1 July 1898, the regiment sustained casualties of ten killed and two wounded. On 2 July it was moved east of Santiago to occupy the defensive line vacated by the sailors of Adm. **Pascual Cervera's Squadron**. Those stationed at **Fort Canosa** were relieved on 3 July by members of the **Alcántara Peninsular Regiment**. On 9 July one company was reassigned to the Fort Canosa line. Lt. Col. José Cotrina Gelabert represented the regiment at the 15 July military commanders meeting, which unanimously agreed to the **capitulation** of Santiago.

ASIATIC SQUADRON. When Com. **George W. Dewey** took command at Nagasaki, Japan, on 3 January 1898, it included only four vessels: the **protected cruisers** *Olympia* and *Boston*, the **gunboat** *Petrel*, and the *Monocacy*, an antique paddle-wheel steamer. After the gunboat *Concord* arrived with much needed ammunition on 9 February, the squadron moved to **Hong Kong**, where it remained stationed until the outbreak of the war. In Hong Kong, the squadron was augmented by the arrival of the revenue cutter *McCulloch* and protected cruisers *Baltimore* and *Raleigh*, and the purchase of the steamers *Nanshan* and *Zafiro*. Upon the outbreak of war and **Great Britain**'s official declaration of neutrality, the squadron moved to **Mirs Bay** in Chinese territory, where on 25 April it received orders to commence operations against the Spanish navy in the **Philippines**. After **Oscar F. Williams** arrived on 27 April, bringing intelligence information on the Philippines, the squadron, consisting of 1,743 officers and enlisted men, sailed to the Philippines and decisively defeated Adm. **Patricio Montojo's Squadron** in the naval **Battle of Manila Bay** on 1 May 1898. Anchored in **Manila Bay** during the following four months, the squadron suffered 12 deaths (none in battle), had 159 men in the hospital, sent 24 home, averaged a sick rate of around 2 percent, and was joined by other vessels, including the *Charleston*, *Monadnock*, and the *Monterey*.

ASOMANTE HILLS, PUERTO RICO, SKIRMISH AT (12 AUGUST 1898). Hills located near the town of Aibonito on the main military road from **Ponce** to **San Juan**, where, following the loss of Ponce, a Spanish force of 1,280 men and two Plasencia guns, including troops from the **Patria Battalion** and Provisional Battalion No. 6 of Puerto Rico, took up positions under the command of Lt. Col. **Francisco Larrea** in an attempt to stop advancing U.S. forces under the command of Maj. Gen. **James H. Wilson**.

On 12 August a brief skirmish was fought near the hills between entrenched Spanish forces and a U.S. artillery reconnaissance force composed of Battery F, **Third U.S. Artillery**, and the **Third Wisconsin Infantry**, resulting in two U.S. dead and five wounded. After news of the **Armistice Protocol** arrived, Lt. Col. **Tasker Bliss**, under a flag of truce, informed the Spanish defenders; however, they refused to believe it until official word came the next day.

ASSOCIATED PRESS. Under the direction of general manager Melville E. Stone, who initially had pacifist leanings and hesitated stirring up public sentiment for war, the Associated Press (AP) provided news dispatches to most American newspapers at the time of the war. However, its record was scarcely better than that of the "**yellow press**" in objective journalism because, in spite of the fact that it sent out a blanket denial of rumors abounding after the *Maine* disaster, it later provided an abundance of false information. Its summary of the report of the U.S. investigation of the *Maine* came out before the report was given to **Congress**. The AP never revealed how it got the report even though an investigation was conducted by the U.S. government, and a 4 May 1898 dispatch reported that Adm. **Pascual Cervera's Squadron** had returned to Cádiz, Spain.

During the war against Spain, the AP used 23 **correspondents**, who were based throughout the Caribbean, and four **press boats**, which included the *Dauntless*. William A. M. Goode, who was on board the *New York* during the **Naval Battle of Santiago** on 3 July, Alfred C. Goudie, and **George E. Graham** covered the **Santiago**,

Cuba, **campaign**. Harry L. Beach was with the **First Marine Battalion** at **Guantánamo**, **Cuba**.

Charles Sanford Diehl, who was in charge of the AP's Cuban coverage during the war, estimated in his book *The Staff Correspondent* (1931) that war coverage from March to October 1898 had cost the AP $284,210, which included $141,402 spent on press boats, and salaries and expenses of correspondents. Cable tolls from the war zone had cost $124,554, and extra costs in distributing news over leased wires in the United States had cost $18,154.

ASTOR, JOHN JACOB IV (1864–1912). Lieutenant Colonel (USV). Inventor, author, and one of the richest men in the world, Astor, who was one of the first to offer his services to the U.S. government, donated a **yacht** to the **U.S. Navy**, funded and equipped the **Astor Battery**, and offered the use of two of his railroads to transport war supplies to Florida. Volunteering for service, he initially served on the staff of Maj. Gen. **Joseph C. Breckinridge**, inspecting **Camp Thomas** at Chickamauga Park, Georgia. Later, while on the staff of Maj. Gen. **William R. Shafter**, Astor attended the **Aserraderos Conference**, fought in the **Santiago**, **Cuba**, **campaign**, and was promoted to colonel. He died on the *Titanic* on 15 April 1912.

ASTOR BATTERY. A $100,000 mountain artillery battery funded and equipped by **John Jacob Astor IV**, who imported the guns and ammunition from abroad at his own expense. It was commanded by First Lt. Peyton C. March (Fifth U.S. Artillery) who trained the battery. Organized and mustered into service at New York City on 1 June 1898 with three officers and 98 enlisted men, it was popularly known as the "Asteroids." Many of its members had seen military service in other countries and included a notable list of college graduates, mostly athletes of some reputation. Arriving at San Francisco on 19 June from New York City, the battery sailed on 27 June with the third expedition of the **Eighth Corps**. While crossing the Pacific, the battery's chorus sang the unit's song "We're Natural-Born Soldiers," composed by Charles C. Webster. After arriving at **Manila, Philippines**, it was assigned to the **First Brigade** and participated in the **Battle of Manila** on 13 August.

The battery sailed from Manila on the steamship *Senator* 16 December 1898, arriving at New York City on 22 January 1899. Its members were mustered out of service on 2 February 1899, with one officer and 85 enlisted. Total casualties during the war were three enlisted killed in action, seven wounded, one died from wounds, and two died from disease.

ATLANTA CONSTITUTION. A Democratic newspaper edited by Capt. Evan P. Howell, who served on the **Dodge Commission**. In competition with the *Atlanta Journal*, which was also a Democratic paper, it strongly supported U.S. intervention in **Cuba**, and immediately discarded the accident theory of the *Maine* explosion, declaring "the hand of a Spaniard did the work," and carried a poll on 17 February 1898, which showed that 90 percent of those questioned blamed Spanish treachery for the *Maine* disaster. On 12 March, it called for a declaration of war, not on the basis of the *Maine* but on the humane demand that the United States end the Cuban "butchery."

During the war its main correspondents were Robert B. Cramer, who covered the Caribbean theater, and Joseph Ohl, who was based in Washington, D.C., and was one of the first to question the competency of Secretary of War **Russell A. Alger** and Maj. Gen. **William R. Shafter**. As part of its flamboyant coverage of the war, it claimed, after the U.S. naval bombardment of **San Juan**, **Puerto Rico**, on 12 May 1898, that Puerto Rico had been captured by Rear Adm. **William T. Sampson**. On 4 July, one day after the **Naval Battle of Santiago**, **Cuba**, its bannered headlines read "Sampson Burns and Sinks Cervera's Ships; Shafter Demands Santiago's Surrender," beneath which were drawings of the Confederate and the U.S. flags.

AUGUSTÍN Y DÁVILA, BASILIO (1840–1910). Lieutenant general, Spanish governor general, and captain general of the **Philippines** (9 April 1898–4 August 1898). After replacing Gov. Gen. **Fernando Primo de Rivera**, Augustín issued a proclamation on 23 April 1898 stating that the North American people "constituted of all the social excrescences," had provoked the war. He warned that a U.S. squadron was coming to the Philippines to destroy Catholicism, and rob and kidnap people to be exploited in agricultural or industrial labor. Calling upon Filipinos to unite under the "glorious Spanish flag," he predicted that Spain would win a short war. Com. **George W. Dewey** had the captain of each ship in the **Asiatic Squadron** read a copy of Augustín's proclamation to his crew, whereupon it was greeted with laughter.

Believing the **Spanish Navy** could defeat Dewey's squadron, Augustín refused to scatter his ships and opposed Adm. **Patricio Montojo**'s request for his squadron to leave **Manila**. Hoping to prevent the insurgents from gaining control of the countryside, he left most of the **Spanish Army** scattered throughout the islands in their garrisons instead of bringing them to Manila; however, many were soon overpowered by the insurgent forces. After the naval **Battle of Manila Bay** on 1 May, he evacuated civilians from the walled city of Manila, and on 4 May formed a **Consultative Assembly** and organized a

Filipino militia to gain popular support. Both efforts had failed by the end of May.

During May Augustín intimated through British Consul **E. H. Rawson-Walker** a willingness to surrender to the United States, but Adm. Dewey did not have sufficient land forces, and Augustín would not consider surrendering to the insurgents, whom he viewed as uncivilized. In July, upon learning that Adm. **Manuel Cámara's Squadron** had been recalled, he secretly began negotiations with the United States for the surrender of Manila and cabled Madrid that his situation was doomed. Relieved of command for "defeatism" on 4 August 1898, he was succeeded by Gen. of Division **Fermín Jáudenes y Álvarez** and was surreptitiously evacuated by the German ship *Kaiserin Augusta* on 5 August 1898.

AUÑÓN Y VILLALÓN, RAMÓN (1844–1925). Captain, Spain's minister of the marine during the war. Auñón had commanded a **battleship**, was considered a good manager, and had supported sending Adm. **Pascual Cervera's Squadron** to the West Indies. Succeeding **Segismundo Bermejo y Merelo** as minister of the marine on 18 May 1898, his tenure was marked by sudden changes of strategy owing to Spanish defeats and his own unrealistic appraisal of the military situation.

Because of political pressure, Auñón cancelled Bermejo's 12 May 1898 order, allowing Adm. Pascual Cervera's Squadron to return to Spain. On 27 May 1898, he ordered part of the Spanish home fleet to attack U.S. Atlantic coastal cities only to change direction on 15 June when he ordered Adm. **Manuel Cámara's Squadron** to the **Philippines**. Within weeks he ordered its recall to protect Spain against a possible U.S. naval attack. In response to repeated appeals from Cuban Gov. Gen. **Ramón Blanco y Erenas** for reinforcements, Auñón informed Adm. **Pascual Cervera** on 3 June that his squadron, which was blockaded at **Santiago**, **Cuba**, would be detached only temporarily for duty in the Philippines, soon to return to the West Indies with reinforcements. Later he agreed with Gov. Gen. Ramón Blanco y Erenas and ordered the sortie from Santiago, Cuba, which resulted in the annihilation of Adm. Cervera's Squadron in the **Naval Battle of Santiago** on 3 July 1898.

AUSTRIA-HUNGARY. Because Spain's Queen Regent **María Cristina** came from Austria-Hungary, Emperor Franz Josef sympathized with Spain. Directed by Foreign Minister Count Agenor von Goluchowsi and ambassadors Viktor Dubsky and Hengervar von Hengelmüller, all of whom were sympathetic to Spain, Austria-Hungary undertook actions to forestall war. However, with little influence in

Washington, it worked to promote and coordinate joint European initiatives such as the **Great Powers Note**.

AUTONOMIST PARTY—CUBA (*PARTIDO AUTONOMISTA CUBANO*). Led by José María Gálvez, Antonio Govin, Dr. Francisco Zayas, and the Marquís de Montoro, its goal was an autonomous status for **Cuba** within the Spanish empire. After the outbreak of the **Cuban Revolt** in February 1895, its offer of mediation was rejected by the insurgents. Furthermore, Spain rejected its request for greater home rule to keep the revolt from spreading. By the time party leaders formed part of the **autonomous government** in January 1898, the party had been politically neutralized by the revolt.

AUTONOMOUS GOVERNMENT—CUBA. Formed by a coalition of the **Autonomist Party** and the Reformist Party, which was led by Dr. Eduardo Dolz, the government began to function on 1 January 1898, with José María Gálvez as president of the cabinet. Composed of a two-chambered parliament, which was headed by the governor general who appointed for life 17 out of the 35 members of the upper chamber, the government controlled domestic affairs while Spain retained jurisdiction over the courts, foreign relations, military authority, and church-state relations. The party's success was minimal because it was rejected by the majority of Spaniards in **Cuba**, including most army officials, who saw it as an attempt to placate the insurgents, and by the insurgents, who saw it as a threat to their goal of independence. It was disbanded when Cuba came under U.S. military control after the war.

AUTONOMOUS GOVERNMENT—PUERTO RICO. After a cabinet led by Francisco Mariano Quiñones began functioning on 15 January 1898, the government was formally inaugurated on 9 February 1898. On 27 March 1898, a 32-member parliament dominated by **Muñocistas** was elected. Upon the outbreak of the war against the United States, the cabinet proclaimed its allegiance to Spain and asked the government to arm the people. After the convening of the parliament under the presidency of Herminio Díaz Navarro on 17 July, virtually nothing was accomplished, and it disbanded when U.S. forces landed at **Guánica**, **Puerto Rico**, on 25 July. After the war many of the cabinet members stayed on and briefly served under the U.S. military government. The cabinet was abolished by Brig. Gen. **Guy V. Henry** in February 1899.

AUTONOMY. On 25 November 1897, Spain's government published three decrees that granted autonomy to **Cuba** and **Puerto Rico**. The decrees extended all the rights of peninsular Spaniards to Spanish citizens in the Antilles, applied Spain's electoral law to Cuba and Puerto Rico, and provided for the formation of parliaments in the islands, which were granted significant control over domestic concerns while Spain retained control over foreign relations and defense.

Prior to the outbreak of war against the United States in April 1898, Spain argued that autonomy was working, but the U.S. failure to take action against the Cuban insurgent **Junta** in New York City was impeding its complete success. In Puerto Rico it was more workable than in war-torn Cuba. However, most U.S. officials and newspapers dismissed autonomy as unworkable and unacceptable.

AUTONOMY RIOTS (12 JANUARY 1898). Riots against **autonomy** broke out in **Havana, Cuba**, on 12 January 1898, when a mob, organized by Spanish officers, attacked the offices of three pro-autonomy newspapers—*El Reconcentrado, La Discusión,* and *El Diario de la Marina.* Although all was quiet by 14 January, the "**yellow press**" depicted the riots as a revolution. The **McKinley administration** briefly considered sending a naval force to Havana, and a stormy U.S. congressional debate ensued. For many American politicians the riots were proof that autonomy in Cuba had already failed after less than two weeks of government.

In the United States the story played in papers across the country and shook public confidence in Spain's ability to cope with the **Cuban Revolt**. Papers such as the *Chicago Tribune, New York Journal, New York Sun,* and *New York World* frequently ran scare headlines calling for war, predicting revolution, or demanding that U.S. warships be sent to **Havana** to protect American lives and property, whereas the *New York Herald, Richmond Dispatch,* and *San Francisco Chronicle* cautioned the public against overreacting.

AUXILIARY NAVAL FORCES. Upon the outbreak of war, both the Spanish and U. S. navies scrambled for auxiliary ships to be used in coaling, dispatch work, repair, resupply, troop transport, and scouting. Such ships were chartered, donated, leased, or purchased by both navies. Spain acquired many from the **Transatlantic Company**, whereas the United States acquired many **yachts** from the wealthy, leased ocean liners, and incorporated tugboats and cutters from the **Revenue Cutter Service**.

AZCÁRRAGA Y PALMERO, MARCELO DE (1832–1915). Lieutenant general and senator for life who served various times as president of the Senate in the **Cortes**, interim president of the cabinet, and captain general of the **Spanish Army**. A member of the **Liberal-**

Conservative Party, Azcárraga, a career soldier who had fought in Mexico, Santo Domingo, and the Carlist Wars, served as minister of war in the conservative government of **Antonio Cánovas** and for a few weeks served as interim president of the cabinet after the assassination of Cánovas in August 1897, until replaced by **Práxedes M. Sagasta** on 4 October 1897. Consulted by Sagasta before he authorized the signing of the **Armistice Protocol** on 12 August 1898, Azcárraga replied that it was tragic that the Spanish troops in central and western **Cuba** had not been tested against the U.S. forces, but if the government was determined to sign, then he would support the effort for peace. When the Conde de las Almenas severely chastised the **Spanish Army** in the Cortes on 7 September 1898, he rose to defend the army, blaming the politicians for losing the war. After the war he served as interim president of the cabinet in 1901 and 1904 and retired from the army in 1904.

"AZORÍN." See **MARTÍNEZ Y RUIZ, JOSÉ**

—B—

BACON AMENDMENT. Introduced by Democratic Senator Augustus O. Bacon of Georgia on 11 January 1899, it disclaimed any intention to exercise permanent U.S. sovereignty, jurisdiction, or control over the **Philippines** and advocated recognition of an early Philippine independence. After vigorous debate, it was defeated in the Senate on 14 February, by a vote of 30–29, with Vice President **Garret Hobart** casting the tiebreaking vote.

BACOOR BAY, PHILIPPINES. An inlet on **Manila Bay** about ten miles south of **Manila**. Before the naval **Battle of Manila Bay** on 1 May 1898, the Spanish **gunboats** *General Lezo* and *Velasco* and the transport *Manila* were moored there for repairs. After the battle these ships were burned, except the *Manila*, which was captured. A small town named Bacoor was located near the bay, and in August 1898, it served as a temporary headquarters for **Emilio Aguinaldo** and his nationalist forces.

BADGER. (USN) Auxiliary **cruiser**, commanded by Comdr. A. S. Snow. Formerly the passenger steamer *Yumuri* of the Ward Line, it was purchased by the **U.S. Navy** on 19 April 1898 and assigned to the **Northern Patrol Squadron**. On 25 June, it moved to **Key West, Florida**, became part of the **North Atlantic Fleet**, and was used to patrol the Cuban coast and in convoy duty in the Caribbean. On 12

July, it was assigned to the **Eastern Squadron**. After being transferred to the **War Department** in 1900, it was returned to the navy in 1902 and served as a supply ship until transferred to mercantile service in 1907. It was converted into a barge in 1930.

La. 1889, com. 22 April 1898, dis. 4,784, hp. 3,200, sp. 16
Armament: 6–5″, 6–3pdr.
Cc. 836, comp. 235

BAGLEY, WORTH (1874–1898). Ensign (USN), second in command of the **torpedo boat *Winslow***. A U.S. Naval Academy graduate from Raleigh, North Carolina, he was killed in a naval engagement at **Cárdenas, Cuba**, on 11 May 1898. Bagley was the first and only U.S. naval officer killed by the Spanish during the war. Posthumously he achieved fame as over 2,000 soldiers and the entire community attended his funeral in Raleigh, North Carolina, and Josephus Daniels wrote *The First Fallen Hero: A Biographical Sketch of Worth Bagley* (1899). Bagley became a martyr for the cause of a **North-South Reunion**. The *Atlanta Constitution* commented, in its editorial "The First Blood of Two Wars" on 13 May 1898, that "the blood of this martyr freely spilled upon his country's altar seals effectively the covenant of brotherhood between North and South."

BAKER, EDWARD LEE JR. (1865–1913). Sergeant major, **Tenth U.S. Cavalry (colored)**. A veteran black American soldier who had served on the frontier with the **Ninth** and Tenth U.S. Cavalries, Baker fought in the **Battle of Las Guásimas** on 24 June 1898 and was wounded twice on 1 July in the assault on the **San Juan Heights**. He was awarded the **Congressional Medal of Honor** for saving a wounded comrade. His diary tells of the heroism of his fellow black soldiers. Later, as a captain in the Philippine Scouts, he served in the **Philippine Insurrection**, commanding the Forty-Ninth Volunteer Infantry (colored).

BALER, PHILIPPINES, SIEGE OF (1 JULY 1898–2 JUNE 1899). A somewhat remote coastal town on the island of Luzon in the province of Nueva Ecija became the site of one of the proudest moments in Spanish military history when an isolated group of 47 Spanish soldiers held out for 337 days before capitulating to Filipino insurgents. Initially under the command of Capt. Enrique de las Morenas, who died of **disease** on 22 November 1898, and then Lt. Saturnino Martín Cerezo, this small force came under attack by Filipino insurgents on 1 July 1898. Persevering against overwhelming odds, hunger, and disease, they continued to resist even after the Spanish-American War was over.

On 12 April 1899, a group of **marines** under a naval officer, Lt. James C. Gilmore, went out to relieve Baler, but the unit was ambushed by Filipino rebels and its members taken prisoner. The garrison, reduced to a mere 30 soldiers, eventually capitulated on 2 June 1899, on the condition that it be allowed to march out and return to Spain. **Emilio Aguinaldo** issued a decree in tribute to their gallantry and granted them safe conduct. Lt. Martín Cerezo later recounted the siege in his book *Under the Red and Gold: Being Notes and Recollections of the Siege of Baler* (1909).

BALFOUR, ARTHUR JAMES (1848–1930). Conservative leader of the House of Commons and acting foreign secretary of **Great Britain**. Frequently dealing with foreign affairs on his own initiative because of the absences of Prime Minister **Robert Cecil**, who was his uncle, Balfour consistently rejected Spanish overtures because he wanted future U.S. support for British interests in the Far East. He assured **John Hay**, U.S. ambassador to Great Britain, that all measures taken by Britain relating to the Cuban situation would first have to be acceptable to the United States. He also refused the request of **Julian Pauncefote**, British ambassador to Washington, for a second Great Power representation in Washington, D.C., to forestall war in April 1898 because he believed it would undermine President **William McKinley**.

BALLOON OPERATIONS AT SANTIAGO, CUBA. A balloon detachment, which was part of the **Signal Corps**, was ordered east from Fort Logan, Colorado, when the war began. Under the command of Lt. Col. **Joseph E. Maxfield**, the detachment, which consisted of the observation balloon *Santiago*, three officers, and 23 enlisted men, went to New York City, then to **Tampa, Florida**, where it was almost lost because of railroad congestion. The detachment went with the **Fifth Corps** on the transports *Rio Grande* and *Segurança* to **Daiquirí, Cuba**.

After the detachment disembarked on 28 June 1898, the balloon was immediately pressed into service. Moved to the front on 29 June on a train of six wagons, five of which carried 180 tubes of hydrogen gas, the torn and patched balloon ascended three times on 30 June. On 1 July, it accompanied U.S. troops in their attack on **San Juan Heights**. Towed by four enlisted men, the balloon, with both Maxfield and Lt. Col. **George M. Derby** aboard, was hauled down to treetop level as it moved through a forested area. Upon arriving within 650 yards of the heights, its guide ropes got tangled in the treetops, and the balloon, dangling 50 feet above the trees, immediately disclosed the U.S. line of march. Consequently, the Spanish troops on the heights poured a withering fire into the area. The balloon was shot out of the sky, and both Derby and Maxfield escaped unhurt.

Col. **Leonard Wood** later called the operation "one of the most ill-judged and idiotic acts" he had ever seen. But the balloon, during its brief flight, had discovered an unknown trail turning left (south) off the road, so the U.S. advance on the heights could continue. After his first balloon was shot out of the sky, Maxfield returned to Tampa to assemble another balloon unit, but the war ended before he could complete it. The detachment left **Santiago**, **Cuba**, on 23 August 1898, on the transport *Minnewaske* for **Camp Wikoff** at Montauk Point, Long Island, New York.

BALTIMORE. (USN) **Protected cruiser** commanded by Capt. Nehemiah M. Dyer. Previously serving as the flagship of the Pacific Station, it had been in **Hawaii** since October 1897, when on 25 March 1898, it left Honolulu with ammunition for the **Asiatic Squadron**. After reaching **Hong Kong** on 22 April, it sailed with Com. **George W. Dewey**'s squadron for the **Philippines**, where it fought in the naval **Battle of Manila Bay** on 1 May. During the battle it fired 1,434 shots while sustaining eight wounded; subsequently, its detachment of **marines** secured the arsenal at **Cavite**. On 3 May, together with the *Raleigh*, it compelled the surrender of the Spanish batteries at the bay's entrance. During the **Battle of Manila** on 13 August, it was stationed off **Manila**, opposite the Luneta batteries. After the war it remained on Asiatic Station until May 1900 and served as a minelayer in World War I. Decommissioned in 1922, it lay inactive at Pearl Harbor from 1922 to 1942, when it was sold.

La. 1888, com. 1890, dis. 4,413, hp. 10,064, sp. 20
Armor: d. 2.5″, sl. 4″, ct. 3″
Armament: 4–8″, 6–6″, 4–6pdr., 4–1pdr., 2 C. mgs.
Cc. 490, comp. 386

BANCROFT. (USN) **Gunboat** commanded by Comdr. **Richardson Clover**. Originally laid down as a barquentine-rigged training ship for the U.S. Naval Academy, it was used as a gunboat after 1896. Called home from the Mediterranean upon the outbreak of war, it was assigned to the North Atlantic Station. During the war it convoyed the **Fifth Corps** to **Daiquirí**, **Cuba**, served on **blockade** duty at **Havana** and the **Isle of Pines**, seized a small schooner on 28 July, and sustained one killed in an engagement on 2 August while trying to free a grounded Spanish schooner near Cortes Bay on the southern Cuban coast. After the war it served as a survey vessel in the Caribbean. Subsequently, it was transferred to the **Revenue Cutter Service** in 1906. It was scrapped in 1922.

La. 1892, com. 1893, dis. 839, hp. 1,213, sp. 14.5
Armor: d. 1/4–5/16″
Armament: 4–4″, 8–3pdr., 1–1pdr., 2–18″ tt. (aw.)
Cc. 139, comp. 148

BARBOSA, JOSÉ CELSO (1857–1921). Puerto Rican autonomist and later pro-statehood leader. After graduating from the University of Michigan with a medical degree, Barbosa, a descendant of African slaves, returned to **Puerto Rico** to practice medicine and became a leader in the autonomist movement. When the movement divided over the issue of fusion with Spain's **Liberal Party**, Barbosa, who had opposed the pact, helped form the **Orthodox-Historical Autonomist Party**. Briefly serving as a minority member in the **autonomous government**, he withdrew shortly before the U.S. invasion. In July 1898, Barbosa jovially received the news from Madrid newspapers that he had been executed by Spanish authorities for treason. By the end of August 1898, Barbosa was ardently advocating self-government and eventual Puerto Rican statehood, insisting that Puerto Ricans needed a preparatory period in order to learn self-government. To attain this goal, he helped found the Republican Party. He later served for ten years on the governor's Executive Council, established by the Foraker Act, and was elected to the Puerto Rican Senate.

BARBOSISTAS. Name given to the followers of **José Celso Barbosa**. Also known as *puros*, to distinguish them from the followers of **Luis Muñoz Rivera**, they won four seats out of 32 in the parliamentary elections of 27 March 1898. During the war they refused to participate in the insular parliament, which met from 17 July to 25 July 1898.

BARKER, ALBERT SMITH (1845–1916). Captain (USN), commanded the **cruiser** *Newark*. Barker, a U.S. Naval Academy graduate, was an initial member of the **Naval War Board** in March 1898. He soon left to command the *Newark*. While commanding the *Newark*, he participated in the bombardment of **Santiago, Cuba**, on 1 July 1898. In August 1898, Barker assumed command of the *Oregon* and later succeeded Adm. **George W. Dewey** as commander of the **Asiatic Squadron**. Promoted to rear admiral, he commanded the Atlantic Fleet from 1903 to 1905.

BARRETT, JOHN (1866–1938). U.S. minister to Siam (1894–1898). A former journalist, Barrett, who favored taking the **Philippines**, tried to join Com. **George W. Dewey**'s squadron for its journey to **Manila, Philippines**. After arriving in **Hong Kong** too late to join the squadron, he received a message from **William R. Hearst** asking him to report for the *New York Journal* during the war. Barrett accepted, also wrote for *Harper's Weekly*, and served as a diplomatic adviser to Adm. Dewey. A believer that the United States should carry the "White Man's Burden" in guiding Filipinos until they were ready for a large degree of self-government, Barrett wrote "The Value of the Philippines," *Munsey's Magazine* (August 1899). Later he served as a delegate to the Second Pan American Conference and as a U.S. minister to various Latin American countries. He directed the Pan American Union from 1907 to 1920.

BARTON, CLARA HARLOWE (1821–1912). As the founder and president of the **American Red Cross**, Barton led the Red Cross effort throughout the war. Barton, who had advocated Cuban independence so that it could "come to the United States," went to **Cuba** in early 1898 as part of the Central Cuban Relief Committee, which she had helped to establish to aid the victims of Spain's **reconcentration** policy. Working with Gov. Gen. **Ramón Blanco y Erenas**, Barton oversaw the distribution of supplies, particularly in the **Matanzas** area, aided wounded from the *Maine*, and left Cuba on 10 April 1898. She wrote about these efforts in "The Cuban Orphans," *Outlook* (12 August 1899) and in "Our Work and Observations in Cuba," *North American Review* (May 1898).

Upon the outbreak of war, Barton devoted all her attention to the Cuban theater. Hoping to arrange for the landing of supplies under a flag of truce, on 2 May she wrote to Adm. **William T. Sampson** requesting permission for the Red Cross to go to Cuba before the U.S. military. After Sampson denied her request, Barton aided Cuban refugees and Spanish **prisoners of war** at **Key West, Florida**.

In the wake of the landing of the **Fifth Corps** at **Daiquirí, Cuba**, Barton, along with Red Cross **nurses**, arrived at **Siboney** on the Red Cross chartered steamer *State of Texas* on 26 June. However, the army's head surgeon told her that her assistance was "not desired," so she offered her assistance to the Cuban insurgents and set up a field hospital. During the war she strictly censored all reporting on the Red Cross by requiring all **correspondents** to submit all letters and news copy to her. Any unfavorable news did not leave her *State of Texas* headquarters. After the war the U.S. Senate passed a resolution thanking her and the Red Cross for its service during the war. However, Barton, who had been unwilling to delegate responsibility, had widened the rift between the national Red Cross and its local chapters. She resigned in 1904.

BASQUE NATIONALIST PARTY (*PARTIDO NACIONALISTA VASCO*). Founded in 1894 under the leadership of **Sabino de Araña**

y Goiri, it was a Catholic conservative party working for an independent Basque state. Its main newspaper, *Bizkaitarra*, was closed down by the Spanish government, and its leaders were frequently jailed. Nevertheless, the party maintained an antiwar policy, harshly criticized Spain's overseas policy, and had four of its members elected to public office in Bilbao.

BATES, JOHN COALTER (1842–1919). Brigadier general (USV), commanded an independent brigade, Second Division, **Fifth Corps**. The Missouri-born son of Edward Bates, Lincoln's attorney general, Bates, a Civil War veteran, had spent 30 years on the frontier, attaining the rank of lieutenant colonel, when in May 1898, he was appointed a brigadier general (USV) and assigned to command what came to be known as **Bates's Independent Brigade**.

Bates supervised the landing at **Siboney, Cuba**, on 23 June and for a short time commanded Siboney. His brigade fought in the **Battle of El Caney** on 1 July. After the **capitulation** of **Santiago, Cuba**, Bates, now a major general (USV), commanded the Third Division of the Fifth Corps and was placed in charge of guarding thousands of captured Spanish soldiers. He signed the **Round Robin Letter** and briefly returned to the United States only to be reassigned to Cuba in command of U.S. forces in the Santa Clara district. Soon ordered to the **Philippines**, Bates fought in the **Philippine Insurrection**, and was later promoted to lieutenant general, becoming chief of staff of the **U.S. Army**.

BATES'S INDEPENDENT BRIGADE. Commanded by Brig. Gen. **John C. Bates** in the **Fifth Corps**. Consisting of 47 officers and 1,038 enlisted men of the **Third U.S. Infantry** and **Twentieth U.S. Infantry**, it fought in the **Battle of El Caney** on 1 July 1898, sustaining three killed and 11 wounded. On 2 July, while placed on the left of the U.S. line facing **Santiago, Cuba**, the brigade engaged the entrenched Spanish soldiers for two days, sustaining one killed and 18 wounded.

"BATTLE OF ANNISTON" (24 NOVEMBER 1898). After moving from Mobile, Alabama, to Camp Shipp near Anniston, Alabama, in early September 1898, the **Third Alabama Infantry**, a black volunteer regiment, was greeted with so much open hostility by white residents and soldiers that Col. **Robert E. Bullard** requested protection from the **War Department**. Finally, on 24 November 1898, black soldiers, fed up with the insults, attacked a group of whites. The ensuing fight, which came to be known as the "Battle of Anniston," left one black soldier dead and several soldiers and civilians wounded.

Although white officers of the Third Alabama said their men had resorted to violence because of accumulated grievances against the free-wheeling activities of white volunteers, Alabama Democratic Senator **John T. Morgan** condemned Alabama Gov. Joseph F. Johnston for putting "guns in the hands of negroes as soldiers" and for his policy of defending the nation's honor "with members of the dependent race."

BATTLESHIP. The principal fighting ship of the navies, it was more heavily armored than an **armored cruiser** and seldom exceeded 17 knots. U.S. battleships, which were armed with 12- and 13-inch guns, cost around $3 million to build and around $547,000 a year to maintain. Spain had one battleship, the *Pelayo*, and the United States had five: four first-class—the *Iowa*, *Indiana*, *Massachusetts*, and *Oregon*—and one second-class—the *Texas*.

BAY STATE. A hospital ship purchased for $50,000 and outfitted for $113,000 by the citizens of Boston and the Massachusetts Volunteer Aid Association for medical use. During the war the *Bay State* transported large amounts of medicines and stores furnished by the society and brought 336 ill soldiers back to the United States from **Santiago, Cuba**, and **Puerto Rico**. On 15 November 1898, it was sold to the U.S. government.

"BEEF COURT." Hoping to nullify the **Dodge Commission**'s findings against his **"embalmed beef"** accusations, Maj. Gen. **Nelson A. Miles**, stating that he had new evidence, asked President **William McKinley** to appoint a military court of inquiry on beef. The court, which came to be known as the "Beef Court," opened with Miles as the first witness on 20 February 1899. Miles produced no new evidence, repudiated former newspaper interviews, and altered so many of his statements that the court had a hard time figuring out what the charges were. The court issued its report on 29 April 1899. Although declaring that canned beef was wholesome, the report stated that its large-scale use in the tropics had been a "colossal error"; furthermore, it dismissed Miles's accusations of tainted refrigerated beef as groundless and severely criticized Miles for not having immediately reported his concerns about the beef and for not having "sufficient justification" for his allegations.

BELLIGERENT RIGHTS. During the **Cuban Revolt**, the "**yellow press**" and many politicians such as senators **Henry C. Lodge** and **John T. Morgan**, and Joseph W. Bailey, House of Representatives minority leader from Texas, supported the recognition of the belligerent rights of the Cuban insurgents. Such a recognition, which was not a recognition of Cuban independence, would have recognized the insurgents as a legitimate political force and allowed the United States to treat them as such. Although it would have allowed American arms merchants to legally supply the insurgents, such a recognition would have permitted Spain to stop and inspect U.S. ships on the high seas and absolved Spain from any obligation to protect U.S. property in **Cuba**. Overall, such a recognition was more of a political statement in support of the Cuban insurgents than a concrete measure to aid them because such a recognition would have extended few benefits to them that they did not already enjoy. Although many resolutions in support of such recognition were introduced into the **Congress** before the war, most were buried in the House of Representatives by Speaker of the House **Thomas B. Reed** and effectively opposed by the **Big Four** in the Senate and by the **Cleveland** and **McKinley administrations**.

BENJAMIN, ANNA NORTHEND (1874–1902). A magazine writer and lecturer. Benjamin, while reporting for *Leslie's Weekly* during the war, pointed out in "The Truth about Army Rations" (30 July 1898) that rations were insufficient for troops traveling to **Tampa, Florida**, and in "Yellow Fever at Key West" (28 July 1898), she reported that **yellow fever** was not a serious problem. When the **Fifth Corps** left Tampa, Florida, for **Daiquirí, Cuba**, on 14 June 1898, Benjamin was left behind because of the government's ban on women reporters in the war zone. After paying her own way on a collier, she arrived at **Guantánamo, Cuba**, where Capt. **Bowman McCalla**, not knowing what to do with a female reporter, sent her to **Santiago**. Benjamin arrived the day before the city capitulated and subsequently entered the harbor on the *State of Texas*. She later wrote about her experiences at Santiago in "The Darker Side of War," *Leslie's* (4 August 1898), and in "A Woman's Visit to Santiago," *Leslie's* (25 August 1898). While returning to New York on a transport, she served as a nurse, the only female nurse, to 111 soldiers and correspondents. Billed as a female war correspondent after the war, Benjamin became a popular lecturer and later went to the **Philippines** to cover the **Philippine Insurrection**.

BERMEJO Y MERELO, SEGISMUNDO (1832–1899). Rear admiral, Spanish minister of the marine (4 October 1897–16 May 1898). After entering the navy at the age of 14, Bermejo saw service in **Cuba** and the **Philippines** and served as the director of the Torpedo School, creating Spain's first division of **torpedo boats**. A multilingual author, he thought **Valeriano Weyler y Nicolau** should not have been recalled, because if the **Cuban Revolt** had been quelled by Weyler, then **autonomy** might have been accepted.

Before becoming minister of the marine, Bermejo commanded the squadron at Cádiz until replaced by his friend Adm. **Pascual Cervera y Topete**. In February and March 1898, with war approaching, he corresponded with Cervera and expressed his confidence in the **Spanish Navy** and deprecated the **U.S. Navy**, calling U.S. sailors mercenaries and pointing out that they were of many different nationalities. When Cervera wrote that Bermejo's plans for blockading the U.S. Atlantic coast and destroying **Key West**, **Florida**, were dreams, Bermejo remained optimistic; nevertheless, he never let Cervera's warnings get past his desk to others in the government. On 13 March, the navy began to deploy according to his plan of retaining one squadron to protect Spain while another was to be sent to Cuba. Accordingly, on 23 April 1898, he ordered Adm. **Cervera's Squadron** to the West Indies.

After Spain's overwhelming defeat at the naval **Battle of Manila Bay** on 1 May, Bermejo came under severe criticism. Although he sent a message on 12 May allowing Adm. Cervera to return to Spain, Bermejo was soon replaced as minister of the marine by Capt. **Ramón Auñón y Villalón**, who canceled the order.

BERNADOU, JOHN BAPTISTE (1858–1908). Lieutenant (USN), commanded the **torpedo boat** *Winslow*. A U.S. Naval Academy graduate, Bernadou was wounded in the engagement at **Cárdenas, Cuba**, on 11 May 1898 and advanced ten numbers in rank for gallantry. He later wrote about the engagement in "The *Winslow* at Cárdenas," *The Century Magazine* (March 1899). After the war he was promoted to commander, worked in the Bureau of Ordnance, and authored several treatises.

BETANCES, RAMÓN EMETERIO (1827–1898). Puerto Rican independence leader. An abolitionist and physician trained in **France**, Betances had been banished several times for his outspoken advocacy of Puerto Rican independence since the 1850s. While exiled to the Dominican Republic, he established a Puerto Rican Revolutionary Committee, which eventually became a section of the **Cuban Revolutionary Party**. Later, while in exile in Paris, France, he was named general delegate of the Puerto Rican Section of the Cuban Revolutionary Party. He always insisted that the Cuban and Puerto Rican independence struggles should be combined. An ardent activist, Betances sent agents into Spain to lead demonstrations, rejected Spanish bribes and offers of **autonomy**, and met with the anarchist who later assassinated Spanish Prime Minister **Antonio Cánovas del Castillo**

in August 1897. After the Spanish-American War began, he wrote, on 1 July 1898, to Dr. **José Julio Henna**, advocating that Puerto Ricans rise up so that **Puerto Rico** would be independent before U.S. troops landed. Because if they did not, Betances was convinced Puerto Rico would be a U.S. colony forever. After the U.S. conquest of the island, he was one of the few to urge armed resistance. He died the same year in Paris, France.

BEVERIDGE, ALBERT JEREMIAH (1862–1927). Ardent expansionist and Republican senator from Indiana (1899–1911). A lawyer who believed that the United States was God's chosen nation to bring Christianity to the world, Beveridge, an eloquent orator and advocate of Anglo-Saxon superiority, called the Teutonic peoples the "master organizers of the world." Upon the outbreak of the war against Spain, he advocated the immediate seizure of the **Philippines** as a gateway to the China market. After the **Armistice Protocol** of 12 August 1898, he continued to champion American expansion, calling the war against Spain a "holy" war, "a war for civilization," and a war that had opened "to the republic the portals of the commerce of the world." On 16 September 1898, during his campaign for the Senate, Beveridge made a speech at Indianapolis, Indiana, in which he stated "Hawaii is ours, Porto Rico is to be ours; at the prayer of her people Cuba finally will be ours." Three hundred thousand copies of the speech were distributed in an attempt to influence President **William McKinley** during the **Treaty of Paris** negotiations. After he won election to the Senate, Beveridge toured the Philippines in November 1899 and returned to the United States still justifying the American conquest and urging the United States to civilize the Filipinos.

BIAK-NA-BATÓ, PHILIPPINES. A town 30 miles from **Manila**, which served as **Emilio Aguinaldo**'s headquarters in late 1897. Here Aguinaldo reinstituted guerrilla warfare since his insurgent forces had suffered reverses in the summer of 1897. On 1 November 1897, a constituent assembly was convened and approved a revolutionary constitution that established the same day what came to be known as the Biak-na-bató Republic. Aguinaldo served as president of the republic until the signing of the **Pact of Biak-na-bató** in December 1897.

"BIG FOUR." A group of Republican senators who successfully blocked attempts at granting **belligerent rights** or other recognition of the Cuban insurgents. It included Nelson W. Aldrich (Rhode Island), William B. Allison (Iowa), Orville H. Platt (Connecticut), and John C. Spooner (Wisconsin). Sometimes they were referred to as the

"Big Six" when Republican Senators **Marcus A. Hanna** (Ohio) and **George F. Hoar** (Massachusetts) were included.

BIGELOW, JOHN JR. (1854–1936). Captain, commanded D Troop in the **Tenth U.S. Cavalry**. A West Point graduate and brother of journalist **Poultney Bigelow**, John Bigelow was a veteran of frontier Indian campaigns and a professor of military science at MIT from 1894 to 1898. He was severely wounded in the taking of the **San Juan Heights** on 1 July 1898. Later in his book *Reminiscences of the Santiago Campaign* (1899), he described the battles of 1 July as "uncoordinated bravery" on the part of his black soldiers, who advanced without any commands. He extolled the record of black American troops in **Cuba**, which he felt had enhanced "the self-respect and stimulated the aspirations" of all black citizens, and claimed the lack of discretion and subtlety in race relations by white Floridians was the principal cause of friction with black troops. After the war he retired at his own request.

BIGELOW, POULTNEY (1855–1954). Correspondent for *Harper's Weekly* and the *Times* (London) during the war. Born into a newspaper family, his father was the managing editor of the *New York Evening Post*. Bigelow, the brother of Capt. **John Bigelow**, was on the farcical *Gussie* **Expedition**. But he achieved fame and condemnation when he reported the truth on 28 May 1898 from **Tampa, Florida**, about the **Fifth Corps**. Although he praised the patriotism and qualities of the individual soldier and officer, he criticized the competency of senior officers, pointed out that political influence was rampant, and cited a complete lack of adequate supplies because of mismanagement and Tampa's lack of sufficient railroad lines. His report set off a national firestorm of criticism that questioned his patriotism and resulted in his losing his credentials to travel as a correspondent with the **army** to **Cuba**. Nevertheless, Bigelow continued to write, frequently criticizing **Theodore Roosevelt** and the **volunteer** armed forces while supporting the regular army.

BIVINS, HORACE WAYMAN (1862–1937). Sergeant in G Troop, **Tenth U.S. Cavalry**. Born to slave parents in Virginia, Bivins later reported in his *A Narrative Written during the Cuban Campaign* (1899) the ovations by crowds throughout the North as the Tenth Cavalry moved to **Camp Thomas**. Even though race problems arose as the regiment entered the South, it was cheered by crowds of blacks and whites in Nashville, Tennessee. Together with his full-blooded Irish water spaniel named Booth, Bivins went with the **Fifth Corps** to **Daiquirí, Cuba**, in command of the regiment's Hotchkiss guns.

An ardent advocate of black patriotism, on 22 June 1898, while off the southern Cuban coast delivering supplies to Cuban insurgents, he wrote a letter to a friend stating, "There is no people on earth more loyal and devoted to their country than the Negro." During the **Battle of San Juan Hill** on 1 July, Bivins was wounded while operating a Hotchkiss gun alone after the other men of his unit had been wounded. After the battle, he planted one of the flags given to him by the women of Madison, Wisconsin, on the crest of San Juan Hill. Commended for his bravery, Bivins remained in the trenches at the front until **Santiago** capitulated on 17 July 1898. By 26 July, he was sick with dysentery and thought almost dead; nevertheless, he returned to duty on 10 August and left **Cuba** a few days later for **Camp Wikoff** at Montauk Point, Long Island, New York. Bivins later saw service in the **Philippine Insurrection**.

BLACK AMERICAN NEWSPAPERS. Although most black newspapers approved of the insurgent struggle to free **Cuba** from the Spanish, they were generally wary of a possible war against Spain until the *Maine* disaster. Upon the outbreak of the war against Spain, the *New York City New York Age*, edited by Timothy Thomas Fortune, and the *Washington D.C., Colored American*, edited by Edward E. Cooper, supported the war effort, arguing that black participation would certainly bestow benefits. Even antiexpansionist or antiwar papers such at the *Kansas City American Citizen*, edited by George Dudley, the *Washington Bee*, edited by William C. Chase, and the *Richmond Planet*, edited by John Mitchell Jr., counseled their readers to support the war effort, arguing that all loyal citizens must do their duty. A few papers, such as *Parson's Weekly Blade*, edited by Monroe Dorsey, and the *Cleveland Gazette*, edited by Harry C. Smith, remained adamantly opposed to the war.

During the war the papers regularly received letters directly from soldiers who openly aired their successes and complaints, and black emigration schemes to the newly won lands filled the pages of the *Topeka, Kansas, Colored Citizen*. However, most newspapers began to question the war on the basis of race. As blacks were denied commissions, William C. Chase called the war a "Jim Crow War," and John Mitchell Jr. began a highly publicized and supported "no officers, no fight" campaign. Beginning with the annexation of **Hawaii** in July, more papers criticized the fact that a war to liberate Cuba had turned into a war of conquest, a point of view that exploded in black newspapers throughout the United States upon the outbreak of the **Philippine Insurrection** and was bolstered by the argument that the United States could not deal humanely with minorities at home much less abroad.

BLACK AMERICAN REGULAR SOLDIERS, U.S. ARMY. Although they fought in a segregated army that prohibited their becoming officers, black soldiers were overwhelmingly patriotic. All four of the regular army units, which included the **Ninth** and **Tenth U.S. Cavalry** and the **Twenty-Fourth** and **Twenty-Fifth U.S. Infantry**, were commanded by white officers and fought in the **Santiago, Cuba, campaign,** earning five **Congressional Medals of Honor** and 26 certificates of merit. There were no black artillery units.

BLACK AMERICAN VOLUNTEER SOLDIERS, U.S. ARMY. Upon President **William McKinley**'s first call for 125,000 **volunteers** on 23 April 1898, **black Americans** rushed to volunteer. Recruiting stations were established and mass meetings held; however, blacks' participation quickly became a political issue. The size of most preexisting black militia units, which belonged to separate or unattached battalions and companies, posed a problem because, unless a state's quota included units of less than regimental strength, their admission would require consolidation of black and white units to form mixed regiments. Few governors were willing to do this. Many simply refused to accept black volunteers and rejected all requests by black militia units to be mobilized. And although a few individuals served in white volunteer units in Maine and Iowa, almost all who were accepted for service were segregated into all-black units.

Initially, only three states had black units available for duty. These included the **Third Alabama Infantry,** Company L of the otherwise all-white **Sixth Massachusetts Infantry,** and the **Ninth Ohio Infantry Battalion**. A second call for 75,000 volunteers on 25 May 1898, saw the admission of more units because of President McKinley's pressuring various governors, or from the failure of whites to fill their state's quota. Republican governor Daniel L. Russell mustered in the **Third North Carolina Infantry,** and four other states mustered in black units for the first time: the **Eighth Illinois Infantry,** First Indiana Infantry, **Twenty-Third Kansas Infantry,** and **Sixth Virginia Infantry**. All totaled, around 10,000 black Americans entered the volunteer army, either serving in their state's unit or in the federally sponsored "**immune**" regiments; however, only Company L of the Sixth Massachusetts saw combat during the war. After the war the Eighth Illinois, Twenty-Third Kansas, and the Ninth Immunes were dispatched to **Cuba** as part of the U.S. occupation army.

A particularly contentious issue during the war was the call initiated by John Mitchell Jr., editor of the *Richmond Planet*, for black officers for black units. Mitchell's theme was taken up by blacks across the country; however, only three volunteer units had complete rosters of black commissioned officers: the Eighth Illinois, the

Twenty-Third Kansas, and the Third North Carolina. Although some blacks were promoted in the "immune" regiments, these were temporary promotions. Eventually 259 blacks would hold commissions; yet, with the mustering out of the last black volunteers in May 1899, no black held a commission except for Lt. **Charles Young** and several chaplains. Also, governors across the South abolished the black companies of their state militias, and many volunteers returned home only to lose the right to vote.

BLACK AMERICANS. At a time of increasing segregation, most of the 7.5 million black Americans sympathized with the independence struggles in **Cuba** and the **Philippines** and were quick to emphasize the racial kinship with Cuba's fight for independence with their own struggle for first-class citizenship. The prospect of a full-fledged war with Spain after the *Maine* disaster, in which 22 black Americans died, marked a turning point in their attitude, and although most believed it was their civic obligation to serve in the event of war, they began to question how such a war would affect their status at home.

Upon the outbreak of war, the sight of black troops going to war momentarily united the community, and most black Americans, like **Booker T. Washington** and the members of the **Pinchback Delegation** offered their support and organized committees to coordinate the enlistment of the thousands who rushed to volunteer. Although many argued that patriotic black participation would bestow benefits upon black Americans, most agreed with the pragmatic words of the editor of the *Wisconsin Weekly Advocate*, who wrote on 9 July 1898, "It is highly probable that out of the nation's necessity will spring the race's opportunity and from between the dragons teeth of cruel war may be wrung concessions that years of sulking could never bring about. At least it is the Negro's business to be on the safe side."

However, when the war turned into a war of conquest, opposition quickly grew, especially over the issue of retaining the Philippines. Vocal critics included clergymen, such as African Methodist Episcopal Church Bishops Henry McNeal Turner and Alexander Walters, lawyer Frederick L. McGhee of Minnesota, newspaper editors John Mitchell Jr. of the *Richmond Planet* and William C. Chase of the *Washington Bee*, scholars William S. Scarborough of Wilberforce University and Kelly Miller of Howard University, poet Paul L. Dunbar, and Booker T. Washington.

BLACK POWDER. A holdover from the Civil War, it was considered archaic because of its corrosive nature and the clouds of smoke it emitted after being ignited, which obscured vision and revealed troop and artillery positions. Nevertheless, because of a shortage of modern weapons and ammunition at the onset of the war, U.S. military forces were forced to use black powder in many of their naval guns, artillery, and almost all rifles for the volunteer forces. The Spanish-American War was the last sizable war to use black powder.

BLANCO Y ERENAS, RAMÓN (1836–1906). Lieutenant general, Spanish captain general, and governor general of **Cuba**. Blanco, the Marqués de Peña Plata, was a career soldier who fought in Santo Domingo, the **Philippines**, and the Carlist Wars. He served as captain general of Cataluña, governor general of Cuba (1879–1881), and governor general of the Philippines (1893–1896). During his tenure in the Philippines, Blanco undertook a policy that was viewed as too moderate by Spaniards, especially the friars living in the Philippines. Consequently, he was replaced by Lt. Gen. **Camilo García de Polavieja y del Castillo** on 13 December 1896.

After assuming the position of governor general of Cuba on 31 October 1897, Blanco announced he had come to offer self-government, replaced Lt. Gen. **Valeriano Weyler y Nicolau**, issued an amnesty proclamation on 8 November 1897, assumed a defensive military posture, and oversaw the establishment of an **autonomous government**. Prior to the war against the United States, Blanco pressured the Spanish government to send Adm. **Pascual Cervera's Squadron** to Cuba, and upon the outbreak of war, he issued a proclamation on 23 April calling the people to arms and blaming the United States for the war. After Cervera's Squadron arrived at **Santiago, Cuba**, on 19 May, he demanded that it remain in Cuba, predicting a possibly fatal shattering of public morale if it left.

Shortly before the beginning of the land campaign of the U.S. **Fifth Corps** at Santiago, Blanco wrote to Cuban insurgent commander Maj. Gen. **Máximo Gómez y Báez** about an alliance against the United States. His offer was immediately rejected by Gómez. On 24 June, he was given supreme command of all Spanish land and naval forces in Cuba. On 1 July, Blanco ordered Cervera's Squadron to breakout of Santiago. So confident was he of a successful breakout, that on 3 July, the day of the **Naval Battle of Santiago**, Blanco sent a telegram to the military commander at **Cienfuegos, Cuba**, advising him to prepare for the squadron's arrival and to congratulate Cervera on his victory. After learning of Cervera's disastrous defeat, Blanco cabled Cervera through Washington, D.C., calling him and his men "heroic defenders of the Fatherland."

In spite of Cervera's disastrous defeat and the critical situation at a besieged Santiago, Blanco reported to the government that even though most of the Cuban people were sympathetic to the United States, the army was loyal and ready to continue the fight. After the government responded on 12 July that peace was imperative, he polled 18 generals about negotiations and reported to Spain on 14 July that although the army wished to continue the war, it would accept the government's decision.

BLISS, TASKER HOWARD (1853–1930). Lieutenant colonel (USV), chief of staff in Brig. Gen. **James H. Wilson**'s First Division in the **Puerto Rican campaign**. A West Point graduate, Bliss had taught at West Point and at the **Naval War College**, and served as a special assistant to the secretary of war and as a military attache to Madrid (1897–1898), where he served as the chief advisor to U.S. Minister Gen. **Stewart L. Woodford**. Prior to the war, Bliss counseled caution and attempted to prevent a conflict with Spain.

With war imminent, Bliss was recalled, promoted to lieutenant colonel, and went to **Puerto Rico** along with Brig. Gen. James H. Wilson's forces, where he personally carried the news of the **Armistice Protocol** of 12 August to Spanish troops at the Asomante Hills. He was promoted to colonel on 12 August 1898 and served on the board of officers that selected campsites for U.S. occupation troops in **Cuba**. As chief of the Cuban Customs Service (December 1898–May 1902), Bliss rooted out corruption. After serving as the first commandant of the newly established Army War College in 1903, Bliss was promoted to major general, served as chief of staff of the U.S. Army, and was a delegate to the Versailles Peace Conference that ended World War I.

BLOCKADE. Under international law an officially declared blockade was an act of war, which to have legal force, had to be both declared and effective. During the war the United States officially declared blockades of selective Cuban and Puerto Rican ports. However, Spain, which had issued decrees on blockading along with its **declaration of war** on 23 April, consistently challenged the legality of the U.S. blockades, declaring that they were both ineffective and illegal on the basis that many of the northern Cuban ports had been declared blockaded even before the official U.S. declaration of war on 25 April 1898. On 26 April President **William McKinley** issued a proclamation on the rules of blockading. Significantly, the laws pertaining to **prizes of war** made blockade duty profitable because ships and cargoes obtained through blockade duty were often sold and the money divided among the crew of the capturing vessel.

BLOCKADE OF CUBA. With the goal of preventing Spain from reinforcing and resupplying its army and to avoid an extensive deployment of U.S. troops, Secretary of the Navy **John D. Long** issued a detailed plan on 23 March 1898 to close the western half of **Cuba**'s northern coast. It was followed on 18 April by Capt. **William T. Sampson**'s memorandum detailing the duties for U.S. naval forces and on 21 April by President **William McKinley**'s proclamation, which declared a **blockade** of the northern Cuban coast from Cárdenas to Bahía Honda.

Later written about by **Stephen Bonsal** in "How the War Began. With the Blockading Fleet Off Cuba," *McClure's Magazine* (June 1898), Adm. William T. Sampson's ships left **Key West, Florida**, on 22 April, and the blockade began when the first Spanish ship, the *Buenaventura*, was captured off Key West by the U.S. **gunboat** *Nashville*. By 23 April, U.S. ships were blockading Cabañas, Cárdenas, **Havana**, Mariel, and **Matanzas**. On 27 April, a desultory blockade of **Cienfuegos** on the southern coast began. However, owing to the lack of ships, the United States was unable to maintain a continuous blockade of the more easterly ports on the northern coast, and this forced McKinley to withhold a blockade proclamation of the southern coast until 28 June, when, seeking to end blockade running into Cuba from **Mexico** and Central America, McKinley extended the blockade to the southern Cuban coast. Nevertheless, ports such as Caibarién, Cayo Frances, Nuevitas, Sagua la Grande, and **Santiago** were never declared blockaded.

By early May, Spain declared the blockade ineffective, because ships were entering and leaving supposedly blockaded ports. Moreover, Com. **John A. Howell**, who was later in charge of blockading the northern Cuban coast, had only 14 ships to watch 400 miles of coastline. Nevertheless, no less than 15 engagements between U.S. naval forces and Spanish ships and land forces took place at Cuban ports other than Santiago during the war, and although the exploits of blockade runners such as the *Montserrat* were lionized by the Spanish press, a significant number of ships were captured and others, such as the *Alfonso XII*, were destroyed while trying to run the blockade.

Although the United States was compelled to abandon the blockade of Havana and several other ports frequently for other duties such as the search for Adm. **Cervera's Squadron**, Spain was unable to capitalize on this because of its naval weakness. Consequently, the blockade imposed hardship, cut off some supplies, and only a few ships succeeded in blockade running. Had the war lasted longer it would have caused widespread deprivation inside Cuba.

BLOCKADE OF MANILA, PHILIPPINES. Although President **William McKinley** never officially proclaimed a **blockade**, Com. **George W. Dewey**, immediately following the **Battle of Manila Bay** on 1 May 1898, instituted a blockade of **Manila**. From 1 May until

13 August 1898, Dewey's naval forces maintained a rigid blockade to cut off Manila from outside assistance. All ports remained closed, and trade between Manila and the outside world came to a standstill.

Problems arose with the arrival of German naval units in June, and on 11 July, Dewey claimed full powers to identify all warships entering **Manila Bay**, maintaining that ships' flags were not sufficient because false flags had been a common ruse. Both the German commander, Vice Adm. **Otto von Diederichs**, and the British commander, Capt. **Edward Chichester**, acknowledged the U.S. right to identify ships in the bay but denied that a blockading belligerent could board a neutral warship to establish its identity. Dewey subsequently backed down while maintaining the right to communicate with any vessel.

After 13 August, Dewey opened the port of Manila, and major coastal ports were opened to international commerce as they came under U.S. control. However, the prospect of conflict with **Emilio Aguinaldo**'s nationalist forces prompted the navy to restrict interisland trade that could support Filipino military units. Consequently, only six ports were opened to international trade by 26 December 1899.

BLOCKADE OF SANTIAGO, CUBA. Although the United States never officially proclaimed it blockaded, **Santiago** was visited by few Spanish ships after the outbreak of war. Beginning with the arrival of the **Flying Squadron** on 28 May, the **blockade** was sealed with the arrival of Adm. **William T. Sampson**'s force on 1 June. Sampson divided his force into two divisions. The eastern division was under the command of Sampson and consisted of Sampson's flagship the *New York*, the **battleships *Iowa*** and *Oregon*, the **cruiser *New Orleans***, the **torpedo boat *Porter***, and armed **yacht *Mayflower***. The western division, under the command of Com. **Winfield S. Schley**, consisted of Schley's flagship the ***Brooklyn***, the battleships *Massachusetts* and *Texas*, the cruiser *Marblehead*, and the yacht *Vixen*.

Putting his fastest ships on his flanks, Sampson placed his force in a semicircle facing the harbor entrance, maintaining a distance of six miles from the entrance during the day and moving closer at night. After beginning the bombardment of shore-based fortifications on 6 June, Sampson modified his blockade on the night of 8 June by using the battleships' **searchlights** to illuminate the harbor entrance.

Immediately following the **Naval Battle of Santiago** on 3 July 1898, the British man of war *Pallas* and the Austrian ship *María Teresa* were allowed to carry their respective subjects out of Santiago. The blockade came to an end with the **capitulation** of Santiago on 17 July 1898.

BLUE, VICTOR (1865–1928). Lieutenant (USN) on the converted **yacht** *Suwanee*. A U.S Naval Academy graduate from North Carolina, Blue, an engineer, was involved in a 31 May 1898 effort to land munitions for Cuban insurgents. He later volunteered for two scouting missions at **Santiago, Cuba**. From 11 June until 13 June, Blue, in uniform and wearing his sword so as not to be confused as a spy, went ashore after the sighting of the **"Ghost Squadron"** and verified the presence of all of Adm. **Cervera's Squadron** in Santiago harbor. His report allowed the **Fifth Corps** to leave **Tampa, Florida**, for Santiago, Cuba. From 25 June until 27 June, he went ashore again and verified the position of each of Cervera's ships for a projected **torpedo** attack. After the **capitulation** of Santiago on 17 July, Blue was assigned to command the former Spanish **gunboat** *Alvarado*. Promoted five numbers for "extraordinary heroism" during the war, Blue was later the chief of the Bureau of Navigation (1913–1916) and was promoted to rear admiral.

BONIFACIO, ANDRÉS (1863–1897). Filipino revolutionary who founded the **Katipunan** on 7 July 1892. Espousing radical change, Bonifacio became the Katipunan's president on 1 January 1896. He penned a compendium *The Duties of the Sons of the People* (1896) and issued the "Cry of Balintawak," calling Filipinos to armed revolt against Spain in August 1896. Due to internal divisions in the revolutionary movement, **Emilio Aguinaldo** ordered his arrest, and despite Aguinaldo's commutation of his death sentence, Bonifacio was executed, along with his brother Procopio, by order of Gen. Mariano Noriel on 10 May 1897.

BONSAL, STEPHEN (1865–1951). Correspondent and writer. A widely traveled correspondent, Bonsal served in the U.S. diplomatic corps in Korea, Madrid, Peking, and Tokyo before signing on with the *New York Herald* and *Harper's Weekly* to cover the **Cuban Revolt**. Upon returning from **Cuba** in April 1897, he testified to the Senate Foreign Relations Committee and later in the year published *The Real Condition of Cuba Today* (1897), in which he severely criticized Spain's **reconcentration** policy. During the war, Bonsal, writing for *McClure's Magazine*, was on the *Gussie* **Expedition**, attended the **Aserraderos Conference** on 20 June 1898, and covered the **Santiago, Cuba, campaign** of the **Fifth Corps** in "The Fight for Santiago. An Account of an Eye-witness," *McClure's Magazine* (October 1898) and "The Night after San Juan. Stories of the Wounded on the Field and in the Hospital," *McClure's Magazine* (December 1898). After the war Bonsal wrote *The Fight for Santiago: The Story of the Soldier in the Cuban Campaign, from Tampa to the Surrender* (1899), in which he extolled the bravery of **black American regular soldiers**. He also wrote a fiction novel, *The Golden Horseshoe* (1900), as a plea for benevolent imperialism, and served as President Woodrow Wilson's interpreter at the Versailles Peace Conference that ended World War I.

BOSTON. (USN) **Protected cruiser** commanded by Capt. Frank Wildes. As part of the original **Asiatic Squadron**, the *Boston* fought in the naval **Battle of Manila Bay** on 1 May 1898, was hit four times, fired 1,086 shots, and sustained one wounded. During the **Battle of Manila** of 13 August, it was stationed off the city's front, opposite the Luneta batteries. Returning to San Francisco in August 1899, it was later used as a training vessel for the Oregon Naval Militia (1911–1916) and as a receiving ship at Mare Island in San Francisco Bay from 1918 until 1946. On 8 April 1946, it was towed out to sea and sunk off the coast of San Francisco.

La. 1884, com. 1887, dis. 3,189, hp. 4,030, sp. 15.6
Armor: d. 1.5″, b. 2″
Armament: 2–8″, 6–6″, 2–6pdr., 2–3pdr., 2–1pdr.
Cc. 490, comp. 278

BREAKFAST MYTH. Resulting from a dispatch by **Joseph L. Stickney**, an eyewitness to the naval **Battle of Manila Bay** on 1 May 1898, it was initially believed that a confident Com. **George W. Dewey**, after the initial phase of the battle, had ordered that his men be given breakfast. The myth was later discounted by Lt. Carlos G. Calkins, the navigating officer of the *Olympia*, in his "Historical and Professional Notes on the Naval Campaign of Manila" and "Naval Campaign of Manila Bay" in *Proceedings of the Naval Institute* (June 1899). In fact, Dewey, after being informed about a shortage of ammunition, had ordered a pause to ascertain the correctness of the report. During this pause, Dewey ordered that his men be given something to eat, and upon learning that the report was false, he ordered his squadron to return to battle.

BRECKINRIDGE, JOSEPH CABELL (1842–1920). Major general (USV) and inspector general of the **U.S. Army** (1889–1904). Breckinridge left his administrative duties to go to **Santiago, Cuba**, with the **Fifth Corps**. During the fighting on 2 July 1898, he had his horse shot out from under him. Upon returning to the United States, Breckinridge was ordered to restore order at **Camp Thomas**. Consequently, he took command of the **First Corps** on 2 August 1898 and commanded Camp Thomas until its practical abandonment in September 1898. He then moved his forces to Lexington, Kentucky, and was relieved of command on 20 October 1898 by Maj. Gen. **James H. Wilson**. His support of his old friend Maj. Gen. **Nelson A. Miles** during the **"Embalmed Beef" controversy** ruined his reputation, and he retired in 1904. In analyzing the war, Breckinridge pointed out that the Cuban insurgents, who had little organization, needed to be supervised by U.S. officers to fully perform a specific duty. Moreover, bayonets had been useless while **smokeless powder** was an absolute necessity. He praised **black American regular soldiers** for their courage under fire.

BRODIE, ALEXANDER OSWALD (1849–1918). Major in the **Rough Riders**. Upon the outbreak of war, Brodie, a West Point graduate, Arizona cattleman, miner, Indian fighter, and former Yavapai County official, tried to get his own volunteer regiment accepted. However, he soon joined the Rough Riders and went with the **Fifth Corps** to **Daiquirí, Cuba**. He was wounded while commanding the left flank during the **Battle of Las Guásimas** on 24 June 1898. After being promoted to lieutenant colonel on 11 August 1898, Brodie returned to Arizona and served as governor.

BROOKE, JOHN RUTTER (1838–1926). Major general, commanded the **First Corps** (16 May–23 July 1898). Upon the outbreak of war, Brooke, a Civil War veteran, assumed command of both **Camp Thomas** at Chickamauga, Georgia, and the First Corps. Reassigned to the **Puerto Rican Campaign**, his 5,000-man force left Newport News, Virginia on 28 July and began landing at **Arroyo, Puerto Rico**, on 3 August. Commanding the right flank in the U.S. advance across the island, his force fought a sharp skirmish at **Guayama** on 5 August and advanced northwest in an attempt to cut off the Spanish retreat from **Ponce** and isolate the Spanish troops at Aibonito.

After the war, Brooke chaired the Puerto Rican **evacuation commission**, and after taking official possession of **San Juan, Puerto Rico**, on 18 October 1898, he served as the military governor of **Puerto Rico** until 9 December 1898. During his tenure, Brooke allowed former **autonomous government** officials to remain in power and appointed a new supreme court. He then served as the first military governor of **Cuba**, receiving the formal Spanish **capitulation** in **Havana** on 1 January 1899. Brooke reorganized the island's government, initiated a huge relief effort to help the sick and hungry, and negotiated the dismantling of the **Cuban Revolutionary Army**. He was succeeded by Maj. Gen. **Leonard Wood** on 13 December 1899.

BROOKLYN. (USN) **Armored cruiser** commanded by Capt. **Francis A. Cook**. Having an improved design over the *New York*, it commanded greater offensive power than any other armored cruiser at the time of its commissioning and incorporated the use of electrically operated turrets. During the war the *Brooklyn* served as the flagship in the **Flying Squadron** of Com. **Winfield S. Schley**. The fastest U.S. ship in the **Naval Battle of Santiago** on 3 July 1898, it overtook the *Cristóbal Colón*. Firing 1,973 shots during the battle, it was hit about 25 times, sustaining the only American casualties: one dead (Chief Yeoman G. H. Ellis) and one wounded (Fireman J. Burns). Later, Pvt. Harry L. MacNeal (USMC) was awarded the **Congressional Medal of Honor** for his conduct during the battle. After the war the *Brooklyn* served as the flagship of the **Asiatic Squadron** and later went to **France** to bring back the body of John Paul Jones. It was decommissioned at Mare Island, San Francisco on 9 March 1921 and sold.

La. 1895, com. 1896, dis. 9,215, hp. 18,700, sp. 21.9
Armor: s. 3″, d. 3″, sl. 6″, b. 8 & 4″, t. 5.5″, ct. 8.5″
Armament: 8–8″, 12–5″, 12–6pdr., 4–1pdr., 4 C. mgs., 4 tt. (aw.)
Cc. 1,461, comp. 480

THE *BRUIX* INCIDENT (5 MAY 1898). At the same time as the *Bruix*, a French **armored cruiser** coming from Saigon, was arriving at **Manila Bay, Philippines**, on 5 May, the *McCulloch*, which was carrying Com. **George W. Dewey**'s dispatches to **Hong Kong**, and the *Boston* and the *Concord* were leaving the bay. When the *Bruix* appeared beyond the island of Corregidor, its flag could not be made out by the U.S. ships and its hull was painted black like a warship. The *Boston* quickly opened fire. After the wind shifted, the *Bruix*'s flag was seen and the firing ceased.

BRUMBY, THOMAS MASON (1855–1899). Flag lieutenant (USN) on the *Olympia*. A U.S. Naval Academy graduate, Brumby had been at the Naval Observatory and the **Naval War College** before being assigned to the *Olympia* in January 1898. While serving as Com. **George W. Dewey**'s flag lieutenant, he was sent by Dewey to German Vice Adm. **Otto von Diederichs** to complain about perceived German violations of the **blockade of Manila**, witnessed Dewey threatening war with **Germany** over the *Irene* incident, and was assigned by Dewey to serve as the newspaper censor. However, Dewey, upon appeal from the **correspondents**, frequently overruled Brumby's decisions. After the **Battle of Manila** on 13 August 1898, Brumby, along with Lt. Col. Charles Whittier of Maj. Gen. **Wesley Merritt**'s staff, went ashore to arrange the initial terms of the **Capitulation of Manila Agreement**. Terms were drawn up, and Brumby lowered the Spanish flag and hoisted the U.S. flag over Manila at 5:43 p.m.

BRYAN, WILLIAM JENNINGS (1860–1925). Democratic Party leader and presidential candidate. Defeated by **William McKinley** in the 1896 election, Bryan believed expansion was antagonistic to American ideals. However, after war was declared, Bryan, viewing the war as a crusade to free **Cuba**, was appointed by the governor of Nebraska to colonel (USV) and placed in command of the **Third Nebraska Infantry**. He conducted affairs with a minimum of military protocol, drew few distinctions between officers and enlisted men, and entrusted some decisions to a vote of his unit. Encamped in Florida, Bryan, who never left the United States during the war, became disgruntled as a war to free Cuba turned into a war for colonial empire. Discharged on 12 December 1898, he hastened to Washington, D.C., to lobby the Senate against the ratification of the **Treaty of Paris**. However, Bryan soon changed his mind and supported its ratification, arguing that a speedy conclusion to the war would bring about the independence of the **Philippines**. During his second campaign for the presidency in 1900, Bryan harshly criticized the **McKinley administration**'s imperialistic policy and lost the election.

BUCCANEER. **Yacht** owned by **William R. Hearst**. While previously serving as a **press boat** for the *New York Journal*, it had been temporarily seized by Spain and was being held in the harbor of **Havana**, **Cuba**, when the *Maine* blew up. Upon the outbreak of war, Hearst donated it to the **U.S. Navy**. When a small detachment of soldiers took possession of the yacht on 7 June, the *New York World* ran a story on 8 June, entitled "Zeal by Theft in Newsgetting Thwarted at Port Tampa," which stated that reporters on the vessel were suspected of having obtained government plans and documents and had intended to sail for some port where they could send the matter by wire. Hearst immediately sued the *World* for $500,000 for libeling his patriotic efforts by accusing him of trying to betray military secrets and published his correspondence in which he had offered the boat as a donation. The yacht finally joined the U.S. fleet on 6 August 1898.

BUCK, WILLIAM HENRY (1868–1924). Ensign (USN). A U.S. Naval Academy graduate, Buck and Ens. **Henry H. Ward** were sent to Europe by the **Office of Naval Intelligence** to gather information on Adm. **Manuel de la Cámara's Squadron**. After leaving the United States on 30 April 1898, they arrived in Liverpool, England, on 8 May and assumed disguises as British subjects. Quickly leaving

England they arrived at Lisbon, Portugal, and went to Gibraltar on a chartered yacht to observe Cámara's Squadron. After reaching Gibraltar on 23 May, Buck and Ward separated, and Ward went to the Madeiras and the Caribbean while Buck cruised the Mediterranean and provided some useful information on Cámara's Squadron.

BUENAVENTURA. A 1,741-ton, Spanish merchant ship under the command of Lt. Juan de Río. Loaded with Texas timber, it became the first **prize of war** when it was captured by the **gunboat *Nashville*** within sight of **Key West, Florida,** on 22 April 1898, at 5:30 a.m. Lt. de Río, who did not know that war had begun, raised the standard of Spain upon seeing so many warships. When the *Nashville* fired a shot across the *Buenaventura's* bow, it was the first shot of the war. A second shot from the *Nashville* followed and the *Buenaventura* stopped. Its cargo, which was neutral property, was restored to its owners.

BUFFALO. (USN) Auxiliary **cruiser**. Formerly the *Nictheroy*, it was purchased by the **U.S. Navy** from the Brazilian government for $575,000 and accompanied the ***Oregon*** during its voyage past Brazil. It was convoyed by the *Marietta* to the Pará River, where it had to be left for repairs to its machinery. After the completion of the repairs, the *Buffalo* steamed alone to Newport News, Virginia, where it was fitted for service. However, it did not see service during the war. Commissioned on 25 September 1898, it later served as a transport during World War I, a destroyer tender, and finally as a barracks ship until it was sold in 1927.

BULLARD, ROBERT E. LEE (1861–1947). Captain who commanded the **Third Alabama Infantry**, a black regiment. An Alabama native and West Point graduate with frontier service, Bullard made the Third Alabama a well-disciplined regiment. He believed blacks made good soldiers only when commanded by white officers and vigorously defended his troops, complaining that journalists exaggerated black incidents so that "a fist fight became 'a riot' and a plain drunk 'a mutiny.'" Promoted to colonel (USV) in August 1898, Bullard later served in the **Philippine Insurrection**, fought in World War I, and rose to the rank of lieutenant general.

BÜLOW, PRINCE BERNHARD VON (1849–1929). German foreign minister (1897–1900). Von Bülow, who wanted to maintain a neutral course, repeatedly cautioned Kaiser **Wilhelm II** against openly siding with Spain prior to the war, because he believed that **France** and **Great Britain** might exploit such a policy for their own purposes in the Far East and Africa. Yet, wary of driving Spain into a closer relationship with France and wanting to preserve the Spanish monarchy without running the risk of diplomatic complications with the United States, he supported prewar efforts to forestall war, such as the **Great Powers Note** and **Vatican** mediation. However, he opposed Germany's taking a leading role in such efforts. Instead, he favored concerted European action.

On 5 April 1898, in the midst of the Vatican's mediation attempt, Von Bülow, believing that Spain would accept papal mediation and the United States would reject it, suggested a trade-off to prevent war: Spain would leave **Cuba** immediately if the United States would agree to allow the Pope to arbitrate the *Maine* dispute. The proposal was not attractive in either Washington or Madrid. After the outbreak of war, Von Bülow, who believed in the ultimate victory of the United States, proposed, on 14 May 1898, the sending of a German naval force to **Manila**, **Philippines**, to gather information. Vice Adm. **Otto von Diederichs** was soon ordered to Manila. He later served as chancellor of Germany (1900–1909).

BUSTAMANTE Y QUEVEDO, JOAQUÍN (1847–1898). Captain, chief of staff for Adm. **Cervera's Squadron**, and foremost torpedo expert in the **Spanish Navy**. Bustamante had been the director of the Torpedo School at Cartegena and invented a torpedo that bore his name. During the war, Bustamante, who was esteemed by both Spanish and U.S. sailors, favored a sortie of Cervera's Squadron from **Santiago, Cuba**, for **San Juan, Puerto Rico**, at a council of commanders meeting on 26 May 1898 and later developed a plan for a night sortie, which was rejected on 8 June.

On 3 June, Bustamante personally went to inform Adm. **William T. Sampson** that the men on the *Merrimac* had survived their attempt to block the Santiago channel and were prisoners. In command of Adm. Cervera's forces, which disembarked at Santiago, Cuba, on 22 June, Bustamante was mortally wounded on 1 July during the battles for the **San Juan Heights**. In the hospital during the **Naval Battle of Santiago** on 3 July, he felt that the squadron had been deliberately sacrificed by the government. He died on 19 July 1898 and was later buried at San Fernando, Spain, in the Pantheon of Distinguished Sailors.

—C—

CABAÑAS BAY, CUBA. Located three miles west of the entrance to the harbor at **Santiago, Cuba**. Only ten miles by road from Santiago, it was reconnoitered in May and June 1898 by U.S. forces as a possible landing site for the **Fifth Corps**. On 17 June, steam cutters from the *New York* and *Massachusetts* faced heavy fire upon entering the bay. After the *Texas* and *Vixen* directed supporting fire at Spanish positions, the cutters withdrew without a casualty. Not chosen as a landing site because of its being in range of the guns of Adm. **Pascual Cervera's Squadron**, which was anchored in Santiago harbor, Cabañas Bay was bombarded on 22 June by the *Scorpion*, *Texas*, and *Vixen* and attacked on land by Cuban insurgents under the command of Gen. **Jesús Rabí** as a feint attack to assist the landing of the Fifth Corps at **Daiquirí**.

CABLE-CUTTING OPERATIONS. Even before the war began, **cables** had been selected as an important target by the **U.S. Navy**. On 30 April 1898, orders were given to cut the cables at **Cárdenas**, **Cienfuegos**, **Guantánamo**, and **Santiago**, **Cuba**. Spain soon protested that such actions were a violation of international law. Cable-cutting operations frequently proved hazardous to U.S. sailors, because, by moving close enough to shore to grapple the cable, they exposed themselves to Spanish fire. Moreover, such operations, which had to be done by hand, took time because the cables were usually covered with layers of tarred rope and armored with another sheath of wire. Despite numerous attempts, the U.S. Navy never completely severed cable communications between Spain and **Cuba**, the **Philippines**, and **Puerto Rico**.

One of the most significant cable-cutting operations occurred after the **Battle of Manila Bay** on 1 May 1898. Although Com. **George W. Dewey** had applied to representatives of the Eastern Extension Telegraph Company at **Manila**, **Philippines**, for permission to send telegrams, the Spanish captain general of the Philippines refused because by rights of contract the Spanish government could deny usage. Consequently, on 2 May, Dewey had the *Zafiro* cut the cable connecting Manila with **Hong Kong**. Without direct communications to Hong Kong, Dewey was forced to send his dispatches by boat to Hong Kong, thereby delaying his official reports throughout the war. Even though the Spanish government expressed its willingness on 11 July 1898 for a complete neutralization of the cable and freedom of usage, the United States postponed any decision. The cable was not reopened until 22 August 1898, after the U.S. **Eighth Corps** had taken Manila.

CABLES. Although telegraph cables did not extend across the Pacific Ocean by 1898, they did cross the North Atlantic Ocean and extended throughout the Caribbean. During the war their usage raised significant issues of international law, ushered in a revolution in journalism as news was quickly carried back to the United States, and facilitated diplomatic initiatives. Moreover, cables were used before and during the war by both Spain and the United States in deploying and maintaining rapid communications with their respective military forces. Faster communications proved expensive, and newspapers spent huge sums to transmit their stories. Although the normal rate from **Key West, Florida**, to New York was five cents a word, urgent rates from the war zones cost much more. The **Associated Press** paid $8,000 in tolls for its account of the destruction of Adm. **Pascual Cervera's Squadron** in the **Naval Battle of Santiago** on 3 July 1898. Although both Spain and the United States instituted **censorship** over cable traffic during the war, they, by joint agreement, allowed the Havana–Key West cables to be kept open. Consisting of four submarine cables owned by a subsidiary of the Western Union Telegraph Company, they were used by the **Hellings-Villaverde Network** to provide intelligence information to the U.S. military.

CADARSO Y REY, LUIS (1844–1898). Captain who commanded the *Reina María Cristina*. As a youth he had served in the **Philippines**, returned to Spain and was named lieutenant fiscal of the Supreme Council of War and the Marine. He returned to the Philippines in 1897 and commanded the *Reina María Cristina* in Adm. **Patricio Montojo's Squadron**. He was killed during the **Battle of Manila Bay** on 1 May 1898, while directing the rescue of his men.

CALHOUN, WILLIAM J. (1848–1916). A former congressman and judge in Danville, Illinois, Calhoun, a political friend of President **William McKinley**, was sent to **Cuba** in May 1897 by McKinley to gather information. He knew nothing about Cuba and didn't speak Spanish; yet, after a three-week tour, he reported back to McKinley on 22 June 1897. Comparing Spain's role in Cuba to that of an octopus either slowly strangling its prey or quickly killing it when it resists, Calhoun depicted an island utterly devastated by war and by Spain's **reconcentration** policy. According to Calhoun, U.S. trade and investments were threatened. Spanish corruption was rampant, and the war was stalemated. Calhoun believed there would be no permanent peace in Cuba unless Cuba was "made free commercially, if not politically."

CALLAO. (SPN) **Gunboat.** Its commander unaware that war had begun, the *Callao* arrived at **Manila, Philippines**, from Palawan after the **Battle of Manila Bay** on 1 May 1898 and was impounded by the **U.S. Navy**. Commissioned into the **Asiatic Squadron** on 2 July, it served as a tender to the *Olympia*, and during the **Battle of Manila** on 13 August, it fired on **Fort San Antonio Abad**. It was sold in 1923.

La. 1888, dis. 243, sp. 10
Armament: 4–3pdr., 2–1pdr.
Comp. 31

CÁMARA Y LIBERMOORE, MANUEL DE LA (1836–1920). Rear admiral, commanded the Spanish squadron at Cádiz. Having previously served in the Caribbean and the **Philippines**, Cámara headed naval commissions to Washington and London and directed the general staff at **Havana, Cuba**. At the 23 April 1898 meeting that decided the fate of Adm. **Pascual Cervera's Squadron**, he favored immediately sending the squadron to the West Indies.

As a result of Minister of the Marine **Ramón Auñón y Villalón**'s orders of 27 May, Cámara, in command of a naval force that included the **armored cruiser** *Emperador Carlos V,* three auxiliary cruisers, and a despatch boat, was to attack a U.S. coastal city, preferably Charleston, South Carolina, and then go to **San Juan, Puerto Rico**, **Santiago, Cuba**, or Havana, Cuba. However, on 15 June, he was ordered to the Philippines by Auñón and began his voyage on 16 June.

CÁMARA'S SQUADRON. Commanded by Rear Adm. **Manuel Cámara y Libermoore**, the squadron was based at Cádiz, Spain. Although first formed by orders of 27 May 1898, for raiding the eastern coast of the United States, on 15 June it was ordered to Mindanao to ensure Spanish sovereignty in the **Philippines**, but to avoid "notoriously unfavorable encounters" so as to preclude a "useless sacrifice of the squadron." It consisted of the **battleship** *Pelayo*; the **armored cruiser** *Emperador Carlos V*; the auxiliary unprotected cruisers *Patriota* and *Rápido*; three **torpedo-boat destroyers** *Audaz, Proserpina*, and *Osado* (which had orders to return to Spain after reaching Suez); the transports *Buenos Aires* and *Isla de Panay* (carrying about 4,000 troops); and four colliers with 20,000 tons of coal. In response to its formation, the United States formed the **Eastern Squadron** and conducted a **disinformation** campaign intent on forcing the recall of Cámara's Squadron to Spain.

The squadron left Cádiz on 16 June and arrived off Port Said, Egypt, on 26 June. However, **Great Britain**, maintaining a strict neutrality, had instructed Lord Cromer, the British proconsul in Egypt, to prevent delivery of coal to the squadron on the grounds that it had a supply sufficient to return to Spain. Moreover, Ethelbert Watts, U.S. deputy consul general at Cairo, had secured a lien upon all coal available at Suez. On 29 June, Cámara was informed he could not coal in British territory and had to leave Port Said within 24 hours.

By 5 July the squadron had passed through the Suez Canal and proceeded a short distance into the Red Sea. Within days it was recalled to Spain to prevent its possible destruction in the Philippines and to protect Spanish shores from possible U.S. attack. The squadron arrived at Cartagena, Spain, on 23 July and, in order to help maintain public confidence, was ordered to keep close to shore, exhibit the flag, and use its **searchlights** while proceeding to Cádiz.

CAMBON, JULES MARTIN (1845–1935). French ambassador to Washington D.C. (1897–1902), who frequently referred to the Americans as ignorant barbarians. Formerly the governor general of Algeria (1891–1897), Cambon arrived in Washington, D.C., in December 1897 and presented his credentials on 15 January 1898. The guiding force of French policy prior to and during the war, his central objectives were to prevent an Anglo-American alliance and to keep the United States out of European affairs, fearing the United States could "set fire to the four corners of Europe." Therefore, he signed the **Great Powers Note** of 6 April 1898 and, upon the outbreak of war, recommended French involvement to end the war and thus limit American military successes.

Although Cambon believed President **William McKinley** to be a weak man, having given in to **Congress** and let the war happen, he felt that McKinley wanted peace. In charge of Spain's interests in Washington, D.C., he served as Spain's intermediary in beginning, negotiating, and signing the **Armistice Protocol** of 12 August 1898. Although Cambon consistently tried to limit Spain's losses, he advised his government that a quick settlement was best. He suggested to McKinley that Paris be the site of the formal negotiations for a treaty of peace, and McKinley accepted. Cambon later felt his efforts had been successful because he had ended "the hostilities by leaving the Americans in America."

CAMP ALGER, VIRGINIA. Named after Secretary of War **Russell A. Alger**, it was established on 18 May 1898, seven miles from Washington, D.C., and placed under the command of Maj. Gen. (USV) **William M. Graham**. As the **Second Corps** was organized, the camp quickly swelled with troops, so that by the end of May there were 18,308 men in camp. Because the nearest adequate bathing facilities were seven miles from camp in the Potomac River, filthy sanitary conditions soon developed. Moreover, the water supply was limited until about 40 wells were sunk by the end of June, and an initial scarcity of tents forced six to eight men into shelters for four. The camp soon acquired a dirty fringe of bordellos, gambling dens, greasy restaurants, and saloons. Furthermore, a burlesque theater continued on the camp's edge until Maj. Gen. Graham, disgusted by its "immoral exhibitions," ordered it closed. Only two brigades under the command of Brig. Gen. **Henry M. Duffield** and Brig. Gen. **George A. Garretson** ever left the camp for war. When the camp was discontinued in early September 1898, the remaining troops moved to **Camp Meade**. Throughout the war there were 31,195 men encamped here, and by the end of September, there were 107 deaths in camp from all causes.

CAMP CUBA LIBRE, JACKSONVILLE, FLORIDA. Established on 29 May 1898, on the banks of the St. Johns River about three miles from the business district, it was placed under the command of Maj. Gen. **Fitzhugh Lee**. Because the camps at **Tampa, Florida,** quickly became overcrowded, the **Seventh Corps** moved here. The camp was one of the best-run and better-equipped camps. Healthy water was carried from Jacksonville's waterworks by pipes to the camp, bathing houses were built, and an efficient waste-disposal system transferred human waste to the river and out to sea. Although there was plenty of food, an initial scarcity of utensils forced men to eat with their fingers while using shingles and pieces of board for plates. Throughout the war 28,842 men, all **volunteers**, were encamped here, and by the end of September, there were 246 deaths in camp from all causes. With the transfer of the Seventh Corps to Savannah, Georgia, the abandonment of the camp began on 23 October 1898.

CAMP DEWEY, PHILIPPINES. Upon the arrival on 30 June 1898 of the **Eighth Corps'** first expedition, Brig. Gen. **Thomas M. Anderson** selected a campsite on an old peanut farm near the beach a few miles south of **Manila, Philippines**. After the **First California Infantry** occupied the site in early July, it was christened Camp Dewey and served as a base of operations for the Eighth Corps' campaign to take Manila. By the end of September 1898, there were 63 deaths in camp from all causes.

CAMP McCALLA, GUANTÁNAMO, CUBA. Named after Comdr. **Bowman H. McCalla**, it was established by the **First Marine Battalion** on 10 June 1898, after it landed at the eastern side of the outer harbor of **Guantánamo**. The first U.S. base on Cuban soil, it was located on a 150-foot-high hill and was later moved near the beach after the fighting of 11–13 June. The battalion remained here until 5 August, protecting U.S. ships that coaled in the bay. The camp was extremely well maintained, sustaining no deaths and only a 2 percent sickness rate.

CAMP MEADE, MIDDLETOWN, PENNSYLVANIA. The camp was established on 24 August 1898, near Middletown, Pennsylvania. In early September 1898, about 22,000 men of the **Second Corps** under the command of Maj. Gen. **William M. Graham** were moved here from **Camp Alger**. Even though there were 64 deaths from all causes by the end of September, camp conditions were good. At times discipline was lacking; for although officers took the drastic step of forbidding the sale of alcohol in the regimental canteen of the Fifteenth Minnesota Infantry (USV), the ban quickly fell apart as the surrounding regiments continued drinking. The camp was discontinued in November 1898, and the remaining troops were distributed to various camps in the South.

CAMP MERRIAM AND CAMP MERRITT, SAN FRANCISCO, CALIFORNIA. Established on 7 May 1898, for the mobilization of the **Eighth Corps**, Camp Merriam, which was commanded by Maj. Gen. Henry C. Merriam, was located at the Presidio reservation. Although it was a model camp for around 10,000 men, its area was limited and crowded. Therefore, when it was learned that the Eighth Corps was to be increased, the camp was moved to Camp Merritt, near the northern boundary of Golden Gate Park. Around 18,000 men were encamped here until the Eighth Corps began to leave for **Manila** in late May. By the end of September 1898, there were 139 deaths from all causes in both camps.

CAMP THOMAS, CHICKAMAUGA PARK, GEORGIA. Officially named Camp George A. Thomas, it was established on 14 April 1898, at Chickamauga National Park, nine miles from Chattanooga, Tennessee. Encompassing 7,000 acres, it was commanded by Maj. Gen. **John R. Brooke** (20 April–23 July), Maj. Gen. **James F. Wade** (23 July–2 August), and Maj. Gen. **Joseph C. Breckinridge** from 2 August until its practical abandonment in September 1898.

The **First** and **Third Corps** were organized here, and the camp, averaging 46,947 men, had the largest concentration of troops among all the camps. During the war a total of 69,161 **volunteers** and 7,283 regulars were encamped here. Unlike in most other camps, units here practiced large-scale combat maneuvers; however, discipline was questionable. An Illinois regiment mutinied and a Wisconsin regiment refused to drill or eat in protest over the bad food. A dirty fringe of bordellos, gambling dens, greasy restaurants, and saloons quickly sprung up near the camp. Because of poor sanitary conditions owing to an unsatisfactory water supply and the swelling numbers of ill-disciplined volunteers and a shortage of medical supplies and facilities, disease was rampant. By August there were 4,400 reported typhoid cases. Consequently, in late August many soldiers were either mustered out or sent to other camps. By the end of September 1898, only a small detachment of troops remained encamped. Of the 425 total deaths in camp from all causes by the end of September, most were from **disease**.

CAMP WIKOFF, MONTAUK POINT, LONG ISLAND, NEW YORK. Located 125 miles from New York City on the eastern end of Long Island, it was established on 7 August 1898 and named after Col. **Charles Wikoff**, who was killed at the **Battle of San Juan Hill** on 1 July 1898. On 5 August, Maj. Gen. **Samuel B. M. Young** arrived with orders to establish the camp as a quarantine station and hospital site. Two days later troops began to arrive from Florida at the 15,000-acre site, and on 14 August, the first troops of the **Fifth Corps** began to arrive. After his arrival on 15 August, Maj. Gen. **Joseph Wheeler** assumed command of the camp.

Although in less than a week after Maj. Gen. Young's arrival, wells had been sunk, water had been piped to the site, and 10,000 tents had been erected, the camp was far from prepared to receive the sudden influx of troops. Critical press reports soon surfaced, and the **Democratic Party** began to criticize the **Republican Party** for the camp's situation. Private benefactors and charitable organizations launched an extensive campaign to supply food, clothing, and other necessities, and the camp soon showed marked improvement. By 28 September 1898, when the last units had been processed through the camp, it had received over 21,800 soldiers, one-half of whom were suffering from **disease**. Of these, only 257 died, mostly from the effects of diseases contracted in **Cuba**. On 3 October, the Fifth Corps was formally disbanded here.

CAMPS—UNITED STATES. On 14 May 1898, the U.S. government abandoned plans to retain the **U.S. Army** regiments in their states and ordered their concentration in camps in the southeastern United States and at San Francisco, California. The regular army moved first and was soon followed by volunteer units. The largest camps were **Camp Thomas** at Chickamauga Park, Georgia, and **Camp Alger** in Virginia. Whereas troops destined for **Manila, Philippines**, assembled at San Francisco, those destined for **Cuba** assembled at **Tampa, Florida**.

Since most commanders believed they would soon go to war, they made few provisions for the long term. The filthy and overcrowded conditions that soon developed in many camps were exacerbated by supply shortages, and dirty fringes of bordellos, gambling dens, and saloons sprung up near the camps. Racial incidents were frequent, and discipline was poor among the **volunteers**, especially after the **Armistice Protocol** of 12 August ended hostilities. Knowing they were not going to war, many units voted to demobilize, and some even mutinied.

Owing to outbreaks of **disease** and demobilization, many camps were abandoned and soldiers were sent to Camp Hamilton at Lexington, Kentucky, Camp Poland at Knoxville, Tennessee, Camp Shipp at Anniston, Alabama, Camp Wheeler at Huntsville, Alabama, and **Camp Wikoff, Montauk Point, Long Island, New York.**

CANADA. As part of the British Empire, Canada, under the leadership of Prime Minister Wilfrid Laurier, was officially neutral during the war; however, its policy leaned toward the United States. The U.S. **Secret Service** was allowed to conduct counterespionage operations on Canadian soil in its attempt to break up the Spanish-run **Montreal Spy Ring**, and despite Spanish protests, the Great Lakes-based U.S. revenue cutter *Gresham* was allowed to pass through Canadian waters en route to wartime service on the U.S. east coast.

After the spy ring's existence erupted in the Canadian press on 6 June 1898, with the publication of a purloined incriminating letter by Spanish Lt. Ramón Carranza, a debate ensued in the House of Commons on 13 June. Carranza and **Juan Du Bosc**, who were directing the ring, were expelled, leaving Eusebio Bonilla Martel, Spain's consul general, to continue directing the ring while supervising Spain's consular employees in Canada, Bermuda, and the West Indies and coordinating the repatriation of Spanish **prisoners of war**.

CANALEJAS Y MÉNDEZ, JOSÉ (1854–1912). Leader of Spain's **Liberal Party** and editor-owner of the newspaper *El Heraldo de Madrid*. A former minister and member of the **Cortes**, Canalejas objected to the Liberal Party's manifesto of June 1897. He considered reforms as a sign of Spanish weakness and predicted the Cuban insurgents would reject **autonomy**. After his wife died unexpectedly during the summer, he decided to travel to **Cuba** and left Madrid in late October. For two months Canalejas visited Paris, where he met with **Ramón Betances**; New York City, where he attempted to negotiate with the Cuban **Junta**; Washington, D.C., where he met with President **William McKinley**, and **Havana, Cuba**. Although a private citizen, Canalejas was acting as Prime Minister **Práxedes M. Sagasta**'s eyes and ears and reported to Sagasta that McKinley was committed to peace, autonomy would never succeed, a war against the United States was unwinnable, and Cuba was "lost." While he was in New York City, **Enrique Dupuy de Lôme**, Spain's ambassador in Washington, D.C., wrote to him. His temporary secretary Gustavo Escoto, an insurgent agent, took the letter and gave it to the Junta. It soon became known as the **De Lôme Letter**.

During the war Canalejas rose in the Cortes on 22 June to berate both the Sagasta and former **Antonio Cánovas** governments for failing to prepare for war. When he was consulted by Sagasta before the signing the **Armistice Protocol** of 12 August, he stated he was not opposed to peace and that the government should make peace without any excuse. He reserved the rights of all to discuss the war's results. In September 1898, he spoke out against government **censorship**, opposed those government officials who blamed the press for Spain's defeats, and pointed out the tragic situation of returning soldiers. Canalejas later served as president of the Cortes and prime minister of Spain, and on 12 November 1912, he was assassinated by an anarchist.

CÁNOVAS DEL CASTILLO, ANTONIO (1828–1897). Conservative prime minister of Spain (23 March 1895–8 August 1897). Leader of the **Liberal-Conservative Party** and former prime minister, Cánovas, who instituted the *turno pacífico* system of alternating the **Liberal** and **Conservative Parties** in power, was one of the most prominent political figures in nineteenth century Spain. Fearing the prospect of revolt at home and confronted by the **Cuban** and **Philippine Revolts**, he adopted a policy to quell the revolts by force and then institute reforms. Desiring to pacify **Cuba** before the United States intervened, Cánovas sent Lt. Gen. **Valeriano Weyler y Nicolau** to Cuba to win the war and undertook European diplomatic initiatives through **Carlos O'Donnell y Abreú**, his minister of state, to head off U.S. intervention. His administration rejected U.S. Secretary of State **Richard Olney**'s 4 April 1896 offer of U.S. mediation, announced reforms for the pacified areas of Cuba on 29 April 1897, and failed in its attempts to bribe Cuban rebel leaders. He was assassinated on 8 August 1897 by Miguel Angiolillo, an anarchist.

CAPITULATION (*CAPITULACIÓN*). The term was used in the **Capitulation of Manila** and **Capitulation of Santiago Agreements** because it was less pejorative than surrender, especially because by Spanish military law many Spanish military leaders were to be court-martialed upon their return to Spain for having been defeated.

CAPITULATION OF MANILA AGREEMENT (14 AUGUST 1898). Signed two days after hostilities had officially ended with the **Armistice Protocol**, the agreement was based on a document signed by Maj. Gen. **Wesley Merritt** and Gov. Gen. **Fermín Jáudenes** the previous day. Its relatively liberal provisions allowed Spanish troops, after depositing their arms, to remain in quarters under their own commanders until a formal peace treaty was signed. Spanish officers remained in their own homes and retained their side arms, mounts, and private property. All public property was surrendered to the United States, and although reparation questions were to be referred to Washington, families of Spanish military personnel were allowed to depart at their own convenience. All public funds, which amounted to over $1 million, were turned over to the United States, and **Manila** was placed under U.S. military guard.

The agreement, whose last paragraph was almost identical to that of General Winfield Scott's famous order issued in Mexico City at the end of the Mexican-American War, was signed by Brig. Gen. **Frances V. Greene**, Capt. **Benjamin P. Lamberton**, Lt. Col. Charles A. Whittier, and Lt. Col. Enoch H. Crowder for the United States; and Lt. Col. Nicolas de la Peña (auditor-general), Col. Carlos Reyes (colonel of engineers), and Col. José María Olaquén Felia (general staff) for Spain.

CAPITULATION OF SANTIAGO, CUBA, AGREEMENT (16 JULY 1898). After the wording of a preliminary document was changed to make it read as the final document, the agreement was signed at 6:00 p.m. by Spanish commissioners Brig. Gen. **Federico Escario** Lt. Col. Ventura Fontán, interpreter Robert Mason, who was the English consul at Santiago, and U.S. commissioners Maj. Gen. **Joseph Wheeler**, Maj. Gen. **Henry W. Lawton**, and First Lt. **John D. Miley**.

By its terms, Spanish commanders capitulated not only their forces and material at **Santiago, Cuba**, but also the brigade at **Guantánamo** and the garrisons at Alto Songo, Baracoa, El Cristo, Palma Soriano, Sagua de Tánamo, and San Luís. Consequently, although the agreement did not include the Spanish military forces at Holgíun and **Manzanillo**, the **U.S. Army** effectively controlled eastern **Cuba**. Furthermore, the Spanish commanders promised to deliver an inventory of forces and material and to remove or assist in removing all mines and other obstacles from the harbor. Allowed to retain their military records, they received a U.S. guarantee that their officers could retain their side arms and their troops, their personal possessions, and a U.S. promise to pay for the repatriation of all these forces to Spain. Cubans who had served with the Spanish forces could remain in Cuba upon delivering up their arms and accepting a parole not to bear arms against U.S. forces. Finally, Spanish forces would march out of Santiago, Cuba, with full military honors.

Significantly, the **U.S. Navy** neither was represented at the meetings preceding the agreement nor signed it. Adm. **William T. Samp-**

son only learned of the agreement the day it was signed and was sent a copy for his "information," not for his approval. Because the agreement said nothing about the Spanish ships in Santiago's harbor, Sampson moved to seize them as **prizes of war**. On 19 July, Maj. Gen. **William R. Shafter**, adopting a more diplomatic approach to the navy's complaints, informed Secretary of War **Russell A. Alger** that it was not too late for the navy to sign. The next day Sampson received authority to sign the agreement from Naval Secretary **John D. Long**, but when he attempted to take this step, Shafter reversed his position. Sampson reported Shafter's new position to Long and left the question to the U.S. government in Washington, D.C.

CAPRON, ALLYN K. (d. 1898). Captain, commanded light artillery battery E, **First U.S. Artillery**, **Fifth Corps**. A liberal drinker and grizzled veteran, Capron, whose father had died in the Mexican-American War, landed near **Santiago, Cuba**, in late June 1898, and while moving his battery up, filed past his son **Allyn Capron Jr.**'s grave. On 1 July his battery, which consisted of four 3.2-inch light guns and 82 men, was attached to Brig. Gen. **Henry W. Lawton**'s division in the **Battle of El Caney**. Initially posted about 2,300 yards south of El Caney, the battery's fire was ineffective until it was moved to within 1,000 yards of the Spanish lines. It then began to breach the stone fort *El Viso* about 2:00 p.m. After the battle of El Caney, Capron's battery was placed in support of the U.S. right on the **San Juan Heights** and later fired a 21-gun salute at the **capitulation** of Santiago ceremonies on 17 July 1898. Capron returned to the United States and died of typhoid fever on 18 September 1898 at Fort Meyer, Virginia. A wreath from President **William McKinley** was placed on his grave.

CAPRON, ALLYN K. JR. (1871–1898). Captain, commanded L Troop in the **Rough Riders**. Born in Brooklyn and famous as a great shot and hunter, Capron, a fifth-generation soldier and son of **Allyn K. Capron**, had spent years among the Apaches, knew sign language, and frequently told tall tales. Called by **Theodore Roosevelt** "the best soldier in my regiment . . . the archtype of the fighting man," Capron was in the advance unit of the Rough Riders on 24 June 1898 when the **Battle of Las Guásimas** began. Hit in the chest, he fell mortally wounded on his 27th birthday.

CÁRDENAS BAY, CUBA, BATTLE OF (11 MAY 1898). A thriving seaport with a population of 17,550 on Cuba's northern coast, Cárdenas, which was 12 miles from its bay's entrance, marked the eastern end of the initial U.S. **blockade of Cuba**. On 8 May 1898, the *Wins-*

low entered the bay and fired at the Spanish **gunboats** and armed tugs that were present, in an effort to draw them outside the bay, where the *Wilmington* and *Machias* were waiting. Although the attempt failed, the *Winslow, Wilmington, Machias,* and the revenue cutter *Hudson* returned on 11 May. A one-hour engagement ensued between the American ships and Spanish shore batteries, the gunboats *Alerta* and *Ligera,* under the command of Lt. Antonio Pérez, and the armed tug *Antonio López.* After the *Winslow* was disabled, it was towed out of action by the *Hudson* and the U.S. ships were forced to withdraw at 3:30 p.m. With part of Cárdenas in flames, approximately seven townspeople had been killed and two Spanish ships damaged. All the U.S. casualties of five dead and three wounded were sustained by the *Winslow.* Among the dead was Ens. **Worth Bagley.**

CARLISTS. An ultraconservative political movement that rejected the "liberal" monarchy of the Queen Regent **María Cristina** and **Alfonso XIII** and advocated traditional Catholicism. Taking its name from Don Carlos, the pretender to the throne, it lost three civil wars in the nineteenth century. By the 1890s it was a weakened force struggling to survive. Carlists were united in rejecting U.S. demands concerning **Cuba.** On 27 January 1898, *El Correo Español,* a Madrid-based Carlist newspaper, demanded that the government stand up against "Yankee" provocations, and on 13 April, it called on Spaniards to unite against the monarchy if it agreed to the "dishonorable" loss of Cuba. After initial Spanish defeats in the war against the United States, many Carlists still believed the Spanish soldiers' innate superiority would guarantee victory and opposed any negotiations. Consequently, in November 1898, as the **Treaty of Paris** negotiations were under way, Juan Vázquez de Mella—Carlism's theoretician—demanded that Spain throw the **Armistice Protocol** of 12 August in President **William McKinley**'s face, take advantage of Latin America's dislike of the Anglo-Saxons, and launch a common army against the United States.

CARLOS V. See *EMPERADOR CARLOS V*

CARROLL, HENRY KING (1848–1931). Author, Methodist clergyman, and editor of *The Independent,* Carroll was sent by President **William McKinley** as a special commissioner to study **Puerto Rico** and prepare a report on its postwar conditions. After visiting Puerto Rico in late 1898, where he held lengthy hearings, he concluded in his *Report on the Island of Porto Rico* (1899) that the Puerto Ricans had welcomed the U.S. invasion and advocated self-government for Puerto Rico, recommending that Washington grant it full territorial status and allow Puerto Ricans to elect their own legislature. However, General George W. Davis, the U.S. military governor of the island, won out as he urged the **War Department** to overrule Carroll's views, and Puerto Rico continued under U.S. military rule.

CASTELAR Y RIPOLL, EMILIO (1832–1899). Spanish Republican leader, journalist, professor of history and president of Spain's Republic (1873–1874). After returning from exile, Castelar led the more traditional branch of **Republicans**, which became the left wing of Spain's regime, and he vocally opposed U.S. congressional attempts to grant **belligerent rights** to the Cuban insurgents. After Spain's initial defeats in May 1898, he advocated the abdication of Queen Regent **María Cristina** and soon warned about U.S. imperialism's designs to annex **Cuba**, the **Philippines**, and **Puerto Rico**. Consulted by Prime Minister **Práxedes M. Sagasta** in early August 1898, Castelar favored a negotiated settlement. By September 1898 he was blaming everyone for having caused Spain's defeat and advocated the renovation of the **Liberal Party**.

CASTILLA. (SPN) Unprotected **cruiser**, commanded by Capt. Alonso Morgado Pita da Viega. A wooden cruiser built in Spain with an auxiliary sailing bark rig, it was part of Adm. **Patricio Montojo's Squadron** at **Manila, Philippines**. Owing to a leak in its propeller shaft, it could only move by sail and had to be towed to **Subic Bay** and back to Manila. Hit a recorded 37 times during the **Battle of Manila Bay** on 1 May 1898, the *Castilla* quickly caught fire and hauled down its flag at 10:15 a.m. Sustaining casualties of 23 killed and 80 wounded, it sank and burned for two days.

La. 1881, dis. 3,289, hp. 4,400, sp. 13
Armament: 4–5.9″, 2–4.7″, 2–3″, 4–75mm, 10 mgs., 2–14″ tt.
Cc. 470, comp. 401

CASTINE. (USN) A single-funneled, two-masted **gunboat**, commanded by Comdr. R. M. Berry. Previously stationed in the South Atlantic, it joined the **North Atlantic Squadron** and participated in the **blockade of Cuba**, capturing the schooner *Antonio y Paco* off Mariel on 2 May 1898. Later in May, as part of the **Flying Squadron**, it patrolled off **Cienfuegos, Cuba**. In June the *Castine* helped convoy the **Fifth Corps** to **Daiquirí, Cuba**, and shelled the beach at Daiquirí before the Fifth Corps landed there on 22 June. After the war it was posted to the Asiatic Station, and from 1908 to 1913 it was commanded by Lt. Chester W. Nimitz while it served as a submarine tender. It was sold in 1921.

La. 1892, com. 1894, dis. 1,177, hp. 1,900, sp. 15.5
Armor: 3/8″
Armament: 8–4″, 4–6pdr., 2–1pdr., 2 G. mgs., 1 tt.
Cc. 290, comp. 154

CATALANISM. The 1890s saw the emergence in Cataluña, Spain, of a political movement demanding home rule for a Catalan-speaking state. Prominent among its supporters were Enric Prat de la Riba, the theoretician of Catalan nationalism, Juan Sallares of the **Fomento de Trabajo Nacional**, and the Catalan Union. Because 60 percent of Cataluña's external commerce was with **Cuba**, the economic effects of the **Cuban Revolt** and the war against the United States exacerbated the political crisis. After Spain's overwhelming defeat at the **Battle of Manila Bay** on 1 May 1898, Prat de la Riba, in his manifesto *Als Catalans*, called for immediate peace. His call was supported on 12 June by the Catalan Union, and on 6 July by *La Renaixensa*, the principal organ of Catalanism. Although a postwar attempt to form a party with Lt. Gen. **Camilo de Polavieja** failed, Catalanism was a powerful force in Spanish politics in the postwar era.

CAVITE, PHILIPPINES. A town, province, and narrow peninsula south of **Manila** on the eastern side of **Manila Bay**, Cavite was the principal Spanish naval station in the **Philippines**. Under the command of Com. Enrique Sostoa y Ordóñez, the arsenal and naval station were defended by two 64-pounder Armstrong muzzle-loading rifles, three 6.3-inch rifles (two of which were breech-loading Hontorias), and one 4.7-inch breech-loading Hontoria taken from the *Don Antonio de Ulloa*.

After the **Battle of Manila Bay** on 1 May 1898, the *Petrel* fired on its government buildings. A white flag was raised at 12:15 p.m. However, on 2 May the Spanish flag was again flying over Cavite; consequently, a small U.S. force under the command of Com. **Benjamin P. Lamberton** landed. Cavite surrendered, and the Spanish troops were allowed to leave for Manila. On 3 May, a landing party of **marines** took possession of the arsenal. After the war Sostoa was jailed upon his return to Spain, court-martialed, and acquitted, even though he had raised the white flag at Cavite without orders.

CAZADORES DE LA PATRIA BATALLÓN. **See PATRIA BATTALION NO. 25**

CECIL, ROBERT (MARQUIS OF SALISBURY) (1830–1903). Conservative prime minister of **Great Britain**. After Queen Victoria had received a 17 March 1898 letter from Spain's Queen Regent **María Cristina** pleading for British assistance in forestalling U.S. encroachment on **Cuba**, Lord Salisbury, while agreeing that María Cristina was in a "lamentable and grievous" position, convinced Queen Victoria that such action was not expedient for Great Britain. He doubted the wisdom of prewar collective European diplomatic action to bring about a resolution of the Cuban situation because he believed it might strengthen rather than weaken the "war party" in the United States. However, after the outbreak of war between Spain and the United States and consultations with U.S. Ambassador **John Hay**, Salisbury informed **Austria-Hungary** in June 1898 of the possibility of collective European action in negotiating an end to the war. The effort came to naught because President **William McKinley** was adamantly opposed to any European intervention, and Spain was not yet ready to negotiate.

CENSORSHIP. With the outbreak of the **Cuban** and **Philippine Revolts**, Spanish authorities imposed a strict censorship that continued on through the Spanish-American War. To circumvent its enforcement in **Cuba** prior to the war, U.S. newspapers established codes, hired secret **correspondents** in **Havana**, and used **press boats** and cable stations in Haiti and Jamaica. In **Puerto Rico**, on 7 April 1898, before the outbreak of the war, Spanish authorities imposed regulations that were subsequently strengthened on 21 and 22 April when constitutional guarantees were suspended and martial law proclaimed. Nevertheless, the **press**, with and without government authorization, belatedly published news of Spanish defeats, and upon the beginning of the U.S. invasion on 25 July, letters from **Yauco** and **Ponce** were published. After the signing of the **Armistice Protocol** on 12 August, censorship was softened, and officially ended on 17 October and then reimposed the next day with the official U.S. takeover of Puerto Rico.

Although the Spanish press outside of Madrid had been frequently subject to governmental censorship before the war, the Madrid press remained relatively unfettered. Even with the outbreak of the war against the United States, Spain's government intermittently held up publication of the news of Spanish defeats only for a few days. On 27 May, *El Imparcial* criticized the government for letting information flow freely. During an open debate on censorship in June and July, many Barcelona and Madrid newspapers openly criticized other newspapers for printing fictitious information. After having decided to proceed to a negotiated settlement of the war, Prime Minister **Práxedes M. Sagasta** suspended freedom of the press on 14 July. *El Nacional*, **Francisco Romero Robledo**'s newspaper, proposed an act of protest, and some Madrid newspapers proposed to suspend publication in protest. Romero Robledo and the directors of *El Tiempo* and *El Imparcial* met with Sagasta to protest; however, censorship remained in force as Spain negotiated an end to the war.

Despite the efforts by U.S. military authorities to impose censorship regulations from the beginning of the war, most newspapers avoided and ignored the regulations and set up codes to bypass the censors. Moreover, many local newspapers received uncensored letters and reports from their hometown soldiers and sailors. After Adm. **William T. Sampson** invoked censorship at **Key West, Florida**, on 23 April, full details of the **blockade of Cuba** were published. Furthermore, when Maj. **William R. Shafter** ordered all dispatches from **Tampa, Florida**, to be cleared first by a censor after the *Gussie* debacle in mid-May, his **Fifth Corps**'s expedition to **Daiquirí, Cuba**, in June was accompanied by 89 correspondents, who, despite the fact they had been instructed not to publish anything until the expedition was concluded, continued to report the war on a daily basis, including avoiding Shafter's ban on their presence at the **capitulation** of **Santiago**. In the **Philippines**, Com. **George W. Dewey** assigned Lt. **Thomas M. Brumby** as censor. However, Dewey let correspondents travel about at will and frequently overruled Brumby on appeal from the correspondents, allowing their reports to pass. Even though the **Signal Corps** had been effective in placing censors in cable offices in key U.S. cities, Capt. **Alfred T. Mahan** pointed out after the war that in the next war a close supervision of the press, "punitive as well as preventative," would be one of the first military necessities.

CERERO Y SÁENZ, RAFAEL (1834–1906). General of division, member of Spain's **Peace Commission**, which negotiated the **Treaty of Paris**. An engineer, Cerero directed the building of the first *trocha* in **Cuba**. After returning to Spain in 1881, he was promoted to brigadier general and named inspector of engineers in the **Philippines**. Subsequently Cerero returned to Spain, was promoted to general of division, commanded at Melilla, and served as captain general of Castilla Nueva. Early in 1898, he returned to the Philippines and in September was appointed to the Peace Commission. During the negotiations of the Treaty of Paris, he opposed the $20 million U.S. offer for the Philippines. After signing the Treaty of Paris, Cerero was promoted to lieutenant general in 1899 and in 1903 retired to the reserve list. He authored various works on military engineering.

CERVERA BAVIERA, JULIO (1854–?). Commander, commanded engineers and aid to Gov. Gen. **Manuel Macías y Casado** of **Puerto Rico**. An engineer, African explorer, and career soldier, Cervera authored various scientific and geographic articles and works, received honorary titles from geographic societies, and served as Macías's assistant in Melilla, the Canaries and then in Puerto Rico. During the war Cervera commanded Spanish forces that attempted to detain Maj. Gen. **John R. Brooke**'s forces after they had landed at **Arroyo** on 3 August 1898. Subsequently, he was decorated for his valor and wrote *La defensa militar de Puerto Rico* (1898). After the war Cervera served as the director of the Superior School of the Arts and Industry in Madrid and as a deputy in the **Cortes** from Valencia.

CERVERA Y TOPETE, PASCUAL (1839–1909). Spanish rear admiral. A much decorated nobleman, Cervera was Spain's foremost sailor, having served as Spain's naval attaché in Washington, as the adjutant of the queen regent, and as minister of the marine in the **Práxedes M. Sagasta** government until, having failed to receive support for his naval reform program, he resigned. He then took command of the naval squadron at Cádiz on 30 October 1897. Worried about a possible war with the United States, Cervera wrote to his cousin on 30 January 1898, warning of impending defeat and disaster in the event of such a war. During February and March 1898, he repeatedly expressed the same opinions to Minister of the Marine **Segismundo Bermejo y Merelo**, advising him that **Cuba** was already lost and that he should avoid war because the offensive power of the **Spanish Navy** was a little less than two-fifths that of the **U.S. Navy**. Nevertheless, upon the outbreak of the Spanish-American War, Cervera was ordered to lead his squadron to the West Indies, where it was destroyed in the **Naval Battle of Santiago** on 3 July 1898. After the battle he was taken prisoner and then transported to the Naval Academy at Annapolis, Maryland, where he was received with honors and allowed to move about freely. U.S. public opinion viewed him as a gallant gentleman. He was even offered a home in Florida, which he declined.

After the cessation of hostilities, Cervera was repatriated to Spain on the *City of Rome*. Arriving at Santander on 19 September, he received a telegram from the queen regent welcoming him home; however, the **Spanish press** vilified him and demanded his punishment for being responsible for his defeat at Santiago. He was followed by the police, and the conde de Almenas, in a speech in the Cortes on 20 February 1899, called him "sick and crazy." Most of his critics were silenced when his official correspondence with the government was published by *La Epoca*. Cervera's views were translated and published by the U.S. Navy as *Views of Admiral Cervera Regarding the Spanish Navy in the Late War, November 1898* (1898).

After the Sagasta government fell at the end of April 1899, the Supreme Council of War and the Marine exonerated Cervera. Promoted to vice admiral in 1901, he was named chief of the general staff of the navy in 1902 and made a senator for life in 1903. However, his popularity in the United States fell overnight, when upon responding to a U.S. newspaper request to write about the recent assassination of President **William McKinley**, Cervera, after condemning the assassination, protested the United States having declared war on Spain.

CERVERA'S SQUADRON. Named after its commander, Adm. **Pascual Cevera y Topete**, it consisted of the **armored cruisers** *Infanta María Teresa*, *Vizcaya*, *Almirante Oquendo*, and *Cristóbal Colón*, and the **torpedo-boat destroyers** *Furor*, *Plutón*, and *Terror*. After arriving at the Cape Verde Islands on 7 April 1898, Cervera held a four-hour-long captains council on 20 April, during which all disagreed with the proposed sending of the squadron to the West Indies. Capt. **Víctor Concas y Palau** wrote a report of their views and Adm. Cervera sent the report along with his own letter, calling the proposed mission a "useless sacrifice." Nevertheless, on 23 April a majority of a government council, composed of Minister of the Marine **Segismundo Bermejo y Merelo**, one admiral, four vice admirals, eight rear admirals, and five captains, decided to send the squadron. Accordingly, on 24 April Bermejo ordered the squadron to the West Indies.

The squadron left the Cape Verde Islands on 29 April bound for **Puerto Rico**. On 13 May the *Terror* was left at **Martinique** because of mechanical problems, and the squadron stopped at **Curaçao** on 14 May before it arrived at **Santiago**, **Cuba**, on 19 May. Bermejo's message of 12 May, which allowed the squadron to return to Spain, had been withdrawn by the time Cervera received it at Santiago on 19 May. Although the **U.S. Navy** failed to intercept the squadron, it was plagued by problems: a shortage of coal and **torpedoes**, fouled bottoms, mechanical problems, faulty guns and ammunition, and no adequate facilities at Santiago to complete repairs. Proposals for leaving Santiago were either opposed by the majority of captains because of the squadron's condition or deferred by the sighting of U.S. naval vessels. By 29 May the squadron was blockaded in Santiago harbor by U.S. naval forces.

On 22–23 June, the sailors disembarked and took up positions in defense of Santiago. Although the captains unanimously agreed that any sortie was impossible owing to the U.S. blockade, on 28 June, Gov.-Gen. **Ramón Blanco y Erenas** ordered the squadron to leave. The squadron's sailors sustained casualties of 31 killed and wounded during the battles of 1 July, and on 2 July, after Blanco had ordered him to leave immediately, Cervera commanded the squadron to leave the next day. On 3 July, the squadron was completely destroyed in the **Naval Battle of Santiago**.

CHADWICK, FRENCH ENSOR (1844–1919). Captain (USN), commanded the *New York* and served as Adm. **William T. Sampson**'s chief of staff. A U.S. Naval Academy graduate, Chadwick served as chief of the **Office of Naval Intelligence** and on the U.S. board of inquiry into the *Maine* explosion. Although he initially believed the disaster had been caused by an internal explosion, the evidence presented to him made him change his mind to support the board's finding of an external explosion. During his service on the board, Chadwick sent private missives to **Theodore Roosevelt**, then assistant secretary of the navy, which outlined scenarios for possible future engagements against Spain. When Com. William T. Sampson was appointed to command the **North Atlantic Squadron**, he chose Chadwick as his chief of staff.

Chadwick initially advocated attacking and taking **San Juan, Puerto Rico**, before taking action in **Cuba**, supported Adm. Sampson's view of attacking **Havana** with an overwhelming naval force in order to attain a decisive victory early in the war, and argued against Maj. Gen. **William R. Shafter**'s effort to have the navy force the channel at **Santiago** without the army's having taken the heights near the channel. On 6 July, Chadwick arranged with Shafter for a joint army-navy assault on the channel and heights, but it was never implemented. After the war he supported Sampson during the **Sampson-Schley Controversy**, served as president of the **Naval War College**, was promoted to rear admiral in 1903, and retired in 1906. He later wrote *The Relations of the United States and Spain: The Spanish-American War* (1911), a multivolume history of the war. Chadwick believed that Spain had been defeated but not dishonored, pointed out that there was not any definite plan to seize and hold **Manila** or the **Philippines** before the war, and opined that in demanding the Philippines, which he supported, the United States had altered its moral position from one of altruism to one of self-interest.

CHAFFEE, ADNA ROMANZA (1842–1914). Brigadier general, commanded the Third Brigade, Second Division, **Fifth Corps**. A veteran of the Civil War and Indian campaigns in the southwest, Chaffee, a lieutenant colonel, was promoted to brigadier general (USV) in May 1898. His brigade, which included the **Seventh Infantry**, **Twelfth Infantry**, and **Seventeenth Infantry**, went to **Santiago, Cuba**, with the Fifth Corps, and fought in the **Battle of El Caney** on 1 July 1898. Promoted to major general (USV), Chaffee signed the **Round Robin Letter** of 3 August. With the cessation of hostilities, he served briefly in the United States commanding the First Division of the **Fourth Corps**, only to return to Cuba where he served as chief of staff of the U.S. military government of **Leonard Wood** until 1900. He later commanded U.S. forces in China during the Boxer Uprising. Becoming army chief of staff in 1904, Chaffee was the only soldier to have enlisted as a private in the Civil War and subsequently to have held every rank up to and including lieutenant general.

CHANLER, WILLIAM ASTOR (1867–1934). Captain, assistant adjutant general of volunteers on Maj. Gen. **Joseph Wheeler**'s staff. A New York assemblyman and great-great-grandson of John Jacob Astor, Chanler was a world traveler, an African explorer, and a commander of the New York Guard in 1898. A sympathizer of the Cuban insurgents, he helped **Johnny O'Brien** organize a **filibuster**ing expedition in 1897. On 11 March 1898, Chanler resigned from the New York Assembly to raise a regiment of **volunteers**, and at about the same time President **William McKinley** signed the congressional joint resolution authorizing U.S. intervention in **Cuba**, Chanler placed an advertisement in several New York newspapers calling for volunteers for his regiment. Over 1,500 men signed up at a recruitment office on Sixth Avenue. Chanler served with the **Fifth Corps** in the **Santiago, Cuba, campaign**, receiving special commendation for his efforts. Discharged from volunteer service on 30 September 1898, he was elected to the House of Representatives.

CHAPMAN, CARLTON THEODORE (1860–1925). Artist and correspondent. A specialist in marine- and landscapes, Chapman, an eyewitness to the **Santiago, Cuba,** and **Puerto Rican campaigns**, contributed various drawings and articles on the war to *Harper's Weekly*, including "After the Great Sea-Fight off Santiago" (6 August 1898), and his painting "The Naval Battle of Santiago" appeared in *Harper's Monthly* (January 1899).

CHARLESTON. (USN) **Protected cruiser**, commanded by Capt. Henry Glass. Formerly the flagship of the **Pacific** and the **Asiatic Squadrons**, the *Charleston*, which had been stationed at San Francisco, joined the first expedition of the **Eighth Corps** to **Manila, Philippines**, at Honolulu, Hawaii, on 1 June 1898. During the trip it seized the island of **Guam** on 21 June 1898. Upon arriving at Manila on 30 June, it joined the Asiatic Squadron and participated in the **Battle of Manila** on 13 August, being deployed off the city front opposite the Luneta batteries. On 2 November 1899, it ran aground on an uncharted reef and was damaged beyond salvage.

La. 1888, com. 1889, dis. 3,730, hp. 6,666, sp. 18
Armor: d. 2″, sl. 3″
Armament: 2–8″, 6–6″, 4–6pdr., 2–3pdr., 2–1pdr, 4–37mm., 2 C. mgs.
Cc. 757, comp. 300

CHICHESTER, EDWARD (1849–1906). Captain, commanded the British cruiser *Immortalité*. Chichester had been friendly with Com. **George W. Dewey**, paying him courtesy visits, when Com. Dewey and the **Asiatic Squadron** were anchored at **Hong Kong**. After Dewey's overwhelming victory in the naval **Battle of Manila Bay** on 1 May 1898, Chichester, in overall command of the *Immortalité*, the **cruiser** *Iphigenia*, and the **gunboat** *Linnet*, arrived at Manila Bay. He was punctilious in observing Dewey's **blockade** of the city and made it known that his sympathies were with the United States. On 13 August, as Dewey's squadron moved into position prior to the **Battle of Manila**, Chichester moved his ships to a position between the German and U.S. ships in order to obtain a better view and to be out of the way of any fire. His action gave rise to the myth that he had done so in order to prevent the Germans from interfering in the battle. The myth found its way into many texts, including a history of the war written by **Henry Cabot Lodge**. After U.S. forces took **Manila** on 13 August, Chichester ordered the *Immortalité* to fire a 21-gun salute to the U.S. flag then flying over Manila.

CHRISTY, HOWARD CHANDLER (1873–1952). Illustrator, painter, and journalist. An eyewitness to the **Santiago, Cuba, campaign**, Christy achieved his first major success during the war. Among his works were the sketch *Wounded Rough Riders Coming over the Hill at Siboney* and the painting *An Awful Tragedy of the Spanish War*, which depicted a domestic casualty at **El Caney** and appeared in *Leslie's* on 20 October 1898. Christy, who had slowly acquired a contempt for the Cuban insurgents, also wrote articles for *Leslie's* and *Scribner's*, such as "An Artist at El Pozo," *Scribner's Magazine* (September 1898). He adroitly used his war-won fame to become a prominent illustrator, created the "Christy Girl" for *Scribner's*, and painted portraits of Benito Mussolini and President Calvin Coolidge. His best-known painting, *Signing the Constitution* (1940), hangs in the U.S. Capitol.

CIENFUEGOS, CUBA. A sugar port of 65,000 on the southern Cuban coast. Cienfuegos, a center of **cable** communications between Spain and **Cuba** that remained open throughout the war, was the headquarters of one of the corps of the **Spanish Army** in Cuba. On 27 April 1898, a desultory U.S. **blockade** began, and two days later the *Mar-*

blehead and *Eagle* exchanged fire with the Spanish launches and gunboats *Satélite*, *Lince*, and *Gaviota*. After 30 minutes the Spanish vessels withdrew. After a major naval engagement on 11 May, U.S. ships were withdrawn on 13 May, and until mid-June the blockade was virtually nonexistent, except for the brief arrival at the end of May of the **Flying Squadron** in search of Adm. **Pascual Cervera's Squadron**. On 1 June two groups of Spanish blockade runners entered the harbor. The last naval engagement took place on 13 June when the *Yankee* suffered one wounded against the *Galicia* and land batteries.

CIENFUEGOS, CUBA, BATTLE OF (11 MAY 1898). After Adm. **William T. Sampson** ordered the underseas **cables** at **Cienfuegos** cut, the *Marblehead*, *Nashville*, *Eagle*, and revenue cutter *Windom*, under the immediate command of Comdr. **Bowman H. McCalla**, arrived on 7 May 1898. In the early morning of 11 May, the U.S. ships opened fire and two team cutters and four launches carrying 56 sailors and **marines** under the command of Lt. **Cameron M. Winslow** left the ships and headed for shore. As they were hoisting cables with grapnels, they came under intense fire from an estimated 1,500 Spanish troops as they closed to within 50 feet of shore. A three-hour battle ensued. Although Winslow and his men had destroyed two of the three cables before withdrawing, they had sustained casualties of two dead and 11 wounded. These were the first U.S. casualties of the war. Estimates of Spanish casualties ran as high as almost 300. Later, 54 **Congressional Medals of Honor** were awarded, the second largest number ever earned in a single engagement in U.S. military history.

CINCINNATI. (USN) **Protected cruiser**, commanded by Capt. Colby M. Chester. A sister ship to the *Raleigh*, it was stationed in the South Atlantic before the war. As part of the **North Atlantic Squadron** during the war, it saw service on the **blockade of Cuba**, shelling the area near **Matanzas** on 27 April 1898. Detailed to Com. **John C. Watson**'s squadron, the *Cincinnati* scouted for Adm. **Pascual Cervera's Squadron**, patrolling the Yucatan Passage. After convoying troops in Maj. Gen. **Nelson A. Miles**'s expedition to **Puerto Rico**, it patrolled off **San Juan**, **Puerto Rico**, and on 2 August shelled the hills and beaches between **Arroyo** and Guayama. It was sold in 1921.

La. 1892, com. 1894, dis. 3,213, hp. 10,000, sp. 19
Armor: d. 2.5″, sl. 2.5″, ct. 2″
Armament: 1–6″, 10–5″, 8–6pdr., 2–1pdr., 4–18″ tt. (a.w.)
Cc. 460, comp. 312

CISNEROS, EVANGELINA, INCIDENT. Called by the *New York Journal* the "Cuban Joan of Arc," Evangelina Cosio y Cisneros was the daughter of a Cuban insurgent who had been sentenced to life imprisonment on the **Isle of Pines.** While living on the island to be close to her father, Cisneros was allegedly assaulted by a Spanish military commander. However, Spanish officials contended that the commander had been deliberately lured into her home and an attempt had been made on his life. She was convicted of sedition and transferred to a women's prison in **Havana, Cuba,** where, in August 1897, she was discovered by George E. Bryson, a correspondent for the *New York Journal.* In early October, Karl Decker, another *Journal* correspondent, rescued Cisneros and smuggled her out of Cuba. Her rescue, which was headlined "Evangelina Cisneros Rescued by the Journal" on 10 October 1897, became one of the *Journal*'s most sensational stories as she was brought to New York City, where an extravagant celebration in her honor was held in Madison Square Garden. Later she was taken to Washington, D.C., where she met various political leaders.

CITY OF WASHINGTON. A 2,683-ton commercial steamer. Launched in 1877, it was purchased by the Ward Line in 1888. In the harbor of **Havana, Cuba,** when the *Maine* exploded on 15 February 1898, the *City of Washington*'s crew assisted in rescuing the survivors. Its dining room was turned into a makeshift hospital, and Capt. **Charles W. Sigsbee** retired to the captain's room where he composed his cable on the disaster. Chartered by the **U.S. Army** from April to September 1898, during the war it transported troops of the **Fifth Corps** to **Daiquirí, Cuba,** at a rate of $450 per day, and got lost prior to the landing. Subsequently, the *City of Washington* carried discharged employees back to **Tampa, Florida,** transported Maj. Gen. **John R. Brooke**'s forces to **Arroyo, Puerto Rico,** and carried troops of the Fifth Corps to **Camp Wikoff** at Montauk Point, Long Island, New York, after the war. It was taken out of service as a commercial steamer in 1908, converted into a coal barge, and was wrecked in Florida in 1917.

CLARK, CHARLES EDGAR (1843–1922). Captain (USN), commanded the **battleship** *Oregon.* A Vermont U.S. Naval Academy graduate, Clark had commanded the *Monterey* before assuming command of the *Oregon* on 17 March 1898. As a result of the *Oregon*'s highly publicized 15,000-mile voyage from the west coast of the United States to **Key West, Florida,** Clark became known as "Clark of the Oregon." After commanding the *Oregon* in the **Naval Battle of Santiago** on 3 July 1898, Clark was temporarily appointed chief of staff for a proposed squadron to attack Spain, but he was forced to step down because of illness in early August. In 1899 Clark commanded at the Navy Yard in Philadelphia, Pennsylvania, was promoted to rear admiral in 1902, and retired in 1905. He wrote about his life in the navy in his memoir *My Fifty Years in the Navy* (1917).

CLEVELAND, STEPHEN GROVER (1837–1908). Democratic president of the United States (1885–1889 and 1893–1897). An antiexpansionist, Cleveland called the Cuban insurgents "the most inhuman and barbarious cutthroats in the world," did not believe the Cuban issue was worth U.S. involvement, and personally opposed any recognition of the Cuban insurgents. After he was succeeded by **William McKinley** in 1897, Cleveland believed that McKinley's amiable weakness, mixed with his political ambition, was helping to lead the United States into a war against Spain. After the Spanish-American War he viewed the imperialistic "craze" as "un-American" and became a vice president of the **Anti-Imperialist League**.

CLEVELAND ADMINISTRATION. Although President **Grover Cleveland** believed the United States had legitimate interests in its investments and trade, his administration, guided by his anti-expansionist views, withdrew a treaty to annex **Hawaii** and preferred continued Spanish sovereignty over **Cuba** to the possibility of an independence that could lead to European intervention. Moreover, the Cleveland administration consistently and effectively opposed congressional resolutions recognizing the **belligerent rights** of the Cuban insurgents and the **Cuban Republic**. On 12 June 1895, Cleveland issued a proclamation of neutrality, and his administration attempted to stop **filibuster**ing expeditions from the United States. However, owing to increasing congressional concern and damage to U.S. investments, on 4 April 1896, Secretary of State **Richard Olney** issued a note offering the good offices of the United States to mediate the Cuban conflict. The offer was rejected by Spain. By December, Cleveland viewed the Cuban situation as one of chaos, where neither Spain nor insurgent forces had established definite authority. Consequently, on 7 December 1896, in his fourth state of the union message, Cleveland moved away from strict neutrality. He still opposed the recognition of the Cuban Republic; however, he called for Cuban **autonomy** and mentioned that the United States might take action at some future point should Spain fail to resolve the Cuban situation in a reasonable amount of time. American public reaction was generally unfavorable. Claiming Cleveland's action was "too little," many newspapers criticized Cleveland for a policy of procrastination, and the **"yellow press"** branded him an ally of Spain. An angry **Congress**

passed the Cameron Resolution, a concurrent resolution that only expressed congressional opinion in recognizing Cuban independence. It was thwarted by Secretary of State Olney. During his final months in power, Cleveland authorized two U.S. planters with interests in Cuba to privately discuss autonomy with the insurgent leaders, but nothing came of his final initiative to avoid war.

CLOVER, RICHARDSON (1846–1919). Commander (USN) of the gunboat *Bancroft*. A U.S. Naval Academy graduate, Clover served as chief of the **Office of Naval Intelligence** (1897–1898). After having commanded the *Bancroft* throughout the war, he returned to the Office of Naval Intelligence, served as a naval attaché in London (1900–1902), was promoted to rear admiral, and retired in 1908.

CLUB BORIQUEN. A New York City-based Puerto Rican independence organization established on 28 February 1892. Led by Juan de Matta Terreforte and Domingo Collazo, its efforts to spark armed revolt in **Puerto Rico** failed miserably, and its weekly newspaper *Puerto Rico* circulated little in Puerto Rico because of effective government **censorship.** In 1895 it became the Puerto Rican section of the **Cuban Revolutionary Party.**

COAMO, PUERTO RICO, BATTLE OF (9 AUGUST 1898). Located in south-central **Puerto Rico** about 17 miles east-northeast of **Ponce,** Coamo was a town that saw the first serious combat of the **Puerto Rican campaign.** As U.S. forces under the command of Brig. Gen. **Oswald H. Ernst** advanced from Ponce, they were confronted by Spanish forces numbering 248 men under the command of Capt. **Rafael M. Illescas.** Without artillery, Illescas's command consisted of two companies of the **Patria Battalion** and some civil guards and **guerrillas.** After the **Sixteenth Pennsylvania Infantry,** led by Col. **Willis J. Hullings,** executed a nighttime flanking maneuver, fighting broke out in the morning of 9 August. After Illescas was killed at 9:00 a.m., Spanish resistance crumbled. U.S. casualties consisted of six wounded, all in the Sixteenth Pennsylvania Infantry, and Spanish casualties amounted to five killed, eight wounded, and 167 prisoners. Later in the day, U.S. forces took possession of the town.

COASTAL DEFENSE—UNITED STATES. Although an 1886 board recommend the expenditure of $125 million to replace masonry forts and add breech-loading rifles and mortars, construction lagged because **Congress** appropriated only around 10 percent of the recommended funds. By 1898, the **War Department** had only emplaced 151 of 2,000 heavy guns and mortars, when Brig. Gen. John M. Wilson, chief of engineers of the **U.S. Army,** ordered on 25 January the emplacement of all coastal guns as soon as possible. However, the first monies for coastal defense were not approved until $15 million of the **Fifty Million Dollar Bill** of 9 March was allotted to coastal fortifications. Owing to the lack of modern guns, the War Department was forced to improvise. Seventy-five temporary batteries were set up at 21 different harbors by the engineers and the **Ordnance Department** by mounting obsolete muzzle-loading rifles and reconditioned Civil War–era guns and mortars.

Extra shifts at ordnance factories and arsenals began, the **Signal Corps** began installing electric communications systems at selected coastal points, and engineers began to lay mine fields in the principal harbors, eventually mining 28 American harbors. Immediately upon the outbreak of the war, the Coastal Signal Service, which was staffed by the **naval militia,** manned 36 coastal signal stations. During the war the Coast Artillery Corps of the U.S. Army manned the coastal defenses, the **United States Auxiliary Naval Forces** patrolled the mine fields and protected the principal harbors, and the **Flying Squadron, Northern Patrol Squadron,** and **Pacific Squadron** were assigned to patrol the coastal waters. By mid-summer 1898, the War Department had installed 185 cannon and mortars, completed emplacements for 550 more, tripled ammunition reserves, and blocked every major port with mines. When the war ended none of the guns had fired a shot against Spanish ships. They were eventually dismounted and placed in storage for a future emergency.

COGHLAN, JOSEPH BULLOCK (1844–1908). Captain (USN), commanded the *Raleigh.* A U.S. Naval Academy graduate, Coghlan was in command of the *Richmond* before being assigned to the *Raleigh,* which was part of the **Asiatic Squadron.** For his conduct during the naval **Battle of Manila Bay** on 1 May 1898, he was advanced six numbers. On 7 July, he went to **Subic Bay** to investigate reports that the German **cruiser *Irene*** was interfering with Filipino insurgent efforts to take **Isla Grande.** He found no conclusive evidence. After his ship and the *Concord* fired on Spanish positions, the Spanish soldiers surrendered. Coghlan then handed over his prisoners and their munitions to the Filipino insurgents. After the war he commanded the naval station at Puget Sound and was promoted to rear admiral in 1902.

COLLAZO Y TEJADA, ENRIQUE (1848–1921). Brigadier general, commanded the Mayarí Brigade in the **Cuban Revolutionary Army.** Collazo, who had graduated from the artillery school in Segovia, Spain, fought against Spain in the Ten Years' War and was serving under Maj. Gen. **Calixto García** when he achieved renown as the guide and companion who accompanied Lt. **Andrew S. Rowan** on his return to the United States. After the Spanish-American War, Collazo was elected to the Cuban House of Representatives, founded the newspaper *La Nación*, and wrote several volumes on Cuban history, including *Los americanos en Cuba* (1905) and *La guerra en Cuba* (1926).

COLT RAPID-FIRE (MACHINE) GUN. The weapon was first adopted by the **U.S. Army** in 1890, and when the war began, the 1895 model was the latest in automatic weapons. Colt guns were used by the **Fifth Corps** at **Santiago, Cuba**, on board various U.S. ships, by the **marines** at **Guantánamo, Cuba**, and by the **Rough Riders** at Santiago. It was called "Colt's potato-digger" by the troops because of its peculiar downward recoil. Those that accompanied the Fifth Corps proved less effective than the **Gatling gun** because, being mounted on tripods, they were less mobile, did not use U.S.-manufactured ammunition, and frequently broke down.

COLUMBIA. (USN) **Protected cruiser**, commanded by Capt. J. H. Sands. Designed as a commerce raider, the four-funneled ship crossed the Atlantic Ocean at an average speed of 18.5 knots, the best showing for a man of war at the time. Initially attached to the **Northern Patrol Squadron**, upon the outbreak of war the *Columbia* was assigned to the **Flying Squadron**. It served on the **blockade of Cuba** and convoyed Maj. Gen. **Nelson A. Miles**'s forces, which landed at **Guánica, Puerto Rico**, on 25 July 1898. After the war it was out of commission from 1907 to 1915, and was sold in 1922.

La. 1892, com. 1894, dis. 7,375, hp. 21,000, sp. 21
Armor: d. 2.5″, sl. 4″, ct. 5″
Armament: 1–8″, 2–6″, 8–4″, 12–6pdr., 2–1pdr., 2 C. mgs., 4–14″ tt. (aw.)
Cc. 1,670, comp. 477

COLWELL, JOHN CHARLES (1856–?). Lieutenant commander (USN), naval attaché in London, England. Prior to the war, Colwell procured the *Albany* and *New Orleans* for the **U.S. Navy**. During the war while working for the **Office of Naval Intelligence**, he spent $27,000 in establishing and running an extensive network of spies in Belgium, Egypt, London, Madrid, and Paris. Concerned that he might be upstaged by his rival Lt. **William S. Sims**, U.S. naval attaché in Paris, France, Colwell also paid agents to inform him of Sims's activities. His agents tracked Adm. **Manuel Cámara's Squadron** and planted **disinformation** to mislead the Spanish.

COMMANDING GENERAL OF THE UNITED STATES ARMY.
Position occupied by Maj. Gen. **Nelson A. Miles** during the war. He
exercised direct control only over the **adjutant general's** and inspector general's departments and had nominal command over the troops
in the field. No one knew to what extent Miles was subject to the
direction of Secretary of War **Russell Alger**, who controlled fiscal
and supply matters. Each was supposed to act independently of the
other. However, without an adequate staff, the commanding general
was frequently impotent in planning and execution.

COMMODORE. A **filibuster** boat. After leaving Jacksonville, Florida,
carrying a cargo of arms and ammunition for the Cuban insurgents,
it was damaged on 31 December 1896, after grounding on sandbars
in the St. Johns River; nevertheless, it headed out to open seas and
flooded. The boat was abandoned, and **Stephen Crane**, who had
signed on as a seaman for $20 a month along with three others, landed
in a dinghy on Daytona Beach on 3 January 1897. The incident gave
birth to Crane's story "The Open Boat."

COMPAÑÍA TRANSATLÁNTICA. See TRANSATLANTIC COM-
PANY

COMPETITOR INCIDENT. Named after the *Competitor*, a **filibuster**
schooner engaged in gun running between **Cuba** and the United
States, the incident was reported in the American **press** after its crew
of five men, two of whom were U.S. citizens, was captured by the
Spanish, tried as pirates, and sentenced to be shot in May 1896. U.S.
officials pressured the Spanish government, and as a result of a
change in Spanish policy, the men remained in jail, the case was reopened, and on 16 November 1897, the Queen Regent **María Cristina** pardoned them.

COMPOSITE GUNBOAT. Gunboat with a composite construction,
which was a steel frame with wood planking. They were plated with
steel above and planking below the waterline or with a complete steel
shell. The underwater plating was wood-sheathed and coppered to do
away with the expense and trouble caused by the rapid accumulation
of barnacles and marine vegetation on steel-bottomed ships. Composite gunboats in the **U.S. Navy** included the *Annapolis*, *Marietta*,
Newport, *Princeton*, *Vicksburg*, and *Wheeling*. Their construction
cost was around $250,000.

CONCAS Y PALAU, VÍCTOR MARÍA (1845–1916). Captain, commanded the *Infanta María Teresa*. Concas y Palau, who later became

the vice president of the Geographical Society of Madrid, opposed the military's decision to send Adm. **Pascual Cervera's Squadron** to the West Indies. He wrote an opinion, which was sent along with Adm. **Pascual Cervera y Topete**'s letter of protest, in which he pointed out that the American naval forces were "immensely" superior to Spain's and that sending the squadron was a strategic error because it should be retained to defend Spain's coasts.

After the squadron arrived at **Santiago, Cuba,** on 19 May 1898, Concas advocated a sortie by the squadron in two council of commanders meetings but was outvoted. He was wounded while serving as Adm. Cervera's chief of staff during the disastrous **Naval Battle of Santiago** on 3 July 1898. After the war he served as Adm. **Patricio Montojo**'s counsel at Montojo's court-martial and wrote *La escuadra del Almirante Cervera* (1899), which was translated and published by the U.S. **Office of Naval Intelligence** as *The Squadron of Admiral Cervera* (1900), and *Sobre las enseñanzas de la guerra hispano-americana* (1900). Concas castigated the Spanish **press** and believed that Adm. Cervera's Squadron was deliberately sacrificed to keep the government in power. He pointed out that little if anything was done to prevent it because Spanish politicians were living in denial. **Cuba** was lost even before the war began, and to enter the war was "madness" since its outcome was a foregone conclusion. The only way to avoid the war was to have abandoned Cuba.

CONCORD. (USN) **Gunboat**, commanded by Comdr. **Asa S. Walker**. A *Yorktown* class gunboat originally rigged as a three-masted schooner, it joined the **Asiatic Squadron** on 9 February 1898 at Yokohama, Japan, bringing a much-needed supply of ammunition. During the naval **Battle of Manila Bay** on 1 May the *Concord* fired 582 shots and sustained no damage. On 12 May, while off **Cavite**, the ship was in danger after the blowing out of a lower manhole plate joint on a boiler. The ship was saved by the actions of Watertender William A. Crouse and Firemen John W. Ehle and James L. Hull; subsequently, Crouse, Ehle, and Hull were awarded the **Congressional Medal of Honor** for their actions. On 7 July, the *Concord* steamed with the *Raleigh* to **Subic Bay** to confront the German **cruiser** *Irene*, which allegedly had been interfering with insurgent operations against **Isla Grande**. During the **Battle of Manila** on 13 August, the *Concord* was deployed off the mouth of the Pasig River. After the war it served as an accommodation ship from 1909 to 1914 and then as a quarantine vessel under the Treasury on the Columbia River. It was sold in 1929.

La. 1890, com. 1891, dis. 1,710, hp. 3,400, sp. 16.8
Armor: d. .3″, ct. 2″

Armament: 6–6″, 2–6pdr., 2–3pdr., 3–1pdr., 2–37 mm.
Cc. 370, comp. 195

CONGRESS—U.S. After the outbreak of the **Cuban Revolt** in February 1895 and lasting until the outbreak of the Spanish-American War in April 1898, a Republican-controlled Congress, with the support of many Democrats, attempted to assert its control over U.S. foreign affairs. Resolutions were introduced recognizing the **Cuban Republic** and the **belligerent rights** of the Cuban insurgents, asking the U.S. government to offer its good offices for a negotiated settlement, advocating the annexation of **Cuba** and the protection of American citizens and demanding information about the Cuban situation. Such efforts were effectively countered by both the **Cleveland** and **McKinley administrations**, House Speaker **Thomas B. Reed**, and the "**Big Four**" in the Senate. **See also Republican Party** and **Democratic Party.**

However, in 1898 increasingly deteriorating relations between the United States and Spain, congressional pressure, and public outcry over the *Maine* disaster forced the McKinley administration to accede to congressional opinion because its diplomatic options were exhausted. On 9 March 1898, Congress passed the **Fifty Million Dollar Bill**, intended to bolster the national defense, and a **Peace Faction** of Republican senators assisted in crafting diplomatic policy. However, with perceived diplomatic alternatives exhausted, President **William McKinley** delivered his war message to the Congress on 11 April. After a week of vigorous debate and conference committees, the **Turpie-Foraker Amendment** was rejected and the **Teller Amendment** was added to a final resolution, which was approved on 19 April in the House by a vote of 311 for, six opposed, one present, and 38 not voting, and in the Senate by a vote of 42 for, 35 opposed, with 12 not voting. It was not an official declaration of war, but rather it authorized President McKinley to use U.S. military forces to ensure that Spain relinquish its authority and withdraw its military forces from Cuba. McKinley signed it the next day.

Subsequently, in April Congress approved the organization of the **U.S. Army** into a regular army and a **volunteer** army, authorized the recruitment of three volunteer cavalry regiments, approved a **declaration of war**, and authorized the enlargement of the regular army. During May, it approved the recruitment of three regiments of volunteer engineers and authorized the "**immunes**" regiments. In June Congress approved the **War Revenue Bill**, and in July it approved the annexation of **Hawaii**. After the cessation of hostilities in August, the Republicans retained control over Congress in the fall elections. After an intense debate, the Senate ratified the **Treaty of Paris** on 6

February 1899 and rejected efforts to modify the treaty in defeating the **Bacon Amendment** and passing a watered-down **McEnery Resolution** on 14 February.

CONGRESSIONAL MEDAL OF HONOR. Officially known as the Medal of Honor, a total of 112 were awarded for meritorious service during the war. Sixty-seven were awarded to the **U.S. Navy**, 30 to the **U.S. Army**, and 15 to the **Marines**.

CONSERVATIVE PARTY—SPAIN. See **LIBERAL-CONSERVATIVE PARTY—SPAIN**

CONSTITUTION REGIMENT. Also called the Twenty-Ninth Regiment, it was part of the **San Luis Brigade** at **Santiago, Cuba**. Six companies totaling 822 men from the regiment were stationed in the Santiago area. Three companies fought in the **Battle of El Caney** on 1 July under the command of Brig. Gen. **Joaquín Vara del Rey y Rubió** and were later lionized by U.S. forces for their gallantry. Lt. Col. Juan Puñet, who organized the retreat from El Caney, agreed with all the other military commanders at a 15 July meeting that Santiago should capitulate.

CONSULTATIVE ASSEMBLY—PHILIPPINES (28 MAY–13 JUNE 1898). Created by Gov. General **Basilio Augustín y Dávila** on 4 May 1898, it was intended to attract Filipino support for Spain during its war against the United States. Composed of Filipino notables, it was an advisory body presided over by the governor general. Among the assembly's members were **Pedro A. Paterno**, its president, and several Filipinos who had been identified with the **Katipunan** or would later serve in the insurgent Philippine Republic government. Although the assembly did draw up a plan for **autonomy**, it never accomplished anything of note, and met for the last time on 13 June 1898.

CONVERSE, GEORGE ALBERT (1844–1909). Commander (USN) of the **cruiser *Montgomery***. A U.S. Naval Academy graduate, Converse pioneered in the use of electricity on board ships and in the introduction of **smokeless powder** in the **torpedo** service, commanding the U.S. Navy's Torpedo Service from 1893 to 1897. While commanding the *Montgomery* before the war, he had suppressed **filibuster**ing expeditions, wrote a frightening report on Spain's **reconcentration** policy in **Cuba**, and testified to the *Maine* court of inquiry that he believed there had been two explosions and that the internal explosion alone could not have caused the structural damage to the *Maine*. Upon the outbreak of war against Spain, Converse captured several Spanish vessels in the Bahamian Channel and suggested using the **Merrimac** to block the **Santiago, Cuba,** harbor entrance. After commanding the *Montgomery*, he served in the Bureau of Navigation and was chief of the Bureau of Equipment, Ordnance and Navigation. In 1904 he was promoted to rear admiral.

COOK, FRANCIS AUGUSTUS (1843–1916). Captain (USN), commanded the **armored cruiser** *Brooklyn*. A U.S. Naval Academy graduate and Civil War veteran, Cook commanded the *Brooklyn*, Com. **Winfield S. Schley**'s flagship in the **Flying Squadron**, throughout the war. He fought in the **Naval Battle of Santiago** on 3 July 1898, during which he ordered the turn that became known as **"Schley's Loop."** After the battle, Cook went on board the Spanish **cruiser** *Cristóbal Colón* to accept its surrender. Advanced five numbers in rank for his service during the war, Cook later served as a member of the Naval Examining and Retiring Board (1893–1903), was promoted to rear admiral, and retired in 1903.

COPPINGER, JOHN JOSEPH (1834–1909). Major general, commanded the **Fourth Corps**. An Irish-born Civil War veteran, Brig. Gen. Coppinger commanded the First Independent Division, composed of troops assembled at Mobile, Alabama, until 16 May 1898, when he was appointed major general (USV) and his forces were designated as the Fourth Corps. Even though he had been slated to participate in the **Puerto Rican campaign**, Coppinger never left the United States during the war. After the war he married the daughter of James G. Blaine and served with the army in the West.

CORBIN, HENRY CLARK (1842–1909). Brigadier general, adjutant general of the **U.S. Army**. A veteran of the Civil War and the Indian wars, Corbin, a Republican, served as a military advisor to Presidents Rutherford Hayes, James Garfield and Chester Arthur. In February 1898, he was appointed adjutant general of the U.S. Army, and as such, became one of the most powerful bureau chiefs in the **War Department** because he had control of personnel matters. A talented administrator, Corbin reported to **Commanding General Nelson A. Miles** but could take orders only from Secretary of War **Russell A. Alger**. By June Corbin had become President **William McKinley**'s de facto chief of staff, because McKinley had lost confidence in both Alger and Miles. Therefore, Corbin coordinated the mobilization of U.S. forces, and all orders to the U.S. Army passed through his office during the war. He kept his office open around the clock and worked on Sundays and holidays. After the war Corbin was promoted to major general, stayed free from postwar criticism, was promoted to lieutenant general in 1906, and wrote a history of the army's general staff.

CORREA Y GARCÍA, MIGUEL (1830–1900). Lieutenant general, minister of war in the **Sagasta administration**. A career artillery soldier, Correa had served for over 50 years when he was appointed minister of war on 4 October 1897. By March 1898, he believed war with the United States was inevitable and opposed the **Vatican**'s mediation effort. Pointing out that it was against the army's wishes, he threatened to resign when Sagasta's government ordered a suspension of hostilities in **Cuba** in April 1898. Although he knew the **Spanish Navy** was ill-matched against the United States, Correa had confidence in the **Spanish Army**'s defensive policy. During the war he served on the council that decided Spanish strategy, and he attempted to influence public opinion because he believed it was necessary to maintain the public's respect for the army. His 3 June 1898 request that Adm. **Pascual Cervera's Squadron** be sent to the **Philippines** was turned down by the government. After the disastrous defeat of Adm. Cervera's Squadron in the **Naval Battle of Santiago** on 3 July, Correa pleaded with Gov. Gen. **Ramón Blanco y Erenas** to hold firm in Cuba and ordered Capt. Gen. **Manuel Macías y Casado**, the governor general of **Puerto Rico**, to strongly resist a U.S. invasion, partly to improve probable future peace negotiations. Nevertheless, he opposed the **Armistice Protocol** of 12 August 1898.

CORRESPONDENTS—UNITED STATES. The Spanish-American War period was a golden age for correspondents in the field. Among the major U.S. newspapers, the *New York Journal* had about 50, the *New York Herald*, about 30, the **Associated Press** had 23, the *New York World* had 18, *Harper's Weekly* employed 14 correspondents and artists, the *New York Sun* and the Scripps-McRae League had 13 each, the *Chicago Record* had 12, the Publisher's Press Association had 10, the *Chicago Tribune* and *Leslie's Weekly* had eight each, the *Brooklyn Eagle* had five, and about 35 other newspapers and magazines had from one to four correspondents in the field. Approximately 300 correspondents, photographers, and artists covered the Spanish-American War. Few had any experience in covering a war, and many avoided criticism of the U.S. military while showing a reckless disregard for national security by writing about ship and troop movements. Moreover, many mixed up their role as reporter/patriot and directly participated by fighting in combat and engaging in **espionage** and intelligence gathering. Some, such as **Stephen Crane** and **Richard**

H. Davis, were designated as a "special correspondent" to distinguish the literary correspondent from the general reporter.

Over 75 correspondents covered the **Cuban Revolt**, and at least 15 joined the insurgents. During the war, 89 sailed with the **Fifth Corps** to **Daiquirí, Cuba**, and over 150 covered the **Santiago, Cuba, campaign**. Although female correspondents were banned by the U.S. military from war zones, Mrs. Kathleen B. Watkins of the *Mail and Express* (Toronto), Katherine White of the *Chicago Record*, and **Anna N. Benjamin** of *Leslie's Weekly* circumvented the ban and covered the Santiago campaign. Whereas the war in **Cuba** and **Puerto Rico** received mass coverage, fewer than 30 correspondents made it to the **Philippines**. Although a handful went with the expeditions of the **Eighth Corps** to **Manila**, most did not arrive until the outbreak of the **Philippine Insurrection** in February 1899.

Although the war saw the emergence of a war correspondent as a comedy type in American **literature**, Richard H. Davis summed up their patriotic role in his article "Our War Correspondents in Cuba and Porto Rico," *Harper's Monthly Magazine* (May 1899) writing, "They kept the American people informed of what their countrymen—their brothers, fathers, and friends—were doing at the front. They cared for the soldiers when they were wounded, and, as Americans, helped Americans against a common enemy by reconnoitering, scouting, and fighting. They had no uniform to protect them; they were under sentence to be shot as spies if captured by the Spaniards; and they were bound, not by an oath as were the soldiers, but merely by a sense of duty to a newspaper, and by a natural desire to be of service to their countrymen in any way that offered."

CORTES. Composed of two houses—a Senate and a Congress of Deputies—Spain's parliament included representatives from **Cuba** and **Puerto Rico**. It approved **autonomy** legislation in March 1897, and during the Spanish-American War was dominated by the **Liberal Party**. Prime Minister **Práxedes M. Sagasta** suspended it in June 1898, to dampen fierce criticism stemming from Spain's early defeats in the war, and on 14 July, to avoid criticism while the government proceeded to a negotiated solution to the war. Because the constitution required authorization by the Cortes to cede Spanish territory, it met in a closed and secret session in early September 1898 and authorized such a cession so that Spain's **Peace Commission** could negotiate the **Treaty of Paris**. The scene of vociferous debate and accusations during the negotiations, it failed to ratify the Treaty of Paris.

CRANE, STEPHEN (1871–1900). Special correspondent for the *New York World* and later for the *New York Journal*. Already famous as the author of *The Red Badge of Courage* (1895), Crane engaged in **filibustering** on the *Commodore* before the war. After being rejected by the **U.S. Navy** when the war began, he signed up as a reporter for the *New York World*. During the war Crane wrote almost 50 dispatches, most of which were long, descriptive articles that expressed his interest in the regular soldier. He went on **press boats** in attempts to find Adm. **Pascual Cervera's Squadron** and covered the **marines'** campaign at **Guantánamo, Cuba**, where he was decorated for valor, and later wrote about in "Marines Signaling under Fire at Guantánamo," *McClure's Magazine* (February 1899).

Crane went ashore with **Harry Sylvester Scovel** in mid-June and verified the presence of Cervera's Squadron at **Santiago, Cuba**, and covered the landing of the **Fifth Corps** at **Daiquirí** on 22 June. Although he missed the **Battle of Las Guásimas** on 24 June, he took the wounded **David Edward Marshall**'s dispatch for the *New York Journal*, walked five miles to the coast and filed it for him. An eyewitness to the 1 July battles for the **San Juan Heights**, his dispatch was printed as "Stephen Crane's Vivid Story of the Battle of San Juan," *New York World* (14 July 1898). Extolling the role of the regular army soldier he wrote **"Regulars Get No Glory,"** *New York World* (29 July 1898). Ill with fever, Crane left **Siboney** on 8 July and arrived in New York only to be greeted by an angry *World* management for having filed Marshall's dispatch and for a dispatch that he did not write on the **Seventy-First New York Infantry**'s cowardice. When the *World* refused to reimburse him for his expenses, he signed a contract with the *New York Journal* and covered the **Puerto Rican campaign**, writing two articles and personally capturing the town of **Juana Díaz**. After the signing of the **Armistice Protocol** on 12 August, Crane slipped into **Havana, Cuba**, and while remaining there for four months, wrote 17 articles for the *Journal*.

Crane, who agreed with the U.S. conquest of the **Philippines** and **Puerto Rico** as a military necessity and believed that the Cubans would get their independence when they had matured politically, went to live in England. Subsequently, he wrote "War Memories" *Anglo-Saxon Review* (December 1899), *Wounds in the Rain* (1900), and 14 short stories that chronicled his wartime experiences, impressions, and opinions.

CREELMAN, JAMES (1859–1915). A special correspondent for the *New York Journal*, Creelman, already an experienced Canadian-born war correspondent, arrived in **Cuba** in March 1896 as a correspondent for the *New York World* and wrote sensationalist stories that vividly described Spanish atrocities. He was expelled from Cuba and, upon returning to the United States, was hired by the *New York Journal*, which sent him to Europe in 1897. After the outbreak of war, **William R. Hearst** ordered him in June 1898 to purchase "some big English steamer" and sink it in the Suez Canal to prevent Adm. **Manuel Cámara's Squadron** from reaching the **Philippines**. After Creelman failed to purchase a ship, he returned to the United States and went to cover the **Santiago, Cuba, campaign**. Wounded after having been one of first U.S. combatants inside the stone fort during the **Battle of El Caney** on 1 July, he captured a Spanish flag as "a glorious prize for my newspaper." After the war he returned to the *World*, then back to the *Journal*, and died on his way to cover World War I. In his memoir, *On the Great Highway: The Wanderings and Adventures of a Special Correspondent* (1901), Creelman defended the **"yellow press"** because it had never "deserted the cause of the poor and downtrodden" and justified the war because it had emancipated Cuba "from the bloody rule of Spain."

CRISTÓBAL COLÓN. (SPN) Armored cruiser commanded by Capt. **Emilio Díaz Moréu**. Formerly the Italian-made *Giuseppe Garibaldi*, it was purchased by Spain in May 1896 and delivered on 16 May 1897 without its two 10-inch guns. As the finest ship in Adm. **Pascual Cervera's Squadron**, it fought in the **Naval Battle of Santiago** on 3 July 1898. With Com. José de Paredes y Chacón, second-in-command of the squadron, on board, it was the third ship to leave Santiago harbor and almost escaped. After steaming west, the ship ran out of its supply of good coal and began to use an inferior grade, which it had taken on at **Santiago**. Subsequently, its boiler pressure began to decline around 1:00 p.m., and the *Cristóbal Colón* was overtaken by the *Oregon*, followed by the *Brooklyn* and *Texas*. When a shell from the *Oregon* passed over the ship, Capt. Díaz Moréu fired a gun leeward as a sign of surrender, and the colors were hauled down. The *Cristóbal Colón* turned to shore at 1:15 p.m., and ran aground 48 miles west of Santiago near Río Turquino around 1:30 p.m., having sustained casualties of one dead and 16 wounded. The captain ordered the valves opened, and the ship soon filled with water. When its survivors were rescued, U.S. officers were surprised that most of its firemen and coal-passers were drunk. After having been ashore in the trenches outside of Santiago for 36 hours without food, in the depths of the ship, where the temperature was never under 110 degrees, they had "liberally dosed" themselves with brandy to brace themselves for the ardor of battle. Although virtually undamaged by shell fire, because it was hit only a countable six times, the ship turned over on its side at 10:30 p.m. Owing to the extent of the damages, the ship was abandoned because no company thought it could be recovered.

La. 1895, dis. 6,840, hp. 14,000, sp. 20.25
Armor: s. 6″, d. 1.5″, t. 5″
Armament: 2–10″ (not mounted), 10–5.2″, 6–4.7″, 10–2.25″ N., 10–1.46″,
    2 mgs., 5 tt.
Cc. 1,200, comp. 511

CROWNINSHIELD, ARNET SCHUYLER (1843–1908). Captain
(USN), chief of the Bureau of Navigation and member of the **Naval
War Board** during the war. A U.S. Naval Academy graduate from a
seafaring family, Crowninshield was a Civil War veteran and commanded the *Maine* from 1895 to 1897. He served a chief of the Bureau of Navigation from 1897 to 1902 and was promoted to rear
admiral.

CRUISER. Built for more speed than a **battleship**, a cruiser was lightly
armored. There were auxiliary cruisers, ships chartered or purchased
immediately prior to or during the war; **armored cruisers**; **protected
cruisers**; and unprotected cruisers, which had no effective deck protection. The **Spanish Navy** had two old armored iron cruisers, two
large wooden cruisers, six armored cruisers, five protected cruisers,
ten unprotected cruisers, and 11 smaller cruisers. The **U.S. Navy** had
one large wooden cruiser, one dynamite cruiser (the *Vesuvius*), two
armored cruisers, 14 protected cruisers, and 15 small cruisers.

CUBA. After the *Maine* disaster of 15 February 1898, Cuba became
the primary issue of U.S. foreign policy. Devastated by the **Cuban
Revolt**, an **autonomous government** was installed on 1 January
1898, only to be greeted by the **Autonomy Riots** of 12 January. Although the government was supported by the Catholic Church, it controlled only those areas where Spanish military forces were stationed.
Under the control of Gov.-Gen. **Ramón Blanco y Erenas**, a 197,000-
man army consisted of 155,000 regular forces and 42,000 irregular
forces, which were divided into corps stationed at **Havana**, **Cienfuegos**, Puerto Principe, in Eastern Cuba, and on the *trochas*. These
soldiers were dispersed throughout the island to protect key economic
and urban centers. Of the 57 vessels in the navy, 32 were small
launches and craft of little use except to patrol the coast. Most were
based in Havana and were in bad condition.

During the Spanish-American War, a U.S. naval **blockade** was imposed, and because Spain could not control the sea, no substantial
reinforcements or supplies were delivered. Most of the army was
never involved in the war because the major land engagements occurred at **Santiago**, and although Gov.-Gen. Blanco and many army
commanders wished to continue the fight, the signing of the **Armi-**

stice Protocol on 12 August ended the war. Over the next few months Spanish forces were repatriated to Spain, with the United States paying the cost of repatriating its **prisoners of war.** On 1 January 1899, Lt. Gen. Adolfo Jimenez Castellanos, the last Spanish captain general of Cuba, was replaced by Maj. Gen. **John R. Brooke.** A U.S. government of military occupation was installed, and **volunteer** regiments from the United States served as occupation forces.

CUBA REGIMENT. Also known as the Santiago Regiment, 12 companies totaling 1,644 men were stationed in the **Santiago, Cuba,** area upon the outbreak of the Spanish-American War. One company was stationed at the harbor entrance at **Socapa,** six companies were between **Aguadores** and the **San Juan Heights,** and five companies occupied various points along the bay and in the mountain passes surrounding Santiago.

CUBAN BOND CONSPIRACY. A conglomeration of theories developed among **Silver Republicans,** pro-Bryan members of the **Democratic Party,** and **Populist Party** members that Cuban bondholders, international bankers, and the **McKinley administration,** in order to ensure their own investments, were conspiring to deprive the Cuban people of their freedom by restraining the United States from going to war against Spain to liberate **Cuba** or by purchasing Cuba outright. Moreover, they intended to burden the United States with a substantial debt by assuming responsibility for "Cuban bonds," which the Spanish government had issued over the centuries to meet colonial obligations.

CUBAN DEBT ISSUE. Upon the opening of negotiations for the **Treaty of Paris** on 1 October 1898, the Cuban debt issue proved the most contentious, occupying nearly a month of discussions. The debt, which was estimated at $400–$500 million, was the result of Spain's charging its overseas wars and wars against the **Carlists,** the annual cost of its diplomatic corps for the Western Hemisphere, a pension paid to the heirs of Columbus, and the administration of **Cuba** to Cuba's budget. Spain wanted the United States to assume Cuba's debt, and **William R. Day,** head of the U.S. **Peace Commission,** suggested a U.S. concession by forming a mixed commission to determine obligations. But the **McKinley administration** steadfastly refused. The disagreement almost caused the negotiations to fall apart until an American ultimatum on 24 October forced Spanish acquiescence to the U.S. position at the end of October.

CUBAN JUNTA. See JUNTA

CUBAN LEAGUE OF THE UNITED STATES. Founded by William McDowell, a New York businessman, the league, under the supervision of the **Junta** and directed by its president Col. Ethan Allen, consisted of affiliated pro-Cuban insurgent clubs. By November 1895, it had affiliates, composed of American citizens, in most of the larger cities in the United States. It cooperated with the Junta in establishing a close working relationship with the **press**, provided material and moral support for the insurgents, and raised money for the cause at public speeches, fairs, and carnivals, which it sponsored.

CUBAN REPUBLIC—GOVERNMENT. Formed after the outbreak of the **Cuban Revolt** in February 1895, the Cuban insurgent government was led by President Bartolomé Masó upon the outbreak of the Spanish-American War in April 1898 and represented in the United States by **Tomás Estrada Palma** in New York City and **Gonzalo de Quesada de Arostequia** in Washington, D.C. In order to leave U.S. policy free from entanglements, the **McKinley administration** refused to officially recognize the republic. After the war the United States installed a military government of occupation and the Cuban government, which opposed the dismemberment of the army, lost out to Maj. Gen. **Máximo Gómez**. The army was disbanded in 1899, and an already fragmented government dissolved.

CUBAN REVOLT (1895–1898). After its outbreak in February 1895, **José Martí y Pérez**, the founder of the **Cuban Revolutionary Party**, and Maj. Gen. **Máximo Gómez** signed the *Manifesto of Montecristi* on 25 March 1895, calling their followers to arms. Although Martí was killed shortly after landing in **Cuba** on 11 April 1895, the revolt spread as Gómez implemented a scorched earth policy and conducted a guerrilla war intended to wear down Spain. Under the command of António Maceo (1848–1896), insurgent forces extended the war to western Cuba in late 1895. The insurgent cause was trumpeted by many U.S. politicians and newspapers, particularly the **"yellow press,"** and aided by **filibusters**, and American citizens, such as **Frederick Funston**, fought in the insurgent ranks. Although Spain sent 214,000 soldiers to Cuba during the revolt, by its forces only controlled the major towns and ***trocha***s, and the insurgents roamed the countryside at will. By the time of the outbreak of the Spanish-American War, Cuban insurgent casualties amounted to 5,180 killed in combat and 3,427 dead from disease, whereas Spanish casualties amounted to 2,161 killed in combat, 8,600 wounded, and 53,000 dead from disease. In its effort to suppress the revolt, Spain spent over a billion pesetas.

CUBAN REVOLUTIONARY ARMY. Under the overall command of Maj. Gen. **Máximo Gómez**, the insurgent army, numbering from 25,000 to 40,000, was led by wealthy planters and business and professional men and recruited from plantation workers, small tradesmen, and urban laborers. Its forces in eastern Cuba, known as the Liberating Army, were under the command of Maj. Gen. **Calixto García** and, at the time of the Spanish-American War, contained around 15,000 troops, of which 6,500 were in the immediate environs of **Santiago, Cuba,** and 1,000 others were near **Guantánamo**. Although they assisted American forces in their campaigns at Santiago and Guantánamo by pinning down isolated Spanish forces and providing intelligence information, they were not used as frontline troops in the major battles at Santiago and were excluded from any participation in negotiations and the resulting **capitulation** of Spanish forces. After the war many insurgents continued under arms, carrying out police duty, and although many resented the U.S. intervention, Maj. Gen. Gómez won out in a disagreement with the insurgent government, and the army was disbanded in 1899, with the United States paying each soldier $75 to lay down his arms.

CUBAN REVOLUTIONARY PARTY (*EL PARTIDO REVOLUCIONARIO CUBANO*). Formed in 1892 by members of clubs of exiled Cubans in the United States under the direction of **José Martí y Pérez**, the party's goal was Cuban independence. With funding coming from Cuban tobacco workers in Florida and Cubans abroad, it established the **Junta** in New York City. **Gonzalo de Quesada Arostequia** represented the party in Washington, D.C., and it was assisted by the **Cuban League**. It was the political base of support in the United States for the **Cuban Revolutionary Army** upon the outbreak of the **Cuban Revolt** in February 1895. In December 1895, a Puerto Rican section of the party was formed under the direction of Dr. **José Julio Henna** and was dissolved on 6 August 1898. The party's appeals for aid from Latin American governments were rejected. After the Spanish-American War, the party was formally dissolved in December 1898.

CURAÇAO. A Dutch island in the West Indies, which, owing to the Dutch proclamation of neutrality, only allowed Adm. **Pascual Cervera's Squadron** 48 hours in port and limited coaling upon its arrival from **Martinique** on 14 May 1898. On 15 May the U.S. consul cabled

Washington, D.C., about Cervera's presence, and Cervera's Squadron left for **Santiago, Cuba**.

CUSHING. (USN) **Torpedo boat**, commanded by Lt. Albert Gleaves. The first torpedo boat built for the "New Navy," it was built of galvanized steel and initially used for experimental work. Stationed at **Key West, Florida**, prior to the war, the *Cushing* was used in the suppression of **filibuster**ing expeditions. In the **North Atlantic Squadron** during the war, the *Cushing* patrolled the **Havana, Cuba**–Key West, Florida **cable**. It captured four small vessels on 7 August 1898 in the Cayman Islands and along with the torpedo boat *Gwin*, captured two more on 11 August. After the war, it was in the Reserve Torpedo Flotilla until it was sunk as a target on 24 September 1920.

La. 1890, com. 1890, dis. 116, hp. 1,600, sp. 22.5
Armament: 3–1pdr., 3–18″ tt.
Cc. 35.4, comp. 22

CUZCO HILL, CUBA, BATTLE OF (14 JUNE 1898). Situated east of the entrance to the bay of **Guantánamo, Cuba**, Cuzco Hill, the location of the only water supply on the eastern side of the bay, was attacked by forces of the **First Marine Battalion**, which included 160 marines under the command of Capt. **George F. Elliott** and 50 Cuban insurgents on 14 June 1898. Assisted by gunfire from the *Dolphin*, the four-hour battle began at 11:00 a.m. Spanish forces were routed and retreated having sustained 60 casualties with 20 taken prisoner. U.S. casualties totaled three wounded and 12 overcome by heat prostration, and the Cuban insurgents sustained two killed and four wounded. The battle was the first serious land fighting of the war and was covered by **Stephen Crane**, a correspondent for the *New York World*. The eastern side of the lower bay was cleared of Spanish resistance. Later, Pvt. John Fitzgerald and Sgt. John H. Quick were awarded the **Congressional Medal of Honor** for their actions under fire.

—D—

DAGGETT, AARON SIMON (1837–1938). Lieutenant colonel, commanded the **Twenty-Fifth U.S. Infantry**, Second Brigade, Second Division, **Fifth Corps**. Daggett, a career soldier who had enlisted in the Civil War as a private, commanded his **Black American** regiment in the **Battle of El Caney** on 1 July 1898 in the **Santiago, Cuba, campaign**. After being promoted to brigadier general (USV) on 12

September 1898, he fought in the **Philippine Insurrection** and in China. He retired in 1901 with the rank of brigadier general.

DAIQUIRÍ, CUBA. Located on the southern Cuban coast 14 miles east of **Santiago**, Daiquirí was a shipping port of the Spanish-American Iron Company, a subsidiary of the Carnegie Corporation. It had no real harbor and two piers: one high iron pier unfit for landing purposes and one small forty-foot wooden pier. Prior to the landing of the **Fifth Corps** on 22 June 1898, it was defended by about 300 Spanish soldiers. After the landing of the Fifth Corps, it served as a supply base during the **Santiago, Cuba, campaign**.

DAIQUIRÍ, CUBA, LANDING AT (22 JUNE 1898). Prior to the landing of the **Fifth Corps** on 22 June 1898, **Daiquirí**'s 300 Spanish defenders withdrew under orders to shorten their defensive line. At 9:40 a.m., U.S. naval forces, under the overall command of Capt. **Caspar F. Goodrich**, bombarded the area for 30 minutes. Even though the civilian captains of the **transports** refused to move close to shore, shortly before 10:00 a.m., Brig. Gen. **Henry W. Lawton**'s division began to land in 52 makeshift **landing craft**; nevertheless, by nightfall, 6,000 men had landed. The next morning the landing began again, and after Lawton's forces had occupied **Siboney** on 23 June, the Fifth Corps began to land there the same night. Casualties were extremely light. One Spanish soldier was killed and five wounded, and two U.S. soldiers, Cpl. Edward T. Cobb and Pvt. John English, of the **Tenth U.S. Cavalry** drowned. However, more than 30 horses and mules drowned as the side hatches of the transports were opened and they were dropped overboard and forced to swim ashore.

DALY, WILLIAM HUDSON (1842–1912). Major, chief surgeon of U.S. Volunteers on the staff of Maj. Gen. **Nelson A. Miles**. A Pittsburgh, Pennsylvania, physician, Daly was appointed to his position upon the outbreak of the war and assigned to the staff of his longtime friend Maj. Gen. Miles. Trusted by Miles and accused by others of trying to extract bribes from would-be army contractors, Daly investigated various army **camps** and troop ships in the United States and **Puerto Rico**. In August and September 1898, he informed Miles that refrigerated beef was "apparently preserved with secret chemicals" that were detrimental to the health of the troops and that he had thrown such beef overboard at **Ponce, Puerto Rico**. Miles used Daly's report to initiate the **"Embalmed Beef" Controversy**. On 20 January 1899, Daly appeared as a sworn witness in front of the **Dodge**

Commission; however, his charges were refuted by the commission's report of 9 February 1899.

DAUNTLESS. Oceangoing tug that under the command of Capt. **Johnny "Dynamite" O'Brien**, made more successful **filibuster**ing landings than any other ship between 1895 and 1898. While serving as a **press boat** for the **Associated Press** during the war, it was used to clandestinely carry dispatches between Adm. **William T. Sampson** and Secretary of the Navy **John D. Long**.

DAVIS, CHARLES HENRY (1845–1921). Captain (USN), commanded the auxiliary **cruiser** *Dixie* from April to September 1898. A U.S. Naval Academy graduate, Davis, an avowed expansionist, had been the superintendent of the Naval Observatory and was instrumental in getting **Theodore Roosevelt** appointed as assistant secretary of the navy. During the war he was in charge of the initial U.S. naval forces that landed and occupied the port of **Ponce, Puerto Rico**, on 27 July 1898. On 2 August, Davis suggested to Adm. **William T. Sampson** that the navy seize **San Juan, Puerto Rico**. After Sampson had broached the idea with Secretary of the Navy **John D. Long**, it was rejected because of pressure from Maj. Gen. **Nelson A. Miles**, who wanted the army to take the city. After the war Davis returned to the Naval Observatory and was promoted to rear admiral in 1904.

DAVIS, CUSHMAN KELLOGG (1838–1900). Republican senator from Minnesota, chairman of the Senate Foreign Relations Committee, and member of the U.S. **Peace Commission** that negotiated the **Treaty of Paris**. A former governor of Minnesota, Davis, an outspoken expansionist, was a staunch supporter of the Cuban insurgents. He favored retaining coaling stations in the Ladrones and Caroline Islands and believed the acquisition of the **Philippines** was a great opportunity for American trade in East Asia. During the Treaty of Paris negotiations, Davis supported Cuban independence and favored retaining **Guam**, Philippines, and **Puerto Rico** without paying any compensation to Spain. He voted to ratify the treaty and later wrote *The Treaty of Paris* (1899).

DAVIS, OSCAR KING (1866–1932). Correspondent for the *New York Sun* and *Harper's Weekly*. After covering the **Flying Squadron** at the beginning of the war, Davis was ordered west by the *Sun* to cover the expeditions of the **Eighth Corps** to **Manila, Philippines**. He took a train across country, joined the first expedition to the Philippines, and was an eyewitness to the taking of **Guam** on 22 June 1898. Based on the diary of Belgian Consul **Edouard C. André**, Davis wrote

"Dewey's Capture of Manila," *McClure's Magazine* (June 1899), an accurate account of the negotiated **Battle of Manila** on 13 August 1898. Justifying U.S. expansionism, he later wrote *Our Conquest of the Pacific* (1898).

DAVIS, RICHARD HARDING (1864–1916). Most famous newspaper correspondent of the time. A novelist and playwright, Davis, a romantic dandy who supported U.S. expansionism and the liberation of **Cuba**, went, along with **Frederic S. Remington**, to Cuba in January 1897 for the *New York Journal*. Among his many articles were **"The Death of Rodríguez"** on 2 February 1897, and on 12 February, "Does Our Flag Shield Women?", which gave rise to the infamous *Olivette* **Incident**, after which Davis refused to work for **William R. Hearst**, the owner of the *Journal*, for the rest of his life.

Upon the outbreak of war between Spain and the United States, the **U.S. Army** offered him a captaincy. Davis declined and covered the **Santiago, Cuba,** and **Puerto Rican campaign**s for the *New York Herald* and wrote articles for the *Times* (London) and *Scribner's Magazine*. Initially he covered the **blockade of Cuba** and the formation of the **Fifth Corps** at **Tampa, Florida**. Davis attached himself to the **Rough Riders** and was present at the **Aserraderos Conference** and the landing at **Daiquirí**, where he began a personal feud with Maj. Gen. **William R. Shafter**, because Shafter refused to let him land with the first troops. He fought in the **Battle of Las Guásimas** on 24 June 1898, and later extolled the Rough Riders in his article "The Rough Riders' Fight at Guásimas," *Scribner's* (September 1898). His dispatch after the **Battle of San Juan Hill** on 1 July, which criticized the Fifth Corps's expedition as having been prepared "in ignorance and conducted in a series of blunders," was withheld from publication by the *New York Herald* until 7 July because it was "too inflammatory"; moreover, Davis had written, "Another such victory as that of July 1 and our troops must retreat."

After participating in the Puerto Rican campaign, Davis credited Maj. Gen. **Nelson A. Miles** for its overwhelming success and advocated U.S. retention of the island in "The Porto Rican Campaign," *Scribner's* (November 1898). After the war Davis summed up his personal experiences and opinions on the war in his book *The Cuban and Porto Rican Campaigns* (1898), extolled the patriotic role of the war **correspondents** in "Our War Correspondents in Cuba and Porto Rico," *Harper's Monthly Magazine* (May 1899), and wrote four short stories on the war based on the themes of love, honor, duty, and self-sacrifice.

DAY, WILLIAM RUFUS (1849–1923). U.S. secretary of state (25 April 1898–16 September 1898). A neighbor and close friend of President **William McKinley** from Canton, Ohio, Day, a judge whose ambition was to be on the Supreme Court, had no Washington or foreign experience when he was appointed assistant secretary of state by McKinley in April 1897. Owing to the failing health of Secretary of State **John Sherman**, Day was deeply involved in all prewar matters concerning the Cuban situation and sought out the advice of Assistant Secretary of State Alvery A. Adee, a career diplomat, and **John B. Moore**, a scholar of international law. Upon Sherman's resignation in April 1898, Day became secretary of state.

Although his duties during the war were not onerous because most policy was decided by McKinley, Day directed efforts to secure the annexation of **Hawaii** and the drafting of the **Armistice Protocol** of 12 August. Upon McKinley's request, he resigned his office and chaired the U.S. **Peace Commission**, which negotiated the **Treaty of Paris**. While serving on the commission Day mediated differences in the U.S. delegation; initially favored only retaining a naval station at **Manila, Philippines**; and favored retaining **Cuba** and **Puerto Rico**. Day returned from Paris, was appointed to the U.S. Court of Appeals for the Sixth Circuit, and in 1903 was appointed to the Supreme Court by President **Theodore Roosevelt**.

DE LÔME LETTER. Displeased with President **William McKinley**'s annual message of December 1897, **Enrique Dupuy de Lôme**, Spain's minister to the United States, wrote a five-page letter to **José Canalejas**, the editor of *El Heraldo de Madrid* who was touring **Cuba**. The letter was stolen by Canalejas's secretary and given to the Cuban insurgents. A facsimile of the letter appeared on the front page of the *New York Journal* on 9 February 1898, under the headline "The Worst Insult to the United States in History." The letter, which had criticized McKinley as "weak and a bidder for the admiration of the crowd" and called him a "would-be politician," appeared on front pages throughout the country. More importantly, the letter seemed to reveal Spain's insincerity with respect to its pledge of reforms and **autonomy**.

Although McKinley reacted calmly, de Lôme was recalled, and Spain officially apologized, the letter's publication caused a public and congressional outcry. **Congress** passed a resolution calling for the **McKinley administration** to publish U.S. consular reports from Cuba. The **"yellow press"** demanded intervention, and the *New York Herald*, the *Wall Street Journal* and the *Washington Post* called for restraint. Whereas the northern **press** generally was more vocal in denouncing the letter, the midwestern press was restrained and many southern **Democratic Party** papers agreed with de Lôme's opinion of McKinley.

Although the U.S. public was not ready to go to war over the letter, its publication marked the beginning of the Cuban situation receiving paramount consideration in the American press. On 11 February 1898, the *Savannah, Georgia, Morning News* asked, "What will be the next important incident?" The answer was only four days away when the *Maine* exploded in **Havana** on 15 February.

"THE DEATH OF RODRÍGUEZ" (2 FEBRUARY 1897). An article written by **Richard H. Davis** after witnessing the predawn execution of 20-year-old Cuban insurgent Adolfo Rodríguez by a Spanish firing squad on 19 January 1897. Rodríguez, the only son of a farmer, had joined the insurgents, was captured, and found guilty of bearing arms against the government. Davis's long and moving account of the execution became a classic after it appeared in the *New York Journal* on 2 February 1897.

DECLARATION OF WAR—SPAIN (23 APRIL 1898). For the Spanish government, the resolution of 19 April 1898 by the U.S. **Congress** was a virtual declaration of war. Through the process of a letter from Prime Minister **Práxedes M. Sagasta** to the Queen Regent **María Cristina** and the queen regent's concomitant decree, Spain declared war on the United States on 23 April 1898. Sagasta's letter blamed the United States for starting the war and announced the formal break in diplomatic relations, and the Royal Decree abrogated the treaty of peace and friendship of 27 October 1795, the protocol of 12 January 1877, and all other agreements between Spain and the United States. It also proclaimed Spain's rules of war with respect to **neutral rights**, pronounced that **blockades**, to be obligatory, had to be effective, maintained Spain's right to commission privateers and auxiliary ships for the **Spanish Navy,** defined contraband, and stated that non-American vessels that committed acts of war against Spain would be considered and judged as pirates even if they had letters of marque from the United States.

DECLARATION OF WAR—UNITED STATES (25 APRIL 1898). A House bill declaring war on Spain had been introduced on 25 February 1897, but it was not moved to a vote. After President **William McKinley** formally announced the withdrawal of Spain's minister from Washington and recommended a declaration of war on 25 April 1898, a joint resolution declaring war was immediately introduced and passed the same day in both the House and the Senate. There was no debate in the House, and the discussion in the Senate was behind closed doors. Although the declaration was approved on 25 April 1898, it was made retroactive to 21 April 1898, because McKinley had ordered a **blockade** of northern **Cuba** on the twenty-first. The declaration also authorized McKinley to call into service the militia of the states and empowered him to use the land and naval forces of the United States. Significantly, no mention was made of the **Philippines**. On 11 May 1898, Spain's foreign minister protested the illegality of making the declaration retroactive, stating that all seizures or captures of Spanish ships prior to 25 April were therefore not valid.

DELCASSÉ, THÉOPHILE (1852–1923). French minister of foreign affairs (28 June 1898–1905). A former governor of Algeria and an under secretary of state for colonies, Delcassé, a known champion of French expansionism, succeeded Gabriel Hanotaux on 28 June 1898 and adopted a basic hands-off policy with respect to direct involvement in the war. After negotiations began on the **Armistice Protocol**, he advised Spain to accept the harsh terms and give up its possessions in the West Indies in the hope of saving the **Philippines**. Later, after officially welcoming the Spanish and U.S. **Peace Commissions**, which had arrived in Paris to negotiate the **Treaty of Paris**, Delcassé pushed Spain to accept the U.S. annexation of the Philippines, arguing that it was better than prolonging the war.

DEMOCRACIA, LA. Puerto Rican newspaper founded by **Luis Muñoz Rivera** in 1890. An ardent prewar opponent of union with the United States, it called for Puerto Rican unity in support of Spain upon the outbreak of war, claiming on 4 May 1898, "We prefer death, rather than lose our nationality." However, in August 1898, after Spain's defeat, it called for harmony between Puerto Ricans and U.S. occupation forces. Later, it became critical of U.S. occupation when self-government was not forthcoming and was censored by Maj. Gen. **Guy V. Henry**.

DEMOCRATIC PARTY—UNITED STATES. Its 1896 party platform expressed sympathy for the Cuban people in their struggle for liberty and independence, and many Democratic newspapers such as the *Atlanta Constitution* and the *Boston Daily Globe* were strongly interventionist. By the spring of 1898 many Democrats had become **jingoes** on the basis of liberating **Cuba**. Although 77 House Democrats opposed the annexation of **Hawaii**, most state party platforms in October 1898 implicitly favored retaining the **Philippines**. Even though a *New York Herald* poll showed 71.3 percent of the Democratic newspapers to be against the **Treaty of Paris**, Democratic leaders, such as **William Jennings Bryan**, helped to narrowly ratify it in February 1899, although others, such as Senator Arthur P. Gorman of Maryland, failed in their attempt to defeat the treaty. However, divisions soon disappeared as the **McKinley Administration**'s policy in confronting the **Philippine Insurrection** brought most Democrats together. Consequently, the party's 1899 platform severely denounced McKinley for involving the United States in an unnecessary war.

DENBY, CHARLES (1830–1904). Member of the **Dodge** and **Schurman Commission**s. A lawyer and Civil War veteran, Denby, who served as the U.S. minister to China (1885–1898), believed the business of diplomacy was to advance commerce and was an ardent supporter of U.S. expansion into the Far East. During the **Treaty of Paris** negotiations, he argued in "Shall We Keep the Philippines?" *The Forum* (November 1898) that the United States had the right as conquerors to hold the **Philippines**, which he saw as a U.S. foothold in the Far East. After the war, Denby served as vice president of the Dodge Commission and on the Schurman Commission.

DEPARTMENT OF WAR. See WAR DEPARTMENT

DERBY, GEORGE McCLELLAN (1856–1948). Lieutenant colonel, chief engineer of the **Fifth Corps**. Born at sea and educated privately in Paris, Dresden, and Switzerland, Derby, a West Point graduate, fought in the **Santiago, Cuba, campaign**, hiring spies and directing army reconnaissance efforts after the Fifth Corps landed at **Daiquirí, Cuba**, on 22 June 1898. He also participated in **balloon operations** to gain tactical intelligence and was shot out of the sky on 1 July during the battles for the **San Juan Heights**. He later served as the chief engineer of the **Second Corps**. Before he retired in 1907, he was promoted to colonel.

DETROIT. (USN) Unprotected **cruiser**, commanded by Comdr. James H. Dayton. Previously used in the suppression of **filibuster**ing expeditions, the *Detroit*, as part of the **North Atlantic Squadron**, participated in the **blockade of Cuba**, capturing the steamer *Catalina* on 24 April 1898, and in the bombardment of **San Juan, Puerto Rico**, on 12 May. After convoying the **Fifth Corps** to **Daiquirí, Cuba**, it shelled the beach area at Daiquirí before the Fifth Corps landed on 22 June. After the war it served in the North Atlantic and was sold in 1910.

La. 1891, com. 1893, dis. 2,094, hp. 5,400, sp. 19
Armor: d. 5/16", sl. 7/10"
Armament: 2–6", 8–5", 6–6pdr., 2–1pdr., 2 C. mgs., 3–18" tt. (aw.)
Cc. 340, comp. 250

DEWEY, GEORGE W. (1837–1917). Commodore (USN), commanded the **Asiatic Squadron**. A U.S. Naval Academy graduate, Dewey served as president of the Board of Inspection and Survey, and in October 1897, he was appointed to command the Asiatic Squadron through the political influence of **Theodore Roosevelt** and Senator **Redfield Proctor**. After assuming command on 3 January 1898, at Nagasaki, Japan, Dewey was in command on his flagship *Olympia* during the **Battle of Manila Bay** on 1 May. The battle, which Dewey believed made the United States a world power, made him a national hero, and he was promoted to rear admiral on 7 May.

During the remainder of the campaign in the **Philippines** Dewey stayed on the *Olympia* in **Manila Bay**, maintained a lenient policy toward newspaper **correspondents**, and after inviting **Emilio Aguinaldo** to return to the Philippines, he met with Aguinaldo on 19 May and later provided him with arms and ammunition. When instructed by the U.S. government on 26 May not to have political alliances with Aguinaldo's insurgents, Dewey responded on 3 June, stating he had made no commitments or promises of alliance. On 10 July, Dewey threatened war against **Germany** for **blockade** violations when German Vice Adm. **Otto von Diederichs** sent Capt. Lt. Paul von Hintze to the *Olympia* to protest the boarding of the *Irene* by an officer from the revenue cutter *McCulloch*.

After the **Armistice Protocol** of 12 August, Dewey advocated a liberal policy of increasing self-government for the Filipinos and did not believe that they would fight the United States almost up to the outbreak of the **Philippine Insurrection** in February 1899. Remaining in the Philippines, he testified in front of the **Schurman Commission** and denied that any promises had been made to Aguinaldo; rather, he said his actions were merely an "act of courtesy." He returned to the United States in September 1899 and was greeted as a national hero as **Dewey mania** swept the land. He became president of the newly created General Board of the Navy.

DEWEY MANIA. After the Spanish-American War, Adm. **George W. Dewey** remained in the **Philippines** for a little more than a year. Upon his return to New York City in September 1899, Dewey was given a hero's welcome. "Welcome Dewey!" was spelled out in a 36 foot-high electric sign on the Brooklyn Bridge. An enormous parade was held, a Dewey medal struck, a Dewey triumphal arch erected, Dewey flags were everywhere, and ices à la Dewey were served molded like **battleships**. New York City presented him with a gold loving cup, and **Congress** awarded him a $10,000 sword of honor and invented a brand-new lifetime rank for him: "Admiral of the Navy." He was offered a house in Washington, D.C., and works of art were sent to him from all over the country. His name appeared everywhere: babies, chewing gum (Dewey's chewies), cigar boxes, cocktails, hats, horses, and in the then latest jingle, "How Did Dewey Do It?" Unfortunately for Dewey, fame proved fleeting as his inauspicious remark about the presidency not being a very difficult job sank any hope he had for the office.

DEWEY-MONTOJO CORRESPONDENCE. A brief correspondence took place in late September 1898 between Adm. **George W. Dewey**, the victor of the **Battle of Manila Bay** of 1 May 1898, and Adm. **Patricio Montojo**, the loser. While Montojo was being court-martialed in Spain, he wrote to Dewey for answers to certain questions. He hoped to use Dewey's answers in his defense and to secure the transfer of Spanish **prisoners of war** from Filipino insurgent hands into U.S. hands. Montojo asked if Dewey agreed that there had been no defenses at **Subic Bay** and that the depth of the water at Subic Bay would have caused greater casualties than at **Cavite**. Dewey agreed. When Montojo asked if the Spanish defeat was due not to his unreadiness but to his poor ships, Dewey hedged in responding that the defense was "gallant in the extreme." Dewey then expressed his regrets that Montojo was under such duress. However, Dewey later criticized Montojo severely for not remaining with his ships the night before the battle and for not launching a **torpedo** attack during the battle.

DEWEY'S DISPATCH ON THE NAVAL BATTLE OF MANILA BAY (1 MAY 1898). Com. **George W. Dewey** was in no hurry to report his overwhelming victory at the **Battle of Manila Bay** on 1 May. After being refused the use of the **cable** to **Hong Kong**, Dewey ordered the cable cut on 2 May. Finally, on 5 May, Dewey signed his dispatches—one that reported his victory and another, the taking possession of the arsenal at **Cavite**—put them on board the *McCulloch*, and sent them, carried by Lt. **Thomas M. Brumby**, to Hong Kong. The 650-mile trip took two days.

Earlier, on 2 May 1898, the first legitimate news of the battle had come from Madrid via London, in Gov.-Gen. **Basilio Augustín y Dávila**'s report. Augustín stated that U.S. ships had taken refuge behind foreign shipping and Spanish ships had suffered "severe loss." The *New York Herald* immediately ran the report beneath the headline "Spain's Asiatic Fleet Destroyed by Dewey," and the *New York Journal* proclaimed "Victory, Complete! . . . The Maine is Avenged." President **William McKinley**, believing that victory had been achieved, telegraphed Dewey on 3 May, congratulating him on his victory; however, days passed and there was no word from Dewey.

Four days later, on 7 May, at 3:00 a.m. **Edward Harden**'s eyewitness account arrived. Although Harden worked for the *New York World*, his account was picked up and published first by the *Chicago Tribune* in that morning's edition. Finally, at 8:45 a.m. Secretary of the Navy **John D. Long** received Dewey's coded dispatches. While Long was telephoning President McKinley for permission to make an official announcement to the **press**, **Theodore Roosevelt**, who had been reading the message over the shoulders of the decoders, immediately took it and read it to a room full of reporters. Later, Long emerged from his office and gave out a carefully censored version. Both Roosevelt's uncensored and Long's censored versions appeared side by side in that day's newspaper accounts.

DÍAZ MORÉU, EMILIO (1846–1913). Captain, commanded the *Cristóbal Colón*. Entering the navy at ten years of age, Díaz Moréu, while a liberal deputy in the **Cortes**, initiated a debate in June 1894 on the navy's poor condition by stating that Spain was lacking a complete ship capable of combat. Prior to the war against the United States, he opposed sending Adm. **Pascual Cervera's Squadron** to the West Indies. During the **Naval Battle of Santiago** on 3 July 1898, Díaz Moréu commanded the *Cristóbal Colón*. After running his ship into shore to avoid destruction, he and Com. José de Paredes y Chacón were in the wardroom with a tureen of soup in front of them when they formally surrendered to Capt. **Francis A. Cook** of the *Brooklyn*. Briefly held as a **prisoner of war**, he left the United States on 20 August 1898 for Spain on a French mail steamer. After the war Díaz Moréu retired in 1901 and was made a senator for life in 1911.

DIEDERICHS, OTTO VON (1843–1918). German vice admiral. Assuming command of the German Asiatic Fleet on 14 November, 1897, von Diederichs directed German troops that landed at Kiachow Bay, China, and while refitting in Nagasaki, Japan, he received orders on 2 June 1898 to proceed to **Manila, Philippines**. He arrived on 12 June aboard his flagship *Kaiserin Augusta*, met with Com. **George W. Dewey**, and officially visited Lt. Gen. **Basilio Augustín y Dávila**, Spanish governor general of the Philippines. He diplomatically ignored Adm. Dewey's threat of war against **Germany** over the *Irene* on 10 July. After the war, von Diederichs's "A Statement of Events in Manila Bay . . . , May–October 1898" was published in the *Journal of the Royal United Service Institution* in November 1914. Intended as an answer to accusations in Adm. Dewey's autobiography, von Diederichs's statement claimed his intentions at Manila were strictly neutral. He had no political instructions and had not interfered with the U.S. **blockade of Manila**.

DISEASE. Medical science in 1898 had no knowledge about the origins or transmission of malaria, typhoid, and **yellow fever**, and although yellow fever was the source of principal alarm, malaria and typhoid were the principal killers. For U.S. forces in the **Philippines** they caused few casualties because of the efficiency of military programs. On 13 August 1898, only 124 out of 8,000 troops were in the hospital, and one-half of those were for wounds; moreover, typhoid only caused 14 deaths.

The Cuban situation was far different. Although only 3,437 Cuban insurgents died from disease from 1895 to 1898, both Spanish and U.S. forces were devastated. From 1895 through 1898, 53,000 Spanish soldiers died from disease, yellow fever being credited with 13,000 deaths and other diseases, with 40,000. Although the **First Marine Battalion** at **Guantánamo, Cuba**, had no deaths from disease, the **Fifth Corps** was devastated by malaria during the **Santiago, Cuba, campaign**. By 2 August, its sick list totaled 4,290 and caused the publication of the **Round Robin Letter** and the quick removal of the corps from **Cuba**. Although only 514 died from disease in Cuba during the war, many sick were transported to the United States and subsequently died.

For the **U.S. Army** diseases did the greatest damage in the U.S. **camps** during the war. According to Dr. Nicholas Senn, chief surgeon of U.S. volunteers, in his *Medical and Surgical Aspects of the Spanish-American War* (1900) and the **Reed/Vaughn/Shakespeare Commission**, typhoid was prevalent in all the camps, caused 86 percent of the deaths from disease, and killed around 1,500 soldiers. Typhoid epidemics in the overcrowded and unsanitary camps caused hospital systems to collapse and proved deadly, killing 425 at **Camp Thomas**, 107 at **Camp Alger**, and 246 at **Camp Cuba Libre**. It was never really brought under control but merely burned itself out. Although a great public and journalistic clamor arose over the issue, death rates from disease were quite a bit lower than those of training camps during the Civil War.

For the U.S. military, diseases proved far more deadly than bullets during the war. Whereas only 379 deaths out of a total of 5,452 in 1898 resulted from combat, disease killed nearly ten times as many as bullets. According to **French E. Chadwick**, from 1 May to 30 September 1898, diseases killed 80 officers and 2,485 enlisted men in the army, and 56 in the navy. Of the Spanish soldiers who were repatriated to Spain after the war, it is estimated that over 20,000 died from diseases that they had contracted overseas.

DISINFORMATION. Both the Spanish and American governments conducted disinformation campaigns during the war. Any consistent

Spanish effort was thwarted by military reverses from the beginning of the war. However, the government did attempt to confuse U.S. authorities by circulating "private" information in mid-June that Adm. **Pascual Cervera's Squadron**, which was blockaded at **Santiago, Cuba**, would steam to the **Philippines**. In **Puerto Rico**, Spanish Gov.-Gen. **Manuel Macías y Casado** ordered the *Gaceta de Puerto Rico*, the official newspaper, to give out false information that Adm. **Patricio Montojo's Squadron** had defeated Com. **George W. Dewey's Asiatic Squadron** in the **Battle of Manila Bay** on 1 May 1898, in order to bolster public opinion. The *Gaceta* also published news that the Cuban insurgents had given up their fight to join Spain against the United States in the war. However, when the real news soon circulated in Puerto Rico, its effects were devastating to public morale.

After Lt. **William S. Sims**, naval attaché in Paris, informed Washington in May 1898 that his agent in Paris could plant false information with **Fernando de León y Castillo**, Spain's ambassador to Paris, the **Navy Department** quickly ordered naval attaches abroad to conduct a deliberate disinformation campaign. Sims soon leaked a false report that the **Fifth Corps** intended to land at either **Cienfuegos** or **Matanzas, Cuba**. However, the main disinformation effort was meant to deter Adm. **Manuel de la Cámara's Squadron** from leaving Spain for the Philippines. On 1 June, Sims received instructions from the **Naval War Board** to give out false information about the preparation of a U.S. fleet to attack the Spanish coast. Later in June, Sims passed information that charts of the Spanish coast had been issued to American ships. Subsequently, Sims reported that the information was "apparently causing great anxiety in Madrid." During the formation of the **Eastern Squadron**, U.S. agents kept Spain apprised of its planned attack on the Spanish coast.

DIXIE. (USN) Auxiliary **cruiser**, commanded by Capt. **Charles H. Davis**. Formerly the *El Río* of the South Pacific Company, it was purchased by the **U.S. Navy** on 15 April 1898. Staffed in part by ten officers and 267 men from the Maryland **naval militia**, it was initially assigned to the **Northern Patrol Squadron** and transferred to the **blockade of Cuba** on 13 June. On 21 June, the *Dixie* bombarded one blockhouse east of **Santiago, Cuba**, and another southeast of **Cienfuegos**. After its assignment to the **Eastern Squadron** on 7 July, it captured the French steamer *Manoubia* bound for Sagua la Grande, Cuba, as a prize on 25 July; however, the steamer was later released because Sagua la Grande had not been proclaimed officially blockaded. It convoyed Maj. Gen. **Nelson A. Miles**'s expedition to **Guánica, Puerto Rico**, arriving there on 25 July. On 27 July, Lt. G. A.

Merriam, its executive officer, arranged the surrender of **Ponce**. After the war, the *Dixie* served as a training platform for fleet and landing exercises, as a transport, and later as a destroyer tender until it was sold in 1922.

La. 1893, com. 9 April 1898, dis. 6,114, hp. 3,800, sp. 16
Armament: 10–6″, 6–6pdr., 2 C. mgs.
Cc. 1,371, comp. 211

DODGE, GRENVILLE MELLEN (1831–1916). President of the **Dodge Commission**. An engineer, Civil War major general, and railroad tycoon, Dodge, a personal friend of President **William McKinley** and Secretary of War **Russell A. Alger**, believed a war would cause economic instability. Therefore, after the *Maine* explosion on 15 February 1898, he advised McKinley to keep the peace and not go to war unless to defend the nation's integrity. Upon the outbreak of war, Dodge was offered the command of the **First Corps**, but he turned it down, preferring to tend to his business affairs. After hostilities had ceased, he reluctantly agreed to serve as the president of the Commission to Investigate the War Department, which came to be known as the Dodge Commission. He later retired to Council Bluffs, Iowa.

DODGE COMMISSION (26 SEPTEMBER 1898–9 FEBRUARY 1899). Upon request of Secretary of War **Russell A. Alger**, President **William McKinley** appointed a commission to investigate the conduct of the **War Department** during the war with Spain on 24 September 1898. Its members included president **Grenville M. Dodge**; Col. James A. Sexton, a Chicago businessman and commander of the Grand Army of the Republic; Col. **Charles Denby**; Capt. Evan P. Howell, the editor of the *Atlanta Constitution*; Urban A. Woodbury, former governor of Vermont; Brig. Gen. John M. Wilson, chief of engineers; James A. Beaver, former governor of Pennsylvania; Maj. Gen. Alexander McDowell McCook; Dr. Phineas S. Conner, professor of surgery; Lt. Col. F. B. Jones, **Quartermaster Corps**; secretary Richard C. Weightmann, *Washington Post* journalist; and recorder Maj. Stephen C. Mills.

While conducting its investigation from 26 September until 9 February 1899, it came to be known as the Dodge Commission. In Washington, D.C., its sessions in the Lemon Building were open to the public, and further testimony was collected by subcommittees during visits to military **camps** and cities in 12 states. A total of 595 witnesses were called. However, because it was not a legal court of inquiry, it could not compel witnesses to attend or force them to make statements under oath, and although military officials were granted immunity from prosecution, most of them were reluctant to criticize higher-ranking officers or government officials.

In its eight-volume report, which was issued on 9 February 1899, the Dodge Commission concluded that Maj. Gen. **Nelson A. Miles**'s charges on **"embalmed beef"** lacked substantiation and rebuked Miles for withholding his suspicions from the proper authorities; moreover, it found that canned beef was an acceptable ration although it was unsuitable for the tropics. Although the commission found no evidence of corruption or criminal incompetence in the War Department, its report, without naming Alger, found that the department lacked a "complete grasp of the situation" in managing its affairs. It blamed most administrative mistakes and supply shortages on the country's historic aversion to maintaining a large standing army and cited the divided authority in the department for having produced friction for many years. However, it concluded that "notwithstanding the haste with which the nation entered upon the war with Spain," the United States should be proud of its military for ending Spanish colonial power in less than three months and teaching the world at large "the strength and the nobility of a great Republic."

DOLPHIN. (USN) Dispatch boat and **gunboat**, commanded by Com. Henry W. Lyon. With a three-masted schooner rig, it was the first vessel of the new steel navy to be completed. It circumnavigated the globe from 1885 to 1888. Assigned to the **North Atlantic Squadron** during the war, the *Dolphin* served on the **blockade of Cuba** at **Havana** and **Santiago**, and on 22 May 1898, along with the *Wasp*, it provided protective fire in a failed attempt to land two companies of infantry at Cabañas to make contact with Cuban insurgents. On 6 June, it participated in the bombardment of the Spanish forts at the Santiago harbor entrance, and later shelled the shore in support of the **First Marine Battalion** during the **Battle of Cuzco Hill** on 14 June near **Guantánamo, Cuba**. After the war, it served as a special dispatch ship for the secretary of the navy. Purchased by the Mexican navy in 1922, it was scrapped in 1925.

La. 1884, com. 1885, dis. 1,486, hp. 2,255, sp. 16
Armament: 2–4″, 2–6pdr., 4–47 mm. rev.
Cc. 265, comp. 152

DON ANTONIO DE ULLOA. (SPN) **Gunboat**, commanded by Capt. José de Iturralde. Designated by the Spanish as an unprotected **cruiser**, it was built in Cartagena, Spain. Stationed at **Manila, Philippines**, it was part of Adm. **Patricio Montojo's Squadron**. Two of its 4.7-inch guns had been removed and installed in shore batteries. During the **Battle of Manila Bay** on 1 May 1898, it was hit a countable

37 times and sustained casualties of eight dead and ten wounded. It was sunk by gunfire in some five fathoms of water but did not burn.

La. 1887, dis. 1,152, hp. 1,500, sp. 12.5
Armament: 4–4.7″, 2–3″, 6–2.25″–1.46″, 1 mg., 2–14″ tt.
Cc. 220, comp. 190

DON JUAN DE AUSTRIA. (SPN) **Gunboat**, commanded by Comdr. Juan de la Concha. Designated by the Spanish as an unprotected **cruiser**, it was built in Cartagena, Spain. Stationed at **Manila, Philippines**, it was part of Adm. **Patricio Montojo's Squadron**. During the **Battle of Manila Bay** on 1 May 1898, it sustained 22 wounded and was deliberately sunk by its crew. After being fired by the *Petrel*, its magazines blew up in the night of 1 May. After being raised, it was taken to **Hong Kong**, repaired, and placed into U.S. service in Chinese waters by the end of November 1898. From 1907 until 1917 it served with the Michigan **naval militia** and was sold in 1919.

La. 1887, dis. 1,159, hp. 1,200, sp. 14.5
Armament: 4–4.7″, 2–3″, 6–2.25″–1.46″, 1 mg., 2–14″ tt.
Cc. 220, comp. 207

DORST, JOSEPH HADDOX (1852–1915). Captain, Fourth U.S. Cavalry. A West Point graduate and veteran of the Indian campaigns on the frontier, Dorst, promoted to lieutenant colonel (USV) on 9 May 1898, led expeditions during May to land supplies for the Cuban insurgents. His efforts were all the army could point to by way of land operations during the first two months of the war. The most famous of these expeditions were the *Gussie* and *Florida* **expeditions**. During the **Santiago, Cuba, campaign**, while serving as the adjutant to Maj. Gen. **Joseph Wheeler**, Dorst fought in the **Battle of Kettle Hill** on 1 July and two days later carried Maj. Gen. **William R. Shafter**'s first surrender demand to Spanish General of Division **José Toral y Velázquez**. After the war he fought in the **Philippine Insurrection** and was promoted to colonel in 1903.

DU BOSC, JUAN. Spanish charge d'affaires in Washington (11 February 1898–21 April 1898). After **Enrique Dupuy de Lôme** resigned, Du Bosc served as Spain's Interim Minister to Washington until the arrival of **Luis Polo de Bernabé** in March 1898. Upon being replaced by Bernabé, Du Bosc wrote a final report which predicted "inevitable war by May 1". After leaving Washington along with Bernabé when the war began, he went to **Canada** where he assisted in developing Spain's **Montreal Spy Ring**. After Bernabé was expelled from Canada in late May for **espionage** activities, Du Bosc, now serving as Spain's acting consul general, directed Spain's espionage activities until he was expelled on 9 July 1898. Before he left he turned over operations to Eusebio Bonilla Martel and then returned to Spain.

DUFFIELD, HENRY MARTYN (1842–1912). Brigadier general (USV), commanded an independent brigade in the **Fifth Corps**. A lawyer, Civil War veteran, and former city counsellor of Detroit, Michigan, Duffield, who was promoted to brigadier general (USV) on 27 May 1898, commanded the First Brigade, Third Division, in the **Second Corps**. After leaving **Camp Alger** on 15 June, the 2,500-man brigade, which included the **Ninth Massachusetts Infantry**, the **Thirty-Third Michigan Infantry**, and the **Thirty-Fourth Michigan Infantry**, arrived at **Siboney**, **Cuba**, after the landing of the Fifth Corps. Subsequently, Duffield commanded the Siboney area until his brigade fought a feint engagement at **Aguadores** on 1 July as a planned diversion to assist in the main assault on the **San Juan Heights**. After returning to the United States in August, Duffield resigned his commission on 30 November 1898 and returned to civilian life. From 1910 to 1911, he served as commander-in-chief of the Naval and Military Order of the Spanish American War.

DUKE OF TETUÁN. See O'DONNELL Y ABREÚ, CARLOS MANUEL

DUNNE, FINLEY PETER (1867–1936). Preeminent turn-of-the-century American humorist. A Chicago-born newspaper man, Dunne, who had graduated at the bottom of his high school class, became a conscience that told Americans they were acting stupidly or running to extremes through his comic creation Mr. Martin Dooley, a genial Irish bartender from the south side of Chicago. In his nearly 50 pieces on the Spanish-American War and the **Philippine Insurrection**, Dunne showed great respect for the common soldier and sailor; however, he mocked imperialism and "Anglo-Saxonism," denounced the stay-at-homes who used the war for political power and financial gain, referred to Maj. Gen. **Nelson A. Miles**'s **Puerto Rican campaign** as a "gran' picnic an' moonlight excursion," and satirized **Emilio Aguinaldo**, Senator **Albert J. Beveridge**, and **Theodore Roosevelt**'s book *The Rough Riders*. Collections of his writings, such as *Mr. Dooley in Peace and in War* (1898), *Mr. Dooley in the Hearts of His Countrymen* (1898), and *Mr. Dooley's Philosophy* (1900), became popular throughout the United States because of the war.

DUPONT. (USN) **Torpedo boat**, commanded by Lt. Spencer Shepard Wood. While stationed at **Key West, Florida**, it was engaged in the suppression of **filibuster**ing expeditions and brought the orders to the

Maine to go to **Havana**, **Cuba**, on 24 January 1898. Assigned to the **North Atlantic Squadron** during the war, it served as a dispatch and patrol boat on the **blockade** off Havana, **Matanzas**, and **Santiago, Cuba**. Upon returning to New York City on 9 August, the *Dupont* had proved very dependable during the war, logging more than 9,000 miles without a mechanical failure. After the war, it served at Newport, Rhode Island, and was sold in 1920.

La. 1897, com. 1897, dis. 165, hp. 3,200, sp. 28.5
Armament: 4–1pdr., 3–18″ tt.
Cc. 76, comp. 24

DUPUY DE LÔME, ENRIQUE (1851–1904). Spain's minister to the United States (1895–10 February 1898). A member of the **Liberal-Conservative Party** and career diplomat, de Lôme was a skillful, patient, and indefatigable enemy of the Cuban insurgents. Although he loathed the uncouth Americans, he stayed on as Spain's minister under the liberal administration of **Práxedes M. Sagasta**. Predicting that Cuban independence would mean a black republic, he believed even war against the United States was preferable to a negotiated humiliation that resulted in the loss of **Cuba**. In his correspondence with U.S. diplomatic officials, he consistently blamed the insurgents for causing all the problems in Cuba, rejected U.S. intervention, advocated Cuban reforms only after the insurrection had been pacified, and supported allowing U.S. charities to assist Cuban civilians. Because of the publication of the **De Lôme Letter**, he resigned, was replaced by **Luis Polo de Bernabé**, and returned to Spain.

D.W.H.B. The international code for surrender that was hoisted on the *Olympia* at 11:00 a.m. during the **Battle of Manila** on 13 August 1898. A sketch of the flags to be hoisted had been given prior to the battle to **Edouard C. André**, the Belgian consul, who passed it on to Spanish Gov.-Gen. **Fermín Jáudenes y Álvarez**.

DYER, GEORGE LELAND (1849–1914). Lieutenant (USN), naval attaché in Spain. A U.S. Naval Academy graduate, Dyer, who had been the head of the U.S. Naval Academy's modern language department for four years, was a naval intelligence officer and served for nine months as the naval attaché in the U.S. legation at Madrid, Spain. After arriving in Spain with U.S. Ambassador **Stewart L. Woodford** in September 1897, Dyer opposed going to war against Spain. Upon leaving Spain on 23 April 1898 for Paris, he wrote "War is a horrible grisly thing and yet our people are mad for it! They will get it now, by **Jingo!**" During the war Dyer commanded the **gunboat** *Stranger* and served on the **blockade** off **Havana, Cuba**. He was the naval governor of **Guam** (1904–1905). In 1908, Dyer was promoted to commodore and retired.

DYER, NEHEMIAH MAYO (1839–1910). Captain (USN), commanded the *Baltimore*. After joining the merchant marine at the age of 15, Dyer entered the volunteer navy as a mate, was promoted to ensign for bravery, and served on various vessels patrolling the South Atlantic and Caribbean. After being promoted to commander, he served at the **Naval War College**, was promoted to captain on 13 July 1897, and was assigned to command the *Baltimore* in October 1897. While serving in the **Asiatic Squadron** during the war, Dyer was advanced seven numbers in rank for his meritorious conduct during the **Battle of Manila Bay** on 1 May 1898. After the war the citizens of Baltimore presented Dyer with a golden sword. He was promoted to rear admiral in 1901.

DYNAMITE GUNS. The Sims-Dudley version was used on the *Vesuvius*, a U.S. dynamite **cruiser**, during the war. A pocket-sized land version was used by Cuban insurgents under the command of **Frederick Funston** in the **Cuban Revolt**. During the Spanish-American War a dynamite gun was used by the **Rough Riders** in the **Santiago, Cuba, campaign** and by soldiers under the command of Maj. Gen. **John R. Brooke** during the **Puerto Rican campaign**. The land-based wheeled version had two barrels. The lower barrel fired a cartridge that pushed a piston, compressing the air, which fired the explosive gelatine charge in the upper barrel. The fuse on the charge could be set to explode on impact or to delay up to seven seconds; its range varied between one and two miles; and it could be fired up to six times a minute. However, it was not frequently fired because of its tendency to jam. The Rough Riders' gun tried one shot during the battles for the **San Juan Heights** on 1 July 1898, sprung its breech, and was useless for the rest of the day. Dynamite guns were soon made obsolete by advances in explosives.

—**E**—

EAGAN, CHARLES PATRICK (1841–1919). Brigadier general, commissary general of the **U.S. Army**. An Irishman famous for gallantry in the Indian Wars, Eagan, who was appointed commissary general in May 1898, was in charge of the **Subsistence Department** during the war. After the war Eagan's career was destroyed in the **"Embalmed Beef" Controversy**. Although the **"Beef Court"** absolved him of wrongdoing, it censured him for purchasing unduly large quantities of refrigerated beef. Moreover, Eagan, who had a notorious temper, openly accused Maj. Gen. **Nelson A. Miles** of having fabricated the entire "embalmed beef" episode and offered to "force the lie down his throat covered with the contents of a camp latrine." Consequently, Eagan was court-martialed and forced from active duty for conduct unbecoming an officer and conduct prejudicial to military discipline. Later President **William McKinley** commuted the sentence to one of suspension from rank and duty until Eagan retired in 1905.

EAGLE. (USN) **Gunboat**, commanded by Lt. William Henry Hudson Southerland. Formerly the yacht *Almy*, it was purchased by the **U.S. Navy** on 2 April 1898 and assigned to the North Atlantic Station. During the war the *Eagle* participated in Cuban **cable-cutting operations**, briefly engaged Spanish gunboats at **Cienfuegos, Cuba**, on 29 April, and destroyed a light vessel and lighthouse at Diego Perez Island 65 miles west of Cienfuegos on 11 May. While serving as a dispatch boat for Adm. **William T. Sampson**, it carried information to Com. **Winfield S. Schley** on 24 May that Adm. **Pascual Cervera's Squadron** was at **Santiago, Cuba**. However, when the **Flying Squadron** left Cienfuegos for Santiago, its bow compartment filled with water, and because no appliances were aboard, it was bailed out with buckets, slowing down the entire squadron. On the night of 7 June, it sighted the **"Ghost Squadron,"** which delayed the voyage of the **Fifth Corps** to Santiago, Cuba. The *Eagle* later escorted the **Fifth Corps** to **Daiquirí, Cuba**, and on 12 July, it captured the Spanish merchantman *Santo Domingo*, suffering one wounded in the engagement and destroying the grounded steamer.

La. 1890, com. 26 March 1898, dis. 434, hp. 850, sp. 15.5
Armament: 4–6pdr., 2 C. mgs.
Cc. 85, comp. 64

EASTERN SQUADRON, U.S. NAVY. In response to the departure of Adm. **Manuel de la Cámara's Squadron** from Spain for the **Philippines** on 16 June 1898, preparations were made to send a special U.S. naval force to raid in Spanish waters, thereby hoping to force Spain to order Adm. Cámara's return. On 18 June, **John D. Long**, secretary of the navy, ordered Adm. **William T. Sampson** to detail the **battleships** *Iowa* and *Oregon* and the **cruisers** *Brooklyn*, *Dixie*, *Harvard*, *Yale*, and *Yosemite* to attack Spain if Adm. Cámara's Squadron passed Suez; and a **disinformation** campaign was undertaken to persuade Spain that the threat was real.

Adm. Sampson was loath to accept the order because he believed it would diminish his ability to sustain the **blockade of Cuba** and diminish the force necessary to fight Adm. **Pascual Cervera's Squadron** at **Santiago, Cuba**. Moreover, after the defeat of Adm. Cervera's Squadron in the **Naval Battle of Santiago** on 3 July, Adm. Sampson insisted that the ships be reassigned to the **Puerto Rican campaign**. Nevertheless, the Eastern Squadron was officially formed on 7 July, and placed under the command of Com. **John C. Watson**.

Although Adm. Cámara's Squadron began its return voyage to Spain, preparations continued, and on 9 July, Com. Watson hoisted his flag on the *Oregon*; furthermore, the squadron's mission was broadened. To accompany the squadron to Spain, a covering squadron was organized, and upon their arrival in Spanish waters, the Eastern Squadron would continue on to the Philippines because of concerns about the German naval presence at **Manila Bay** while the covering squadron harassed the Spanish coast. In late July, some of the vessels were detailed to accompany Maj. Gen. **Nelson A. Miles**'s expedition to **Puerto Rico**, and the Eastern Squadron's departure was postponed on 4 August, pending the outcome of armistice negotiations. As a result of the **Armistice Protocol** of 12 August, the squadron never left the Caribbean.

EBERLE, EDWARD WALTER (1864–1929). Lieutenant (USN). A U.S. Naval Academy graduate from Texas, Eberle commanded the *Oregon*'s forward main turret during the war. After the war he wrote "The *Oregon*'s Great Voyage," *Century Magazine* (November 1899) and "The '*Oregon*' at Santiago," *Century Magazine* (May 1899) in which he covered the *Oregon*'s voyage around South America and its participation in the **Naval Battle of Santiago** on 3 July 1898. After the war, Eberle continued to serve on the *Oregon* in the **Philippines** and later commanded the Atlantic Torpedo Fleet. While serving as superintendent of the naval academy (1915–1919), he was promoted to rear admiral, and later served as chief of naval operations (1923–1927).

ECONOMICS OF WAR—SPAIN. Prior to and during the Spanish-American War, Spain was economically weak. Its currency, the peseta, began to depreciate in 1891, and with the outbreak of the **Cuban Revolt** in 1895, an inflationary period began. Although the declining peseta and the revolt stimulated external commerce, the cost of the war, which was 1.5 billion pesetas from 4 May 1895 to 30 June 1898, proved to be insurmountable for the government. Because the administration of **Antonio Cánovas del Castillo** was unable to secure an international loan in 1896 to help cover the costs, Spain was forced to rely on an internal loan that was successful because wealthy Spaniards participated, thanks to the speculative economic conditions of the time. Nevertheless, the cost of a two-front war in confronting both the Cuban and **Philippine Revolts** proved overwhelming. In 1897 the government ran a deficit of 143 million pesetas. As food prices rose, riots began; moreover, unemployment increased and strikes occurred as factories closed. When **Práxedes M. Sagasta** took power on 4 October 1897, the treasury was empty, and the public debt was $1.7 billion. Although private fund-raising functions, such as those undertaken by the newspaper *El Imparcial*, assisted returning sick and wounded soldiers, more than one-fourth of Spain's budget of 1897–1898 was allocated to war expenditures, the peseta continued to drop, bread riots took place in a few cities, and workers protested.

During April 1898, public patriotic functions were held to raise money to finance the upcoming war against the United States. By royal decree on 14 April, a national board was established and a national subscription drive was launched with the help of the Catholic Church. However, upon the outbreak of the war, Spanish bonds dropped 29 percent of their issue value, and the government failed to float another international loan. In May the economic crisis reached a breaking point. The peseta was devalued, and riots over increasing food prices continued in a few towns; moreover, international bankers refused to extend more credit until Spain sued for peace. In the postwar period, Spain did not experience a great economic slump because the **Treaty of Paris** did not close its former markets, a new demand was created with the return of 100,000 Spaniards from the colonies, and a large amount of capital was repatriated from the colonies between 1898 to 1902.

ECONOMICS OF WAR—UNITED STATES. The Spanish-American War was an economic showcase for the United States with an inflation rate of only 8 percent and war revenue receipts far surpassing needs. By 1897 the United States was just beginning to come out of the 1893 depression and business leaders, with few exceptions, were opposed to U.S. intervention in the **Cuban Revolt**. In March 1898, **Congress** approved the **Fifty Million Dollar Bill** for defense without having to borrow.

Upon the outbreak of war, the U.S. government raised money through taxation and borrowing. Lyman J. Gage, secretary of the treasury, popularized the issue of $200 million in short- and long-term government bonds in June 1898. Because both Congress and President **William McKinley** favored the experiment of attracting large numbers of small lenders, the long-term bonds were issued in denominations as low as $20, subscriptions were received by mail, every bid under $500 was immediately accepted, and no submission above $4,500 was allowed. The public responded overwhelmingly to both the short- and long-term bonds as the total amount tendered reached an astonishing $1.3 billion. Such a "popular loan" became the precursor of the massive marketing of war bonds done during World War I. In addition to bond sales, taxes were increased as the **War Revenue Bill** was signed by McKinley on 13 June 1898. The rates of several existing excise taxes were increased and some taxes levied during the Civil War were reimposed.

The direct cost of the three-month war was around $150 million. Eventually the totals reached $283 million in net costs, $83 million in debt interest, and $4.1 billion in veterans' benefits, for a total of $4.4 billion.

EFEELE. See LARREA Y LISO, FRANCISCO [EFEELE]

EIGHTEENTH U.S. INFANTRY, U.S. ARMY. After leaving Fort Bliss, Texas, the regiment, under the command of Col. D. D. Van Valzah, arrived in New Orleans, Louisiana, and was then ordered to San Francisco, California, where it joined the **Eighth Corps**. Companies A, B, E, and G left on 15 June 1898, with the first expedition to **Manila, Philippines**, and companies C, D, F, and H left on 27 June with the third expedition. Assigned to the **Second Brigade**, the regiment, with an effective strength of 48 officers and 749 enlisted men, fought in the **Battle of Manila** on 13 August, sustaining no combat casualties during the Manila campaign. After companies I, K, L, and M joined the regiment, it fought in the **Philippine Insurrection** and returned to the United States in 1901.

EIGHTH CORPS, U.S. ARMY. Officially constituted at San Francisco 21 June 1898, it was placed under the command of Maj. Gen. **Wesley Merritt**. Originating from President **William McKinley**'s 2 May order to send an expeditionary force to the **Philippines**, regular and **volunteer** regiments were ordered on 6 May to concentrate at San Francisco. Under the direction of Brig. Gen. Henry C. Merriam, the corps began to leave San Francisco on 25 May, in seven well-organized expeditions, the first of which captured **Guam** on 22 June and arrived in the Philippines on 30 June. The entire corps had not yet arrived in the Philippines by the end of July; consequently, Merritt renamed his combined force the First Division of the **Eighth Corps** and made Brig. Gen. **Thomas M. Anderson** the divisional commander. He placed its two brigades, totaling 641 officers and 15,058 enlisted men, under the command of Brig. Gen. **Arthur MacArthur** and Brig. Gen. **Francis V. Greene**. Its artillery component consisted of 16 light field guns, six small mountain guns, and an assortment of **Gatling guns** and other rapid-fire weapons.

The corps established **Camp Dewey** south of **Manila**, and after the **Battle of Manila** on 13 August, received the **capitulation** of Manila. On 30 August 1898, Merritt was replaced as commander by Maj. Gen. **Elwell S. Otis**, who upon taking command, reorganized it into two divisions commanded by Maj. Gen. Anderson and Maj. Gen. MacArthur. The corps fought in the **Philippine Insurrection** and was discontinued on 13 April 1900.

EIGHTH CORPS'S EXPEDITIONS TO THE PHILIPPINES.

Under the direction of Brig. Gen. Henry C. Merriam, the **Eighth Corps** left San Francisco, California, in seven well-organized expeditions. On carefully prepared **transports**, each expedition sailed on a month-long 7,000 voyage to **Manila, Philippines**, using Honolulu, **Hawaii**, as a stopover en route.

The first expedition, under the command of Brig. Gen. **Thomas M. Anderson**, included 117 officers and 2,382 enlisted men. Regular units included five companies of the **Fourteenth U.S. Infantry**; and **volunteer** units included the **First California Infantry, Second Oregon Infantry**, and a detachment of California Volunteer Artillery. Carrying 400 tons of ammunition for Adm. **George W. Dewey's Asiatic Squadron**, it left San Francisco on 25 May 1898 on the transports *Australia*, *City of Pekin*, and *City of Sydney*. Included among the passengers were reporters **Oscar King Davis** of the *New York Sun*, Douglas White of the *New York Journal*, and John Fay of the *Chicago Tribune* and the *New York World*. After arriving at Honolulu, Hawaii, on 1 June, it was joined by the *Charleston*, left Honolulu on 4 June, captured **Guam** on 21 June, arrived at Manila on 30 June, and landed at **Cavite** on 1 July.

The second expedition, under the command of Brig. Gen. **Francis V. Greene**, included 3,586 officers and men. Regular units included a battalion of the **Eighteenth U.S. Infantry**, a battalion of the **Twenty-Third U.S. Infantry**, and 23 men of the Engineer Corps. Volunteer units included the **First Colorado Infantry, First Nebraska Infantry, Tenth Pennsylvania Infantry**, and batteries A and B of the **Utah Light Artillery**. It left San Francisco on 15 June, on the transports *China*, *Colon*, *Senator*, and *Zealandia*. Included among the passengers was reporter John F. Bass of *Harper's Weekly*. After arriving at Honolulu on 23 June, it coaled for two days and arrived at Manila on 17 July.

The third expedition, under the command of Brig. Gen. **Arthur MacArthur**, included 197 officers and 4,650 enlisted men. Regular units included a battalion of the Eighteenth U.S. Infantry, a battalion of the Twenty-Third U.S. Infantry, batteries G, H, K, and L of the **Third U.S. Artillery**, company A of the Engineer battalion, company

A of the **Signal Corps**, and 36 officers and 65 enlisted men of the **Hospital Corps**. Volunteer units included the **Thirteenth Minnesota Infantry**, two battalions of the **First Idaho Infantry**, two battalions of the **First North Dakota Infantry**, a battalion of the **First Wyoming Infantry**, and the **Astor Battery**. Among the passengers were 32 civilian clerks and messengers, Maj. Gen.**Wesley Merritt,** magazine writer Murat Halstead, and **Frank D. Millet** of *Harper's Weekly* and the *Times* (London). The expedition left San Francisco 27–29 June on the transports *City of Pará, Indiana, Morgan City, Newport, Ohio,* and *Valencia.* It arrived at Manila on 25–31 July.

The remaining four expeditions arrived after hostilities had ceased because of the **Armistice Protocol** of 12 August. The fourth expedition, under the command of Maj. Gen. **Elwell S. Otis**, included 3,030 soldiers. It left San Francisco on 15–19 July and arrived at Manila on 21 August. The fifth expedition, under the command of Col. H. C. Kessler, included 1,735 soldiers. It left San Francisco on 19 July and arrived at Manila on 24 August. The sixth expedition, under the command of Brig. Gen. Harrison G. Otis, included 1,735 soldiers. It left San Francisco on 23–29 July and arrived at Manila on 24 August. The seventh expedition, under the command of Lt. Col. Lee Stover, included 839 soldiers. It left San Francisco on 29 July and arrived at Manila on 31 August.

EIGHTH ILLINOIS INFANTRY (USV). Upon the second call for **volunteers**, Republican Governor John R. Tanner promptly moved to fulfill his promise to organize an all-black regiment. On 18 June 1898, the regiment was designated as the Eighth Illinois and had a complete roster of black officers. Commanded by Col. John R. Marshall, the first **Black American** Col. in the **U.S. Army**, the regiment was mustered in at Springfield, Illinois, on 12–21 July 1898, with 43 officers and 1,226 enlisted men. Although Gov. Tanner tried to have the regiment sent into combat, it saw no combat during the war. However, the regiment arrived at **Santiago, Cuba**, on the *Yale* on 16 August and performed occupation duty at San Luis, guarding Spanish **prisoners of war**. After leaving Santiago on 19 March 1899, the regiment was mustered out at Chicago, Illinois, on 3 April 1899, with 46 officers and 1,180 enlisted. Casualties sustained while in service included 16 dead from **disease**, two killed by accident, one murdered, and nine deserted.

EIGHTH OHIO INFANTRY (USV). Commanded by Col. Curtis V. Hard, it was organized and mustered into service at Columbus, Ohio, on 13 May 1898, with 48 officers and 838 enlisted men. The regiment came to be known as the "President's Own" because, by request of

President **William McKinley**, his two nephews—**James F. McKinley** and John D. Barker—were admitted to the regiment on 23 June. After arriving at **Camp Alger**, it was assigned to the Second Brigade, First Division, of the **Second Corps**. The regiment left **Camp Alger** on 5 July, and after arriving in New York City, it sailed on the *St. Paul*, and arrived at **Santiago, Cuba**, on 10 July. After briefly participating in the **Santiago, Cuba, campaign**, the regiment left Santiago on the *Mohawk* on 18 August for **Camp Wikoff, Montauk Point, Long Island, New York**. After leaving Camp Wikoff on 6 September, the regiment was furloughed for sixty days and then mustered out of service at Wooster, Ohio, on 21 November, with 50 officers and 1,180 enlisted men. Casualties sustained while in service included 75 dead from **disease** and two deserted. Col. Hard wrote of the regiment's service in his memoirs, which were later published as *Banners in the Air: The Eighth Ohio Volunteers and the Spanish-American War* (1988).

EIGHTH U.S. INFANTRY, U.S. ARMY. Commanded by Maj. C. H. Conrad, the regiment left Cheyenne, Wyoming, went to **Camp Thomas, Chickamauga Park, Georgia**, and then to **Tampa, Florida**, where it was assigned to the First Brigade, Second Division, in the **Fifth Corps**. After steaming to **Daiquirí, Cuba**, on the transport *Seneca*, the regiment, which consisted of 19 officers and 487 enlisted men, fought in the **Battle of El Caney** on 1 July, sustaining six killed and 46 wounded. On 12 August, it left on the transport *Mobile* for **Camp Wikoff, Montauk Point, Long Island, New York**.

EL CANEY, CUBA. A small village about six miles northeast of **Santiago, Cuba**, that was close to the reservoir that supplied water to Santiago, its main defenses, which were supported by trenches and rifle pits and surrounded by barbed wire, consisted of wooden blockhouses to the west and north, a stone church, and its strong point, a stone fort, *El Viso*, which was on a hill about 450 yards southeast of the hamlet. Three companies of the **Constitution Regiment**, one company of dismounted **guerrillas**, 40 soldiers of the **Cuba Regiment**, and 50 soldiers of the mobilized forces, totaling 521 men, were stationed here under the command of Brig. Gen. **Joaquín Vara del Rey**. As part of Santiago's outer defensive line, it was attacked and taken after a ten-hour battle on 1 July 1898, by the Second Division of the **Fifth Corps**.

After a 3 July meeting between the foreign consuls in Santiago and U.S. officials, Santiago's civilians were allowed to evacuate Santiago and move to El Caney. Subsequently, close to 20,000 civilians arrived. Horrible conditions soon developed, and **Frederick W. Rams-**

den, British consul at Santiago, reported starvation at El Caney by 8 July. On 14 July, the refugees drew up a petition asking to return to Santiago. Their request was granted by American and Spanish authorities, and by 16 July they had returned to Santiago.

EL CANEY, CUBA, BATTLE OF (1 JULY 1898). According to the plan of Maj. Gen. **William R. Shafter**, **El Caney** was to be attacked and taken within two hours by the 6,653-man Second Division under the command of Brig. Gen. **Henry W. Lawton**, and then Lawton's force would join in the main attack on the **San Juan Heights** on 1 July 1898. However, the Spanish 521-man defending garrison, commanded by Brig. Gen. **Joaquín Vara del Rey** and armed only with **Mauser rifles**, held off the U.S. attack for ten hours before succumbing.

With Brig. Gen. **William Ludlow**'s brigade on the U.S. left, Brig. Gen. **Adna R. Chaffee**'s brigade on the right, and Col. **Evan Miles**'s brigade held in reserve in the center, the U.S. attack, which took the form of a gradually closing in semicircle, began at 6:35 a.m. when Capt. **Allyn Capron**'s battery of four light artillery pieces opened fire on the village. Even though Lawton's force was reinforced with the arrival of Brig. Gen. **John C. Bates's Independent Brigade**, the U.S. forces failed to carry the position; moreover, Lawton was ordered to break off the attack. His request to continue was granted, and at 2:00 p.m. Capron's battery, which had been moved to within 1,000 yards of the Spanish positions, began to breach the walls of the stone fort. After the stone fort was taken by the **Twelfth Infantry** and **Twenty-Fourth Infantry** shortly after 3:00 p.m., fighting continued until 5:00 p.m.

Having run out of ammunition, the Spanish forces, reduced to 80 effectives, retreated. They had sustained 235 casualties, including the deaths of Brig. Gen. Vara del Rey and his two sons. About 100 men managed to get back to **Santiago**, and 126 were taken prisoner. U.S. casualties included 81 dead and 360 wounded. As Lawton's division moved out for the San Juan Heights at 8:00 p.m., the battle had produced a feeling of mutual respect between Spanish and American soldiers.

EL POZO, SANTIAGO, CUBA. A high hill known as "the well" 2,500 yards in front of the **San Juan Heights**. Prior to the battles of 1 July 1898, Maj. Gen. **Joseph Wheeler**'s Dismounted Cavalry Division and Brig. Gen. **Jacob F. Kent**'s First Division of the **Fifth Corps** were encamped near here. From here they assaulted the San Juan Heights on 1 July, while Capt. **George Grimes**'s battery of four 3.2-inch guns, which was posted near here, opened fire on the heights. Lt. Col. **Edward J. McClernand**, adjutant of the Fifth Corps, was stationed here on 1 July, in order to relay messages between Maj. Gen. **William R. Shafter**, who was ill at his headquarters one mile east of El Pozo, and the forces attacking **El Caney** and the heights. Although a system of messengers and telephone lines was set up, it failed to work properly, resulting in many commanders directing their units on 1 July without directions from their superior officers. After the battles of 1 July, two batteries of light artillery were established here to support the American entrenchments on the heights. On 2 July, a council of commanders of the Fifth Corps was held here. Maj. Gen. William R. Shafter was dissuaded from retreating and the corps remained entrenched in front of **Santiago, Cuba**.

ELLICOTT, JOHN MORRIS (1859–1955). Lieutenant (USN), served on the *Baltimore*. After serving in the **Asiatic Squadron** and fighting in the **Battle of Manila Bay** on 1 May 1898, Ellicott conducted a careful investigation of the destroyed Spanish ships. In his *Effect of the Gun Fire of the United States Vessels in the Battle of Manila Bay (May 1, 1898)*, which was published by the **Office of Naval Intelligence** in 1899, he concluded that the iron and steel plates on the sides of the Spanish vessels did not slow down the U.S. projectiles enough to explode them. Moreover, it was apparent that 8-inch shells had much greater effect for their size than those of lesser caliber, and gun shields struck from a distance of over 2,500 yards were dangerous to those supposedly protected by them. Ellicott concluded that the Spanish ships had broken off action because of conflagration and casualties to personnel rather than sinking, which occurred later on. An eyewitness to the surrender of Corregidor, he also wrote about the surrender, the **marines'** participation in the war, and the defenses of **Manila Bay, Philippines**. His observations influenced later naval construction.

ELLIOTT, GEORGE FRANK (1846–1931). Captain (USMC), commanded Company C in the **First Marine Battalion**. From Alabama, Elliott left West Point after two years to take a 2nd Lt. commission in the Marine Corps. By 1894 he was the fleet marine officer on Asiatic station on the *Baltimore*. After the outbreak of war, Elliott went to **Guantánamo, Cuba**, where he commanded two marine companies during the **Battle of Cuzco Hill** on 14 June 1898. His conduct advanced him three numbers in grade, and he was written about by **Stephen Crane** in "The Red Badge of Courage Was His Wig-Wag Flag," *New York World* (1 July 1898). Promoted to major, Elliott fought in the **Philippine Insurrection** and became commandant of the Marine Corps in 1903. Promoted to major general in 1908, he retired in 1910.

ELLIS, GEORGE HENRY (1875–1898). Chief yeoman (USN) of the *Brooklyn*. From Peoria, Illinois, Ellis enlisted in the navy in 1892. While aboard the *Brooklyn* he had distributed religious literature, and during the **Naval Battle of Santiago, Cuba,** on 3 July 1898, Ellis was the only American killed when a shell from the *Vizcaya* decapitated him while he was standing on the bridge ten feet from Com. **Winfield S. Schley**, reporting to the navigator on the distances of the Spanish ships. Schley ordered his body taken below, and he was buried later.

"EMBALMED BEEF" CONTROVERSY. Stemming from charges by Maj. Gen. **Nelson A. Miles** that refrigerated beef had been prepared with chemicals in order to preserve it, the controversy erupted when Miles appeared in front of the **Dodge Commission** on 21 December 1898 and gave sensational testimony about the "embalmed beef," which had supposedly been fed to the **U.S. Army** during the war. Based on information from Dr. **William H. Daly**, who had made several inspections of **camps** and troopships, Miles reported the use of "secret chemicals" to preserve the beef. Even though Miles and Daly were the only witnesses in front of the Dodge Commission to make the charges, their accusations filled the headlines, and the political enemies of the **McKinley administration** made the most of it. However, the Dodge Commission ruled the charges unfounded, stating that refrigerated beef was pure, sound and had not been treated with chemicals.

The army suffered serious political damage. The high command fragmented, and although Secretary of War **Russell A. Alger** and **Grenville M. Dodge** demanded the removal of Miles, President **William McKinley** refused, not wanting a bigger scandal. Officers, such as Inspector Gen. **Joseph C. Breckinridge**, who supported Miles, and others who criticized Miles, such as Commissary Gen. **Charles P. Eagan**, had their careers ruined. Subsequently, Miles, claiming to have new evidence, demanded and got another inquiry, which came to be known as the **"Beef Court."**

EMERSON, EDWIN JR. (1869–1959). A correspondent for *Leslie's Weekly* and spy for the **Military Information Division** of the **U.S. Army**. Upon the outbreak of the war, the German-born Emerson resigned his job as a secretary of the School of Education at Columbia University in New York City and tried to volunteer for army service. However, he was rejected because of poor eyesight and hired by *Leslie's* as a correspondent, even though he had no real journalistic experience. As a correspondent he sent public reports to his employer and secret reports to the Military Information Division.

As a spy Emerson carried out a courier mission to Cuban insurgent commanders and went to **Puerto Rico** in May 1898, along with Lt. **Henry Whitney**. Emerson entered **San Juan** as a German reporter, crossed the island by foot and on horseback, was arrested, and escaped by bribing his guard and stealing a horse. After he escaped to St. Thomas, Emerson returned ragged and penniless to New York City on 8 June, only to find that his employer had gone into receivership, and no one had the authority to issue him back pay. Yet, within a week Emerson was in Washington, D.C., briefing President **William McKinley**, Secretary of War **Russell A. Alger**, and Maj. Gen. **Nelson A. Miles**. Nevertheless, his exploit became one of the most publicized missions of the war as he wrote "Porto Rico as Seen Last Month," *Review of Reviews* (July 1898), and "Alone in Porto Rico: A War Correspondent's Adventure," *The Century Magazine* (September 1898). After receiving a letter from **Theodore Roosevelt** asking him to join the **Rough Riders**, he took passage on a naval ship to **Santiago, Cuba**, where he was sworn in as a trooper on 10 July. After the war Emerson recounted his war adventures in his autobiography, *Pepy's Ghost* (1900), and wrote *Rough Rider Stories* (1900).

EMPERADOR CARLOS V. (SPN) **Armored cruiser** in Adm. **Manuel de la Cámara's Squadron**. Usually called the *Carlos V,* it was being overhauled upon the outbreak of the war and was unable to sail with Adm. **Pascual Cervera's Squadron**. Quickly completed by mid-May 1898, it then joined Adm. Cámara's Squadron.

La. 1895, dis. 9,235, hp. 15,000, sp. 19
Armor: s. 2″, d. 6.5″, b. 9.75″, hoods 3 7/8″, ct. 12″
Armament: 2–11″, 8–5.5″, 4–3.9″, 2–12pdr., 4–6pdr., 4–1pdr., 2 mgs., 6 tt.
Cc. 1800, comp. 600

ENGINEERS, UNITED STATES ARMY. One of ten agencies in the **War Department**, the Corps of Engineers was under the direction of Brig. Gen. John M. Wilson (1897–1901). It was increased in April 1898, so that upon outbreak of the war the corps consisted of 109 officers and a battalion of 752 engineers organized into five companies. During the war, the War Department spent $5.5 million through the corps in its efforts to protect the United States. The corps supervised the construction of hundreds of coast artillery emplacements and mined 28 harbors. After the war, it cleared the **mines** from the harbors.

The corps also participated in overseas operations. In **Cuba** companies C and E, consisting of eight officers and 192 enlisted men under the command of Capt. Edward Burr, went on the transport

Alamo with the **Fifth Corps** to **Daiquirí, Cuba**. They built a small pier at **Siboney**, worked on the road from Siboney to **Santiago**, and Lt. Col. **George M. Derby** served as the Chief Engineer on the staff of Maj. Gen. **William R. Shafter**. After sustaining casualties of only one wounded during the campaign, they left Santiago on the *Minnewaske* on 23 August for **Camp Wikoff, Montauk Point, Long Island, New York**.

Company A, consisting of two officers and 100 enlisted men under the command of First Lt. Charles P. Echols, went with the third expedition of the **Eighth Corps** to **Manila, Philippines**, on 26 June 1898. Assigned to the **Second Brigade**, the company, with an effective strength of one officer and 58 enlisted men, fought in the **Battle of Manila** on 13 August and sustained no casualties. Subsequently, under the direction of William L. Sibert, chief engineer of the Eighth Corps, the engineers rebuilt and operated railroads around Manila.

In addition to the regular army corps of engineers, a **volunteer** brigade, consisting of three regiments, was raised by act of **Congress** on 11 May. The first regiment, consisting of 50 officers and 1,098 enlisted men, saw postwar service in **Puerto Rico** where 18 men died from **disease** and four deserted. The second regiment, consisting of 49 officers and 1,087 enlisted men, had its first and second battalions assigned to postwar Cuban occupation duty and its third battalion was sent to **Hawaii**, where it served from August 1898 to April 1899. Casualties sustained during the regiment's service included 12 dead from disease, 22 deserted, and one drowned. The third regiment, consisting of 53 officers and 1,094 enlisted men, did postwar Cuba occupation duty from December 1898 to April 1899 and sustained casualties of ten dead from disease and 29 deserted.

ERICSSON. (USN) **Torpedo boat**, commanded by Lt. Nathaniel Reilly Usher. Prior to the war it was involved in the suppression of **filibustering** expeditions while patrolling between **Key West, Florida**, and **Havana, Cuba**. Assigned to the **North Atlantic Squadron** during the war, the *Ericsson* continued to patrol the area between Havana and Key West, capturing a Spanish fishing schooner off Havana on 22 April 1898. After convoying the **Fifth Corps** to **Daiquirí, Cuba**, it served on the **blockade of Santiago, Cuba**. On 3 July, it was accompanying the **cruiser** *New York*, which was carrying Adm. **William T. Sampson** to a meeting with Maj. Gen. **William R. Shafter**, when the **Naval Battle of Santiago** began. Along with the *New York*, it steamed back to Santiago and rescued 11 Spanish officers and 90 sailors from the *Vizcaya* by laying itself alongside the exploding *Vizcaya*. It also towed small craft to pick up survivors from other Spanish ships and patrolled off Cuba until mid-August 1898. It was sunk during target practice in 1912.

La. 1894, com. 1897, dis. 120, hp. 1,800, sp. 24
Armament: 4–1pdr., 3–18″ tt.
Cc. 36, comp. 23

ERNST, OSWALD HERBERT (1842–1926). Brigadier general (USV), commanded the First Brigade, First Division, of the **First Corps** during the **Puerto Rican campaign**. A Harvard and West Point graduate, Ernst, a Civil War veteran, was superintendent of West Point from 1893 to 1898. His brigade, which consisted of the **Second** and **Third Wisconsin Infantry** and the **Sixteenth Pennsylvania Infantry**, left **Camp Thomas**, Georgia, on 8 July 1898, sailed on the transport *Grande Duchesse*, and landed at **Ponce**, **Puerto Rico**. Guided by Carlos Patterne, a young Puerto Rican, his force moved toward **Juana Díaz** and fought in the **Battle of Coamo** on 9 August. On 10 August, Ernst issued a proclamation to the people of Coamo stating no actions would be taken against its citizens who accept U.S. sovereignty. On 12 August, his brigade fought briefly in the skirmish at the **Asomante Hills**. Ernst later served as inspector general of U.S. troops stationed in postwar **Cuba** and in 1899 worked on a commission to determine the best route for a canal through the isthmus of Panama. He retired in 1906 with the rank of major general.

ESCARIO GARCÍA, FEDERICO (1854–?). Colonel of Spanish infantry. After beginning his military career in the **Philippines**, Escario returned to Spain in 1872, was gravely wounded fighting against the **Carlists**, and returned to **Matanzas, Cuba**, in 1895, where he fought against Cuban insurgents. Upon the outbreak of war against the United States in April 1898, he was based at **Manzanillo, Cuba**, and in late June led what came to be known as **Escario's Column** from Manzanillo to **Santiago, Cuba**, to aid Spanish forces fighting against the U.S. **Fifth Corps**. Promoted to brigadier general, Escario served as a commissioner and negotiated and signed the **Capitulation of Santiago Agreement** of 16 July 1898. After the war he was repatriated to Spain and served as the military governor of Alicante and as a deputy in the **Cortes**.

ESCARIO'S COLUMN. Led by Col. **Federico Escario García**, a relief column of 3,752 Spanish soldiers, left **Manzanillo, Cuba**, on 22 June 1898 and after an arduous 11-day, 160-mile march through jungle and mountains, arrived at **Santiago, Cuba**, on the night of 2 July. The column consisted of 3,300 infantry, 35 men of the medical corps, a company of transportation troops, a 250-man contingent of mounted **guerrillas**, a detachment of sappers, a section of mountain artillery with two three-inch Plasencia guns, and about 200 pack animals. The infantry, composed of five battalions of regular infantry, included the first battalion of the Andalusia Regiment under the command of Comdr. Julián Llorens, the first and second battalions of the **Isabel Católica Regiment**, a battalion of Puerto Rican Chasseurs under the command of Lt. Col. Ramón Arana, and a battalion of the **Alcántara Peninsular Regiment**.

During its epic journey, the column fought over 40 skirmishes with Cuban insurgents and sustained a 10 percent casualty rate owing to bullets, **disease**, and desertion, which included three officers and 68 soldiers wounded and 27 soldiers killed in action. The most severe fighting occurred at Aguacate on 1 July, when the column sustained seven killed and 43 wounded. Although Maj. Gen. **Calixto García** had proposed sending 2,000 of his insurgent troops to intercept the column, Maj. Gen. **William R. Shafter** ordered most of the insurgents to remain at Santiago to assist in the siege. Nevertheless, Shafter quickly blamed the Cuban insurgents for failing to stop the column.

"ESCUCHAS." Puerto Ricans led by Eduardo Lugo Viña, who assisted Brig. Gen. **Theodore Schwan**'s brigade during its seven-day campaign from 7 August to 13 August 1898 in driving the Spanish forces out of western **Puerto Rico**. Consisting of 11 men, some of whom were arrested as spies by the Spanish, they took possession of Sábana Grande in the name of the United States and then moved on San Germán, where they tried to obligate the mayor to exercise his authority for the United States.

ESPIONAGE. Prior to the war, Spain contracted the Pinkerton Detective Agency to spy on the Cuban **Junta** and to break up **filibuster**ing expeditions. Although the early overwhelming defeats put Spain on the defensive during most of the war, it conducted a minor **disinformation** campaign and established the **Montreal Spy Ring** in Montreal, **Canada**. At the Paris Peace Conference, which negotiated the **Treaty of Paris**, Sarah Atkinson, a stenographer attached to the U.S. delegation, provided Spain with information.

For some U.S. officials espionage was ungentlemanly. Secretary of the Navy **John D. Long** declined to run a secret operation from his office. Moreover, the **U.S. Army** refrained from outright espionage until the actual **declaration of war** because such action was considered unethical in time of peace. During the Spanish-American War, however, the United States had better information than Spain.

The **Signal Corps** routinely intercepted Spanish **cable** traffic and the Post Office searched the mail. Overseas, U.S. consulates monitored Spanish military activities. Of particular concern was the progress of Adm. **Manuel de la Cámara's Squadron**. The **Office of Naval Intelligence** was informed of its development by Lts. **John C. Colwell** and **William S. Sims**, and the **Navy Department** sent Ensigns **William H. Buck** and **Henry H. Ward** to Europe to monitor the squadron.

In **Cuba**, the **Hellings-Villaverde Network** provided direct intelligence from the Spanish govenor-general's palace in **Havana**, and the **Military Information Division** sent Lt. **Andrew S. Rowan** to Cuba. In the **Philippines**, Com. **George W. Dewey** established his own network. William Doherty, an American ornithologist and entomologist, took copious notes prior to the war as he walked around **Manila**. Hiding his plans of Spanish fortifications in a newly laundered shirt, which he placed in the bottom of his trunk, Doherty later gave the notes to Dewey in **Hong Kong**. Dewey also received valuable information from **Oscar F. Williams**, the former U.S. consul in Manila, **Frank B. Upham**, and an unknown businessman who made frequent trips between Manila and Hong Kong. In **Puerto Rico**, valuable information was obtained by Lt. **Henry H. Whitney** of the Military Information Division and **Edwin Emerson Jr.**; moreover, U.S. forces, upon landing were assisted by Puerto Ricans such as the **"Escuchas"** and Carlos Patterne, who accompanied Brig. Gen. **Oswald H. Ernst**'s brigade, journeyed behind Spanish lines, and carried secret information between Puerto Rican informers and U.S. commanders.

Significantly, newspapers frequently outperformed the government's intelligence agencies and then delivered their information to the U.S. authorities while at the same time sometimes publishing it. Particularly adept was the *New York Herald*, which through its worldwide network of stringers, accurately reported the journey of Adm. **Pascual Cervera's Squadron** across the Atlantic Ocean. Foremost among the reporters were **James Hare** of *Collier's Weekly*; **George B. Rea**, **Stephen Crane**, and **Harry Sylvester Scovel** of the *New York World*; Charles H. Thrall, also of the *New York World*, who spied in Havana during the war, gathered information on gun emplacements, became a wanted man with a $2,000 price on his head, was captured and later released in a prisoner exchange; Fred O. Somerford, of the *New York Herald*, who served as a liaison with Cuban insurgent Maj. Gen. **Máximo Gómez**; and William Freeman Halstead, a young Canadian who worked for the *Herald* and was arrested in Puerto Rico before the war, sentenced to nine years in jail for spying, and was freed after the war.

After the war the **U.S. Navy** aborted its network, and **Whitelaw Reid**, a member of the U.S. **Peace Commission**, recorded in his diary that the commissioners were quite satisfied with the suspension of espionage since several of them had expressed a "strong dislike for this whole spy business."

ESTRADA PALMA, TOMÁS (1835–1908). Delegate plenipotentiary and foreign representative of the **Cuban Revolutionary Party** in the United States. Estrada Palma had risen to the rank of general during the Ten Years' War against Spain, was captured, imprisoned and released upon the war's end. Eventually landing in New York, he became a naturalized citizen and ran a Quaker school. When the **Cuban Revolt** broke out in February 1895, Estrada Palma, who had long considered the annexation of **Cuba** to the United States an option, directed the insurgent **Junta** in New York City, and was an official representative of the **Cuban Republic**. He opposed **autonomy**, approved a scheme through bankers Samuel M. Janney and John J. McCook in the spring of 1897 for the sale of bonds in exchange for Cuban independence, and released the **De Lôme Letter** to the *New York Journal*. Upon the outbreak of the Spanish-American War, Estrada Palma supported U.S. intervention in Cuba, enjoining Maj. Gen. **Calixto García** to provide assistance to the invading U.S. forces. After the war he became the first president of the Cuban Republic (1902–1906), and as such, leased **Guantánamo, Cuba**, to the **U.S. Navy**.

EULATE Y FERY, JUAN ANTONIO (1845–1932). Captain, commanded the Spanish **armored cruiser** *Vizcaya*. After joining the navy at 15, he served in **Cuba** and returned to Spain to fight against the **Carlists**. Promoted to captain, Eulate returned to Cuba and in 1895 became the commander of the arsenal at **Havana**. He left Cuba on 1 January 1897 to take command of the *Cristóbal Colón*. During the war against the United States, he commanded the *Vizcaya* and served with Adm. **Pascual Cervera's Squadron**. During the **Naval Battle of Santiago** on 3 July 1898, Eulate was wounded three times, and after being blown overboard, was rescued by U.S. sailors and brought to the *Iowa*. When the *Iowa*'s guards presented arms, Eulate unbuckled his sword-belt, kissed the hilt, and offered it to Capt. **Robley Evans**, who out of respect refused to accept the sword. As Capt. Evans was escorting him to his cabin, Eulate turned toward his burning ship and exclaimed "Adios, Vizcaya!" At that moment the *Vizcaya* blew up. After being detained as a **prisoner of war** at the naval academy in Annapolis, Maryland, Eulate returned to Spain in September 1898. A military tribunal exonerated him, and he served in various naval positions, being promoted to vice admiral. Finally, in 1911, Eulate, a highly decorated veteran, retired.

EVACUATION COMMISSIONS. As part of the **Armistice Protocol** of 12 August 1898, three-man commissions were appointed on 16 August by the United States and on 22 August by Spain to arrange within 30 days for the evacuation of Spanish troops from **Cuba** and **Puerto Rico** and the transfer of the sovereignty of Puerto Rico. The U.S. commissioners for Cuba were Maj. Gen. **James F. Wade**, Rear Adm. **William T. Sampson**, and Maj. Gen. Matthew C. Butler; and for Puerto Rico Maj. Gen. **John R. Brooke**, Rear Adm. **Winfield S. Schley**, and Brig. Gen. William W. Gordon. Spain's commissioners for Cuba were General of Division Gonzalez Parrado, Rear Adm. Pastor y Landero, and the Marquís de Montoro; and for Puerto Rico General of Division **Ricardo Ortega y Díaz**, First Class Naval Capt. Vallarino y Carasco, and Auditor of Division Sanchez del Águila y León.

EVANS, ROBLEY DUNGLISON (1846–1912). Captain (USN), commanded the *Iowa*. A U.S. Naval Academy graduate, Evans, a Civil War veteran and advocate of building a new navy, earned his nickname "Fighting Bob" after using force to thwart mob violence in Chile in 1881. Evans opposed the formation of the **Flying Squadron** because it would divide U.S. naval forces, and on 26 March 1898 he took command of the *Iowa* when Capt. **William T. Sampson** was appointed to lead the **North Atlantic Squadron**. Evans supported Sampson's plan to begin the war by bombarding the forts at **Havana, Cuba**, believing it would produce an early end to the war.

In command of the *Iowa* during the **Naval Battle of Santiago** on 3 July, Evans later gave credit for the overwhelming victory to Sampson and disparaged Com. **Winfield S. Schley** for failing to quickly find Adm. **Pascual Cervera's Squadron**. Promoted to rear admiral in 1901, Evans wrote *A Sailor's Log: Recollections of Forty Years of Naval Life* (1901). Later he commanded the around-the-world cruise of the Great White Fleet of the **U.S. Navy** in 1907–1908. He retired in 1908 and wrote *An Admiral's Log* (1910).

EWERS, EZRA PHILETUS (1837–1912). Lieutenant colonel, commanded the **Ninth U.S. Infantry**, Third Brigade, First Division of the **Fifth Corps**. A career soldier, Ewers, a veteran of the Civil War and Indian wars on the frontier, commanded the Ninth U.S. Infantry during the **Battle of San Juan Hill** on 1 July 1898. After Col. **Charles Wikoff**, the brigade commander, was killed early in the battle, Ewers took command of the brigade and led it in successfully attacking and taking San Juan Hill. He was promoted to brigadier general (USV) on 12 July 1898 and retired in 1901 with the rank of brigadier general.

—F—

FAIRBANKS, CHARLES WARREN (1852–1918). Republican senator from Indiana (1897–1904) on the Senate Foreign Relations Committee. A former railroad lawyer, Fairbanks, who wanted to avoid war, was in the **"Peace Faction"** of Republican Senators. However, upon the outbreak of war, he worked with Indiana Governor James A. Mount to gain the **War Department**'s approval to organize a black battalion commanded by black officers and successfully pressured the War Department to send an Indiana regiment to **Puerto Rico** by pointing out that other states had troops in the Caribbean whereas Indiana had none. He voted for the **Treaty of Paris**, and was later elected vice president of the United States (1905–1909).

FAJARDO, PUERTO RICO. A cape and a town of 8,794 in northeastern **Puerto Rico**. Only about 35 miles from **San Juan**, Fajardo was practically undefended. It had neither permanent fortifications nor artillery batteries and was defended by two companies of Provisional Battalion No. 3. Therefore, it had initially been the destination of the U.S. expeditionary force under the command of Maj. Gen. **Nelson A. Miles** until Miles's destination was published in the U.S. **press**.

Two boats from the *Puritan* landed at the lighthouse here on 1 August and then left. The *Puritan* returned the next day with the *Amphitrite* and *Leyden*. A detachment of U.S. sailors landed and took control of the lighthouse. A local landowner arrived and convinced them to send a detachment to town. Accompanied by Dr. Santiago Veve, 13 sailors occupied the town and raised the American flag. Owing to the impossibility of reinforcements, the detachment, unable to confront nearby Spanish forces, left Fajardo the same day. The next day, 3 August, Spanish forces arrived, took down the American flag and raised the Spanish flag. Ironically, crowds cheered both flag raisings. After the war *partidas* entered Fajardo on the night of 21 September 1898 and destroyed Spanish-owned stores. On 30 September, U.S. forces formally took possession of the town.

FIFTH CORPS, U.S. ARMY. Organized at **Tampa, Florida**, it was placed under the command of Maj. Gen. **William R. Shafter** on 16 May 1898. Composed mostly of regular infantry and cavalry, the Fifth Corps left Tampa on 29 **transports** on 14 June for **Daiquirí, Cuba**. After many soldiers had been left behind because of a lack of transports, the force only included 819 officers and 16,058 enlisted men, of which on 2,465 were **volunteers**. The Fifth Corps landed at Daiquirí and **Siboney, Cuba**, beginning 22 June, and subsequently fought in the **Battles of Las Guásimas** (24 June), **El Caney** (1 July),

Kettle Hill (1 July), and **San Juan Hill** (1 July) and received the **capitulation** of **Santiago, Cuba,** on 17 July.

Beginning 7 August, because of the prevalence of **disease,** the corps was withdrawn to **Camp Wikoff, Montauk Point, Long Island, New York**. Numbering 1,109 officers and 20,761 enlisted in August, its regular units were quickly reassigned, so that by September it consisted of 218 officers and 5,136 enlisted. It was formally disbanded on 7 October 1898 at Camp Wikoff. During the war the corps sustained 243 killed in action, 1,445 wounded, and lost 771 men to disease.

FIFTH CORPS'S EXPEDITION TO SANTIAGO, CUBA. On 30 May 1898, Maj. Gen. **William R. Shafter** was ordered to proceed under convoy to **Santiago, Cuba,** and capture or destroy the garrison and with the aid of the navy to capture or destroy Adm. **Pascual Cervera's Squadron**. By 6 June, the 29 **transports** and six support vessels had been loaded with ordnance. It was then discovered that the carrying capacity was 18,000–20,000 troops, not 27,000 as had been planned; therefore, many troops were left behind as they began to board the transports during the evening of 6 June. A mad scramble to get to the docks ensued. The **Ninth U.S. Infantry** stole a wagon train to get to the docks. The **Seventy-First New York Infantry** commandeered a train at bayonet point. **Theodore Roosevelt** stole both a train to get to the docks and a ship for his **Rough Riders** upon arriving at the docks. On 8 June, the Fifth Corps left **Tampa, Florida,** only to be ordered to halt by Secretary of War **Russell A. Alger** at 2:00 p.m. because of a report of a Spanish squadron in the Bahamas Channel. After the mystery of the **"Ghost Squadron"** was cleared up, the corps finally departed on 14 June escorted by 13 naval vessels.

In addition to the Fifth Corps, the expedition included 30 civilian clerks, 272 teamsters and packers, 107 stevedores, 89 correspondents, and 11 **foreign military observers**. No fewer than 2,295 animals accompanied the expedition: 959 horses, of which 381 were private, and 1,336 pack and draft mules. Along with 112 six-mule and 81 escort wagons, there were seven ambulances, and one observation **balloon**. Artillery was in short supply as only four batteries of light artillery, two batteries of siege guns, one Hotchkiss rapid-fire revolving cannon, one pneumatic **dynamite gun,** and four **Gatling guns** were carried in the expedition. The expedition steamed east along the northern Cuban coast, rounded the eastern end of the island, and began to land on 22 June at **Daiquirí**.

FIFTY MILLION DOLLAR BILL (9 MARCH 1898). On 6 March 1898, President **William G. McKinley** called Joseph G Cannon, Republican of Illinois and chairman of the House Appropriations Committee, to the White House to discuss funding national defense. After McKinley wrote a single sentence "for national defense, fifty million dollars," Cannon, who knew the treasury could stand an outright appropriation of $50 million, retired to his hotel, and the bill for appropriating the requested funds was prepared the same evening. It was introduced in the House Appropriations Committee on 7 March and was unanimously approved by both houses of **Congress** on 9 March. There had been no debate in the Senate and only four hours of patriotic speeches in the House.

Although McKinley had hoped the appropriation would improve the nation's defenses and as a show of strength halt Spanish diplomatic intransigence, he was informed by **Stewart L. Woodford**, U.S. minister to Spain, that the bill, according to well-placed sources in the Spanish government, had killed **autonomy** in **Cuba** and only encouraged the insurgents. Madrid was stunned. Without a loan the money had been raised, and it appeared as if it had been raised for war. The *New York Journal* agreed as it announced on 8 March "For War $50,000,000"; however, the *New York Tribune* labeled it "the peace appropriation." Of the $50 million, the **U.S. Army**, which was confined by the language of the bill, spent most of its $20 million on **coastal defenses**, whereas the **U.S. Navy** spent most of its $30 million to augment its fleet.

FILIBUSTER. A corruption of the Dutch word *vrijbuiter* for freebooter, it was applied to those who ran supplies from the United States to the Cuban insurgents during the **Cuban Revolt**. Only 27 of the 71 expeditions between 1895 and 1898 reached Cuba, but they did entangle the United States in the revolt. Although U.S. officials intercepted 33 expeditions and the Supreme Court increasingly upheld convictions, Spain consistently maintained that the U.S. government was not enforcing its own neutrality laws against these expeditions. Among the most notable incidents was that of the *Competitor* in 1896. The most successful filibustering boat was the *Dauntless*, which was commanded by **Johnny "Dynamite" O'Brien**.

FIRST BRIGADE, EIGHTH CORPS, U.S. ARMY. Commanded by Brig. Gen. **Arthur MacArthur**, it was organized on 1 August 1898 and included the **Thirteenth Minnesota Infantry**, two battalions of the **Twenty-Third U.S. Infantry**, two battalions of the **First North Dakota Infantry**, two battalions of the **First Idaho Infantry**, one battalion of the **Fourteenth U.S. Infantry**, one battalion of the **First Wyoming Infantry**, and the **Astor Battery**, totaling 196 officers and 4,904 enlisted men. During the **Battle of Manila** on 13 August 1898, the brigade was on the U.S. right and sustained casualties of five killed and 38 wounded.

FIRST CALIFORNIA INFANTRY (USV). Commanded by Col. James S. Smith, the regiment was organized and mustered into service at San Francisco on 6 May 1898, with 51 officers and 986 enlisted men. As part of the first expedition of the **Eighth Corps** to **Manila, Philippines**, it sailed from San Francisco for Manila on the *City of Pekin* on 25 May. After arriving on 30 June, it disembarked on 3 July and established **Camp Dewey**. Assigned to the **Second Brigade**, the regiment sustained casualties of two dead and eight wounded during the trench engagement on 31 July, and with an effective strength of 48 officers and 904 enlisted men, the regiment participated in the **Battle of Manila** on 13 August, sustaining combat casualties of one dead and two wounded. Upon the **capitulation** of Manila, the regiment did guard and patrol duty in Manila. These events were recorded by the unit's poets O. H. Fernbach and W. O'Connell McGeehan and songwriter/poet John M. Miller. During the Spanish-American War the regiment sustained total combat casualties of three dead and ten wounded. After fighting in the **Philippine Insurrection**, the regiment left Manila on 26 July 1899 and arrived at San Francisco on 24 August. It was mustered out of service on 21 September 1899, with 50 officers and 999 enlisted men. Casualties sustained while in service included one officer and nine enlisted killed in action, three officers and 45 enlisted wounded, 24 died of **disease**, two were accidentally killed, one drowned, and seven deserted. The regiment's history was later chronicled by Charles R. Detrick in his *History of the Operations of the 1st Regiment California United States Volunteer Infantry in the Campaign in the Philippines* (1900).

FIRST COLORADO INFANTRY (USV). Commanded by Col. Irving Hale, the regiment was organized and mustered into service at Denver on 1 May 1898, with 46 officers and 970 enlisted men. It left Denver on 17 May and arrived at San Francisco on 21 May. Part of the second expedition of the **Eighth Corps** to **Manila, Philippines**, it left San Francisco on the steamship *China* on 15 June and arrived at Manila on 17 July. Assigned to the **Second Brigade**, the regiment, with an effective strength of 43 officers and 941 enlisted men, fought in the **Battle of Manila** on 13 August, sustaining combat casualties of four wounded. The regiment, which sustained total combat casualties of one dead and seven wounded during the Spanish-American War, remained in Manila doing camp, garrison, and outpost duty until 15 March 1899. Its exploits were extolled by George F. Taylor, the unit's poet, in "Colorado's Advance on Manila." After fighting in the **Philippine Insurrection**, the regiment left Manila on 17 July 1899. After arriving in the United States on 16 August, the regiment was mustered out of service on 8 September 1899, with 46 officers and 938 enlisted men. Casualties sustained while in service included 12 killed, 41 wounded, 22 died from **disease**, one drowned, one committed suicide, and three deserted. The official history of the regiment by Arthur C. Johnson is recorded in Karl Irving Faust's *Campaigning in the Philippines* (1899).

FIRST CORPS, U.S. ARMY. Organized at **Camp Thomas**, Georgia, it was placed under the command of Maj. Gen. **John R. Brooke** on 16 May 1898. During May it consisted of 1,294 officers and 23,349 enlisted. Brooke was relieved by Maj. Gen. **James F. Wade** on 23 July, and Wade was soon replaced by Brig. Gen. **Royal T. Frank**, who retained commanded until the arrival of Maj. Gen. **Joseph C. Breckinridge** on 2 August 1898.

In July 1898, with the corps numbering 1,449 officers and 35,140 enlisted, its First Division, under Maj. Gen. **James H. Wilson,** was detailed for duty in **Puerto Rico** and saw action in the **Puerto Rican campaign**. On 21 and 22 August the Second Division was sent to Camp Hamilton, Lexington, Kentucky, and the Third Division to Camp Poland, Knoxville, Tennessee. On 20 October 1898, Gen. Wilson relieved Gen. Breckinridge of the command of a reorganized First Corps, and the troops were moved to **camps** in the South. Gen. Wilson moved his headquarters to Macon, Georgia.

Under the command of Gen. Wilson, the remaining units of the corps performed Cuban occupation duty, mainly in the provinces of Matanzas and Santa Clara, during December 1898 and January 1899. The corps was discontinued by orders of 16 January 1899, and the few troops remaining in the United States belonging to the corps were assigned as separate brigades to the **Second Corps, U.S. Army**.

FIRST IDAHO INFANTRY (USV). The only regiment organized by Idaho, it was mustered into service on 7 May 1898, with 32 officers and 644 enlisted men. After leaving Boise on 19 May, it arrived in San Francisco, and the first and second battalions, under the command of Lt. Col. John W. Jones, left San Francisco on the *Morgan City* on 27 June, as part of the third expedition of the **Eighth Corps** to **Manila, Philippines**. After arriving at Manila on 31 July, the regiment was assigned to the **First Brigade** and participated in the **Battle of Manila** on 13 August 1898. After the war it did outpost and garrison duty and then fought in the **Philippine Insurrection**. After leaving Manila on 30 July 1899, it arrived in the United States on 29

August 1899 and was mustered out of service on 25 September 1899, with 32 officers and 444 enlisted men. Casualties sustained while in service included seven killed, 27 wounded, 13 died from **disease**, one was killed by accident, one drowned, and two deserted. The regiment's exploits were chronicled by James Camp in his *Official History of the Operations of the First Idaho Infantry, U.S.V. in the Campaign in the Philippine Islands* (1899).

FIRST MARINE BATTALION. On 16 April 1898, the battalion was organized for service in **Cuba** under the command of Lt. Col. **Robert W. Huntington**. Consisting of 24 officers and 623 enlisted men, it was organized into five rifle companies and an artillery battery that included four three-inch rapid-fire guns. After leaving Brooklyn, New York, on the *Panther* on 22 April, the battalion remained at **Key West, Florida**, for four weeks until it left for **Guantánamo, Cuba**, on 7 June. On 10 June, the battalion landed on the east side of Guantánamo Bay, and engaged in five days of fighting, which included the **Battle of Cuzco Hill** on 14 June.

At the end of July, the **Naval War Board** directed the battalion to seize the **Isle of Pines**; consequently, the battalion left Guantánamo on the *Resolute* on 9 August. However, the mission digressed as the naval escort bombarded **Manzanillo** on 12 August. News of the **Armistice Protocol** forced the mission's cancellation, and the battalion was disbanded in mid-September. During its service in Cuba, no one in the battalion died from **disease** and only 2.5 percent of the command became ill; moreover, it sustained only six combat deaths.

FIRST NEBRASKA INFANTRY (USV). Commanded by Col. John P. Bratt, it was organized and mustered into service on 9–10 May 1898, with 51 officers and 983 enlisted men. The regiment left San Francisco on the *Senator* on 15 June in the second expedition of the **Eighth Corps** to **Manila, Philippines**. After arriving at Manila on 17 July, the regiment was assigned to the **Second Brigade**, and with an effective strength of 39 officers and 837 enlisted men, it fought in the **Battle of Manila** on 13 August, sustaining no combat casualties. During the Spanish-American War the regiment sustained total combat casualties of one dead and nine wounded. Subsequently, it fought in the **Philippine Insurrection**. Ira Kellogg, the regiment's songwriter/poet, wrote "Nebraska's Battle Song" and the poems "A Lonely Soldier" and "Nebraska's Boys in the Trenches." After leaving Manila on 1 July 1899, the regiment arrived in the United States on 29 July 1899 and was mustered out of service on 23 August 1899. Casualties sustained while in service included 35 killed, 168 wounded, 28 died of **disease**, one drowned, and two deserted.

FIRST NORTH ATLANTIC SQUADRON, U.S. NAVY. Commanded by Com. **John C. Watson** from 1 May 1898 until 1 July when replaced by Com. **John A. Howell**, the squadron, which was known as the Blockading Squadron from 6 May to 21 June, was used to **blockade** the northern Cuban coast. According to Adm. **William T. Sampson**'s orders of 11 July, it consisted of the **cruisers** *San Francisco*, the flagship, and *Montgomery*; **monitors** *Amphitrite*, *Miantonomoh*, *Puritan*, and *Terror*; **gunboats** *Annapolis*, *Bancroft*, *Castine*, *Dolphin*, *Machias*, *Nashville*, *Newport*, and *Vicksburg*; armed **yachts** *Hawk*, *Mayflower*, and *Wasp*; armed tugs *Leyden*, *Tecumseh*, and *Uncas*; revenue cutters *Hamilton*, *Hudson*, *McLane*, *Morrill*, *Windom*, and *Woodbury*; and the lighthouse tender *Armeria*.

FIRST NORTH DAKOTA INFANTRY (USV). Organized and mustered into service on 13–16 May 1898, with 30 officers and 642 enlisted men, the first and second battalions, under the command of Lt. Col. W. C. Treumann, left San Francisco on the steamships *Indiana* and *Valencia* on 28 June, with the third expedition of the **Eighth Corps** to **Manila, Philippines**. After arriving at Manila on 31 July, the battalions were assigned to the **First Brigade**, fought in the **Battle of Manila** on 13 August, and subsequently performed garrison and outpost duty. The regiment's poet Edward S. Peterson wrote "Three Cheers for All" extolling patriotism and the flag. After fighting in the **Philippine Insurrection**, the battalions left Manila on 30 July 1899, arrived in the United States on 29 August 1899, and were mustered out of service on 25 September 1899, with 31 officers and 507 enlisted men. Casualties sustained while in service included seven killed, 14 wounded, nine died from **disease**, one was killed by accident, and one drowned. The regiment's participation in the war was chronicled by Phil H. Shortt in his *Official History of the Operations of the First North Dakota Infantry, U.S.V. in the Campaign in the Philippine Islands* (1899).

FIRST UNITED STATES CAVALRY, U.S. ARMY. Commanded by Lt. Col. C. D. Viele, it was assigned to the Second Brigade, Dismounted Cavalry Division, **Fifth Corps**. Eight troops went to **Daiquirí, Cuba** on the transport *Leona*. Consisting of 20 officers and 503 enlisted men, the troops fought in the **Battle of Las Guásimas** on 24 June, sustaining casualties of seven enlisted killed and three officers and five enlisted wounded. During the fighting for the **San Juan Heights** on 1–3 July, the troops sustained casualties of one officer and 12 enlisted killed and 47 enlisted wounded. The troops left **Santiago** on the transports *Gate City* and *Vigilancia* on 7 and 9 August, for **Camp Wikoff, Montauk Point, Long Island, New**

York. During their service in the **Santiago, Cuba, campaign**, the troops sustained 75 total casualties.

FIRST UNITED STATES INFANTRY, U. S. ARMY. Commanded by Col. **Evan Miles**, it was ordered from San Francisco, California, to New Orleans, Louisiana. Upon being transferred to **Tampa, Florida**, it was assigned to the Second Brigade, Second Division, **Fifth Corps**. While at Tampa, companies E and G participated in the *Gussie* Expedition. The regiment went on the *Segurança* as part of the Fifth Corps to **Daiquirí, Cuba**, and after Miles assumed command of the Second Brigade, the regiment, which consisted of 14 officers and 438 enlisted men, was commanded by Lt. Col. William H. Bisbee. Briefly engaged during the **Battle of El Caney** on 1 July, it sustained one wounded enlisted man. After sustaining casualties of two wounded in the **Santiago, Cuba, campaign**, the regiment left **Santiago** on the **transports** *D. H. Miller* and *Mexico* on 19 and 25 August, for **Camp Wikoff, Montauk Point, Long Island, New York**.

FIRST U.S. ARTILLERY, U.S. ARMY. As part of the **Fifth Corps**'s artillery battalion, which was under the command of Maj. John H. Dillenback, two light artillery batteries fought in the **Santiago, Cuba, campaign**. Battery E, of three officers and 79 enlisted men, was commanded by Capt. **Allyn Capron**, and Battery K, of two officers and 78 enlisted men, was commanded by Capt. C. L. Best. Only one enlisted man was killed in combat during the campaign.

FIRST U.S. VOLUNTEER CAVALRY. See ROUGH RIDERS

FIRST WYOMING INFANTRY (USV). Commanded by Major F. M. Foote, it was organized and mustered into service on 7 May 1898, with 14 officers and 324 enlisted men. The battalion arrived in San Francisco, California, on 24 May and sailed on the transport *Ohio* on 27 June, as part of the third expedition of the **Eighth Corps** to **Manila, Philippines**. As part of the **First Brigade**, it fought in the **Battle of Manila** on 13 August and later in the **Philippine Insurrection**. It left Manila on 30 July 1899, and after returning to the United States, it was mustered out of service on 23 September 1899. Casualties sustained while in service included three killed, five wounded, ten died from **disease**, and four deserted. The battalion's exploits were chronicled by Madison Stoneman in his *Official History of the Operations of the 1st Battalion Wyoming Infantry United States Volunteers in the Campaign in the Philippine Islands, 1899* (1899).

FISKE, BRADLEY ALLEN (1854–1942). Lieutenant (USN), executive officer on the *Petrel*. A U.S. Naval Academy graduate, Fiske was an inventor, had over 60 patents, and invented a telescopic sight for naval guns, which was standard equipment throughout the **U.S. Navy** by the outbreak of the Spanish-American War. During the **Battle of Manila Bay** on 1 May 1898, he directed the *Petrel*'s gunfire from a specially built wooden observation tower. After the battle, Fiske's ship fired the remaining Spanish ships. The first American to go ashore after the battle, Fiske used broken French to communicate with the Spaniards who merely wanted to surrender. They assisted him in untying tugs and launches, which he then took as **prizes of war**, and the *Petrel* steamed away with her string of prizes in tow astern. Promoted to lieutenant commander in March 1899, he fought in the **Philippine Insurrection** and in 1911 was promoted to rear admiral. Fiske believed the Spanish-American War marked the rise of the United States to the ranks of world power and wrote *Wartime in Manila* (1913) and an autobiographical account, *From Midshipman to Rear Admiral* (1919).

FLINT, GROVER (1867–1909). Correspondent for the *New York Journal*. A son-in-law of John Fiske and an ardent Anglo-Saxonist, Flint was handpicked by **William R. Hearst** to report from **Cuba** because he had actual combat experience in the Indian wars, was fluent in Spanish, and had lived in Spain. Arriving in Cuba in late March 1896, Flint spent four months in the field with insurgent forces under the command of Maj. Gen. **Máximo Gómez** and was named an honorary commander in the **Cuban Revolutionary Army** on 20 May 1896. Although only able to send four dispatches from inside Cuba, Flint had met Paulina Ruíz Gonzalez, the 21-year-old wife of an insurgent captain, and wrote about how she carried the flag into battle, personally leading charges with a machete in ten battles. During the war against Spain, Flint continued working for the *Journal*, reporting from **Tampa**, **Florida**, before the **Fifth Corps** left for the **Santiago**, **Cuba**, **campaign**. He also wrote *Marching with Gomez* (1898), a review of his experiences while in Cuba that created sympathy for the Cuban insurgents and elevated Gen. Gómez a status comparable to that of George Washington.

***FLORIDA* EXPEDITIONS.** The *Florida*, a 1,307-ton **transport**, was used during the Spanish-American War to deliver supplies to the Cuban insurgents. On 17 May 1898, it left **Tampa**, **Florida**, under the command of Lt. Col. **Joseph H. Dorst** and successfully landed 400 Cuban insurgents, 7,500 rifles, 1.3 million cartridges, and provisions at Port Banes on the northeastern Cuban coast on 26–27 May. It returned to Tampa, but was unable to go with the **Fifth Corps** to

Daiquirí, Cuba, on 14 June because it had been damaged in a collision on 9 June.

After being repaired, the *Florida* left **Key West, Florida**, under the command of Lt. C. P. Johnson, of the **Tenth U.S. Cavalry**, on 25 June. Along with the transport *Fanita*, it carried 65 animals, large cargoes of ammunition and provisions, 50 men of troop M of the Tenth U.S. Cavalry, 15 volunteers under Lt. Winthrop Chanler, and 375 Cuban insurgents. On 29 June, a landing east of **Cienfuegos, Cuba**, failed after Spanish forces arrived. The next day a repeated attempted 40 miles farther east failed after a brief skirmish; moreover, the *Florida* was grounded on a reef within a mile of the beach and had to be towed off by the *Helena* on 1 July. Finally, after sailing farther east to Palo Alto, the entire force and supplies were successfully landed.

FLYING SQUADRON, U.S. NAVY. Although U.S. naval authorities did not want to divide the fleet, public pressure to protect the east coast of the United States against possible Spanish attack forced the formation of the Flying Squadron on 17 March 1898. Stationed at Hampton Roads, Virginia, under the command of Com. **Winfield S. Schley**, its mission was to protect the east coast and to be ready to deploy to the Caribbean. The squadron was initially composed of its flagship the **armored cruiser *Brooklyn*, battleships *Massachusetts*** and *Texas*, **protected cruisers *Columbia*** and *Minneapolis*, and the collier *Merrimac*.

After arriving at **Key West, Florida**, on 18 May, the squadron blockaded **Cienfuegos, Cuba**, and by the end of May, it was blockading **Santiago, Cuba** because of the presence of Adm. **Pascual Cervera's Squadron**. By then the battleship *Iowa*, the **cruisers *Harvard*, *Marblehead***, and *New Orleans*, and the collier *Sterling* had been added to the squadron. On 21 June the squadron ceased to officially exist, and it became the second squadron of the newly designated **North Atlantic Fleet**.

FOMENTO DE TRABAJO NACIONAL, EL. Founded in Barcelona, Spain, in 1889, it was a powerful organization of Catalan industrialists, and it consistently defended the protection of its lucrative West Indies market; consequently, it opposed **autonomy** in its newspaper *El Trabajo Nacional* and by lobbying the Spanish government. Under the presidency of Juan Sallares y Plá, *El Trabajo Nacional*, on 15 January 1897, advocated the reconquest of **Cuba** by force of arms, and viewed Spaniards as a superior race. On 5 August 1898, it analyzed Spain's defeat by the United States by pointing out the failings of Spanish industrial development as having been the root cause of the defeat.

FOOTE. (USN) **Torpedo boat**, commanded by Lt. William L. Rodgers. Assigned to the **North Atlantic Squadron** during the war, it served on the **blockade of Cuba** and on 25 April 1898 briefly engaged the Spanish gunboat *Ligera* at **Cárdenas, Cuba**, which resulted in little damage to either ship. After being renamed Coast Torpedo Boat No. 1 in 1918, it was sold in 1920.

La. 1896, com. 1897, dis. 142, hp. 2,000, sp. 25
Armament: 3–1pdr., 3–18″ tt.
Cc. 44, comp. 20

FORAKER, JOSEPH BENSON (1846–1917). Republican senator from Ohio (1897–1909). A Cincinnati lawyer and former governor of Ohio, Foraker submitted resolutions calling for Cuban independence, the immediate recognition of the Cuban insurgent government, the immediate withdrawal of Spain from **Cuba**, and authorizing President **William McKinley** to use force. After **McKinley's War Message** of 11 April 1898, Foraker feared that American intervention would be turned "from intervention on the ground of humanity into an aggressive conquest of territory." However, after the easy U.S. conquest of **Puerto Rico**, he favored its retention as "simple business policy" because the Puerto Ricans had no experience in organizing a government. Foraker later authored the Foraker Act (1900), which established U.S. civilian rule in Puerto Rico. However, he wanted the United States to leave Cuba as soon as possible. Nevertheless, he voted for the **Treaty of Paris**.

FOREIGN MILITARY OBSERVERS WITH THE FIFTH CORPS. They included Colonel Yermoloff of **Russia**; Major Clement de Grandpré of **France**; Major G. Shiba and Lieutenant Saneyuki Akiyama of **Japan**; Commander Dahlgren, Captain Wester, and Captain Abildgaard of Sweden and Norway; Captain **Arthur H. Lee** of **Great Britain**; Capt. Count von Goetzen and Lieutenant Commander von Rebeur Paschwitz of **Germany**; and Lieutenant J. Roedler of **Austria-Hungary**. They were later joined by Captain Alfred Paget of Great Britain.

FORT CANOSA, SANTIAGO, CUBA. Located about a mile behind the **San Juan Heights**, 140 mounted **guerrillas** were stationed in the vicinity on 1 July 1898, when the fort served as the headquarters of Lt. Gen. **Arsenio Linares y Pombo** during the **Battles of El Caney, Kettle Hill**, and **San Juan Hill**.

FORT SAN ANTONIO ABAD, MANILA, PHILIPPINES. Located on **Manila Bay** to the south of **Manila**, its battery contained three 3.6-inch and four 3.2-inch bronze guns. During the **Battle of Manila** on 13 August 1898, the fort was briefly fired on by U.S. ships, but no fire was returned. Soon after, it was easily taken by the **Second Brigade** of the **Eighth Corps**, because it was unoccupied as a result of negotiations that preceded the battle.

FOURTEENTH UNITED STATES INFANTRY, U.S. ARMY. After arriving in San Francisco, California, five companies left on 25 May 1898, as part of the first expedition of the **Eighth Corps** to **Manila, Philippines**. After arriving at Manila on 30 June, the companies (A, C, D, E, and F), under the command of Capt. John Murphy and consisting of eight officers and 327 enlisted men, were assigned to the **First Brigade** and fought in the **Battle of Manila** on 13 August, sustaining no combat casualties. During the Spanish-American War, the regiment's total combat casualties included two dead and three wounded. Joined by companies G, I, K, L, and M, the regiment fought in the **Philippine Insurrection** and returned to the United States in 1900 and 1901.

FOURTH ARMY CORPS, SPANISH ARMY. Officially formed on 20 June 1898, it was composed of the division of **Santiago, Cuba**, and the division of **Manzanillo, Cuba**, and was initially commanded by Lt. Gen. **Arsenio Linares y Pombo** and later by General of Division **José Toral y Velázquez**. Its chief of staff was Lt. Col. Ventura Fontán. Although the forces at Manzanillo were part of the corps, they were not included in the **Capitulation of Santiago Agreement** of 16 July 1898.

FOURTH CORPS, U.S. ARMY. Organized at Mobile, Alabama, it was placed under the command of Maj. Gen. **John J. Coppinger** on 16 May 1898. Initially composed of one division under the command of Brig. Gen. **John C. Bates**, the division moved to **Tampa, Florida**, and upon moving to Miami, Florida, on 20 June, it was transferred to the **Seventh Corps**. Two more divisions were formed at Tampa, and the regular regiments were sent with the **Fifth Corps** to **Santiago, Cuba**. On 20 July, the remaining troops were moved to Fernadina, Florida. On 11 August, in an attempt to diminish **disease**, the corps, consisting of 534 officers and 12,009 enlisted, was ordered to Camp Wheeler at Huntsville, Alabama, where it was commanded by Maj. Gen. **Joseph Wheeler** from 13 October until 14 December 1898. Wheeler was replaced by a series of commanders until Brig. Gen. **Royal T. Frank** assumed command on 29 December 1898 and its headquarters was moved to Anniston, Alabama. The corps was discontinued on 16 January 1899, and its remaining units were constituted as a separate brigade in the **Second Corps**.

FOURTH OHIO INFANTRY (USV). Originally the Fourteenth Ohio National Guard, the regiment was organized and mustered into service with 50 officers and 842 enlisted men and went to **Camp Thomas**, where it became part of the **First Corps**. After arriving at **Ponce, Puerto Rico**, on 1 August 1898, it fought a **skirmish at Guayama** on 5 August. After leaving Puerto Rico on 30 October, it was mustered out of service on 20 January 1899, with 49 officers and 1,210 enlisted men. Casualties sustained while in service included one killed, nine wounded, 23 died from **disease**, and five deserted. Its wartime experience was chronicled by Charles E. Creager in his *The Fourteenth Ohio National Guard—the Fourth Ohio Volunteer Infantry: A Complete Record of This Organization From Its Foundation to the Present Day* (1899).

FOURTH UNITED STATES INFANTRY, U.S. ARMY. Commanded by Lt. Col. A. H. Bainbridge, it left Fort Sheridan in Chicago, Illinois, on 1 April and went to **Tampa, Florida**, where it was part of the Second Brigade, Second Division, of the **Fifth Corps**. Consisting of 21 officers and 444 enlisted, the regiment went to **Cuba** on the **transport** *Concho* and fought in the **Battle of El Caney** on 1 July, sustaining casualties of one officer and six enlisted killed and two officers and 33 enlisted wounded. It left **Santiago, Cuba**, on the *Seneca* on 13 August, for **Camp Wikoff, Montauk Point, Long Island, New York**. During the war, the regiment sustained 46 total combat casualties.

FOURTH U.S. ARTILLERY, U.S. ARMY. As part of the **Fifth Corps**'s artillery battalion, which was under the command of Maj. John H. Dillenback, two batteries of siege artillery commanded by Capt. William Ennis fought in the **Santiago, Cuba, campaign**. Battery G consisted of two officers and 53 enlisted men, and battery H consisted of one officer and 65 enlisted. The batteries sustained no combat casualties during the campaign.

FOX, JOHN WILLIAM JR. (1863–1919). Novelist and journalist. A Kentuckian who had graduated from Harvard and reported for the *New York Sun* and *New York Times*, Fox was already famous for *A Cumberland Vendetta* (1896), the first of a series of fictional novels on life in the mountains of Kentucky. Upon the outbreak of war, he enlisted as a private in the **Rough Riders** but was persuaded to be a reporter for *Harper's Weekly*. During the war Fox reported from **Camp Thomas** and from **Santiago, Cuba**, writing "Santiago and Caney" (30 July 1898) and "The Surrender" (13 August 1898) *Harper's Weekly*. After the war he wrote *Crittenden: A Kentucky Story of Love and War* (1899). Based on the **Santiago, Cuba, campaign**, it flowed with extravagant patriotism and national reunification.

FRANCE. Under the leadership of President Francois-Félix Faure, France declared its neutrality on 27 April 1898. Prior to the Spanish-American War, France acted to forestall war. In 1896, together with **Great Britain** and **Germany**, France sent a secret note to Spain urging it to accept a U.S. offer to mediate the Cuban conflict. In 1897, the government encouraged French holders of Spanish government bonds to support **autonomy**, and in April 1898, it participated in the **Great Powers Note**. Although sympathetic to Spain, France was not willing to act alone because its main ally, **Russia**, opposed any such course and impending difficulties with Great Britain over African problems suggested restraint.

Upon the outbreak of war, public and press opinion were overwhelmingly pro-Spanish, and it was generally believed that Spain would win owing to the inferiority of U.S. military personnel. Out of 52 newspapers in Paris, only three were pro-United States. However, opinion quickly changed after initial Spanish defeats. By the end of June, *Le Temps* and *Le Figaro* described Spain's situation as hopeless and urged an end to the war.

Under the direction of Foreign Minister Gabriel Hanotaux, the government resisted Spanish attempts to abandon neutrality, and discussed a negotiated settlement in June with U.S. Ambassador **Horace Porter**. After Hanotaux was replaced by **Théophile Delcassé** on 27 June, the government, working with **Jules M. Cambon**, its ambassador to Washington, D.C., began a concerted effort to bring about a negotiated settlement by pressuring Spain to end the war in order to limit U.S. involvement in Europe and the Mediterranean area. Cambon worked to bring about the **Armistice Protocol** of 12 August, and the government hosted the **Treaty of Paris** negotiations.

FRANK, ROYAL THAXTER (1836–1908). Brigadier general (USV), commanded the **First Corps**. Appointed to brigadier general (USV) on 4 May 1898, Frank replaced Maj. Gen. **James F. Wade** as commander of the First Corps at **Camp Thomas**, Georgia. He was relieved on 2 August by Maj. Gen. **Joseph C. Breckinridge**. In September Frank commanded Camp Shipp at Anniston, Alabama, and the **Third Corps**, which was stationed at the camp. Frank assumed command of the **Fourth Corps** on 29 December 1898 at Anniston, Alabama, and commanded the corps until it was discontinued on 16 January 1899.

FRYE, WILLIAM PIERCE (1831–1911). Republican senator from Maine (1881–1911) and president pro tempore of the Senate. An outspoken expansionist who favored the U.S. conquest of **Cuba** before the war, Frye, a member of the Committee on Foreign Relations, requested a **battleship** to patrol the Maine coast upon the outbreak of the Spanish-American War. After having openly advocated the conquest of the **Philippines** and **Puerto Rico** during the war, Frye served on the U.S. **Peace Commission** that negotiated the **Treaty of Paris**. When the negotiations were stalled by a formal U.S. demand for all of the Philippines on 31 October 1898, Frye suggested paying Spain $10–20 million dollars for the islands. After returning to the United States, he voted to ratify the Treaty of Paris.

FUNSTON, FREDERICK. (1865–1917). Known as "Fightin' Fred," Funston joined the **Cuban Revolutionary Army** and rose to a lieutenant colonel in command of artillery. Because of illness, Funston returned to the United States early in 1898. Upon the outbreak of the Spanish-American War, he was appointed to command the Twentieth Kansas Infantry (USV), and although he did not see action in the war, he later fought in the **Philippine Insurrection**, becoming famous for his capture of **Emilio Aguinaldo** on 23 March 1901. He later wrote *Memories of Two Wars: Cuban and Philippine Experiences* (1911), in which he recounted his experiences as a **filibuster** in **Cuba** and fighting in the Philippine Insurrection. He was promoted to major general in 1914.

FUROR. (SPN) **Torpedo-boat destroyer**, commanded by Comdr. Diego Carlier. As part of Adm. **Pascual Cervera's Squadron**, it was destroyed in the **Naval Battle of Santiago** on 3 July 1898. After leaving the harbor it moved east, and upon seeing the armed **yacht** *Gloucester* moving in, it turned west. Coming under intense fire, the *Furor*'s engine and steering were quickly disabled. A white flag was displayed and the order was given to abandon ship. Within 20 minutes after having left the harbor entrance, it was sunk in the surf close to **Cabañas Bay** by the *Gloucester* at 10:45 a.m.

La. 1896, dis. 380, hp. 6,000, sp. 28
Armament: 2–14pdr., 2–6pdr., 2–1pdr. M., 2–14″ tt.
Cc. 100, comp. 67

—G—

GALICIA. (SPN) Torpedo **gunboat**, commanded by Lt. Aurelio Matos. A steel-hulled, single-funnel, two-masted rig based at **Cienfuegos**,

Cuba, it engaged the *Yankee* on 13 June 1898, escaping with the help of shore batteries.

La. 1891, dis. 530, hp. 2,600, sp. 18
Armor: d. .5″
Armament: 6–2.25″ N., 1 mg., 2 tt.
Cc. 106, comp. 96

GAMAZO, GERMÁN (1838–1901). Spanish minister of production and **Liberal Party** leader. The foremost representative of the Castilian wheat growers, Gamazo, who closely collaborated with his brother-in-law **Antonio Maura y Montaner**, split with **Práxedes M. Sagasta** over Sagasta's support of free trade. He was a moderate leader of the right wing of the Liberal Party and supported **autonomy** for the colonies. In October 1897, Gamazo refused to join Sagasta's recently formed government and later opposed Spain's going to war against the United States. In the reshuffling of the Sagasta government in May 1898, he accepted the position of minister of production and pressed for an early peace. After Spain's disastrous defeat in the **Naval Battle of Santiago** on 3 July, Gamazo demanded peace no matter what the terms. In the postwar period he competed with **Segismundo Moret y Prendergast** for the leadership of the Liberal Party.

GARCÍA, PANTALEON T. (1856–1936). A prominent military and political leader in the Filipino insurgent movement. From **Cavite**, García joined the **Katipunan** in 1896. Fighting in many battles against the Spanish, he was promoted to brigadier general and presided over the board that tried **Andres Bonifacio** and his brother Procopio during April and May 1897. He recommended a court-martial, which sentenced the Bonifacio brothers to death.

As part of the **Pact of Biak-Na-Bató** settlement, García left the **Philippines** with **Emilio Aguinaldo** for **Hong Kong** in late December 1897. Subsequently, he returned to the Philippines, and after the outbreak of the Spanish-American War, he was appointed by Gov. Gen. **Basilio Augustín y Dávila** to the **Consultative Assembly** in early May 1898. García soon left the assembly, and shortly after Aguinaldo's return on 19 May, he served as an insurgent commander near **Manila**. In July, García, along with Artemio Ricarte, attempted to negotiate Manila's surrender, but nothing came of it because the Spanish refused to surrender to the insurgents. He was a delegate to the **Malolos Congress** in September 1898, which established the Philippine Republic. After the outbreak of the **Philippine Insurrection**, García was promoted to general of division and was the supreme commander in Central Luzon. After being captured in 1900, he accepted amnesty, took the oath of allegiance to the United States, and occupied several positions in the U.S.-controlled government.

GARCÍA IÑIGUÉZ, CALIXTO (1839–1898). Major general in the Cuban insurgent forces. A veteran of previous wars for Cuban independence, García, a tall, elderly man, left Spain to join the **Cuban Revolt** when it began in 1895. During the revolt, García, whose son was an insurgent general, commanded the Liberating Army in eastern **Cuba**. When Spain declared a suspension of hostilities on 11 April 1898, he immediately rejected the offer and continued campaigning, forcing the Spanish into defensive positions throughout eastern Cuba. He met with Lt. **Andrew S. Rowan** on 1 May, and after Maj. Gen. **Nelson A. Miles** requested his assistance, he agreed to help the **Fifth Corps** when it landed in eastern Cuba. García attended the **Aserraderos Conference** on 20 June, and although he cooperated with U.S. forces, he informed **Tomás Estrada Palma** on 27 June that he suspected that the United States did not intend to recognize the **Cuban Republic** after the expulsion of the Spanish army. However, he felt American public opinion, despite the **McKinley administration**'s policy, would work on behalf of Cuban independence.

During the siege of **Santiago, Cuba**, by the Fifth Corps, García deployed his forces northwest of the city and on 17 July wrote a letter to Maj. Gen. **William R. Shafter** protesting the insurgent exclusion from the **capitulation** of Santiago and the temporary retention of Spanish officials in office. In protest over U.S. actions, he submitted his resignation and retired with his forces to Jiguaní. Subsequently, Brig. Gen. **Leonard Wood** tried to placate him by inviting him to the United States. He accepted, was honored with a public ceremony in New York City, and went to Washington, D.C., where he met President **William McKinley**. While in Washington, D.C., García died on 11 December, and a state funeral was held for him in **Havana, Cuba**, in February 1899.

GARRETSON, GEORGE ARMSTRONG (1844–1916). Brigadier general (USV), commanded the Second Brigade, First Division, **Second Corps**. A West Point graduate, Garretson had resigned from the army and spent his life as a banker and staunch Republican in Cleveland, Ohio, until the outbreak of war. Promoted to brigadier general (USV) on 4 May 1898, he took command of a brigade at **Camp Alger**. His brigade, which consisted of the **Sixth Illinois Infantry**, **Sixth Massachusetts Infantry**, and the **Eighth Ohio Infantry**, left camp on 5 July 1898, arrived at **Siboney, Cuba**, on 11 July, and then landed at **Guánica, Puerto Rico** as part of Maj. Gen. **Nelson A. Miles**'s invasion force. His brigade, which was part of Brig. Gen.

Guy V. Henry's division, immediately moved on **Yauco** and on 26 July, before reaching Yauco, fought a brief skirmish against Spanish forces. His force occupied Yauco on 28 July. Arriving at **Ponce** on 4 August, his brigade moved north to Adjuntas and was aptly assisted by **engineers** in crossing the difficult country between Adjuntas and Utuado, which it reached on 16 August.

GATLING GUN. A multiple-barrel, rapid-fire gun invented by Richard J. Gatling, it was officially adopted by the **U.S. Army** in 1866 and used in the west. Consisting of six to ten .30-caliber barrels in a rotating cylindrical mount, the gun could fire up to 1,200 rounds per minute when a gunner turned the crank, and 3,000 per minute when it was motor driven. The gun was drawn by a pair of mules, and because it was mounted on wheels, it was more mobile than the **Colt Rapid-Fire Gun**. The gun was used as a close support machine gun for the first time during the Spanish-American War in the **Santiago**, **Cuba**, and **Puerto Rican campaigns**.

GEIER. German light **cruiser**. Built for colonial work, it had a barkentine rig, ram bows, and wooden sheathing. On 9 December 1897, it left Kiel, **Germany**, arriving in Port-au-Prince, Haiti, on 9 January 1898. Its mission was to enforce a German indemnity demand on Haiti. After the *Geier* had visited **Havana**, **Cuba**, U.S. Consul General **Fitzhugh Lee** advised President **William McKinley** that its visit to Havana would provide an excellent pretext for sending a U.S. warship there. Soon the *Maine* was dispatched to Havana. During the war the *Geier* cruised the Caribbean, visiting **San Juan**, **Puerto Rico**, and Havana and **Cienfuegos**, **Cuba**. During World War I, it was captured by the **U.S. Navy** in 1917 and sunk in 1918.

La. 1894, dis. 1,888, hp. 2,800, sp. 15.5
Armament: 8–105 mm., 2 tt.
Comp. 160

GENERAL LEZO. (SPN) **Gunboat**, commanded by Lt. Comdr. Rafael Benavente. Designated by the Spanish as a third-class **cruiser**, it was an iron-hulled, single-funneled boat with a light schooner rig designed for colonial duty. Stationed at **Manila**, **Philippines**, the *General Lezo* was part of Adm. **Patricio Montojo's Squadron**, and its 4.7-inch guns had been removed before the war to strengthen the shore batteries at the entrance to **Manila Bay** while its crew was assigned to other ships. Anchored in **Bacoor Bay**, it was undergoing repairs and therefore was not engaged in the **Battle of Manila Bay** on 1 May 1898. Nevertheless, it was fired by the *Petrel* after the battle.

La. 1885, dis. 524, hp. 600, sp. 11
Armament: 2–4.7″, 1–3.5″, 3 mgs., 1 tt.
Cc. 80, comp. 135

"GENERATION OF 98." Spain's defeat in the Spanish-American War presented many Spanish writers with the perception of a national catastrophe that provided the context for their criticisms. First called the "Generation of the Disaster" by historian Gabriel Maura y Gamazo, the name was popularized by **José Martínez Ruiz, "Azorín,"** in an article "The Generation of 1898″ in his collection of essays *Clásicos y modernos* (1913). Although it was a misnomer because 1898 did not mark a crisis in Spanish letters, it represented a long Spanish tradition of social and political criticism. However, the war, which writers frequently referred to as "The Disaster," gave them the opportunity to call for national regeneration through European ideals while retaining Spanish traditional virtues. The result was a literary revival that impacted succeeding generations and included, among others, novelists Pío Baroja y Nessi, Vicente Blasco Ibáñez, and Ramón María del Valle-Inclán; playwright Jacinto Benavente; poets Ramón Jimenez and Antonio Machado y Ruiz; and writers Jose Martínez Ruiz, Jose Ortega y Gasset, and **Miguel de Unamuno.**

GERMAN-SPANISH UNDERSTANDING (10 SEPTEMBER 1898). Unbeknownst to the U.S. **Peace Commission** at the **Treaty of Paris** negotiations, Spain and **Germany** concluded a secret understanding on 10 September 1898 that called for the cession of **Kusaie,** Yap, and Ponape in the Caroline Islands in the Pacific Ocean to Germany provided Spain achieved its aims in the Treaty of Paris negotiations. Although Spain did not achieve its aims, eventually Germany purchased the Carolines in 1899.

GERMANY. Although Kaiser **Wilhelm II** had frequently and vociferously expressed his support for Spain prior to and during the war, under the guidance of Foreign Minister **Bernhard von Bülow** Germany worked to preserve the Spanish monarchy, expand its influence in the Far East, and rejected Filipino insurgent appeals for help against Spain. Although unwilling to take the lead in any concerted European diplomatic prewar action that would antagonize the United States, Theodor Ludwig von Hollenben, Germany's Ambassador to Washington, D.C., signed the **Great Powers Note** of 6 April 1898.

Upon the outbreak of the Spanish-American War most of the German press and public sided with Spain; nevertheless, through official statements by Kaiser Wilhelm and Foreign Minister von Bülow, Germany declared its official neutrality. German warships, under the command of Vice Admiral **Otto von Diederichs**, were sent to **Manila Bay**, **Philippines**, to observe the war, because German policy hoped to bring about a neutralization of the Philippines and possibly pick up some colonial crumbs to be used as naval fulcra. After the signing of the **Armistice Protocol** on 12 August, Germany entered into a secret **German-Spanish Understanding** on 10 September concerning islands in the Caroline Islands.

"GHOST SQUADRON". On the night of 7 June 1898, the *Eagle* reportedly sighted a Spanish **cruiser** and destroyer while passing through the St. Nicholas Channel off the northern Cuban coast. The departure of the **Fifth Corps** from **Tampa, Florida**, for **Santiago, Cuba**, was immediately halted. A skeptical Adm. **William T. Sampson** soon sent Lt. **Victor Blue** ashore at Santiago to verify the presence of Adm. **Pascual Cervera's Squadron** in the harbor. On 10 June, the *Yankee* arrived at Santiago and reported sighting eight vessels, including a **battleship**. The mystery was solved on 11 June when the *Armeria*, *Panther*, *Scorpion*, *Supply*, and *Yosemite* arrived at Santiago. Sampson realized that three of the ships, along with the English ship *Talbot*, which had been in the vicinity of the sighting, had been mistaken for the enemy. Sampson's opinion was confirmed by Lt. Victor Blue's report that all of Adm. Cervera's Squadron was anchored in Santiago harbor. The incident caused a six-day delay in the departure of the Fifth Corps.

GIBBS, JOHN BLAIR (1859–1898). Ens. (USN), acting assistant surgeon for the **First Marine Battalion** at **Guantánamo, Cuba**. A graduate of the University of Virginia Medical School, Gibbs was a well-known and respected surgeon in New York City. Upon the outbreak of war, he volunteered and reported to **Key West, Florida**, where he was assigned to the First Marine Battalion. At Guantánamo, Gibbs treated **Stephen Crane** for fever and was shot and killed, possibly by friendly fire, the night of 11–12 June 1898. His death was an intensely personal experience for Crane, who subsequently wrote about Gibbs in "The Red Badge of Courage Was His Wig-Wag Flag" *New York World* (1 July 1898).

GLASS, HENRY (1844–1908). Captain (USN), commanded the **cruiser** *Charleston*. A U.S. Naval Academy graduate, Civil War veteran, and author of *Marine International Law* (1885), Glass had commanded the *Texas* and was captain of the Navy Yard at Mare Island when appointed to the *Charleston*, which he commanded from May to December 1898. He commanded the U.S. naval forces that captured **Guam** on 22 June 1898. After the **capitulation** of **Manila, Philip-**

pines, on 13 August 1898, Glass served as captain of the Port of Manila through October. Later, while commanding the Naval Training Station at San Francisco, he was promoted to rear admiral in 1901. After briefly commanding U.S. naval forces in the Pacific, he retired in 1906.

GLOUCESTER. (USN) **Gunboat**, commanded by Lt. Comdr. **Richard Wainwright**. Formerly J. Pierpont Morgan's **yacht** *Corsair*, it was purchased by the **U.S. Navy** for $225,000 on 23 April 1898 and assigned to the North Atlantic Station. It carried information concerning U.S. plans to attack **Santiago, Cuba**, from Maj. Gen. **Nelson A. Miles** to Cuban insurgent Maj. Gen. **Calixto García** on 6 June and transported Cuban insurgents to Sigua, near Santiago, Cuba, on 21 June. While serving on the **blockade of Santiago, Cuba**, the *Gloucester* was assigned to intercept the Spanish **torpedo-boat destroyers** as they emerged from the harbor. During the **Naval Battle of Santiago** on 3 July, it was nearly hit by friendly fire as it moved across the line of fire of the *Indiana*, and it fired 1,369 shots, pounding the Spanish torpedo-boat destroyers *Furor* and *Plutón*. After the battle it rescued Spanish survivors from the *Furor*, *Plutón*, and *Infanta María Teresa*, who included Adm. **Pascual Cervera**, Cervera's son Lt. Angel Cervera, and Capt. Pedro Vásquez. After convoying Maj. Gen. Nelson A. Miles's expedition to **Guánica, Puerto Rico**, it was the first ship into Guánica harbor. Later Howard Sprague painted the *Gloucester at the Naval Battle of Santiago*, which appeared in the *Century Magazine* in May 1899, and *The Log of the U.S. Gunboat Gloucester* was published by the U.S. Naval Academy in 1899. The *Gloucester* was sold in 1919.

La. 1891, com. 20 May 1898, dis. 786, hp. 2,000, sp. 17
Armament: 4–6pdr., 4–3pdr., 2 C. mgs.
Cc. 120, comp. 94

GODKIN, EDWIN LAWRENCE (1831–1902). Editor of the *New York Evening Post* and *The Nation*. The Irish-born Godkin, an ardent antiexpansionist, harshly criticized the **"yellow press"**, calling the yellow journals "the nearest approach to hell," "a national disgrace," and "public evils" in his many editorials. He directly accused the *New York Journal* and *New York World* of gross misrepresentation of the facts concerning the *Maine* disaster. Opposed to a war with Spain, Godkin blamed the yellow journals for causing the war in their efforts to sell newspapers and criticized the U.S. **press** for deliberately hushing up the seamy side of the war. He opposed the conquest of **Puerto Rico** and subsequently demanded self-government for the island. Furthermore, he opposed the annexation of **Hawaii** and the retention of the **Philippines** on racial grounds and supported the **Anti-Imperialist League**.

GÓMEZ Y BÁEZ, MÁXIMO (1836–1905). Major general and general-in-chief of the **Cuban Revolutionary Army**. Born in the Dominican Republic, Gómez served in the **Spanish army** and then dedicated three decades of his life to fighting for Cuban independence. After the outbreak of the **Cuban Revolt** in February 1895, he landed in **Cuba** on 11 April 1895, and believing the Cubans could win without U.S. intervention, he conducted a scorched earth campaign of economic sabotage that intended to eventually force Spain to withdraw from Cuba when the cost of maintaining its control exceeded its yield. Gómez rejected Spain's offer of **autonomy**, ordering his men to shoot anyone who accepted, and upon the outbreak of the Spanish-American War, he rejected Gov. Gen. **Ramón Blanco**'s proposal of a Spanish-Cuban alliance against the United States.

Following the landing of the **Fifth Corps** at **Daiquirí, Cuba**, on 22 June 1898, Gómez was troubled by the racism and arrogance of the U.S. soldiers; however, he supported a policy of accommodation with the United States. After the signing of the **Armistice Protocol**, which ended hostilities on 12 August, Gómez agreed that his men would disband upon being paid by the United States. He retired from the political scene, wrote articles warning of American designs on Cuba, and believing the first Cuban president should be native born, he rejected an invitation to run for the Cuban presidency in 1900. He died in **Havana, Cuba**, in 1906.

GÓMEZ NÚÑEZ, SEVERO (1859–?). Captain of Spanish artillery at **Havana, Cuba**. Having studied artillery in Spain, Gómez Núñez, upon assignment to Havana, became a faculty member in the sciences at the University of Havana. An authoritative Spanish commentator on the war, he covered the war in **Cuba**, the **Philippines**, and **Puerto Rico** in his five-volume *The Spanish-American War (La guerra hispano-americana)* (1899–1902). Protesting the "deathlike silence" of many Spaniards following the war, he maintained there was a moral obligation to speak out. While pointing out mistaken Spanish policies in the colonies, Gómez Núñez maintained that the Cuban insurrection could not have existed without U.S. support; moreover, tragically Spain had erroneously believed a conflict with the United States could be avoided by diplomacy. Upon the outbreak of war, Spain had gone to war with a mistaken conception of its own strength, had sent the already doomed Adm. **Pascual Cervera's Squadron** to the West Indies merely for political motives, and had failed to concentrate its forces at **Manila, Philippines**. Consequently, it was unjust to throw all the blame on the military, because a disorganized government had directly caused a disorganized military, and Gómez Núñez believed that Spain's defeat should serve as a warning for Spain to become strong at home. After the war, Gómez Núñez served as a deputy in the **Cortes** and as a civil governor of Cádiz, Coruña, and Seville.

GOMPERS, SAMUEL (1850–1924). President of the **American Federation of Labor** until his death. A sympathizer of the Cuban insurgents, Gompers supported the U.S. war effort against Spain so that labor's demands would be helped by the government. Although he declared it was "a glorious and righteous" war, Gompers soon changed his mind as the war to liberate **Cuba** became one of retaining conquered lands. He opposed the annexation of **Hawaii** and believed such expansion by the United States would threaten the United States with "an inundation of Mongolians" that would overwhelm the U.S. labor force; moreover, he described the Filipinos as "savages and barbarians." Fearing mass immigration from newly conquered lands as a threat to U.S. labor, Gompers became a vice president of the **Anti-Imperialist League**.

GOODRICH, CASPAR FREDERICK (1847–1925). Captain (USN), commanded the *St. Louis*. A U.S. Naval Academy graduate, Goodrich, who was president of the **Naval War College** in early 1898, drew up a plan for establishing a coastal signal service, which was implemented upon the outbreak of the Spanish-American War. Commanding the *St. Louis* during the war, he directed **cable-cutting operations** in Cuban waters, participated in the search for Adm. **Pascual Cervera's Squadron**, and was in command of the naval aspects of the landing of the **Fifth Corps** at **Daiquirí** and **Siboney, Cuba**, beginning 22 June 1898. On 10 July, he wrote to Secretary of the Navy **John D. Long** complaining that the **U.S. Army** did not appreciate the navy's work. Stating the army was as helpless as "a babe" in landing in **Cuba** until the navy stepped in, he called the army a "spoiled child" that viewed the navy as its "handmaid". After taking command of the *Newark* on 6 August, Goodrich commanded the naval force that took possession of **Manzanillo, Cuba**, on 12 August. Promoted to rear admiral in 1904, he wrote *Rope Yarns from the Old Navy*, which was published by the Naval Historical Society in 1931.

GRAHAM, GEORGE EDWARD (1866–?). Correspondent for the **Associated Press**. Graham went to war on Com. **Winfield S. Schley**'s flagship the *Brooklyn*, and went ashore as Schley's personal representative to confer with Cuban insurgent commanders to work out their assistance for U.S. troops landing at **Daiquirí** and **Siboney**,

Cuba. After his first intimate contact with the Cuban insurgents, he later wrote "The Truth about the Insurgents" *Leslie's* (28 July 1898), in which he expressed his shock at their comparative nudity, disdained their filthy conditions, and advised U.S. soap manufactures to get a "splendid advertisement by cleaning the Cuban army." On board the *Brooklyn* next to Com. Schley during the **Naval Battle of Santiago** on 3 July 1898, Graham later wrote "The Destruction of Cervera's Fleet—As seen by an Eye-Witness on the *Brooklyn*, Commodore Schley's Flagship" *McClure's Magazine* (September 1898), in which he extolled Schley's command and falsely claimed that Adm. **Pascual Cervera's Squadron** was superior to that of the U.S. naval force. After the war when the **Sampson-Schley Controversy** erupted in the **press**, Graham, who ardently supported Schley, wrote *Schley and Santiago: An historical account of the blockade and final destruction of the Spanish fleet under command of Admiral Pasquale Cervera, July 3, 1898* (1902).

GRAHAM, WILLIAM MONTROSE (1834–1916). Major general (USV), commanded the **Second Corps** at **Camp Alger**. A Civil War veteran and career soldier, Graham was a brigadier general (Fifth U.S. Artillery), commanding the Department of the Gulf until he was promoted to major general (USV) on 4 May 1898 and assigned to command the Second Corps at Camp Alger. During August and early September his corps moved to **Camp Meade**, and he was relieved of command on 2 November 1898.

GRANT, FREDERICK DENT (1850–1912). Brigadier general (USV), commanded the Third Brigade, First Division, **First Corps**. A son of Ulysses S. Grant and a West Point graduate, Grant, who had been a U.S. minister to **Austria-Hungary** and the police commissioner of New York City, was appointed colonel of the Fourteenth New York Infantry (USV) on 2 May 1898. Promoted to brigadier general (USV) on 27 May, he briefly commanded the First Brigade, First Division, of the **Third Corps** at **Camp Thomas**, Georgia. By the end of July, Grant, now commanding the Third Brigade, which consisted of the First and Third Kentucky Infantry (USV) and the Fifth Illinois Infantry (USV), in the First Division, of the First Corps, began to prepare his troops for the **Puerto Rican campaign**. However, by the time his brigade arrived at **Ponce, Puerto Rico**, hostilities had ceased. Subsequently he commanded the **San Juan, Puerto Rico** military district until April 1899 and harshly criticized U.S. military officials for being too lenient on the Puerto Ricans. He later commanded U.S. forces in the **Philippine Insurrection**, and became a major general in 1906.

GRAY, GEORGE (1840–1925). Democratic senator from Delaware (1885–1899) and ranking minority member on the Senate Foreign Relations Committee. A former judge and attorney general of Delaware, Gray, an antiexpansionist, was a member of the U.S. **Peace Commission** that negotiated the **Treaty of Paris**. He opposed taking the entire **Philippines** because it would reverse U.S. continental politics, introduce the United States into European politics and entangling alliances, increase taxes, and necessitate a large navy and a greatly increased military establishment. However, he signed the Treaty of Paris and supported its ratification, arguing that the treaty's failure would compel the United States to be a ruthless conqueror and that there was ample time after the treaty's ratification to make concessions. Subsequently he served as a U.S. circuit court judge.

GREAT BRITAIN. Under the control of the Conservative Party, Great Britain was guided by Prime Minister and Foreign Secretary **Robert Cecil**, the marquis of Salisbury, and Acting Foreign Secretary **Arthur J. Balfour**. Although Queen Victoria sympathized with her relative, Spain's Queen Regent **María Cristina**, she was dissuaded by Cecil from any open support of Spain. Openly sympathetic to the United States and concerned about rising German power, Britain consistently countered Spanish requests to rally the European powers to its side despite requests from **Julian Pauncefote**, Britain's ambassador to Washington, D.C. Upon the outbreak of the Spanish-American War, Britain declared its neutrality on 26 April 1898, took over the U.S. legation in Madrid, Spain, during the war, and served as a conduit in forwarding U.S. peace proposals in June 1898.

The **press** was generally sympathetic to the United States during the war, and various British correspondents provided first hand coverage of the war. E. F. Knight of the *Times* (London), H. C. Seppings Wright of the *Illustrated London News*, George C. Musgrave of the *Daily Chronicle* (London), and John B. Atkins of the *Manchester Guardian* covered the Cuban theater. Atkins later wrote *The War in Cuba: The Experiences of an Englishman with the U.S. Army* (1899).

After the U.S. naval victory at the **Battle of Manila Bay** on 1 May 1898, British ships, under the command of Capt. **Edward Chichester**, arrived at **Manila Bay, Philippines**. With the objective of keeping China open to British penetration, the British government viewed the establishment of a U.S. presence in the **Philippines** as a buffer to the actions of other powers in the Far East. However, the British press, which had initially approved of U.S. actions during the war, became increasingly critical of the United States during the **Philippine Insurrection**.

GREAT POWERS NOTE (6 APRIL 1898). On 25 March 1898, Spain launched a diplomatic offensive abroad, requesting the European powers to employ their good offices on Spain's behalf to forestall increasing U.S. intervention in **Cuba**. **Austria-Hungary**, acting under pressure from her ally **Germany**, led in preparing a joint remonstrance; however, **Great Britain** instructed **Julian Pauncefote**, its ambassador to Washington, D.C., to make sure the presentation by the Great Powers was not offensive to the United States. Consequently, Pauncefote worked with U.S. Assistant Secretary of State **William R. Day** in writing the note. Although President **William McKinley** was adamant against any European intervention in U.S. Cuban policy, he hoped that a European appeal for a peaceful solution would slow the congressional rush to war.

On 7 April, six diplomats—Pauncefote, Theodor Ludwig von Holleben for Germany, **Jules Cambon** for **France**, Hengervar von Hengelmüller for Austria-Hungary, De Wollant for **Russia**, and G. C. Vinci for **Italy**—met with McKinley and delivered an innocuous note, predated to 6 April. McKinley expressed his appreciation of the humanitarian and disinterested character of their note. However, it had little effect on **Congress**. With a comparable message, six representatives of the Great Powers met with Spain's Queen Regent **María Cristina** and Minister of State **Pío Gullón y Iglesias** on 9 April. Their request for an armistice in Cuba resulted in the 10 April proclamation of a suspension of hostilities in Cuba. A second effort by the Great Powers on 18 April in Washington, D.C., never took place because it was torpedoed by **Arthur J. Balfour**, acting foreign secretary of Great Britain.

GREELY, ADOLPHUS WASHINGTON (1844–1935). Brigadier general, commanded the U.S. **Signal Corps**. During the war against Spain, Greely, an author, explorer, scientist, soldier, and Civil War veteran, directed the Signal Corps. Therefore, he was in overall command of the White House **Operating Room**, the corps's establishing communications networks as part of the nation's **coastal defense**, and the corps's **censorship** and intelligence efforts. After the war, Greely wrote "The Signal Corps in War Time," *Century Magazine* (1903) and his autobiographical account *Reminiscences of Adventure and Service* (1927). He was promoted to major general in 1906.

GREENE, FRANCIS VINTON (1850–1921). Brigadier general (USV), commanded the second expedition of the **Eighth Corps** to **Manila, Philippines**. A West Point graduate, engineer, historian and former military attaché to the Russian army, Greene was a colonel of the **Seventy-First New York Infantry** when Maj. Gen. **Wesley Mer-**

ritt requested him for the **Philippine campaign**. Appointed a brigadier general (USV) on 27 May 1898, he left **Tampa, Florida**, and arrived in San Francisco, California, on 4 June.

Greene's expedition left San Francisco on 15 June, briefly landed on **Wake Island** on 4 July, and arrived at Manila on 17 July. After landing, he worked out a deal with Filipino insurgent Brig. Gen. Mariano Noriel on 28 July, whereby on 29 July the insurgents evacuated a section of trenches facing Manila that was then occupied by U.S. forces, allowing them to directly attack Manila. Greene commanded the **Second Brigade** during the **Battle of Manila** on 13 August and later worked out and signed the **Capitulation of Manila Agreement** on 14 August. He subsequently wrote "The Capture of Manila" *The Century Magazine* (March, April 1899). On 17 August, Greene was placed in charge of the fiscal affairs of Manila.

After returning to the United States, Maj. Gen. (USV) Greene met with President **William McKinley** from 27 September to 1 October and was influential in convincing McKinley to retain all of the **Philippines**. His report, which argued that returning the Philippines to Spain would lead to civil war, whereas handing them over to the insurgents would result in anarchy, was then forwarded to the U.S. **Peace Commission** that was negotiating the **Treaty of Paris**. From October to December, he commanded the Second Division of the **Seventh Corps** at Jacksonville, Florida, and during Cuban occupation duty. On 10 January 1899, he was asked by McKinley to speak to Filipino insurgent representative **Felipe Agoncillo** in order to get him to sign a prepared telegram to be sent to **Emilio Aguinaldo** asking Aguinaldo to prevent the outbreak of hostilities. Agoncillo replied that he was powerless to prevent such a conflict. On 28 February 1899, Greene resigned, returned to civilian life and directed power companies, worked as the police commissioner of New York City, and wrote several books on military policy.

GRESHAM. (USN). Revenue cutter based in Milwaukee, Wisconsin, on Lake Michigan. When the conde de Rascón, Spain's ambassador to **Great Britain**, protested its being allowed to pass through Canadian waters on the St. Lawrence River to the Atlantic Ocean in June 1898, the British stated that the government had promised this before the war; therefore, the promise would be kept. During the war, the *Gresham* was used to patrol northern coastal waters.

La. 1896, com. 1896, dis. 1,098, sp. 14.5
Armament: 4—3", 2 mg.
Comp. 103

GRIDLEY, CHARLES VERNON (1844–1898). Captain (USN), commanded the *Olympia*, flagship of the **Asiatic Squadron**. A U.S.

Naval Academy graduate and Civil War veteran, Gridley had served as an instructor at the U.S. Naval Academy and on the European Station before he was promoted to captain and assigned to the command of the *Olympia* in March 1897. Although he had already been declared medically unfit before the Spanish-American War, Gridley refused to return to the United States and commanded the *Olympia* during the **Battle of Manila Bay** on 1 May 1898. At the beginning of the battle, Com. **George W. Dewey**, aboard the *Olympia*, turned to Gridley and at 5:40 a.m. gave what became the most famous command of the war: "You may fire when ready, Gridley." Gridley left Manila Bay for the United States on 25 May, but he did not live to enjoy his fame. He died on his way home at Kobe, Japan, on 5 June.

GRIGSBY'S COWBOYS. Officially known as the Third U.S. Volunteer Cavalry, the regiment took its name from its commander, Col. Melvin (Milt) Grigsby (USV), the attorney general of South Dakota. Organized and mustered into service in Montana, Nebraska, North Dakota, and South Dakota, on 12–23 May 1898, with 45 officers and 961 enlisted men, the regiment arrived at **Camp Thomas**, Georgia, on 23 May and was assigned to the **First Corps**. While the regiment sat out the war at Camp Thomas despite Grigsby's efforts, 270 men contracted typhoid, and its members frequently composed doggerel laments about army life. On 8 September 1898, the regiment was mustered out of service at Camp Thomas with 45 officers and 936 enlisted men. Casualties sustained while in service included nine died from **disease** and four deserted. The regiment's wartime exploits were later chronicled by its Adjt. Otto L. Sues in his book *Grigsby's Cowboys, Third United States Volunteer Cavalry, Spanish-American War* (1900).

GRIMES, GEORGE SIMON (1846–1920). Captain, commanded Battery A, **Second U.S. Artillery**, Light Artillery Battalion of the **Fifth Corps**. An English-born career soldier and Civil War veteran, Grimes fought in the **Santiago, Cuba, campaign** during the Spanish-American War. His four-gun battery, which consisted of three officers and 79 enlisted men, was located near **El Pozo** and fought in the battles for the **San Juan Heights** on 1 July 1898. Before opening fire at 8:20 a.m. Grimes chased the newspapermen and foreign attaches away from the battery. The fire of his battery proved ineffective; moreover, since it was using **black powder**, its position was soon disclosed and it was quickly silenced by the opposing Spanish guns. After the war Grimes was promoted to major in 1899 and finally to brigadier general in 1907.

GUAM. The first overseas possession conquered by the United States in the war, Guam, the largest and most southern of the Marianas Islands, had been a Spanish possession since 1668 and was strategically located in the middle of the western Pacific Ocean, 1,500 miles east of the **Philippines** and 3,300 miles west of **Hawaii**. With a population of 9,630, Guam was under the control of the governor-general of the Philippines. Virtually defenseless, its 60-man Spanish garrison had not manned its forts for years.

At daylight on 20 June 1898, the first expedition of the **Eighth Corps** to **Manila**, **Philippines**, consisting of the **cruiser *Charleston*** and three **transports**—*Australia, City of Pekin,* and *City of Sydney*—carrying 2,500 troops, entered Port San Luis d'Apra harbor. The *Charleston,* under the command of Capt. **Henry Glass,** fired a few shots at the abandoned Fort Santa Cruz. Soon a boat carrying Frank Portusach, a naturalized U.S. citizen, Lt. José García y Guttiérrez, who commanded the port, and Dr. José Romero, a physician, came out to the *Charleston.* Because Guam had not had any news from Manila since 14 April, the authorities did not know that a state of war existed and had come out to the ship to apologize for not being able to return the *Charleston's* salute. Glass informed them they were prisoners and then released them on parole to carry the news to the governor of the island. Later in the day the governor's secretary arrived bringing a courteous letter, requesting an interview ashore. The following morning a group of **marines** and two companies of the **Second Oregon Infantry** were sent ashore under a flag of truce with a written demand for surrender. Lt. Col. Juan Marina y Vega, the island's governor, quickly drew up the surrender document. At 2:15 p.m. the U.S. flag was hoisted over the island.

Lt. Col. Juan Marina y Vega and five officers and 54 non-commissioned officers and privates were put on the *City of Sydney,* because it was the only ship with proper accommodations. Frank Portusach told Capt. Henry Glass that he would look after things until U.S. forces returned, and the local Chamorro population was left in charge of its island. The expedition left on 22 June and continued on to Manila. **Oscar K. Davis** covered the episode in "The Taking of Guam" *Harper's Weekly* (20 August 1898).

As a result of the **Treaty of Paris,** the island became a U.S. possession, and from 1899 to 1949, it was under the control of the **U.S. Navy.** During the **Philippine Insurrection,** Filipino revolutionaries were deported to Guam until 24 August 1902, when they were given permission to return to the Philippines.

GUÁNICA, PUERTO RICO. On the southwest coast of Puerto Rico, 15 miles west of **Ponce,** Guánica, one of the better Puerto Rican ports, was where the U.S. invasion force under the command of Maj. Gen. **Nelson A. Miles** first landed. In the early morning of 25 July 1898, a small force of 28 sailors, under the command of Lt. **Harry M. P. Huse,** the executive officer of the *Gloucester*, was briefly shot at by a small force of 11 Spanish **guerrillas** while it attempted to land. The *Gloucester* opened fire and quickly dispersed the few Spanish defenders who fled to **Yauco** to raise the alarm. No shots were fired as they entered the city and raised the U.S. flag at 11:00 a.m. Huse's force captured ten lighters and put them into use as U.S. regulars, the **Sixth Massachusetts Infantry** and **Sixth Illinois Infantry** landed unopposed. Local officials remained at their posts, and on 26 July, the mayor designated the town "Guánica, PR, United States of America." After landing, the American forces immediately began to move on Yauco.

GUANTÁNAMO, CUBA. Located on the southwestern Cuban coast about 46 miles east of **Santiago, Cuba**, Guantánamo, a town of 8,000, some 12 miles inland from a 15-mile long bay, was seen by the **U.S. Navy** as a necessary coaling and repair station that would be needed to support the landing of the **Fifth Corps** at Santiago, Cuba.

Although the entrance to the bay was mined, the **mines** proved ineffective because of marine growth and poor construction; moreover, a handful of contact mines were located in the channel between Caimanera, Guantánamo's port, and Fort Toro, on the island Cayo de Toro, on the west side of the bay. A 5,992-man division under the command of Brig. Gen. Félix Pareja Mesa defended the area but had been isolated by the Cuban insurgents. Pareja, who believed Guantánamo would be a main landing area for U.S. troops, established extensive defensive works around the town.

After the *St. Louis* and *Wompatuck* had failed, on 10 May 1898, to cut the **cable** that ran to Haiti, Secretary of the Navy **John D. Long** asked Adm. **William T. Sampson** about the possibility of seizing Guantánamo and using it as a coaling station. Sampson ordered a reconnaissance of the area and that the **First Marine Battalion** at **Key West, Florida**, prepare for action. Subsequently, the **Naval War Board** recommended, on 3 June, that the marine battalion seize the entrance to the bay.

On 7 June, the *Marblehead* and *Yankee* reduced the Spanish fortifications at the bay's entrance, drove away the gunboat *Sandoval*, and a landing party of marines from the *Marblehead* destroyed the cable station near the bay's entrance. Three days later, on 10 June, the First Marine Battalion, under the command of Lt. Col. **Robert W. Huntington,** landed on the eastern side of the bay's entrance and met no resistance. They established **Camp McCalla**, and the **Associated**

Press reported "The invasion of Cuba by the American forces began today." With a brief Spanish attack on the camp the following day, the first land fighting of the Spanish-American War began. The fighting lasted three days, and the marines, supported by naval gunfire and reinforced by 60 Cuban insurgents, sustained casualties of three dead and three wounded. **Stephen Crane**, who was later decorated for his participation, subsequently wrote about the fighting in "Marines Signaling Under Fire at Guantánamo" *McClure's Magazine* (February 1899).

As a result of the **Battle of Cuzco Hill** on 14 June and U.S. naval shelling of Spanish positions, the Spanish were driven from the eastern coast of the lower bay by 15 June. For the remainder of the war no more fighting took place. With total marine combat casualties of six dead and 16 wounded, the lower bay had been secured. Forty-eight mines were removed on 21–22 June during a systematic search of the bay, and the bay was put to use as an anchorage for coaling, resupplying, and maintenance operations for U.S. ships involved in the **Santiago, Cuba, campaign** and as a departure point on 21 July for Maj. Gen. **Nelson A. Miles**'s force to invade **Puerto Rico**.

On 22 July, a launch from the *Marblehead*, under a flag of truce, landed U.S. negotiators. Because the garrison was severely short on food, an agreement was quickly reached to deliver food to the Spanish defenders, one-third of whom were ill. Three days later, on 25 July, Guantánamo capitulated.

GUAYAMA, PUERTO RICO, SKIRMISH AT (5 AUGUST 1898).

A town of 14,000 located five miles inland in southeastern **Puerto Rico**, Guayama was served by its seaport **Arroyo**. At the end of May 1898, one company of Provisional Battalion No. 6 was stationed here with 123 effectives. Although patriotic military parades of *voluntarios* were held in June, after the 25 July American landing at **Guánica**, the town's mayor sent a delegation to inform Maj. Gen. **James H. Wilson** at **Ponce** that the Spanish had abandoned the town; however, because he feared that they would return and burn the town, the mayor asked for U.S. protection.

On 4 August, U.S. forces under the command of Brig. Gen. Peter C. Haines, which were part of Maj. Gen. **John R. Brooke**'s command at Arroyo, were ordered to take Guayama so Brooke's forces could then move on to Cayey and get behind the Spanish forces at **Aibonito**. Consisting of the **Fourth Ohio Infantry** and the **Third Illinois Infantry**, Haines's force left Arroyo early on the morning of 5 August. At 11:00 a.m., it briefly skirmished outside of Guayama with a 40-man Spanish **guerrilla** force led by Capt. Salvador Acha. Acha's command sustained casualties of two dead and 15 wounded, and the

U.S. casualties amounted to five wounded, all from the Fourth Ohio Infantry.

Upon entering the town after the skirmish, American troops found what appeared to be a deserted town; however, when Haines and his staff entered, the people came out and cheered. When the Spanish briefly shelled the town, they were driven off by two **dynamite guns** firing three shots. Then the bands played, Mayor Celestino Domínguez Gómez welcomed the American troops, and the U.S. flag was raised.

GUERRILLAS. Loyalists who served in the **Spanish Army** in **Cuba** and **Puerto Rico**. They were called "irregulars" to distinguish them from the regulars and were usually mounted. Cubans, Puerto Ricans and Spaniards could enlist. In Cuba guerrillas had fought against the insurgents since the beginning of the **Cuban Revolt** in 1895. Upon the outbreak of the Spanish-American War in late April 1898, there were eight companies, totaling 1,000 men, in the **Santiago, Cuba**, area. In Puerto Rico guerrillas were organized by Capt. Salvador Acha throughout the island beginning on 24 April 1898. By the end of May most towns in Puerto Rico had guerrilla forces, but the army general staff in **San Juan** had denied them arms.

GULLÓN Y IGLESIAS, PÍO (1835–1916). Spain's minister of state (4 October 1897–15 May 1898) and **Liberal Party** leader. A newspaper editor and writer, Gullón served as a deputy and a senator in the **Cortes** and in various governmental positions under **Práxedes M. Sagasta**. Although he had only a limited knowledge of foreign affairs, Gullón was appointed minister of state when Sagasta formed his cabinet on 4 October 1897. Pro-French in outlook, Gullón, who considered a war against the United States as hopeless for Spain, officially refused U.S. offers of mediation, announced Spain's **autonomy** policy, and tried to enlist the Great Powers and the **Vatican** in forestalling U.S. policy in March 1898. On 16 April he even asked the Pope to suggest to the Great Powers that they undertake a naval demonstration against the U.S.; however, the Pope refused. After Spain's early military defeats in the war, Gullón came under serious criticism for having advocated concessions to the United States prior to the war and was replaced by the Duke of **Almodóvar del Río** on 15 May 1898.

GUNBOAT. Although almost any small boat fitted with one or more guns was often called a gunboat, most were usually between 800 and 2,000 tons, without protective decks, had shallow drafts, and were regarded as expendable compared with major ships. Upon the outbreak of the Spanish-American War, the **Spanish Navy** had 23 gunboats, ten torpedo gunboats and six gun vessels. The **U.S. Navy** had 16 gunboats, and although they saw more action than any other ships in the U.S. Navy during the war, few except the *Concord* and *Petrel* were well known.

GUSSIE. A 576-ton, side-wheel steamer, it gained fame during the *Gussie* **Expedition** and was used in June 1898 to transport teamsters, packers, mules, and horses of the **Fifth Corps** to **Daiquirí, Cuba**, at a rate of $350 per day. Subsequently, it carried sick and discharged soldiers back to **Tampa, Florida**, and returned with supplies for the Fifth Corps.

GUSSIE EXPEDITION (10 MAY–16 MAY 1898). In accordance with the 6 May 1898 order to expedite arms and stores to the Cuban insurgents, the fire-engine red *Gussie*, under the command of Lt. Col. **Joseph H. Dorst**, left **Tampa, Florida**, on 10 May 1898, with Companies E and G of the **First U.S. Infantry**, artist **Rufus F. Zogbaum**, and correspondents **Poultney Bigelow** of *Harper's Weekly*, Charles E. Akers of the *Times* (London), James F. J. Archibald of the *San Francisco Post*, and **Stephen Bonsal** of the *New York Herald*. However, the expedition was no secret because it had been heralded in the **press** even before its departure, with the *Atlanta Constitution* headlining the story as "Cuban Invasion Commences Today" on 10 May.

By the morning of 12 May, the *Gussie* was off **Havana, Cuba**, and accompanied by the revenue cutter *Manning* and the *Wasp*, it was frequently fired on by Spanish shore batteries. A little west of Cabañas, a landing was made by Company E in the early afternoon. However, no Cuban insurgents were found, and when local Spanish forces attacked, there was no opportunity to unload the supplies. During the brief beach engagement, correspondent Archibald was wounded while commanding U.S. troops. Upon the arrival of the *Dolphin*, the troops were removed from the beach. After drifting during the night, another attempt was made to land the supplies three miles east of Mariel; however, this attempt also failed when it was fired on by Spanish forces. On 16 May, the *Gussie* returned to Tampa, Florida, with its supplies still aboard. Maj. Gen. **William R. Shafter** was incensed; consequently, he tightened up **censorship** regulations, ordering that no dispatches be sent from Tampa without being cleared and stamped by a military censor. Bonsal later wrote about the expedition in "The First Fight on Cuban Soil" *McClure's Magazine* (July 1898).

—H—

HALE, EUGENE (1836–1918) Republican senator from Maine (1881–1911). A conservative lawyer who as a senator had opposed measures for political and social reform, Hale opposed the recognition of **belligerent rights** for the Cuban insurgents and belabored them for the destruction of American property. He was part of the **"Peace Faction"** of Republican senators in March 1898, and later voted against the **Treaty of Paris**.

HALL, HARRY ALVAN (1861–1917). Captain, Company H, **Sixteenth Pennsylvania Infantry**. A former general counsel in the United States of the governments of **Austria-Hungary** and **Italy** and a U.S. attorney in Pennsylvania, Hall fought in the **Puerto Rican campaign**, and was promoted to major for his bravery during the **Battle of Coamo** on 9 August 1898. Believing it was his duty to render a tribute to the memory of a hero, Hall wrote to the widow of Spanish Capt. **Rafael Martínez Illescas** on 20 August, extolling her late husband's valor in the battle of Coamo. Calling Illescas a "legendary model of the ideal soldier," Hall believed that the Spanish forces would never have surrendered had her husband lived. After the war he served as a district judge in Pennsylvania.

HANNA, MARCUS ALONZO (1837–1904). Republican senator from Ohio (1897–1904). A wealthy businessman who had managed **William McKinley**'s 1896 presidential campaign, Hanna succeeded **John Sherman** as senator from Ohio in 1897. He opposed the recognition of **belligerent rights** for the Cuban insurgents, was part of the **"Peace Faction"** of Republican senators, and opposed going to war against Spain. However, upon the outbreak of war, Hanna reversed his stance, helped expedite the acceptance of the **Ninth Ohio Infantry Battalion** into volunteer service, promoted the expansion of the United States in the newly conquered territories, and was a senate leader in the fight for the ratification of the **Treaty of Paris**.

HARDEN, EDWARD (EDWIN) W. Correspondent for the *New York World*. A former treasury agent, Harden was sent by President **William McKinley** to the **Philippines** to assess the commercial potential of the islands. Inviting his close friend and reporter **John T. McCutcheon** to join him, Harden and McCutcheon sailed on the *McCulloch* on 8 January 1898. Upon joining Com. **George W. Dewey**'s **Asiatic Squadron** at **Hong Kong** on 17 April, Harden arranged to cover the war for the *New York World*. He was an eyewitness to the **Battle of Manila Bay** on 1 May 1898, and his dispatch, claiming a "great

American triumph," was the first in print in the United States; however, it appeared in the *Chicago Tribune* and not the *World*. Harden went ashore on 3 May and observed the United States taking control of **Cavite**, observed the **Battle of Manila** on 13 August 1898, left the Philippines in October 1898, and returned to the United States to report to the government on his mission.

Harden later wrote "Dewey at Manila: Observations and Personal Impressions Derived from a Service with the American Fleet in the Philippines from April, 1898, to October, 1898," *McClure's Magazine* (February 1899), in which he recounted the battles, discounted the **breakfast myth**, viewed the Germans as a constant menace, and complimented Com. George Dewey for his command in battle and for his diplomacy in treating **Emilio Aguinaldo** with courtesy while never officially recognizing his government.

HARE, JAMES H. (1856–1946). Photographer and correspondent. The British-born Hare came to New York City in 1889 and worked as a photographer for the *Illustrated American*. During the Spanish-American War, Hare, a photographer for *Collier's Weekly*, did intelligence work by mapping the Cuban coastline for Adm. **William T. Sampson** and by searching for Adm. **Pascual Cervera's Squadron** on the *Sommers N. Smith* in May 1898. However, Hare became famous as one of the most daring and resourceful battlefield news photographers when with his small box camera he photographed the **blockade of Cuba** and the **Santiago, Cuba, campaign**. After the war he continued working for *Collier's*, photographing and reporting on Latin American revolutions and the Russo-Japanese War. A pioneer in aerial photography, Hare worked for *Leslie's Weekly* during World War I.

HARVARD. (USN) Auxiliary **cruiser**, commanded by Capt. Charles S. Cotton. Formerly the ocean liner *New York*, it was leased from the American Line by the **U.S. Navy** on 26 April 1898 and attached to the North Atlantic Station on 30 April with a civilian crew. During the war it scouted for Adm. **Pascual Cervera's Squadron** and discovered part of the squadron at **Martinique** on 11 May 1898. Subsequently, the *Harvard* delivered the **Navy Department** order to Com. **Winfield S. Schley** on 27 May to **blockade Santiago, Cuba**, and then carried Schley's telegram about his squadron's coal shortage to Jamaica, where it arrived on 28 May.

In late June, the *Harvard* transported two battalions of the **Thirty-Fourth Michigan Infantry** and the **Ninth Massachusetts Infantry** to **Siboney, Cuba**, and rescued the survivors of the *Infanta María Teresa* and *Almirante Oquendo* after the **Naval Battle of Santiago** on 3 July. On 10 July, it left **Guantánamo, Cuba**, and transported Spanish **prisoners of war** to Portsmouth, New Hampshire. After returning to Santiago, Cuba, on 18 August, the *Harvard* transported the **Thirty-Third Michigan Infantry** to **Camp Wikoff, Montauk Point, Long Island, New York**. Decommissioned on 2 September 1898, it was returned to its owners and was later used as a transport during World War I. It was scrapped in 1923.

La. 1888, com. 26 April 1898, dis. 13,000, hp. 20,600, sp. 21.8
Armament: 8–5″, 8–6pdr.
Cc. 2,656, comp. 407

HARVARD INCIDENT (4 JULY 1898). Spanish **prisoners of war** from the **Naval Battle of Santiago** on 3 July 1898 were placed aboard the auxiliary **cruiser *Harvard***. Around midnight on 4 July, when a prisoner either passed or attempted to pass a line marked on the deck beyond which prisoners were not to pass, a sentry fired. The other prisoners were brought to their feet, and guards responded to an alarm by pouring a volley into the massed prisoners. Six Spanish sailors were killed and 13 wounded. The incident marred an otherwise effective policy of good treatment of the prisoners. Upon the request of Spanish Adm. **Pascual Cervera y Topete** an inquiry was conducted, and the U.S. government stated the incident, while regrettable, was an accident caused by a misunderstanding during an altercation with the sentry.

HARVEYIZED STEEL ARMOR. Dating from 1890, Harveyized steel armor, which was an alloy nickel-steel plate, was used extensively on U.S. warships, but not very extensively on Spanish warships. A six-inch plate was more than twice as resistant as the same size iron plate and better than the best steel plate not treated by the process. In 1895 an even newer Krupp process of toughening armor was developed. It was rated 20 to 30 percent more effective than Harveyized steel, and although it was adopted by the **U.S. Navy** in 1898, it did not make its appearance in time for the Spanish-American War.

HAVANA, CUBA. With a population of 198,000, Havana was the foremost city of the West Indies and possessed one of the finest harbors in the world. Serving as the headquarters of the governor-general of Cuba, **Ramón Blanco y Erenas**, and the *Gaceta de Habana*, the official newspaper, its defenses were extensive. Although many artillery batteries were not completed when the war began, 31,500 regular Spanish troops were in the vicinity and a total of 153 artillery pieces were in place. The most powerful battery included 12- and 11-inch guns in the Santa Clara fort. Three lines of 28 electrical and mechanical **mines** defended the harbor entrance; moreover, two tubes for firing **Whitehead torpedoes** were mounted on the mole of the captain of the port. At night **searchlights** illuminated the harbor entrance and two heavy hawsers with floats were stretched across the entrance. All stations were connected by telegraph and telephone systems.

However, the naval vessels in the harbor were of negligible quality. Frequently under repair were the **cruisers** *Alfonso XII*, *Infanta Isabel*, and *Marques de la Ensenada*. Of the four **torpedo boats**, which included the *Filipinas*, *Martín Alonso Pinzón*, *Nueva España*, and the *Vincente Yañez Pinzón*, the *Filipinas* was useless. The **gunboat** *Magallanes* could not light its fires. The unprotected cruiser *Conde de Venadito* was one of the few ships in working order. Blockaded from the beginning of the war, only a few vessels succeeded in running the **blockade**; moreover, the Spanish vessels in port never seriously challenged the blockade. There were frequent parleys under a flag of truce between U.S. and Spanish naval forces, one resulting in a prisoner exchange of Spanish soldiers for two U.S. reporters on 28 May.

Havana was never the site of serious combat owing to the war's brevity. U.S. forces entered Havana on 31 December 1898, and on 1 January 1898, Capt. Gen. Adolfo Jimenez Castellanos, in compliance with the **Treaty of Paris**, transferred power to Maj. Gen. **John R. Brooke**.

HAWAII. A republic, under the presidency of Sanford B. Dole, was established by a revolution led by American planters and business leaders in 1893, which overthrew the regime of Queen Liliuokalani. From its inception, the republic pushed for its annexation by the United States as its leaders became increasingly alarmed by the steady rise in the Japanese population and by the islands' vulnerability to attack by **Japan** or European powers; however, such efforts were rejected by the **Cleveland administration**. After the inauguration of **William McKinley**, a treaty of annexation was submitted to the Senate. It brought forth an immediate Japanese protest, which claimed that the maintenance of the status quo in Hawaii was essential to maintain good U.S.-Japanese relations. After Secretary of State **John Sherman** rejected Japanese claims, Japan withdrew its objection. Unbeknownst to either Japan or the American public, secret instructions had been sent to the U.S. naval commander in the area to hoist the American flag and establish a provisional protectorate should Japan manifest warlike intentions.

Even with the support of the **Republican Party** and McKinley, the treaty of annexation languished in the Senate. Following the destruction of the *Maine* on 15 February 1898, annexationist strategy shifted.

Believing it was easier to obtain a simple majority rather than a two-thirds vote in the Senate, on 16 March, a joint resolution for annexation was introduced by Senator **John T. Morgan**, who pointed to the danger of Japanese influence and the necessity of acquiring the "Key to the Pacific." However, it failed to stir any action until Com. **George W. Dewey**'s victory at the **Battle of Manila Bay** on 1 May.

The outbreak of the Spanish-American War served as a catalyst. On 4 May, a joint resolution for annexation was introduced in the House of Representatives; however, Speaker of the House **Thomas B. Reed** kept it from the floor until 10 June. Meanwhile, while critics questioned its constitutionality and argued that annexation was a departure from U.S. traditions, support for annexation grew. The *New York Sun* claimed on 1 June that "To maintain our flag in the Philippines, we must raise our flag in Hawaii," and the *New York Tribune* argued that the U.S. success in the **Philippines** had made Hawaii "imperative" as a halfway station to the Philippines. Upon the arrival of the first expedition of the **Eighth Corps** to the Philippines on 1 June, the islands became a base of operations and were used by subsequent expeditions.

Although opposed by Speaker Reed, the resolution passed the House on 15 June by a vote of 209–91 and the Senate on 6 July by a vote of 42–21, with 26 abstentions. McKinley signed it on 7 July. According to the resolution, Hawaii ceded all rights of sovereignty; ownership of all public, government, or crown lands, public buildings, ports, harbors and military equipment reverted to the United States; power was to be exercised by persons appointed by McKinley; existing treaties with foreign nations by the previous government were terminated; the United States assumed the public debt of the previous government, not to exceed $4 million in liability; no further Chinese immigration to the islands was allowed without U.S. approval; and no Chinese in Hawaii were allowed to enter the United States.

The formal transfer of power took place on 12 August 1898, and Sanford Dole, upon the congressional provision for a territorial government in 1900, became the first governor of the territory of Hawaii.

HAWK. (USN) Armed **yacht**, commanded by Lt. John Hood. Formerly the *Hermione*, it was purchased by the **U.S. Navy** on 2 April 1898 and assigned to the North Atlantic Station. During the war the *Hawk* blockaded **Havana**, **Cuba**, and carried Adm. **William T. Sampson**'s orders to Com. **Winfield S. Schley**, informing him on 23 May that Adm. **Pascual Cervera's Squadron** was probably at **Santiago**, **Cuba**. On 5 July, the *Hawk* attacked and destroyed the *Alfonso XII*

off Havana. After the war it served off and on as a training vessel
until the eve of World War II.

La. 1891, com. 5 April 1898, dis. 375, hp. 1,000, sp. 14.5
Armament: 2–6pdr., 2–1pdr., 2 C. mgs.
Cc. 70, comp. 50

HAWKINS, HAMILTON SMITH (1834–1910). Brigadier general
(USV), commanded the First Brigade, First Division, **Fifth Corps**. A
West Point graduate and former commandant of cadets at West Point,
Hawkins commanded the army's infantry and cavalry school (1894–
1898), and was appointed brigadier general (USV) on 4 May 1898.
His brigade, which included the **Sixth U.S. Infantry, Sixteenth U.S.
Infantry**, and the **Seventy-First New York Infantry**, fought in the
Battle of San Juan Hill on 1 July, with Hawkins, who was wounded,
leading the charge. Promoted to major general (USV) on 8 July,
Hawkins became a regular brigadier general on 28 September and
was discharged from volunteer service in November 1898.

HAY, JOHN MILTON (1838–1905). U.S. ambassador to Great Britain
and secretary of state (30 September 1898–1905). A novelist, poet,
historian, and lawyer, Hay was President Lincoln's private secretary
and served in the U.S. legation in Madrid, Spain. A harsh critic of
Spanish despotism, Hay, an advocate of Anglo-Saxon harmony and
U.S. expansion, was appointed by President **William McKinley** as
U.S. ambassador to **Great Britain**. During the war he arranged for
Britain to handle U.S. consular affairs in Spain, advocated the conquest of the **Philippines** and **Puerto Rico** and the independence of
Cuba, believed the Germans had no desire to provoke a conflict over
the Philippines, and wrote to **Theodore Roosevelt** on 27 July, calling
the war "a splendid little war."

On 30 September, Hay succeeded **William R. Day** as secretary of
state. He informed the U.S. **Peace Commission** of McKinley's late
October decision to take all of the Philippines and later cabled the
commission authorizing it to pay between $10 and $20 million to
Spain in lieu of the Philippines issue. After the war he authored the
Open Door Policy with respect to China.

HEARST, WILLIAM RANDOLPH (1863–1951). Owner of the *New
York Journal*. After turning the *San Francisco Examiner* into a
profitable newspaper through sensationalism, Hearst took over the
New York Journal in October 1895 and made it into the epitome of
the **"yellow press."** A Democrat and avowed expansionist, Hearst
championed the Cuban insurgents and consistently demanded a war
against Spain to liberate **Cuba** from Spanish tyranny. Ecstatic upon

the outbreak of war, Hearst was turned down when he offered to finance a cavalry regiment, donated his **yacht *Buccaneer*** to the **U.S. Navy**, and tried to secure a commission. The commission as an ensign in the navy, which was delayed on purpose by President **William McKinley** because Hearst had supported **William J. Bryan**, came through on 7 August when hostilities had almost ceased.

As the owner of the *Journal*, Hearst, who was already operating at a loss when the war broke out, spent more money than any other newspaper in covering the war. For Hearst, the war was "The *Journal*'s War." His order to **George B. Rea**, a *Journal* correspondent, to buy a steamer and sink it in the Suez Canal to stop Adm. **Manuel de la Cámara's Squadron**, was not carried out. Hearst chartered the steamship *Sylvia*, and personally led the *Journal* to **Santiago**, **Cuba**. After arriving there on 18 June, he interviewed U.S. and Cuban military leaders, brought out a Cuban edition of the *Journal*, and while dressed in a black business suit, observed the **Battle of El Caney** on 1 July. After the **Naval Battle of Santiago** on 3 July, he picked up Spanish survivors, personally reported their capture to Adm. **William T. Sampson** and was given a receipt upon delivering them to the *St. Louis*. After returning to the United States on 18 July, Hearst had his receipt framed and hung on his office wall along with a bullet-torn flag given to him by Cuban Maj. Gen. **Calixto García**.

HELENA. (USN) Single-masted **gunboat**, commanded by Comdr. William T. Swinburne. Costing $280,000, it was designed with a very shallow draft of nine feet and with twin screws and oversize rudders for maneuverability in river operations. Part of the **North Atlantic Squadron** during the war, the *Helena* served on the **blockade of Cuba**, capturing the steamer *Miguel Jover* on 23 April 1898, the smack *Do Septembre* on 27 April, and the schooner *Oriente* on 5 May. It convoyed the **Fifth Corps** to **Daiquirí, Cuba**, fought a brief engagement on 1–2 July at Fort Tunas, and participated in the naval engagement at **Manzanillo, Cuba**, on 18 July. It was sold in 1932.

La. 1896, com. 1897, dis. 1,397, hp. 1,900, sp. 15
Armor: d. 5″, sl. 3/8″
Armament: 8–4″, 4–6pdr., 4–1pdr., 2 G. mgs.
Cc. 277, comp. 170

HELLINGS, MARTIN LUTHER (1841–1908). Manager of the International Ocean Telegraph Company's office at **Key West, Florida**. A Civil War veteran and one of Key West's most respected citizens, Hellings, a personal friend of Capt. **Charles D. Sigsbee**, supervised an intelligence gathering network before the war. He arranged for confidential messages to be sent on passenger ships between **Havana**,

Cuba, and Florida, and established the **Hellings-Villaverde Network**. Promoted to captain in the **Signal Corps** during the Spanish-American War, his clandestine network provided useful information that was sent directly to the office of President **William McKinley**.

HELLINGS-VILLAVERDE NETWORK. Prior to the explosion of the *Maine* on 15 February 1898, **Martin L. Hellings**, the manager of the International Ocean Telegraphic Company's office in **Key West, Florida**, routinely received intelligence information from Domingo Villaverde, a telegraph operator in the **Havana, Cuba, cable** office located in the governor-general's palace. Essentially a one-way communication, Villaverde, who had access to most official Spanish governmental telegrams, usually telegraphed Hellings after the Spanish censor retired at 9:00 p.m. Because the International Ocean Telegraphic Company was a subsidiary of the Western Union Telegraph Company, the network was established with the full knowledge and approval of Thomas T. Eckert, chairman of the board of Western Union. Even though the network got the first message out of Havana about the *Maine* disaster, its existence was almost completely secret.

Owing to a mutual agreement by the Spanish and U.S. governments to keep the Havana to Key West cable open during the war, the network continued. It became part of the **Signal Corps** and came under the overall direction of Brig. Gen. **Adolphus W. Greely**. Messages were directly relayed to the **operating room** in the White House; however, its existence was kept secret. Not even Secretary of War **Russell A. Alger**, Secretary of the Navy **John D. Long**, Adm. **William T. Sampson**, or the **Naval War Board** knew of its existence.

The network kept President **William McKinley** informed on almost a daily basis of the Spanish governmental cable traffic passing through Havana. It immediately reported the arrival of Adm. **Pascual Cervera's Squadron** at **Santiago, Cuba**, on 19 May; however, nobody believed the information. Consequently, Greely informed Long of the network's existence. Long then cabled Sampson strongly advising him to send Com. **Winfield S. Schley**'s **Flying Squadron** to Santiago.

HEMMENT, JOHN C. Photographer for the *New York Journal*. One of the best photographers of his day, Hemment, while in **Cuba** before the war, photographed the *Maine* as it passed Morro Castle entering **Havana** harbor on 25 January 1898. He was shocked by the destruction of the *Maine* on 15 February, because he personally knew many of the crew. During the war Hemment photographed the **Seventy-First New York Infantry** in camp at Hempstead, Long Island; went with **William R. Hearst** on the *Sylvia* to **Santiago, Cuba**; and interviewed members of the **American Red Cross** and U.S. and Cuban military leaders. He photographed the graves of the **Rough Riders** killed during the **Battle of Las Guásimas** on 24 June, and in the midst of the battles for the **San Juan Heights** on 1 July, Hemment shared a "luxurious" picnic lunch with **James Hare** of *Collier's Weekly*. He later covered the return of the Rough Riders to **Camp Wikoff, Montauk Point, Long Island, New York**, and wrote *Cannon and Camera: Sea and Land Battles of the Spanish-American War in Cuba, Camp Life, and the Return of the Soldiers* (1898), in which he extolled the bravery of Spanish troops, Rough Riders, Seventy-First New York Infantry, and **black American regular troops**.

HENNA, JOSÉ JULIO (1848–1924). President of the Puerto Rican section of the **Cuban Revolutionary Party**. A physician and independence advocate, Henna was expelled from **Puerto Rico** and became the spokesman for Puerto Rican independence in the United States. The Puerto Rican section of the Cuban Revolutionary Party was founded at his New York City residence on 8 December 1895, and he maintained a correspondence with **Ramón Betances** in Paris, France. Beginning in March 1898, Henna and **Roberto H. Todd** lobbied in Washington, D.C., for the inclusion of Puerto Rico in American war plans and offered their services for the liberation of Puerto Rico. Henna provided the **Navy Department** with maps and information and supported the annexation of Puerto Rico by the United States after a period of tutelage. On 18 October 1898, he telegraphed President **William McKinley**, welcoming American control of Puerto Rico and assuring him of his loyalty and devotion.

HENRY, GUY VERNOR (1839–1899). Brigadier general (USV), commanded the First Division, **Seventh Corps**. A West Point graduate and recipient of the **Congressional Medal of Honor** during the Civil War, Henry, a veteran of the Indian wars on the frontier, was promoted to brigadier general (USV) on 4 May 1898. In command of the First Division of the Seventh Corps at **Tampa, Florida**, Henry and his corps remained there when the corps moved to **Camp Cuba Libre** at Jacksonville, Florida.

Ordered to **Santiago, Cuba**, to assist in the reduction of the city, Henry's 3,300-man force arrived on the *St. Paul* on 10 July. After Santiago capitulated on 17 July, his force sailed on the *Comanche* on 21 July for **Guánica, Puerto Rico**. After landing at Guánica, his force, which consisted of the **Sixth Massachusetts Infantry** and **Sixth Illinois Infantry**, moved through **Yauco** and arrived at **Ponce**. Ordered to march from Ponce to Arecibo on 6 August, Henry's force arrived at Utuado on 13 August, where he received orders to suspend hostilities. He had conducted a seven-day campaign without firing a shot.

Promoted to brigadier general in October 1898, Henry commanded the military district at Ponce after the war. On 9 December 1898, he succeeded Maj. Gen. **John R. Brooke** as military governor of **Puerto Rico** and was promoted to major general (USV). During his brief tenure, he strictly enforced the law, promoted the spread of English, viewed **Luis Muñoz Rivera** as a subversive, and allowed no freedom of the press. He was replaced on 9 May 1899 by Brig. Gen. George W. Davis.

HERALDO DE MADRID, EL. A Madrid-based liberal newspaper edited by **José Canalejas y Méndez.** Ardently pro-Spanish, on 9 March 1896, in the midst of the **Cuban Revolt**, it stated, "We are ready for anything, including a conflict with the United States." It opposed **autonomy**, criticized Lt. Gen. **Valeriano Weyler**'s methods in **Cuba**, and denounced President **William McKinley's Ultimatum** of 26–28 March 1898, stating on 31 March, "to abandon Cuba . . . offended the nation's dignity; to give it to the Yankees . . . would be even more humiliating."

The *Heraldo* remained pro-war against the United States until after the defeat of Adm. **Pascual Cervera's Squadron** in the **Naval Battle of Santiago, Cuba**, on 3 July. Then it demanded that the government negotiate a peace as soon as possible and, on 22 August 1898, published Adm. Cervera's account of the naval battle of Santiago.

HERCULES. *Chicago Record*'s **press boat** during the war. It saw 110 days of duty off **Cuba** and **Puerto Rico** during the war while covering the **Santiago, Cuba, campaign**, the **blockade of Cuba**, and the U.S. invasion of Puerto Rico.

HIGGINSON, FRANCIS JOHN (1843–1931). Captain (USN), commanded the **battleship** *Massachusetts*. A U.S. Naval Academy graduate and Civil War veteran, Higginson had commanded the Navy Yard at New York City before assuming command of the *Massachusetts* in 1897. During the war he participated in the **blockade of Cuba**, commanded the naval expedition that transported Maj. Gen. **Nelson A. Miles**'s forces to **Guánica, Puerto Rico**, and was promoted to commodore on 10 August 1898. After the war he served as chairman of the Lighthouse Board and was promoted to rear admiral in 1899.

HIST. (USN) Armed **yacht**, commanded by Lt. Lucien Young. Formerly the *Thespia*, it was purchased by the **U.S. Navy** on 22 April 1898 and assigned to the North Atlantic Station. During the war, it served on the **blockade of Cuba**, capturing the Spanish schooner *Nickerson* on 29 June. On 30 June, it engaged Spanish forces at **Manzanillo, Cuba**, and rescued 142 Spanish survivors after the **Naval Battle of Santiago** on 3 July. After serving in **cable-cutting operations**, the *Hist* fought in the U.S. naval attack on Manzanillo on 18 July, and on 12 August, while escorting the **First Marine Battalion** to seize the **Isle of Pines**, it and the other ships digressed and bombarded Manzanillo.

La. 1895, com. 13 May 1898, dis. 413, hp. 500, sp. 14.5
Armament: 1–3pdr., 4–1pdr., 1 C. mg.
Cc. 60, comp. 56

HOAR, GEORGE FRISBIE (1826–1904). Republican senator from Massachusetts (1877–1904). A Harvard graduate and lawyer, Hoar was closely associated with the founding of the **Republican Party** in Massachusetts. He served as a congressman (1869–1877), was elected to the Senate, opposed any attempt to officially recognize the Cuban insurgents, and became a highly vocal opponent of U.S. imperialism. However, upon the outbreak of war, Hoar supported the war effort, calling the war, "The most honorable single war in all history." Although he supported the annexation of **Hawaii** to forestall **Japan**'s acquisition of the islands, he joined the **Anti-Imperialist League**, and despite his personal affection for President **William McKinley**, Hoar became the chief Senate spokesman in opposing the ratification of the **Treaty of Paris**. Basing his arguments on constitutional grounds, he argued that the United States could not govern a foreign territory against its will and presented a resolution on 14 January 1899 that granted independence to the **Philippines**. Such actions caused **Theodore Roosevelt** to label him a traitor.

HOBART, GARRET AUGUSTUS (1844–1899). Vice president of the United States (1897–1899). A former New Jersey legislator and corporation director, Hobart presided over the Senate debates on **belligerent rights** and informed President **William McKinley** in early April 1898 that he could no longer hold back the Senate, predicting that if McKinley did not act soon, the Senate would declare war on its own. After the ratification of the **Treaty of Paris**, he cast the deciding vote that rejected the **Bacon Amendment** on 14 February 1899.

HOBSON, RICHMOND PEARSON (1870–1937). Lieutenant (USN), led the volunteer crew of the *Merrimac* on 3 June 1898 in its attempt to block the harbor entrance of **Santiago, Cuba**. A U.S. Naval Academy graduate from Alabama, Hobson, a specialist in naval architecture, was promoted to lieutenant and assigned to Adm. **William T.**

Sampson's flagship the *New York*. Although not officially eligible to command at sea because he was not a line officer, Hobson directed the *Merrimac*'s attempt on 3 June to block the harbor entrance at Santiago. Although the attempt failed and Hobson was taken prisoner, he became a national hero overnight. After he was freed in a prisoner exchange on 6 July, he directed the raising of the *Infanta María Teresa* and was sent to **Manila, Philippines**, to direct the raising of Spanish vessels sunk by Com. **George W. Dewey's Asiatic Squadron**. Returning to the United States, Hobson's popularity was immense. He was known as "the most kissed man in America," and after retiring from the navy in 1903, Hobson, an ardent prohibitionist, became a highly paid speaker. He was elected to **Congress** as a Democrat, awarded the **Congressional Medal of Honor** in 1933, and promoted to rear admiral on the retired list in 1934. He recounted his experience directing the *Merrimac* episode writing "The Sinking of the Merrimac," *Century Magazine* (December 1898; January, February, and March 1899), and *The Sinking of the "Merrimac": A Personal Narrative of the Adventure in the Harbor of Santiago de Cuba, June 3, 1898, and of the Subsequent Imprisonment of the Survivors* (1899).

HONG KONG. A British colony, governed by Gov.-Gen. Wilsone Black, Hong Kong, the home base of the Filipino insurgent **Hong Kong Revolutionary Committee**, briefly served as an anchorage for Com. **George W. Dewey's Asiatic Squadron** prior to the war and as the site for meetings between **Emilio Aguinaldo**, Filipino insurgent leader, and **Rounsevelle Wildman**, U.S. consul. Upon the outbreak of war between Spain and the United States, Gov.-Gen. Black informed Dewey, his personal friend, on 23 April of **Great Britain**'s declaration of neutrality; therefore, Dewey's squadron had to leave Hong Kong by 25 April. At the bottom of the official note, Black wrote a personal note stating, "God knows, my dear Commodore, that it breaks my heart to send you this notification." Dewey responded on 24 April with a note thanking him for his many courtesies. Although overwhelmingly sympathetic to the United States, most of those at the Hong Kong Club bet against the success of Dewey's forthcoming attack on the Spanish squadron anchored in **Manila Bay**; nevertheless, Dewey's squadron was cheered as it left Hong Kong on 24 April for **Mirs Bay, China**.

HONG KONG REVOLUTIONARY COMMITTEE. Initially known as the Hong Kong Junta, it was organized in November 1897 and later directed by **Felipe Agoncillo**. When **Emilio Aguinaldo** arrived in **Hong Kong**, the committee was composed of Felipe Agoncillo, Galiciano Apacible, José Ma Basa, Mariano Ponce, and Teodoro Sandiko. Upon the outbreak of the Spanish-American War, the committee issued a proclamation forecasting Philippine independence and asking Filipinos not to fire on the soon-to-arrive U.S. squadron because it was coming in the name of humanity to help liberate the **Philippines**. The committee's opinion soon changed. On 5 May 1898, it decided to prepare Filipino insurgent forces for war with the United States should the United States reject Philippine independence. Later on 10 August, the committee organized an executive board to serve as the diplomatic corps for the Filipino insurgents and sent Felipe Agoncillo to Washington, D.C., in September to negotiate with the U.S. government. After the suppression of the **Philippine Insurrection** by American forces, it was officially dissolved on 31 July 1903.

HOOD, JOHN (1859–1919). Lieutenant (USN), commanded the *Hawk*. A U.S. Naval Academy graduate, Hood had been on the *Maine* when it blew up on 15 February 1898. After commanding the *Hawk* during the war, he served on the *Nero*, made a survey for the Pacific Cable from 1899 to 1900, and was promoted to rear admiral in 1916.

HORMIGUEROS, PUERTO RICO, ENGAGEMENT AT (10 AUGUST 1898). Located seven miles south of **Mayagüez**, Hormigueros was the site of a brief skirmish on 10 August between Spanish forces under the command of Capt. José Torrecillas and the U.S. forces of Brig. Gen. **Theodore Schwan**. Schwan's column of 1,447 men was marching from San Germán en route to Mayagüez when Torrecillas's force, consisting of the Sixth Company of the **Alfonso XIII Battalion** and a company of **guerrillas** moved to meet them at Hormigueros. After a brief two-hour clash, Spanish forces withdrew, sustaining casualties of one dead and nine wounded, according to Spanish officials, and around 50 in U.S. reports. American casualties were one killed and 16 wounded. Schwan's force then occupied Mayagüez the following day, and Torrecillas was later awarded the Red Cross of Military Merit by Spain. U.S. forces formally took possession of Hormigueros on 16 August 1898.

HORNET. (USN) Armed **yacht**, commanded by Lt. James Meredith Helm. Formerly the *Alicia*, it was purchased by the **U.S. Navy** from Henry M. Flagler for $117,500 on 6 April 1898 and assigned to the North Atlantic Station. During the war it convoyed the **Fifth Corps** to **Daiquirí, Cuba**, and while engaging Spanish forces at **Manzanillo** on 30 June, it was disabled and had to be towed out of action by the *Wompatuck*. After engaging in **cable-cutting operations**, the *Hornet* fought in the U.S. naval attack on Spanish naval forces at Manzanillo on 18 July. It was sold in 1910.

La. 1890, com. 12 April 1898, dis. 425, hp. 800, sp. 15
Armament: 3–6pdr., 2–1pdr., 2–37 rev. cannons, 2–6 mm. C.
Cc. 65, comp. 55

"HORROR SHIPS." Name given by U.S. newspapers to the first **U.S. Army transports** that brought ill and wounded soldiers back from **Santiago, Cuba**. On 8 July 1898, Lt. Col. Benjamin F. Pope, chief surgeon of the **Fifth Corps**, began sending the sick and wounded home; however, the transports were not adequately equipped or staffed. After the first of these transports, the *Seneca*, arrived in New York City on 20 July, sensationalist reports of the pathetic conditions on the ship filled newspapers throughout the country and generated an uproar. President **William McKinley** ordered an immediate investigation. From August to September 1898, 87 men died at sea while the Fifth Corps was transported from Santiago to **Camp Wikoff, Montauk Point, Long Island, New York**.

HOSPITAL CORPS, U.S. ARMY. Founded in 1887, it was part of the **War Department** and consisted of 791 enlisted medical corpsmen in early 1898; however, the war caused its rapid increase to almost 6,000 men by the end of August 1898. Nevertheless, throughout the entire war it lacked sufficient trained personnel necessary to carry out its missions in **Cuba**, the **Philippines**, and **Puerto Rico**. Thirty-six officers and 65 enlisted men served with the **Eighth Corps** in the **Philippine campaign**, and 275 corpsmen served with the **Fifth Corps** in the **Santiago, Cuba, campaign**.

HOSPITAL SHIPS. Owing to a lack of hospital ships, **Congress**, on the eve of war, voted war funds for both the **U.S. Army** and **U.S. Navy** to furnish ships for hospital duty. **Transports** such as the *Breakwater*, *Cherokee*, and *Olivette* were converted for use. Other hospital ships included the ***Bay State***, ***Relief***, ***Solace***, and ***State of Texas***.

HOSPITALS. The Spanish-American War saw the introduction of permanent general hospitals for soldiers' care and medical research. Although there were serious problems with the hospitals established at the various **camps** throughout the United States because of a lack of supplies and trained personnel, there were few complaints about the 11 general hospitals established in the United States during the war. Moreover, large numbers of sick were sent to civilian hospitals in New York City and Philadelphia, Pennsylvania, to relieve the pressure of numbers, especially with the return of the **Fifth Corps** from **Santiago, Cuba**, during August 1898. Several hospitals were established with private funds. Foremost among the donors was Helen Miller Gould Shephard (1868–1938), the eldest daughter of millionaire Jay Gould (1836–1892). Not only did she turn her own mansion on the Hudson River into a hospital, but she established others with her own funds.

Contrary to the overall excellent medical record of the **Eighth Corps** in the **Philippines campaign**, the experience of the Fifth Corps in the **Santiago, Cuba, campaign** quickly became a travesty. The corps's principal medical facility was an improvised base hospital that was set up at **Siboney** soon after it landed. It was not sufficiently supplied owing to a lack of boats to bring the supplies ashore; moreover, the army refused the direct assistance of the **American Red Cross nurses**, so the Red Cross established its own hospital of 25 beds and six nurses at Siboney. Only one field hospital with five surgeons existed. Established through the efforts of Maj. M. W. Wood, chief surgeon of the First Division, all of its food had been brought ashore in Wood's private baggage. When faced with over 1,400 wounded from the battles for the **San Juan Heights** on 1 July, the hospital system was overwhelmed. Nevertheless, few soldiers died from their wounds, and a field hospital was quickly established in a church at **El Caney**. Here Dr. Bangs, an army veteran surgeon who had a habit of popping his glass eye of its socket and then cleaning it on his pants, tended to both U.S. and Spanish wounded by operating on them on the altar. The outbreak of **disease** quickly paralyzed an already inadequate system.

HOSTOS Y BONILLA, EUGENIO MARÍA DE (1839–1903). Puerto Rican educator, philosopher, and writer. A great admirer of republicanism and federalism, Hostos was originally a monarchist favoring an independent confederation in the West Indies attached to Spain. He founded teacher training schools in the Dominican Republic and helped reform Chile's educational system. After joining the Puerto Rican section of the **Cuban Revolutionary Party**, Hostos arrived in the United States from Chile in the summer of 1898 and gave an interview that appeared in the *New York Times* on 22 July as "Senor E. M. Hostos Talks." He denied that Puerto Ricans would resist a U.S. invasion, wanted an interview with President **William McKinley**, and stated that if **Puerto Rico** were to be annexed to the United States, it should be done with the consent of its population expressed through a plebiscite. Although he preferred an independent Puerto Rico as part of a West Indies federation, Hostos was willing to accept a 20-year period of U.S. tutelage, after which the people would choose between statehood and independence. Subsequently, he presented his idea of tutelage when he met with McKinley.

Hostos, believing the cession of Puerto Rico to the United States was illegal, returned to Puerto Rico after the U.S. conquest and launched the Liga de Patriotas on the southern coast, advocating that the United States should prepare the country for republican democracy and eventual independence. Believing Puerto Rico had merely changed one master for another, Hostos left Puerto Rico and died in the Dominican Republic, a broken and disillusioned man.

"HOT TIME IN THE OLD TOWN TONIGHT." The most popular song during the war. The **First Colorado Infantry**'s regimental band played it while the regiment pursued fleeing Spaniards during the **Battle of Manila** on 13 August 1898.

HOWELL, JOHN ADAMS (1840–1918). Commodore (USN), commanded the **Northern Patrol Squadron** and then the First Squadron in the **North Atlantic Fleet**. A U.S. Naval Academy graduate, Howell served in the Civil War, did survey work with the U.S. Coast and Geodetic Survey, and patented the **Howell torpedo**. He commanded the U.S. European squadron from February to April 1898.

Howell returned to the United States on his flagship *San Francisco* and commanded the Northern Patrol Squadron from 20 April to 1 July. On 1 July, he assumed command of the First Squadron in the North Atlantic Fleet and directed the **blockade** of the northern Cuban coast. Promoted to rear admiral on 10 August 1898, he was president of the Examining and Retiring Board after the war and retired in 1902.

HOWELL TORPEDO. Patented by **John A. Howell** in 1885 and completed in 1889, it was the first U.S. service torpedo and armed U.S. **battleships** for about a decade. Powered by a small steam turbine that drove a 132-pound flywheel, it was 14 inches in diameter, had a length of 132 inches, and weighed 580 pounds while carrying a 100-pound warhead. Its 400-yard range was limited by the strength of its flywheel. The **Whitehead torpedo** had almost replaced it as the primary torpedo of the **U.S. Navy** by the time of the Spanish-American War.

HUBBARD, ELBERT (1856–1915). Editor of *The Philistine*, a monthly magazine. Hubbard, who retired at 36, having made a fortune in a mail-order business out of Buffalo, New York, was an advocate of an elite business class that was to redeem the world from sickness, want, and distress. In February 1899, needing a piece to fill his magazine's March issue, Hubbard, who had read a piece on Lt. **Andrew S. Rowan**'s mission to Cuban insurgent Maj. Gen. **Calixto García** during the war, sat down and within an hour wrote "A Message to Garcia, being a preachment." Published in *The Philistine*, it was an instantaneous success.

Although he got nearly all the facts wrong, Hubbard immortalized both Rowan and García by using Rowan's dedication to completing his mission in a work intended to inspire employees' loyalty and morale. It was translated into 20 languages, many U.S. and foreign companies distributed it to their workers, and governments passed it out to their employees. By 7 May 1915, when he died on the *Lusitania*, Hubbard had made $250,000 in royalties. By 1952 its circulation was estimated to have reached 80 million.

HUDSON. (USN) Armed revenue cutter, commanded by Lt. Frank H. Newcombe R.C.S. It was loaned to the **U.S. Navy** by the Treasury Department on 24 March 1898 and, armed with 2–6pdr. guns, it was assigned to the North Atlantic Station. During the naval action at **Cárdenas**, **Cuba**, on 11 May 1898, the *Hudson* towed the disabled *Winslow* out of the bay under heavy fire. After serving on **blockade** duty off **Havana**, **Cuba**, it convoyed the **Fifth Corps** to **Daiquirí**, **Cuba**. After the war it was returned to the Treasury Department.

HULL, JOHN ALBERT TIFFIN (1841–1928). Republican representative from Iowa (1891–1911) and chairman of the House Military Affairs Committee. A Civil War veteran and former lieutenant governor of Iowa, Hull was a longtime advocate of army reform. In early 1898, the **War Department** worked through him to try and expand the regular army. Consequently, on 17 March 1898 he introduced the **Hull Bill**, which was soon defeated.

Hull, who was sympathetic to **black American** demands to volunteer for service during the war, welcomed the opportunity to assist in getting approval from the War Department and on 10 May 1898, enacted a bill that provided for the enlistment of 10,000 **volunteers** or **"immunes"** that would allow blacks to enlist. However, when only four black regiments were allowed and it was prohibited for a black to rise above the level of a lieutenant, Hull tried but failed to get the restrictions removed.

HULL BILL. Introduced in the House of Representatives by **John A. T. Hull** on 17 March 1898, it proposed to increase the regular army to 104,000 men and proposed changes in the organization of infantry regiments. Although supported by President **William McKinley**, Secretary of War **Russell A. Alger**, and Maj. Gen. **Nelson A. Miles**, the bill encountered insurmountable opposition from legislative supporters of the **National Guard** or state militias. The bill's opponents knew that, if it passed, the bill would largely exclude the militia from service in a probable Cuban campaign and, over time, would minimize the role of the state militias. On 7 April, it was defeated 155–61 by an unlikely coalition of pro-militia legislators, generally southern Democrats who still resented the army's role in Reconstruction, and Populists, who opposed the then current use of the army against strikers. The defeat referred the bill to committee, where it died, and left no alternative to that of the use of the state militias.

HULLINGS, WILLIS JAMES (1850–19?). Colonel, commanded Third Brigade, First Division, **First Corps**. A state representative and senator (1881–1911), Hullings, a Republican, was a member of the state's **National Guard**. During the war he initially commanded a brigade that included the **Sixteenth Pennsylvania Infantry**, **Second Wisconsin Infantry**, and Third Kentucky Infantry. Subsequently, he commanded the Sixteenth Pennsylvania during the **Puerto Rican campaign** in Brig Gen. **Oswald H. Ernst**'s brigade. His regiment performed well in the **Battle of Coamo** on 9 August 1898. Promoted to brigadier general (USV) for his conduct during the war, Hullings directed the National Association of Spanish-American War Veterans for two years. He later served in the House of Representatives.

HUNKER, JOHN JACOB (1844–1916). Commander (USN), commanded the *Annapolis*. A U.S. Naval Academy graduate and Civil War veteran, Hunker, who was the senior naval officer present at **Tampa, Florida**, on 8 June 1898, organized and commanded the ships that transported the **Fifth Corps** from Tampa to **Daiquirí, Cuba**. He later commanded the naval expedition that captured **Nipe Bay, Cuba**, on 21 July. For his actions during the war, Hunker was advanced three numbers, was promoted to captain in 1900, and to rear admiral in 1906.

HUNTINGTON, ROBERT W. (1840–1917). Lieutenant colonel (USMC), commanded the **First Marine Battalion**. A Civil War veteran, Huntington served in the cavalry on the frontier and commanded the New York barracks immediately before the war. One of the toughest and most demanding officers in the Marine Corps, Huntington was ending his career when called upon to command the First Marine Battalion during its campaign at **Guantánamo, Cuba**. Promoted to colonel, he was en route to take the **Isle of Pines** when the **Armistice Protocol** was signed on 12 August 1898. Huntington retired in 1900.

HUSE, HARRY McLAREN PINCKNEY (1858–1942). Lieutenant (USN), executive officer on the *Gloucester*. Born at West Point and a graduate of the U.S. Naval Academy, Huse was advanced five numbers for his courage during the **Naval Battle of Santiago, Cuba**, on 3 July 1898. After the battle when defeated Spanish Adm. **Pascual Cervera** was brought to the *Gloucester*, he told Cervera in French "Victory is ours, but the glory is yours."

Participating in the U.S. conquest of **Puerto Rico**, on 25 July Huse commanded a party of 28 sailors who were the first to land at **Guánica**, and his group raised the first U.S. flag on Puerto Rican soil. After the war he taught at the U.S. Naval Academy, commanded U.S. Naval Forces in European waters, and was promoted to vice admiral.

—I—

IGLESIAS, PABLO (1850–1925). Leader of the **Spanish Socialist Workers Party**. The son of a washerwoman, Iglesias imprinted the party with French Marxism, was a strident critic of Spanish **Republicans**, and served as president of the party's National Committee and director of its paper *El Socialista*.

Before the war, Iglesias maintained the impossibility of Spain's winning a war against the United States, and after the war had begun, he was one of the first to call for a negotiated settlement when he wrote on 9 July 1898, "to sustain that Spain should continue fighting the United States is true insanity." After the signing of the **Armistice Protocol** of 12 August 1898, he defended the Socialist Party's consistent anti-war policy.

ILLESCAS, RAFAEL MARTÍNEZ (1854–1898). Captain, Spanish commander of the **Patria Battalion** in **Puerto Rico**. After fighting against the **Carlists**, Martínez Illescas arrived in Puerto Rico in 1886. During the Spanish-American War, he commanded Spanish forces at the **Battle of Coamo** on 9 August 1898. He was eating breakfast in the house of Florencio Santiago, the mayor of Coamo, when the shooting started, and he later led his troops on horseback until he was shot through the heart at 9:00 a.m. Upon his death, Spanish resistance collapsed. On 20 August 1898, Capt. **Harry A. Hall** of the **Sixteenth Pennsylvania Infantry** wrote to Illesca's widow, Eugenia Bugallo, commending her husband's valor. His body, accompanied by U.S. troops, was taken to **Ponce**, where it was buried with full military honors. On 15 May 1915, his remains were exhumed and reburied with honors in Cartagena, Spain.

ILOILO, CEBU, PHILIPPINES. A city on the island of Cebu in the middle **Philippines** some 300 miles south of **Manila**. Communications between Spain and the Philippines remained open through here after the Manila to **Hong Kong cable** was cut by the *Zafiro* on 2 May 1898. From here small ships took messages to a cable station on the small island of Labuan off the north coast of Borneo. After the **capitulation** of Manila on 13 August 1898, the Spanish seat of government, under the command of Gov.-Gen. **Diego de los Ríos y Nicolau**, was transferred here.

After Spanish officials had offered to surrender, a task force under Brig. Gen. Marcus P. Miller was readied. On 25 December 1898, the city, which had been besieged by Filipino insurgents, was evacuated by Spanish forces, and it was occupied by insurgents without bloodshed or disorder. Two days later Brig. Gen. Miller's forces arrived on **transports**. Upon the outbreak of the **Philippine Insurrection** on 4 February 1899, the city was bombarded by the *Boston* and *Petrel* and occupied by Miller's forces.

IMMORTALITÉ. British **armored cruiser**, commanded by Capt. **Edward Chichester**. Having served in Chinese waters since 1895, it arrived at **Manila Bay, Philippines**, on 7 May 1898. Before the **Battle of Manila** on 13 August 1898, Chichester moved it and the *Iphigenia* between the U.S. and German naval forces. This gave rise to the groundless legend that the British had saved Adm. **George W. Dewey's Asiatic Squadron** by serving notice to the German navy, which allegedly was about to attack Dewey's squadron. Later in the day when the American flag was raised over **Manila**, the cruiser's band struck up Adm. George Dewey's favorite march "Under the Double Eagle," and the ship fired a 21-gun salute. From 1899 to 1902 it was reduced to subsidiary duties and placed in reserve. It was sold in 1907.

La. 1887, dis. 5,600, hp. 5,500, sp. 17
Armor: s. 10″, d. 2–3″, ct. 12″
Armament: 2–9.2″, 10–6″, 6–6pdr., 10–3pdr, 6–18″ tt. (4 aw. & 2 sub.)
Cc. 900, comp. 484

"IMMUNES." Formerly known as the First through Tenth U.S. Volunteer Infantry, these ten regiments were authorized on 11 May 1898. Not to exceed 10,000 men, they were to be made up of men from the southern states who were supposedly "immune" to "diseases incident to the tropics." The concept was soon abandoned in practice as the regiments included companies from the hill regions of the South as well as from northern states, such as New Jersey. Four of the regiments—the Seventh, Eighth, Ninth, and Tenth—were composed of 4,000 **black Americans**.

The Second, Third, Fourth, Fifth, and Ninth regiments served as garrison troops occupying **Cuba** after the war, and the Sixth did garrison duty in postwar **Puerto Rico**.

IMPARCIAL, EL. The Spanish **Liberal Party**'s newspaper in Madrid. One of Spain's largest and most prestigious newspapers, it was edited by Manuel Troyano, provided broad news coverage, and had a circulation of 120,000 in 1898. Before the Spanish-American War, it had been highly critical of Capt. Gen. **Valeriano Weyler y Nicolau**'s methods in **Cuba**, opened a subscription drive to collect funds for wounded and ill soldiers returning from Cuba, and in November 1897 concluded that because of casualties and **disease**, the **Spanish Army** in Cuba was too small to end the **Cuban Revolt**.

Highly critical and disdainful of American interference and power before the war, *El Imparcial* was infuriated that the U.S. government held Spain responsible for sinking the *Maine*, believed U.S. policy was based solely on removing Spain from Cuba for eventual U.S. annexation, and called upon Spain's government to defend Spanish honor after President **William McKinley's War Message** of 11 April 1898. During the war it was such a vocal supporter of Spain's war effort that it was called "the champion of the war with the United States." However, after the overwhelming defeat of Adm. **Pascual Cervera's Squadron** at the **Naval Battle of Santiago**, **Cuba**, on 3 July, it demanded a negotiated peace.

IMPERIALISTS—UNITED STATES. Although in general agreement over U.S. expansion, their motivations varied. **Albert J. Beveridge** and Josiah Strong, believers in Anglo-Saxon superiority, defended expansion as the U.S. duty to spread American institutions and to "civilize" the heathen. Senator **Henry C. Lodge** and **Alfred T. Mahan** emphasized the need for coaling stations and ports to support the new American navy. Others, such as **Theodore Roosevelt**, simply wanted to follow the example of the times and establish the United States as a world power. Although many were motivated by genuine humanitarian concerns, business interests, which had initially opposed going to war, saw the U.S. victories and conquests as a means to open markets, particularly for entrance into the Chinese market. They were supported in their opinion by Brooks Adams, a Boston historian, who wrote in "The Spanish War and the Equilibrium of the World" *The Forum* (August 1898) that the war's results had clearly demonstrated that the United States was ready for economic supremacy.

INDIANA. (USN) First-class **battleship**, commanded by Capt. **Henry C. Taylor**. A sister ship to the *Massachusetts* and *Oregon*, it had an armored belt that extended about three-fifths of its length and was mechanically unsound throughout the war because of bad boilers, which affected its speed. Assigned to the North Atlantic Station, the **marine** detachment on board was commanded by Capt. Littleton W. T. Waller, who was later a major general.

During the war the *Indiana* participated in the 12 May 1898 **bombardment of San Juan**, **Puerto Rico**, and convoyed the **Fifth Corps** to **Daiquirí, Cuba**. During the **Naval Battle of Santiago** on 3 July 1898, it could not exceed ten knots because of a fouled bottom and a forward 13-inch turret that was out of order. Hit only twice and suffering minor damage, the *Indiana* directed most of its 1,876 shots fired during the battle at the *Almirante Oquendo*. It later bombarded **Santiago** on 10–11 July and was scheduled to be part of the covering squadron for the **Eastern Squadron**. Decommissioned in 1919, it was sunk in target practice on 1 November 1920, and its hulk was sold for scrap.

La. 1893, com. 1895, dis. 10,288, hp. 9,000, sp. 15
Armor: s. 18″, d. 2.75″, t. 15″ & 6″, b. 8–17″, ct. 9″
Armament: 4–13″, 8–8″, 4–6″, 20–6pdr., 6–1pdr., 2 C. mgs., 3–18″ tt.
  (aw.)
Cc. 1,600, comp. 473

INFANTA MARÍA TERESA. (SPN) **Armored cruiser**, commanded by Capt. **Víctor M. Concas**. Spanish-built and patterned on the British *Aurora* class, it was a sister ship to the *Vizcaya* and *Almirante Oquendo*. It had an armored belt that extended two-thirds of its length and a protective deck that was flat over the belt and curved at the extremities, leaving a high unprotected freeboard. Its 11-inch guns were mounted fore and aft in single barbettes with lightly armored hoods, and its 5.5-inch guns were without any armored protection except shields.

While serving as Adm. **Pascual Cervera**'s flagship, the *Infanta María Teresa* was destroyed in the **Naval Battle of Santiago** on 3 July 1898. The first ship out of the harbor at 9:35 a.m., it withstood the fire of all U.S. ships for ten minutes with only its two bow-turret guns usable against more than 100 U.S. guns. It headed for the U.S. **cruiser** *Brooklyn*, intending to ram it, but heavy fire forced it to turn westward. With Capt. Concas wounded and its men unable to extinguish the on board fires, Adm. Cervera took command and beached it 6.5 miles west of the harbor entrance at 10:35 a.m.

Plagued with faulty equipment during the brief battle, it had been hit a countable 29 times. Its crew was rescued by the *Harvard* and the *Gloucester*. Floated and taken to **Guantánamo**, **Cuba**, for repairs on 24 September, it later left Guantánamo under its own steam for Norfolk, Virginia, under convoy of the repair-ship *Vulcan*. En route it was driven ashore in the Bahamas during a gale on 1 November 1898 and abandoned.

La. 1890, dis. 6,890, hp. 13,700, sp. 20.2
Armor: s. 12–10″, d. 2–3″, b. 9″, ct. 12″
Armament: 2–11″, 10–5.5″, 8–2.2.″, 8–1.4″, 2 M. mgs., 8 tt. (2 sub.)
Cc. 1,050, comp. 484

INGLATERRA HOTEL. The top hotel in **Havana**, **Cuba**. It was located on the ocean front near the center of town on the west side of the Parque Central. U.S. Consul **Fitzhugh Lee** lived here. A favorite haunt where journalists stayed, and from which they reported the **Cuban Revolt**, and a meeting ground for diplomats and spies, it was staffed by Spanish loyalists.

INSULAR CASES. After a short period of military government in **Puerto Rico**, the United States established a civilian government. However, the Foraker Act of 1900 did not give the citizens of Puerto Rico all the privileges and protections of the U.S. Constitution. It was tested in the Insular Cases, the most decisive of which was *Downes v. Bidwell* (1904).

Downes brought the case against Bidwell, a port collector, to recover back duties paid under protest on a consignment shipped to him from Puerto Rico. Dealing with the vexing question of constitutional relations with the territories acquired in the war, the Supreme Court, with four members dissenting, ruled that the Constitution did not automatically follow the flag, and Downes lost his case. Puerto Rico was held to be territory "foreign to the United States in a domestic sense."

IOWA. (USN) First-class **battleship**, commanded by Capt. **Robley D. Evans**. Assigned to the North Atlantic Station during the war, the *Iowa* participated in the **bombardment of San Juan**, **Puerto Rico**, on 12 May 1898 and served in Adm. **William T. Sampson**'s division in blockading **Santiago**, **Cuba**. Every sailor volunteered to go on the *Merrimac*'s attempt to block the Santiago harbor entrance on 3 June. It bombarded Spanish fortifications at the entrance to Santiago harbor on 6 June and on 8 June began night duty training its **searchlights** on the harbor entrance. Firing 1,473 shots during the **Naval Battle of Santiago** on 3 July 1898, it destroyed Adm. **Pascual Cervera**'s flagship, the *Infanta María Teresa*, and was hit 11 times, causing no serious damage. After the battle, it assisted in the rescue of survivors from the *Vizcaya*. The *Iowa* was later assigned to the covering squadron for the **Eastern Squadron**. As a result of their heroic efforts during a boiler room explosion on 20 July, Coppersmith Philip B. Keefer and Fireman Robert Penn were awarded the **Congressional Medal of Honor**. Decommissioned in 1920, it was sunk as a gunnery target on 22 March 1923.

La. 1896, com. 1897, dis. 11,340, hp. 11,000, sp. 17
Armor: s. 14″, t. 15″ & 8″, b. 6–15″, d. 2.75″, ct. 10″
Armament: 4–12″, 8–8″, 6–4″, 20–6pdr., 4–1pdr., 4 C. mgs., 4–14″ tt.
 (aw.)
Cc. 1,795, comp. 486

IRELAND, JOHN H. (1838–1918). Archbishop of St. Paul, Minnesota. An Irish-born lifelong champion of the **Republican Party** and personal friend of President **William McKinley**, Ireland was selected by Cardinal Rampolla, foreign minister of the **Vatican**, to serve as an emissary of **Pope Leo XIII** in the brief March–April 1898 Vatican mediation effort to avoid war between the United States and Spain. Ireland met with McKinley on 1 April to ascertain if McKinley would welcome the Vatican's effort. He reported that McKinley desired peace and wanted help to obtain it; moreover, McKinley would accept either a proposal to purchase **Cuba** or an armistice leading to Cuban-Spanish negotiations. McKinley, who had no intention of accepting Vatican intervention, merely wanted to exert additional pressure on Spain through Ireland to accept his ultimatum of 27 March. Based on Ireland's report, the Vatican continued its efforts. When Spain granted an armistice in Cuba on 9 April, Ireland felt peace was assured.

IRENE. German, wood-sheathed, **protected cruiser**. One of the first German protected cruisers, it arrived at **Manila Bay, Philippines**, on 6 May 1898, from Nagasaki, Japan, and ignored Com. **George W. Dewey's blockade**. On 27 June an American naval party from the *McCulloch* boarded the *Irene* to verify compliance with blockade regulations. Dewey later claimed that the *Irene* had only stopped after the U.S. ships fired across her bow; however, neither the logs nor the commanders of the U.S. ships confirmed Dewey's version. On 7 July another supposed incident occurred at **Isla Grande**. When German Vice Adm. **Otto von Diederichs** sent an emissary on 10 July to protest the boarding of the *Irene* by U.S. naval forces, Dewey exploded and threatened war against **Germany**. By 1914 the *Irene* was serving as a U-boat depot ship and was broken up in 1921.

La. 1887, dis. 4,947, hp. 8,000, sp. 18
Armor: d. 3″
Armament: 4–150 mm, 8–105 mm, 6–50 mm, 3–350 mm. tt.

Comp. 365

ISABEL CATÓLICA REGIMENT. A Spanish infantry regiment stationed at **Manzanillo, Cuba**. Its first battalion, under the command of Comdr. Luis Torrecilla, and its second battalion, under the command of Comdr. Eugenio Briceño, were part of **Escario's Column**. Soon after their arrival in **Santiago, Cuba**, six companies relieved the units of the **Alcántara Peninsular Regiment** in the **Fort Canosa** area in the front lines.

ISABELLA II. (SPN) Unprotected **cruiser**, commanded by Capt. José Boado. Stationed at **San Juan, Puerto Rico**, its rapid-fire battery of 4.7″ guns had been removed and installed near the San Fernando Battery. During the naval engagement between the *Terror* and the *St. Paul* outside San Juan on 22 June 1898, the *Isabella II* retreated to San Juan harbor after the *Terror* was damaged. On 14 September 1898, it left San Juan for Spain.

La. 1886, dis. 1,130, hp. 1,550, sp. 14
Armament: 4–4.7″, 2–2.7″, 3 mgs., 2 tt.
Cc. 220, comp. 130

ISLA DE CUBA. (SPN) Small **protected cruiser**, commanded by Capt. José Sedrach. Built in England with a two-masted schooner rig, it was the sister ship of the *Isla de Luzón*. Called from **Iloilo, Philippines**, to **Manila**, it joined Adm. **Patricio Montojo's Squadron**. During the **Battle of Manila Bay** on 1 May 1898, Adm. Montojo transferred his flag to it after the *Reina María Cristina* was sunk. Having sustained two wounded during the battle, the *Isla de Cuba* was aground and full of water after the battle when it was fired by the *Petrel*. Later raised, it was sent to **Hong Kong** for major repairs. Taken into U.S. service, it was sold to Venezuela in 1912. Renamed the *Mariscal Sucre*, it survived until 1940.

La. 1886, dis. 1,045, hp. 2,200, sp. 14
Armor: d. 2.5″, ct. 2″
Armament: 4–4.7″, 2–2.25″, 3–1.46″, 1 mg., 3–14″ tt.
Cc. 160, comp. 187

ISLA DE LUZÓN. (SPN) Small **protected cruiser**, commanded by Comdr. I. L. Human. Built in England with a two-masted schooner rig, it was the sister ship of the *Isla de Cuba* and part of Adm. **Patricio Montojo's Squadron** at **Manila, Philippines**. Having sustained six wounded during the **Battle of Manila Bay** on 1 May 1898, it was aground and full of water after the battle when it was fired by the *Petrel*. Later raised, it was sent to **Hong Kong** for major repairs. Taken into U.S. service, it served with the Louisiana and Illinois

naval militia (1903–1918) and with the Naval Torpedo Station as a yard craft. It was sold in 1920.

La. 1886, dis. 1,045, hp. 2,200, sp. 14
Armor: d. 2.5″, ct. 2″
Armament: 4–4.7″, 2–2.25″, 3–1.46″, 1 mg., 3–14″ tt.
Cc. 160, comp. 187

ISLA DE MINDANAO. A 4,195-ton, lightly armed, merchant transport of the **Transatlantic Company**. After arriving in the **Philippines** on 22 April 1898, it served as a mail-boat steamer and transported munitions. Part of Adm. **Patricio Montojo's Squadron**, it was anchored in **Bacoor Bay**. During the **Battle of Manila Bay** on 1 May, it caught fire from U.S. shelling, and its 125-man crew sustained no casualties before it was abandoned. After the battle it was destroyed by gunfire from the *Concord*.

ISLA GRANDE, PHILIPPINES. Located in **Subic Bay**, its Spanish garrison held out against Filipino insurgent attack until 7 July 1898, when the *Raleigh* and *Concord* arrived to investigate the reported interference of the German **cruiser *Irene*** in Filipino insurgent efforts to take the island. Capt. **Joseph B. Coghlan** of the *Raleigh* found no conclusive evidence of such interference, and the *Irene* left with the women and children it had come to evacuate. The *Raleigh* and *Concord* then shelled the island and the garrison surrendered to U.S. naval forces. Capt. Coghlan then turned the captured Spanish **prisoners of war** over to the Filipino insurgents but did not allow the insurgents to capture and hold the island. **Edward W. Harden**, a correspondent for the *New York World*, soon wrote "Dewey Scared Off a Meddling German Warship" (14 July 1898), in which he reported that while there was not any overt act on the part of the Germans, there was always the danger of it.

ISLE OF PINES. Located 30 miles off the southwest coast of **Cuba**, it was seen in the prewar plans of the **Naval War College** as a possible naval base. Prior to the Spanish-American War, it was the only land proposed for annexation by the United States in compensation for freeing Cuba from Spanish control. On 1 July 1898, Maj. Gen. **Nelson A. Miles** proposed using the island as a base for U.S. cavalry action on the Cuban mainland as well as for hospitals, a supply base, and departure point for an expedition to conquer **Puerto Rico**. Secretary of War **Russell A. Alger** rejected the plan.

ITALY. The weakest of the six great European powers who signed the **Great Powers Note** on 6 April 1898, Italy, although its government was sympathetic to Spain and its press was highly critical of the United States, never contemplated a vigorous American policy and could only promise to cooperate with the initiatives of others. Its foreign policy followed a delicate balancing act that supported diplomatic initiatives to negotiate peace while trying to keep Spain from leaning toward **France**.

—J—

JACKIES. Contemporary slang for U.S. sailors.

JACOBSON, HERMANN. Commander of the German **cruiser** *Geier*. An eyewitness to the war while visiting Spanish ports throughout the Caribbean, Jacobson wrote about the war. His work was published by the U.S. **Office of Naval Intelligence** in 1899 as *Sketches from the Spanish-American War by Commander J.* In it he praised the courage of Spanish soldiers while criticizing Adm. **Pascual Cervera y Topete** for not having left the harbor of **Santiago**, **Cuba**, under the cover of darkness. Jacobson also criticized the bombardment of **San Juan**, **Puerto Rico** on 12 May 1898, by U.S. naval forces under the command of Adm. **William T. Sampson** for having been conducted without properly warning the civilian population in advance.

JAMES, WILLIAM (1842–1910). Harvard psychologist, theologian, philosopher, and anti-imperialist. Even though he believed that the American motivation for the war stemmed from an honest humanitarianism, James deplored the "war fever" that had gripped the country, viewed **Congress** as "entirely mad," and felt **Theodore Roosevelt** was still "mentally in the Sturm und Drang period of early adolescence." In a private letter about the ratification of the **Treaty of Paris**, James, a vice president of the **Anti-Imperialist League**, wrote that the country had "puked up its ancient principles" when tempted to retain the lands it had conquered during the war. During the **Philippine Insurrection** he excoriated the United States, exclaiming "God damn the United States for its vile conduct in the Philippine Isles."

JAPAN. Although a significant part of its press, political establishment, and public viewed the United States as an interloper in Asia, Japan officially declared its neutrality on 30 April 1898. In a period of growing militarism, nationalism, and expansion in China, Japan was unwilling to provoke a crisis with the United States at a time of intense rivalry with European powers in China; nevertheless, Japan officially protested the U.S. annexation of **Hawaii**. A Japanese

protected cruiser, the *Itsukushima*, was present in **Manila Bay, Philippines**, during the war. After the defeat of Spanish forces in the **Philippines**, a quiet offer was made to the United States on 8 September 1898, for Japan to participate in governing the islands. A quick American refusal did not change policy, for although official policy had supported Spain's retention of the Philippines, U.S. possession was preferred to any other possible alternative short of cession to Japan.

JÁUDENES Y ÁLVAREZ, FERMÍN. Spanish general of division in the **Philippines**. Second in command of Spanish forces in the Philippines, Jáudenes replaced **Basilio Augustín y Dávila** on 4 August 1898, and became governor-general and captain general of the Philippines. Terrified that the Filipino insurgents would torture and execute every Spaniard in **Manila** and without knowledge of the signing of the **Armistice Protocol**, he negotiated the prearranged **Battle of Manila** on 13 August 1898 and the subsequent **Capitulation of Manila Agreement**. Jáudenes was succeeded by Gen. Francisco Rizzo, returned to Spain, and jailed in the San Francisco Prison in Madrid during his court-martial. During the trial, he blamed his defeat on Spain's disregard for the Philippines and stated that only his prudence had saved Manila from "pillage and devastation" by the Filipinos. Although the judges declined to reach a verdict, he was removed from service, placed on the reserve list, and forbidden to discharge any public duties.

JINGO. A bellicose, chauvinistic term that formed the chorus of a popular music-hall ditty. It had come into popular use in 1878 in **Great Britain** when it was on the verge of intervening in the Russo-Turkish War, being applied to members of the British Conservative Party who urged the government to support the Turks. Picked up in the United States, it was applied to those individuals who boasted of their patriotism and favored an aggressive, warlike foreign policy.

JORGE JUAN. (SPN) An old, wooden-hulled **gunboat**. Located at **Nipe Bay, Cuba**, it had been anchored so long that it could no longer get under way. It was sunk during the naval engagement at Nipe Bay on 21 July 1898, when after getting off a few shots, it was scuttled by its crew who then escaped by rowing to shore.

La. 1876, dis. 935, hp. 1,100, sp. 13
Armament: 3–4.7″, 2–3.15″, 2 rev. cannon
Cc. 128, comp. 146

JUANA DÍAZ, PUERTO RICO. Located about ten miles northwest of **Ponce**, this town of 21,000 surrendered to **Stephen Crane** on 3

August 1898. Soon after the U.S. occupation of Ponce, Crane and **Richard H. Davis**, who were discussing how quickly Puerto Rican towns were surrendering to U.S. forces, decided to capture a town on their own. After selecting Juana Díaz, they agreed to go together the next morning, but Crane left early, passed through U.S. lines, and arrived at Juana Díaz where he was presented with the keys to the town jail by the mayor. Crane organized a celebration, and the next day, while he was sitting sipping coffee, U.S. forces marched into the town and were welcomed by both the townspeople and Crane.

JUNTA. Popular name for the Cuban insurgent organization in New York City. It was first appointed in September 1898 by the **Cuban Republic**, which authorized it to conduct diplomatic relations. The Junta represented the confederated clubs of Cuban revolutionaries in the United States and was led by **Tomás Estrada Palma**. Composed chiefly of Cuban-born naturalized American citizens, it carried on highly successful propaganda activities through public events and newspapers such as *Patria* and *El Porvenir*, organized prewar **filibuster**ing expeditions, organized and oversaw the work of the **Cuban League**, and got considerable support from U.S. labor unions and the **"yellow press"**. Its influence in the East and Midwest was significant, little in the South, and almost non-existent in the West. Although Spain viewed it as the primary cause of the **Cuban Revolt**, many in the organization feared that a war between Spain and the United States would result in a U.S. military occupation and annexation of **Cuba**.

—K—

KAISERIN AUGUSTA. German, wood-sheathed, **protected cruiser** that served as Vice Admiral **Otto von Diederich**'s flagship. On 12 June 1898, it arrived at **Manila Bay, Philippines**, and on 5 August 1898 surreptitiously evacuated the Spanish Gov.-Gen. **Basilio Augustín y Dávila** after he had been relieved from office. It left after the 13 August **Battle of Manila** for **Hong Kong**. In 1914 it became a gunnery school ship and was broken up in 1920.

La. 1892, dis. 6,218, hp. 15,650, sp. 21.5
Armor: d. 2.75″
Armament: 12–150 mm, 8–105 mm, 8–88 mm, 4 rev. cannon, 5–350 mm tt.
Comp. 430

KATAHDIN. (USN) A 250-foot-long antiquated armored harbor defense ram. Commanded by Comdr. George F. Wilde, it was recommissioned from March to October 1898. The only vessel of its type in the **U.S. Navy**, the *Katahdin* was built at a cost of $930,000 for the express purpose of ramming other vessels. Employing a double bottom that was flooded to lower its already low hull to six inches above the water, it had to remain sealed while at sea, thereby causing poor ventilation and a suffocating heat.

Although ordered to join the Cuban **blockade** in late June 1898, it saw no combat action during the war because it did not arrive at **Santiago, Cuba**, until after the **Naval Battle of Santiago** on 3 July 1898. Briefly used in naval operations around **Cuba** following the war, it was soon decommissioned, and eventually sunk by naval gunfire as an experimental target in September 1909.

La. 1893, com. 1896, dis. 2,155, hp. 5,068, sp. 16
Armor: s. 6–3″, d. 6–2.5″, ct. 18″
Armament: 4–6pdr.
Cc. 202, comp. 97

KATIPUNAN. A clandestine Filipino insurgent organization established in 1892 by **Andres Bonifacio**. Loosely based on Masonic rites and principles, it led the fight for independence during the **Philippine Revolt**, which broke out in August 1896. In March 1897, the Katipunan was absorbed into the movement led by **Emilio Aguinaldo** when representatives of several revolutionary factions voted at the Tejeros Convention to form a new revolutionary government. Bonifacio and his brother, who opposed such a move, were executed in May 1897.

KENNAN, GEORGE (1845–1924). Correspondent, author, and grandfather of future diplomat George F. Kennan. A foreign correspondent for *The Century Magazine* who had extensively covered Russia, Kennan accepted an invitation to go to **Cuba** as a correspondent for *The Outlook*, a weekly New York journal, to report on the work of the **American Red Cross** during the Spanish-American War. Arriving at **Tampa, Florida**, on 6 May 1898, he described the situation at the Tampa Bay Hotel as a "brilliant military ball at a fashionable seaside summer resort" and pointed out the complete lack of any plan of operations for embarking the **Fifth Corps**. He went to Cuba, along with **Clara Barton**, on the steamer *State of Texas*.

A judicious observer and harsh critic of Maj. Gen. **William R. Shafter**, Kennan, in his articles for *The Outlook* and in his subsequent book *Campaigning in Cuba* (1899), strongly criticized the **U.S. Army** for its inadequate **disease** prevention and care of the wounded, described the bravery of both Spanish and U.S. combatants, praised **black American regular soldiers** for their courage, poignantly wrote of the courtesy and concern of wounded U.S. soldiers for their more seriously wounded comrades, and depicted the filthy conditions of **Santiago, Cuba**, after its **capitulation**. After Kennan caught malaria, he left Cuba in August 1898, only to return in December to report on the U.S. military occupation.

KENT, JACOB FORD (1835–1918). Brigadier general (USV), commanded the First Division, **Fifth Corps**. A West Point graduate, Civil War veteran, and instructor at West Point, Kent spent thirty years on the frontier until the outbreak of the war. After a brigade under his command conducted a feint landing on 22 June at **Cabañas, Cuba**, in support of the landing of the Fifth Corps at **Daiquirí, Cuba**, Kent and his brigade were forgotten by Maj. Gen. **William R. Shafter** and they were not recalled for three days.

After landing at **Siboney, Cuba**, on 25 June, Kent's division, which consisted of 272 officers and 4,924 enlisted men, sustained 89 killed and 489 wounded in the **Battle of San Juan Hill** on 1 July 1898. Later promoted to major general (USV), he signed the **Round Robin Letter** of 3 August 1898. After brief service in the **Philippines**, Kent was promoted to permanent brigadier general on 4 October 1898 and retired 11 days later.

KETTLE HILL, SANTIAGO, CUBA. Part of the **San Juan Heights** and located about 400 yards to the northeast of San Juan Hill, it was named after a large sugar-boiling cauldron, that looked like a great tea kettle, located on its summit. At its base was the San Juan River. Spanish forces here totaling 137 soldiers were minimally reinforced before the **Battle of Kettle Hill** on 1 July.

KETTLE HILL, CUBA, BATTLE OF (1 JULY 1898). As part of the general attack by U.S. forces on the **San Juan Heights**, **Kettle Hill** was the first objective of the Dismounted Cavalry Division, which was temporarily under the command of Brig. Gen. **Samuel S. Sumner** owing to the illness of Maj. Gen. **Joseph Wheeler**.

Initiated by the **Ninth U.S. Cavalry**, the attack up a low rise quickly became intermingled as the **Rough Riders**, and the **First U.S. Cavalry** joined the main attack up the hill, while the **Third U.S. Infantry**, **Sixth U.S. Infantry**, and **Tenth U.S. Cavalry** advanced partially up the hill. By the time U.S. forces reached the top of the hill, with **Theodore Roosevelt** among the leaders, the outnumbered Spanish forces had already retreated.

After reaching the summit, U.S. forces poured fire into the Spanish forces on **San Juan Hill**, charged down the western slope across the low ground and up the northern extension of San Juan Hill, and captured part of the San Juan Heights just north of the El Pozo-Santiago

Road. By the end of the day, Brig. Gen. Sumner's division had sustained casualties of 35 killed and 328 wounded.

KEY WEST, FLORIDA. Located 90 miles from **Havana**, **Cuba**, the city of 22,000 and the island had been selected as early as 1895 in **Naval War College** planning as an advanced base in a war against Spain. Although minimally fortified upon the outbreak of war, its naval base, under the command of Com. **George C. Remey**, became the naval headquarters of the Cuban theater for the **North Atlantic Squadron** and the **Flying Squadron**, served as a coaling and repair station, and held the 22 Spanish ships that were captured during the opening weeks of the war.

As a center for **cables** between the U.S. and **Cuba**, Key West quickly became a news distribution center, and even though Adm. **William T. Sampson** invoked **censorship** on 23 April 1898 by taking possession of the local cable offices, numerous **correspondents**, using the Key West Hotel as their headquarters, frequently sent the full details of the war to their respective offices. Unbeknownst to either Adm. Sampson or the **press**, the **Hellings-Villaverde Network**, which gathered intelligence directly from Havana, Cuba, operated out of the local telegraph office.

KIMBALL, WILLIAM WIRT (1848–1930). Lieutenant (USN), commanded the Atlantic Torpedo Boat Flotilla during the war. A U.S. Naval Academy graduate, Kimball studied at the Naval Torpedo Station at Newport, Rhode Island, promoted the development of a submarine designed by John P. Holland, prepared the final draft of the **Kimball Plan** while serving in the **Office of Naval Intelligence**, and organized the first **torpedo boat** flotilla in the **U.S. Navy**. An exponent of the theories of **Alfred T. Mahan**, Kimball favored offensive naval warfare. Decorated for his service during the war, he was promoted to commander in 1899 and later to rear admiral.

KIMBALL PLAN. An 1896 war plan worked out at the **Naval War College** in collaboration with the **Office of Naval Intelligence**, the plan was named after Lt. **William W. Kimball** because he prepared the final draft. Officially called "The War with Spain 1896: General Considerations of the War, the Results Desired and the Consequent Kind of Operations to be Undertaken," it advocated the Caribbean as the principal theater of operations with the goal of liberating **Cuba** from Spanish rule. Included were two supplementary campaigns: one of harassment in Spanish waters to keep the **Spanish Navy** at home and another to capture **Manila, Philippines**. Since Manila was to be captured as a supply base, no thought was given to the annexation of the **Philippines**. Foreseeing a strictly naval war, the land war in Cuba was left to the Cuban insurgents, and if any U.S. forces were to be used ashore, they were to be used only for a limited purpose such as the reduction of **Havana**, which it was believed would end the war. The Naval War College was not content with the plan so other options were considered.

KRAG-JÖRGENSEN RIFLE. Named after its Norwegian designers, it was adopted as the standard **U.S. Army** rifle in 1892 and used by all regular army forces in all theaters of the war. It was also used by the **Rough Riders** in the **Santiago, Cuba, campaign** and by a few **volunteer** regiments in the **Puerto Rican campaign**. A bolt-action, .30-caliber, magazine-fed rifle that used smokeless ammunition, it was later replaced by the Model 1903 **Springfield rifle.**

KUSAIE (UALAN). A Pacific island in the eastern Carolines only eight miles in diameter, it was included in the secret **German-Spanish Understanding** of 10 September 1898, which called for its cession conditioned upon the outcome of the **Treaty of Paris**. However, during the treaty negotiations, the United States included it in its 21 November 1898 ultimatum as a result of naval considerations impressed upon the U.S. **Peace Commission** by Comdr. Royal B. Bradford and Secretary of State **John Hay**'s order to the Peace Commission on 1 November to acquire Kusaie for **cable** purposes. The resulting U.S. offer of $1 million for the island on 30 November was rejected by Spain. Nothing came of a later Spanish offer to cede it to the United States in exchange for commercial concessions in the Antilles; subsequently, the United States sought to compensate for its failure to acquire Kusaie by laying claim to **Wake Island**.

—L—

LABRA Y CADRAMA, RAFAEL MARÍA DE (1841–1918). Spanish **Republican** leader. A Cuban-born journalist, lawyer, and writer, Labra served as a republican deputy and a senator in the **Cortes**, opposed the fusion of the Puerto Rican autonomists with Spain's **Liberal Party**, preferring that they ally with Spanish republicans rather than the Liberal Party, and championed **autonomy** for **Cuba** and **Puerto Rico**, writing in "El problema económico cubano" *La Justicia* (9 April 1897) that autonomy would guarantee continued Spanish control over Cuba. After supporting Spain in the war against the United States, he remained in Spain and wrote extensively. He contributed to the **"Literature of the Disaster,"** writing *El pesimismo* *de última hora* (1899), and in his book *La reforma política de Ultramar* (1900), Labra stated that American propaganda had dishonored Puerto Ricans when it stated that they all had acclaimed the U.S. invader. He later represented Spain at the International Tribunal at the Hague.

LAMBERTON, BENJAMIN PEFFER (1844–1912). Commander (USN), served as Com. **George W. Dewey**'s chief of staff. A U.S. Naval Academy graduate who, after lighthouse board assignments, was ordered to the **Asiatic Squadron** in the spring of 1898, Lamberton joined the squadron just before it sailed for **Manila** and was on the bridge of the *Olympia* next to Dewey during the **Battle of Manila Bay** on 1 May. The next day Lamberton went ashore and accepted the formal surrender of the **Cavite** arsenal. Promoted to captain on 17 May, he assumed command of the *Olympia* on 25 May and served as the naval representative on the commission that drew up the **Capitulation of Manila Agreement** of 14 August. Advanced seven numbers for his actions, his duty was cut short by eye trouble caused by his close proximity to the guns of the *Olympia* during the battle of Manila Bay. He was later promoted to rear admiral.

LANCASTER. (USN) An old, 3,250-ton, wooden steam vessel, commanded by Comdr. Thomas Perry. Assigned to the North Atlantic Station, it served as Com. **George C. Remey**'s flagship at **Key West, Florida**.

LANDING CRAFT, U.S. MILITARY. Despite the experience of the **marines** and **U.S. Navy** in occasional amphibious training operations before the war, the U.S. military was caught completely unprepared for the logistical demands of the **Fifth Corps** when it landed at **Daiquirí** and **Siboney, Cuba**, beginning on 22 June 1898. Because no real landing craft existed, barges, lifeboats, naval launches, steam lighters, tugs, and whaleboats were used to ferry munitions, provisions, and soldiers to shore. Upon the arrival of the expeditions of the **Eighth Corps** at **Manila, Philippines**, lifeboats, steam launches, and native craft "cascos" were used to land soldiers and munitions.

LARREA Y LISO, FRANCISCO [EFEELE] (1855–1913). Lieutenant colonel, on the general staff of the **Spanish Army** at **San Juan, Puerto Rico**. He commanded Spanish forces at the 12 August 1898 skirmish at the **Asomante Hills**. After the war, Larrea wrote, under the pseudonym Efeele, *El desastre nacional y los vicios de nuestras instituciones militares* (1901). In it he criticized Spain's war effort and stated that the Puerto Rican ruling group was cowardly and had run to support the United States merely for monetary profit in their businesses. He fought in North Africa and in 1911 was promoted to general of division.

LAS GUÁSIMAS, CUBA, BATTLE OF (24 JUNE 1898). A deserted village about three miles northwest of **Siboney, Cuba,** Las Guásimas was the scene of the first major land engagement of the **Santiago, Cuba, campaign.** Maj. Gen. **Joseph Wheeler,** who wanted to get his troops into combat as soon as possible, exceeded Maj. Gen. **William R. Shafter**'s directions and ordered Brig. Gen. **Samuel B. M. Young** to move his forces inland. Consisting of soldiers from the **First** and **Tenth U.S. Cavalry** regiments and the **Rough Riders,** Young's forces, numbering 1,000 men, fought an early morning two-hour battle against approximately 1,500 Spanish troops under the command of Brig. Gen. **Antero Rubín Homent,** which consisted of three companies of the Provisional Battalion of Puerto Rico No. 1, three companies of the **San Fernando Regiment** and two Plascenia guns. Even before the battle began, Rubín was ordered to fall back to **Santiago** to avoid being cut off by arriving U.S. forces.

Dividing his command, Wheeler sent the Tenth U.S. Cavalry and three Hotchkiss revolving cannons along the main road while the Rough Riders moved along a wooded and tangled trail about a mile west of the road. With Sgt. Hamilton Fish Jr., a scion of one of New York's wealthiest families, leading on point, the Rough Riders came under intense fire. Capt. **Allyn Capron Jr.** and Fish were killed. Correspondent **David Edward Marshall** was severely wounded, and Thomas Isbell, part-Cherokee Indian, was wounded seven times before being carried from the field. Correspondent **Richard H. Davis** quickly picked up a gun and fought alongside **Theodore Roosevelt** and the rest of the Rough Riders. James Robb Church, assistant surgeon of the Rough Riders, was later awarded the **Congressional Medal of Honor** for his heroism in treating and evacuating the wounded. At 9:00 a.m. a two-pronged charge by both the regulars and Rough Riders carried the day as Maj. Gen. Wheeler, who was ill, left his ambulance to lead a charge. By 10:00 a.m. the battle was over when reinforcements arrived. Whereas Rubín's forces sustained casualties of ten killed and 25 wounded, Wheeler's forces sustained casualties of 16 dead and 52 wounded.

Opinions of the battle varied. The initial U.S. newspaper accounts extolled the Rough Riders' role and depicted the battle as an ambush of U.S. troops; however, it was not an ambush because Wheeler knew where the Spanish forces were. Most U.S. commanders saw it as a victory that forced the Spanish to retreat and boosted morale for their troops, not knowing that Rubín, after reporting the U.S. forces had been repulsed, conducted a planned retreat. **Stephen Crane** wrote of it as a "gallant blunder." Already deteriorating relations between U.S. forces and Cuban insurgents got worse as Cuban insurgents, although providing intelligence and acting as guides, had failed to show up in force as promised. After the war, the **Dodge Commission** concluded that the battle had played an "unimportant role" in the campaign. Although Wheeler did not pursue the retreating Spanish forces, the results of the battle reinforced an already convinced Maj. Gen. Shafter to attack Santiago from the interior rather than attacking the heights at the harbor entrance.

LAS MARÍAS, PUERTO RICO, SKIRMISH AT (13 AUGUST 1898). The last combat of the war, the skirmish took place on 13 August 1898, one day after the **Armistice Protocol** had been signed, between the rear guard of the **Alfonso XIII Battalion** under the command of Lt. Col. Antonio Osés, who were retreating from **Mayagüez**, and U.S. forces under the command of Brig. Gen. **Theodore Schwan**. After a U.S. reconnaissance force consisting of six infantry companies, a platoon of cavalry, and a section of artillery cut off the retreating Spanish forces, they pressed forward and opened fire. In a drenching rain, the Spanish forces scattered among the hills, and a number drowned in the rising Prieto River. There were no American casualties; however, the Spanish sustained casualties of five killed, 14 wounded, and 56 were taken prisoner, including Lt. Col. Osés. The planned pursuit was called off the next day when word of the Armistice Protocol arrived.

LAWTON, HENRY WARE (1843–1899). Brigadier general (USV), commanded the Second Division in the **Fifth Corps**. A Civil War veteran, Lawton fought in various Indian campaigns, personally leading the column that captured Geronimo. During the war, Lawton, a highly competent and experienced commander, supervised the Fifth Corps's initial landing at **Daiquirí, Cuba**, on 22 June 1898 and moved the next day to occupy **Siboney**. On 1 July he commanded U.S. forces in the **Battle of El Caney** and in a conference of commanders on 2 July, opposed Maj. Gen. **William R. Shafter**'s suggestion of retreat. Promoted to major general (USV) on 8 July, he favored allowing Spanish soldiers to return home with their arms and signed both the **Capitulation of Santiago Agreement** of 16 July 1898 and the **Round Robin Letter** of 3 August 1898. Having served briefly as the military governor of **Santiago** and then of the entire province, Lawton was relieved of command in October 1898 because of "ill health" caused by heavy drinking. He later swore off liquor and commanded U.S. soldiers in the **Philippine Insurrection**, dying in combat against insurgents under the command of an officer named Geronimo.

LAZAGA Y GARAY, JOAQUÍN MARÍA (d. 1898). Spanish Captain, commanded the **armored cruiser** *Almirante Oquendo*. Present at the 23 April 1898 military conference that decided to send Adm. **Pascual Cervera's Squadron** to the West Indies, Lazaga argued that the squadron should first be strengthened and then sent to **Puerto Rico**. Furthermore, he went outside the military by arranging for **Francisco Silvela** to visit Prime Minister **Práxedes M. Sagasta** in an effort to postpone the decision. Although it is known he died in the **Naval Battle of Santiago** on 3 July 1898, reports vary as to how. Spanish survivors reported he drowned while trying to swim to the beach, whereas others reported he was incinerated in the pilot house or died of heart failure after the battle while trying to evacuate the wounded.

LEE, ARTHUR HAMILTON (1868–1947). British captain in the Royal Artillery, created as Viscount Lee of Fareham in 1922. As military attaché to the British Embassy in Washington, D.C., he served as a foreign observer with the **Fifth Corps**. Lee was present at the **Aserraderos Conference** of 20 June 1898 and the **Battle of El Caney** of 1 July. He later wrote about this battle in "The Regulars at El Caney," *Scribner's Magazine* (October 1898), vividly describing the gruesome sight of the Spanish dead and reporting that the Spanish prisoners expected to be shot by their American captors.

LEE, FITZHUGH (1835–1905). Major general (USV), commanded the **Seventh Corps**. The portly nephew of Robert E. Lee and former major general in the Confederate cavalry, Lee, who had been the Democratic governor of Virginia, was appointed U.S. consul to **Havana, Cuba**, in 1896. He detested the Spanish, openly supported the Cuban insurgent cause, and advocated U.S. intervention. Although he felt President **William McKinley**'s prewar policy was "cowardly, heartless, and idiotic," he was retained by McKinley as U.S. consul.

Lee rejected Spain's policy of **autonomy** as unworkable because of loyalist Spaniards and his belief that a Spanish military victory over the Cuban insurgents was impossible. Although he had previously requested that the *Maine* be sent to Havana during the **Autonomy Riots**, he advised the **McKinley administration** to wait after the riots subsided. Lee was surprised when the *Maine* arrived in Havana on 24 January 1898. He did not believe that the Spanish authorities at Havana had anything to do with the destruction of the *Maine*. When Spain suggested that he be recalled on 1 March 1898, the McKinley administration refused. Lee left Havana on the steamship *Fern* on 10 April, returned to Washington, D.C., on 12 April, and testified to **Congress** that he now believed Spain had sunk the *Maine*.

Appointed to command the Seventh Corps upon the outbreak of war, Lee selected the site for **Camp Cuba Libre, Jacksonville, Florida**, and ran a model **camp** even though his corps never saw action. After the war, Lee and the Seventh Corps went to Cuba to serve as an occupational force in January 1899. He became military governor of Havana Province. Subsequently Lee wrote *Cuba's Struggle against Spain with the Causes for American Intervention and a Full Account of the Spanish-American War, Including Final Peace Negotiations* (1899) to justify both the war and its result. He retired from the army in March 1901.

LEE RIFLE. Also known as the Winchester-Lee rifle, it was adopted by the **U.S. Navy** in the mid-1890s. A .236-caliber bolt-action rifle with a five-cartridge magazine, the rifle fired **smokeless powder** and was regarded as one of the best small arms in existence, especially after its use by the **First Marine Battalion** at **Guantánamo, Cuba**, during the Spanish-American War. With each man carrying 180 rounds, the rifle's particular advantages were its high muzzle velocity of 2,400 feet per second and its penetrating power.

LEO XIII, POPE (1810–1903). Gioacchino Vincenzo Pecci served as Pope from 1878 until his death. Fearing that a disastrous war might topple the Spanish monarchy, Leo, who was the godfather to **Alfonso XIII**, the son of Spain's Queen Regent **María Cristina**, offered to mediate the escalating crisis between the United States and Spain over the **Cuban Revolt** in late March and early April 1898; however, the United States rejected the offer. On 3 April he asked María Cristina to grant an armistice in **Cuba**, and Spain promptly announced it would suspend hostilities.

LEÓN Y CASTILLO, FERNANDO DE, MARQUÉS DEL MUNÍ (1842–1918). Spain's ambassador to **France** (1897–1910). A lawyer by training, León y Castillo had previously served as ambassador to France, colonial minister, and minister of the interior. His attempt to negotiate a joint resolution by several European powers during the crisis surrounding the destruction of the *Maine* on 15 February 1898 failed when **Great Britain** and **Germany** would not comply.

When the cabinet of **Práxedes M. Sagasta** was changed in mid-May, León y Castillo refused the post of foreign minister, arguing that because France might be willing to mediate the war at a proper time, he would be most helpful in France. On 9 July, he continued to hope for European assistance in resolving the war by proposing that

Spain seek diplomatic help, and upon receiving authorization, León y Castillo officially approached the French government on 18 July to see if it would act as an intermediary in proposing a negotiated settlement. Within days the French accepted. During the **Treaty of Paris** negotiations he worked through his old friend **Whitelaw Reid**, who was a member of the U.S. **Peace Commission**, to smooth out disagreements between the Spanish and U.S. Peace Commissions even though he was not an official delegate. León y Castillo later wrote about his diplomatic experiences in his memoirs *Mis tiempos* (1921).

LERROUX GARCÍA, ALEJANDRO (1864–1949). Spanish radical **Republican**. The son of an army veterinary surgeon, Lerroux directed *El País*, the mouthpiece of the Progressive Republican Party, and soon became a leading figure on the far left of Spanish republicanism. In 1897 he left *El País* and established his own paper, *El Progreso*. Virulently anticlerical, he advocated the establishment of a working-class base. Lerroux was imprisoned for supporting the **Cuban Revolt**, and after the overwhelming defeat at the **Naval Battle of Santiago, Cuba**, on 3 July 1898, he accused the government of Spain of "high treason." After the war he moved to Barcelona and built the strongest republican movement in Spain, which dominated Barcelona politics until World War I. He later wrote an autobiographical account *Mis memorias* (1963).

LEYDEN. (USN) Armed tug, commanded by Ensign Walter S. Crosley. Fitted with six- and three-pound guns, it was assigned to the **North Atlantic Squadron**. After participating in the U.S. naval attack on **Nipe Bay**, **Cuba**, on 21 July 1898, it served in Puerto Rican waters.

LIBERAL-CONSERVATIVE PARTY—SPAIN (*PARTIDO LIBERAL CONSERVADOR*). Established and led by **Antonio Cánovas del Castillo**, the party came to power in 1875 and alternated in power with the **Liberal Party** owing to a power-sharing agreement, the *turno pacífico*. The party opposed **autonomy** for the colonies and supported military pacification of the **Cuban** and **Philippine Revolts**. After the assassination of Cánovas in August 1897, the party was led by **Francisco Silvela** until his death and then by **Antonio Maura**.

LIBERAL-FUSIONIST PARTY—PUERTO RICO (*PARTIDO LIBERAL FUSIONISTA PUERTORRIQUEÑO*). Founded on 14 February 1897, in **San Juan** after the autonomist movement fractured over the issue of a pact with Spain's **Liberal Party**. Under the presidency of **Luis Muñoz Rivera**, the party affiliated with the Spanish

Liberal-Fusionist Party, and its newspaper *La Democracia* continued to espouse **autonomy**. In the 27 March 1898 general elections for a Puerto Rican legislature, the party won 26 seats. After the U.S. conquest, it was dissolved.

LIBERAL PARTY—SPAIN (*PARTIDO LIBERAL*). Also known as the Liberal-Fusionist Party, it grew out of a merger of parties in the 1880s. Led by **Práxedes M. Sagasta**, it first came to power in 1881 as part of the *turno pacífico*. On 24 June 1897, the party called for Cuban **autonomy**, and opposed to Cuban independence, it pledged political reforms as well as military force to end the **Cuban Revolt**. Spain's defeat in the Spanish-American War and the death of Sagasta in 1903 dealt the party a heavy blow, and although led by **Segismundo Moret**, it split into various factions.

LINARES Y POMBO, ARSENIO (1848–1914). Lieutenant general, chief of division of the Spanish division at **Santiago, Cuba**. Linares fought against Cuban insurgents, against the **Carlists**, and against Filipino insurgents before returning to **Cuba** as the commander of Spanish forces at Santiago, Cuba. Promoted to lieutenant general in May 1898, he organized the defenses of Santiago. Instead of concentrating all his forces at Santiago, Linares left garrisons, totaling almost 24,000 men, intact at Baracoa, **Guantánamo**, Holguín, **Manzanillo**, and Sagua de Tánamo. Establishing his headquarters at **Fort Canosa**, Linares opposed the leaving of Adm. **Pascual Cervera's Squadron** until **Escario's Column** had arrived. He was severely wounded during the battles for the **San Juan Heights** on 1 July 1898 and was replaced by Gen. **José Toral y Velázquez**. In response to Gov.-Gen. **Ramón Blanco**'s suggestion that his army break out of Santiago, Linares sent a telegram to Gov.-Gen. Blanco on 12 July advising him that surrender was inevitable and offering to take full responsibility for such an action. After the war Linares was criticized for not concentrating his forces at Santiago, defended the army against criticism in the **Cortes**, was appointed senator for life, and served as minister of war in the administration of **Francisco Silvela**.

LISCUM, EMERSON H. (d. 1900). Lieutenant colonel, commanded the **Twenty-Fourth U.S. Infantry** in the **Fifth Corps**. A Civil War veteran and career soldier famous for his poor treatment of **black American** soldiers, he fought in the **Santiago, Cuba, campaign** and was promoted to brigadier general (USV). During the **Battle of San Juan Hill** on 1 July 1898, Liscum briefly took command of the Third Brigade in Brig. Gen. **Jacob F. Kent**'s division after Lt. Col. W. S.

Worth was wounded. Liscum was wounded five minutes later. He was discharged from volunteer service on 31 December 1898.

LITERARY DIGEST. A weekly U.S. magazine that reprinted many of the best cartoons from domestic and foreign newspapers and magazines. It also collected humor and satire in weekly "Topics in Brief" and "More or Less Pungent," reprinted a compilation of views from various newspapers on various topics, and produced surveys of opinions, one of which pointed out that from 9 July 1898 on, a majority of the U.S. **press** favored expansion.

LITERATURE—SPAIN. Among the few writers who consistently questioned Spain's colonial policy were Ángel Ganivet García, whose *Idearium español* (1897) castigated Spain for its colonial politics, and **José Martínez y Ruiz "Azorin,"** whose "Gaceta de Madrid" *Madrid Cómico* (10 April 1898) satirized vociferous nationalists. However, most writers, and especially short-story writers who included the issues in their works, supported Spain. Even though dramatist Jacinto Benavente y Martínez satirized the Spanish aristocracy, most plays were patriotic, especially the zarzuelas, immensely popular satirical and humorous one- and three-act operettas such as *Cuadros disolventes* (1896), which referred to the "yankee pigs," and *Cádiz* by Javier de Buergos y Chueca, from which came the **"March of Cádiz,"** a patriotic song.

Upon the outbreak of the Spanish-American War, many poets such as Federico Balart in his poem "Canto a la guerra" *El Imparcial* (23 April 1898), extolled Spain's going to war, certain of eventual Spanish victory. After Spain's initial overwhelming defeats, many poets, however, became critical and disillusioned. For example, Vicente Medina y Tomás, a regionalist poet from Murcia, wrote the very popular "Cansera" *Blanco y Negro* (18 July 1898); moreover, Francisco "Zeda" Fernández de Villegas, Madrid's most prominent theater critic, pointed out on 9 July in *La Epoca* the frivolous and minimum Spanish reaction to the defeats.

After the war Rubén Darío, a Nicaraguan poet, returned to Spain in 1898 a national hero for proclaiming his faith in Spain in his article "The Triumph of Caliban" *La Epoca* (20 August 1898) and referring to the United States as the "monster" that had gobbled up **Cuba**. However, other poets were disillusioned by Spain's defeat. Antonio Machado y Ruiz, soon to become Spain's most popular poet, wrote the poem "A Young Spain" (1898), calling the era a "a time of lies, of infamy" and "an evil hour—pregnant with grim prophecy." Juan Maragall, a Catalan poet, reproached Spain for its warlike madness in his poem "Canto del Retorno" (1899). Such disillusionment and a long tradition of criticism gave rise to a group of writers that later became known as the **"Generation of 98,"** and a demand for renewal came from the **"Literature of the Disaster"** and the use of the **Quijote Motif** by novelists Benito Pérez Galdós and Juan Valera y Alcalá Galiano.

LITERATURE—UNITED STATES. Many famous and not-yet-famous writers were directly affected by the war. Sherwood Anderson enlisted in the Ohio Volunteer Infantry; Damon Runyon, a reporter, went with a Colorado regiment to the **Philippines**; Carl Sandburg enlisted in the **Sixth Illinois Infantry** and went to **Puerto Rico**; **Theodore Roosevelt** turned down an eager young cowboy from Idaho, Edgar Rice Burroughs, because the **Rough Riders** had too many **volunteers**; **Stephen Crane**, **Richard Harding Davis**, and **Frank Norris** participated in the **Santiago**, **Cuba**, and **Puerto Rican campaigns**.

Prior to, during, and after the war most writers confidently supported U.S. policy, weaving the themes of the nation's divinely inspired destiny and Anglo-Saxon supremacy into their works. The short story "A Brief History of Our Late War with Spain" appeared in *Cosmopolitan Magazine* (November 1897–February 1898) even before the war had been fought. Probably written by Frank R. Stockton, it was full of sanguinary battles as Europe unified against the United States; nevertheless, the United States, led by the businessmen who directed the war effort, won and established itself as the greatest power in the world. After the *Maine* explosion on 15 February 1898, Richard Hovey wrote the poem "The Word of the Lord from Havana" *New York World* (20 March 1898), championing U.S. intervention in **Cuba**, and Clinton Scollard wrote the poem "The Men of the *Maine*," whose sacrifice had created a bond of national unity.

The war provided dramatists, novelists, and poets with an abundance of heroes: the Rough Riders, Adm. **George W. Dewey**, Lt. **Richmond P. Hobson**, Com. **Winfield S. Schley**, and Maj. Gen. **Joseph Wheeler**. Themes such as revenge for the *Maine*, the righteousness of the U.S. cause in freeing Cuba, doggerel humor about bad army food and lost loves, the **North-South reunion**, and the "duty and destiny" of the United States appeared in dramas such as Frank E. Chase's *In the Trenches, a Drama of the Cuban War in Three Acts* (1898), and John A. Fraser's *Dewey, the hero of Manila* (1898) and *Santiago, or, For the red, white and blue: a war drama in four acts* (1898), and in novels and poems. Moreover, soldiers in various military units frequently had their works published in newspapers throughout the country.

There were few who took exception and opposed U.S. policy. William Dean Howells, the dean of American letters, who thought the war "an abominable business," condemned U.S. action in the Philippines as a war of conquest and joined the **Anti-Imperialist League**. Ambrose Bierce, an antiexpansionist, wrote short stories indirectly connected to the war in his *Fantastic Fables* (1899), criticizing false newspaper accounts and satirizing both forces as incompetent at **Santiago, Cuba**. Paul Laurence Dunbar, a **black American** poet, wrote "The Conquerors," extolling the heroism of black American soldiers during the war, yet turned strident critic when blacks did not gain rights for having fought. F. B. Coffin, a black pharmacist in Little Rock, Arkansas, wrote the poem "Santiago de Wilmington" *Indianapolis Freeman* (7 January 1899), a poem that expressed the overwhelming sentiment of blacks at the end of the war in pointing out that blacks had valiantly fought in the war while racial violence against blacks occurred at home in Wilmington, North Carolina.

In the postwar era, however, most writers supported the war effort and used its results to justify U.S. expansion. Of the 50 novels written about the war by 1950, the majority were stories for juveniles in the form of a series of novelettes sometimes known by their respective heroes. Among them were the *Young Glory* series written by A. Pottow and W. E. Mott, the *Yankee Doodle* series written by H. K. Shackleford, the *True Blue* series with its hero Clif Faraday written by Upton Sinclair, the *Starry Flag* with its hero Hal Maynard by Douglas Wells, and the *Old Glory* and *Bound to War* series written by Edward L. Stratemeyer. Also justifying U.S. expansion were **John Fox**, Richard Hovey's poem "Unmanifest Destiny," and the short stories by Stephen Crane, Richard Harding Davis, and humorists Frank R. Stockton and John K. Bangs.

Almost unknown to white Americans but enjoying a wide circulation among black Americans was Sutton E. Griggs's *Imperium in Imperio: A Study of the Negro Problem* (1899). Griggs, a Baptist minister in Nashville, Tennessee, wrote about a secret black organization that united all black Americans in an attempted revolt against the white racist government during the war to throw off racist oppression.

"LITERATURE OF THE DISASTER." After the Spanish-American War, Spanish writers, motivated by **regenerationism**, criticized Spain's decadence and called for Spanish renewal. Included among these writers were Damián Isern y Marco (*Del desastre nacional y sus causas* [1899]), **Rafael María de Labra**, Ricardo Macías Picavea (*El problema nacional: hechos, causas, remedios* [1899]), J. Rodríguez Martínez (*Los desastres y la regeneración de España* [1899]), and **Luis Morote**.

LODGE, GEORGE CABOT (1873–1909). Ensign (USN), on the *Dixie*. The son of **Henry Cabot Lodge**, he had served as his father's secretary, and his first volume of poetry was published in the spring of 1898. While serving under the command of his uncle Capt. **Charles H. Davis** on the *Dixie*, Lodge commanded a gun crew, and after landing on 27 July at **Ponce, Puerto Rico**, he returned the following day and raised the American flag over the city. After the war, Lodge served as a secretary of a United States Senate committee. His sonnets were published, and he published "The Song of the Wave" (1898), *Cain, A Drama* (1904), and "Herakles" (1908). After his death, his collected poems and dramas were issued in 1911.

LODGE, HENRY CABOT (1850–1924). Republican senator from Massachusetts (1893–1925) and member of the Senate Foreign Relations Committee. An articulate spokesman and author, Lodge consistently advocated in articles such as "Our Blundering Foreign Policy" *The Forum* (March 1895) and "Our Duty to Cuba" *The Forum* (May 1896) a blueprint for American prosperity that included a strong fleet, the acquisition of strategically located territories such as **Hawaii**, and an Isthmian canal to link the east and west coasts. He deprecated Spain as medieval and tyrannical, and demanded U.S. action in **Cuba** to bring an end to hostilities and to give Cuba its independence.

During the war Lodge turned his house at Nahant, Massachusetts, over to the **U.S. Army** as a signal station, and one of his sons, **George C. Lodge**, served on the *Dixie*. After the war Lodge led the fight to ratify the **Treaty of Paris** and wrote *The War with Spain* (1899), which justified the expansionist course of the **McKinley administration**.

LONG, JOHN DAVIS (1838–1915). Secretary of the navy (March 1897–April 1902). A former Massachusetts Republican governor and congressman and member of the Massachusetts Peace Society, Long, who readily admitted his ignorance of naval affairs, was appointed secretary of the navy because he was an able administrator. He called the **De Lôme Letter** "an unfortunate occurrence" because **Enrique Dupuy de Lôme** was "a man of a good deal of ability who had rendered excellent service," and believed the *Maine* explosion was an accident. Shortly before the war, Long organized the **Naval War Board** to advise him on naval matters, and he defended the **McKinley administration**'s efforts at diplomatically resolving the Cuban situation.

However, upon the outbreak of war, Long favored its vigorous prosecution, participated in the almost daily strategy conferences with President **William McKinley** at the White House, and cabled the first definite instructions on the **Philippines** to Adm. **George W. Dewey** on 26 May 1898, that with respect to **Emilio Aguinaldo**'s nationalist Filipino movement, it was desirable "not to have political alliances with the insurgents." Long was furious with Com. **Winfield S. Schley** for his dilatory tactics in pursuing Adm. **Pascual Cervera's Squadron** and authorized a **disinformation** campaign. When Spain's initial offer for negotiations arrived at the end of July, he favored only retaining a naval station at **Manila, Philippines**.

After the war Long wrote *The New American Navy* (1903), in which he credited Adm. **William T. Sampson** for the victory at the **Naval Battle of Santiago** on 3 July 1898, criticized Com. Winfield S. Schley for his delay tactics in pursuing Adm. Pascual Cervera's Squadron, and castigated journalists for their distortions of the naval aspects of the war.

LÓPEZ DE CASTILLO'S LETTER (21 AUGUST 1898). Pedro López de Castillo, a Spanish infantry soldier at **Santiago, Cuba**, wrote a letter to the **U.S. Army** before going home. In the letter López expressed his best wishes to the U.S. troops, congratulating them for having fought valiantly. However, he excoriated the Cuban insurgents, calling them a people "without a religion, without morals, without conscience, and of doubtful origin." While expressing his gratitude for the United States's healing the sick and treating **prisoners of war** well, López warned that the Cubans, who would find it "a burden to comply with the laws which govern civilized humanity," were now an American problem. Maj. Gen. **William R. Shafter** cabled the letter to Washington, D.C., on 22 August 1898, and, after reading it, President **William McKinley** authorized its publication.

LUDINGTON, MARSHALL INDEPENDENCE (1839–1919). Brigadier general and quartermaster general of the **U.S. Army**. A Civil War veteran, Ludington assumed command over the **Quartermaster Corps** in February 1898. Worried about the likelihood of war, he suggested immediate preparation. Despite his planning, the changing circumstances of war repeatedly changed his plans and made new demands. After a 3 April 1898 meeting with the **War Department**, Ludington contracted out for the needed supplies, but he rejected several bids for experimental canvas uniforms, insisting that they should be made from khaki. He tried in vain to secure the lightweight cotton cloth called khaki; however, when it became obvious that the demand for clothing and tentage would outstrip capacity, he improvised with below-standard army cloth. Consequently, Ludington and his corps were heavily criticized by the U.S. **press** and by politicians, despite the fact that other options were few or nonexistent. Promoted to major general in 1903, he retired soon after.

LUDLOW, WILLIAM (1843–1901). Brigadier general (USV), chief engineer on the staff of Maj. Gen. **William R. Shafter**. A West Point graduate and Civil War veteran, Ludlow, a career engineer, served on the frontier, surveyed the Yellowstone and the Black Hills regions, and served as the military attaché at the U.S. Embassy in London, England. Favoring a direct attack on **Havana, Cuba**, by landing the army at Mariel, Ludlow opposed the plan to attack **Santiago, Cuba**, as wasting forces on a secondary objective. Promoted to brigadier general (USV) in May 1898, he commanded the First Brigade of the Second Division of the **Fifth Corps** during the **Santiago, Cuba, campaign**. He attended the **Aserraderos Conference** on 20 June, commanded his brigade during the **Battle of El Caney** on 1 July, and signed the **Round Robin Letter** of 3 August. Appointed major general (USV) in September, Ludlow commanded the Second Division of the **First Corps** and in December became the military governor of the city and department of Havana, Cuba. In 1901 he went to the **Philippines** but soon returned because of illness and died shortly thereafter.

LUNA DE ST. PEDRO, ANTONIO NARCISO (1868–1899). Commander in chief of the Army of the Philippine Republic. Initially an advocate of reforms, Luna had obtained a Doctor of Pharmacy degree in Madrid, Spain, studied chemical engineering in Belgium, and worked in Paris, France, as an assistant in a histology and bacteriology laboratory. Upon returning to **Manila** in 1894, Luna was appointed chemist of the Municipal Laboratory. After being implicated in the **Philippine Revolt**, he was deported to Spain. While imprisoned in Madrid, Luna studied military tactics. After returning to the **Philippines**, he was appointed brigadier general, and repeatedly urged **Emilio Aguinaldo** not to trust U.S. military and political maneuvers. After the **capitulation** of Manila to American forces on 13 August 1898, Luna served as a representative in the Philippine Republic and published *La Independencia*, the principal insurgent newspaper. Upon the signing of the **Treaty of Paris** on 10 December 1898, Luna urged Aguinaldo to attack U.S. forces. On 20 February 1899, after the outbreak of the **Philippine Insurrection**, Luna was appointed to the rank of commander in chief of the Army of the Republic. Because of a power struggle within the insurgent ranks, he was murdered on Aguinaldo's orders on 5 June 1899.

—M—

MABINI, APOLINARIO (1864–1903). Intellectual leader of the Filipino insurgent movement and **Emilio Aguinaldo**'s private counsellor. Crippled by poliomyelitis, Mabini, a lawyer, had been imprisoned by Spanish authorities for political activities. Pardoned in July 1897, he immediately rejoined the insurgent movement. Immediately after the outbreak of the Spanish-American War, Mabini wrote an open letter to Filipino revolutionaries predicting Spain's defeat; however, he cautioned them about American intentions, pointing out that the United States, like Spain, coveted the **Philippines**. In July he wrote *The True Decalogue*, a political tract in the form of ten commandments, and later drafted a constitutional program, which, while granting Emilio Aguinaldo full powers during the war, envisioned the establishment of a national legislature, open elections in which women could vote and hold office, and freedom of the press, religion, and speech. Mabini believed the outbreak of the **Philippine Insurrection** on 4 February 1899 was a coup prepared by the **McKinley administration** to aid in the passage of the **Treaty of Paris**. Having served as prime minister in the Philippine Republic, Mabini was captured by U.S. forces, deported to **Guam**, and freed in February 1903, after signing an oath of allegiance to the United States. He returned to **Manila, Philippines**, and died on 13 May 1903.

MacARTHUR, ARTHUR (1845–1912). Brigadier general (USV). A decorated Civil War veteran with 20 years of frontier duty, MacArthur, a lieutenant colonel, was promoted to brigadier general (USV) in May 1898 and commanded the third expeditionary force of the **Eighth Corps**, which arrived in the **Philippines** at the end of July. During the **Battle of Manila** on 13 August, MacArthur commanded the **First Brigade**, and on 15 August he was appointed military commandant and provost marshal of **Manila**. Cited for gallantry, he was promoted to major general (USV), commanded U.S. forces during the **Philippine Insurrection**, and served as military governor of the islands from 1900 to 1901. The father of Douglas MacArthur, he retired in 1909 with the rank of lieutenant general.

MACHIAS. (USN) **Gunboat**, commanded by Comdr. John F. Merry until 27 June 1898, and then by Comdr. W. W. Mead. A single-funneled, two-masted ship, it was part of the **North Atlantic Squadron** and served in Cuban waters throughout the war. During early May while off the Cuban coast, it almost rammed the *New York World*'s **press boat** *Three Friends* and on 11 May was involved in a naval engagement at **Cárdenas, Cuba**. It was sold to Mexico on 29 October 1920, renamed, and disposed of in 1935.

La. 1891, com. 1893, dis. 1,177; hp. 1,900, sp. 15.5
Armor: d. 5/16″
Armament: 8–4″, 4–6pdr, 2–1pdr.
Cc. 193; comp. 154

MACÍAS Y CASADO, MANUEL (1845–?). Lieutenant general, governor-general, and captain general of **Puerto Rico**. A decorated veteran of previous campaigns in the Caribbean and northern Africa, Macías arrived in Puerto Rico on 3 February 1898 with the mission to implement an **autonomous government**. Therefore, Macías delegated his military functions to Col. Juan Camó, the chief of the general staff. Upon the outbreak of war with the United States, he called for resistance, requested reinforcements, suspended constitutional guarantees on 21 April, and declared martial law on 22 April. During the war he ordered a **disinformation** campaign meant to keep public morale high in spite of early Spanish defeats. However, he **cable**d Spain on 23 May that the majority of the population was indifferent, some towns sympathized with the United States, most *voluntarios* were vacillating, and because the people's spirit had fallen, they would not resist the U.S. invaders. When **Luis Muñoz Rivera** requested that the people be armed to fight the United States, Macías refused because he doubted their loyalty. Because he expected the main U.S. invasion force to land on the north coast, he kept most of his forces there and believed the U.S. landing at **Guánica** on 25 July was merely a feint. After the war Macías assisted American authorities in suppressing *partidas*, and on 16 October 1898, as he left for Spain on the steamship *Covadonga*, both Spanish and U.S. guns fired farewell salutes.

MAHAN, ALFRED THAYER (1840–1914). Captain (USN), member of the **Naval War Board**. A graduate of the U.S. Naval Academy and former president of the **Naval War College**, Mahan, the philosopher of sea power, was famous for his book *The Influence of Sea Power upon History, 1668–1783* (1890), which was admired by the British, German, Japanese, and American navies. He argued that sea power had been and would continue to be the prime factor in making and breaking nations and empires. In his article "The United States Looking Outward" *Atlantic Monthly* (December 1890), he maintained that sea power was essential for national greatness and that the United States "must now begin to look outward." In his book *The Interest of America in Sea Power, Present and Future* (1897), he wrote that sea power was essential for national greatness; therefore, the nation should build a powerful navy, expand its trade, and obtain naval bases in strategic areas, not large colonies, to be used as coaling stations.

After he retired from the navy in 1896, Mahan believed the annexation of **Hawaii** was necessary for national defense. However, he did not support intervention in **Cuba** and did not blame Spain for the *Maine* explosion. Because he did not expect a war against Spain, Mahan left the United States with his family for a vacation in **Italy**. In Rome when war was declared, he was recalled and served on the Naval War Board. Asked by reporters how long the war would last, he replied about three months. While on the Naval War Board, his suggestions were incorporated into the plan for blockading Cuba. He advocated the seizure of **Puerto Rico** before Cuba to control the Caribbean, believed initially that the United States should only take a coaling station in the **Philippines**, and criticized dividing the fleet and using it against shore installations. After the war he wrote *Lessons of the War with Spain and Other Articles* (1899). According to Mahan, the aim of the war had been "to enforce the departure" of Spain from Cuba. He was surprised that trouble in Cuba had led onward to Asia and warned "We cannot expect ever again to have an enemy so entirely inapt as Spain showed herself to be." Subsequently, he supported Secretary of State **John Hay**'s Open Door Policy in China and was promoted to rear admiral in 1906.

MAINE. (USN) Second-class **battleship**, commanded by Capt. **Charles D. Sigsbee**. Built at a contract price of $2,500,000, it was originally designated as an **armored cruiser**; however, upon commissioning, it was designated a battleship and was one of the first modern steel battleships in the **U.S. Navy**. Because of the possibility of disturbances at **Havana, Cuba**, endangering U.S. citizens, the *Maine* arrived at **Key West, Florida**, on 15 December 1897. It was ordered to Havana on 24 January 1898 under the pretext of a friendly visit; however, it arrived at Havana at 11:00 a.m. on 25 January, unexpected by Consul **Fitzhugh Lee** and the Spanish government. There were formal visits to and from the *Maine*. Spanish officials sent a case of sherry to the ship's officers, and U.S. officers in civilian clothing attended baseball games and a bullfight. Although naval officials were considering withdrawing the *Maine* to New Orleans for Mardi Gras, Capt. Sigsbee cautioned against leaving, arguing that leaving might stir things up. The officials agreed, and the *Maine* stayed.

At 9:40 p.m. on 15 February, the *Maine* exploded, killing 266 officers and men. The next day the Spanish government expressed its sympathy as the entire Spanish delegation in Washington, D.C., visited President **William McKinley**, and on 17 February, a state funeral was held in Havana. The *Maine* lay at the bottom of Havana harbor for many years. Finally in 1911, **Congress** appropriated the money to remove it and recover the bodies still believed to be trapped in its hull. The **U.S. Army Engineers** recovered the remains of 64 men, who were then buried in Arlington Cemetery. After the hulk was salvaged, its remains were towed out to sea and sunk in the Straits of Florida on 16 March 1912.

La. 1889, com. 1895, dis. 6,682, hp. 9,000, sp. 17
Armor: s. 12″, d. 2″, t. 8″, b. 12″, ct. 10″
Armament: 4–10″, 6–6″, 7–6pdr., 8–1pdr., 4 G. mgs., 4–14″ tt. (aw.)
Cc. 896; comp. 354

MAINE **INVESTIGATIONS.** Although President **William McKinley** and Secretary of the Navy **John D. Long** initially believed the *Maine* explosion on 15 February 1898 was accidental, the American public, **Congress**, and **Theodore Roosevelt** quickly blamed Spain. Overnight the slogan **"Remember the *Maine*, to Hell with Spain!"** caught hold in spite of the fact that before the *Maine* explosion the **U.S. Navy** had experienced more than 20 ship fires associated with spontaneous combustion of coal during the 1890s, and in two instances these fires nearly caused the powder magazines to explode.

On 16 February, Secretary Long ordered a court of inquiry into the disaster, and the U.S. government rejected Spain's offer of a joint investigation. Consequently, two investigations—one by the United States and one by Spain—were conducted.

The American investigation was conducted by a court of inquiry composed of its president Capt. **William T. Sampson**, Capt. **French E. Chadwick**, Lt. Comdr. **Adolph Marix**, and Lt. Comdr. William P. Potter, the executive officer of the *New York*. It opened its investigation on the lighthouse tender *Mangrove* in **Havana** harbor on 21 February, and the first witness was Capt. **Charles D. Sigsbee** of the *Maine*. Because the meetings were conducted in secrecy, witnesses pointed out the precautions that had been taken prior to the explosion, and no Spaniards were called to testify. On 25–27 February, Ens. William Van Nest Powelson, who had directed the diving operations investigating the site, testified that he believed a submerged mine had sunk the *Maine*. On 1 March, the court moved to **Key West, Florida**, to interrogate the surviving crew members. By 17 March the investigation was completed, and the full sealed report was sent to McKinley on 22 March. It arrived in Washington on 24 March and was delivered to McKinley the next day. The report, which did not fix responsibility on any person or persons, presented a unanimous verdict that there had been two explosions. According to the report, the first explosion had been an external one caused by a submarine mine, which then set off a second, internal, explosion. After the report was delivered to

Congress on 28 March, numerous resolutions and speeches called for Cuban independence, driving Spain out of **Cuba**, and a U.S. **declaration of war**.

Spain's investigation began almost immediately after the explosion. Adm. Vicente Manterola, who commanded the Havana naval station, appointed a board of inquiry composed of Capt. Pedro del Peral y Caballero, acting as judge, and Lt. Francisco Javier de Salas y Gonzalez, as secretary. Although the U.S. officials refused to let Spanish divers examine the wreck, Spanish officials, after rowing around the wreck, composed an interim report on 20 February that found all evidence pointing to an internal explosion. On 22 March, its official report found that an explosion in the forward magazine had caused the ship's destruction. After Spain officially released its findings on 27 March, Spain offered to submit the issue to arbitration. The offer was rejected by the U.S. government.

Later, during the **Treaty of Paris** negotiations, Spain once again requested an international commission to investigate the *Maine*; however, the U.S. **Peace Commission** rejected the request, stating that the case was closed. In 1911 the Vreeland Board conducted a 12-day slipshod investigation before the *Maine* was towed out to sea and sunk. This investigation supported the notion of external causation. However, in 1976, Rear Adm. Hyman G. Rickover's book *How the Battleship Maine Was Destroyed*, using a modern engineering analysis, not only criticized the initial investigations by U.S. officials but concluded there had been no external explosion and that the explosion had been precipitated by an internal explosion in the six-inch reserve magazine, which caused a partial detonation of other forward magazines.

MAINE **NEWSPAPER COVERAGE.** The trip of the *Maine* to **Havana**, **Cuba**, received widespread publicity and was overwhelmingly approved of in the U.S. **press**; moreover, most accepted the government's reason for sending the *Maine* as a voyage of a friendly nature. On 26 January the *Washington Post* opined that instead of provoking hostilities, the trip would "go far toward preventing the very occurrence which might precipitate it."

After the explosion of the *Maine* on 15 February 1898, Spanish **censorship** held up news dispatches. The only dispatches which made it out that night were Capt. **Charles D. Sigsbee's Cable**, a 100-word **Associated Press** dispatch, and **Harry Sylvester Scovel**'s dispatch paying tribute to the efforts of Spanish rescuers, which went out on a stolen cable blank containing the censor's stamp of approval.

Subsequently, the Spanish press was generally horrified by the disaster, expressed its general sympathy, and rejected the idea of any

Spanish involvement. *El País*, a Madrid-based republican socialist newspaper, opined that accusations of Spain's culpability were "infamies." *El Imparcial* was infuriated that Spain was held responsible for the disaster, and *El Correo Militar*, a Madrid-based military newspaper, stated on 24 March 1898 that the *Maine* had been sunk by the "ineptness and laxity of its crew."

In the United States the reaction was immediate. Many journals urged caution, including the *New York Times, New York Herald*, *Wall Street Journal, Washington Post, Philadelphia Public Ledger, Minneapolis Journal, Milwaukee Sentinel, Baltimore Sun*, and *Chicago Times-Herald*. The *Army-Navy Journal* printed a reasoned comment on the tendency toward "self-ignition" in modern vessels because of electrical systems, faulty boilers, or the spontaneous combustion of stores, and the *Washington Evening Star* found, in a 17 February survey of naval officers, that most of these officers leaned toward the accident theory. However, more newspapers quickly assumed Spanish complicity.

Almost every major newspaper in the West held Spain directly responsible. The *Boston Daily Globe*, the *Atlanta Constitution*, and the *Birmingham Age-Herald* blamed Spain, and although the *St. Louis Post-Dispatch* urged caution on 16 February, the next day it reported the *Maine* had been torpedoed. By 17 February, both the *New York Journal* and the *New York World* were blaming Spain for the *Maine* disaster, with vivid drawings of the exploding ship, descriptions of supposed plots, and abundant misquotations. The *Journal* even offered a $50,000 reward for detection of the perpetrator. On 24 February, the *Philadelphia Inquirer* ran a huge banner headline that read "INQUIRY COURT ON *MAINE* DISASTER WILL SAY A TORPEDO DID THE WORK," and on 25 February another headline read "INDISPUTABLE EVIDENCE FOUND OF SPANISH MINE UNDER *MAINE*." Such coverage brought forth the first nationwide outburst of criticism of the **"yellow press."**

By the end of February the U.S. press was still divided over the cause of the disaster and what action the government should pursue; however, any reservations were quickly dispelled by the release of the *Maine* report at the end of March. The report, which had been leaked to the press, was published in over 100 newspapers even before it had been formally submitted to **Congress**. Although many southern newspapers refused to accept the report's findings, eastern and western papers generally supported the findings and an overwhelming majority of western papers held Spain responsible for the disaster. The *Los Angeles Times*, which had previously urged caution, fell into line on 29 March, opining "we have tangible, direct, and definite cause for war," and the *St. Louis Post-Dispatch* headlined on

28 March "Spain's Guilt is Not Fixed by Verdict . . . But Only One Conclusion Can Be Drawn from it: That Spaniards Blew Up the Maine." On 30 March, the *Washington Post*, now wanting a more aggressive policy, exclaimed that "in the minds of American people this is not regarded as a 'mere incident' to be subordinated to any other."

MALOLOS, PHILIPPINES. A town 25 miles north of **Manila**, it was the capital of Bulacan Province, Luzon. After the proclamation of a revolutionary government on 23 June 1898, it served as the capital of **Emilio Aguinaldo**'s government, which came to be known as the Malolos Republic. In September 1898, it served as the meeting place of the **Malolos Congress** and later as the capital of the Philippine Republic. It was taken by U.S. forces on 31 March 1899 and garrisoned by U.S. forces throughout the **Philippine Insurrection**.

MALOLOS CONGRESS. Convened at **Malolos, Philippines**, on 15 September 1898, under the presidency of **Pedro A. Paterno**, it consisted of 85 congressmen, partly elected and partly appointed. Later the number of members rose to 110. The congress framed the **Malolos Constitution**.

MALOLOS CONSTITUTION. Written by Felipe Calderon, it was framed in **Malolos, Philippines**, by the **Malolos Congress** from September to November 1898 and was adopted by the congress on 29 November 1898. Signed by **Emilio Aguinaldo** on 23 December 1898, it was promulgated on 21 January 1899. Modeled on the American, French, Belgian and Latin American constitutions, it established a unicameral legislature and a council of state composed of a president and his secretaries. However, contrary to the wishes of **Apolinario Mabini**, the president was subordinated to the national legislature. The constitution included a lengthy enumeration of the rights and liberties of individuals.

MANGROVE. (USN) Lighthouse tender, commanded by Lt. Comdr. W. H. Everett until 7 June 1898 and then by Lt. Comdr. D. D. V. Stuart. Pressed into service, it arrived at **Havana, Cuba**, on 21 February 1898 and served as the meeting place for the U.S. board that investigated the *Maine* explosion. In March the *Mangrove* moved to **Key West, Florida**, when the court moved there to interview *Maine* survivors. During the war, it was attached to the North Atlantic Station. With only one revolver among its entire crew, on 25 April it captured the faster and more heavily armed Spanish liner *Panamá*. After blockading **Matanzas, Cuba**, the *Mangrove* attacked the Spanish gunboat *Hernán Cortes* on 14 August at Caibarien. A Spanish launch came out under a white flag to inform its crew that the **Armistice Protocol** had been signed two days before.

MANILA. (SPN) Transport. Built in England, it was purchased by Spain and sent to the **Philippines**, where it transported troops and materiel during the **Philippine Revolt**. Armed with three small guns, it was stationed at **Bacoor Bay** during the **Battle of Manila Bay** on 1 May 1898. On 4 May it was taken over as a **prize of war** by the **U.S. Navy** and used to transport U.S. forces.

MANILA, PHILIPPINES. A city of 154,000, with over 300,000 in the greater Manila area, Manila served as the capital and was the residence of Gov.-Gen. **Basilio Augustín y Dávila**. Because Spanish forces were scattered throughout the islands, only 13,000 Spanish soldiers were in the Manila area. Its artillery defenses were wholly inadequate. Of the 100 guns on the city's shore defenses only four were modern breech-loaders, and of the 226 guns of all types, only 12 were modern breech-loaders and 164 were muzzle-loaders. Moreover, its land defenses, which consisted of a line of 15 blockhouses connected by a more or less continuous line of entrenchments around the outskirts of the city, were vulnerable. It was also the home base of Adm. **Patricio Montojo's Squadron**.

After the U.S. victory at the **Battle of Manila Bay** on 1 May 1898, the city was blockaded by Adm. **George W. Dewey's Asiatic Squadron** and later in May came under siege on land by **Emilio Aguinaldo**'s 12,000-man insurgent forces, who were soon joined by the U.S. **Eighth Corps**. By early August, the city's water supply was cut off, food was running out, refugees were massed in the city, and there was no hope of reinforcements. Therefore, newly appointed Gov.-Gen. **Fermín Jáudenes y Álvarez**, using Belgian Consul **Edouard C. Andre** as an intermediary, negotiated a sham battle to save Spanish honor with Maj. Gen. **Wesley Merritt** and Adm. **George W. Dewey**. On 13 August, the prearranged **Battle of Manila** took place according to plan. Later in the day Flag. Lt. **Thomas M. Brumby** and Lt. Col. Charles Whittier landed, and in consultation with Gov.-Gen. Jáudenes and Adm. **Patricio Montojo**, drew up preliminary articles of **capitulation**. At 5:43 p.m. the American flag was raised over Manila, the U.S. squadron fired a salute, and the **Second Oregon Infantry** took up duty as a provost guard.

The next day the 13,000 Spanish troops were officially surrendered, and a victory parade was held; however, no Filipino insurgents were allowed to enter the city. Brig. Gen. **Arthur MacArthur** was appointed military commandant and provost marshal general of Manila.

Upon the arrival of news of the **Armistice Protocol** having been signed on 12 August, Gov. Gen. Jáudenes protested the **Capitulation of Manila Agreement** but to no avail. The total combat casualties sustained by American forces during the investment and capture of the city were 20 dead and 106 wounded.

MANILA, PHILIPPINES, BATTLE OF (13 AUGUST 1898). Prior to the battle, negotiations were conducted on two fronts. First, because Filipino insurgents had the city surrounded, a deal was made allowing forces of the U.S. **Eighth Corps** to occupy certain trenches in order to directly attack the city. Second, Adm. **George W. Dewey** and Maj. Gen. **Wesley Merritt**, through the assistance of Belgian Consul **Edouard C. André**, concluded a **capitulation** agreement with Gov.-Gen. **Fermín Jáudenes y Álvarez** whereby, in order to save the city from bombardment, keep the Filipino insurgents out, and maintain Spanish military honor, Dewey would conduct a token bombardment of one of the unoccupied forts, and U.S. forces would then enter the city. However, the agreement was never put in writing and U.S. military commanders directing the attack had no knowledge of its terms.

On 13 August, the battle opened when Adm. Dewey's ships, deployed off the city, slowly bombarded **Fort San Antonio Abad** for an hour, beginning at 9:35 a.m. At 10:25 a.m. the **Second Brigade**, consisting of 3,800 men under the command of Brig. Gen. **Francis Greene**, attacked from the south. At 11:00 a.m. the **First Brigade**, consisting of 5,000 men under the command of Brig. Gen. **Arthur MacArthur**, attacked from the southeast, and Adm. Dewey, according to plan, hoisted **D.W.H.B.**, the international signal asking surrender, and a white flag was raised by Spanish officials.

Flag. Lt. **Thomas M. Brumby** and Lt. Col. Charles Whittier landed, and in consultation with Gov.-Gen. Jáudenes and Adm. **Patricio Montojo**, drew up preliminary articles of capitulation. At 5:43 p.m. the American flag was raised over Manila. Before dark, U.S. forces had occupied the city. Total U.S. combat casualties during the brief battle were six dead and 43 wounded, whereas Spanish forces sustained 49 dead.

MANILA BAY, PHILIPPINES. The entrance to the 770-square-mile bay consisted of two channels—the Boca Chica and the Boca Grande—divided by the island of Corregidor, which had three eight-inch muzzle-loading rifles. The 17 guns at the bay's entrance were manned by 293 men under the command of Col. Maximiano Garcés de las Fayos. To the north of Corregidor, the Boca Chica, which was about two miles in width, was defended by three seven-inch muzzle-loading rifles at Punta Gorda, and two 6.3-inch breech-loading rifles at Punta Lassisi. To the south of Corregidor, the Boca Grande, the three-mile-wide main passage to the bay, was defended by three 5.9-inch breech-loading rifles on Caballo Island, three 4.7-inch breech-loading rifles on El Fraile Rock, and three 6.3-inch muzzle-loading rifles at Punta Restinga. Moreover, **mines**, improvised from **Whitehead torpedoes**, were planted off Caballo Island.

Adm. **Patricio Montojo** rejected fighting at the bay's entrance because the water was too deep for mines to be effective and the land batteries in the area could only briefly detain the U.S. squadron. After Montojo's disastrous defeat at the **Battle of Manila Bay** on 1 May 1898, the *Baltimore* and the *Raleigh* compelled the batteries at the entrance to the bay to surrender on 3 May. While Adm. **George W. Dewey** conducted a naval **blockade** of the bay and city of **Manila**, warships from other countries arrived. By the end of June these ships included the Japanese **cruiser** *Itsukushima*; the French cruiser *Bruix*; the British cruisers *Immortalité* and *Iphigenia*, and **gunboat** *Linnet*; and, under the command of Vice Adm. **Otto von Diederichs**, the German **battleship** *Kaiser*, the cruisers *Cormoran*, *Irene*, *Kaiserin Augusta*, and *Prinzess Wilhelm*, and the transport *Darmstadt*. The German squadron, which was more powerful than Dewey's, moved about the bay at will, interfered with Filipino insurgent operations against the Spanish, landed men at former Spanish positions, and its officers met with Spanish officials. Moreover, Dewey repeatedly accused them of violating his blockade and on 10 July threatened war against **Germany**. After the **capitulation** of Manila on 14 August, these ships departed.

MANILA BAY, PHILIPPINES, BATTLE OF (1 MAY 1898). It was no secret that Com. **George W. Dewey's Asiatic Squadron** would attack Adm. **Patricio Montojo's Squadron** upon the outbreak of war between the United States and Spain. The Spanish government was aware of U.S. plans in early March 1898. On 2 March, the German consul in Hong Kong informed his government that he had been informed by the U.S. consul of the plan; accordingly, Kaiser **Wilhelm II** passed the information on to the Spanish government. On 6 March the *New York Sun* informed its readers of the plan, and on April 28, the *New York World* printed that Dewey's squadron was headed to **Manila, Philippines**.

After Dewey's squadron left **Mirs Bay, China**, on 27 April, Montojo, whose squadron returned to Manila from **Subic Bay** on 29 April, anchored his squadron in eight meters of water at Cañacao Bay behind the naval base at **Cavite**, south of the city of Manila, in order to reduce his casualties in the upcoming fight, which he expected to lose. The squadron consisted of the flagship *Reina María Cristina*, *Castilla*, *Don Antonio de Ulloa*, *Don Juan de Austria*, *Isla de Luzón*, *Isla de Cuba*, and *Marqués del Duero*. Informed at 7:00 p.m. on 30 April that Dewey had reconnoitered Subic Bay and left for Manila, Montojo and his officers went to Manila for a night of festivities. Unconcerned about **mines**, owing to the depth of the channel and the likelihood that they had deteriorated in the tropical waters, Dewey led his squadron into the bay around midnight. After a battery at El Fraile briefly fired on the squadron, Dewey's squadron, having sustained no damage, steamed on toward Manila. After a report arrived at 2:00 a.m. confirming that Dewey had entered the bay, Montojo ordered his squadron to prepare for battle.

Dewey's squadron, which was better protected, armored, and armed than Montojo's, approached Cavite and was fired on by Montojo's Squadron at 5:15 a.m. Dewey then closed his column into a single file with a 200-yard interval between ships. At 5:41 a.m., as the *Olympia*, *Baltimore*, *Raleigh*, *Petrel*, *Concord*, and *Boston* closed within 5,000 yards of Montojo's Squadron, Dewey gave the order to Capt. **Charles Gridley** of the *Olympia* to open fire, stating "You may fire when ready, Gridley." Passing from east to west, Dewey's squadron made five runs past Montojo's Squadron. When the *Reina María Cristina* left its moorings and attempted to attack the *Olympia* at 7:00 a.m., it was hit by fire from the entire U.S. squadron. Mortally wounded, it was forced to return to the Spanish anchorage.

Shortly after 7:30 a.m., with most of the Spanish ships ablaze, Dewey received a false report from Capt. Gridley that the *Olympia* was low on ammunition. He immediately broke off action, retired to confer with his captains, and ordered that his men be given breakfast since they had not eaten. Because the targets on both sides had been almost completely obscured by thick clouds of **black-powder** smoke from the naval guns, Dewey, after the smoke had cleared, unexpectedly saw that Montojo's Squadron had been devastated. To everyone's surprise not one U.S. ship had been seriously damaged. Only the *Baltimore* had sustained casualties. The American squadron returned to action at 11:16 a.m., and, with Montojo's entire squadron ablaze, ceased firing at 12:30 p.m. and anchored off Manila. Dewey then ordered the *Petrel* to fire and finish off any Spanish ships still afloat.

The entire Spanish squadron had been destroyed while sustaining casualties of 161 dead and 210 wounded, and Dewey's squadron, while suffering only minor damage, sustained casualties of nine wounded. Although Dewey's squadron had scored only 142 hits out of more than 5,000 shots fired, Spanish gunfire had only scored 15 hits on the U.S. squadron.

News of the overwhelming defeat stunned the Spanish public, and street demonstrations broke out in 18 cities, with one crowd going to Prime Minister **Práxedes M. Sagasta**'s home to demand an end to his government. Although **Dewey's dispatch** on the battle did not reach U.S. officials until 7 May, U.S. newspapers carried news of the victory on 3 May.

MANZANILLO, CUBA. Located on the southwestern coast of Oriente Province in eastern **Cuba**, Manzanillo, a city of 23,000, was 150 miles overland from **Santiago, Cuba**. Its 8,668-man garrison consisted of troops from the **Isabel Católica Regiment** and the Andalusia Regiment. Naval forces under the command of Capt. Joaquín Gómez de Barredo included **gunboats** *Delgado Perrado* (Lt. Ubaldo Serís), *Estrella* (Lt. Joaquín Rivero), *Guantánamo* (Lt. Bartolome Morales), and *Guardían* (Lt. Carlos del Camino); an armed launch *Centinela* (Ens. Alejandro Arias Salgado); and two disabled gunboats: *María* and *Cuba Española* (Lt. Luis Pou).

A headquarters for **blockade** runners, Manzanillo was declared blockaded by the United States at the end of June 1898, and a series of naval engagements occurred here on 30 June, 1 July, and 18 July. After 18 July the port was effectively closed by U.S. naval forces, and on 12 August, U.S. naval forces under the command of Capt. **Caspar F. Goodrich** demanded the town's surrender. Upon receiving a refusal, the *Alvarado*, *Hist*, *Newark*, *Osceola*, and *Suwanee* bombarded the town. After the garrison's commander received news of the **Armistice Protocol**, which was signed the same day, a number of white flags flew over Manzanillo on 13 August, and the port's captain came out and delivered news of the armistice to the U.S. naval forces. During the bombardment U.S. forces sustained no casualties whereas Spanish casualties totaled six dead and 31 wounded.

MANZANILLO, CUBA, BATTLE OF (18 JULY 1898). On 18 July 1898, U.S. naval forces returned in force to **Manzanillo**. The **gunboats** *Helena* and *Wilmington*, the armed **yachts** *Hist*, *Hornet*, and *Scorpion*, and the armed tugs *Osceola* and *Wompatuck* entered the harbor, and while systematically staying out of range of Spanish guns, they destroyed ten ships in the harbor. Three gunboats (*Delgado Perrado*, *Estrella*, and paddle-wheeler *María*) were burned and sunk, and two gunboats (*Guantánamo* and *Guardían*) were forced ashore and destroyed. The transports *Gloria* and *Jose García* were burned and sunk, and the steamer *Purísima Concepción* was burned and sunk at the dock. Not one American ship was seriously damaged and no casualties were sustained. Spanish casualties included three dead and 14 wounded.

MANZANILLO, CUBA, BATTLES OF (30 JUNE 1898 AND 1 JULY 1898). On 30 June 1898, a one-hour exchange of naval gunfire took place between Spanish naval forces, under the command of Capt. Joaquín Gómez de Barredo, and U.S. naval forces. The Spanish force included the **gunboats** *Delgado Perrado, Estrella, Guantánamo*, and *Guardían*, and two disabled gunboats: *María* and *Cuba Española*. The U.S. force included the armed **yachts** *Hist* and *Hornet*, and the armed tug *Wompatuck*. The outgunned U.S. ships were forced to retreat after a damaged *Hornet* had to be towed out of range by the *Wompatuck*. The following day, 1 July, the armed yacht *Scorpion* and the armed tug *Osceola*, having replaced the three ships engaged the previous day after they had gone to **Guantánamo** for coal, entered the harbor and were immediately fired on by shore batteries and naval vessels. After 23 minutes, the two U.S. vessels withdrew.

MARBLEHEAD. (USN) Unprotected **cruiser**, commanded by Comdr. **Bowman H. McCalla**. Assigned to the **North Atlantic Squadron**, the *Marblehead* cut **cables** and fought in the engagement at **Cienfuegos, Cuba**, on 11 May 1898. As a result of their actions during the engagement, 21 sailors and five **marines** were awarded the **Congressional Medal of Honor**. While serving on the **blockade of Santiago, Cuba**, the *Marblehead* shelled Santiago on 6 June and then moved to **Guantánamo** on 7 June. On 14 June it helped drive the Spanish forces from the eastern coast of the lower bay. Before the landing of the **Fifth Corps** at **Daiquirí** on 22 June, the *Marblehead* was cruising close to the Cuban coast between **Morro Castle** and **Aguadores**, when the entire U.S. squadron, mistaking a railroad train running along the coast for a Spanish torpedo boat, opened fire. The *Marblehead* was not hit, and later Comdr. McCalla bragged that he was the only man in the navy who had been fired on by an entire fleet of **battleships** and cruisers and had lived. During 26–27 July its crew disabled 27 contact **mines** at Guantánamo Bay, and four sailors were later awarded the Congressional Medal of Honor for their actions. During August the *Marblehead*'s crew raised the Spanish **gunboat** *Sandoval*. Posted to the Pacific Ocean after the war, it was sold in 1921.

La. 1892, com. 1894, dis. 2,094, hp. 5,400, sp. 17
Armor: d. 5/16″, sl. 7/16″
Armament: 9–5″, 6–6pdr., 2–1pdr., 2 C. mgs., 3–18″ tt. (aw.)
Cc. 340, comp. 274

"MARCH OF CADIZ" *(MARCHA DE CÁDIZ).* A song from the operetta *Cádiz* by Javier de Buergos y Chueca. Although it was not about Spain's wars, it came to function as a patriotic symbol when it was sung at patriotic demonstrations and by soldiers going to war to fight against the Cuban insurgents.

MARÍA CRISTINA (1858–1929). Queen regent of Spain (1885–1902). From **Austria-Hungary**, María Cristina was the wife of King Alfonso XII, and when he died, she was pregnant with the future **Alfonso XIII**. Her primary goal as regent was to conserve the throne for her son. After U.S. Secretary of State **Richard Olney** offered the U.S. good offices to mediate the **Cuban Revolt**, María, who was adamant that Spain should retain its colonial possessions, opposed any reforms until the revolt had been suppressed. However, on 25 November 1897, she signed the decrees that granted **autonomy** to **Cuba** and **Puerto Rico**.

During a 17 January 1898 private social visit with U.S. Minister **Stewart L. Woodford**, María, who spoke fluent English, appealed directly to President **William McKinley** to break up the Cuban insurgent **Junta**. Stating that Spain had met all of McKinley's demands, she pointed out the changed government, autonomy decrees, and the institution of relief for suffering Cubans. However, when Woodford turned her request aside, she broke off the interview.

In March 1898 she began a personal diplomacy, through which she hoped to obtain the support of the European powers to forestall war. She asked her native Austria-Hungary to get involved, and on 17 March, she sent a letter to her relative Queen Victoria of England stating "the Americans intend to provoke us and bring about a war." Even though Victoria sympathized with María's plight, she was dissuaded by Prime Minister **Robert Cecil**. Upon the initiation of a national drive to assist injured soldiers returning from Cuba and the **Philippines**, María personally donated one million pesetas.

Upon the outbreak of the Spanish-American War, María called in the **Cortes** for the support of Spain against the "unjust attacks made upon us," and after the overwhelming U.S. victory at the **Battle of Manila Bay** on 1 May, she suggested to foreign diplomats that if the United States offered peace in exchange for Cuba, the government would accept. She supported Spain's signing of the **Armistice Protocol** of 12 August and the **Treaty of Paris** on 10 December. However, when it became known that the vote to ratify the Treaty of Paris in the Cortes was too close to be passed, she used her constitutional powers and ratified the treaty on 19 March 1899.

MARINES, U.S. NAVY. Under the command of Col. Commandant Charles Heywood, the marine corps, which totaled 2,728 men, was part of the **U.S. Navy**. On 16 April 1898, Heywood received orders to form two marine battalions; however, the two were reduced to one and then augmented by 200 men to become the **First Marine Battalion**. During the war the battalion played a key role in the seizure of the bay at **Guantánamo, Cuba**. Most of the corps, 2,055 men, served on board 57 naval vessels as guards and manned secondary batteries during the **Battle of Manila Bay** on 1 May and the **Naval Battle of Santiago, Cuba**, on 3 July. They provided landing parties that destroyed **cable** stations in **Cuba**, took possession of **Guam** on 21 June, and occupied the naval station at **Cavite, Philippines**. Nevertheless, at the end of the war, marine corps leaders still believed the primary role of the corps in the future would be manning secondary batteries on ships. However, the war provided the marine corps with many of its future commandants. First Lt. John A. Lejeune served on the *Cincinnati*; First Lt. Wendell C. "Buck" Neville served at Guantánamo, Cuba; First Lt. Ben H. Fuller served on the *Columbia*; Capt. William P. Biddle commanded the marine detachment on the *Olympia*; Capt. George Barnett served on the *New Orleans*; and Second Lt. John H. Russell served on the *Massachusetts*.

MARIX, ADOLPH (1848–1919). Lieutenant commander (USN), commanded armed **yacht** *Scorpion* during the war. A German-born graduate of the U.S. Naval Academy who had served as the executive officer of the *Maine* until months before its destruction, Marix served as the judge advocate on the *Maine* board of inquiry. Besieged by reporters as he traveled north with the *Maine* Report, he arrived in Washington, D.C., on 24 March 1898 and delivered the report to the **McKinley administration**. During the war Marix participated in the bombardment of **Cabañas Bay, Cuba**, as a feint to the **Fifth Corps**'s landing at **Daiquirí** on 22 June. Involved in the 1 July and 18 July naval engagements at **Manzanillo**, Marix was promoted for conspicuous bravery. After the war, he served as captain of port of **Manila** (1901–1903). Promoted to rear admiral in 1908, he retired in 1910.

MARQUÉS DEL DUERO. (SPN) **Gunboat** commanded by Lt. Comdr. Salvador Moreno de Guerra. An iron-hulled, schooner-rigged gunboat, it was stationed at **Manila, Philippines**, as part of Adm. **Patricio Montojo's Squadron**. During the **Battle of Manila Bay** on 1 May 1898, the *Marqués del Duero* remained behind the main Spanish battle line and therefore was only hit five times. After the battle it was fired by the *Petrel* and was entirely gutted by fire.

La. 1875, dis. 492, hp. 550, sp. 10
Armament: 1–6.4″, 2–4.7″, 1 mg.
Cc. 89, comp. 114

MARSHALL, DAVID EDWARD (1869–1933). Correspondent for the *New York Journal*. After arriving at **Daiquirí, Cuba**, with the **Fifth Corps**, Marshall attempted to raise the *Journal*'s flag ahead of the U.S. flag but failed. Accompanying the **Rough Riders**, he was shot through the spine in the **Battle of Las Guásimas** on 24 June 1898 and told his story in "A Wounded Correspondent's Recollections of Guásimas" *Scribner's Magazine* (September 1898) and "How It Feels to Be Shot" *Cosmopolitan* (September, 1898). Because he was wounded, Marshall could not deliver his dispatch of the battle, so **Stephen Crane**, who was reporting for the *New York World*, took Marshall's dispatch, walked to **Siboney**, and filed the dispatch for him. Crane later lost his job over this. Marshall became the Rough Riders' historian with his book *The Story of the Rough Riders, 1st U.S. Volunteer Cavalry* (1899).

MARTÍ Y PEREZ, JOSÉ (1853–1895). Cuban essayist, journalist, poet, and revolutionary. Martí was imprisoned as a youth for his political activities. His sentence was commuted to confinement within Spain, where he studied law at the universities of Madrid and Zaragoza. After returning to Cuba, he was deported and fled to the United States, where he remained until 1895. While living in the United States he founded the **Cuban Revolutionary Party** in 1892 and edited the insurgent newspaper *Patria* in New York City. On 25 March 1895, Martí, along with Maj. Gen. **Máximo Gómez**, issued the *Manifesto of Montecristi*, calling their followers to arms to fight for Cuban independence. After landing in **Cuba** in April 1895, Martí was killed in battle at Dos Rios on 19 May 1895.

MARTÍNEZ CAMPOS, ARSENIO (1831–1900). Captain general and governor-general of **Cuba**. A member of the **Liberal-Conservative Party**, Martínez Campos was Spain's most illustrious soldier. He supported the monarchy and defeated the Cuban insurgents during the Ten Years' War in Cuba. After the outbreak of the **Cuban Revolt**, he became governor-general of Cuba in April 1895. He issued an amnesty proclamation and promised reforms. Adopting an essentially defensive military strategy, he used the *trocha* system, distributed sufficient forces to various points all over Cuba to suppress the spread of the revolt, and attempted to contain the insurgents in the eastern province of Oriente. When his strategy failed, he realized that only total war would defeat the insurgents, and, reluctant to engage in such a war, he sent in his resignation on 7 January 1896. After being replaced by Lt. Gen. **Valeriano Weyler y Nicolau** in February, Martínez Campos returned to Spain and warned Queen Regent **María Cristina** that his heart told him that this would be the last war that

Spain had to endure in America. He wrote to his friends predicting that Weyler's methods would be the end of Spanish rule in Cuba, for "even the dead will rise out of their graves to fight Weyler." Before Prime Minister **Práxedes M. Sagasta** ordered the signing of the **Armistice Protocol** on 12 August 1898, he consulted with Martínez Campos. Martínez Campos informed Sagasta that although he supported negotiations, he believed that Sagasta should not be the one involved. He believed that a leader who had failed to avoid a war should not be the one to sign the peace.

MARTÍNEZ ILLESCAS, RAFAEL. See ILLESCAS, RAFAEL MARTÍNEZ

MARTÍNEZ Y RUIZ, JOSE "AZORÍN" (1873–1967). Spanish critic, essayist, journalist, and novelist. Having abandoned his legal studies and moved to Madrid in 1896 to make a career as a journalist, Martínez Ruiz, who came to be known as "Azorín," briefly worked as a journalist, but he was dismissed owing to his anarchistic views, his strident attacks on the church and marriage, and his defense of divorce and free love. He published satirical works, such as *Charivari* (1897) and *Pecuchet, demagogo* (1898), which caused a furor. Opposed to the Spanish-American War, he wrote "Gaceta de Madrid," *Madrid Cómico* (10 April 1898), which satirized vociferous Spanish nationalists. After the war he published *El alma castellana* (1900), and, in a series of articles in 1913, he pinned the name **"Generation of 98"** on the writers of the Spanish-American War period. He later became a conservative, served as undersecretary of the ministry of education, and was elected to the *Academia Española* in 1924.

MARTINIQUE. A French island in the West Indies, Martinique served as a **cable** terminus. While searching for Adm. **Pascual Cervera's Squadron**, the *Harvard* arrived at St. Pierre, Martinique, at 9:30 a.m. on 11 May 1898. While ashore, Capt. Charles S. Cotton was informed around 6:00 p.m. that at 4:00 p.m. the Spanish **torpedo-boat destroyer** *Furor* had arrived at Fort de France, the naval station and capital. In fact, the *Furor* and the *Terror* under the command of Capt. **Fernando Villaamil** had arrived, trying to obtain coal and information.

Owing to French neutrality, the governor prohibited the Spanish vessels from obtaining coal and delayed their leaving because of the *Harvard*'s presence. Villaamil was informed by the captain of the Spanish hospital steamer *Alicante*, which had arrived on 23 April, of the disastrous defeat suffered at the **Battle of Manila Bay** on 1 May and of the position of Adm. **William T. Sampson**'s ships at **San**

Juan, Puerto Rico. Meanwhile, Cotton was also informed that the *Harvard* could not leave until 7:00 p.m. on 12 May. Wishing to verify the presence of one of Cervera's ships, Cotton requested that the U.S. consul, accompanied by a **marine** lieutenant, go to Fort de France to obtain complete information. They made the 12-mile journey in a rowboat, arriving at 2:00 a.m. on the 12th and returned by local steamer at 9:00 a.m. Cotton's information regarding the presence of Cervera's Squadron reached Washington during the night of 12 May. In fact, only the *Terror* remained at Martinique, because Villaamil, anxious to inform Adm. **Pascual Cervera** of the latest news, decided to leave the *Terror* because it had bad boilers and weighed anchor on the *Furor* at midnight on 11 May. Assisted by the *Alicante*, which illuminated the harbor buoys, Villaamil left at full speed and informed Cervera at 3:00 a.m. on 12 May of Sampson's proximity to San Juan, Puerto Rico. Consequently, Cervera decided it would be madness to go to San Juan and instead steamed to **Curaçao** for coal.

MASSACHUSETTS. (USN) First-class **battleship**, commanded by Capt. **Francis J. Higginson**. A sister ship of the *Indiana* and *Oregon*, the *Massachusetts* had been built for **coastal defense** and thus stressed guns and armor over speed. Initially it served in the **Flying Squadron**, searching for Adm. **Pascual Cervera's Squadron**, and later blockaded **Santiago, Cuba**, using its **searchlights** to illuminate the harbor entrance at night. Although it participated in the bombardments of Spanish positions at the harbor entrance, it missed the **Naval Battle of Santiago** on 3 July 1898, because it was coaling at **Guantánamo**. Briefly detailed to the **Eastern Squadron**, it served as the command ship for Maj. Gen. **Nelson A. Miles**'s invasion of **Puerto Rico**. It was destroyed in 1920 when it was used for target practice by shore batteries at Pensacola, Florida.

La. 1893, com. 1896, dis. 10,288, hp. 10,000, sp. 16.2
Armor: s. 18″, d. 2.75, t. 15″ & 6″, b. 8–17″
Armament: 4–13″, 8–8″, 4–6″, 20–6pdr., 6–1pdr., 2 C. mgs, 3 tt.
Cc. 1,600, comp. 473

MATANZAS, CUBA. The second largest city of **Cuba** with a population of 87,800, Matanzas was located on a bay about 50 miles east of **Havana** on the northern Cuban coast. Defended by 17,000 regular Spanish troops in the area, Matanzas was **blockade**d by U.S. naval forces from the beginning of the war. On 27 April 1898, Adm. **William T. Sampson**, who had received reports of the erecting of shore batteries 52 miles east of Matanzas, decided to reconnoiter the area and arrived shortly before 1:00 p.m. with the **cruisers *New York*** and *Cincinnati*, and the **monitor *Puritan***. For 19 minutes the supposed fortifications were bombarded, and U.S. official reports claimed the forts were destroyed. However, Gov.-Gen. **Ramón Blanco y Erenas** stated that only a mule had been killed. Dubbed the "Matanzas Mule," it was buried with military honors, and the U.S. action was lampooned by Puerto Rican poet Jose Mercado "Momo" in his poem "The Burro of Matanzas."

MAURA Y MONTANER, ANTONIO (1853–1925). Spanish **Liberal Party** leader. A Majorcan self-made lawyer, Maura served as a member of the **Cortes**, and while minister of overseas territories in the cabinet of **Práxedes M. Sagasta**, he presented a project for a law on Cuban **autonomy** in 1893. After it was defeated, Maura resigned. Upon Sagasta's ascension to power in October 1897, Maura refused to join the cabinet. After the war, Maura, a member of the conservative wing of the Liberal Party, led a faction into the **Liberal-Conservative Party**, rose to the party's leadership, served as prime minister of Spain, and sought to regenerate Spain through "reform from above," succeeding **Francisco Silvela** as the proponent of **regenerationism**.

MAUSER RIFLE. Designed by Paul and Wilhelm Mauser of **Germany**, it was considered the finest military rifle of its time. A bolt-action .276-inch caliber repeating rifle, it was clip-loaded with a five-cartridge magazine, fired **smokeless powder**, and weighed 9.7 pounds with its bayonet. Spain began using it in 1891, and 30,000 rifles and carbines were delivered to Spanish troops in **Cuba**. A good rifleman could squeeze off eight aimed shots in 20 seconds with the Mauser. Although the Mauser was superior to the **Krag-Jörgensen** rifle because of its rapid fire and higher degree of accuracy, the **U.S. Army** had rejected it and adopted the Krag-Jörgensen before the war.

MAXFIELD, JOSEPH EDWIN (1860–1926). Lieutenant colonel (USV), in the **Signal Corps**. Assigned to command the only observation **balloon** in the Signal Corps, Maxfield reached **Tampa, Florida**, on 31 May 1898 and barely located his equipment at the railroad yard. Along with his balloon detachment, Maxfield left on the *Segurança*, disembarked at **Daiquirí, Cuba**, on 28 June, and was in charge of balloon operations during the **Santiago, Cuba, campaign**. Although there was only enough gas to fill the balloon once, it was immediately pressed into service and made three ascents the first day. During the **Battle of San Juan Hill** on 1 July, Maxfield, accompanied by Col. **George Derby**, ascended in the balloon and accompanied the soldiers into battle. The balloon was shot out of the sky, and neither Maxfield nor Derby was injured. Both were recommended for brevet promotions for their extraordinary heroism. Maxfield quickly returned to the United States to secure another balloon, but the war was over before he could return to action.

MAYAGÜEZ, PUERTO RICO. Located on the western coast of **Puerto Rico**, Mayagüez, with a population of 28,000, was unfortified and on 30 May 1898 was defended by four companies of the **Patria Battalion** and 40 artillerymen, which meant about 500 effectives. Under the overall command of Col. Julio Soto Villanueva, the district was defended by 1 August by 1,362 soldiers, most of whom were regulars from the **Alfonso XIII Battalion** under the command of Lt. Col. Antonio Osés. Upon the approach of U.S. forces under the command of Brig. Gen. **Theodore Schwan** and the resulting skirmish at **Hormigueros** on 10 August, Col. Soto chose not to defend the town and ordered a retreat. The town was occupied by American forces on 11 August, and they were greeted by many prominent citizens in a public reception. The next day part of Schwan's command followed the retreating Spanish forces and moved toward **Las Marías**, where a skirmish was fought on 13 August.

MAYFLOWER. (USN) Armed **yacht**, commanded by Comdr. M. R. S. Mackenzie. Purchased on 19 March 1898 by the **U.S. Navy** for $430,000 from the Ogden Goelet estate, its lavish fittings were almost all removed, except for one of the original four solid marble bathtubs. Torpedo tubes were installed in the former dining room and steel plates were added amidships to protect the engines and boilers. During the war it served on the **blockade of Cuba** and was later assigned to the **Eastern Squadron**. After the war, it served as the presidential yacht for 25 years, was sold in 1931, and later carried Jewish refugees to Palestine as late as 1948.

La. 1896, com. 24 March 1898, dis. 2,690, hp. 4,700, sp. 16.8
Armament: 2–5", 12–6pdr., 2–6 mm. C. mgs.
Cc. 584, comp. 171

McCALLA, BOWMAN HENDRY (1844–1910). Commander (USN), commanded the *Marblehead*. A U.S. Naval Academy graduate and strict disciplinarian, McCalla took command of the *Marblehead* in 1897 and upon the outbreak of the war, commanded naval forces blockading **Havana** and **Cienfuegos, Cuba**. While directing **cable-cutting operations**, McCalla was in overall command of U.S. naval forces at the engagement at Cienfuegos on 11 May 1898. In mid-June he commanded the expedition that seized the bay at **Guantánamo, Cuba**, after which he established and commanded a naval base there until the end of the war. The **First Marine Battalion** named its camp at Guantánamo after him. Promoted to captain in August 1898, he later served in the **Philippine Insurrection** and in the Boxer Rebellion in China, reaching the rank of rear admiral in 1903.

McCASKEY, WILLIAM SPENCER (1843–1914). Major, commanded the **Twentieth U.S. Infantry**, Independent Brigade, in the **Fifth Corps**. A career soldier who rose from a volunteer private in the Civil War to major general in 1907, McCaskey commanded his regiment in the **Battle of El Caney** on 1 July 1898. After the war he served in the **Philippine Insurrection** from March 1899 until February 1902.

McCLERNAND, EDWARD JOHN (1848–1926). Lieutenant colonel and adjutant of the **Fifth Corps**. A West Point graduate, McClernand was present at the **Aserraderos Conference** on 20 June 1898. At 3:00 a.m. on 1 July, Maj. Gen. **William R. Shafter**, who was ill and could not go to the front to command, called him in and ordered him forward to **El Pozo** so that McClernand could coordinate messages between Shafter's headquarters and the U.S. forces attacking **El Caney** and the **San Juan Heights**. Although a series of messengers and telephone lines were used to transmit information and orders, the system did not function well. On 2 July, McClernand suggested to Shafter that he demand the surrender of **Santiago, Cuba**, rather than withdraw. After the war, he served in the **Philippine Insurrection** and attained the rank of brigadier general in 1912.

McCULLOCH. (USN) Converted revenue cutter, commanded by Capt. Daniel B. Hodgson, R.C.S. Named the *Hugh McCulloch*, it was sent on a round-the-world trip for service on the Pacific Coast. After leaving the United States on 8 January 1898, it joined the **Asiatic Squadron** on 17 April at **Hong Kong**. At the rear of the squadron when it entered **Manila Bay, Philippines**, on the night of 30 April/1 May, its smokestack caught fire, and Spanish guns at El Fraile briefly opened up. Although it took no part in the **Battle of Manila Bay** on 1 May, its chief engineer died from heat prostration. Subsequently, it was used as a dispatch boat, carrying Com. **George W. Dewey**'s initial dispatches to Hong Kong on 5 May and transporting **Emilio Aguinaldo** when he returned to the **Philippines** on 19 May. In September the *McCulloch* captured the steamer *Pasig*, which was running guns for Filipino insurgents. By executive order, it was returned to the Treasury Department on 29 October, left Manila on 6 November, and arrived at San Francisco on 4 January 1899.

La. 1897, com. 1897, dis. 1,432
Armament: 4–3″, or 4–6pdr., 2–3″

Comp. 68

McCUTCHEON, JOHN TINNEY (1870–1949). An artist and reporter for the *Chicago Record*. Invited by his close friend, reporter **Edward W. Harden**, to take a trip around the world on the *McCulloch*, McCutcheon and Harden left the United States on 8 January 1898, arrived at **Hong Kong** on 17 April, and joined Com. **George W. Dewey's Asiatic Squadron**. An eyewitness to the **Battle of Manila Bay** on 1 May 1898, McCutcheon photographed and sketched Dewey's squadron during the battle. He believed the United States should retain the **Philippines** because the German squadron at Manila was there to secure the Philippines as colonies if the United States did not retain them. After the war he recounted his experiences in "The Surrender of Manila," *The Century Magazine* (April 1899), and the *Chicago Record* reprinted his articles in *The Chicago Record's War Stories* (1899). His autobiography, *Drawn from Memory* (1950), contained many of his famous cartoons and sketches.

McENERY RESOLUTION (14 FEBRUARY 1899). Democratic Senator Samuel D. McEnery of Louisiana, an anti-imperialist, switched sides five minutes before roll call and voted to ratify the **Treaty of Paris** on 6 February 1899, because he had been promised that his resolution endorsing Philippine independence would be approved in "due time." After the **Bacon Amendment** failed on 14 February, McEnery introduced his resolution, which declared that the United States would not permanently annex the **Philippines** but intended to establish a government suitable to the wants and conditions of the inhabitants, preparing them for local self-government and "in due time to make such disposition of said islands as will best promote the interests of the citizens of the United States and the inhabitants of said islands." It was passed without amendment by a vote of 26–22, but was never brought up in the House of Representatives for a vote.

McINTOSH, BURR (1862–1942). Correspondent-photographer for the *New York Journal* and *Leslie's Weekly*. McIntosh covered the **Fifth Corps** at **Tampa, Florida**, and the Fifth Corps's **Santiago, Cuba, campaign**. He was present at the Fifth Corps's landings at **Daiquirí** and **Siboney**, blamed Maj. Gen. **Joseph Wheeler** for the **Battle of Las Guásimas** on 24 June 1898, which he felt was an "ill-judged victory," and was present at the **Battle of San Juan Hill** on 1 July. McIntosh wrote "Perils of the Front" *Leslie's* (18 August 1898) in which he pointed out that Maj. Gen. **William R. Shafter**'s order restricting reporters from landing along with the corps at Daiquirí was "the fundamental cause of a great deal of the unkind criticism" directed at Shafter by the **press**. Having lost 58 of his 250 pounds, McIntosh returned to the United States and wrote *The Little I Saw of Cuba* (1899).

McKIBBEN, CHAMBERS (1841–1919). Lieutenant colonel, commanded the **Twenty-First U.S. Infantry**, Second Brigade, First Division, in the **Fifth Corps**. Promoted to brigadier general (USV) 8 July 1898, McKibben participated in the formal **capitulation of Santiago, Cuba**, was promoted to brigadier general (USV), assigned to command the Second Brigade of the Second Division, and signed the **Round Robin Letter** of 3 August. After the war he was military governor of Santiago and commanded the First Brigade, First Division, in the **Second Corps** until April 1899. After commanding the Department of Texas, he retired after 40 years of service.

McKINLEY, JAMES F. (1880–1941). Private, nephew of President **William McKinley**. Having lived with McKinley's mother and family for many years, he arrived at **Camp Alger** on 23 June 1898, along with John D. Barker, another of McKinley's nephews, with a letter of introduction from the president, requesting their being assigned to Company I of the **Eighth Ohio Infantry**. After landing near **Santiago, Cuba**, on 10 July, both nephews were detailed as orderlies to Brig. Gen. **Guy V. Henry** and accompanied him to **Puerto Rico**. After the war, McKinley fought in the **Philippine Insurrection** and advanced through the grades to major general by 1935.

McKINLEY, WILLIAM (1843–1901). President of the United States 1897–1901. A former Republican congressman and governor of Ohio, McKinley, a religious man whose character was beyond reproach, was horrified by war because of his experiences serving in the Civil War. As president, McKinley, who was an avid newspaper reader, established an institutionalized relationship with the **press** by holding press conferences and dispersing press releases. Moreover, he was a charitable man. After he made a national appeal for charity for Cuban relief efforts on 24 December 1897, he personally donated $5,000 to begin the program, a fact unknown until after his death.

Later stating that the "march of events" had forced his administration into war against Spain, McKinley believed that, had he been left alone to diplomatically resolve the Cuban situation, it could have been done without war. Nevertheless, as commander in chief during the war, he was fully involved and in command in pursuing victory in the quickest and least-costly manner. He held almost daily conferences with his principal military advisers to coordinate operations of the army and navy and to decide overall strategy; moreover, he established an **Operating Room** or "war room" in the White House to direct the war. Although he mainly appointed officers from the regular army to command positions (19 out of 26 major generals, and 66 out of 102 brigadier generals), he did bow to political pressure in granting commissions to the sons of prominent Republicans.

McKinley supported the annexation of **Hawaii**, believing he was continuing a long-standing **Republican Party** policy, and personally directed all U.S. negotiations, writing out the conditions that became the **Armistice Protocol** of 12 August, and appointing the U.S. **Peace Commission** to negotiate the **Treaty of Paris**. After returning from a cross-country speaking tour in October 1898, he ordered the Peace Commission to take all of the **Philippines**. Because they could not be abandoned or given to a European power, "duty and destiny" required the United States to keep the islands. According to **James F. Rusling**, McKinley later claimed divine inspiration for the decision. On 6 September 1901, McKinley was assassinated, and **Theodore Roosevelt** became president.

McKINLEY ADMINISTRATION. Under the direction of President **William McKinley**, the cabinet was composed of Vice President **Garret A. Hobart**; Secretaries of State **John Sherman, William R. Day**, and **John Hay**; Secretary of War **Russell A. Alger**; Secretary of the Navy **John D. Long**; Secretary of the Treasury Lyman J. Gage; Attorneys General Joseph McKenna and John W. Griggs; Secretary of the Interior Cornelius N. Bliss; Secretary of Agriculture James Wilson; and Postmaster General Charles E. Smith.

After **William J. Calhoun** reported on the Cuban situation, the administration undertook its first diplomatic initiative concerning **Cuba** on 26 June 1897 in a note by Secretary of State John Sherman and shortly after in the 16 July instructions from Sherman to U.S. Minister to Spain **Stewart L. Woodford**, offering the good offices of the United States to help resolve the Cuban situation. In his first state of the union message on 6 December 1897, McKinley expressed cautious optimism because of Spanish reforms, rejected the recognition of **belligerent rights** for the Cuban insurgents, and argued that Spain be given a reasonable amount of time to implement its reform program (using the phrase "near future" in reference to a deadline for Spain to settle its affairs in Cuba, which suggested possible future U.S. intervention). On 27 March 1898, because of an increasing public and congressional clamor for war after the *Maine* disaster on 15 February 1898 and Spain's policy of diplomatic delay, **McKinley's Ultimatum** was delivered to Spain. Because subsequent Spanish concessions were too few and too late, **McKinley's War Message** was delivered to **Congress** on 11 April.

During the war the administration refused to officially recognize the Cuban and Filipino insurgents and soon developed a policy of maintaining control over any conquered territories. While maintaining a policy of no European interference, the administration rejected French and British overtures for peace negotiations in early June and did not allow the Cuban or Filipino insurgents to participate in negotiations. Rather, the administration pursued a course of direct negotiations with Spain, which resulted in the signing of the **Armistice Protocol** on 12 August and the **Treaty of Paris** on 10 December. Subsequently, the administration was confronted by the **Philippine Insurrection**.

McKINLEY'S ULTIMATUM TO SPAIN (27 MARCH 1898). After the release of the board of inquiry's report on the *Maine*, the political situation in the United States demanded immediate action concerning the Cuban situation. Accordingly, the **McKinley administration**, confronted by Spain's delaying tactics, issued an ultimatum to Spain. After procedural arrangements were worked out in a meeting with the **"Peace Faction"** of Republican senators on 25 March 1898, the administration, on 27 March, set the following conditions: 1) an armistice in **Cuba** until October 1 while negotiations between Spain and the insurgents were conducted through the offices of the president of the United States; 2) an immediate revocation of the **reconcentration** policy with U.S. assistance in relieving the suffering of the civilian population; 3) if possible, if terms of peace were not satisfactorily settled by 1 October, the U.S. president would be the final arbiter between Spain and the insurgents. Although **Stewart Woodford**, U.S. minister to Spain, had been informed on 28 March that Cuban independence was to be part of the conditions, he did not explicitly mention Cuban independence when he delivered the conditions to Spain's government on 29 March.

On 31 March, Spain responded, offering arbitration on the *Maine* issue and announcing that an order had been given to revoke reconcentration in the western provinces of Cuba. Moreover, the governor-general was provided with funds to relieve the suffering of the civilian population and American cooperation would be accepted. However, the armistice issue would be turned over to Cuba's **autonomous government**, which would not assemble until 4 May, and a suspension of hostilities would be granted if the insurgents requested it. *El Imparcial* commented on 31 March, "It is better to weep over lost loved ones than to live in shame and dishonor."

McKINLEY'S WAR MESSAGE TO CONGRESS (11 APRIL 1898). After having postponed the message once because he wanted more time to negotiate, on 11 April 1898, President **William McKinley**, who had been informed by Republican legislators that a delay would divide the party and bring about electoral defeat in the fall elections, sent his "War Message" to **Congress**. The 7,000-word message began with a review of recent Cuban history, moved on to refuse recognition of the **Cuban Republic**, and supported the judgment of the *Maine* board of inquiry, citing it as "proof of the state of things in Cuba that is intolerable." McKinley asked for congressional authorization to intervene in **Cuba** based on a humanitarian cause to end the bloodshed and suffering in Cuba and to protect American citizens' lives and property. Citing the serious injury the war had caused to U.S. commerce, trade, and business, the present Cuban situation was a constant menace to peace and entailed upon the U.S. government an enormous expense. Although he briefly mentioned Spain's recent concession in granting a suspension of hostilities at the end of his message, McKinley effectively turned the Cuban issue over to Congress.

Many Republicans applauded, and the message was praised by the *New York Times*, *Wall Street Journal*, and *New York Herald*; the *Los Angeles Times* called it on 12 April a "calm, candid, judicial review of the situation." However, many congressmen reacted in disbelief, thinking the message ambiguous, contradictory, and indecisive. The *Washington Post*, on 12 April, gave it partial support but found it disappointing because "it makes no definite and concrete recommendations." The *New York Sun*, *New York Journal*, the *Boston Daily Globe*, the *St. Louis Post-Dispatch*, and Denver's *Rocky Mountain News* denounced the speech. The *New York World* editorialized, stating "Mr. McKinley's Quibbles and Straddles," and a survey of 145 newspapers found that 74 viewed it as a distinct disappointment and 71 found it acceptable. In Spain there was outrage. Street demonstrations took place in Madrid, Barcelona, Valencia, and Zaragosa. The Spanish **press** excoriated McKinley. *El Correo Militar*, a Madrid-based military newspaper, reacted on 12 April, accusing McKinley of "vomiting" humiliation on Spain, and *El Imparcial* called upon the government to defend Spanish honor since McKinley's message was ignoble.

McKINNON, WILLIAM D. (1858–1902). Chaplain of the **First California Infantry**. After arriving at **Manila**, **Philippines**, with the **Eighth Corps**, McKinnon was asked by Brig. Gen. **Thomas Anderson** to enter Manila and ask Archbishop **Bernardino Nozaleda** to assist in ending the war. On 9 August, on the spur of the moment, McKinnon walked up to the Spanish lines without a flag of truce and was taken to Archbishop Nozaleda, with whom he had a long conversation. Nozaleda denied having authored a proclamation against the United States and believed the city would not surrender without a fight. McKinnon returned to the U.S. lines, informed U.S. military officials of his conversation, and Maj. Gen. **Wesley Merritt** and Adm. **George W. Dewey** then made plans to attack. After the war McKinnon briefly served as superintendent of schools in Manila.

MERCHANT MARINE, UNITED STATES. Because of the brevity of the war and overwhelming American naval victories early on, the merchant marine played a small role in the war. Although the **U.S. Navy** chartered 12 of the finest ocean liners and converted them into warships manned by the **naval militia**, and purchased and kept eight smaller merchant ships, they were inadequate for the vital tasks of coaling the navy, transporting the army, and resupplying U.S. forces; therefore, the U.S. armed forces purchased and chartered foreign ships at high prices. For example, Com. **George W. Dewey** purchased the British collier *Nanshan* and steamer *Zafiro* at **Hong Kong**. Frequently the foreign ship's crew and officers refused to take the ship into a combat zone, therefore delaying operations until an American crew arrived. Although marine insurance rose rapidly, no U.S. merchant ships were lost in the war.

MERRIMAC. (USN) Collier, commanded by Comdr. James M. Miller. Formerly the *Solveig*, it was purchased by the **U.S. Navy** on 12 April 1898 from the Hogan Line for $342,000 and assigned to the **Flying Squadron**. Because it frequently broke down and had to be towed to **Santiago, Cuba**, the *Merrimac* was placed on the list of expendable vessels. Consequently, it was chosen to be used in an attempt to block the Santiago harbor entrance in order to prevent Adm. **Pascual Cervera's Squadron** from leaving.

When a call was made for volunteers for what was viewed as a suicide mission, hundreds of men volunteered. However, only six were selected to go under the command of Lt. **Richmond P. Hobson** of the *New York*, and one other stowed away. Commanded by Lt. Hobson, the crew consisted of Coxswains Claus K. Clausen, John E. Murphy, and Osborn Deignan; Chief Master-at-Arms Daniel Montague; Gunner's Mate First Class George Charette; Watertender Francis Kelly; and Machinist First Class George F. Phillips. All were later awarded the **Congressional Medal of Honor**.

The plan was for the *Merrimac* to steam past **Morro Castle**, swing crosswise of the channel, drop the anchors, open the valves, and explode the attached **torpedoes**, and for the crew to escape in a lifeboat that was towed astern. After a first attempt on the night of 1 June was called off because the sun rose before they were ready, a second attempt began at 3:00 a.m. on 3 June. Hit by torpedoes and with its steering-gear shot away by gunfire, the ship settled inside the harbor entrance, failing to block the channel. The uninjured crew was picked out of the water at 6:00 a.m. by a Spanish steam launch with Adm. **Pascual Cervera** aboard. That afternoon, Capt. **Joaquín Busta-mante** came out under a flag of truce and informed Adm. **William T. Sampson** that the crew was uninjured and were prisoners. They were later released in a prisoner exchange on 6 July.

MERRITT, WESLEY (1834–1910). Major general, commanded the **Eighth Corps**. A West Point graduate and Civil War and frontier veteran, Merritt was the superintendent of West Point (1882–1887), and before the war, was a brigadier general commanding the Depart- ment of the East. Nearing the age of retirement, Merritt, an avowed expansionist, had written *Armies of Today* (1893) and articles advo- cating the need for a large, modern regular army.

Upon the outbreak of the war, he asked to command the Eighth Corps and then regretted it, thinking that the **Philippine campaign** would be a side show. Assigned to command the Eighth Corps on 16 May 1898, Merritt received his instructions on 19 May, telling him not to ally with the insurgent forces of **Emilio Aguinaldo** and to defeat the Spanish and bring order and security to the islands while they were in U.S. possession. Although his instructions left unclear the long-range goals of U.S. policy, Merritt, who personally advo- cated taking all of the **Philippines**, read them as meaning conquest of the islands.

After leaving San Francisco with the third expedition of the Eighth Corps on the *Newport* on 29 June, he arrived at **Manila** in late July. Believing Aguinaldo was a "Chinese half-breed adventurer" with no claim to govern the Philippines, Merritt, after the **Battle of Manila** on 13 August, issued an official proclamation establishing a govern- ment of military occupation, promising that all who cooperated with the United States would receive its support and protection. At the end of August he transferred command of the Eighth Corps to Maj. Gen. **Elwell S. Otis** and went to Paris, **France**, to brief the U.S. **Peace Commission**, which was negotiating the **Treaty of Paris**. Merritt ad- vised them that the American flag should fly over the Philippines "forever," and in his opinion, the Filipinos wanted to be annexed to the United States. In December 1898 he resumed command of the Department of the East and retired in 1900.

"A MESSAGE TO GARCÍA". See HUBBARD, ELBERT

MEXICO. Under the dictatorship of President Porfirio Díaz, Mexico declared its neutrality on 22 April 1898. Although there was much public support for Spain, Mexico, intent on maintaining good relations with the United States, took steps to restrict open support for Spain, refused Cuban insurgent requests to organize a Latin American demarche, and its semiofficial press, such as *El Mundo* and *El Imparcial* in Mexico City, refrained from anti-U.S. invective. Nevertheless, its numerous and wealthy Spanish colonies in Mexico City and Puebla held patriotic meetings, raised money, and although its press vehemently criticized the United States, its **blockade** runners left Mexico for **Cuba**.

MIANTONOMOH. (USN) Double-turreted **monitor**, commanded by Capt. Mortimer L. Johnson. A sister ship to the *Amphitrite*, *Monadnock*, and *Terror*, it was never designed for sea duty. It had a double bottom, was limited in fuel supply, and was very poorly ventilated. Attached to the North Atlantic Station, it served on the **blockade of Cuba** during the war. It was stricken in 1915 and sold in 1922.

La. 1876, com. 1891, dis. 3,990, hp. 1,600, sp. 12
Armor: s. 7″, d. 1.75″, t. 11.5″, ct. 9″
Armament: 4–10″, 2–6pdr., 2–3pdr., 2–1pdr, 2–37 mm.
Cc. 270, comp. 150

MILES, EVAN (1838–1908). Colonel, commanded the Second Brigade, Second Division, in the **Fifth Corps**. A Civil War veteran, Miles was a career soldier who had served on the frontier and been the major of the **Twenty-Fifth U.S. Infantry**. During the war, Miles, formerly a commander of the **First U.S. Infantry**, commanded a brigade during the **Santiago, Cuba, campaign**. His brigade, which included the **First U.S. Infantry**, **Fourth U.S. Infantry**, and **Twenty-Fifth U.S. Infantry**, was held in reserve until the afternoon of 1 July 1898, when it was ordered into action to fight in the **Battle of El Caney**. On 6 October 1898, Miles was promoted to brigadier general (USV) and retired in 1899.

MILES, NELSON APPLETON (1839–1925). Major general, **commanding general of the U.S. Army**. A Civil War veteran and famed Indian fighter, Miles became the commanding general in 1895 and was known as a pompous soldier who designed his own uniforms, which regularly paraded a chest full of medals. He initially questioned the need for a war over **Cuba** and after the war contended the issues could and should have been settled by peaceful means. From the beginning of the war Miles advocated operations on Spain's periphery designed to obtain important victories at a small cost. He therefore favored conquering **Puerto Rico** first instead of Cuba and favored the occupation of only **Manila**, not the entire **Philippines**.

Concerned over the effects of **disease** in Cuba during the rainy season, Miles suggested a naval **blockade** and the use of a small force to harass the Spanish while supplying the insurgents. Owing to his intense rivalry with Secretary of War **Russell A. Alger**, he lost favor with President **William McKinley** early on in the war.

After participating in the negotiations for the **capitulation** of **Santiago, Cuba**, Miles left **Guantánamo** on 21 July with a 3,415-man expeditionary force, which would eventually number 15,000, to invade Puerto Rico. After landing at **Guánica** on 25 July, Miles issued two proclamations. The first, on 28 July, claimed the U.S. was fighting in the cause of liberty, justice, and humanity, and had not come to make war against the Puerto Ricans but to promote their prosperity and bestow the "blessings of the liberal institutions of our government." On 29 July, Miles issued a second proclamation; however, this was directed to his commanding officers and declared U.S. military power supreme on the island, established martial law, and declared that the private rights and properties of Puerto Ricans would be respected as soon as they demonstrated their obedience.

In the midst of conducting a highly successful four-pronged campaign to conquer Puerto Rico, Miles was angered that the **Armistice Protocol** of 12 August had denied him the capture of **San Juan**. A day earlier he issued his first public attack on his perceived enemies in an interview with the *Kansas City Star*. He accused Secretary Alger of undermining his authority at Santiago, Cuba, and claimed the **War Department** had ignored his plans for suppressing the **yellow fever** epidemic and withheld ships and landing craft for his **Puerto Rican campaign**. On 7 September, Miles claimed that the war had been fought according to his plan.

After he received a warning in August from Major Dr. **William H. Daly** about the possibility of chemically treated beef being used by the **U.S. Army**, Miles did not immediately inform the War Department; instead, he waited, lodged a formal complaint on 9 September, built his case for two months, and then gave sensational testimony to the **Dodge Commission** on 21 December, which became known as the **"Embalmed Beef" Controversy** and ended with the **"Beef Court."** Promoted to lieutenant general in 1901, Miles retired in 1903. He wrote about the war in a series of articles entitled "The War with Spain," which appeared in the *North American Review* in May, June, and July 1899, and in his memoirs *Serving the Republic: Memoirs of the Civil and Military Life of Nelson A. Miles, Lieutenant-General United States Army* (1911).

MILEY, JOHN DAVID (1862–1899). First lieutenant, Maj. Gen. **William R. Shafter's** aide-de-camp. Shafter's most trusted aide, Miley was present at the **Aserraderos Conference** on 20 June 1898. In his book *In Cuba with Shafter* (1899), he wrote that Shafter had rejected Adm. **William T. Sampson**'s request that the army storm the heights at the harbor entrance of **Santiago, Cuba**. Because Shafter was ill, Miley was sent to the front carrying the orders to begin the attack and to coordinate the 1 July operations that attacked the **San Juan Heights**. On 4 July he met with the foreign consuls stationed at Santiago to hear their request that civilians be allowed to evacuate the city for **El Caney**. Miley served as a commissioner when **Richmond P. Hobson** and others from the *Merrimac* were freed on 6 July in a prisoner exchange. Acting as a commissioner during the negotiations for the **capitulation** of Santiago, Miley favored allowing the Spanish soldiers to retain their arms and signed the **Capitulation of Santiago Agreement** of 16 July 1898. After Santiago formally capitulated on 17 July, Miley, who had been assigned the task of gathering in all the Spanish garrisons in the Division of Santiago, went with a Spanish representative and secured the surrender of six neighboring garrisons at Dos Caminos, El Cristo, Morón, Palma Soriano, San Luis, and Songo.

MILITARY INFORMATION DIVISION (MID), U.S. ARMY. Organized in 1885, the Military Information Division (MID), as part of the **War Department**, was subordinate to the **Adjutant General's Department**. By 1898, the MID, headed by Maj. **Arthur L. Wagner**, had a budget of $40,000 and consisted of 12 officers, ten clerks and two messengers in Washington, D.C., working with 40 officers attached to the **National Guard** and 16 attaches operating abroad in Berlin, London, Madrid, Paris, St. Petersburg, Tokyo, Vienna, and in several Latin American countries. The MID gathered intelligence information, particularly on the Cuban insurgents, and prepared maps and mobilization plans; however, during peace time it did not engage in espionage. During the Spanish-American War, the MID assisted the **Signal Corps** and, attempting to gather intelligence behind enemy lines, sent Lt. **Andrew S. Rowan** to **Cuba**, and Lt. **Henry H. Whitney** and correspondent **Edwin Emerson** to **Puerto Rico**.

MILLET, FRANCIS [FRANK] DAVIS (1846–1912). Correspondent for *Harper's Weekly* and the *Times* (London), Millet, an Englishman and experienced war correspondent, left San Francisco with the third expedition of the **Eighth Corps** on the *Newport* on 27 June 1898. He participated in the 4 July celebrations aboard the *Newport* toasting and speaking on "Nations Friendly to the U.S. and the Queen of England." After arriving in the **Philippines** at the end of July, Millet covered the **Battle of Manila** on 13 August, attended the opening of the **Malolos Congress** on 15 September, and left Manila on 22 September. Subsequently, he wrote *The Expedition to the Philippines* (1899), the best popular work on the Eighth Corps's campaign. In it he wrote that the Filipino insurgents were "extraordinary conceited" and resented the presence of U.S. troops because their presence deprived them of "plundering the rich town of Manila." Moreover, he defended Adm. **George W. Dewey's blockade** regulations, pointing out that only the Germans had protested.

MINES. Although mines were employed by both sides during the war, they were almost universally ineffective or ineffectively used.

Initially the Coast Artillery Corps of the **U.S. Army** mined various U.S. harbors; however, the mines soon caused shipping problems, so the **United States Auxiliary Naval Forces** assisted ships through the minefields. Protests from shipping concerns and the improbability of a Spanish naval attack resulted in their removal beginning in mid-July 1898. The mines were never tested because not one Spanish warship ever attempted an attack on a U.S. port during the war.

Spain attempted to protect its colonial harbors using contact and electrical mines, which could be exploded from a station on shore, and by cannibalizing **torpedoes**, such as the **Whitehead torpedoes**, which were placed at the entrance to **Manila Bay**, **Philippines**. However, many of these mines did not work because of bad fuses and their being thickly overgrown with barnacles and seaweeds in the tropical climate. However, the mining of the entrance to the harbor of **Santiago**, **Cuba**, kept Adm. **William T. Sampson**'s naval forces from storming the harbor's entrance.

MINNEAPOLIS. (USN) **Protected cruiser**, commanded by Capt. Theodore F. Jewell. Built as a commerce destroyer, it was in bad condition when it was assigned to the **Flying Squadron**. During the search for Adm. **Pascual Cervera's Squadron**, the *Minneapolis* captured the Spanish bark *María Dolorosa* off **San Juan**, **Puerto Rico**. On 9 June 1898, it joined the **Northern Patrol Squadron** and was stationed at Newport News, Virginia, to guard the **battleships** being built there. While at Newport News, the *Minneapolis* was under repair from 11 June to 17 August 1898. After the war it served as a training ship until it was decommissioned in 1906. Recommissioned for convoy duty during World War I, it was decommissioned and sold in 1921.

La. 1893, com. 1894, dis. 7,375, hp. 21,000, sp. 21
Armor: d. 2.5″, sl. 4″, ct. 5″
Armament: 1–8″, 2–6″, 8–4″, 12–6pdr., 2–1pdr., 2 C. mgs., 4–18″ tt. (aw.)
Cc. 1,891, comp. 477

MIRS BAY, CHINA. A small bay 25–30 miles east of **Hong Kong**, it was in Chinese territory. When Com. **George W. Dewey** moved his **Asiatic Squadron** from Hong Kong to here on 24–25 April, China, which had not yet declared its neutrality, was too weak to protest. On 25 April, Dewey received his orders informing him that war between the United States and Spain had commenced. After **Oscar F. Williams**, former U.S. Consul at **Manila**, arrived on the morning of 27 April and gave Dewey the latest intelligence information, Dewey's squadron left the bay at 2:00 p.m. for the **Philippines**.

MONADNOCK. (USN) Double-turreted **monitor**, commanded by Capt. William H. Whiting. A sister ship to the *Amphitrite*, *Miantonomoh*, and *Terror*, it was part of the **Pacific Squadron**. Although it was not built for interoceanic travel, it was ordered to **Manila, Philippines**, on 25 June 1898, to reinforce Adm. **George W. Dewey's Asiatic Squadron**. After crossing the Pacific Ocean, it reached Manila on 16 August and joined the Asiatic Squadron. After the war it served in the Far East until it was sold in 1923.

La. 1883, com. 1896, dis. 3,990, hp. 3,000, sp. 11.6
Armor: s. 9″, d. 1.75″, b. 11.5″, t. 7.5″, ct. 7.5″
Armament: 4–10″, 2–4″, 2–6pdr., 2–3pdr., 2–1pdr., 2–37 mm.
Cc. 386, comp. 171

MONITOR. Although Spain had none, the **U.S. Navy** had 13 single-turreted monitors and six double-turreted monitors. The single-turreted monitors, which dated from the Civil War period and carried muzzle-loading smooth-bore guns, were brought into service to protect U.S. harbors, and all except one, which was on the Pacific Coast, were stationed on the Atlantic Coast. The six double-turreted, iron-hulled monitors were highly unreliable at sea. They rolled so quickly that they were poor gun platforms; moreover, their slow speed and poor fuel capacity meant they were usually towed. The *Amphitrite*, *Miantonomoh*, *Puritan*, and *Terror* served in Cuban waters, and the *Monterey* and *Monadnock* journeyed from California to **Manila, Philippines**, to augment Com. **George W. Dewey's Asiatic Squadron**.

MONOCACY. (USN) An antique paddle-wheel steamer that served as a **gunboat**, it was commanded by Comdr. Oscar W. Farenholt. Long stationed in the Far East, it was nicknamed the "Jinricksha of the Navy." It served as a base of procurement at Shanghai, China, for Com. **George W. Dewey's Asiatic Squadron**. Dewey assigned three officers and 50 men from it to fill vacancies throughout his squadron after the purchase of the *Nanshan* and the *Zafiro*. Left behind when the squadron steamed for **Manila**, the *Monocacy* did not participate in the **Battle of Manila Bay** on 1 May 1898. Deemed unfit, it was sold to a Japanese firm in 1903.

La. 1864, com. 1866, dis. 1,370, hp. 850, sp. 11.2
Armament: 6 guns
Comp. 159

MONTEREY. (USN) Double-turreted **monitor**, commanded by Comdr. Eugene H. C. Leutze. The first monitor to be laid down for the new steel navy of the 1880s, it served in the **Pacific Squadron**. Although it was not built for interoceanic travel, it was ordered to **Manila, Philippines**, in late May 1898, to reinforce Adm. **George W. Dewey's Asiatic Squadron**. After leaving San Diego, California, on 11 June, it crossed the Pacific Ocean, under tow by the collier *Brutus* for more than half the voyage, and upon reaching Manila on 4 August, it joined the Asiatic Squadron. During the **Battle of Manila** on 13 August, it was deployed off the city front. After serving in the Far East until 1917, it became a station ship at Pearl Harbor until it was sold in 1922.

La. 1891, com. 1893, dis. 4,084, hp. 5,250, sp. 13.6
Armor: s. 13–5″, d. 3″, t. 8–7.5″, b. 13–11.5″, ct. 10″
Armament: 2–12″, 2–10″, 6–6pdr., 4–1pdr., 2 G. mgs.
Cc. 230, comp. 190

MONTERO RÍOS, EUGENIO (1832–1914). President of the Senate and president of Spain's **Peace Commission** that negotiated the **Treaty of Paris**. One of the most powerful members of Spain's **Liberal Party** and a former minister. Montero Ríos proposed on 8 May 1898, that Spain begin immediate negotiations with the United States to end the war. Prime Minister **Práxedes M. Sagasta** briefly considered his proposal and then rejected it. Upon the signing of the **Armistice Protocol** on 12 August, Montero Ríos remarked that the protocol had "made the catastrophe definitive and irreparable." On 20 September, his article "Quién mató a Meco?" appeared in *El Liberal*. Explaining why Spain had lost the war, Montero Ríos, using Meco in reference to Spain's overwhelming defeat in the war, blamed everyone for Spain's loss in writing "We all killed him." As president of Spain's Peace Commission, he favored offering **Cuba**, the **Philippines**, and **Puerto Rico** free if the United States absorbed all their debts, and was the commission's main strategist in trying to provoke a European intervention and possible arbitration. After receiving his government's order on 25 November to sign the treaty, Montero Ríos protested and offered his resignation rather than continue; however, he was persuaded to continue and signed the treaty. After Sagasta's death he led the Liberal Party and published *El Tratado de Paris* (1904), a compilation of his speeches on the treaty.

MONTGOMERY. (USN) Unprotected **cruiser**, commanded by Comdr. George A. Converse. It was involved in the suppression of **filibustering** expeditions while stationed at **Key West, Florida**, and called on several Cuban ports while the *Maine* was in **Havana**. On 8 March 1898, the *Montgomery* was ordered to Havana to assist the *Maine* court of inquiry. Assigned to the **North Atlantic Squadron** during the war, it escorted the *Panther*, which carried the **First Marine Battalion**, to Key West, Florida. Subsequently, it served on the **blockade of Cuba**, searched for Adm. **Pascual Cervera's Squadron**, participated in the bombardment of **San Juan, Puerto Rico**, on 12 May, and was part of Maj. Gen. **Nelson A. Miles**'s invasion of **Puerto Rico**.

La. 1891, com. 1894, dis. 2,094, hp. 5,400, sp. 19
Armor: d. 5/16″, sl. 7/16″
Armament: 9–5″, 6–6pdr., 2–1pdr., 2 C. mgs., 3–18″ tt. (aw.)
Cc. 340, comp. 274

MONTOJO Y PASARÓN, PATRICIO (1839–1917). Spanish rear admiral defeated by Com. **George W. Dewey** at the **Battle of Manila Bay** on 1 May 1898. Montojo studied in Cádiz, entered the navy in 1852, and served in the **Philippines, Puerto Rico**, and **Cuba**. In 1897, he was awarded the Grand Cross of María Cristina. In a 15 March 1898 conference of commanders, he openly stated that his squadron could not defeat Dewey's squadron or prevent the bombardment of **Manila**. Therefore, Montojo proposed fighting at **Subic Bay**. His suggestion was accepted by Gov.-Gen. **Fernando Primo de Rivera**. On 11 April, he **cabled** Madrid stating, "I am without resources or time." Minister of the Marine **Segismundo Bermejo** responded that deficiencies were to be made up for by "zeal and activity." After his squadron returned from Subic Bay to Manila, Montojo attended a reception in Manila instead of remaining with his squadron the night before the Battle of Manila Bay. During the battle on 1 May, Montojo, on his flagship the *Reina María Cristina*, was wounded in the leg, and after half of his crew was disabled, he ordered the ship to be abandoned and sunk before the magazines could explode. He then transferred his flag to the *Isla de Cuba*.

In September 1898, Montojo was suspended from further military functions and left Manila in October for Spain, where he presented himself on 11 November. Because of the destruction of his squadron he was court-martialed. Along with his counsel, Capt. **Víctor M. Concas**, Montojo defended his decision to fight off **Cavite** on 1 May.

Arguing that Subic Bay was not fortified, he stressed the failure of Spain's government to provide supplies and reinforcements, pointed out that he had anchored off Cavite in order to save Manila from bombardment, and reminded the court that any thought of moving his squadron away from Manila was opposed by governmental authorities. In September 1899, he was convicted and ordered retired from active service, placed on the reserve list, and forbidden to discharge any public duties. A lover of literature, Montojo translated James Fenimore Cooper's *The Two Admirals*, wrote critical essays, a novela, nautical manuals, and technical and literary articles. He wrote about his defeat at the battle of Manila Bay in "El desastre de Cavite, sus causas y sus efectos" *La España Moderna* (1909).

MONTOJO'S SQUADRON. Under the command of Rear Adm. **Patricio Montojo y Pasarón**, the squadron, composed of 1,796 men, consisted of the unprotected **cruiser *Reina María Cristina***, the wooden cruiser *Castilla*, two small cruisers *Isla de Cuba* and *Isla de Luzón*, and the **gunboats *Don Antonio Ulloa*, *Don Juan de Austria*,** and *Marques del Duero*. On 25 April 1898, the squadron left **Manila, Philippines**, at 11:00 p.m. and arrived at **Subic Bay** on 26 April. Finding the defenses unprepared, a council of captains meeting decided to return to Manila. The council considered three options: 1) it rejected a fight at Corregidor because the water was deep, mines were not available, and the land batteries there could only briefly detain Com. **George W. Dewey's Asiatic Squadron**; 2) it also rejected a stand under the batteries protecting Manila because this would subject the city to bombardment; 3) it decided to anchor in the shallow water off **Cavite** in Cañacao Bay under support of a battery at Sangley Point because the shallow water would minimize casualties. After leaving Subic Bay at 10:30 a.m. on 29 April, the squadron returned to Manila Bay and anchored off Cavite. During the **Battle of Manila Bay** on 1 May 1898, the entire squadron was destroyed. Also destroyed were the *General Lezo* and the *Velasco*, two gunboats undergoing repairs at **Bacoor Bay**.

MONTREAL SPY RING. Upon the outbreak of the Spanish-American War, Spain established a spy ring under the direction of **Luis Polo de Bernabé**, former Spanish minister to Washington, D.C., in the Windsor Hotel in Montreal, **Canada**. Ramón Carranza, military attache, and **Juan Du Bosc** arrived from Toronto on 6 May 1898. Throughout the war the U.S. **Secret Service** attempted to break up the ring by sending agents into Canada to conduct counterespionage.

Angel Cabrejo was sent to Victoria, Canada, where, in the guise of a student and chaperon to his sister, he gathered intelligence, and

Carranza hired a Canadian detective agency to recruit agents. Among Carranza's agents were Frank A. Mellor and George Downing. Mellor, a Canadian-born former artilleryman, was arrested by the Secret Service when he tried to enlist in the **Fifth Corps** at **Tampa, Florida**. Downing, who had been a petty officer on the ***Brooklyn***, was arrested in Washington, D.C. and found dead in his jail cell a few days later.

The existence of the spy ring became public in early June when a 26 May incriminating letter by Carranza to his cousin, Adm. Jose Gómez Ymay, was stolen by the Secret Service and leaked to the **press**. In the letter Carranza admitted his spying activities. Polo de Bernabé was expelled in late May, and Du Bosc took over as acting consul general and directed the spy ring. In July Carranza and Du Bosc were expelled, and operations were turned over to Eusebio Bonilla Martel, the new consul general. Although the Secret Service believed it had effectively smashed the ring, from 23 May to 21 September 1898, 70 messages were sent from Montreal to Madrid. The messages not only revealed contacts in Washington, D.C., but contained accurate information on the departure of the Fifth Corps from Tampa, Florida, and its landing near **Santiago, Cuba**, reported there would be no land attack in **Cuba** until Adm. **Pascual Cervera's Squadron** was destroyed, and identified **Puerto Rico** as a target for invasion.

MONTSERRAT. A 6,932-ton steamer of the **Transatlantic Company** commanded by Capt. Manuel Deschamps. One of the finest steamers of the line, it was taken over for use during the war and armed. Deschamps was lionized in the Spanish **press** because his ship, which carried supplies and troops, ran the U.S. **blockade** of **Cienfuegos, Havana**, and **Matanzas, Cuba**, before returning to Spain.

MOORE, JOHN BASSETT (1860–1947). Assistant secretary of state and secretary to the U.S. **Peace Commission** that negotiated the **Treaty of Paris**. Moore was a Democrat, professor, and prominent scholar of international law at Columbia University in New York City. He assisted the U.S. government on questions of international law and opposed the recognition of the **Cuban Republic** and the granting of **belligerent rights** to the Cuban insurgents in "The Question of Cuban Belligerency" *Forum* (May 1896). **William R. Day**, upon becoming secretary of state at the end of April 1898, appointed Moore as assistant secretary of state.

On 9 May, Moore drafted a memorandum that was the earliest U.S. definition of its peace terms. The memorandum called for Spain to evacuate **Cuba**, demanded the cession of **Puerto Rico** as an "indemnity," and proposed that the United States acquire a coaling station in the **Philippines** or in the Caroline Islands. It was passed on to President **William McKinley**. Later he prepared a draft of peace terms for the **Armistice Protocol**, which regarded the Philippines as a "practical possession" of the United States. His draft did not survive the cabinet's scrutiny, and it was decided to put off any decision on the Philippines. During the negotiations of the Treaty of Paris, Moore drafted many of the articles of the treaty. After the war he wrote "International Law in the War with Spain" *Review of Reviews* (May 1899) and "Maritime Law in the War with Spain" *Political Science Quarterly* (September 1900), which justified the legality of American actions during the war and the subsequent negotiations.

MORET Y PRENDERGAST, SEGISMUNDO (1838–1913). Spain's colonial minister. The **Liberal Party**'s most outspoken proponent of **autonomy** for **Cuba**, Moret, a lawyer and economist, was educated in England, served six times in cabinet offices, and was considered one of Spain's leading experts in foreign affairs. On 4 October 1897, he became colonial minister in the government of **Práxedes M. Sagasta** and was the architect of the autonomy decrees of November 1897. Because he considered a war with the United States as hopeless, he attempted to convince European governments to mediate U.S.-Spanish disagreements over Cuba. Although rejecting the offers by U.S. financiers to pay off Cuba's debt in exchange for the island's independence, Moret favored responding positively to President **William McKinley's Ultimatum** of 27 March 1898, believing an armistice would give Spain more time to resolve the Cuban situation.

After Spain's early defeats in the war, Moret came under attack for having urged concessions to the United States prior to the war. On 15 May, he was dropped from the cabinet and replaced by Vicente Romero Girón. Consulted by Sagasta in early August as his government moved to sign the **Armistice Protocol**, Moret approved of such action, provided the settlement only included Cuba and **Puerto Rico**. After Sagasta's death, Moret led the Liberal Party and served as prime minister.

MORGAN, JOHN TYLER (1824–1907). Democratic senator from Alabama and member of the Senate Foreign Relations Committee. Formerly a Confederate brigadier general, Morgan was an ardent expansionist. He introduced resolutions recognizing the **belligerent rights** of the Cuban insurgents and Cuban independence. After his resolutions passed the Senate, they were shelved by House Speaker **Thomas B. Reed**. On 12 March 1897, in a letter to the *New York Journal*, Morgan wrote that if he were president he "would bombard Havana" and that **Cuba** should become an American colony. On 16

March 1898, he introduced a resolution for the annexation of **Hawaii**.
After the war he voted for the **Treaty of Paris**, believing the United
States should retain the **Philippines** because of its trade potential and
its possible future use to alleviate U.S. racial problems by allowing
U.S. blacks to emigrate there.

MOROTE Y GREUS, LUIS (1862–1913). Spanish **republican** journalist and writer. Previously decorated by the army for his actions in
combat in North Africa, Morote, who wrote for *El Liberal*, went to
Cuba, and in February 1897 interviewed Cuban insurgent Maj. Gen.
Máximo Gómez. Gómez had him detained as a spy, and upon being
freed, Gov.-Gen. **Valeriano Weyler** wanted him court-martialed. A
deputy in the **Cortes** in 1898, Morote responded to Spain's defeat in
the war by writing *La moral de la derrota* (1900) and later wrote
Sagasta, Melilla, Cuba (1908).

MORRO CASTLE, SANTIAGO, CUBA. Located 260 feet above sea
level on heights on the eastern side of the harbor entrance, the for-
tress, which was called a "castle," dated from the sixteenth century
and was commanded by Comdr. of Infantry Antonio Ros. It was defended by a battery of seven muzzle-loading rifled bronze guns and
howitzers, which bore dates in the 1700s, and three companies totaling 411 soldiers. Along with **Socapa**, it was the main objective of
U.S. naval bombardments. Consequently, during the siege of **Santiago, Cuba**, the Morro area sustained total casualties of four killed
and 84 wounded.

**"MOSQUITO SQUADRON." See UNITED STATES AUXILIARY
NAVAL FORCES**

MOTION PICTURES. The Spanish-American War was the first U.S.
war to be captured in motion pictures, and although the first commercial cinema appeared in Spain in 1896, geographical distance and lack
of control of the sea precluded films on the war from reaching Spanish audiences during the war. Shortly after the explosion of the *Maine*
on 15 February 1898, Albert E. Smith and James Stuart Blackton of
Vitagraph Pictures filmed a Spanish flag being torn down from a
flagpole and replaced with the Stars and Stripes. Shown throughout
the upper East Coast to vaudeville audiences, the one-minute "Tearing Down the Spanish Flag" was a sensation. The Edison Company
followed with similar scenes as well as footage of the sunken *Maine*.
Both studios filmed the funeral parade and burial of the ship's victims.

After the U.S. declared war, Edison, Vitagraph, and Biograph studios filmed scenes of soldiers and sailors training, in battle, and returning home. Some scenes were authentic, whereas others were staged, and a flood of spurious films filled the insatiable demand of vaudeville audiences. Two Biograph cameramen accompanied **William R. Hearst** to **Cuba**, but their film was lost. Smith and Blackton filmed the **Fifth Corps** at **Tampa, Florida,** accompanied the Fifth Corps to **Santiago,** and filmed the **Rough Riders**'s charge during the **Battle of Kettle Hill** on 1 July. Their footage was put together in the 30-minute "Fighting with Our Boys in Cuba." After returning to New York in July, Smith and Blackton, who had told people they had filmed the **Naval Battle of Santiago** of 3 July, secretly shot a staged naval battle on the roof of the Morse Building in New York City with toy boats, dashes of gunpowder, and tobacco smoke. The two-minute "The Battle of Santiago," which cost $1.98 to produce, was an instant success. In a similar fashion, they also produced "The Battle of Manila Bay," starring the **cruiser** *New Orleans*, which had been stationed in the United States and Caribbean during the war. The popularity of such Spanish-American War films continued into 1899 and then quickly died out.

MÜLLER Y TEJEIRO, JOSÉ. Lieutenant, second in command of Spain's naval forces at **Santiago, Cuba.** From 19 May to 17 July 1898, he kept a war diary, which was compiled into a book by 10 August 1898 and published as *Combates y capitulación de Santiago de Cuba* (1898) and translated by the **Office of Naval Intelligence** and published as *Battles and Capitulation of Santiago de Cuba* (1899). In his book Müller blamed the U.S. government and the **jingoes** for using the **Cuban Revolt** as a pretext for the war and defended the spreading out of Spanish forces by Lt. Gen. **Arsenio Linares.** Because no outside help could be expected because of U.S. command of the sea and insurgent control of the countryside, the army, which could not move to another city, had to protect its food and water supply. He believed the **Naval Battle of Santiago** on 3 July was futile but it was "the greatest act of valor imaginable." While poignantly expressing the situation of poorly fed and paid Spanish soldiers, he harshly criticized the merchants of Santiago for hoarding supplies for their own financial gain and cowardly fleeing to **El Caney** as refugees on 5 July.

MUÑOCISTAS. Term applied to followers of **Luis Muñoz Rivera.** They favored **autonomy** and linkage with Spain's **Liberal Party.** They won 24 seats in the 32-member parliament in the 27 March 1898 parliamentary elections in **Puerto Rico.**

MUÑOZ RIVERA, LUIS (1859–1915). Leader of the Puerto Rican **Liberal-Fusionist Party** and editor of *La Democracia*. At various times in his political career he endorsed **autonomy**, commonwealth status, independence, and statehood; however, prior to the Spanish-American War, he supported a merger with Spain's **Liberal Party** and advocated for autonomy. Upon the outbreak of the war, Muñoz Rivera, a cabinet member in the **autonomous government**, exhorted his countrymen to support Spain. At the opening of the autonomous parliament on 17 July 1898, he exclaimed: "We are Spaniards, and wrapped in the Spanish flag we will die." However, his request that the people be armed to fight the United States was refused by Gov.-Gen. **Manuel Macías y Casado**. When he saw Maj. Gen. **Nelson A. Miles**'s proclamation of 27 July, Muñoz Rivera changed sides and supported the invading American forces. After the war, Muñoz Rivera, while serving as the president of the autonomous cabinet, which was allowed to continue by U.S. military authorities, called for a brief U.S. military occupation, founded the Federal Party, and favored statehood for Puerto Rico.

—N—

NANSHAN. A 5,059-ton British steamer, it was purchased by Com. **George W. Dewey** on 6 April 1898, in **Hong Kong**. Dewey assigned one U.S. officer, Lt. W. B. Hodges, to command while retaining its British captain and mainly Chinese crew. During the war it served as a collier in the **Asiatic Squadron** and was armed with 1–6pdr. gun. After the war it continued to serve in the Pacific and was sold in 1922.

NASHVILLE. (USN) **Gunboat**, commanded by Comdr. Washburn Maynard. A two-masted and two-funneled gunboat, it was assigned to the **North Atlantic Squadron** and fired the first shot of the war when it captured the Spanish lumber craft *Buenaventura* on 22 April 1898. Days later, while serving on **blockade** duty off **Cienfuegos** and **Havana**, **Cuba**, the *Nashville* captured the Spanish steamers *Pedro* and *Argonauta*. Because of its participation in the 11 May engagement at Cienfuegos, 19 of its sailors and seven of its **marines** were awarded the **Congressional Medal of Honor**. After the war it was ordered to the Asiatic Station. Sold in 1921, it was converted into a barge and was scrapped in 1957.

La. 1895, com. 1897, dis. 1,371, hp. 2,530, sp. 16.3
Armor: d. 5/16″, s. 3/8″
Armament: 8–4″, 4–6pdr., 2–1pdr.
Cc. 395, comp. 180

NATIONAL GUARD, UNITED STATES. Composed of 45 independent state militia organizations totaling 115,627 men, of whom 9,376 were officers, the National Guard units were under the control of the governors of the respective states. Because the governors viewed any federal control as a states-rights issue, the guard lacked a coordinating organization. Consisting of mostly infantry with a scattering of cavalry and artillery, most units were under strength, poorly trained and equipped, and usually functioned as social clubs.

Deeply involved in politics, the guard opposed the **Hull Bill** to enlarge the regular army, and after conferences with the **McKinley administration**, a compromise was worked out in the 22 April 1898 volunteer army bill. While the guard retained its organizations and the governors their powers of appointment, the president could appoint high commanders; moreover, units were permitted to be sworn in en masse, retaining their officers. When President **William McKinley** issued his call for 125,000 **volunteers** on 23 April, the number nearly equaled the entire enlisted strength of the guard. A later call on 25 May for 75,000 volunteers brought the total to 200,000, a number designed to accept all prewar guardsmen willing to enlist.

Equipped with .45-caliber **Springfield rifles**, most states mobilized their volunteers around their guard units; however, Maine and Rhode Island established new regiments and recruited individual guardsmen from other units to fill their ranks. John W. Leedy, **Populist Party** governor of Kansas, unlike other governors, ignored the **War Department**'s instructions and bypassed the state's guard units and recognized units organized by citizens throughout the state. Electing their own captains and lieutenants, most guard units accepted service. However, some did not, the most important case being that of the Seventh New York, one of the best units, which objected to being commanded by West Pointers. Consequently, it remained home during the war.

Many units, such as the First Missouri, which showed up without shoes and socks, arrived in **camps** poorly equipped. Towns sent delegations and doctors to the camps to check on their soldiers, some assigned newspaper reporters to enlist and go with the units even though prohibited by law, and many soldiers openly wrote to their local newspapers about everything. However, most of the units never saw action. Of the more than 200,000 men who were mobilized in 140 state-sponsored regiments, only some 35,000 were sent overseas or even included in units that had been assigned to overseas duty when the **Armistice Protocol** was signed on 12 August. Although a few units performed occupation duty in **Cuba** and **Puerto Rico** after the war, most returned home and were mustered out during the fall and winter of 1898.

NAVAL MILITIA, UNITED STATES. Totaling 4,445 petty officers and enlisted men, it was organized in 17 states: California, Connecticut, Florida, Georgia, Illinois, Louisiana, Maryland, Massachusetts, Michigan, New Jersey, New York, North Carolina, Ohio, Pennsylvania, Rhode Island, South Carolina, and Virginia. Under the jurisdiction of the assistant secretary of the navy, who dealt with the governors and adjutants general of the various states, its duty was to man the coast and harbor defense vessels; thus, it freed the regular navy to go to sea.

Initially called on in March 1898, 1,600 of its men served on single-turret **monitors**, tugs, and **yachts**, which patrolled **mine**fields and provided personnel for the coastal signal service. Subsequently, 2,600 of its men were mustered into the regular navy. The Illinois militia furnished the largest number, 19 officers and 709 enlisted men, who served on 58 vessels in Cuban waters. The New Jersey militia furnished 34 officers and 373 men, of whom 20 officers and 261 men served on the *Badger* and *Resolute*. Men from the Maryland, Massachusetts, Michigan, and New York naval militias served as officers and men on the merchant steamers *Dixie*, *Prairie*, *Yankee*, and *Yosemite*.

NAVAL WAR BOARD (23 MARCH 1898–24 AUGUST 1898). Stemming from ad hoc groups that had developed war plans, it was organized by Secretary of the Navy **John D. Long** to serve as his advisory body. Without orders or specific authority, it first formally met on 23 March 1898. Its initial membership consisted of **Theodore Roosevelt** (president of the board and assistant secretary of the navy), Capt. **Arnet S. Crowninshield** (chief of the Bureau of Navigation), and Capt. **Albert S. Barker** of the naval secretary's office. After Roosevelt resigned to join the **Rough Riders** and Barker was sent to command the *Newark*, Long appointed Rear Adm. **Montgomery Sicard** as president of the board and called Capt. **Alfred T. Mahan** back to active duty to serve on the board. Although Long kept the board's formal powers vague, he accepted most of its advice in ordering major naval movements throughout the war. In March the board enunciated the basic principle that governed U.S. naval operations through the war: the concentration of the navy's forces against **Cuba** and **Puerto Rico** and the conduction of operations against Spain only after the defeat of Spain's naval forces in the Caribbean. Although Mahan recommended the abolition of the board in May and its replacement by one officer, the board continued throughout the war until its adjournment on 24 August.

NAVAL WAR COLLEGE. Established in 1884 at Newport, Rhode Island, it began planning for a possible war against Spain when in 1894 students took the question of war with Spain as a training problem. While one group discussed strategy for a war in which the United States and **France** were allied against **Great Britain** and Spain, and another considered a war of the United States against Spain, Lt. Comdr. **Charles J. Train** developed a comprehensive plan.

An 1895 plan entitled "Situation in the Case of War with Spain" was sent to the navy early in 1896. It considered three options: 1) a direct attack by the United States against Spain was deemed risky and unduly expensive; 2) an attack against Spain's possessions in the Pacific, although inexpensive and safe, would not bring the enemy to terms; and 3) an attack against **Cuba** and **Puerto Rico**, even though it might not end the war, would place the burden of continuing the war on Spain while U.S. land forces would seize **Havana, Cuba. Key West, Florida**, would serve as the advance naval base and **Tampa, Florida**, would be the principal port of embarkation for an advance corps of 30,000 regulars and 250,000 **volunteers**.

In 1896 when the War College was unsatisfied with the **Kimball Plan**, other options were considered and summarized by Capt. **Henry C. Taylor**, who was president of the Naval War College from 1893 to 1896. In the summer of 1897, another plan was crafted which emphasized American **coastal defense** to counter possible Spanish operations against the eastern coast of the United States, advocated the concentration of U.S. naval forces to defeat any naval force that Spain would send to the West Indies, and recommended assisting the Philippine insurgents.

NAVY, SPAIN. Under the overall command of the Minister of the Marine **Segismundo Bermejo y Merelo** until mid-May 1898 and then **Ramón Auñón y Villalón**, Spain's navy was, on paper, the world's seventh largest, ranked just behind the **U.S. Navy**. Its engineers had produced the first practical submarine and first **torpedo-boat destroyer**, and its merchant marine was the world's fifth largest at more than 200 ships. In 1898 the navy had one **battleship**: the *Pelayo*; six **armored cruisers**: the *Almirante Oquendo, Cristóbal Colón, Emperador Carlos V, Infanta María Teresa, Vizcaya*, and *Princesa de Asturias*; five **protected cruisers**; ten unprotected **cruisers**; 19 **torpedo boats**; ten torpedo **gunboats**; six torpedo-boat destroyers; two obsolete iron cruisers; two large wooden cruisers; 11 small cruisers; two dispatch boats; 23 gunboats; and six gun vessels.

Based on a conscriptive system, the navy's personnel consisted of regular and reserve forces, totaling around 15,000 officers and men, which included 830 line officers on the active list, 127 line officers on the reserve list, 90 engineer officers, 252 pay officers, 127 medical officers, and 14,000 warrant officers and seamen. Also, there was a corps of marine infantry of 451 officers and 8,500 men; however, it served in the insular possessions and not aboard ships.

The navy's problems exceeded its attributes. Because its building and repair yards were either closed or poorly equipped, Spain was forced to purchase and repair many of its ships in foreign shipyards. Moreover, there was an almost total absence of general target practice, drill was neglected, and munitions and equipment were frequently lacking or faulty. Despite the purchase of a few ships from **Germany** and **Great Britain** prior to the war, they were not ready for service until mid-May, and although Spain's merchant fleet contributed 154 ships for wartime use, most were not quickly readied for service.

Upon the outbreak of the Spanish-American War, it was divided into two fleets. One remained in home waters and included the *Pelayo*, and the other was Adm. **Pascual Cervera's Squadron**. In mid-June the home fleet was divided as Adm. **Manuel Cámara's Squadron** was ordered to the **Philippines**. During the navy's disastrous defeats suffered at the **Battle of Manila Bay** on 1 May and the **Naval Battle of Santiago** on 3 July, captains were under general naval orders to fight honorably; however, if defeated, they were to direct their ships to shore and scuttle them to prevent the enemy from taking possession. Total naval losses in the war included 14 cruisers and a large number of smaller vessels, and combat casualties of about 500 killed and 300–400 wounded.

NAVY, UNITED STATES. Under the overall command of the Secretary of the Navy **John D. Long**, the navy, which was the sixth largest in the world, consisted of four first-class **battleships**: the *Indiana*, *Iowa*, *Massachusetts*, and *Oregon*; one second-class battleship: the *Texas*; two **armored cruisers**: the *Brooklyn* and *New York*; 14 **protected cruisers**; 15 small **cruisers**; one wooden cruiser; one dynamite cruiser: the *Vesuvius*; six double-turreted **monitors**; 13 single-turreted monitors; 15 **torpedo boats**; 16 **gunboats**; one dispatch boat; and one harbor defense ram: the *Katahdin*. Prior to and during the war 123 vessels were added to the navy by purchase or charter. They included five warships, 15 revenue cutters, 11 fast auxiliary cruisers, 28 armed **yachts**, 27 armed tugs, 19 colliers, one **hospital ship**, five supply and one repair ship, four lighthouse tenders, and two steamers from the U.S. Fisheries Commission. Totaling 196 ships, the wartime navy consisted of 73 fighting ships and 123 auxiliaries. Consisting of 1,232 officers and 11,750 enlisted men upon the outbreak of the war, the navy doubled in size during the war to 2,088 officers and 24,123 enlisted men, including the **marines** and the **naval militia**.

In April 1898, the navy was divided into the **Northern Patrol**

Squadron under the command of Com. **John A. Howell, United States Auxiliary Naval Forces, Pacific Squadron, Flying Squadron** under the command of Com. **Winfield S. Schley, North Atlantic Squadron** under the command of Adm. **Willliam T. Sampson**, and **Asiatic Squadron** under the command of Com. **George W. Dewey**. Although there was a complete lack of landing craft and no joint operations with the **U.S. Army** had been conducted since the Civil War, the navy won overwhelming victories at the **Battle of Manila Bay** on 1 May and the **Naval Battle of Santiago** on 3 July, and took control of the sea from the beginning of the war. Total casualties sustained during the war included 85 killed, of which 29 were from injuries and 56 from disease. Only 18 were killed in battle or died subsequently from their wounds, and 68 were wounded.

NAVY DEPARTMENT, UNITED STATES. Directed by Secretary of the Navy **John D. Long**, and assisted by **Theodore Roosevelt** until he resigned and was replaced by Charles H. Allen in May 1898, the department, dissatisfied with the **Kimball Plan** and the war plan by Capt. **Henry C. Taylor**, convened an ad hoc group of planners that developed a war plan on 17 December 1896. Supported by Rear Adm. Francis M. Ramsey, who strongly opposed the activities of the **Naval War College**, the plan assumed a war only against Spain, emphasized the establishment of a **blockade** against **Cuba** and **Puerto Rico**, placed greater stress on providing the Cuban insurgents with assistance, proposed that the **Asiatic Squadron** proceed to European waters where it would join the European Squadron and, operating from a base seized in the Canary Islands, they would engage Spain's navy in Spanish waters and operate against commerce. Reconsidered in June 1897, the plan was revised. A naval attack on the **Philippines** was restored, and although the plan retained the idea of sending a squadron to Spanish waters, it also provided for the early capture of Puerto Rico. If the United States went to war against both Spain and **Japan**, then defensive operations would be conducted to protect **Hawaii** and the west coast of the United States.

Assisted by the **Office of Naval Intelligence** the Navy Department ordered Comdr. Willard H. Brownson to Europe, where he used $19 million of the **U.S. Navy**'s $29 million from the **Fifty Million Dollar Bill** of 9 March 1898 to purchase the *Albany* and the *New Orleans*. The department also conducted intelligence-gathering operations through its attachés, who were stationed abroad, and by sending special agents Ens. **William H. Buck** and **Henry H. Ward** to Europe to monitor Adm. **Manuel Cámara's Squadron**. Moreover, the department, through the orders of Assistant Secretary Charles Allen, conducted a **disinformation** campaign.

NEUTRAL RIGHTS. Because neither Spain nor the United States had allies during the war, the rights of neutrals was a key legal principle during the war, particularly in naval incidents involving the *Adria* and the *Wanda*.

According to international law, belligerent ships of war had to vacate neutral ports in time of war. **Great Britain**'s declaration of neutrality forced Com. **George W. Dewey's Asiatic Squadron** to leave **Hong Kong**, and French and Dutch neutrality affected Adm. **Pascual Cervera's Squadron** at **Martinique** and **Curaçao**. Moreover, each power that declared itself neutral adopted measures of its own. **Japan**, which proclaimed a strict neutrality on 30 April 1898, restricted both Japanese subjects and foreigners resident in the empire by not permitting them to obtain letters of marque or commission for capturing merchantmen by means of privateers. And they could not accept service in the armed forces of Spain or the United States, sell, charter, purchase, or equip ships, or supply arms or ammunition for either power. Also, no man-of-war or other ship of the belligerents could commit any act of war, visit, search, or capture merchantmen in Japanese waters. Although they could only obtain the necessary supplies to take the ship to the nearest non-Japanese port, they could not stay in Japanese ports longer than 24 hours, and if ships from the belligerent powers were in port at the same time, one was not allowed to leave until 24 hours after the other's departure.

Both the United States and Spain honored the 1856 Declaration of Paris, which outlawed privateering and maintained that neutral flags covered enemy goods, except for contraband. Noncontraband items, belonging to a neutral and being carried in an enemy ship, were not subject to confiscation. In Spain's **declaration of war** on 23 April 1898, Spain, while allowing U.S. vessels in Spanish harbors five days to leave beginning 24 April, proclaimed that a neutral flag protected the enemy's goods except contraband, which was broadly defined as including firearms, explosives, military equipment, and machinery used in servicing warships. On 26 April, President **William McKinley** issued a proclamation on neutral shipping. Like Spain, he proclaimed that a neutral flag protected the enemy's goods except contraband and then broadly defined contraband. However, the United States allowed enemy merchant shipping 30 days from 21 April to leave U.S. ports, restricting them in that they could not transport members of the armed forces or carry contraband, and could load coal and travel to their home ports.

NEW ORLEANS. (USN) **Protected cruiser**, commanded by Capt. William M. Folger. Formerly the *Amazonas*, it was built in **Great Britain** for the Brazilian navy and was the sister ship of the *Albany*. It was purchased by the **U.S. Navy** from the Brazilian government for $1,429,215 on 16 March 1898, and a reassigned U.S. crew from the **cruiser** *San Francisco* sailed it to New York City, where it arrived on 13 April. After refitting, it joined the **Flying Squadron** from 8 May until 24 May and then served on the **blockade** of **Santiago, Cuba**, bombarding Santiago in early June and shelling **Daiquirí** prior to the landing of the **Fifth Corps** on 22 June. Sent to **Key West, Florida**, on 29 June for repairs, it missed the **Naval Battle of Santiago** on 3 July. On 14 July, it relieved the *Yosemite* as the sole blockading ship off **San Juan, Puerto Rico**, and then shot up the beached *Antonio López* on 16 July. It was then assigned to the **Eastern Squadron**. After the war, it entered San Juan, Puerto Rico, on 29 August, landed U.S. officials, and hosted an onboard party for Puerto Ricans on 20 September. Decommissioned in 1922, it was sold in 1930.

La. 1896, com. March 18, 1898, dis. 3,427, hp. 7,500, sp. 20
Armor: d. 1.5″, sl. 3.5″, ct. 4″
Armament: 6–6″, 4–4.7″, 10–6pdr., 8–1pdr., 3–18″ tt. (aw.)
Cc. 747, comp. 366

NEW YORK. (USN) **Armored cruiser**, commanded by Capt. **French E. Chadwick**. The premier **cruiser** of the new **U.S. Navy**, it set a world speed record at its trials. During the war it served as the flagship of Rear Adm. **William T. Sampson** in the **North Atlantic Squadron**. On 22 April the *New York* captured the steamer *Pedro* and then shelled a supposedly fortified area near **Matanzas, Cuba**, on 27 April. On 12 May it bombarded **San Juan, Puerto Rico**. Although it was not involved in the initial part of the **Naval Battle of Santiago** on 3 July, because Adm. Sampson was going to meet with Maj. Gen. **William R. Shafter**, it quickly turned around as Adm. **Pascual Cervera's Squadron** emerged at 9:35 a.m. After firing only four shots during the battle, it finished the battle near the *Cristóbal Colón* when the *Colón* ran ashore west of Santiago. Michael Quinlan, while serving on board as a printer, published his own history of the war, *The Spanish American War* (1898). After the war the *New York* served in the **Philippines**, was renamed twice, decommissioned in 1933, and stricken in 1938. It was scuttled at **Subic Bay, Philippines**, in December 1941 to avoid capture by the Japanese.

La. 1891, com. 1893, dis. 8,200, hp. 17,000, sp. 21
Armor: s. 4″, d. 3″, sl. 6″, t. 5.5″, b. 10–5″, ct. 7.5″
Armament: 6–8″, 12–4″, 8–6pdr., 2–1pdr., 2 C. mgs., 2–14″ tt. (aw.)
Cc. 1,290, comp. 566

NEW YORK HERALD. A New York City newspaper, the *Herald* was the favorite newspaper of the wealthy and the chief competition of the *New York Journal* and *New York World*. A conservative pro-**Republican Party** newspaper that initially was anti-interventionist, it had its own news service, which was used by the *Boston Herald*, *Chicago Times-Herald*, and *San Francisco Chronicle*, and a circulation of 100,000 in 1897.

Prior to the war, the *Herald*'s **correspondents** in **Cuba**, including **George B. Rea** and Walter S. Meriwether, did not have serious problems with Spanish authorities because the *Herald* was not strongly opposed to Spanish rule in Cuba. Moreover, it gave **autonomy** a chance to succeed, and while urging caution over the **Autonomy Riots** of 12 January 1898, it accused irresponsible *jingo* newspapers of trying to lead the United States into a war against Spain. Subsequently, the *Herald* took a conservative position on both the **De Lôme Letter** and the *Maine* disaster. However, by March its position changed. On 12 March it stated the *Maine* was "Wrecked by Mine—McKinley Knows," and on 2 April, it favored U.S. military action over Cuba.

During the war the *Herald* had about 30 correspondents in the field, and its **press boats**, including the *Golden Rod* and the *Sommers N. Smith*, covered the Caribbean theater. Its correspondents, based on a worldwide network of stringers, frequently outperformed U.S. intelligence agencies, particularly in following Adm. **Pascual Cervera's Squadron**. Although William F. Halstead, a Canadian *Herald* correspondent in **Puerto Rico,** was imprisoned on 14 March 1898 for spying, other *Herald* correspondents assisted the U.S. war effort. Fred O. Somerford carried out intelligence work in maintaining a liaison with Cuban insurgent Maj. Gen. **Máximo Gómez**, Harry Brown was at **Guantánamo, Cuba**, with the **First Marine Battalion**, **Richard H. Davis** fought in the **Battle of Las Guásimas** on 24 June, and **Joseph L. Stickney** served as Com. **George W. Dewey**'s aide during the **Battle of Manila Bay** on 1 May.

NEW YORK JOURNAL. A New York City newspaper owned by **William R. Hearst**, the *Journal* was a pro-**Democratic Party** newspaper with its own news service, which was used by the *Chicago Tribune* and the *San Francisco Examiner*. Its sensationalist reporting, epitomized by the **Evangelina Cisneros Incident**, the *Olivette* **Incident**, and the **Ruíz Incident**, and its ardent support of the Cuban insurgents and U.S. intervention in **Cuba** in editorials, fallacious reporting, and the cartoons of Homer W. Davenport made it a vital part of the **"yellow press."**

The first paper to attempt to use a **press boat** to evade Spanish censors, the *Journal* propagandized the prewar Cuban insurgent cause as **Ralph D. Paine** attempted to deliver a lavish *Journal* sword to

Cuban insurgent Maj. Gen. **Máximo Gómez**, and Frederick Lawrence, a former police court reporter in San Francisco, made up accounts of false insurgent victories and Amazons riding with the insurgent cavalry in combat. Moreover, it consistently depicted Spanish policy in Cuba as barbaric, stridently opposed **autonomy** as a scheme, called the **De Lôme Letter** "The Worst Insult to the United States in Its History" on 9 February 1898, and immediately blamed Spain for the *Maine* explosion, claiming on 17 February that an "Enemy's Secret Infernal Machine" had split the *Maine* in two. By 18 February its circulation rose to 1,025,664, and weeks before the release of the report on the *Maine* investigation, it claimed on 11 March, "The court of inquiry finds that the Spanish government officials blew up the Maine." Openly advocating a war against Spain for the liberation of Cuba, the *Journal* conducted its own opinion polls to bolster its views, paid for the *Anita Expedition* of congressmen to visit Cuba in March, and excoriated President **William McKinley** for his diplomatic efforts to resolve the Cuban situation.

During the Spanish-American War, the *Journal* sold over a million papers a day while spending more money than any other paper in covering the war. It maintained 50 **correspondents** in the field and ten press boats. Among the correspondents covering Cuba were **James Creelman**, **Burr McIntosh**, and **David Edward Marshall**. Douglas White covered the campaign of the **Eighth Corps** at **Manila**, **Philippines**, and **Stephen Crane** covered the **Puerto Rican campaign**.

While asking on 9 May "How Do You Like the *Journal's* War?", Hearst hired a special train and sent Henry J. Pain, the "Fireworks King," on a nationwide tour with his show to support the war effort, accused the *New York Herald* and *New York World* of treason in an 11 July editorial for criticizing the government's management of the war, and engaged in fraudulent war reporting, claiming on 21 May that the **Fifth Corps** was "About to Strike the Death Blow," that the U.S. fleet was victorious on 7 June even though no battle had occurred, and that **Santiago, Cuba**, had been taken on 10 June even though no U.S. troops had landed in the area.

After the signing of the **Armistice Protocol** on 12 August, the *Journal* funded the 20 August celebration when Adm. **William T. Sampson**'s fleet arrived in New York City, advocated retaining the **Philippines**, harshly criticized the **War Department**'s treatment of soldiers, even labeling Secretary of War **Russell A. Alger** a murderer. On 23 December, after interviewing Maj. Gen. **Nelson A. Miles**, the *Journal* headlined "Miles Makes Grave Charges Against Administration—Poisons Used in Beef Made the Soldiers Ill," which propagan-

dized what came to be known as the **"Embalmed Beef"**
Controversy.

NEW YORK SUN. A New York City newspaper, the *Sun*, under the
editorship of Charles A. Dana until 1897, ardently supported the
Cuban insurgents. With a circulation of 150,000, it developed the
"human interest" story, and although not a member of **Associated**
Press, it had its own news service, which was used by the *San Fran-*
cisco Chronicle and the *New Orleans Times-Democrat*. An avowedly
jingo newspaper, the *Sun* disparaged Spain's **autonomy** policy, and
after the passage of the congressional resolution of 19 April 1898,
authorizing the use of force in **Cuba**, it editorialized "We are all
jingoes now; and the head jingo is the Hon. William McKinley, the
trusted and honored Chief Executive of the nation's will."

During the war the *Sun* maintained 13 **correspondents** in the field,
and its **press boats**—the *Kanapaha* and *Hercules*—covered the war
in the Caribbean; moreover, it had one correspondent on the *New*
York and one on the *Brooklyn* during the **Santiago, Cuba, cam-**
paign. John R. Spears, a *Sun* correspondent, later wrote *Our Navy in*
the War with Spain (1898), and **Oscar K. Davis** covered the campaign of the **Eighth Corps** at **Manila, Philippines**. In support of the
annexation of **Hawaii**, on 1 June the *Sun* argued "To maintain our
flag in the Philippines, we must raise our flag in Hawaii."

NEW YORK TIMES. A New York City newspaper under the direction
of Adolph S. Ochs, the *Times*, with a circulation in 1897 of less than
25,000, did not compete with the **"yellow press"**; instead, it claimed
it printed just "strictly news." On 16 February 1898, it declared that
the cause of the *Maine* explosion was undetermined and that it was
probably caused by an accident. On 25 February, it harshly criticized
the "yellow press" coverage of the *Maine*, hoping that a law could be
passed to prevent what it termed "freak journalism," and on 28 February it carried a front-page banner exclaiming "No Evidence the
Ship Was Destroyed by Design." However, on 1 April, after the
Maine report was released, it declared that the United States could
not afford to take "a backward step in regard to Spain"; subsequently,
on 12 April, it praised President **William McKinley's War Message**
to **Congress**.

During the war the *Times*, on 20 July, blamed the Cubans for wors-
ening Cuban-U.S. relations and stated that the insurgents wanted to
sack **Santiago, Cuba**, thereby justifying Maj. Gen. **William R. Shaf-**
ter's excluding them from the city. While providing extensive coverage on the **Puerto Rican campaign** through reporters such as
William Whitelock, it editorialized in favor of taking and retaining

Puerto Rico. Amos K. Fiske, a business writer on its editorial page, advocated American colonization of Puerto Rico on 11 July, writing "It is fortunate for Puerto Rico that Spanish outrages in Cuba have brought about an intervention which will rescue both islands at once." On 27 July, the paper was against immediate self-rule by Puerto Ricans because it was the duty of the United States to instruct them in their civic duties.

NEW YORK TRIBUNE. A New York City newspaper published by **Whitelaw Reid**, the *Tribune* was the leading pro-**Republican Party** newspaper in the nation with a circulation in 1897 around 75,000 and supported the **McKinley administration**. On 19 November 1897, it predicted Cuban **autonomy** would not equal Canada's because the Cubans were not as fit as the Canadians for self-government; moreover, Spain's autonomy policy probably would not satisfy the Cuban insurgents. Taking a conservative approach after the *Maine* explosion, on 19 February 1898, the *Tribune* criticized the **"yellow press"** for its fallacious coverage of the *Maine*.

As the McKinley administration moved toward war with Spain, so did the *Tribune*, headlining on 6 April 1898, "War Almost Inevitable." After Com. **George W. Dewey**'s overwhelming victory at the **Battle of Manila Bay** on 1 May, the *Tribune*, on 5 May, stated that a moral obligation may compel the United States to acquire territory on the other side of the world. Furthermore, it argued that Dewey's success made the annexation of **Hawaii** "imperative" as a halfway station to the **Philippines**. After announcing the embarkation of Maj. Gen. **William R. Shafter's Fifth Corps** one day before Shafter received his orders, the *Tribune* then complained about government **censorship**. During the negotiations of the **Treaty of Paris**, the newspaper's Paris bureau kept Reid, a member of the U.S. **Peace Commission**, informed of current world political developments.

NEW YORK WORLD. A New York City newspaper owned by **Joseph Pulitzer**, the *World* was a key member of the **"yellow press."** It was a pro-**Democratic Party** newspaper with a circulation of 822,804 by early 1898 and with its own news service, which was used by the *Chicago Tribune*. An ardent critic of Spanish policy during the **Cuban Revolt**, it opposed Spain's reform efforts on the grounds that they were only being implemented to get the Cubans to stop fighting and not for real change. **James Creelman** reported on Spanish executions of noncombatants and Nellie Bly announced she planned to recruit a regiment of **volunteers** officered by women to fight for Cuban independence.

On 13 February 1897, the *World* demanded U.S. action concerning the Cuban situation and on 15 May charged that the war in **Cuba** was the most brutal in modern civilized history. On 10 February 1898, it demanded immediate punishment for the **De Lôme Letter** and immediately blamed Spain for the *Maine* explosion, headlining on 17 February "Maine Explosion Caused by Bomb or Torpedo?" An ardent advocate of U.S. intervention in Cuba, it confidently predicted on 24 February that an army of one-half million men would be raised in case of a war with Spain; moreover, a 6 March article, quoting over 100 women, claimed "American Women Ready to Give Up Husbands, Sons and Sweethearts to Defend Nation's Honor." Later, on 3 April it carried an article "How I Could Drive Spaniards from Cuba with Thirty Thousand Indian Braves" by "Buffalo Bill" Cody, who claimed he could do it within 60 days.

During the war, the *World's* **press boats**, which included the *Three Friends*, and its 18 field **correspondents**, who included **George B. Rea**, **Stephen Crane**, and **Harry Sylvester Scovel** in Cuba, and **Edward Harden** and John Fay in the **Philippines**, frequently reported military secrets, engaged in intelligence operations for the U.S. military, and championed the American cause while the *World's* circulation rose to 1,300,000 a day.

NEWARK. (USN) **Protected cruiser**, commanded by Capt. **Albert S. Barker** until 8 August 1898 and then by Capt. **Caspar F. Goodrich**. The *Newark* was the last U.S. **cruiser** to carry a full set of sails and one of the first modern cruisers in the **U.S. Navy**. Assigned to the North Atlantic Station, it served on the **blockade of Cuba**, bombarded **Santiago, Cuba**, on 1 July, but missed the **Naval Battle of Santiago** on 3 July because it was coaling at **Guantánamo, Cuba**. It was later relieved from duty off **Puerto Rico** and assigned to the **Eastern Squadron**. Detached on 3 August, it escorted the **First Marine Battalion** to seize the **Isle of Pines**; however, it digressed and bombarded **Manzanillo, Cuba**, on 12 August. After the war it was posted to the Far East and served in the **Philippine Insurrection** and in Chinese waters during the Boxer Rebellion. Stricken in 1913, it served as a quarantine hulk at Providence, Rhode Island, until it was sold in 1926.

La. 1890, com. 1891, dis. 4,083, hp. 8,500, sp. 19
Armor: d. 2″, sl. 3″, ct. 3″
Armament: 12–6″, 4–6pdr., 4–3pdr., 2–1pdr., 2–37 mm. H. rev. cannon, 3 tt.
Cc. 809, comp. 384

NEWPORT. A 2,200-ton steamer, it was chartered as a **transport** in mid-June 1898 at a rate of $1,000 per day. It was quickly overhauled for carrying troops, ammunition, and supplies. It had electric lights, an ice machine that produced 300 pounds a day, a distilling apparatus for drinking water, and cold storage rooms. As part of the third expedition of the **Eighth Corps** to **Manila, Philippines**, it left San Francisco at the end of June, carrying Maj. Gen. **Wesley Merritt** and his staff, 500 soldiers, including the **Astor Battery**, correspondent **Francis Millet**, one captain of the Salvation Army, and $1.5 million in cash. For most of the trip across the Pacific Ocean, it steamed on alone ahead of the expedition, arriving in Manila on 25 July. During the war it was chartered for 379 days at a total cost of $379,000.

NEWPORT. (USN) **Composite gunboat**, commanded by Comdr. Benjamin F. Tilley. A barquentine-rigged, single-screw steamer with a clipper bow, its hull was sheathed and coppered for work in the tropics. Assigned to the **North Atlantic Squadron**, it served on the **blockade of Cuba** and captured or assisted in capturing nine Spanish vessels, including the schooner *Pireneo* and the sloop *Paquette* on 26 April and the sloop *Engracia* on 28 April. After the war, it served as a U.S. Naval Academy training ship until it was transferred to the city of Aberdeen, Washington, by act of **Congress** in 1914. It was disposed of in 1934.

La. 1896, com. 1897, dis. 1,010, hp. 1,000, sp. 13
Armament: 6–4″, 4–6pdr., 2–1pdr., 1 mg.
Cc. 235, comp. 156

NINTH MASSACHUSETTS INFANTRY (USV). Organized and mustered into service at South Framington 9–12 May 1898, with 47 officers and 896 enlisted men. The all-Irish regiment arrived at **Camp Alger** on 1 June. After leaving Camp Alger, the regiment left Newport News, Virginia on the *Harvard* on 26 June and arrived at **Siboney, Cuba**, on 1 July. Consisting of 40 officers and around 800 enlisted men, it was assigned to Brig. Gen. **Henry M. Duffield**'s independent brigade in the **Fifth Corps**. The regiment occupied the **San Juan Heights** on 2 July. It left Santiago, Cuba, on the *Allegheny*, *Berlin*, *Panther*, and *Roumania* on 24–29 August, for **Camp Wikoff, Montauk Point, Long Island, New York**. After returning to Massachusetts on 6 September, it was furloughed for 60 days and mustered out of service at Boston on 28 November, with 46 officers and 1,151 enlisted men. Casualties while in service included three wounded, 114 died from **disease**, one was killed by accident, and one deserted.

NINTH OHIO INFANTRY BATTALION (USV). Commanded by Maj. **Charles Young**, it was organized upon the first call for **volunteers** and mustered into service at Columbus, Ohio, 14 May–8 July

1898, with 16 officers and 314 enlisted men. The only **black American** unit from Ohio in the volunteer army during the war, it was mustered in as "separate" companies with black officers. After arriving at **Camp Alger** on 21 May, it was assigned to the **Second Corps**. A fourth company was added after the second call for volunteers on 25 May, and the battalion was assigned as corps headquarters guard upon the request of Maj. Gen. **William M. Graham**. After hostilities ceased, the battalion arrived at **Camp Meade** on 17 August and was one of the representative commands at the Peace Jubilee in Philadelphia, Pennsylvania. After leaving Camp Meade on 17 November, it went to Camp Arion at Summerville, South Carolina, where it was mustered out on 28 January 1899, with 16 officers and 395 enlisted men. Casualties sustained while in service included five died from **disease**, one murdered, and 15 deserted.

NINTH UNITED STATES CAVALRY (COLORED). Commanded by Lt. Col. J. M. Hamilton, it left Nebraska, Utah, and Wyoming, and arrived at **Camp Thomas**, Georgia. After arriving at **Tampa, Florida**, on 2 May 1898, it was assigned to the First Brigade, Dismounted Cavalry Division, of the **Fifth Corps**. Its chaplain George W. Prioleau regularly wrote to the *Cleveland Gazette*. On 13 May, he wrote about southern prejudice, which had greeted the unit's arrival, and pointed out the black soldiers' patriotism. On 21 May, Prioleau questioned if the United States was better than Spain with respect to race relations. Eight troops went to **Daiquirí, Cuba**, on the transport *Miami*. Consisting of 12 officers and 207 enlisted men, the troops fought in the **Battle of Kettle Hill** on 1 July and sustained casualties of three dead and 19 wounded from 1–3 July. The first unit to occupy **Santiago, Cuba**, after its **capitulation**, it presented arms at the U.S. flag-raising ceremony on 17 July. The unit's members were later awarded seven Certificates of Merit for their conduct during the **Santiago, Cuba, campaign**. After sustaining 23 total combat casualties, the troops left Santiago, Cuba, on the *Rio Grande* and *Leona* on 13 and 16 August for **Camp Wikoff, Montauk Point, Long Island, New York**. After arriving on 23 August, the troops broke camp on 27 September and left for their new station at Fort Grant, Arizona. Later some troops fought in the **Philippine Insurrection**.

NINTH UNITED STATES INFANTRY. Commanded by Lt. Col. **Ezra P. Ewers**, in the Third Brigade, First Division, of the **Fifth Corps**. The regiment left Madison Barracks, New York, and went to **Tampa, Florida**. During the rush to embark, the regiment stole a wagon train and arrived at Port Tampa, where it left for **Daiquirí, Cuba**. Consisting of 21 officers and 445 enlisted men, it fought in the **Battle of San Juan Hill** on 1 July 1898, sustaining casualties of four dead and 23 wounded. For his actions on 2 July, Second Lt. Ira C. Welborn was later awarded the **Congressional Medal of Honor**. After sustaining total combat casualties of five dead and 27 wounded, the regiment left **Santiago, Cuba**, on the *St. Louis* on 10 August for **Camp Wikoff, Montauk Point, Long Island, New York**.

NIPE BAY, CUBA, BATTLE OF (21 JULY 1898). Located on the northern coast of Oriente Province in eastern **Cuba**, Nipe Bay, a sheltered inlet about 14 miles long and eight miles wide, served as an anchorage for the old gunboat *Jorge Juan* and a small gunboat *Baracoa*. Thirteen **mines** were placed at the bay's entrance. Selected in U.S. prewar planning as a naval coaling facility, rendezvous, and anchorage, Nipe Bay, based on a recommendation of the **Naval War Board**, was ordered seized on 17 July 1898 by Secretary of the Navy **John D. Long** for use during the U.S. invasion of **Puerto Rico**. Accordingly, on 21 July, the **gunboat *Annapolis***, the armed **yacht *Wasp***, the armed tug *Leyden* and the gunboat *Topeka* entered the bay. The *Jorge Juan* was sunk, and the *Baracoa* steamed up the Mayari River, where its crew scuttled it. No casualties were sustained by either side. The expedition went for naught because Maj. Gen. **Nelson A. Miles** used the bay at **Guantánamo, Cuba**, for the rendezvous point of his Puerto Rican invasion force; therefore, the U.S. ships at Nipe Bay were soon ordered to Cape Fajardo, Puerto Rico.

NORRIS, FRANK [BENJAMIN FRANKLIN] (1870–1902). A budding novelist at work on writing *McTeague* (1899), Norris, a realist writer, left all his projects to cover the Spanish-American War for *McClure's Magazine*. Covering the **Santiago, Cuba, campaign**, he accompanied Brig. Gen. **Chambers McKibben**'s party during the **capitulation** of Santiago, Cuba, on 17 July 1898, and later wrote "With Lawton at El Caney" *The Century Magazine* (June 1899), which described the **Battle of El Caney** on 1 July, and "Comida: An Experience in Famine" *The Atlantic Monthly* (March 1899), which described the tragic situation of the refugees at **El Caney**. On board the transport *Iroquois* bound for **Puerto Rico** when the war ended, Norris commented that there was "precious little glory in war" and described it as "nothing but a hideous blur of mud and blood." After the war he worked for Doubleday, Page and Company, finished *McTeague*, and wrote *The Octopus* (1901) and *The Surrender of Santiago: An Account of the Historic Surrender of Santiago to General Shafter, July 17, 1898*, which was published in 1917.

NORTH ATLANTIC FLEET, U.S. NAVY. On 21 June 1898, the **North Atlantic Squadron** was renamed the North Atlantic Fleet and placed under the overall command of Adm. **William T. Sampson**. It was divided into two squadrons: the first under the command of Com. **John A. Howell**, and the second under the command of Com. **Winfield S. Schley**.

NORTH ATLANTIC SQUADRON, U.S. NAVY. Ordered to begin concentrating at the naval base at **Key West, Florida**, in January 1898, the North Atlantic Squadron came under the command of Rear Adm. **William T. Sampson** on 26 March 1898, and its prime assignment was to **blockade Cuba** and **Puerto Rico** and destroy any Spanish naval forces that appeared. Built around the **armored cruiser** *New York*, its flagship, and the **battleships** *Iowa* and *Massachusetts* on 10 May 1898, it also included the battleship *Indiana*; **monitors** *Amphitrite*, *Puritan*, and *Terror*; **cruisers** *Cincinnati*, *Detroit*, *Marblehead*, *Montgomery*, and *Vesuvius*; **torpedo boats** *Cushing*, *Dupont*, *Ericsson*, *Foote*, *Porter*, and *Winslow*; **gunboats** *Castine*, *Helena*, *Machias*, *Nashville*, *Newport*, *Wilmington*, and *Vicksburg*; dispatch boats *Dolphin* and *Samoset*; armed tug *Leyden*; and the supply steamer *Fern*. On 21 June the squadron was reorganized and, with the inclusion of the **Flying Squadron**, renamed the **North Atlantic Fleet**. After the war the squadron entered New York City harbor on 20 August to a tumultuous reception.

NORTH-SOUTH REUNION. A prominent theme of the war was the reconciliation of the North and South. Prior to the war a significant part of the South opposed going to war against Spain, including the *Charleston, South Carolina, News and Courier* and former confederate general Wade Hampton of South Carolina, who argued against fighting Spain on the grounds that Spain had supported the South during the Civil War. However, the South overwhelmingly reacted patriotically to the *Maine* disaster, and as war approached, both Hampton and the *News and Courier* changed their opinions and supported a united war effort. Gen. W. L. Carbell, the commander of the trans-Mississippi Department of Confederate veterans, offered to lead 50,000 ex-Confederates to victory over Spain, and three former Confederate generals were commissioned: Maj. Gen. **Fitzhugh Lee**, Maj. Gen. **Joseph Wheeler**, and Maj. Gen. **Joseph C. Breckinridge**.

Beginning in March 1898, the subject of reconciliation became a focal point of national pride. On 9 March, the *Atlanta Constitution* opined "Still another good result of this threatened rupture with Spain will be the more complete unification of the American people." Significantly, before and during the war **Black Americans** were divided over the effects of such a reconciliation. Theophilus G. Steward, chaplain of the **Twenty-Fifth U.S. Infantry**, in a 28 May 1898 letter

to the *Cleveland Gazette* believed that the black soldier's performance in the war would improve the condition of "the American colored man of the South," and D. Augustus Straker, editor of the
Indianapolis Freeman, believed the war would help solve the race
problem. However, Harry C. Smith, editor of the *Cleveland Gazette*,
John Mitchell Jr., editor of the *Richmond Planet*, and newspapers
such as the *Iowa State Bystander* out of Des Moines, Iowa, and the
Tribune of Savannah, Georgia, pointed out that the dissipation of sec-
tionalism by the war promised only to worsen the predicament of
black Americans everywhere in the United States.

NORTHERN PATROL SQUADRON, U.S. NAVY. Established on 20
April 1898 and commanded by Com. **John A. Howell**, its mission
was to patrol the Atlantic Coast from Bar Harbor, Maine, to the capes
of Delaware. It was initially composed of its flagship the **cruiser** *San
Francisco*, *Dixie*, *Prairie*, *Yankee*, and *Yosemite*. During May the
Badger, *Columbia*, and *Southery* were added while the *Yankee* and
Yosemite were detached. On 9 June the *Minneapolis* was added while
on 13 June the *Dixie* was detached. Because the **Navy Department**
wanted to increase the efficiency of the **blockade of Cuba**, it ordered
Com. Howell on 25 June to move his vessels, with the exception of
the *Minneapolis*, to **Key West, Florida**, where they became part of
the first squadron of the **North Atlantic Fleet**.

NOZALEDA Y VILLA, BERNARDINO (1844–1927). Archbishop
of **Manila, Philippines** (1891–1904). A Spanish Dominican priest,
Nozaleda went to the **Philippines** in 1873, earned a doctorate in
canon law, and was on the faculty of Santo Tomás University in Manila. As Archbishop, he opposed the conciliatory administration of
Gov.-Gen. **Ramón Blanco y Erenas** and helped to get Blanco removed and replaced by Gov.-Gen. **Camilo Polavieja**. Upon the outbreak of the Spanish-American War, he issued an appeal on 26 April
1898 to the Filipino people claiming that U.S. heretics intended to
attack the Philippines. On 8 May Nozaleda issued a circular warning
that the people's Catholic faith would be destroyed by U.S. protes-
tantism and that they would be made to work like "common laborers
or even beasts" under a U.S. government. Serving on Manila's civilian defense board, Nozaleda briefly talked with Father **William D.
McKinnon**, chaplain of the **First California Infantry**, and on 8 August recommended the **capitulation** of Manila. After the **Vatican** refused his request to retire in 1900, Nozaleda returned to Spain. His
1903 nomination to be the archbishop of Valencia caused such an
outcry that he retired.

NUEVITAS, CUBA. Located on the northern shore of eastern **Cuba**, Nuevitas, with its small bay, was the site of **filibuster**ing expeditions before the war. Defended by the gunboat *Pizarro* and the armed launches *Golondrina* and *Yumuri*, it was considered as a staging area for U.S. infantry and cavalry prior to a major overland assault on **Havana, Cuba**, in the war plans of Maj. Gen. **Nelson A. Miles**; however, the plan was never accepted. As the Spanish military concentrated its forces after the fall of **Santiago, Cuba**, on 17 July, Nuevitas was quickly abandoned. The three vessels were scuttled and the port evacuated on 31 July, leaving behind only a string of **mines** at the mouth of the bay.

NURSES, UNITED STATES. Prior to the war, nursing was done by men in the **Hospital Corps** of the **U.S. Army**. Consisting of 800 men, the corps had 99 hospital stewards, 100 acting stewards, and 592 privates upon the outbreak of the war, and although **Congress** increased the number of stewards to 200 on 2 June 1898, the corps was overwhelmed by the war. However, female nurses were not introduced until mid-July.

Initially opposed to the use of female nurses, Surgeon General **George M. Sternberg**, overwhelmed by **disease** in the U.S. **camps** and in **Cuba**, relented, and eventually female nurses served in military **hospitals**, in **camps** such as **Camp Thomas** and **Camp Wikoff**, and at **Santiago, Cuba**. Sternberg brought Dr. Anita N. McGee into his office as chief of nurses, and was assisted by the Daughters of the American Revolution (DAR), the **American Red Cross**, and various religious orders. Until September 1898, the Hospital Corps Committee of the DAR was the principal agency for procuring female nurses for the Hospital Corps. Of the approximately 1,500 nurses who served under army contract during the war, over 1,000 were DAR-recommended. There were also about 150 volunteer nurses assigned to the corps. Twelve of the contract nurses and three **volunteers** died during the war.

Of the nurses recruited from religious orders, approximately 200 were from the Sisters of Charity; 12 from the Sisters of Mercy, 11 from the Sisters of the Holy Cross, 12 from the Sisters of St. Joseph, and five from the Congregated American Sisters, who were Indian women from South Dakota. A number came from two Protestant organizations, the St. Barnabas Guild and the Sisters of St. Margaret. Two of these nurses died during the war: Rubina Walworth, aged 19, in the United States, and Sister Mary Larkin, from the Sisters of Charity, from **yellow fever**.

The American Red Cross recruited approximately 700 nurses for service in the war, and its female nurses served in stateside hospitals, but were initially not allowed to operate with the army at **Siboney, Cuba,** where they landed on 26 June under the direction of **Clara Barton.** Consequently, they offered their services to the Cuban insurgents, who readily accepted, and established their own hospital. However, the outbreak of disease among the **Fifth Corps** soon forced the army to reverse its policy, and Barton was officially welcomed. In July 1898, Mrs. A. M. Curtis, the wife of the chief surgeon of the Freedman Hospital in Washington, D.C., and a member of the Red Cross, was commissioned by the **War Department** to "contract nurses" for duty in Cuba. After establishing her headquarters in New Orleans, Louisiana, she recruited 25 **black American** women, many of whom served with the **"immunes"** that went to Cuba.

Among the prominent women who served as nurses were Annie Wheeler, daughter of Maj. Gen. **Joseph Wheeler,** and Frances Scovel, the wife of correspondent **Harry Sylvester Scovel,** both of whom served in Cuba; and the daughter of Secretary of the Navy **John D. Long,** and Helen Gould, a multimillionaire, who served in the United States. After the war the **Dodge Commission** lauded the performance of female nurses and concluded that the Medical Department of the army should create a permanent reserve corps of trained women nurses, which in 1901 became the Army Nurse Corps.

—O—

O'BRIEN, JOHNNY "DYNAMITE" (1837–1917). Legendary **filibuster.** Born in New York City of Irish immigrant parents, O'Brien, a mild-mannered, thick-set man, began his filibustering career when, while working as a harbor pilot in New York City, he accepted an offer in 1885 to take a cargo of arms and ammunition to Colombian rebels. Other ventures in **Cuba,** Honduras, Haiti, **Mexico,** and Panama soon followed, and he acquired the nickname "Dynamite" in 1888 when he carried a cargo of dynamite to Panama in the middle of an electrical storm.

During the **Cuban Revolt,** O'Brien undertook more than a dozen filibustering expeditions on the *Commodore, Dauntless,* and *Three Friends.* Upon hearing beforehand of one of O'Brien's expeditions, Gov.-Gen. **Valeriano Weyler y Nicolau** announced he was going to "have him hanged from the flagpole at Cabañas in full view of the city" and put a price on his head. O'Brien then landed within plain sight of **Havana** on the *Dauntless* on 24 May 1897 and delivered dynamite to the Cuban insurgents. Even the Pinkerton detectives, who were employed by the U.S. government to stop filibustering expeditions, failed to stop him. After the Spanish-American War, he was the chief of Havana harbor pilots, and in 1912 guided the tugs that towed the raised remains of the *Maine* out to sea and sunk them in deep water.

O'DONNELL MEMORANDUM (SUMMER 1896). A 23-page draft memorandum by Spanish Minister of State **Carlos Manuel O'Donnell y Abreú**, which was Spain's first attempt to request concerted European assistance in thwarting United States policy in **Cuba**. In presenting Spain's case, it argued that Spain was not responsible for the **Cuban Revolt**. The conflict continued because the United States continued to allow the **Junta** to operate and had failed to enforce its own laws in stopping **filibuster**ing expeditions; moreover, although President **Grover Cleveland** had done his job, **Congress** had passed laws favoring the rebels. The memorandum promised that reforms, including local self-government, would be implemented once the revolt was put down. Because the Spanish monarchy would fall if U.S. intervention resulted in the loss of Cuba, other European monarchies would be placed in a precarious position. Finally, the memorandum requested that **Austria-Hungary**, **Great Britain**, **France**, **Germany**, **Italy**, **Russia**, and the **Vatican** explain Spain's situation to Washington and ask Washington to take effective steps to halt aid to the Cuban rebels. However, the memorandum was never formally presented.

Initial enthusiastic reactions by the European powers quickly turned to reserve and indifference. Great Britain and France even recommended abandoning the initiative; moreover, Sir Henry Drummond Wolff, the British ambassador to Spain, leaked it to **Hannis Taylor**, U.S. minister to Spain, and Taylor warned O'Donnell. Even though O'Donnell then suspended its delivery, he continued to believe that he had built a foundation for future diplomacy. The initiative was formally closed in a 10 October 1896 note to Spain's representatives abroad.

O'DONNELL Y ABREÚ, CARLOS MANUEL (1834–1903). Spanish minister of state in the government of **Antonio Cánovas del Castillo** from 28 March 1895 to 29 September 1897. The son of an Irish family long resident in Spain and member of the **Liberal-Conservative Party**, O'Donnell, the Duke of Tetuán, was adamant about crushing the **Cuban Revolt** and supported the granting of local self-government to **Cuba** only after the revolt had been crushed.

O'Donnell attempted to enlist European support for Spain in the **O'Donnell Memorandum** in the summer of 1896 and rejected both Secretary of State **Richard Olney's Note** of 4 April 1896, which offered U.S. mediation in the Cuban Revolt, and U.S. Secretary of

State **John Sherman's Note** of 26 June 1897, which castigated Spain's policy in Cuba.

Although he had expected early Spanish defeats at sea in a war against the United States "from want of preparations," O'Donnell held out hope because Spanish forces in Cuba and **Puerto Rico** consisted of seasoned troops and ample supplies. Before the government of Prime Minister **Práxedes M. Sagasta** signed the **Armistice Protocol** of 12 August 1898, Sagasta consulted with him. O'Donnell was not opposed to peace but doubted that Sagasta's government had the necessary authority to negotiate a peace under favorable conditions. He later refused to serve on Spain's **Peace Commission** that negotiated the **Treaty of Paris** and harshly criticized the Spanish **press** for, in effect, constituting a propaganda agency for Spain's enemies before and during the war against the United States.

OFFICE OF NAVAL INTELLIGENCE (ONI). Founded in 1882, it prepared reports and war plans, such as the **Kimball Plan**, for the **Navy Department** from data gathered by naval attachés posted overseas, such as Lt. **George L. Dyer**. Under the direction of Comdr. **Richardson Clover**, the ONI played a fundamental and crucial role. It provided most of the intelligence that guided U.S. naval war efforts and planning, procured ships for the **U.S. Navy** from European vendors, operated a ciphering and decoding room that intercepted Spanish **cable** and telegraphic communications, conducted a **disinformation** campaign against Spain, tracked the progress of Adm. **Manuel de la Cámara's Squadron**, and conducted covert intelligence operations through Ens. **William H. Buck**, Lt. **John C. Colwell**, Lt. **William S. Sims**, and Ens. **Henry H. Ward**. However, the ONI's efforts failed to ascertain the poor condition of both Adm. **Pascual Cervera's Squadron** and Adm. Manuel Cámara's Squadron.

OLIVETTE. A 1,104-ton, commercial passenger steamer owned by the Plant Line, which, except for **cables**, was the only regular channel of communication between **Cuba** and the United States before the advent of **press boats** in 1896. During its regular route between **Tampa, Florida**, and **Havana, Cuba**, the *Olivette* also served as a mail carrier, making three trips a week. Its pursuer acted as a secret courier for the U.S. government, transmitting messages between U.S. Consul **Fitzhugh Lee** in Havana and U.S. naval authorities at **Key West, Florida**. After lending its name to one of the most famous **"yellow press"** incidents—the *Olivette* **Incident** of February 1897—the ship took uninjured survivors of the *Maine* explosion to Key West and then brought divers to Havana to investigate the disaster. During the war, it transported forces of the **Fifth Corps** to **Daiquirí, Cuba**, at a rate of $500 a day and was converted into a **hospital ship**. It transported the sick and wounded from **Santiago, Cuba**, to the United States and returned with medical supplies. On 31 August 1898, it sank at the wharf at Fernandina, Florida.

OLIVETTE **INCIDENT.** On 12 February 1897, a **Richard H. Davis** article "Does Our Flag Shield Women?" appeared on the front page of the *New York Journal*. Davis, while on board the *Olivette* journeying to **Tampa, Florida**, had been told by Clemencia Arango of an incident in which Arango, a suspected insurgent sympathizer, and two other women had been strip-searched by Spanish officials in **Havana, Cuba**, prior to the ship's departure. An outraged Davis sat down and wrote his dispatch at Tampa, Florida, on 10 February 1897. When the article appeared on 12 February, it was complemented on page two with a five-column drawing by **Frederic S. Remington** showing a young woman with a bare backside standing among several Spanish officers. Remington, who was in New York City when the incident occurred, had been called in to do the drawing. He assumed the searchers were men, when in fact it had been done by women.

The article set off a firestorm. Spain's Minister to the United States **Enrique Dupuy de Lôme** stated that Spain had the right to search the passengers, and resolutions were introduced in the U.S. **Congress** demanding that the secretary of state furnish all the information on the "stripping of three lady passengers." Arango, who had been searched by women in private, was mortified, and publicly corrected the report. The *New York World* interviewed the Cuban women, who denied they had been searched by men, and published its findings on 17 February 1898 in "The Unclothed Women Searched by Men was an Invention of a New York Newspaper."

An outraged Davis, who broke with the *Journal*, defended himself in an explanatory letter to the *World* denying that his dispatch had stated the women had been searched by men and blamed Remington's drawing for the misconception; however, Remington claimed he had illustrated only what Davis had written. It mattered little to **William R. Hearst**, the *Journal*'s owner, because the sensationalist fabrication had sold close to one million newspapers.

OLNEY, RICHARD (1835–1917). U.S. secretary of state (1895–1897) in the **Cleveland administration**. A Boston corporate lawyer and former U.S. attorney general (1893–1895), Olney proclaimed the Olney Corollary to the Monroe Doctrine in 1895 claiming virtual U.S. sovereignty over the Western Hemisphere. Olney, who wanted to help Spain end the **Cuban Revolt**, viewed the Cuban **Junta** in

New York City as merely a propaganda agency, believed that Cuban independence would lead to racial war and anarchy, and felt the insurgents' "scorched earth" policy was nothing but pure arson. Consequently, he maintained U.S. neutrality and authored a diplomatic note on 4 April 1896 that offered the U.S. good offices to mediate the Cuban situation. In late December he effectively countered the Cameron Resolution, which sought to recognize Cuban independence.

After he left office, Olney opined that the **De Lôme Letter** and *Maine* disaster had inflamed "popular passions" against Spain more than anything that had happened during the entire Cleveland administration's term. After the war, he wrote "Growth of Our Foreign Policy," *Atlantic Monthly* (March 1900), in which he pointed out that the U.S. policy of abandoning its isolation had been inevitable and, with or without the Spanish-American War, it would not have been long delayed.

OLNEY'S NOTE TO SPANISH GOVERNMENT (4 APRIL 1896). On 7 April 1896, Secretary of State **Richard Olney** sent a confidential diplomatic note to **Enrique Dupuy de Lôme**, Spain's minister to Washington, D.C. Predated to 4 April to distance it from a just-passed congressional joint resolution that had recognized the Cuban insurgents by granting them **belligerent rights**, the note offered the U.S. good offices to help mediate the **Cuban Revolt**, ruled out direct U.S. intervention, supported continued Spanish sovereignty, and asked for a modicum of self-government. It was the first official U.S. attempt at involvement in the Cuban conflict.

Spanish acceptance was out of the question because pro-Cuban speeches and actions in the U.S. **Congress** had resulted in anti-American demonstrations in Madrid and the stoning of the U.S. consulate in Barcelona. **Carlos O'Donnell y Abreú**, Spain's minister of state, waited to reject the U.S. offer until after the crown had offered local self-government to **Cuba** upon the termination of the revolt. On 22 May, he notified the U.S. government that Spain needed to pacify the insurrection first, and although the U.S. could cooperate by suppressing **filibuster**ing and shutting down the Cuban **Junta**, any effort at mediation would not work because the insurgents had already rejected it.

OLYMPIA. (USN) First-class **protected cruiser**, commanded by Capt. **Charles V. Gridley**. It served as Com. **George W. Dewey**'s flagship of the **Asiatic Squadron**. Capt. William P. Biddle, later the commandant of the marine corps, commanded the **marine** detachment on board. During the **Battle of Manila Bay** on 1 May 1898, the *Olympia* led the squadron into battle, fired 1,678 shells, and was hit but suffered little damage. On 25 May, Capt. **Benjamin P. Lamberton** took command. During the **Battle of Manila** on 13 August, it was deployed off **Fort San Antonio Abad** and briefly fired on the fort. After the war it served as an accommodation ship at Charleston, South Carolina (1912–1916), saw active service in World War I, and was decommissioned in 1922. Unique among U.S. naval vessels in the Spanish-American War, it survived as a shrine and museum at Philadelphia, Pennsylvania.

La. 1892, com. 1895, dis. 5,870, hp. 13,500, sp. 21.68
Armor: d. 2″, sl. 4.75″, t. 3.5″, b. 4.5″, ct. 5″
Armament: 4–8″, 10–5″, 14–6pdr., 7–1pdr., 2 C. mgs, 6–18″ tt. (aw.)
Cc. 1,169, comp. 412

O'NEILL, WILLIAM O. "BUCKY" (1860–1898). Captain of Troop A in the **Rough Riders**. The Irish-born, flamboyant mayor of Prescott, Arizona, O'Neill, who got his nickname from "bucking the tiger" while he was a gambler, had been a cowboy, journalist, miner, and sheriff of Yavapai County. Just before the Rough Riders' charge up **Kettle Hill** on 1 July 1898, O'Neill, characteristically refusing to take cover, was strolling up and down the lines exposing himself to Spanish fire when he was shot through the head and killed by a Spanish sniper. **Theodore Roosevelt** called his loss "the most serious loss that I and the regiment could have suffered." Later the **black American** residents of Phoenix, Arizona, in appreciation of O'Neill's daring attempt to rescue two black soldiers who drowned during the landing of the **Fifth Corps** at **Daiquirí, Cuba**, held a mass meeting and adopted a resolution lamenting his death.

OPERATING ROOM "WAR ROOM." Located on the second floor of the White House, it was under the direct command of Lt. Col. Benjamin F. Montgomery of the **Signal Corps**. Replete with large-scale maps, an elaborate network of 15 telephone lines and 20 telegraph wires, which extended to military bureaus and commanders at the front, and a 24-hour staff, it was the prototype of later national military command posts in allowing a direct presidential presence in the battle zones. At its best, a message to **Cuba** and back took 20 minutes.

ORDNANCE DEPARTMENT. Directed by Brig. Gen. Daniel W. Flagler, a West Point graduate and an experienced ordnance officer, it was one of ten agencies in the **War Department** and was responsible for procuring and distributing supplies for the military. At the beginning of the war, the department consisted of Flagler, 55 officers, 104 ordnance sergeants, and 488 enlisted men. Short of personnel and supplies such as ammunition because of congressional penury in the prewar years, the department worked nonstop in supplying the armed forces. Although **Congress** expanded the department on 8 July 1898 by adding 12 more officers to the department, a chief ordnance officer with the rank of lieutenant colonel for each army corps, and a chief ordnance officer with the rank of major for each division, it was never sufficient to meet the demands of the war.

ORDÓÑEZ Y ESCANDÓN, SALVADOR DÍAZ (1845–1911). Colonel, commanded Spanish artillery at **Santiago, Cuba.** A lifelong artillery designer, Ordóñez designed the artillery that bore his name during years of work at the Trubia factory. Arriving in **Cuba** in 1896, he fought against the Cuban insurgents. During the war against the United States, he was responsible for the artillery positions at the entrance to Santiago's harbor and was wounded during a U.S. naval bombardment. While directing the defenses of San Juan Hill, he was wounded again in the **Battle of San Juan Hill** on 1 July 1898. Promoted to brigadier general and decorated for his bravery, he was repatriated to Spain and immediately returned to designing artillery. Promoted to general of division in 1908, he served as military governor of Cartagena, Spain, and was killed during the wars in Morocco.

OREGON. (USN) First-class **battleship**, commanded by Capt. **Charles E. Clark** (17 March 1898–6 August 1898). Costing over $3 million to build, it was the sister ship of the *Indiana* and *Massachusetts*. Called the "bulldog of the American Navy," its historic, well-publicized 15,000-mile voyage began on 7 March 1898, when it left Bremerton, Washington. Arriving in San Francisco on 9 March, it took on fuel and ammunition and on 12 March was ordered to Callao, Peru. After Capt. Charles E. Clark assumed command on 17 March because of the former captain's illness, the *Oregon* left San Francisco on 19 March and arrived in Callao, Peru, on 4 April, where it remained for three days. Assisted by the **gunboat** *Marietta*, by 16 April it was passing through the Strait of Magellan, and arrived at Rio de Janeiro, Brazil, on 30 April, where Clark was informed that war had broken out. Leaving Rio de Janeiro on 4 May, the *Oregon* arrived at **Key West, Florida**, on 26 May.

Assigned to the North Atlantic Station, the *Oregon* helped **blockade Santiago, Cuba**, during which it bombarded Spanish fortifications and used its **searchlights** to illuminate the harbor entrance at night. On 10 June it assisted in the landing of the **Marines** at **Guantánamo, Cuba**. During the **Naval Battle of Santiago** on 3 July, it was hit only three times and fired 1,903 shots. After destroying the *Furor* and *Plutón*, it overtook the fleeing *Cristóbal Colón*, forced it ashore, and assisted in rescuing the *Colon's* survivors. On 7 July, it was assigned to the **Eastern Squadron**, and on 6 August, Capt. **Albert S. Barker** took command because of Capt. Clark's illness.

After the war, it was refit in the New York Navy Yard and then served in the **Philippine Insurrection**, Boxer Rebellion, and World War I. After remaining in Portland, Oregon, for 16 years as a floating monument, it was reactivated during World War II and served as a munitions barge in the Pacific. Severely damaged in a hurricane, it was eventually sold in 1956 to a Japanese firm and was reduced to scrap iron in a Japanese shipyard.

La. 1893, com. 1896, dis. 10,288, hp. 11,111, sp. 16.8
Armor: s. 18″, d. 2.75″, t. 15″ & 6″, b. 8–17″, ct. 9″
Armament: 4–13″, 8–8″, 4–6″, 20–6pdr., 6–1pdr., 2 C. mgs., 3–18″ tt.
(aw.)
Cc. 1,600, comp. 473

ORTEGA Y DÍAZ, RICARDO (1838–1917).

General of division, military governor of **San Juan**, **Puerto Rico**. Entering the army at age 15, Ortega fought in Africa and the Carlist Wars, and was the military governor of Madrid before going to **Puerto Rico** in 1896 to serve as second in command under the captain general of Puerto Rico and as military governor of San Juan. Overconfident of Spain's ability to defeat the United States, on 25 July he expressed his wish to capture a Yankee in order to see his face and to steal a U.S. ship in order to take a siesta on it every afternoon in San Juan's harbor.

After the signing of the **Armistice Protocol** on 12 August 1898, Ortega directed the Spanish **evacuation commission** for Puerto Rico, did not attend the ceremony that formally transferred Puerto Rico to the United States on 18 October, and left Puerto Rico on 23 October 1898 on the *Montevideo*. After arriving in Cádiz, Spain, on 5 November, he resided in Madrid, was promoted to lieutenant general in 1901, and was captain general of the Balearic Islands until 1910.

ORTHODOX-HISTORICAL AUTONOMIST PARTY *(PARTIDO AUTONOMISTA HISTÓRICO ORTODOXO)*.

Founded on 4 March 1897 by **José Celso Barbosa** when the autonomist movement divided over the issue of a pact with the Spanish **Liberal Party** of **Práxedes M. Sagasta**. The party opposed the pact and won four seats in the 27 March 1898 general elections for an autonomous legislature; however, it refused to participate in the insular parliament when it was called on 17 July 1898. The party was dissolved in 1899.

OSCEOLA.

(USN) Armed tugboat, commanded by Lt. J. L. Purcell. Formerly the *Winthrop*, it was purchased by the **U.S. Navy** on 31

March 1898 from the Staples Coal Company and assigned to the North Atlantic Station. During the war it served on the **blockade of Cuba**, convoyed the **Fifth Corps** to **Daiquirí, Cuba**, and participated in engagements at **Manzanillo, Cuba**, on 1 July and on 18 July 1898.

La. 1897, com. 4 April 1898, dis. 571, sp. 14
Armament: 2–6pdr., 1–47 mm., 1 G.
Cc. 150, comp. 30

OTIS, ELWELL STEPHEN (1838–1909). Major general (USV), second in command of the **Eighth Corps**. A brigadier general, Otis was appointed major general (USV) in May 1898 and effectively prepared the expeditions of the Eighth Corps to **Manila, Philippines**. He commanded the fourth expedition, which left San Francisco on 15 July 1898 and arrived at Manila on 21 August.

On 23 August 1898, Maj. Gen. **Wesley Merritt** transferred command of the Eighth Corps to him. Otis intensely disliked Filipinos and believed **Emilio Aguinaldo**'s insurgents were "a band of looters"; subsequently, he ordered them out of the city of Manila. Otis, who rarely left his office, sent overly optimistic reports to Washington, thereby leading the **McKinley administration** to underestimate Filipino opposition to U.S. control. On 4 January 1899, claiming U.S. sovereignty over the islands, Otis issued his first proclamation as military governor of the **Philippines**. It was challenged the next day by Emilio Aguinaldo's protest against the imposition of U.S. sovereignty over an independent Philippines.

—**P**—

PACIFIC SQUADRON, U.S. NAVY. Stationed at San Francisco under the command of Rear Adm. Joseph N. Miller, it included the **protected cruiser** *Philadelphia* (attached 8 July 1898) and from the beginning of the war the **gunboats** *Bennington* and *Wheeling*; armed revenue cutters *Corwin, Grant, Perry,* and *Rush*; **monitors** *Monadnock* and *Monterey*; old wooden corvette *Mohican*; and Fish Commissioner vessel *Albatross*.

PACT OF BIAK-NA-BATÓ. A three-part agreement negotiated by **Pedro A. Paterno** from August 1897 to December 1897, between the Filipino insurgent forces under the command of **Emilio Aguinaldo** and the Spanish government of the **Philippines**. The pact called for the exile of Aguinaldo and some of his followers, payment of an indemnity by Spain for war damages, and amnesty for those Filipino insurgents who gave up their weapons. However, neither the Spanish nor the Filipino insurgents completely complied with its terms. Although Aguinaldo and his followers went into exile in December 1897, he continued planning the next stage of the revolt, and by February 1898, fighting erupted again in the Philippines. The Spanish, after paying $400,000, reneged on paying a second installment and, according to Aguinaldo, failed to implement promised reforms, promises that Spanish officials denied having made.

PAINE, RALPH D. (1871–1925). Correspondent for the *New York Journal*. From Jacksonville, Florida, Paine, the son of a Presbyterian minister, was enthralled by the derring-do of the **filibusters** when he walked into the *Journal*'s office in May 1896 and offered his services. Hired on the spot by **William R. Hearst**, Paine undertook a two-year career as a filibuster, which included a well-publicized failed attempt on the *Three Friends* to deliver the *Journal*'s ivory-handled $2,000 sword to Cuban insurgent Maj. Gen. **Máximo Gómez**. Subsequently, he was indicted by U.S. authorities and forced to hide out for weeks as a fugitive from justice. Paine returned to his job on the *Philadelphia Press*. The sword finally reached Gómez after the Spanish-American War, and Gómez, who was reported to have been disgusted with the "imbeciles in New York" who could have used the money for shoes and bullets for his insurgents, ordered it taken away.

During the war Paine stowed away on board the *New York*, observed the **blockade of Cuba**, and was on the *Three Friends* when the **First Marine Battalion** landed near **Guantánamo**, **Cuba**. Paine followed the **marines** ashore, carrying a bottle of whiskey to pass among them. While he was on a hill talking and sharing the bottle, a Spanish sniper attack began. Paine went out to get the sniper, but because of Spanish fire, he had to take refuge in an old steam boiler. When the shooting stopped, the marines were surprised that he was still alive when he returned to U.S. lines. He later wrote about his exploits in *Roads of Adventure* (1922).

PANDO Y SÁNCHEZ, LUIS MANUEL DE (1844–1927). Spanish general, chief of operations for the **Spanish Army** in **Cuba**. One of the chief officers of Gov.-Gen. **Ramón Blanco**, Pando was closely identified with Blanco's policies. Maj. Gen. **William R. Shafter**, while conducting the **Santiago, Cuba, campaign**, mistakenly believed that Gen. Pando was bringing reinforcements to Santiago, but it was really **Escario's Column**. Pando left **Havana, Cuba**, on 15 June 1898 and went to **Manzanillo, Cuba**, where he remained for the duration of the war. After the war, Pando presented a memoir justifying Blanco's policies to the Spanish Senate on 22 October 1898. For this he was criticized by Gen. **Valeriano Weyler y Nicolau** in his book *Mi mando en Cuba* (1906).

PANTHER. (USN) Auxiliary **cruiser**. Formerly the merchantman *Venezuela*, the *Panther* was purchased by the **U.S. Navy** at Brooklyn, New York, on 19 April 1898, and commanded by Comdr. G. C. Reiter during the war. Leaving New York on 22 April, it carried the **First Marine Battalion** to **Key West, Florida**, where the **marines** disembarked after arriving on 29 April. After towing the **monitor *Amphitrite*** back out to Cuban **blockade** duty, it transported the First Marine Battalion to **Guantánamo, Cuba**, where the battalion landed on 10 June. After the cessation of hostilities, the *Panther* transported troops of the **Fifth Corps** from **Santiago, Cuba**, to **Camp Wikoff, Montauk Point, Long Island, New York**. After the war it served as a training ship, a repair ship, and then a destroyer tender until it was sold in 1923.

La. 1889, com. 22 April 1898, dis. 4,260, hp. 3,200, sp. 13
Armament: 6–5″, 2–4″, 6–3pdr., 1 C. mg.
Cc. 465, comp. 198

PARTIDAS. Beginning in August 1898 and continuing through October, bands of Puerto Ricans began to attack Spaniards and to sack their property. Operating mainly in the interior coffee areas of the island, the bands were composed of small landowners, field-workers, and former militia members. As they burned rural stores, warehouses, houses of landowners, account books, and machinery, U.S. troops intervened. Called bandits by American military authorities and terrorists by the U.S. **press**, they were frequently protected by local judges even though former Gov.-Gen. **Manuel Macías y Casado** assisted U.S. authorities in their repression until he returned to Spain in October 1898. Several clashes with U.S. troops resulted in the death of several of their leaders and the arrest of about 60 members.

PATERNO, PEDRO ALEJANDRO (1857–1911). Known as the author of the first Filipino novel, *Ninay* (1895), Paterno, a member of a well-to-do Manila family, was one of the first Filipinos to go to Europe for graduate study. After obtaining a Doctor of Laws at the University of Salamanca, Spain, he traveled extensively. Upon returning to the **Philippines**, he was named director of the Philippine Library and Museum. While staying on the sidelines during the **Philippine Revolt**, Paterno served as an arbiter between Spanish officials and **Emilio Aguinaldo**. His efforts resulted in the **Pact of Biak-na-bató** in December 1897.

During the Spanish-American War, Paterno served as president of the **Consultative Assembly** and issued a manifesto on 1 June 1898, urging the Filipino people to support Spain in the war. In response, Aguinaldo personally attacked him in a 9 June manifesto. Nevertheless, Paterno later joined the insurgent movement and served as president of the **Malolos Congress** in September 1898. During the **Philippine Insurrection** he headed a cabinet that replaced **Apolinario Mabini**'s cabinet on 9 May 1899. After he was captured by U.S. forces, Paterno worked to negotiate an end to the insurrection.

PATRIA. Cuban insurgent newspaper in New York City. Established on 4 March 1892, it was edited by **José Martí y Pérez**, and although technically not part of the **Cuban Revolutionary Party**, the front page of its first issue published the party's bases. After Martí was killed in combat in **Cuba** in 1895, Enrique José Varona edited the paper.

PATRIA BATTALION NO. 25. Also known as the Cazadores de la Patria battalion, it was a permanent Spanish battalion of 800 men stationed in **Puerto Rico**. On 30 May 1898, four of its companies were stationed at **Mayagüez**, one at Cabo Rojo, and one at San Germán. Subsequently, under the command of Lt. Col. **Francisco Puig**, two companies were ordered to retreat from **Yauco** after the U.S. landing at **Guánica** on 25 July. Two companies fought in the **Battle of Coamo** on 9 August, and its units later fought in the 12 August skirmish at the **Asomante Hills**. After the war, a huge crowd turned out to say farewell when the battalion left **San Juan** for Spain on the steamship *P. de Satrústegui* on 6 October 1898.

PAUNCEFOTE, JULIAN (1828–1902). British ambassador to the United States. Pauncefote, the first British ambassador to the U.S., arrived in Washington, D.C., on 11 April 1893. He helped U.S. Assistant Secretary of State **William R. Day** draft the **Great Powers Note** of 6 April 1898, which he then signed. Upset over President **William McKinley's War Message** of 11 April, Pauncefote attempted to organize another European demarche to avoid war between the United States and Spain, but **Arthur J. Balfour**, acting foreign secretary, refused to authorize this step.

PAY DEPARTMENT, U.S. ARMY. Under the command of Brig. Gen. Thaddeus H. Stanton, paymaster general, the department, which always had enough money to meet its payroll, was increased by 72 officers and clerks during the war. Since many of these new employees had little or no knowledge of army accounts, a school of instruction was organized, resulting in the prompt payment of troops with few errors.

Eleven paymasters served in **Cuba**, and even though they had $1,500,000 on hand, the commanders of two-thirds of the regiments requested that their troops not be paid until they returned to the United States; consequently, these troops were paid after they arrived at **Camp Wikoff, Montauk Point, Long Island, New York**. Ten paymasters and $1,500,000 were sent to **Puerto Rico**; however, Maj. Gen. **Nelson A. Miles** ordered them to remain at **Santiago, Cuba**, because he feared the money might be infected with **disease** even though it had never been taken off the vessels. A new paymaster and new money were soon sent from New York City to pay the troops in Puerto Rico.

In June 1898, President **William McKinley** appointed John R. Lynch, a **black American**, as paymaster of **volunteers** with the rank of major. When Texas volunteers refused to accept their pay from him, they were told to either take the money or they would receive nothing. They took it. Salaries in the army varied from $13 a month with $1.30 extra for combat pay for a private to $625 a month for a major general. An ordinary seaman in the navy received $19 a month and a rear admiral received around $500 a month, not counting **prize money**.

PEACE COMMISSION—SPAIN. Because members of the **Liberal-Conservative Party** refused to participate, Prime Minister **Práxedes M. Sagasta** was forced to rely on his own **Liberal Party** and professional diplomats in appointing a commission to negotiate the **Treaty of Paris**. The commission was named by Royal Decree on 18 September 1898 and given its instructions on 20 September.

It was composed of its chairman **Eugenio Montero Ríos**, president of the Senate and Liberal Party chief; Buenaventura de Abárzuza, a liberal party senator; José de Garnica y Díaz, a Liberal Party member and associate justice of the Supreme Court; **Wenceslao Ramírez de Villaurrutia**, Spain's minister to Belgium; **Rafael Cerero y Sáenz**, general of division; and secretary Emilio de Ojeda, Spain's minister to Morocco.

Upon the commencement of negotiations on 1 October, the commission adopted a strategy of delay in the hope of obtaining European intervention and possible arbitration and to demonstrate to their countrymen that they had exhausted every possible means of restraining the United States and preserving Spanish honor. They tried to retain Spanish sovereignty over the **Philippines** and **Puerto Rico** and attempted to have the United States assume the **Cuban debt**. However, their efforts failed, and they were ordered on 25 November 1898 to sign the treaty with a protest.

PEACE COMMISSION—UNITED STATES. President **William McKinley** tried to obtain Democratic support for the **Treaty of Paris** negotiations by naming two Supreme Court justices, Chief Justice Melville Fuller and Associate Justice Edward D. White, both with backgrounds in the **Democratic Party**, to the commission, but they refused on the grounds of their public duties as judges. Consequently, he selected men who sought appointment and senators on the Senate Foreign Relations Committee. When the commission was named on 27 August 1898, it was composed of its chairman **William R. Day**, former secretary of state who held moderate views; **Cushman K. Davis**, Republican senator from Minnesota who was an expansionist and chairman of the Senate Foreign Relations Committee; **William P. Frye**, Republican senator from Maine who was an expansionist; **George Gray**, Democratic senator from Delaware who was an antiexpansionist and the ranking minority member of the Senate Foreign Relations Committee; **Whitelaw Reid**, the publisher of the *New York Tribune* and an expansionist; and secretary **John B. Moore**, who was an assistant secretary of state.

After receiving its instructions from McKinley on 16 September, the commission left New York City on 17 September and arrived in Paris on 27 September. At the outset a majority of the commission favored an expansionist position that intended to retain lands conquered during the war. When the commission was unable to reach a consensus in October on taking all of the **Philippines**, each commissioner forwarded his views to McKinley with the request that he provide additional instructions. On 26 October, the **McKinley administration** responded with an order to take the entire Philippines. Although the commission divided in late November over proposals by **Eugenio Montero Ríos**, which tied the cession of the Philippines to the assumption of debts, McKinley again provided direction by ordering the commission to remain firm and reject the proposals. After signing the Treaty of Paris on 10 December, the commission left **France** on 16 December and arrived in New York City on 24 December.

"PEACE FACTION." Name given to Republican senators who in March 1898 favored a diplomatic resolution of U.S.-Spanish differences over **Cuba**. The group included Nelson W. Aldrich of Rhode Island; **Charles W. Fairbanks** of Indiana; **Eugene Hale** of Maine; **Marcus A. Hanna** of Ohio; Orville H. Platt of Connecticut; and John C. Spooner of Wisconsin. Acting on the assumption that Spain would retain nominal sovereignty over Cuba, they helped President **William McKinley** draft procedural arrangements for **McKinley's Ultimatum** of 27 March 1898 to the Spanish government. Unbeknownst to them, McKinley simply added the requirement of outright Cuban independence in a subsequent communication to the Spanish government.

"PEANUT CLUB." Name given to an informal gathering of New York City journalists that met in the law offices of **Horatio Rubens** at 66 Broadway. The group got its name from the large box of peanuts that Rubens kept on hand for snacks. Members of more than 40 daily New York City newspapers attended afternoon sessions, during which they were given the Cuban insurgent **Junta**'s latest news releases in time for their morning papers. The club's most consistent members were the *New York Journal* and *New York World*.

PELAYO. (SPN) **Battleship**, commanded by Capt. José Fernández. Built at La Seyne, near Toulon, France, in 1885, it was undergoing refitting upon outbreak of war. Not ready until mid-May, it became part of Adm. **Manuel de la Cámara's Squadron**. It was scrapped in 1925.

La. 1887, dis. 9,917, hp. 8,000, sp. 16.2
Armor: s. 16.5″, d. 2–2.75″, b. 18″, ct. 6″
Armament: 2–12.5″, 2–11″, 9–5.5″, 5–6pdr, 14 mgs., 7 tt.
Cc. 630, comp. 520

PENSIONS—UNITED STATES. Veterans of the Spanish-American War received no education or vocational training benefits; moreover, there was no service pension until 20 years after the war and no right to hospitalization until 1922. Pensions began in 1920 when a statute gave payments to veterans at or over the age of 62 who had served at least 90 days. Pension levels were increased in 1926 and 1930, and in 1930 a two-tiered system was enacted. Veterans with 90 days or more of service were treated more favorably than a new class of veterans created by the legislation. The new class consisted of veterans with less than 90 but more than 70 days of service. Eventually the cost of veterans' benefits, estimated at $4.8 billion, dramatically exceeded the cost of the war itself.

PERSHING, JOHN JOSEPH (1860–1948). First lieutenant and quartermaster of the **Tenth U.S. Cavalry**. A West Point graduate, Pershing fought in Indian campaigns on the frontier, was a professor of Military Science and Tactics at the University of Nebraska, and obtained a law degree. While serving with the Tenth Cavalry, he was given the derisive nickname "Nigger Jack" because of his constant support of his **black American** soldiers. Upon the outbreak of the war, he quit his teaching post at West Point and rejoined the Tenth Cavalry, barely arriving in time at **Tampa, Florida**, to board the regiment's transport.

During the **Santiago, Cuba, campaign**, Pershing, who considered the Cuban insurgents of little service to the United States, won laurels for his conduct during the **Battle of Las Guásimas** on 24 June 1898 and was later awarded the Silver Star for his courage in guiding the second squadron through barbed-wire entanglements and thickets while attacking with the skirmish line in the **Battle of San Juan Hill** on 1 July. Debilitated by malaria, he returned to the United States, was appointed major (USV) in August, and organized the Insular Bureau in the **War Department** to administer the **Philippines** and **Puerto Rico**. He consistently praised the courage of his black soldiers during the war, believed the United States had fought an honorable war in wresting lands from the misrule of "the proudest monarchy of Europe," advocated a U.S. mission to civilize the conquered peoples, and scorned the anti-imperialists. He later fought in the **Philippine Insurrection**, led a U.S. force into Mexico after Pancho Villa, and commanded the U.S. expeditionary force in France during World War I. **Congress** appointed him general of the armies, a rank never held before, and he served as army chief of staff from 1921 to 1924.

PETREL. (USN) **Gunboat**, commanded by Lt. Comdr. Edward P. Wood. Originally rigged as a barquentine, the *Petrel*, whose executive officer was Lt. **Bradley A. Fiske**, was part of the **Asiatic Squadron** when Com. **George W. Dewey** assumed command on 3 January 1898. **Emilio Aguinaldo**, Filipino insurgent leader, later claimed that he met with Wood in **Hong Kong** during March and early April 1898. According to Aguinaldo, Wood asked him to return to the **Philippines** and stated that the United States would support Philippine independence because it had no need of colonies. Subsequently, the *Petrel* steamed to the Philippines and fought in the **Battle of Manila Bay** on 1 May, firing 448 shots. After the battle it fired the remainder of Adm. **Patricio Montojo's Squadron** and commandeered two large tugs, three steam launches, and several smaller boats. For his actions during the battle, Chief Carpenter's Mate Franz A. Itrich was later awarded the **Congressional Medal of Honor**. On 2 May the *Petrel* forced the surrender of the **Cavite** arsenal. During the **Battle of Manila** on 13 August, it briefly fired on **Fort San Antonio Abad**. After participating in the **Philippine Insurrection**, it was sold in 1920.

La. 1888, com. 1889, dis. 892, hp. 1,095, sp. 11.8
Armor: d. .3"

Armament: 4–6″, 2–3pdr., 2–1pdr., 2–37 mm., 2 mgs.
Cc. 200, comp. 122

PHILIP, JOHN WOODWARD "JACK" (1840–1900). Captain (USN) commanded the *Texas*. A U.S. Naval Academy graduate and Civil War veteran, Philip commanded the six-year Woodruff scientific expedition around the world, and after commanding the Boston Navy Yard from 1894 to 1897, he returned to sea duty in command of the *Texas*. During the war, he fought in the **Naval Battle of Santiago** on 3 July 1898, and as his ship was passing the burning *Vizcaya*, with its men abandoning ship, his men broke into cheers. Philip then directed to his crew a line long after remembered: "Don't cheer, boys! Those poor devils are dying." In his article, "The *Texas* at Santiago," *Century Magazine* (May 1899), he wrote that if Adm. **Pascual Cervera's Squadron** had been able to steam straight out of **Santiago**, radiating the ships of the squadron with the **torpedo-boat destroyers** in advance, one or more of them might have escaped. Promoted to commodore in August 1898, he later commanded the Brooklyn Navy Yard, and was promoted to rear admiral in March 1899.

PHILIPPINE CAMPAIGN. After leaving **Mirs Bay, China**, on 27 April 1898, Com. **George W. Dewey's Asiatic Squadron** attacked and overwhelmingly defeated Adm. **Patricio Montojo's Squadron** in the **Battle of Manila Bay** on 1 May 1898. The next day President **William McKinley** authorized an expeditionary force, which became the **Eighth Corps**, for the **Philippines**. While Adm. Dewey's naval forces blockaded **Manila**, the Eighth Corps arrived during June and July. On 13 August the Eighth Corps and U.S. naval forces fought and won the prearranged **Battle of Manila**, one day after the **Armistice Protocol** had been signed ending hostilities.

PHILIPPINE INSURRECTION (1899–1902). Called the Philippine Insurrection by U.S. officials at the time, it was a full-scale war that broke out on 4 February 1899 between U.S. forces and the nationalist Filipino forces of **Emilio Aguinaldo**. Officially lasting for 41 months until 4 July 1902, it eventually saw the deployment of 126,000 U.S. soldiers to the **Philippines**, with 69,000 being engaged at any one time. During the war over 4,000 U.S. soldiers and between 16,000–20,000 Filipino insurgents died; moreover, over 200,000 civilians died from indirect causes such as famine or **disease**. On 4 July 1902, President **Theodore Roosevelt** declared the "insurrection" officially ended. Its suppression cost the United States $600 million.

PHILIPPINE REVOLT. Beginning in August 1896, the **Katipunan**, led by **Andres Bonifacio**, fought against Spain for the independence of the **Philippines**. Initially Spain had only 7,000 troops in the islands, but by the end of October over 23,000 soldiers had arrived. On 30 December 1896, José Rizal, a nationalist leader and founder of the reformist Liga Filipina, was executed by Spanish authorities. In March 1897, a revolutionary government was established under the leadership of **Emilio Aguinaldo**, and Bonifacio was executed on 10 May because of an internal struggle within the independence movement. A short-lived republic was established at **Biak-na-bató** in June, and with the war stalemated, the **Pact of Biak-na-bató** temporarily halted the fighting in December 1897. However, fighting broke out again in February 1898, and Spanish forces, now numbering 41,000, were spread throughout the islands on the defensive by the time Emilio Aguinaldo returned to the Philippines on 19 May.

By summer most of the outlying garrisons on Luzon had fallen into insurgent hands, **Manila** was surrounded by insurgent forces, and an insurgent assembly proclaimed Philippine independence on 12 June. However, with the arrival of the U.S. **Eighth Corps** in June and July, the insurgent forces were relegated to a secondary position as the United States defeated Spain and occupied Manila on 13 August. Conferences took place between U.S. and Filipino leaders but failed to resolve any issues. In September, with the insurgents in control of almost all of the island of Luzon, a revolutionary congress met at **Malolos**, drafted a constitution, and proclaimed the Philippine Republic on 23 January 1899. After Aguinaldo rejected U.S. claims of sovereignty over the Philippines, the **Philippine Insurrection** broke out on 4 February 1899. By 1902 the nationalist forces had been defeated by the United States.

PHILIPPINES. Since the outbreak of the **Philippine Revolt** in 1896, the islands were the scene of bloody fighting, which was temporarily stalled by the **Pact of Biak-na-bató** in December 1897. Under the direction of Gov.-Gen. **Basilio Augustín y Dávila**, Spain's defenses consisted of a 51,331-man army of regulars and *voluntarios* scattered throughout the islands, of which 23,000 were spread across the island of Luzon. Based on Adm. **Patricio Montojo's Squadron**, the navy totaled 37 ships, but most were small launches of 40 tons or lightly armed vessels of less than 600 tons.

Supported by the Catholic Church, which was the biggest landowner on the islands, the government and the church censored all publications. After the disastrous defeat in the **Battle of Manila Bay** on 1 May, Augustín established a **Consultative Assembly** on 4 May 1898 and attempted to recruit a Filipino volunteer militia to bolster Spain's forces. Both efforts failed by the middle of June. **Blockade**d by Adm. **George W. Dewey**'s naval forces and with the Filipino insurgent forces surrounding Manila and isolating Spanish forces throughout the islands, Augustín began to negotiate with U.S. forces. He was replaced on 4 August by **Fermín Jáudenes**, who subsequently negotiated the prearranged **Battle of Manila** on 13 August and the **Capitulation of Manila Agreement** of 14 August.

Under the direction of Maj. Gen. **Wesley Merritt**, the United States established a government of military occupation that excluded the Filipino insurgents. Jáudenes was replaced by Gen. Francisco Rizzo, who was then succeeded by Gen. **Diego de los Ríos**. On 21 December, President **William McKinley** extended U.S. military control to all the islands under the guise of "benevolent assimilation," and in January 1899 he appointed the **Schurman Commission** to investigate the conditions in the islands. On 4 February, fighting erupted between Filipino insurgent forces and U.S. troops, and the **Philippine Insurrection** began. As a result of the **Treaty of Paris**, the islands came under official U.S. control.

PHOTOGRAPHY. At a time when artists were considered superior to photographers, artists' newspaper etchings, which were commonly called photographs, were more common than actual photos. Dwight L. Elmendorf photographed the U.S. military at **Tampa** and **Key West, Florida**, and at **Camp Wikoff, Montauk Point, Long Island, New York**. However, in photographing the war in the tropics, photographers faced the handicaps of excessive moisture, films and plates of limited latitude, working in improvised darkrooms, and being forced to use alcohol to hasten the drying of negatives. Consequently, the photographs of the **Battle of Manila Bay** were of poor quality. Because no official or professional photographers accompanied the **U.S. Navy** in the Caribbean theater, photographs were taken by officers or sailors. Among those who photographed the war in **Cuba** were members of the medical corps, foreign military observers, professional photographers **John C. Hemment** of the *New York Journal* and **James H. Hare** of *Collier's*; and **correspondents Richard H. Davis** and William Dinwiddie of the *New York Herald*, **Burr McIntosh** of the *New York Journal*, and James Burton of *Harper's Weekly*.

PI I MARGALL, FRANCESC (FRANCISCO) (1824–1901). Catalan intellectual and Federalist-Republican politician. Formerly president of Spain's First Republic in 1873 for a brief period of time, Pi i Margall led one faction of the Federalist Party after it divided in 1880. In 1890 he founded the newspaper *El Nuevo Régimen*, which became his mouthpiece in defense of **Catalanism**. Although he was politically marginalized when the **Cuban Revolt** began in 1895, he demanded **autonomy** for **Cuba** and **Puerto Rico**, protested against forced recruitment, and opposed sending more troops to Cuba. By May 1896, Pi i Margall advocated stopping the revolt even if it meant Cuban independence; however, he believed an independent Cuban government should assume the **Cuban debt** and the costs of the war. Consistently opposed to going to war with the United States, he initially believed that the United States would bring democratic government to Spain's former colonies. However, by the war's end he admitted he had misjudged American intentions and harshly criticized its annexationist policy, believing that by becoming an empire it would lose its own liberty.

PINCHBACK DELEGATION. Led by Pinckney B. S. Pinchback, a delegation of **black American** political leaders visited President **William McKinley** shortly after war had been declared against Spain on 25 April 1898 to pledge their support and to get the restrictions removed on the number and level of black officers in the U.S. military. Along with Pinchback, a mulatto who had helped found the **Republican Party** in Louisiana and had served as lieutenant governor of Louisiana and as a U.S. marshal in New York City, the delegation included Judson Lyons (a register of the treasury), Henry P. Cheatham (a former North Carolina congressman and current recorder of deeds in Washington, D.C.), and George H. White (a congressman from North Carolina). The delegation was unsuccessful in getting the restrictions against black officers removed, and Pinchback later supported the **McKinley administration**'s policy in the **Philippines**.

PLÜDDEMANN, MAX (1846–1910). Rear admiral in the German Navy. During the war Plüddemann was an observer with the **U.S. Navy** in the Caribbean. After the war he wrote a study of the war, which was translated and published by the **Office of Naval Intelligence** in 1898 as *Comments of Rear-Admiral Plüddemann, German Navy, on the Main Features of the War with Spain*. His main conclusions were: 1) No developments during the war led to a radical change of views on the conduct of naval warfare; 2) the **battleship**'s supremacy was evident; 3) **torpedoes** were ineffective overall; 4) U.S. claims of damage inflicted by its naval bombardments were exaggerated; 5) the accuracy of U.S. naval gunfire was much better than that of the Spanish, which was miserable; 6) the failure to remove combustible material had caused the extensive fires on Spanish ships during battle; 7) **monitors** were not reliable; 8) Spanish **mines** frequently failed to operate; 9) the U.S. repair ship *Vulcan* was very useful; and 10) nearly all neutral vessels captured by the United States were released.

PLUTÓN. (SPN) **Torpedo-boat destroyer**, commanded by Comdr. Pedro Vásquez. As part of Adm. **Pascual Cervera's Squadron**, the

Plutón fought, and was destroyed, in the **Naval Battle of Santiago** on 3 July 1898. Almost immediately after emerging from the harbor entrance, it was pounded by the *Gloucester* and *Indiana*. Its forward boilers exploded, and it ran aground, tearing open its bow, and sank at 10:45 a.m. a little west of **Cabañas Bay**. More than half of its crew died in combat or drowned. Lt. Caballero, second in command, led 20–25 sailors from the beach overland back to **Santiago**, and others, including Comdr. Vásquez, were rescued by the *Gloucester*.

La. 1897, com. 1897, dis. 420, hp. 7,500, sp. 30
Armament: 2–14pdr., 2–6pdr., 2–1pdr., 2–14″ tt.
Cc. 100, comp. 70

POLAVIEJA Y DEL CASTILLO, CAMILO GARCÍA DE (1838– 1914). Lieutenant general and governor-general of the **Philippines** (December 1896–April 1897). Polavieja, who was known as the "Christian General," served as captain general of **Cuba** from 1890 to 1892 and replaced Gov.-Gen. **Ramón Blanco y Erenas** in the Philippines in mid-December 1896. He consistently defeated the insurgents on the battlefield, relocated the civilian population to guarded areas, and ordered wholesale executions of any insurgent sympathizers. After he asked to return to Spain because of an attack of hepatitis, his request was reluctantly granted. He was replaced by **Fernando Primo de Rivera** and left for Spain on 15 April 1897.

Returning to cheering crowds and national celebrations, Polavieja, a member of the **Liberal-Conservative Party**, briefly toyed with the idea of political office but decided to remain in the background as Spain's possible savior. He maintained a reserved attitude during the Spanish-American War and served as the president of Spain's Red Cross. In September 1898, he supported a program of **regenerationism** by a nonpartisan movement that would reestablish Spain's role in the world, advocated **Catalanism**, and although he blamed the politicians for losing the war, he did not aspire to a military dictatorship. In 1899, he served as minister of war in **Francisco Silvela**'s cabinet.

POLO DE BERNABÉ, LUIS (1854–1929). Spain's minister to the U.S. (March–21 April 1898). An experienced diplomat whose father had been an admiral and held the same diplomatic position in Washington, D.C., Polo de Bernabé replaced **Enrique Dupuy de Lôme** as Spain's minister to the United States. Suspicious of American intentions and skeptical of finding a diplomatic solution, he, nevertheless, assiduously tried to convince the U.S. government that the Cuban **autonomous government** was functioning successfully and made every effort to assist in the distribution of American relief to civilians in **Cuba**.

On 10 April, Polo de Bernabé wrote a lengthy memorandum to the U.S. government defending Spain's policy. Including an announcement of the suspension of hostilities in Cuba, he pointed out that Spain had established **autonomy**, abolished **reconcentration**, and publicly expressed horror over the *Maine* tragedy, assisted its survivors, and shown a willingness to accept arbitration of the issue. Although the contents of the memorandum were approved of by Prime Minister **Práxedes M. Sagasta** when it was **cable**d to Spain, he was chided for having delivered it without prior governmental approval.

On 20 April, Polo de Bernabé turned over Spain's interests in Washington, D.C., to **Jules Cambon**, the French ambassador, and left Washington the next day. Relocating to Montreal, **Canada**, he ran the **Montreal Spy Ring**. After he was expelled from Canada in late May because of his **espionage** activities, he returned to Spain and continued in the diplomatic service.

PONCE, PUERTO RICO. Located on the southern Puerto Rican coast, Ponce, a town of 37,000, was a center of opposition to Spanish rule and was defenseless. Prior to the U.S. invasion, Col. Leopoldo San Martín y Gil, in command of three companies of the **Patria Battalion**, **guerrillas** and *voluntarios* totaling 500 men, was given orders to defend the town; however, only two-thirds of his men were armed and no reinforcements arrived.

On 27 July 1898, the *Dixie*, under the command of Capt. **Charles H. Davis**, anchored off the port of Ponce, two miles south of the town. Lt. G. A. Merriam and Cadet **George C. Lodge** came ashore and demanded the surrender of the town under threat of bombardment. The *Dixie* was soon joined by the *Annapolis* and *Wasp*, and Col. San Martín asked Gov.-Gen. **Manuel Macías y Casado** for instructions. Commercial interests and foreign consuls residing in Ponce **cable**d Macías advising that the town be surrendered. Macías ordered San Martín to evacuate, and with the same commercial interests and foreign consuls acting as intermediaries, a deal was made. The town would be surrendered provided the Spanish forces could retreat unmolested for 48 hours, and the civil government would continue to function. Macías then annulled his previous order and ordered San Martín's removal from command. San Martín, who had withdrawn his forces to Coamo, was then replaced, arrested, and imprisoned in **San Juan**. Subsequently, a court-martial in Spain later freed him because he had acted under orders.

On 28 July, Merriam and Lodge landed again, took possession of the port, and the American flag was raised over the town. Brig. Gen. **Guy V. Henry**'s force arrived overland from **Guánica**, Maj. Gen. **James H. Wilson**'s force disembarked, and Maj. Gen. **Nelson A.**

Miles issued his first proclamation. After Miles met with the civilian authorities in the afternoon, the town celebrated and fire companies paraded. The U.S. military took possession of 91 vessels in the port; however, only three were considered **prizes of war**, and the rest were returned to their owners. According to **Richard H. Davis** the town surrendered four times, first to Ensign Curtin of the *Wasp*, then to three officers who strayed into town by mistake, then to Capt. Davis of the *Dixie*, and finally to Maj. Gen. Miles. **Carlton T. Chapman** later wrote "The Occupation of Ponce" *Harper's Weekly* (13 September 1898).

POPULIST PARTY—UNITED STATES. Springing to national importance in 1892, it was a party of dissatisfaction based on workers and the farmers of the West. The party supported Cuban independence at its 1896 convention and later advocated the recognition of the **Cuban Republic**. Although populists such as Senator William V. Allen of Nebraska championed Cuban independence, others such as Mary E. Lease held deeply racial opinions, believing that Latins were fit only to be the "tillers of the soil" in a Caucasian-owned tropics. In March 1898, Populists helped block the **Hull Bill** to expand the regular army, and upon the outbreak of war, Governors Silas A. Holcomb of Nebraska and John W. Leedy of Kansas ardently supported U.S. intervention in **Cuba**. Seven Populists in the House opposed the annexation of **Hawaii**, six senators voted for the **Treaty of Paris**, and two voted against.

PORTABLE SHIELDS. According to an idea of Maj. Gen. **Nelson A. Miles**, these massive 1,000-pound steel plates on wheeled carriages were to be pushed ahead of soldiers going into battle. One hundred shields on board the *Gate City* arrived at **Siboney, Cuba**, on 9 July 1898, but could not be used in the Cuban mud; consequently, they were transferred to the *Comanche* and taken to **Puerto Rico**, where they were also not used.

PORTER. (USN) **Torpedo boat**, commanded by Lt. John Charles Fremont. Assigned to the **North Atlantic Squadron**, the *Porter* served on the **blockade of Cuba**, capturing the schooners *Mathilde* and *Sofia* on 23 April 1898, and the schooner *Antonio* on 24 April. Although it participated in the naval bombardment of **San Juan, Puerto Rico**, on 12 May, it had to be towed most of the way to San Juan. It was later used by Adm. **William T. Sampson** to carry dispatches to and from his divided squadron, especially during the search for Adm. **Pascual Cervera's Squadron**. On 21 June, it bombarded the **Socapa** battery at the entrance to the harbor of **Santiago, Cuba**, in support of the landing of the **Fifth Corps** at **Daiquirí, Cuba**. It was sold in 1912.

La. 1896, com. 1897, dis. 165, hp. 3,200, sp. 27.5
Armament: 4–1pdr., 3–18″ tt.
Cc. 76, comp. 24

PORTER, HORACE (1837–1921). U.S. ambassador to **France**. A Civil War general and author of *Campaigning with Grant* (1897), Porter, as ambassador from 1897 to 1905, had extensive discussions with Gabriel Hanotaux, French foreign minister, during the war. In June 1898, he told Hanotaux that the United States did not want to annex additional territories or to secure a financial indemnity from Spain and suggested to Washington that he be allowed to enter into direct negotiations with **Fernando León y Castillo**, Spain's ambassador to France. When Hanotaux informed him that Spain had authorized León y Castillo to initiate peace talks, Porter, on 14 June, without authorization from Washington, informed Hanotaux to inform León y Castillo that Spain would probably lose all the **Philippines** if peace did not come within a week. On 18 June Secretary of State **William R. Day** officially rejected Porter's request to enter into negotiations and empowered him to only receive proposals. During the **Treaty of Paris** negotiations Porter served as a conduit between León y Castillo and Day, who chaired the U.S. **Peace Commission**. Porter later served as a U.S. delegate to the Hague Conference.

POST, CHARLES JOHNSON (1873–1956). Private in Company E, **Seventy-First New York Infantry**. Formerly an illustrator for the *New York Journal*, Post, an artist-soldier, carried a sketchbook along with his gun throughout the war and later wrote *The Little War of Private Post* (1960), his memoir about the war. From the viewpoint of the "little man" in a "little war," he called the plan of attack in the **Battle of San Juan Hill** on 1 July 1898 "a sort of go-ahead-and-when-you-get-shot-at-why-dammit-shoot-right-back," and pointed out military blunders, poor equipment, and the ever-present danger of death from bullets or **disease**. After returning to **Camp Wikoff, Montauk Point, Long Island, New York**, Post got a pass and went home to New York City, where he ended up in the hospital. After he got back on his feet, he faced a court problem because he had been fined $500 for failing to show up for jury duty while he was fighting at **Santiago, Cuba**. The judge let him off. He later worked as a free-lance writer and illustrator.

PRAIRIE. (USN) Unprotected **cruiser**, commanded by Comdr. Charles J. Train. Formerly the *El Sol* of the Southern Pacific Company, it was purchased by the **U.S. Navy** on 6 April 1898 and staffed in part by seven officers and 138 men from the Massachusetts **naval militia**. Initially assigned to the **Northern Patrol Squadron**, on 1 July it was incorporated into **North Atlantic Fleet** and saw service on the **blockade of Cuba** and in Puerto Rican waters. After the war it transported troops from **Santiago, Cuba**, to **Camp Wikoff, Montauk Point, Long Island, New York**. It later served as a training ship, a transport, and as a destroyer tender during World War I. It was sold in 1923.

La. 1890, com. 14 April 1898, dis. 6,872, hp. 3,800, sp. 14.5
Armament: 10–6″, 6–6pdr., 2 C. mgs.
Cc. 1,000, comp. 285

PRATT, E. SPENCER. U.S. consul at Singapore. Howard Bray, an English adventurer and former British official in India, introduced Pratt to **Emilio Aguinaldo**. As a result of their discussions of 24–26 April 1898, Aguinaldo left Singapore for **Hong Kong** and later joined Com. **George W. Dewey's Asiatic Squadron** at **Manila, Philippines**, on 19 May. The discussions later became controversial. According to Aguinaldo, Pratt urged him to quickly return to the **Philippines** and stated that the United States would recognize Philippine independence with a U.S. protectorate. Bray later confirmed Aguinaldo's view. Moreover, Pratt had offered to procure guns for the insurgents for a commission and even proposed to serve as their agent in Washington after independence. However, Pratt denied having made any promises and maintained he had consistently told Aguinaldo he had no authority to speak for the U.S. government.

PRESS—SPAIN. Although the press outside the major cities had long been censored by the government, the Madrid press, with 24 political dailies, and the Barcelona press, with 15 political dailies and three economic dailies, were basically uncensored. Most were identified with a particular politician or party, such as *El Imparcial*, the **Liberal Party**'s paper; *El Heraldo de Madrid*, a Liberal paper; and *El Nacional*, a conservative paper of **Francisco Romero Robledo**. During the **Cuban Revolt** the press became sensationalist, and with increased circulation businessmen rather than politicians began assuming control of the larger papers. Most agreed with defeating the Cuban and **Philippine Revolts** first. A few such as *El Pueblo*, which was edited by Vicente Blasco Ibáñez, supported the granting of **autonomy** to **Cuba**, and fewer still such as *El País*, a Madrid-based **republican** socialist newspaper, proclaimed that Cuba was lost on 20 December 1896.

Prior to the Spanish-American War the press caused unrealistic expectations in glorifying Spanish heroism and patriotism, exalting the Spanish soldier as one of the best in the world, depicting the **Spanish Navy** as superior to the **U.S. Navy**, and characterizing Americans as greedy, cowardly, and lacking in military virtues. *El Ejército Español*, on 25 January 1898, spoke of the possibility of an Indian uprising in the United States, which would help Spain, and on 2 March, *El Correo Militar* predicted the defeat of the **U.S. Army** in Cuba and that the Spanish navy would ravage American shipping in the Atlantic Ocean. Moreover, many urged Spain to go to war because Spain had been humiliated by the United States, which had tried to dictate Spain's Cuban policy. On 14 April, *El Correo de Madrid*, a Liberal Party paper, accused the United States of three years of duplicity, trickery, and slander.

Upon the outbreak of the war, the press overwhelmingly supported Spain's war effort. However, such unanimity was quickly broken by Com. **George W. Dewey**'s overwhelming victory at the **Battle of Manila Bay** on 1 May. Doubts quickly surfaced, and as the politicians floundered in the mid-May shake-up in the government of Prime Minister **Práxedes M. Sagasta**, *El Noticiero Universal*, a Barcelona paper, in a 22 May article "En plena Bizancio," excoriated Spain's politicians for doing nothing but quarreling and discussing trifles. With the press beginning to divide over continuing the war, *El Correo Español*, a Madrid **Carlist** newspaper, on 4 June, continued to proclaim that Spain's innate superiority would guarantee victory. However, the defeat of Adm. **Pascual Cervera's Squadron** at the **Naval Battle of Santiago** on 3 July forced most papers to seek a means to end the war. *El Socialista*, the **Spanish Socialist Workers Party** paper, was the first to call for a negotiated settlement. Soon *El Imparcial*, *El Nacional*, *Heraldo de Madrid*, *El Liberal*, and *El País*, which had ardently supported the war, began to demand a negotiated solution, while *El Diario de Barcelona*, a conservative independent paper, disparaged the Spanish press on 9 July for having promoted the idea of a quick victory in the war and for dispensing fictitious information in order to increase sales. On 14 July, Sagasta decreed press **censorship** as his administration moved to a negotiated solution. After the war many, such as **Carlos O'Donnell y Abreú**, blamed the press for causing Spain's defeat, and many of the party-based newspapers, which were wounded by the war, soon disappeared.

PRESS—UNITED STATES. America in the 1890s was a nation of newspaper readers with about 14,000 weeklies and 1,900 dailies, and it was the heyday of the **"yellow press."** Major news services existed—the Scrips-McCrae League, Publishers' Press Association, and **Associated Press**—and papers such as the *New York Herald, New*

York Journal, *New York Sun*, and the *New York World* had their own services.

Prior to the war much of the business press, such as *Banker's Magazine*, *New York Commercial and Financial Chronicle*, *United States Investor*, and the *Journal of Commerce and Commercial Bulletin* believed that a war with Spain would be bad for business, and *The Nation*, which was edited by **Edwin L. Godkin**, ardently opposed U.S. expansionism. However, the "yellow press," the *American Monthly Review of Reviews*, *New York Financial Record*, *Chicago Tribune*, *Munsey's Magazine*, *New York Sun*, *Leslie's Weekly*, and *Louisville, Kentucky, Courier-Journal* supported U.S. expansionism.

Most of the press dismissed Spain's policy of **autonomy** as unworkable and unacceptable, and upon the outbreak of the **Autonomy Riots** in **Havana**, **Cuba**, on 12 January 1898, several papers and magazines raised the specter of war and the need to send a warship to Havana to protect U.S. lives and property. The riots, which were the first Cuban incident to attract the interest of most of the nation's press, were the first opportunity for the "yellow press" to carry on a concerted scare campaign. Subsequently, most supported sending the *Maine* to Havana, and after the publication of the **De Lôme Letter** on 9 February, the Cuban situation received paramount consideration by most of the press even though it was not considered a *casus belli*. Such a cause came with the explosion of the *Maine* on 15 February, as heavy-typed, multiple-columned headlines blamed Spain for the disaster. The popular phrase of the day was "Spanish treachery," false stories abounded claiming that **torpedoes**, electrical bombs, and time fuses had destroyed the *Maine*, and circulation increased dramatically for those fanning the flames of war. By mid-March most of the business press came to acknowledge that a war with Spain posed no serious danger for business, and newspapers, such as the *Chicago Times-Herald* and the *New York Herald*, became pro-intervention.

During the war newspaper circulation quadrupled. Yet, because of exorbitant costs, Arthur Brisbane, an editor of the *New York Journal*, pointed out in his article "The Modern Newspaper in War Time" *Cosmopolitan* (September 1898), that had the war gone on for two years it would have bankrupted every newspaper in New York City. Nevertheless, the press overwhelmingly supported the war effort. On 12 May, the magazine *Public Opinion* hailed the U.S. rise to world-power status, and in June, Walter H. Page, the editor of the *Atlantic Monthly*, in his article "The War with Spain, and After," called the removal of Spain from the West Indies by the war "a necessary act of surgery for the health of civilization."

As victory followed victory, much of the press, particularly the pro-**Republican Party** press, came to support a colonial policy. On

4 August, a sample of 65 newspapers taken by *Public Opinion* showed that 43 percent were for permanent retention of the **Philippines**, 24.6 percent were opposed, and 32.4 percent were wavering. Although such a colonial policy was challenged by the *Boston Herald*, *Evening Post*, *Baltimore Sun*, and *Philadelphia Ledger*, a December 1898 *New York Herald* poll of 498 newspapers found that 305, or 61.3 percent, favored a colonial policy. New England and the Midwest showed clear margins in favor of expansion; the West, an overwhelming margin in favor; and the South alone, by a thin margin, was opposed. Moreover, 84.2 percent of the Republican press was in favor whereas 71.3 percent of the pro-**Democratic Party** press was opposed.

PRESS BOATS. Also called dispatch boats. Many newspapers bought or chartered boats to cover the **Cuban Revolt**. They were used to quickly deliver news from **Cuba** to **cable** stations such as **Key West, Florida**. **William R. Hearst**, owner of the *New York Journal*, was the first to see the need for a press boat when he chartered the *Vamoose* in November 1896. Eventually the *Journal* had ten, including the *Anita*; the *New York Herald* and the **Associated Press** each had five, including the *Dauntless* and the *Wanda*; the *New York World* had three, including the *Three Friends*; and the *New York Sun* and the *Chicago Record* each had one, including the *Hercules*. The *New York Herald* and the *New York World* jointly chartered the *Sommers N. Smith*. During the war about 20 press boats cruised in Cuban and Puerto Rican waters; moreover, frequently there were almost as many press boats accompanying U.S. naval forces as there were ships in the various squadrons. Ray Stannard Baker, in his article "How the News of the War is Reported" *McClure's Magazine* (September 1898), pointed out that charter costs for boats ranged from $5,000 to $9,000 a month. At a total cost of around $1,000 a day, press boats were one of a newspapers' biggest expenses in war coverage.

PRIMO DE RIVERA, FERNANDO (1831–1921). Governor-general and captain general of the **Philippines** (1897–1898). The Marques de Estrella, Primo de Rivera was appointed governor-general of the Philippines on 22 March 1897, and, after arriving in the Philippines on 23 April, replaced Gov.-Gen. **Camilo Polavieja**. Believing the **Philippine Revolt** was on the wane, Primo de Rivera adopted a conciliatory policy and extended unconditional pardons to insurgents. When his policy received little response, he began an aggressive military offensive against **Cavite** Province. On 17 May, he issued another pardon, which was better received, and while Spanish forces continued to force the insurgents to retreat, he toyed with the idea of a negotiated settlement. When **Pedro A. Paterno** offered his services as a mediator, Primo de Rivera accepted, and Paterno's efforts eventually resulted in the **Pact of Biak-na-bató** in December 1897. For bringing peace to the Philippines, Primo de Rivera was awarded the Grand Cross of San Fernando.

Informed by Spanish intelligence on 3 March 1898 of Com. **George W. Dewey**'s plans to attack **Manila** in the event of war, Primo de Rivera convened a council of war on 15 March, and orders were given to develop 15 strong points around Manila and for Adm. **Patricio Montojo's Squadron** to meet the U.S. squadron at **Subic Bay**. However, Primo de Rivera was replaced by Lt. Gen. **Basilio Augustín y Dávila** on 9 April and left for Spain on 12 April. When consulted by **Práxedes M. Sagasta** in early August about a negotiated settlement, he stated he was not opposed to peace. He later served twice as minister of war.

PRISONERS OF WAR. The number of U.S. military personnel taken prisoner during the war was infinitesimal, and those were usually freed in prisoner exchanges. Two American **correspondents**, Hayden Jones and Charles Thrall, of the *New York World*, who had been arrested for **espionage**, were exchanged for captured Spanish soldiers on 28 May 1898 off **Havana, Cuba**. After Maj. Gen. **William R. Shafter** released four Spanish officers and 24 enlisted men on 5 July without a quid pro quo, on 6 July the crew of the *Merrimac* was exchanged for a like number of Spanish prisoners. At the war's end, Spain held no U.S. prisoners of war.

Because of the overwhelming U.S. victories, the United States retained a sizable number of Spanish prisoners of war. On 22 April, Juan de Río, commanding the steamer *Buenaventura*, became the first. In **Cuba** almost 26,000 soldiers and sailors, most from **Santiago**, were taken prisoner. With the exception of the *Harvard* **Incident** of 4 July 1898, they received good treatment. Adm. **Pascual Cervera** and 78 of his officers and 14 sailors were detained at the U.S. Naval Academy at Annapolis, Maryland, and the officers, having given their word, were free to walk around the city during the afternoon without supervision. Upon their arrival they were greeted with full military honors, welcomed by the local population, furnished cooks and servants by the U.S. government, supplied with beer and light wines, and given "spending money." Most of the sailors in Adm. **Cervera's Squadron** were detained at Camp Long on Seavey's Island near Portsmouth, New Hampshire. Other prisoners were held at Fort McPherson, Georgia. Upon learning that **black American** soldiers of the **Twenty-Fourth U.S. Infantry** were guarding the prisoners, the *Savannah Tribune* declared on 21 May that, "It is an outrage that white men (Spaniards) have been subjected to the humiliation of having negro guards over them."

At first the **McKinley administration** considered detaining Spanish prisoners of war at Galveston, Texas. However, as part of the **Armistice Protocol** negotiations, the United States paid for the **repatriation** of Spanish prisoners in Cuba, the **Philippines**, and **Puerto Rico** back to Spain upon the cessation of hostilities.

PRIZE MONEY. According to U.S. law, both captured ships and cargoes could be sold and the prize money divided, half going to the U.S. government and the remainder being portioned out on a sliding scale according to rank among the officers and men of the vessel responsible for the capture. Moreover, prize money was also given at $100 per head for every person on an enemy's ships sunk or destroyed in action with a superior U.S. ship. If the U.S. ship were the same or inferior in size, the money was increased to $200 per head. If the ship was sunk or destroyed without an armed action, the amount was $50 per head.

By 24 May 1898, Adm. **William T. Sampson**'s naval forces had received $750,000, with Sampson receiving $150,000, and Adm. **George W. Dewey's Asiatic Squadron** received $182,350 from its victory at the **Battle of Manila Bay** on 1 May. Dewey received one-twentieth, and the remainder was distributed to *Olympia* ($45,000), *Baltimore* ($40,000), *Boston* ($25,000), *Raleigh* ($22,000), *Concord* ($20,000), *Petrel* ($12,000), and *McCulloch* ($9,000). Each commander received one-tenth of the amount assigned to his ship. Such distribution of spoils continued in the **U.S. Navy** until 1900.

PRIZES OF WAR. Because according to the rules of war, significant **prize money** was awarded to those who captured enemy vessels, prizes of war became a contentious issue. The first prize was the Spanish merchantman *Buenaventura*, which was captured by the *Nashville* on 22 April 1898. Owing to the imposition of the **blockade of Cuba**, by the end of April, a number of vessels had been captured, aggregating close to $3 million in value. On 11 May, Spain's government declared that all captures prior to the 25 April official U.S. **declaration of war** were invalid and illegal even though the declaration had been made retroactive to 21 April.

Many legal problems arose. The Spanish steamer *Miguel Jover*, which was captured on 22 April by the *Helena* off the Cuban coast, was taken to **Key West, Florida**, and later released. The *Restormel*, a British collier, was captured, and although the ship was released, the cargo was condemned. On 25 July, the *Dixie* captured the French steamer *Manoubia* bound for Sagua la Grande, Cuba; however, it was released since Sagua la Grande had not been proclaimed officially blockaded. Moreover, a number of fishing schooners captured early in the war, which had been detained at Key West, were adjudged prizes by a U.S. district court, only to be released when the U.S. Supreme Court overruled the district court.

As a result of the **capitulation** of **Santiago, Cuba**, on 17 July, a major dispute arose between the **U.S. Army** and **U.S. Navy** over Spanish vessels in the harbor. Both insisted the vessels belonged to their respective service. On July 19, the **McKinley administration** informed the services that joint prizes were not within the law. The *Alvarado* was placed into naval service, and five merchant steamers were turned over to the army transport service; however, eventually the steamers were returned to their owners.

PROCTOR, REDFIELD (1831–1908). Republican senator from Vermont. A Civil War veteran, Proctor practiced law in Vermont and became wealthy as the president of the Vermont Marble Company, the largest marble producer in the country. A former governor, congressman, and secretary of war, Proctor actively campaigned for **William McKinley** and helped to secure the command of the **Asiatic Squadron** for Com. **George W. Dewey**. He arrived in **Havana, Cuba**, on 26 February 1898, on a fact-finding tour. After touring four provinces and meeting with Spanish officials, Proctor returned to Washington, intent on merely writing a report about his visit. However, Senator **William P. Frye** convinced him to speak to the Senate; accordingly, Proctor, a man not known for oratory, delivered a passionless speech that gave no new facts to a packed chamber on 17 March. Describing the situation in **Cuba** as "desolation and distress, misery and starvation," Proctor depicted a failed policy of **autonomy**. Although he claimed to be objective, his speech made the case for humanitarian intervention in Cuba.

Telegraphed by the **Associated Press** across the country, Proctor's speech captured the popular mood and profoundly shifted business opinion in favor of intervention. On 19 March, the *Wall Street Journal* opined, "Senator Proctor's speech converted a great many people on Wall Street, who have hereto taken the ground that the United States had no business to interfere in a revolution on Spanish soil." On 23 March, the *American Banker* concluded that it could not understand "how anyone with a grain of human sympathy within him can dispute the propriety of a policy of intervention, so only that this outraged people might be set free." However, not all reactions were favorable. House Speaker **Thomas B. Reed**, famous for his acerbic wit, remarked, "Proctor's position might have been expected. A war will make a large market for gravestones." Proctor later voted for the

Treaty of Paris and, at the time of his death, was reportedly the wealthiest man in Congress.

PROTECTED CRUISER. A cruiser with an armored deck. The U.S. Navy had 14, including the *Baltimore*, *Boston*, *Charleston*, *Olympia*, and *Raleigh*, and the Spanish Navy had five, including the *Isla de Cuba* and *Isla de Luzón*. The contract price for a U.S. protected cruiser varied from $800,000 for the *Boston* to $2,725,000 for the *Columbia*.

PUERTO RICAN CAMPAIGN. After the McKinley administration made its decision on 26 May 1898 to invade Puerto Rico, Maj. Gen. Nelson A. Miles was ordered to prepare and command the expedition. Miles left Charleston, South Carolina, on the *Yale* on 8 July with a 3,500-man force, steamed to Santiago, Cuba, and on 21 July left Guantánamo, Cuba, with 3,415 infantry, two companies of engineers, and one company of the Signal Corps. Accompanied by a naval escort under the command of Capt. Francis J. Higginson, which included the battleship *Massachusetts*, cruiser *Dixie*, armed yacht *Gloucester*, and armed steamships *Columbia*, *Yale*, and *Macon*, the expedition landed at Guánica on 25 July.

Miles's decision not to use troops already in Cuba because of disease harmonized well with President William McKinley's political needs because he was being pressured to send units from many states into action. Eventually Miles's total force of around 15,000 men consisted of both regulars and volunteers, including regular and volunteer artillery, cavalry, engineers, and infantry. His artillery consisted of 106 mortars, howitzers, field and siege guns, and ten Gatlings.

Miles, who wished to avoid frontal assaults and stressed maneuver to isolate and outflank enemy positions, planned a four-pronged thrust from southern Puerto Rico, which would eventually converge on San Juan. The forces involved were under the command of Maj. Gen. John R. Brooke, Brig. Gen. George A. Garretson, Brig. Gen. Theodore Schwan, and Maj. Gen. James H. Wilson. Many Puerto Ricans openly welcomed the invading U.S. forces, and some acted as guides and spies for the U.S. forces. The 19-day campaign, which consisted of skirmishes at Yauco on 26 July, Guayama on 5 August, Coamo on 9 August, Hormigueros on 10 August, Asomante Hills on 12 August, and Las Marías on 13 August, was halted with half the island in U.S. hands by the signing of the Armistice Protocol on 12 August. Total U.S. combat casualties included three dead and 40 wounded whereas Spanish casualties were about ten times as great.

PUERTO RICAN COMMISSIONERS. Composed of Puerto Ricans selected by Warner P. Sutton, former U.S. consul general in Puerto

Rico, and Capt. **Henry H. Whitney** of the staff of Maj. Gen. **Nelson A. Miles**, they returned to the island along with U.S. troops in support of the U.S. invasion. Aligned because of their desire to drive Spain from the island, the commission left Newport News, Virginia, on the *St. Louis* and included Gen. Antonio Mattei Lluveras, P. J. Besoso, José Budet, Domingo Collazo, Mateo Fajardo, Emilio González, Rafael Marxuach, and Rafael Muñoz.

PUERTO RICO. Called the "ever faithful" isle by Queen Regent **María Cristina**, Puerto Rico was governed by Gov.-Gen. **Manuel Macías y Casado** and an **autonomous government**, which was popular and controlled by **"Muñocistas"** of the **Liberal-Fusionist Party**. Moreover, with the Catholic Church supporting the government, Puerto Rico's peaceful political system was not threatened by the small independence movement led by **Ramón Betances**.

While Gov.-Gen. Macías directed his efforts at implementing **autonomy**, Col. Juan Camó y Soler, chief of staff, directed Spain's military forces. With the exception of the artillery at **San Juan** no artillery was available. The army, which consisted of 8,000 regulars and 9,000 *voluntarios*, was scattered throughout the island. The regular forces, consisting of 5,000 infantry, 700 artillery men, and 2,300 **engineers** and civil guards, was based on six infantry battalions: **Alfonso XIII Battalion**, **Patria Battalion**, Provisional Battalions Nos. 3, 4, 6, and the Principado de Asturias Battalion. The volunteer forces were poorly trained and unreliable. The naval forces, which consisted of 368 men, included six vessels—two unprotected **cruisers**, two **gunboats**, an auxiliary cruiser, and the **torpedo-boat destroyer** *Terror*.

Immediately upon the outbreak of the war, Gov.-Gen. Macías declared martial law, price controls were instituted, a national subscription campaign began to help fund the war, and in spite of the fact that **censorship** was enforced, the press, including *La Correspondencia de Puerto Rico*, overwhelmingly supported Spain. Although the autonomous parliament convened on 17 July, it quickly disbanded when U.S. forces initially landed at **Guánica** on 25 July. In a 19-day campaign, U.S. forces overran half the island, only halting because of the signing of the **Armistice Protocol** on 12 August.

Partidas began to attack Spanish-owned properties in the countryside, and newspapers, such as *La Nueva Era* and *La Correspondencia de Puerto Rico*, welcomed American control. A pro-annexationist press began, and *La Bruja* in **Mayagüez** and *La Bomba* in **Ponce** openly satirized the situation. On 22 August, *The Porto Rican Mail*, the first newspaper written in English, appeared in Ponce.

On 26 August, President **William McKinley** issued confidential instructions to the U.S. **evacuation commission**, which stated that Puerto Rico was to become a conquered territory of the United States. The evacuation commission began its work on 10 September. San Juan was officially handed over to Maj. Gen. **John R. Brooke** on 18 October, and all Spanish troops had left by 21 October. Brooke then became the first U.S. military governor of the island, and the island was ruled by a U.S. military governor until 1900.

PUERTO RICO REGIMENT. One battalion of the regiment, the Provisional Battalion of Puerto Rico No. 1, which consisted of six companies of 822 men, was stationed near **Santiago, Cuba**. Prior to the U.S. landing at **Daiquirí** on 22 June 1898, four companies were stationed at Santiago, one at El Cristo and one at Songo. Subsequently, three companies fought in the **Battle of Las Guásimas** on 24 June, and during the 1 July battles for the **San Juan Heights**, they sustained casualties of 20 killed, 61 wounded, and 33 missing. On 15 July, Lt. Col. José Escudero agreed with all the other military commanders that Santiago should capitulate.

PUIG, FRANCISCO (d. 1898). Lieutenant colonel. After U.S. forces landed at **Guánica, Puerto Rico**, on 25 July 1898, Puig was in command of Spanish forces at **Yauco** which consisted of elements of the **Patria Battalion** and mounted **guerrillas**. He had come to Yauco on a special train and intended to attack the U.S. forces as soon as reinforcements arrived; however, no reinforcements were sent, and he received orders from Gov.-Gen. **Manuel Macías y Casado** to retreat from the area to **Ponce**. At first Puig disregarded the orders, and then protesting them, he obeyed and began a retreat from Yauco on 27 July. After he received a harshly critical telegram from the government that questioned his honor, he went to the beach and shot himself.

PULITZER, JOSEPH (1847–1911). Owner and editor of the *New York World*. The Hungarian-born Pulitzer, a Civil War veteran, began to practice sensationalist journalism when he owned the *St. Louis Post-Dispatch* and continued when he moved to New York and took over the *World* in 1883. Although he had no personal interest in **Cuba**, no personal political motives, and had been a lifelong opponent of imperialism, Pulitzer consistently demanded U.S. intervention in Cuba. Directing his paper from his soundproof rooms at home through a series of memos, Pulitzer, who was nearly blind, consistently supported a war against Spain because the United States had a special mission in world affairs in shunning the imperialistic policies of the Old World and promoting democracy. Having become disaffected with U.S. expansionism after the war, he opposed retaining the **Philippines**.

PURITAN. (USN) Double-turreted **monitor**, commanded by Capt. Purnell F. Harrington until 18 June 1898, then by Capt. Fredrick W. Rodgers. The largest of the "modern" monitors of the **U.S. Navy**, its very low freeboard posed a serious disadvantage at sea. Assigned to the **North Atlantic Squadron** during the war, the *Puritan* served on the **blockade of Cuba**, shelled a fortified area near **Matanzas** on 27 April 1898, and was then under repairs until 21 May when it took up **blockade** duty off **Havana, Cuba**. While participating in the **Puerto Rican campaign**, it blockaded **San Juan** and landed sailors at **Fajardo, Puerto Rico**, in early August. After the war it was seldom in full commission and was finally decommissioned in 1910. Stricken in 1918, it was sold in 1922.

La. 1892, com. 1896, dis. 6,060, hp. 3,700, sp. 12.4
Armor: s. 14–6″, d. 2″, b. 14″, t. 8″, ct. 10″
Armament: 4–12″, 6–4″, 6–6pdr., 2–1pdr., 2–37 mm. mgs.
Cc. 410, comp. 270

—Q—

QUARTERMASTER CORPS. Under the command of Brig. Gen. **Marshall I. Ludington**, it was one of ten agencies in the **War Department**. With its prewar money available only for normal peacetime expenditures and its funds from the **Fifty Million Dollar Bill** earmarked for transporting heavy artillery to the coastal defenses, it was not until 20 April 1898 that the corps received its first funds to equip the **U.S. Army** for war.

The capabilities of the corps frequently lagged behind the needs of a rapidly expanding military; consequently, private contractors were a necessity, providing approximately two-thirds of the U.S. Army's clothing and tentage. Also, **transports** were difficult to obtain because the **U.S. Navy** had preceded the Army into the market and the fact that international law prohibited the transfer of foreign ships to U.S. registry after the outbreak of hostilities. Consequently, the corps, relying on ships flying the U.S. flag, ultimately rounded up 38 ships, most of them run-down coastal trade vessels. Nevertheless, in a few months the corps outfitted and supplied an army of more than a quarter million men.

QUESADA AROSTEQUIA, GONZALO DE (1868–1915). Chargé d'affaires of the **Cuban Republic** in Washington, D.C. A graduate of the University of New York and a naturalized U.S. citizen, Quesada effectively lobbied the U.S. government, testified to congressional committees, and traveling throughout the United States, spearheaded a public relations campaign. Following his address on 14 February 1897, the Michigan legislature passed a resolution in favor of Cuban independence. He received considerable help from Matias Romero, **Mexico**'s ambassador to the United States, and had close contacts with many U.S. senators, including **John T. Morgan** and **Henry Cabot Lodge**. Early in 1898, Quesada, along with Henry D. Northrop, wrote *America's Battle for Cuba's Freedom* (1898). Although the book was intended to promote U.S. intervention, it was not published until after the battles at **Santiago, Cuba**; therefore, it was used to justify the U.S. military campaign.

QUIJOTE MOTIF. Responding to defeat and the publication of a new edition of *Don Quijote*, Spanish writers such as Juan Valera y Alcalá and Benito Pérez Galdós chose the story of Don Quijote to affirm the universal role of a defeated Spain. For even though Spain had lost its colonies, the domain of *Don Quijote* should console Spain in its universal role and identity. This motif was sharply criticized by **Miguel de Unamuno**.

—R—

RABÍ, JESÚS (1846–1915). A Native-American Cuban insurgent major general, commanded the Second Corps of the **Cuban Revolutionary Army**. Rabí, a veteran commander who had a $50,000 price on his head, commanded forces in eastern **Cuba** that included Chinese Cubans. After going aboard the *New York* on 16 June to report to Adm. **William T. Sampson** on the military situation in **Santiago, Cuba**, he attended the **Aserraderos Conference** on 20 June 1898. Subsequently, his 500-man force attacked **Cabañas Bay** west of the Santiago harbor entrance as a feint to assist in the landing of the U.S. **Fifth Corps** on 22 June at **Daiquirí**. On 25 June, Rabí's force of 3,000 embarked on U.S. ships and was landed east of Santiago. Later he accompanied Sampson's envoy, Lt. **Victor Blue**, around Santiago's defenses, pointing out the batteries and Spanish troop dispositions. After the war, when the Cuban Revolutionary Army was being disbanded, he did not want to give up his arms. Yet, in the postwar period he served for a time as a forest inspector in the civil government established by the United States.

RALEIGH. (USN) **Protected cruiser** commanded by Capt. **Joseph B. Coghlan**. A sister ship to the *Cincinnati*, the *Raleigh* arrived from the Mediterranean and joined the **Asiatic Squadron**. During the **Battle of Manila Bay** on 1 May 1898, it fired 631 shots while sustaining only one hit. Immediately following the battle it silenced the battery at Sangley Point. Two days later, on 3 May, together with the *Baltimore*, it compelled the surrender of the batteries at Corregidor. During the **Battle of Manila** on 13 August, the *Raleigh* was deployed off **Fort San Antonio Abad**, and briefly fired on the fort. It was sold in 1921.

La. 1892, com. 1894, dis. 3,213, hp. 10,000, sp. 19
Armor: d. 1″, sl. 2.5″, ct. 2″
Armament: 1–6″, 10–5″, 8–6pdr., 4–1pdr., 4–18″ tt. (aw.)
Cc. 460, comp. 314

RAMÍREZ DE VILLAURRUTIA, WENCESLAO (1850–1933).

Spanish diplomat and historian. A member of the **Liberal Party**, Villaurrutia, a lawyer in canon and civil law and professor of the Royal Academy of Jurisprudence and Legislation, was serving as Spain's minister to Belgium when he was selected to be part of Spain's **Peace Commission** to negotiate the **Treaty of Paris**. After the war he served as minister of state and was granted the title of marqués de Villaurrutia. He continued his diplomatic service as Spain's ambassador to Vienna, London, Paris, and Rome, and represented Spain at the Geneva Conference. He recorded his experiences in his memoirs *Palique diplomático. Recuerdos de un embajador* (1923) and explained Spain's strategy of delay during the Treaty of Paris negotiations, which was intended to encourage European intervention and possibly arbitration.

RAMSDEN, FREDERICK W. (d. 1898).

RAMSDEN, FREDERICK W. (d. 1898). British consul at **Santiago, Cuba**. Arriving at Santiago as a youth, Ramsden worked for a British export firm and as a secretary to the British consul at Santiago. He held the post as British consul for nearly 40 years. When the U.S. consul left Santiago, Cuba, on 7 April 1898, he turned over the archives of the consulate to Ramsden. During the war Ramsden kept a diary that began with the appearance of U.S. warships off the coast and ended with the American possession of the city. Although it was written for his sons and not intended for publication, *McClure's Magazine* published it as "Diary of the British Consul at Santiago During the Hostilities" in October and November 1898. He believed that the U.S. forces could have taken the city had they rushed the city after the 1 July battles for the **San Juan Heights**. Visiting **El Caney** on 5 July, Ramsden recorded the horrid conditions of the refugees who had fled Santiago for El Caney. He died from illness on 10 August 1898.

RANDOLPH, WALLACE F. (1841–1910). Brigadier general (USV), commanded the Fifth and **Fourth U.S. Artillery** in the **Fifth Corps**. Rising from a Civil War private to a lieutenant colonel of artillery by March 1898, Randolph was promoted in May 1898 to brigadier general (USV), and in command of the Fourth and Fifth Artillery, arrived at **Siboney, Cuba,** on 9 July 1898 on the transport *Comanche*. Because of bad roads, he only managed to get two of his light batteries into line before **Santiago** capitulated on 17 July. After becoming chief of artillery in the **U.S. Army** in 1901, he was promoted to major general in 1904 and then retired.

RAWSON-WALKER, E. H. (d. 1898). British consul general at **Manila, Philippines**. On 15 April 1898, he informed the British government that a general uprising would soon break out because none of the promised reforms had been carried out by Spanish officials. After the U.S. victory at the **Battle of Manila Bay** on 1 May, Rawson-Walker began his service as a go-between for the Spanish and U.S. military commanders. He boarded Com. **George W. Dewey**'s flagship *Olympia* to ask that **Manila** be spared bombardment. Com. Dewey accepted his suggestion provided his ships were not fired on by the Spanish. Rawson-Walker then delivered Com. Dewey's decision to Spanish officials, who immediately accepted it. Soon he carried messages to Com. Dewey from Gov.-Gen. **Basilio Augustín y Dávila**, which intimated Gov.-Gen. Augustín's willingness to capitulate to U.S. forces. After Rawson-Walker died of illness during the U.S. siege of Manila, his role as a go-between was taken over and completed by Belgian consul **Edouard André**.

REA, GEORGE BRONSON (1869–1936). Correspondent for the *New York Herald*, *New York Journal*, and *New York World*. While reporting in **Cuba** from 1896 to 1897 for the *Herald*, Rea was in the field with the insurgent forces of Maj. Gen. **Máximo Gómez**, who threatened to have Rea shot. Although Rea wrote articles debunking many of the reports of Spanish atrocities by **correspondents**, he was arrested by the Spanish and later freed. Upon his return to the United States, he testified to the Senate on 11 June 1897. In October, he wrote *Facts and Fakes about Cuba: A Review of Various Stories Circulated in the United States Concerning the Present Insurrection* (1897). It was a critical exposé of the mendacious reporting by American correspondents about the **Cuban Revolt**. He wrote that the U.S. public had been "grossly deceived" by many correspondents of the leading newspapers, which he felt were trying to "embroil the U.S. in a war with Spain." Rea blamed the insurgents' scorched earth policy, not **reconcentration**, for having caused most of the suffering of the Cuban civilian population, called the insurgents "bandits and rapists," and thought Capt. Gen. **Valeriano Weyler y Nicolau** had been much maligned.

Rea, who was seated at a café near Havana's Central Park with **Harry Sylvester Scovel** when the *Maine* exploded on 15 February 1898, took Capt. **Charles D. Sigsbee**'s official notice of the disaster to the **cable** office and cabled both Washington and the *New York Herald*. Subsequently, he reported the incident in "The Night of the Explosion in Havana," *Harper's Weekly* 5 March 1898. During the war Rea served as a correspondent for the *New York World* and engaged in intelligence-gathering for the U.S. military in **Puerto Rico**. Unable to go ashore because the authorities at **San Juan** knew of his presence on a French passenger ship in the harbor, he took photos of harbor fortifications. Only the presence of a French naval vessel in the harbor saved him from being taken off and most likely shot. His photos and report were used by Adm. **William T. Sampson** to direct the naval bombardment of **San Juan** on 12 May 1898. In July, while working for the *New York Journal*, Rea was ordered by **William R. Hearst** to buy a steamer and sink it in the Suez Canal to stop Adm. **Manuel de la Cámara's Squadron**. He was not able to carry out Hearst's order. After the war, Rea served as an adviser to Sun Yat-sen (1911–1913) and to the Japanese-controlled Manchoukou government in northern China (1927–1929).

RECONCENTRATION. In response to the Cuban insurgent scorched earth policy, Lt. Gen. **Valeriano Weyler y Nicolau**, within days of his arrival in February 1896, instituted a pilot program of concentrating Cuban civilians in fortified towns in order to contain the rebels and deprive them of support. Strict control over the movement of population, cattle, and food was instituted. Anyone failing to obey the order was considered a rebel. Initially implemented in four provinces, it was soon extended to the entire island by the end of 1896. Because of inadequate supplies for the reconcentrated civilians, the death toll reached around 200,000 by 1898, and the U.S. **press** published excoriating accounts of the policy. The policy was rescinded on 30 March 1898. Weyler later defended his policy by citing similar British actions against the Boers in South Africa and U.S. actions during the **Philippine Insurrection**.

RED CROSS. See AMERICAN RED CROSS

REED, THOMAS BRACKETT (1839–1902). Republican speaker of the House of Representatives (1889–1891, 1895–1899). A Maine congressman, Reed, who weighed close to 300 pounds, was an irascible, independent, and brilliant parliamentarian. Known as "Czar Reed" by his detractors, he was famous for his acerbic wit and quick rejoinder. Reed, who believed President **William McKinley** was spineless, had no favorites as he proved to be one of the most effective opponents of U.S. expansionism. In his article "Empire Can Wait" *Illustrated American* (4 December 1897), he argued against reckless expansion. Instead, he advocated gradual growth. He buried resolutions granting **belligerent rights** to the Cuban insurgents and the recognition of the **Cuban Republic**.

As **Congress** rushed to war in the spring of 1898, Reed recognized that even his manipulations of parliamentary procedure could not stem the tide, and he remarked that trying to dissuade his colleagues was like trying to "dissuade a cyclone." He refused to celebrate Com. **George W. Dewey**'s victory at the **Battle of Manila Bay** on 1 May 1898. Instead, Reed remarked that Dewey should leave immediately because "It will make us trouble for all time to come if he does not." Subsequently, he opposed the annexation of **Hawaii**, which he saw as a pretext conceived by sugar interests and **imperialists**. When he later learned the United States was paying a $20 million indemnity to Spain for the **Philippines**, Reed remarked, "We have bought ten million Malays at $2.00 a head unpicked. And nobody knows what it will cost to pick them." After resigning his seat, he went into retirement in April 1899. However, he continued with his witticisms, writing acerbic comments and imaginary letters from Gen. **Valeriano Weyler** to Congress in which Weyler asked Congress to give him due credit as the originator of the American methods being used during the **Philippine Insurrection**.

REED/VAUGHN/SHAKESPEARE COMMISSION. Because of the many deaths in the U.S. military during the war from typhoid fever, Surgeon General **George M. Sternberg** appointed a commission composed of Maj. Walter Reed, Edward O. Shakespeare, and Victor C. Vaughn to investigate the origins of typhoid fever in U.S. military **camps** during the war. In its report, which was issued in 1900, the commission found that many units had arrived in camp already infected, pointed out problems of diagnosis in which typhoid was frequently confused with malaria, and stated that the **disease** was spread by poor sanitation. Not finding fault with Sternberg, it called for greater authority for medical officers in site selection and sanitary procedures and recommended basic sanitary practices.

REGENERATIONISM. The name given to a reform movement in Spain, which developed in the 1890s and became prominent after Spain's defeat by the United States in the Spanish-American War.

Coming to prominence through writers such as Joaquín Costa, Ángel Ganivet, Damían Isern y Marco—*Del desastre nacional y sus causas* (1899), and Ricardo Macías Picavea—*El problema nacional: hechos, causas, remedios* (1899), and politicians such as **Camilo Polavieja**, regenerationism lamented Spain's economic, moral, and political decline. Although they blamed Spain's corrupt political institutions for this decline, they were not social revolutionaries. Instead, their various proposals concentrated on the need for reform from above to restore Spain to its rightful position in the world.

"REGULARS GET NO GLORY." Article written by **Stephen Crane** at **Siboney**, **Cuba**, on 9 July 1898. It appeared in the *New York World* on 20 July. Crane was irked that the rich society soldiers, particularly those in the **Rough Riders**, were receiving excessive adulation in the newspapers while the common regular soldier, who he called "Nolan," was being ignored. He called the regular soldier "the best man standing on two feet on God's green earth," even though the "public doesn't seem to care very much for the regular soldier."

REID, WHITELAW (1837–1912). Editor and publisher of the *New York Tribune*, Reid, a **Republican Party** wheelhorse and a former U.S. minister to **France**, was an outspoken expansionist, close friend of President **William McKinley**, and initially not in favor of recognizing the **Cuban Republic**. In September 1898, his article "The Territory with Which We Are Threatened" was published in *Century Magazine*. In it he wrote that the United States had a moral obligation to give the people of **Cuba** a better government than that provided by Spain and that American expansion in the **Philippines** and **Puerto Rico** was justified.

The only French-speaking member of the U.S. **Peace Commission** that negotiated the **Treaty of Paris**, Reid advocated taking the entire Philippines by right of conquest and believed the United States was honor-bound to extend its standards and institutions to others. After the war, he wrote *Problems of Expansion* (1900), a compilation of his talks and articles supporting retention of the Philippines. He was appointed American ambassador to **Great Britain** in 1905.

REINA MARÍA CRISTINA. (SPN) Unprotected **cruiser**, commanded by Capt. **Luis Cadarso y Rey**. A Spanish-built three-masted, two-funneled cruiser built on a cellular system with 12 watertight compartments, it was a sister ship to the *Alfonso XII* and *Reina Mercedes*. Stationed at **Manila**, **Philippines**, the *Reina María Cristina* served as Adm. **Patricio Montojo**'s flagship. During the **Battle of Manila Bay** on 1 May 1898, it briefly tried to attack Com. **George**

W. Dewey's Asiatic Squadron, but was set on fire and driven back by U.S. shelling, sustaining casualties of 130 men killed, including Capt. Cadarso, and 80 wounded. Subsequently, it sunk and burned for two days until nothing was left but a mass of twisted iron and charred wood. Its captured battle flag was returned to Spain three decades later as a gesture of respect for the Spanish sailors who died in the battle.

La. 1887, dis. 3,520, hp. 4,000, sp. 13.98
Armament: 6–6.4″, 8–6pdr. H., 6–3pdr. H. rev., 2 M. mgs., 5–14″ tt.
Cc. 500, comp. 409

REINA MERCEDES. (SPN) Unprotected **cruiser**, commanded by Capt. Rafael Micón. A two-funneled cruiser built on a cellular system with 12 watertight compartments, it was sent to **Cuba** in 1896, and was stationed at **Santiago, Cuba**, where it deteriorated. Practically useless because of its malfunctioning boilers, the *Reina Mercedes* was laid up in the harbor during the war. Four of its 6.4-inch guns were removed and installed at the batteries protecting the harbor entrance. During the U.S. naval bombardment of 6 June 1898, it was hit 35 times and sustained casualties of six killed and 12 wounded. On the night of 4 July, an attempt to block the harbor channel entrance by sinking it failed because of heavy U.S. naval gunfire from the *Texas* and *Massachusetts*, which were using their **searchlights**. Raised in March 1899, it was towed to Norfolk, Virginia, for repairs and was later taken to Newport, Rhode Island, and used as a floating barracks at the naval training station. In 1912 it was moved to the U.S. Naval Academy at Annapolis. For the next 20 years, it served as a signal and harbor-control station, as a brig for erring midshipmen, and as a barracks ship for the stewards of the academy's mess hall. Later refurbished, it provided accommodations for the naval-station commander and his family. In 1957 the Spanish ambassador to the U.S. informally requested the return of the *Reina Mercedes* to Spain; however, owing to its condition, it could not be towed across the Atlantic Ocean. Decommissioned in November 1957, it was sunk at sea.

La. 1887, dis. 3,090, hp. 4,400, sp. 17
Armament: 6–6.4″, 8–6pdr. H., 6–3pdr. H. rev., 2 M mgs., 5–14″ tt.
Cc. 500, comp. 375

RELIEF. (USN) **Hospital ship**. Formerly the steamer *John Englis*, it was purchased by the **U.S. Navy** on 18 May 1898, because no hospital ship could be secured under charter. Plans for fitting it were delayed by the **Quartermaster Corps** for ten days since the estimated cost was thought too great. After more than $130,000 was spent outfitting it, the ship, from July to September, carried medicines and hospital supplies to **Santiago, Cuba**, and transported 1,234 sick soldiers (of whom 49 died en route) and 251 wounded (of whom 16 died en route) to the United States.

RELIGION—SPAIN. In both Spain and its colonies, the Catholic Church, the only official church, supported Spain in its wars against the Cuban and Filipino insurgents and later against the United States. From the beginning of the **Cuban Revolt** in 1895, many church leaders adamantly opposed any reforms and blessed the soldiers as they went to war. Saints' relics were used and specific prayers recommended; moreover, the church solicited money as part of the national subscription drives to finance Spain's war efforts and organized a battalion of volunteers. However, in the spring of 1898 the church supported the idea of selling **Cuba** provided the Catholic Church in Cuba was protected.

Upon the outbreak of the Spanish-American War, officials frequently called the Americans barbarians. Jaime, the Bishop of Barcelona, actively supported the national subscription drive, and on 6 May 1898, he published a circular blaming the United States for its unjustified actions and asking for God's protection for Spanish forces. However, news of Spain's overwhelming defeats early in the war caused some church officials to plead for peace in June 1898.

RELIGION—UNITED STATES. Virtually all denominations supported the United States in the Spanish-American War. On 16 April 1898, the *Literary Digest* found with few exceptions the religious press had become insistent on changing the conditions in **Cuba**, peacefully if possible but through war if necessary. Subsequently, early and overwhelming American victories in the war quickly turned former opponents into supporters in most cases. Many agreed with Rev. Washington Gladden, one of the founders of the social gospel, when he justified the war in his *Our Nation and Her Neighbors* (1898), stating that America was going to war in defense of humanity. The Catholic Church, the largest denomination in the country, gave its unwavering support, and members of religious orders served as **nurses**. Mennonites served as medical **volunteers**, and Jews organized the Hebrew-American Volunteer Bureau in New York City and had 691 men ready to fight by mid-July. In their publications, the Methodists ardently supported U.S. expansion.

After the conclusion of hostilities with the signing of the **Armistice Protocol** on 12 August 1898, sermons were preached giving thanks for victory. Many Protestant publications such as the *Baptist Missionary Review* and *Churchman* saw God's hand in victory and argued that the war's results therefore justified the retention of the **Philippines**. Many denominations such as the African Methodist Episcopal Church, the National Baptists Convention, and the African Methodist Episcopal Zion Church quickly sent missionaries to Cuba.

However, for a minority of church leaders, the war's conquests caused serious concern and moved them to become anti-imperialists. Among them were Charles H. Parkhurst, a nationally famous Presbyterian minister, and Henry C. Potter, the Episcopalian Bishop of New York.

"REMEMBER THE *MAINE*, TO HELL WITH SPAIN." The most popular slogan in the United States during the war. In use by March 1898, some claim that it came from "The Word of the Lord from Havana," a poem written by Richard Hovey immediately after the *Maine* explosion on 15 February 1898 and published in the *New York World* on 20 March 1898. Others believe it was derived from a cartoon caption by Clifford K. Berryman in the *Washington Post* on 2 April 1898, which read, "If the row comes, REMEMBER THE *MAINE*, and show the world how American sailors can fight."

REMEY, GEORGE COLLIER (1841–1928). Commodore (USN), commanded the naval base at **Key West**, **Florida**, from 7 May 1898 to 24 August 1898. A U.S. Naval Academy graduate and Civil War veteran, Remey, who had been in command at Portsmouth, New Hampshire, was appointed to command the Key West naval base after Adm. **William T. Sampson** had received reports of rough treatment of Spanish **prisoners of war**. As commander of the Key West naval base on his flagship *Lancaster*, Remey supervised the supply and maintenance of vessels engaged in the Cuban and **Puerto Rican campaigns**. Promoted to rear admiral in November 1898, he resumed his command at Portsmouth, New Hampshire, and later commanded the **Asiatic Squadron** during the **Philippine Insurrection** and Peking Relief Expedition.

REMINGTON, FREDERIC SACKRIDER (1861–1909). A sculptor, painter, author, and illustrator, Remington signed on as a correspondent for the *New York Journal* and went to **Cuba**, along with **Richard H. Davis**, in January 1897. A **jingo**, Remington sketched scenes that depicted Spanish **guerrillas** as savages. After a week he was bored. According to **James Creelman**'s memoir *On the Great Highway* (1901), Remington wired **William R. Hearst**, the owner of the *Journal*: "Everything is quiet. There is no real trouble. There will be no war. I wish to return." Hearst then responded: "Please remain. You furnish the pictures, and I'll furnish the war." Nevertheless, Remington soon left Cuba with a portfolio of pictures vowing not to return unless with U.S. military forces. Within weeks one of his sketches, which was done while he was in New York, was fundamental in causing the *Olivette* **Incident**. On 11 April 1897, the *Journal* published a supplement containing four full pages of Remington's drawings, which showed Spanish atrocities, and bearing the adage, "Peace on Earth Good Will toward Men As It Is in Cuba."

During the Spanish-American War, Remington sketched military training exercises for *Harper's Magazine*, spent seven days on the **battleship *Iowa*** off the Cuban coast, and wrote "Wigwags from the Blockade," *Harper's Weekly* (14 May 1898). In June he went with the **Fifth Corps** to **Daiquirí, Cuba**. He was present at the **Aserraderos Conference** on 20 June and at the **Battle of San Juan Hill** on 1 July. In addition to sketching events, Remington wrote articles such as "With the Fifth Corps," *Harper's Monthly Magazine* (November 1898), and he immortalized the **Rough Riders** in his painting *Charge of the Rough Riders at San Juan Hill*. For Remington, the war was a disillusioning experience. Instead of the heroics of the west, there were **disease** and death. He returned to Cuba for *Collier's Weekly* in February 1899.

REPATRIATION OF SPANISH FORCES. Although Secretary of War **Russell A. Alger** had initially favored sending captured Spanish soldiers in **Cuba** to **camps** at Galveston, Texas, he changed his mind and cabled Maj. Gen. **William R. Shafter** that the United States would transport them back to Spain at U.S. government expense. To obtain ships for the effort, the **War Department** put the contract up for bids. The Spanish **Transatlantic Company**, with a bid of $55 per officer and $20 per enlisted man or dependent, received the contract at the end of July 1898, even before hostilities had ceased. Between 9 August 1898 and 17 September 1898, it transported 22,137 soldiers and 727 civilians to Spain at a cost to the United States of $513,860.

According to the terms of the **Armistice Protocol** of 12 August 1898, **evacuation commissions** were established for Cuba and **Puerto Rico**. The first troops left Cuba on 8 August on the *Alicante*. By the time the evacuation was finished in February 1899, over 145,000 regulars and 40,000 volunteers had returned to Spain. In Puerto Rico, the repatriation of forces began on 14 September and finished on 23 October 1898. Of those who returned to Spain, over 20,000 later died from **disease**s they had contracted in the former colonies.

REPUBLICAN PARTY—UNITED STATES. In general the party favored U.S. expansion. Its 1896 party platform advocated control of

Hawaii, the construction of an American-owned Nicaraguan canal, and the purchase of the Danish West Indies. With respect to **Cuba**, the platform supported "the heroic battles of the Cuban patriots against cruelty and oppression" and extended the party's hope "for the full success of their determined contest for liberty." Finally, it advised the U.S. government to "actively use its influence and good offices to restore peace and give independence to the Island."

After the party gained control of both the **Congress** and the presidency with the 1896 election of **William McKinley**, Cuba was a minor issue for them, the **Philippines** nonexistent, and any efforts to involve the United States directly in the Cuban situation were blocked by Speaker **Thomas B. Reed** in the House, by the **"Big Four"** in the Senate, and by the **McKinley administration** itself. However, increasing tension over Cuba throughout 1897 and early 1898 divided the party. Although McKinley continued to hope for a diplomatic approach, a large number of congressmen threatened to join the Democrats in declaring war on Spain following the release of the *Maine* Report on 28 March 1898.

However, upon the outbreak of war, the party unified around McKinley, and only upon the acquisition of overseas territory did minimal dissent develop. In October 1898, a *Literary Digest* survey of 27 Republican state platforms for 1898 showed that although none explicitly favored retaining all of the Philippines none opposed annexation. After the Republicans retained control of Congress in the fall 1898 elections, the debate on the ratification of the **Treaty of Paris** saw Republican Senators **Eugene Hale** and **George Hoar** rise in opposition. A *New York Herald* poll prior to the vote on the treaty showed that of 241 Republican newspapers, 84.2 percent were for expansion. Only three Republican senators—Hale, Hoar, and Richard F. Pettigrew of South Dakota—voted against the treaty on 6 February 1899.

REPUBLICANS—SPAIN. Divided by the time of the Spanish-American War, republicans opposed the monarchy, and although they were largely excluded from office, they had leaders of national stature. Upon the outbreak of the **Cuban Revolt** in 1895, a few republicans, such as **Francesc Pi i Margall** and **Alejandro Lerroux García**, took an interest in the insurgent **Cuban Republic** and opposed Spain's policy, but most republicans, such as **Emilio Castelar y Ripoll** and **Nicolás Salmerón**, took a strong stand against the insurgents. Upon the outbreak of the Spanish-American War, only Pi i Margall opposed the war, and with almost all republicans supporting Spain's war effort, only a small workers' movement, socialists, and anarchists remained in opposition.

RESOLUTE. (USN) Auxiliary **cruiser**, commanded by Comdr. Joseph Giles Eaton. Formerly the *Yorktown*, an Old Dominion Line passenger ship launched in 1894, it was purchased by the **U.S. Navy** on 21 April 1898 and armed with two 6-pdr. guns. With a 122-man crew, staffed in part by a contingent from the New Jersey **naval militia**, it was assigned to the North Atlantic Station and served as a transport and store ship in the Caribbean during the war. Immediately following the **Naval Battle of Santiago** on 3 July 1898, as it was steaming for **Guantánamo, Cuba**, it sighted the Austrian ship *María Theresa* off **Daiquirí** and mistakenly reported it as a Spanish ship. The report temporarily set off a scramble as U.S. ships prepared for further combat. It later served to take charge of Spanish **prisoners of war**, returned to **Santiago** with hospital supplies and **nurses** on 24 July, and transported light artillery units of the **Fifth Corps** to **Camp Wikoff, Montauk Point, Long Island, New York**. After the war it was sold to a private transportation company and was sunk in a collision in 1916. Raised and rebuilt, it served as a passenger ship until it burned at Hoboken, New Jersey, in 1927.

RESTORMEL. English collier chartered by the Spanish government to supply Adm. **Pascual Cervera's Squadron** with coal. Out of Cardiff, Wales, it left **Curaçao** for **Santiago, Cuba**, to supply Adm. Cervera's Squadron. On 25 May, 1898, it was captured by the *St. Paul* off Santiago in plain sight of Adm. Cervera's ships. The United States confiscated the cargo but released the ship after the war. Adm. **William T. Sampson** protested its release.

REVENUE CUTTER SERVICE, UNITED STATES. Prior to the Spanish-American War, eight cutters patrolled the Florida straits and adjacent waters. They seized 29 vessels for violating U.S. neutrality laws, detained another dozen in port, and broke up two **filibuster**ing expeditions. During the war, 13 cutters were transferred temporarily to the **U.S. Navy** along with their officers and crews. They fought in all the theaters of combat, and transported troops and supplies in the Pacific Ocean and the Caribbean. Initially seven were used to patrol the Atlantic Coast and four were part of the **Pacific Squadron** that patrolled the Pacific Coast. Eight served under Adm. **William T. Sampson** on the **blockade of Cuba**. The *Hudson* saw action during the **Battle of Cárdenas Bay** on 11 May 1898. The *Windom* participated in the **Battle of Cienfuegos** on 11 May, and the *Manning* participated in the **Santiago, Cuba, campaign**. The *McCulloch* served with the **Asiatic Squadron** in the **Philippines**.

RÍOS Y NICOLAU, DIEGO DE LOS (1850–1911). Last Spanish governor-general of the **Philippines**. A career soldier who had seen service in **Puerto Rico**, the **Carlist** Wars, **Cuba**, and in Africa, he was promoted to brigadier general in 1895 and sent to the Philippines, where he served as chief of division on Mindanao and successfully conducted operations against Filipino insurgents. After the **capitulation** of **Manila** on 13 August 1898, Ríos established his capital at **Iloilo**, **Cebu**, and continued to fight against the Filipino insurgents. Trying to save the Visayas and Mindanao for Spain, he considered asking Spain to grant the reforms demanded by the insurgents in the Visayas and instituted a council of reforms in October 1898. However, such actions came too late, and after being besieged by insurgents, Ríos was forced to evacuate Iloilo on 25 December 1898. He arrived in Manila on 1 January 1899 and oversaw the transfer of power and the **repatriation** of Spanish officials, soldiers, and property to Spain. After returning to Spain, he served as military governor of Seville and in 1907 was promoted to lieutenant general.

RIVERO MÉNDEZ, ÁNGEL (1864–?). Captain of artillery. Born in **Puerto Rico** of Spanish parents, he entered the infantry school in Puerto Rico in 1879, went to Spain in 1885 to study artillery, and returned to Puerto Rico in 1891, where he edited a pro-government newspaper and worked as an engineer. Arrested for intervening in political matters, he was freed on 1 March 1898, ordered to return to active duty because war was approaching, and put in charge of the artillery units stationed at Fort San Cristóbal in **San Juan**. His command fired the first shot of the war in Puerto Rico when on 10 May the battery at San Cristóbal fired on the *Yale*, which was blockading the port, and two days later fired on U.S. ships 185 times during the **U.S. Navy**'s bombardment of San Juan on 12 May.

Upon returning to active duty, Rivero Méndez immediately began writing a diary, which became the most complete record of the war in Puerto Rico when it was published as *Crónica de la guerra hispanoamericana en Puerto Rico* (1922). Calling his work "true justice," he demanded that the truth of the *Maine* catastrophe finally be made known because it had caused the war. Believing that Spain tried its best to defend Puerto Rico, he noted Spanish deficiencies, the flight of the civilian population from San Juan, the psychological impact of the reports of early Spanish defeats, and the cowardice of formerly vocal, patriotic Puerto Ricans. Writing that Maj. Gen. **Nelson A. Miles**'s campaign was a "model of modern, humane, civilized war," he posited that the war marked the birth of an imperialist policy for the United States. After the **Armistice Protocol** was signed on 12 August 1898, he remained in command at San Cristóbal when it was used as a jail for Spanish commanders who had surrendered, and following the lowering of the Spanish flag at San Juan on 18 October 1898, he returned to civilian life after 20 years in uniform.

ROMERO ROBLEDO, FRANCISCO (1838–1906). Leader of the Spanish **Liberal-Conservative Party**. A versatile manipulator of elections, Romero Robledo, who through marriage was tied in with the principal Spanish families in **Cuba**, served as minister of justice in the government of Prime Minister **Antonio Cánovas y Castillo** until a blatantly corrupt municipal election in Madrid caused a public outcry. Through his newspaper *El Nacional*, he opposed any concessions on the Cuban issue and supported Lt. Gen. **Valeriano Weyler y Nicolau**'s policy to completely defeat the Cuban insurgents.

Reacting to Spain's early defeats in the war against the United States, Romero Robledo asked in the **Cortes** on 23 June why Adm. **Pascual Cervera's Squadron** did not go out from the harbor at **Santiago, Cuba**, and fight and became a strident critic of the **Sagasta administration**'s preparations for war. After Prime Minister **Práxedes M. Sagasta** decreed **censorship** on 14 July, Romero Robledo, along with other newspaper directors, met with Sagasta in protest. When Sagasta solicited his opinion in early August as to proceeding to a negotiated settlement, Romero Robledo was emphatic that the war should continue, although his newspaper had already demanded a quickly negotiated peace.

ROOSEVELT, THEODORE (1858–1919). Lieutenant colonel in the **Rough Riders**. An ardent advocate of U.S. expansion and a believer in the superiority of the Anglo-Saxon race, Roosevelt championed a war with Spain as early as 1896. Appointed assistant secretary of the navy in 1897, Roosevelt, together with Senator **Henry C. Lodge,** conspired to get Com. **George W. Dewey** appointed to command the **Asiatic Squadron** and served on the **Naval War Board**. On 14 January 1898, he wrote a several-thousand-page memorandum to Secretary of the Navy **John D. Long** urging preparations for war, and while Long was absent on 25 February, he **cable**d Com. Dewey to attack the **Philippines** in the event of a war with Spain. Following the release of the official report on the *Maine*, Roosevelt demanded action because the "shilly-shallying and half measures at this time merely render us contemptible in the eyes of the world," and lamented that President **William McKinley** "had no more backbone than a chocolate eclair."

Soon after the outbreak of war, Roosevelt resigned, ordered a uniform from Brooks Brothers, and, worried about his poor eyesight, had six spare sets of glasses sewn into his uniform and one pair inside his hat. Taking two of his own horses—Rain-in-the-Face and Little Texas—he joined the Rough Riders at San Antonio, Texas. Although

Secretary of War **Russell A. Alger** had offered the command to him, Roosevelt refused, saying he was not qualified. He then proposed Col. **Leonard Wood** to command the Rough Riders. After arriving at **Tampa, Florida**, with the Rough Riders, Roosevelt, not wanting to miss the war, personally commandeered a train to get his men to the docks and then the ship *Yucatan* to transport them to **Daiquirí, Cuba**.

During the landing at Daiquirí, Rain-in-the-Face drowned. After fighting in the **Battle of Las Guásimas** on 24 June, Roosevelt was placed in command of the Rough Riders because Col. Wood had been promoted to command Brig. Gen. **Samuel B. M. Young**'s brigade. In command of the Rough Riders during the **Battle of Kettle Hill** on 1 July, Roosevelt led the charge on Little Texas, until he had to dismount some 40 feet from the top because of a wire fence. He then continued on foot, accompanied by his orderly Henry Bardshar, and they were among the first to reach the Spanish positions.

By 3 July, Roosevelt was writing to his friend Senator Henry C. Lodge demanding that President William McKinley send every regiment and battery possible, warning that "We are in measurable distance of a terrible military disaster." He further added on 5 July in another letter to Lodge that Maj. Gen. **William R. Shafter** was "criminally incompetent." Subsequently, he instigated the **Round Robin Letter** of 3 August.

After returning to the United States, Roosevelt, a war hero and Republican, was elected governor of New York in November 1898 by 17,000 votes and wrote *The Rough Riders* (1899). Although he had frequently complimented the conduct and courage of **black American** soldiers, he infuriated black Americans when he criticized the cowardly conduct of black soldiers during the battles for the **San Juan Heights** on 1 July in his article "The Rough Riders" *Scribner's Magazine* (April 1899). The article touched off a virulent reaction in the black press and was contradicted by white officers.

ROOSEVELT'S CHARGE UP SAN JUAN HILL. Although the **Rough Riders** charged up **Kettle Hill** on 1 July during the battles for the **San Juan Heights**, their charge up San Juan Hill became one of the most popular myths of the war. Initially **Theodore Roosevelt** never claimed in his book *The Rough Riders* that he had led the charge up San Juan Hill, but the name San Juan sounded better to the newspaper people. Subsequently, Roosevelt did little to dispel the notion of his leading a gallant charge to victory, and contrary to numerous drawings and paintings of the event, there was no massed or cavalry charge. Instead, a mixture of units, including the Rough Riders with Roosevelt in the lead, slowly crept their way up the hill. After fire from the **Gatling guns** had virtually cleared the hill, one last rush carried the day.

ROOSEVELT'S ORDER TO DEWEY (25 FEBRUARY 1898). Days after the *Maine* disaster, a tired and overworked **John D. Long**, secretary of the navy, took the day off on 25 February 1898. He returned the next day to find that **Theodore Roosevelt**, his assistant-secretary of the navy, had issued a multitude of orders. One of his orders to Com. **George Dewey**, who was commanding the **Asiatic Squadron**, told Dewey to move his squadron to **Hong Kong**, and in the event of a war with Spain, to undertake offensive operations against the **Philippines**. Although Long reviewed and then canceled many of Roosevelt's orders, he did not cancel the order to Com. Dewey because it was consistent with **Navy Department** war plans.

ROUGH RIDERS. Commanded by Col. **Leonard Wood**, they were officially designated as the First United States Volunteer Cavalry. However, the nickname "Roosevelt's Rough Riders" was shortened to "Rough Riders," and the name stuck. Organized and mustered into service at San Antonio, Texas, Santa Fe, New Mexico, and Muskogee, Indian Territory, from 1–21 May 1898, with 47 officers and 994 enlisted men, the regiment concentrated at San Antonio, where it trained for two weeks. Its mascots were an eagle named Teddy, a dog named Cuba, and a young mountain lion named Josephine, and its favorite marching song was the "Rough Riders' Roundelay."

The regiment was a rare assortment. More than half came from Texas, New Mexico, and Indian Territory, 90 were from New York, and the foreign-born included 14 Germans, 13 English, ten Canadians, seven Scots, five Irish, five Swedes, two Swiss, two Russians, and one each from Alsace, Australia, Denmark, Monaco, and Wales. Composed of 160 cowboys, 53 farmers, 44 ranchers, 44 clerks, 31 railroad men, New York City policemen, bronco busters, polo players, Indians and Indian fighters, sheriffs, a few professional gamblers, Methodist clergymen, Texas Rangers, baseball players, lawyers, an Ivy League quarterback, and a national tennis champion, they left San Antonio, and upon arriving at **Tampa, Florida**, on 4 June, the citizens of Tampa petitioned Col. Wood to keep them inside the **camp** because their notoriety for stealing food along the way had preceded them.

Assigned to the Second Brigade, Dismounted Cavalry Division of the **Fifth Corps**, the regiment's headquarters and eight troops, leaving their horses behind, left Tampa on the *Yucatan* on 14 June and landed at **Daiquirí, Cuba**, on 22 June. Consisting of 26 officers and 557 enlisted men, the troops fought in the **Battle of Las Guásimas** on 24 June, sustaining casualties of eight killed and 31 wounded. James R. Church, the regiment's assistant surgeon, was later awarded the **Congressional Medal of Honor** for his actions during the battle. After Col. Wood was assigned to command the Second Brigade, Lt. Col. **Theodore Roosevelt** assumed command and led the Rough Riders in the **Battle of Kettle Hill** on 1 July, where they sustained casualties of 15 killed and 72 wounded.

On 8 August, the Rough Riders left **Santiago, Cuba**, on the transport *Miami*. During the voyage, Roosevelt, alerted by the ship's captain that his stokers and engineers were drunk from the liquor given to them by the Rough Riders, asked his men to hand over their liquor. About 70 flasks and bottles were delivered and later returned by Roosevelt after the unit landed at **Camp Wikoff, Montauk Point, Long Island, New York**, on 14 August. The 20 undelivered flasks and bottles that he later found were thrown overboard.

After the troops that had remained at Tampa, Florida, arrived at Camp Wikoff, the regiment was mustered out of service on 15 September 1898, with 47 officers and 1,090 enlisted men. Casualties sustained while in service included 26 killed, 104 wounded, 20 died from **disease**, and 12 deserted. Of those who saw service in Cuba, 37 percent were casualties. This was the highest casualty rate of any American unit during the war.

ROUND ROBIN LETTER (3 AUGUST 1898). By August 2 1898, when Maj. Gen. **William R. Shafter** warned the **War Department** about the toll **disease** was taking on his men at **Santiago, Cuba**, over 4,000 soldiers of the **Fifth Corps** were already ill. Secretary of War **Russell A. Alger**'s response directing that the Fifth Corps move to high ground "where yellow fever is impossible" was met with anger by the commanding officers. At a meeting of these officers on 3 August a letter, which came to be known as the Round Robin Letter, was signed by all divisional and brigade commanders and directed to Maj. Gen. Shafter. It demanded that the Fifth Corps "must be removed at once" from **Cuba** and sent to some point on the northern seacoast of the United States, or "it will perish." Although there was no present epidemic of **yellow fever**, the Fifth Corps was disabled by malaria and could be destroyed by a yellow fever epidemic, which was sure to come in the near future. The Round Robin Letter was accompanied by a letter from the chief surgeons of the Fifth Corps, who unanimously recommended the transporting of "the whole army to the United States as quickly as possible." Lt. Col. **Theodore Roosevelt**, who had signed the letter, wrote his own letter to Maj. Gen. Shafter making the same demands.

Both the Round Robin Letter and Roosevelt's own letter were

leaked to the **Associated Press**. On 4 August, the letters appeared on the front pages of many U.S. newspapers and produced a firestorm of controversy. Maj. Gen. Shafter vehemently denied he had given the letters to the **press**, and President **William McKinley** was irate because the letters appeared while diplomatic negotiations with Spain on the **Armistice Protocol** were in progress. Contrary to the opinion of the day, the Round Robin Letter did not force the War Department to bring the Fifth Corps home, because that decision had already been made. It did, however, hasten the matter, as orders were immediately issued on 4 August.

ROWAN, ANDREW SUMMERS (1857–1943). First Lieutenant, in the Nineteenth U.S. Infantry. A West Point graduate who was working with the **Adjutant General's Office**, Rowan was sent by the **Military Information Division** to **Cuba** to meet with Cuban insurgent Maj. Gen. **Calixto García** and secure information about the strength of the Cuban insurgent forces. After leaving Jamaica on 23 April 1898, he landed on the southern Cuban coast in Oriente Province, crossed the Sierra Maestra Mountains, and met with Maj. Gen. García on 1 May at his headquarters at Bayamo. Rowan left the next day, accompanied by a three-man insurgent commission that included Gen. **Enrique Collazo y Tejeda**. After leaving the northern Cuban coast, Rowan arrived in Washington, D.C., on 13 May, and both Rowan and the insurgent commission briefed Maj. Gen. **Nelson A. Miles**.

In late May 1898, Rowan was appointed lieutenant colonel (USV), served on the staff of Maj. Gen. Miles during the **Puerto Rican campaign**, and wrote about his Cuban journey in "My Ride across Cuba" *McClure's Magazine* (11 August 1898). After serving in the U.S. occupation forces in postwar Cuba, Rowan was mustered out of **volunteer** service in March 1899, served in the **Philippines** until 1902, and became internationally famous with the publication of **Elbert Hubbard's** *A Message to García* (1899). He later taught military science at Arkansas State University and retired in 1909 because of ill health with the rank of major. Awarded the Distinguished Service Cross in 1922, the prudish Rowan, who published a pamphlet *How I Carried the Message to García* (1922), refused to appear in or even see the film made about him, because a pretty Cuban dancer was featured in the film.

RUBENS, HORATIO SEYMOUR (1869–1941). Lawyer for the Cuban insurgent **Junta** in New York City. His law office at 66 Broadway served as the headquarters of the **"Peanut Club,"** which included **correspondents** from New York City newspapers. Rubens was a close friend of **José Martí**, the founder of the **Cuban Revolution-**

ary Party, and did free legal work for the Junta. In early April 1898, upon learning that the **McKinley administration** did not intend to recognize the **Cuban Republic**, Rubens denounced the administration's policy, declaring that if U.S. troops landed on Cuban soil without recognizing the Cuban insurgent government, then it would be considered as a declaration of war against the revolution. His heated outburst embarrassed Junta leaders. After the war he served as a legal counsel to the U.S. military government in Cuba and later wrote *Liberty: The Story of Cuba* (1932).

RUBÍN HOMENT, ANTERO (1853–?). Spanish brigadier general at **Santiago, Cuba**. Entering the army at 15, he served three years in **Cuba** as a private, fought in the **Carlist** Wars in Spain, and was seriously wounded in combat against Cuban insurgents upon the outbreak of the **Cuban Revolt** in 1895. During the war against the United States, Rubín commanded the Spanish troops at the **Battle of Las Guásimas** on 24 June 1898 and reported that he had repulsed the American attack before he obeyed orders to fall back to Santiago. On 1 July, while commanding forces during the **Battle of San Juan Hill**, his horse was shot out from under him. Repatriated to Spain in August 1898, he occupied various military posts, was promoted to lieutenant general in 1916 and retired in 1923.

RUÍZ INCIDENT (FEBRUARY 1897). On 5 February 1897, Ricardo Ruíz, a Cuban dentist and naturalized U.S. citizen, was arrested by Spanish authorities and charged with dynamiting a train. Twelve days later, Ruíz, who had fought against Spain in a previous revolt, died in his cell. Subsequently, George E. Bryson, a correspondent for the *New York Journal*, wrote an account stating that Ruíz had possibly been murdered. Although Spanish officials stated that Ruíz had committed suicide by pounding his head against the wall of his cell, the account appeared on 20 February under the headline "American Slain in Spanish Jail." The *Journal* inflamed the issue two days later by reporting that Secretary of State **John Sherman** was in favor of war with Spain for "murdering Americans" and stated that Ruíz was tortured to death. Moreover, **William R. Hearst**, the *Journal*'s owner, demanded war to avenge the death of Ruíz. Ruíz's widow was brought to New York by the *Journal* and then sent to Washington, D.C., where she met with President **William McKinley** and other officials. The U.S. Senate passed a resolution asking for information on the affair, and Secretary Sherman ordered an investigation. However, the **McKinley Administration** refused to be stampeded into rash action, and the incident disappeared from the headlines.

RUSLING, JAMES FOWLER (1834–1918). Lawyer, author, and Civil War veteran. Rusling, a member of the General Conference of the Methodist Episcopal Church, was a member of a delegation from the church's General Missionary Committee, which met with President **William McKinley** on 21 November 1899. According to Rusling's account "Interview with President William McKinley" *The Christian Advocate* (22 January 1903), as the delegation was leaving the White House, McKinley explained his reasons for taking all of the **Philippines**. Although he had never wanted the Philippines, McKinley believed they had come to the United States "as a gift from the gods" when Com. **George W. Dewey**'s victory at the **Battle of Manila Bay** on 1 May 1898 caused them to drop into the lap of the United States. McKinley walked the floor of the White House night after night, prayed to God for guidance, and then it came to him that it would be cowardly and dishonorable to return the Philippines to Spain; moreover, they could not be turned over to European commercial rivals or left to themselves because the Filipinos were unfit for self-government. Therefore there was nothing left to do but to take them all and to educate, civilize, and Christianize the Filipinos. Rusling's story was never corroborated, and it is questionable if he was even present at the time. Moreover, in a book he published in 1899, Rusling had Lincoln use similar language in recalling divine inspiration just before the Battle of Gettysburg during the Civil War.

RUSSIA. Under the rule of Czar Nicholas II, Russia was primarily concerned with Japanese expansion in Asia and was in the process of acquiring territory in China. Therefore, under the direction of Foreign Minister Mikhail N. Muraviev, Russia performed a balancing act. Although not wanting the United States to have any influence in Europe, Russia was not disposed to take actions that would cause difficulties with the United States. Because it refused to take the lead in any concerted prewar European effort to mediate Spanish-U.S. differences, it acted as a braking influence on its ally **France**; nevertheless, its ambassador De Wollant signed the **Great Powers Note** of 6 April 1898. Although the Russian press was highly critical of the United States, Russia declared its neutrality on 20 April, even before the Spanish-American War had begun. After Com. **George W. Dewey**'s overwhelming victory at the **Battle of Manila Bay** on 1 May, Muraviev met with the Spanish and French ambassadors and urged them to end the war as soon as possible before **Great Britain** annexed the **Philippines** or established military bases there. However, the resulting U.S. occupation of the Philippines did not arouse similar concern by Russia.

—S—

SAGASTA, PRÁXEDES MATEO (1825–1903). Prime minister of Spain and president of the Council of Ministers. From a family of modest means, Sagasta rose to become the leader of the **Liberal Party** until his death. Prime minister upon the outbreak of the **Cuban Revolt** in 1895, Sagasta relinquished power to **Antonio Cánovas del Castillo** as part of the *turno pacífico* and initially supported Cánovas's policy of using military means to suppress the revolt. After two years, however, he began to criticize the war effort, and in his "Manifesto to the Nation" on 24 June 1897, he called for political reforms such as **autonomy** and liberalized trade. Two months after Cánovas was assassinated, Sagasta became prime minister in October 1897.

In bad health, Sagasta was committed to solving the Cuban situation through reforms and not through independence; accordingly, the **Sagasta administration** immediately instituted a policy of reforms. Because he considered a war against the United States a hopeless war for Spain, Sagasta believed that the differences with the United States could be solved through diplomatic means. However, neither events in the United States nor pressure on the home front afforded the necessary time. After the U.S. congressional resolution of 19 April 1898 and the beginning of the **blockade of Cuba** on 21 April, Sagasta signed Spain's **declaration of war** and led Spain into war.

Spain's early defeat at the **Battle of Manila Bay** on 1 May precipitated a crisis in Sagasta's government. His offer to resign was rejected by the Queen Regent **María Cristina**, and he reorganized his cabinet. By mid-July, he concluded that a negotiated settlement was necessary and solicited the views of admirals, generals, and politicians before he authorized the signing of the **Armistice Protocol** on 12 August. In September, Sagasta appointed Spain's **Peace Commission** that negotiated the **Treaty of Paris.** When he was blamed for Spain's disastrous defeat, he defended himself stating that his government had done everything possible to avoid war but that war had been unavoidable because of Spain's humiliation by the United States. He further argued that the monarchy probably would have been overthrown had Spain granted independence to **Cuba** or not gone to war. Furthermore, because Spain had fought, she had not been dishonored. After being replaced by a conservative government in March 1899, Sagasta briefly returned to power in 1901–1902. Upon his death, the Liberal Party factionalized.

SAGASTA ADMINISTRATION. On 4 October 1897, Spanish Prime Minister **Práxedes M. Sagasta,** leader of the **Liberal Party,** formed his new government. Included in his cabinet were Minister of State

Pío Gullón y Iglesias, Minister of War Lt. General **Miguel Correa y García**, Minister of the Colonies **Segismundo Moret y Prendergast**, Minister of Production **Conde de Xiquena**, Minister of the Marine **Segismundo Bermejo y Merelo**, Minister of Justice Alejandro Groizard y Gómez de la Serna, Minister of the Interior Trinitario Ruíz de Capdepón, and Minister of Finance Joaquín López Puigcerver. In an attempt to avoid war with the United States over the issue of **Cuba**, the administration instituted a policy of reforms combined with the military suppression of the **Cuban Revolt**. All manner of concessions were made to American demands except that of Cuban independence. Lt. Gen. **Valeriano Weyler** was recalled, and **autonomy** was granted to Cuba and **Puerto Rico** on 25 November 1897. The closing down of the Cuban insurgent **Junta** by the United States was demanded and offers of U.S. mediation were rejected. Although attempts were made to gain European support, the policy of **reconcentration** was ended and a suspension of hostilities in Cuba was ordered on 9 April 1898.

The shock of Spain's early defeat at the **Battle of Manila Bay** on 1 May caused a crisis in the cabinet. Those who had urged concessions to the United States prior to the war found themselves under attack; consequently, Sagasta reorganized his cabinet on 18 May. Its new members included Minister of State Duke of **Almodóvar del Río**, Minister of Production **Germán Gamazo**, Minister of the Marine Capt. **Ramón Auñón y Villalón**, and Minister of the Colonies Vicente Romero Girón. In an effort to publicize its prewar efforts for peace and to curry favor in European capitals, the government then made public its 10–21 April 1898 prewar diplomatic correspondence with the United States.

Although he suspended the **Cortes** on 24 June because of increasing criticism, Sagasta, nevertheless, was confronted by a divided cabinet after the defeat of Adm. **Pascual Cervera's Squadron** in the **Naval Battle of Santiago** on 3 July. Even though the army opposed negotiations, Sagasta decided in mid-July to proceed toward a negotiated settlement. In order to avoid public criticism, Sagasta suspended freedom of the **press**, closed down the Cortes, imposed cabinet unity by threatening to dissolve the entire body, and secured the reluctant support of the army. Having closed off debate and neutralized the army's objections, he authorized Minister of State Almodóvar del Río to solicit **France**'s assistance in opening negotiations and on 11 August approved the signing of the **Armistice Protocol** of 12 August. Subsequently, he appointed Spain's **Peace Commission** to negotiate the **Treaty of Paris**, which formally ended the war.

ST. LOUIS. (USN) Auxiliary **cruiser**, commanded by Capt. **Caspar F. Goodrich**. A former American Transatlantic Line ocean liner and sister ship to the *St. Paul*, it was leased by the **U.S. Navy** from April to September 1898, attached to the North Atlantic Station, and fitted for scouting, transporting, and cable cutting. During the war it searched for Adm. **Pascual Cervera's Squadron**, engaged in **cable-cutting operations** at **Santiago** and **Guantánamo, Cuba**, and served as the command ship for the landing of the **Fifth Corps** at **Daiquirí** and **Siboney, Cuba**.

After the **Naval Battle of Santiago** on 3 July, the *St. Louis* transported Adm. **Pascual Cervera y Topete** and his staff as **prisoners of war** to the United States and carried the **Puerto Rican Commissioners** and reinforcements for Maj. Gen. **Nelson A. Miles**'s invasion of **Puerto Rico**. In early August it transported U.S. soldiers of the Fifth Corps to **Camp Wikoff** at Montauk Point, Long Island, New York. It was returned to the Transatlantic Line on 2 September 1898. Used as a transport in World War I, it was burned out while reconditioning in 1920 and eventually sold in 1925.

La. 1894, com. 24 April 1898, dis. 14,910, hp. 20,000, sp. 22
Armament: 4–5″, 8–6 pdr.
Cc. 2,677, comp. 377

***ST. PAUL*.** (USN) Auxiliary **cruiser**, commanded by Capt. **Charles Sigsbee**. Formerly an ocean liner of the American Transatlantic Line, it was the sister ship to the *St. Louis*. Chartered by the **U.S. Navy** and fitted for scouting and transporting, during the war it searched for Adm. **Pascual Cervera's Squadron** and captured the British collier *Restormel* near **Santiago, Cuba**, on 25 May 1898. On 22 June, it defeated the *Terror* and *Isabella II* during a brief naval engagement outside of **San Juan, Puerto Rico**. Serving as a transport during July and August, it carried U.S. forces to **Siboney, Cuba**, and **Puerto Rico** and repatriated U.S. forces from Siboney to **Camp Wikoff, Montauk Point, Long Island, New York**. On 2 September 1898, it was returned to the Transatlantic Line, only to return to service as a transport in World War I. After having capsized in the North River, New York, while being towed from dry dock on 28 April 1918, it was raised and reconditioned. Sold in 1923, it was scrapped in **Germany**.

La. 1895, com. 20 April 1898, dis. 14,910, hp. 20,000, sp. 22
Armament: 6–5″, 8–6pdr., 6–3pdr.
Cc. 2,677, comp. 381

SALISBURY, ROBERT CECIL, 3RD MARQUESS (1830–1903). See CECIL, ROBERT

SALMERÓN, NICOLÁS (1838–1908). Spanish **Republican** leader. A former president of the First Republic and later member of the

Cortes from Barcelona, Salmerón, believing colonialism was educational for the colonies, supported the suppression of the **Cuban Revolt**, favored **autonomy** for **Cuba** and **Puerto Rico** and a new regime for the **Philippines** while criticizing the reforms of **Antonio Cánovas y Castillo** in his newspaper *La Justicia*. Upon the outbreak of war with the United States, Salmerón followed a patriotic course until the defeat at the **Battle of Manila Bay** on 1 May 1898. Consequently, on 3 May he began a debate in the Cortes about the war. On 10 May, he openly called for abolishing the monarchy and the establishment of a national government. When he was consulted by Prime Minister **Práxedes M. Sagasta** in early August about proceeding to an armistice, he retained the right to express his opinion only in the Cortes. In the postwar period he severely criticized the **Sagasta administration** for not avoiding, not preparing, and not winning the war.

SAMPSON, WILLIAM THOMAS (1840–1902). Rear admiral (USN), commanded the **North Atlantic Squadron**. A U.S. Naval Academy graduate and an expert on **torpedoes** and ordnance, Sampson was an apolitical, reserved, and strict officer. A former superintendent of the U.S. Naval Academy and chief of the Bureau of Ordnance, Sampson assumed command of the *Iowa* in June 1897, served as president of the court of inquiry into the *Maine* disaster, and on 26 March 1898 assumed command of the North Atlantic Squadron. From his flagship *New York*, Sampson, who was promoted to rear admiral on 21 April 1898, commanded 125 naval vessels in the Caribbean theater during the war. An advocate of bombarding **Havana**, **Cuba**, upon the outbreak of war, Sampson believed that such a powerful strike would force a quick end to the war; however, his plan was vetoed by the **Navy Department**. After initiating the **blockade of Cuba**, his squadron bombarded **San Juan**, **Puerto Rico**, on 12 May and arrived at **Santiago**, **Cuba**, on 1 June to **blockade** Adm. **Pascual Cervera's Squadron** in port.

During the war Sampson came into conflict with Maj. Gen. **William R. Shafter** and Maj. Gen. **Nelson A. Miles**. Beginning at the **Aserraderos Conference** on 20 June, Sampson wanted the army to storm the Spanish fortifications at the entrance to Santiago's harbor so his ships could enter and destroy Adm. Cervera's Squadron; however, Shafter refused and advocated the navy's storming the entrance on its own. Sampson was later excluded by Shafter and Miles from any participation in the capitulation of Santiago. Later, he came into conflict with Miles over the number of ships provided for Miles's invasion of **Puerto Rico**, because Sampson did not want to weaken the Cuban blockade. Moreover, Miles effectively maneuvered to stop the navy from attacking San Juan during his **Puerto Rican cam-**

paign. Although Sampson was not initially present at the **Naval Battle of Santiago** on 3 July, Secretary of Navy **John D. Long** and others credited the victory to his planning, and although Com. **Winfield S. Schley** was extolled in the American **press** for the victory, **Sampson's victory message** of 3 July was also carried by the major papers. After the war the wartime difficulties between Sampson and Schley erupted onto the front pages of the nation's newspapers. On 16 August, he was appointed to the **evacuation commission** for **Cuba** and resumed command of the **North Atlantic Fleet** on December 1898. With his health continuing to deteriorate, Sampson was promoted to permanent rear admiral in March 1899, wrote "The Atlantic Fleet in the Spanish War" *The Century Magazine* (April 1899), and commanded the Boston Navy Yard until he was confined to bed in 1901. He retired in February 1902 and died shortly thereafter.

SAMPSON-SCHLEY CONTROVERSY. After the war supporters of Rear Adm. **William T. Sampson** and Com. **Winfield S. Schley** exacerbated a conflict that resulted from Schley's dilatory actions in blockading Adm. **Pascual Cervera's Squadron** at **Santiago**, **Cuba**. Although President **William McKinley** and Secretary of the Navy **John D. Long** supported Sampson, most of the public and newspapers, such as **William R. Hearst's** *New York Journal*, supported Schley, crediting him for the overwhelming American victory at the **Naval Battle of Santiago** on 3 July 1898. Schley was partially mollified when McKinley appointed him to the Puerto Rican **evacuation commission**, and the conflict was almost over. However, a textbook, which called Schley's actions at Santiago disgraceful, was being used at the U.S. Naval Academy when a review of the book called for a court of inquiry into Schley's actions. Schley called for an inquiry to clear his name, and subsequently the **Schley Board of Inquiry** convened.

SAMPSON'S VICTORY MESSAGE (3 JULY 1898). Although the White House had received prior messages on the overwhelming U.S. victory at the **Naval Battle of Santiago** on 3 July, President **William McKinley** was disinclined to believe them until Adm. **William T. Sampson**'s message arrived on 4 July. The message, which began with "The fleet under my command offers the nation as a Fourth of July present the whole of Cervera's fleet," was intended to parallel General William T. Sherman's famous Civil War message offering Savannah, Georgia, as a Christmas present to the nation. Composed by Lt. **Sydney A. Staunton**, Sampson's assistant chief of staff, it was signed by Sampson as a matter of course and transmitted without clearance. Moreover, Staunton had sent it while not allowing Com.

Winfield S. Schley's message to be sent. It was regarded by many as boastful because it emphasized Sampson's role while not mentioning other officers. Only later was it learned that Sampson had not written the message.

SAN FERNANDO REGIMENT. One battalion, composed of six companies totaling 822 men, was in the **San Luis Brigade** at **Santiago, Cuba**. Three of the companies fought in the **Battle of Las Guásimas** on 24 June 1898, and part of the battalion fought in the 1 July battles for the **San Juan Heights**, sustaining casualties of two wounded. Lt. Col. Segundo Perez, representing the battalion, agreed with all other military commanders at the 15 July meeting that Santiago should capitulate.

SAN FRANCISCO. (USN) **Protected cruiser**, initially commanded by Capt. Mortimer L. Johnson and during the war by Capt. Richard P. Leary. Originally rigged as a three-masted schooner, it convoyed the *New Orleans* from England to New York and then served as the flagship of the **Northern Patrol Squadron**. The *San Francisco*, along with the rest of the squadron, was incorporated into Adm. **William T. Sampson**'s fleet on 1 July 1898. It served off **Havana, Cuba**, on **blockade** duty. After the war, it served as a converted minelayer, and during World War I, laid mines in the North Atlantic. Decommissioned in 1921, it was stricken in 1937 and sold in 1939.

La. 1889, com. 1890, dis. 4,098, hp. 10,500, sp. 19.5
Armor: d. 2″, sl. 3″, ct. 3″
Armament: 12–6″, 4–6pdr., 4–3pdr., 2–1pdr., 4 G. mgs., 3 tt.
Cc. 628, comp. 384

SAN JUAN, PUERTO RICO. With a population of 30,000 and an excellent harbor, San Juan was the residence of Gov.-Gen. **Manuel Macías y Casado**. Based on El Morro, a massive stone fortification guarding the entrance to the harbor, and the Castillo de San Cristóbal, San Juan was defended by various batteries totaling 43 medium caliber guns; however, all were of iron and none were rapid-fire. Not since 1797 had San Juan's artillery fired a shot in war; moreover, practice had been rare owing to a lack of ordnance. Subsequently the guns of the *Isabella II* and *Antonio López* were removed and installed ashore. The harbor entrance was partially obstructed by two sunken ships and a series of **mines**, both contact and electrical, and **torpedoes** were emplaced. During the war the only Spanish men-of-war in the harbor were the *Isabella II*, ***Terror***, and the **gunboat** *Ponce de León*.

Army units within the vicinity included six regular companies—

two from the Third Provisional Battalion, one from the Sixth Provisional Battalion, and three from the Principado de Asturias Battalion—which totaled 1,335 men; however, by the end of May 1898 only 631 men were available for service. There was also the Volunteer Battalion No. 1 under the command of Lt. Col. Pedro Arzuaga. Totaling 1,055 men, of which 829 were *voluntarios*, it was made up of Spanish residents and Puerto Ricans and included a detachment of cyclists, composed of 17 youths from prominent families, whose assigned task was to deliver orders.

Upon the outbreak of the Spanish-American War, people began to leave the city for the countryside, and on 29 April a weak and sometimes nonexistent U.S. **blockade** began. Usually consisting of one ship, the blockade proved ineffective, and both foreign and Spanish ships easily entered and left San Juan harbor early in the war. On 10 May, the artillery fired its first shot of the war at the blockading *Yale*, but it was out of range. Two days later, Adm. **William T. Sampson's North Atlantic Squadron** bombarded the city, causing a mass exodus from the city, which by the end of July was almost deserted except for the military units. On 22 June, the *Terror* and *Isabella II* briefly engaged the *St. Paul* but quickly retreated and took refuge in the harbor. After the signing of the **Armistice Protocol** on 12 August, most of the city's residents returned, and on 18 October San Juan was officially transferred to U.S. military control.

SAN JUAN, PUERTO RICO, BOMBARDMENT OF (12 MAY 1898). While moving east from **Key West, Florida**, in search of Adm. **Pascual Cervera's Squadron**, Adm. **William T. Sampson's North Atlantic Squadron** arrived off **San Juan** and at 5:10 a.m. began a two-hour-35-minute bombardment of the Spanish military positions. With the **cruiser *Detroit*** in the lead, followed by the *Iowa*, *Indiana*, *New York*, *Amphitrite*, *Terror*, and *Montgomery*, the squadron made three circuits firing 1,360 projectiles, some with "Porto Rico 1898" written on them. Although the Spanish batteries in return fired 441 shells, there was little damage to either side. It was estimated that of every 100 shots fired by U.S. ships 20 fell short, 60 went long, and only 20 impacted; moreover, many did not even explode upon impact. U.S. casualties amounted to seven wounded and one killed. Spanish casualties were 13 killed and close to 100 wounded, most of whom were civilians.

Even though international law required prior warning when firing on a noncombatant population, Sampson argued that his ships had not deliberately fired on civilians, and therefore no notification was necessary. Moreover, he believed he could have taken San Juan but was forced to break off the engagement to continue searching for

Adm. Cervera's Squadron, which was his prime objective. The following day Gov.-Gen. **Manuel Macías y Casado** and the San Juan press proclaimed the engagement as the "First Victory," and merchants dispensed gifts of champagne, cognac, sweets, cookies, and cigarettes to the Spanish officers.

SAN JUAN HEIGHTS, SANTIAGO, CUBA. A series of low-lying hills rising 125 feet above the general level of the land, they commanded the eastern approach to **Santiago, Cuba**, and consisted of **San Juan Hill** and **Kettle Hill**. Anchoring his eastern defenses on the heights, Lt. Gen. **Arsenio Linares** built a 4,000-yard-long network of fortifications, consisting of a loopholed brick blockhouse, entrenchments, and barbed-wire entanglements. Before the battles of July 1, they were reinforced by two companies under the command of Col. Jose Vaquero and two Krupp guns. Later joined by 60 *voluntarios* from the city, the total force on both hills was 521 men. Outnumbering the Spanish defenders 16 to one, U.S. forces, consisting of Brig. Gen. **Jacob F. Kent**'s and Brig. Gen. **Samuel S. Sumner**'s divisions, took the heights on July 1 at a cost of 124 dead and 817 wounded, and the Spanish sustained over 350 casualties.

SAN JUAN HILL, CUBA, BATTLE OF (1 JULY 1898). Unknown to U.S. commanders, only 250 Spanish soldiers occupied San Juan Hill on 1 July 1898, when Brig. Gen. **Jacob F. Kent**'s division attacked. After Capt. **George S. Grimes**'s light artillery battery of four guns opened fire at 8:00 a.m., its fire not only proved ineffective but was soon silenced by Spanish artillery, which spotted it quickly because of its use of **black powder**. At 9:00 a.m. the order to advance was given, and the Spanish soon spotted the U.S. positions because an observation **balloon** floated above the treetops, accompanying their advance. As the Spanish poured fire into the area, the **Seventy-First New York Infantry** recoiled; nevertheless, Col. **Charles A. Wikoff**, Brig. Gen. **Hamilton S. Hawkins**, and Col. E. P. Pearson moved their brigades into position.

As the front assault across open ground began around 1:00 p.m. with the **Sixth U.S. Infantry**, **Sixteenth U.S. Infantry**, and **Twenty-Fourth U.S. Infantry** in the lead, the **foreign military observers with the Fifth Corps** believed it to be suicidal. In what **Stephen Crane** later called a "soldiers' battle" fought by those who had no orders and those who disobeyed whatever orders they had, Kent's division advanced without any order as the men charged up the hill through knee-high grass and barbed wire. Because the Spanish defenders had entrenched themselves on the actual crest of the hill, rather than the "military crest," they were unable to fire down effectively on Kent's forces as they advanced up the hill. Moreover, the Spanish defenders were hit by enfilade fire from **Kettle Hill**, which had just been taken by Maj. Gen. **Joseph Wheeler**'s division, and at 1:15 p.m., by eight minutes of fire from Lt. John D. Parker's **Gatling gun** detachment. As the U.S. troops reached the summit, the Spanish troops were already in retreat. However, instead of pursuing the retreating Spanish forces, Kent's troops occupied the entrenchments and dug in to prepare for an expected counterattack. After the battle **Richard H. Davis** penned a dispatch to his paper, the *New York Herald*, stating, "Another such victory as that of July 1 and our troops must retreat." It was withheld from publication. **Stephen Bonsal**, an eyewitness, later covered the battle when he wrote "The Fight for Santiago," *McClure's Magazine* (October 1898).

SAN LUIS, CUBA. Located near **Santiago**, **Cuba**, the small hamlet was occupied by Spanish forces under the command of Brig. Gen. **Joaquín Vara del Rey** before the U.S. **Fifth Corps** landed at **Daiquirí** on 22 June 1898. The Spanish forces included four companies of the **Constitution Regiment**, a foot company of **guerrillas**, and a section of mountain artillery. After the capitulation of Santiago on 17 July, about 5,000 Spanish **prisoners of war** were held here, guarded by **black American volunteer soldiers** of the **Eighth Illinois Infantry**, **Twenty-Third Kansas Infantry**, and the Ninth **"Immunes."**

SAN LUIS BRIGADE. Commanded by Brig. Gen. **Joaquín Vara del Rey**, it was one of two brigades in the **Santiago Division** at **Santiago, Cuba**. The brigade included the **Constitution Regiment**, one battalion of the **San Fernando Regiment**, two battalions of the **Cuba Regiment**, one battalion of the **Asia Regiment**, Provincial Battalion of Puerto Rico No. 1, 12 companies of mobilized troops, two squads of royal cavalry, half a battery of artillery, and a small force of civil guards and engineers. After the outbreak of the war a battalion of the **Talavera Regiment** was added.

SAN MIGUEL ISLAND. Located west of the island of Santa Cruz off the southern California coast, the island formally became part of the United States on 2 June 1898. Upon discovering that by some oversight the island had been omitted from the list of islands given up when Mexican independence was acknowledged by the United States, Captain Waters, the island's occupant and alleged owner, hastened to his little island, hoisted the American flag, and took formal possession in the name of the United States.

SANDOVAL. (SPN) A British-built **gunboat** commanded by Lt. Pablo Scandella. It left **Santiago, Cuba**, on 23 April 1898, and steamed to

Guantánamo to mine the harbor entrance. The *Sandoval* remained at Guantánamo throughout the war. On 7 June it was forced to withdraw to Caimanera in Guantánamo Bay by the arrival of the *Marblehead* and *Yankee*. During the negotiations for the **capitulation** of Guantánamo, U.S. authorities warned its captain not to scuttle the ship; however, on 24 July it was sunk according to Lt. Scandella's orders. Later raised by the *Marblehead*, it was put into U.S. service and used for training purposes. Upon its sale in 1919 by the navy, it was converted into a private yacht.

La. 1895, dis. 106, sp. 12
Armament: 1–2.24″, 1–1 pdr. N. rev.

SANTIAGO, CUBA. Located in Oriente Province on the southeastern Cuban coast, Santiago, with a population of 30,000, was the third largest port of **Cuba**, situated at the upper end of a four-mile-long harbor. Moreover, it was the center of Spanish military strength in eastern Cuba and a center for **cables** to western Cuba, Haiti, Jamaica, **Mexico**, **Puerto Rico**, and South America. Despite U.S. efforts, cable communications with Spain were maintained throughout the war.

Under the overall command of Lt. Gen. **Arsenio Linares y Pombo**, the **Santiago Division** was composed of two brigades commanded by General of Division **José Toral y Velázquez** and Brig. Gen. **Joaquín Vara del Rey**. Total forces in the province in April 1898 consisted of 36,000 regular soldiers. By the end of June 13,096 of these soldiers were within a 400-square-mile area of the city. They included 12 companies of the **Cuba Regiment**, eight companies of the **Asia Regiment**, six companies of the **San Fernando Regiment**, six companies of the **Puerto Rico Regiment**, six companies of the **Talavera Regiment**, six companies of the **Constitution Regiment**, 16 companies of mobilized troops, three companies of engineers and sappers, one company of siege artillery, one battery of mountain artillery, one company of civil guards, two cavalry troops of the King's Regiment, one section of the Signal Corps, six organizations of *voluntarios* and firemen, seven organizations of **guerrillas**, and eight companies of sailors from Adm. **Pascual Cervera's Squadron**. Although the city's garrison totaled 10,429 men by the end of June, the militia and *voluntarios* were not reliable, soldiers were exhausted by three years of war against the Cuban insurgents, and the soldiers' pay was 11 months in arrears.

Under the command of Col. **Salvador Ordóñez**, the city's artillery consisted of a few modern guns. Most were old rifled bronze cannons of various calibers. At the harbor entrance there were batteries on the right side of the channel entrance at **Morro Castle** and on the left side at the **Socapa**. Inside the channel entrance on the right side was the Estrella battery, which consisted of two old howitzers, two old muzzle-loading guns, and two modern breech-loading guns. About a half-mile farther inside the entrance on a small peninsula was the Punta Gorda battery, which consisted of four modern breech-loading guns and two old howitzers. Across the channel stretched a steel cable with 25 planks attached to keep the cable afloat as a means of preventing the passage of **torpedoes** with the entering tide. Additionally, 13 contact and electrical **mines** in two rows were placed at the channel entrance.

Cut off from reinforcements during the war because of U.S. command of the seas and the Cuban insurgents dominating the countryside, Linares placed his men in three lines of defense. A screen of troops was placed north of the U.S. landing sites at **Daiquirí** and **Siboney** with orders to retreat if attacked. A second line of fortifications east of Santiago included **El Caney** and the **San Juan Heights**, and a third line consisted of strong points between the heights and the city itself. Linares established his headquarters at **Fort Canosa** one mile behind the heights.

During the war the city was run by a military junta consisting of Gen. Toral as military governor of the city, Capt. Pelayo Pedemonte of the navy, Col. Florencio Caula of the engineers, Lt. Col. Luis Melgar of the artillery, and Lt. **José Müller y Tejeiro** of the navy.

On 18 May the first U.S. ships appeared off the coast, and with the arrival of Adm. Cervera's Squadron on 19 May, Santiago became the principal scene of land operations in Cuba. By the end of May, Cervera's Squadron was **blockade**d by U.S. naval forces, and beginning 6 June, the batteries guarding the entrance to the harbor were bombarded throughout June and early July, causing casualties of ten killed and 118 wounded. After the **Battles of El Caney**, **Kettle Hill**, and **San Juan Hill** on 1 July, Gen. Toral was hard pressed to defend the city. Ammunition was in short supply, food was rapidly running out while the city's merchants hoarded food and raised prices, and the city's water supply was cut off. Because of an arrangement worked out by the foreign consuls in the city, around 20,000 civilians left the city on 5 July and moved to El Caney.

Finally, after a series of proposals and counterproposals, a council of military commanders decided on 15 July to capitulate. On 16 July, the **Capitulation of Santiago Agreement** was signed, and on 17 July the city was formally handed over to U.S. forces under the command of Maj. Gen. **William R. Shafter**. At the ceremony, the American flag was raised over the city by Capt. William H. McKittrick, Shafter's son-in-law and aide-de-camp, and Lt. Wheeler, the son of Maj. Gen. **Joseph Wheeler**.

SANTIAGO, CUBA, CAMPAIGN. The arrival of Adm. **Pascual Cervera's Squadron** on 19 May 1898 focused most of the U.S. war effort in **Cuba** on **Santiago**. After Cervera's Squadron was **block-ade**d in port at the end of May, the *Merrimac* failed to block the channel entrance on 3 June. The U.S. **Fifth Corps**, under the command of Maj. Gen. **William R. Shafter**, landed at **Daiquirí** and **Sibo-ney** from 22–26 June and fought major battles at **Las Guásimas** on 24 June and **El Caney, Kettle Hill,** and **San Juan Hill** on 1 July. With the city besieged by the Fifth Corps, Adm. Cervera's Squadron was destroyed in the **Naval Battle of Santiago** on 3 July as it sortied from the harbor. On 17 July, the city formally capitulated, and by that time, **disease** had begun to cripple the Fifth Corps.

Throughout the campaign Spanish forces, under the command of Lt. Gen. **Arsenio Linares y Pombo**, were never concentrated at Santiago and were hampered by the lack of reinforcements, food, and ammunition. American forces achieved victory without a unified command, best exemplified by the frequent disagreements between Maj. Gen. Shafter and Adm. **William T. Sampson** on whether the navy should storm the harbor's entrance with or without the army's assistance. Though granted both sides lacked sufficient artillery, the U.S. artillery performance was deplorable. Mostly firing **black pow-der**, it quickly gave its positions away. Moreover, there was only rudimentary cooperation with the infantry in battle, which resulted in U.S. soldiers attacking entrenchments without effective artillery support. And Shafter made no use of the naval guns of Sampson's fleet to support his land forces.

SANTIAGO, CUBA, NAVAL BATTLE OF (3 JULY 1898). The sailors in Adm. **Pascual Cervera's Squadron** were withdrawn from the trenches of **Santiago** and boarded their ships on 2 July 1898. At 9:35 a.m. Sunday 3 July, the heavily outgunned squadron, composed of four **cruisers** and two **torpedo-boat destroyers**, sortied from Santiago harbor. **Signal 250** was raised on the blockading U.S. ships, which consisted of the armed **yachts** *Gloucester, Hist,* and *Vixen;* the **battleships** *Indiana, Iowa, Oregon,* and *Texas;* and the **armored cruiser** *Brooklyn*. Because Adm. **William T. Sampson** had left shortly before on the *New York* to meet with Maj. Gen. **William R. Shafter,** Com. **Winfield S. Schley** on the *Brooklyn* initially was in overall command.

Intending to escape and outrun the U.S. ships, Cervera's Squadron, led by the *Infanta María Teresa*, and followed by the *Vizcaya, Cristóbal Colón, Almirante Oquendo, Plutón,* and *Furor,* cleared the channel entrance and turned west. The *Infanta María Teresa* immediately attacked the *Brooklyn*. But a hail of gunfire from the U.S. ships quickly destroyed most of the squadron. Adm. Sampson, upon hearing the sound of battle, quickly returned to the scene with the *New York* and the **torpedo boat** *Ericsson*; however, the battle became a chase as one after another of the Spanish ships was sunk or run aground west of Santiago. By 1:15 p.m. it was all over as the last Spanish ship, the *Cristóbal Colón*, was overtaken by the *Oregon* and the *Brooklyn*, struck its colors, and ran aground.

Although Spanish shooting was poor, that of the United States was hardly good. Firing 9,429 projectiles, the U.S. ships only scored 120 hits. All the Spanish ships were destroyed whereas only three U.S. ships were slightly damaged, and whereas U.S. casualties totaled one dead and ten wounded, Spanish casualties amounted to 323 killed, 157 wounded, and more than 1,700 taken prisoner.

News of the overwhelming victory was soon sent out as the **Associated Press** cabled the story at the "urgent rate," totaling $8,000 in cable tolls. In Spain the public was disheartened, and there were a few demonstrations, mostly by **Carlists**. Significantly, many Spanish politicians and newspapers soon came to favor a negotiated settlement.

SANTIAGO DIVISION. Spanish military forces at **Santiago**, **Cuba**, were organized into two brigades. One was the **San Luis Brigade**, which was commanded by Brig. Gen. **Joaquín Vara del Rey**, and the other brigade was commanded by General of Division **José Toral y Velázquez**.

SANTIAGO REGIMENT. See CUBA REGIMENT

SARGENT, NATHAN (1849–1907). Lieutenant (USN). A U.S. Naval Academy graduate, Sargent had been a naval attache in Berlin, Rome, and Vienna in the early 1890s and served as an aide to Com. **George W. Dewey** throughout the war in the **Philippines**. Promoted to Lieutenant commmander in 1899, he wrote *Admiral Dewey and the Manila Campaign* (1947), a narrative that covers the period from Dewey's assumption of command of the **Asiatic Squadron** through the capture of **Manila** on 13 August 1898. Sargent viewed the German squadron in **Manila Bay** as a threat and covered the *Irene* incident of 10 July when Adm. Dewey threatened war against **Germany**. He credits Dewey's threat with forcing the Germans to obey the **blockade**. Dewey relied heavily upon Sargent's narrative in preparing his own autobiography.

SAVAGE, RICHARD HENRY (1846–1903). Author. A West Point graduate, Savage briefly served in the Egyptian army 1871–1874 and then left military service to be a lawyer and author. During the war he was appointed senior major of the Second U.S. **Volunteer Engineers** and in November 1898 was ordered to **Havana, Cuba**, where he hoisted the first American flag over Havana when the city was formally surrendered to the United States. In 1903 he was elected commander in chief of the National Spanish American War Veterans.

A voluminous writer, his works, which included *A Modern Corsair* (1897), *The Hacienda on the Hill* (1899), and *Brought to Bay* (1900), dealt mainly with prewar **Cuba**. They depicted a corrupt Spanish government and stated the *Maine* was destroyed by one of Lt. Gen. **Valeriano Weyler**'s mistresses so as to precipitate a crisis that would bring Weyler back to Cuba. Whereas Savage often portrayed Cubans as cowards and slackers, he claimed U.S. intervention had saved the revolution from slow strangulation and ultimate defeat.

SCHLEY, WINFIELD SCOTT (1839–1909). Commodore (USN), commanded the **Flying Squadron**. A U.S. Naval Academy graduate and veteran naval commander, Schley took command of the Flying Squadron on 26 March 1898, being advanced over at least a dozen senior officers. After leaving **Key West, Florida**, on 19 May in search of Adm. **Pascual Cervera's Squadron**, Schley was convinced that Cervera was at **Cienfuegos, Cuba**, and despite Adm. **William T. Sampson**'s cable on 24 May informing him that Cervera was probably at **Santiago, Cuba**, Schley meandered. When he finally arrived off Santiago on 26 May, he failed to reconnoiter and then left for Key West, ostensibly for coal. For 17 hours on 26–27 May, he stopped his squadron, drifted, and disregarded Secretary of the Navy **John D. Long**'s order to proceed to Santiago and **blockade** Cervera's Squadron. Finally on 28 May, Schley returned to Santiago, but failed to fire on Spanish ships at the harbor's entrance.

With the formation of the **North Atlantic Fleet** on 21 June, Schley assumed command of the **Second North Atlantic Squadron**. In tactical command on his flagship *Brooklyn* during the **Naval Battle of Santiago** on 3 July, Schley was acclaimed by the American **press** as a hero. After the war he was appointed to the Puerto Rican **evacuation commission**. Promoted to rear admiral on 3 March 1899, he was given command of the South Atlantic Squadron and retired on 9 October 1901. When the **Sampson-Schley controversy** exploded in the news, Schley asked for an official inquiry to clear his name; however, the **Schley Board of Inquiry** failed to exonerate him. He later wrote his memoir *Forty-Five Years under the Flag* (1904).

SCHLEY BOARD OF INQUIRY (12 SEPTEMBER–14 DECEMBER 1901). After Rear Adm. **Winfield S. Schley** requested a formal inquiry to clear his name, a board of inquiry convened on 12 September 1901 to investigate 14 charges. Composed of its president Adm. **George W. Dewey**, Rear Adm. E. K. Benham, and Rear Adm. Francis M. Ramsey, the board listened to no fewer than 1,700 pages of testimony; however, Adm. **William T. Sampson** did not testify because of illness. On 14 December 1901, the board issued its verdict. By a two-to-one vote, with Dewey dissenting, the board censored Schley for "vacillation and dilatoriness" in his search for Adm. **Pascual Cervera's Squadron**. Schley's report on coaling was judged inaccurate and misleading, he was charged with "lack of enterprise," and cited for failing to obey orders from the **Navy Department**. Although he was commended for his courage during the **Naval Battle of Santiago** on 3 July 1898, he was criticized for **"Schley's Loop"** during the battle. The board also recommended that the U.S. Naval Academy textbook that was critical of Schley be withdrawn and the author dismissed. Dewey subsequently wrote his own opinion supporting Schley, and it was published and widely hailed. Schley then appealed to President **Theodore Roosevelt**; however, Roosevelt, in January 1902, approved the majority report and stated the case was closed.

"SCHLEY'S LOOP." During the **Naval Battle of Santiago** on 3 July 1898, the *Brooklyn*, under the command of Com. **Winfield S. Schley**, made a quick turn or "loop" to starboard as the Spanish warship *Infanta María Teresa* approached and tried to ram the *Brooklyn* at the beginning of the battle. Although the *Infanta María Teresa* was forced by heavy U.S. fire to turn to the coast, Capt. **John W. Philip** of the *Texas* maintained that the turn forced him to order "back both engines hard" to avoid an imminent collision with the *Brooklyn*. Schley, who maintained he had never heard of the incident until six months after the battle, later defended his actions claiming that the turn, which was initially prescribed by the *Brooklyn*'s commanding officer Capt. **Francis A. Cook**, had been undertaken to place his ship in a position to engage the enemy. He claimed the "loop," which placed the *Brooklyn* on a course parallel to that of the Spanish ships, determined the nature of the battle; furthermore, he denied he had run across the *Texas*'s bow and stated that there was never any danger of a collision. Schley later offered a second explanation, maintaining the turn had been made to avoid getting caught in a cross fire from the Spanish warships *Cristóbal Colón* and *Vizcaya*. However, the **Schley Board of Inquiry** criticized Schley for the maneuver.

SCHOFIELD, JOHN McALLISTER (1831–1906). Major general and former **commanding general of the U.S. Army**. A West Point graduate and Civil War veteran, Schofield, as commanding general

(1888–1895) put into effect the doctrine that assigned the **U.S. Army** a limited role in offensive war overseas because the **U.S. Navy** would presumably carry the main burden in such conflicts. In January 1897, he called for a war with Spain, or at least U.S. intervention in **Cuba**, to halt the suffering and restore economic order. Because of conflicts between Maj. Gen. **Nelson A. Miles** and Secretary of War **Russell A. Alger** during the war, President **William McKinley** initially turned to Schofield for advice in April 1898. Schofield favored initial attacks on the **Philippines** and **Puerto Rico**, which might absolve the later necessity of attacking Cuba. However, the continuing conflicts between Miles and Alger caused Schofield to lose favor with McKinley, and he left Washington in June 1898, maintaining contact with McKinley. After the war he declined to serve on the **Dodge Commission** to investigate the **War Department**.

SCHURMAN, JACOB GOULD (1854–1942). President of the **Schurman Commission**. The president of Cornell University (1892–1902), Schurman was appointed by President **William McKinley** to head a commission to investigate the situation in the postwar **Philippines**. A reluctant expansionist who had initially been opposed to taking the Philippines, he concluded that immediate independence was out of the question, recommended the establishment of a civil government as soon as possible, and called for the eventual independence of the Philippines. In his publication *Philippine Affairs: A Retrospect and Outlook* (1902), Schurman wrote that McKinley had stated he did not want the Philippines, but because there was no other alternative, he was compelled to take them in the end to prevent serious international complications.

SCHURMAN COMMISSION. Appointed in January 1899 by President **William McKinley** to investigate the postwar situation in the **Philippines** and establish therein local self-government, the commission was composed of its Chairman **Jacob G. Schurman**, Adm. **George W. Dewey**, Maj. Gen. **Elwell S. Otis**, **Charles Denby**, and Dean C. Worcester, a zoologist and the most knowledgeable American on the Philippines. Previously, Worcester had written "Knotty Problems of the Philippines" *The Century Magazine* (October 1898) in which he argued that the Philippines could not be returned to Spain, left alone, or cast adrift to other nations; therefore, the United States was compelled by duty to govern them. The commission arrived in **Manila** in March and on 4 April issued an address to the people of the Philippines, maintaining that the aim of the U.S. government was the well-being of the people and that the United States accepted sovereignty over the Philippines in fulfillment of solemn obligations. In its report of January 1901, Adm. Dewey and the three civilians advised progressively transferring the responsibility of governing the islands to the Filipinos.

SCHWAN, THEODORE (1841–1926). Brigadier general (USV), commanded an Independent Brigade in the **Puerto Rican campaign**. The German-born Schwan, a Civil War veteran and recipient of the **Congressional Medal of Honor**, was a career soldier. Promoted to brigadier general (USV) on 4 May 1898, he took command of the First Division of the **Fourth Corps**. In late July Schwan's 1,500-man brigade consisted of the Eleventh U.S. Infantry, two companies of the Nineteenth U.S. Infantry, Troop A of the Fifth U.S. Cavalry, and two batteries of light artillery: battery C **Third U.S. Artillery** and battery D Fifth U.S. Artillery. The brigade left **Tampa, Florida**, and arrived at southern **Puerto Rico** on the transport *Cherokee* on 31 July. Receiving orders on 6 August to drive the Spanish out of western Puerto Rico, Schwan's force, assisted by Puerto Rican sympathizers, or *"escuchas,"* moved out of **Ponce**, occupied **Yauco** on 9 August, engaged Spanish forces at **Hormigueros** on 10 August, occupied **Mayagüez** the next day, and fought a brief engagement at **Las Marías** on 13 August, which proved to be the last combat of the Puerto Rican campaign.

Although Schwan was sick throughout his brief seven-day campaign, his forces covered 92 miles, occupied nine towns, and took 362 prisoners, while sustaining casualties of one dead and 16 wounded. The brigade's wartime service was chronicled by Karl S. Hermann in *A Recent Campaign in Puerto Rico by the Independent Regular Brigade under the Command of Brig. Gen. Schwan* (1907). After the war, Schwan, who viewed the war as "transcendental" for American participation "in the world's events," served in the **Philippine Insurrection** as principal assistant to the U.S. military government, retired after 40 years of service in 1901, and was promoted to major general in 1916.

SCORPION. (USN) Armed **yacht**, commanded by Lt. Comdr. **Adolph Marix**. Formerly the *Sovereign*, it was purchased by the **U.S. Navy** on 7 April 1898, and after being initially assigned to the **Flying Squadron**, it was attached to the **North Atlantic Squadron** on 24 May. While serving in Cuban waters during the war, it carried dispatches, formed part of the **"Ghost Squadron,"** bombarded **Cabañas Bay** as a feint for the **Fifth Corps's** landing at **Daiquirí** on 22 June, and fought in naval engagements at **Manzanillo** on 1 and 18 July. It was decommissioned in 1927 and sold in 1929.

La. 1896, com. 11 April 1898, dis. 850, hp. 2,800, sp. 17.85
Armament: 4–5″, 6–6pdr., 2 C. mgs.
Cc. 200, comp. 111

SCOVEL, HARRY SYLVESTER (1869–1905). Correspondent for the *New York World*. Trained as an engineer, Scovel served as a correspondent for the *New York Herald* and *New York World* in **Cuba** during the **Cuban Revolt**. He documented Spanish atrocities, acted as a courier for the Cuban insurgents, was deported, and returned to Cuba only to have a reward of $5,000 placed on his head, dead or alive, by Spanish authorities. Arrested and jailed in February 1897, Scovel became an overnight cause célèbre as the *World* publicized his imprisonment; and he was released and expelled in March.

During the Spanish-American War, Scovel, while reporting for the *World*, gathered intelligence for Adm. **William T. Sampson**, served as a courier between Sampson and the Cuban insurgents, smuggled **correspondents** serving as spies into Cuba, attempted to locate Adm. **Pascual Cervera's Squadron** while on the *Sommers N. Smith* in late May 1898, and landed with **Stephen Crane** near **Santiago, Cuba**, in mid-June and verified the presence of Cervera's Squadron in Santiago's harbor. An eyewitness to the **Battles of San Juan Hill** and **Kettle Hill** on 1 July, Scovel came into open confrontation with Maj. Gen. **William R. Shafter** at the capitulation of Santiago on 17 July, where according to observers, Scovel took a swing at Shafter after Shafter had taunted him. He was jailed and deported from Santiago on 18 July. After the war Scovel turned down an offer from the *World* to be its chief European correspondent and went into business in Cuba as a consulting engineer, and became a supporter of the annexation of Cuba by the United States, arguing that it would at least give the Cubans some voice in the U.S. policies that were shaping their nation's future.

SEARCHLIGHTS. Many ships in both the **U.S. Navy** and **Spanish Navy** were equipped with searchlights. Capt. **Fernando Villaamil** bounced them off the clouds on the night of 10–11 May 1898 as a signal to locate Adm. **Pascual Cervera's Squadron**, and Adm. **Manuel de la Cámara's Squadron** illuminated both its ships and the shore as it returned to Spain in late July in an effort to bolster public opinion. However, their most prominent and decisive use occurred at **Santiago, Cuba**, by the **U.S. Navy**. Beginning on 8 June, the **battleships** *Iowa*, *Massachusetts*, and *Oregon* took turns two miles away from the harbor entrance at night, focusing their 100,000-candlepower searchlights on the entrance in order to prevent Adm. Cervera's Squadron from attempting a night sortie. At the same time, the

Brooklyn and *Texas* to the west of the harbor's entrance and the *New York* and *New Orleans* to the east swept their respective coastlines with their searchlights.

SECOND BRIGADE, EIGHTH CORPS, U.S. ARMY. Commanded by Brig. Gen. **Francis V. Greene**, it was located south of **Manila** on the American left, next to **Manila Bay**. The brigade, consisting of 139 officers and 3,691 enlisted men, included company A of the engineer battalion, two batteries of the **Third U.S. Artillery**, batteries A and B of the **Utah Light Artillery**, **First California Infantry**, **First Colorado Infantry**, **First Nebraska Infantry**, **Tenth Pennsylvania Infantry**, and two battalions of the **Eighteenth U.S. Infantry**. During the **Battle of Manila** on 13 August 1898, it assaulted and took **Fort San Antonio Abad** and sustained total combat casualties of one dead and six wounded.

SECOND CORPS, U.S. ARMY. Organized at **Camp Alger**, it was placed under the command of Maj. Gen. **William M. Graham** on 16 May 1898. Composed entirely of **volunteers**, it consisted of 922 officers and 17,467 enlisted men. During the war two of its brigades left the United States: One under the command of Brig. Gen. **Henry M. Duffield** went to **Santiago, Cuba**, and the other under the command of Brig. Gen. **George A. Garretson** was sent to **Puerto Rico**. Because Camp Alger was to be discontinued, the corps, which consisted of 1,347 officers and 33,765 enlisted men in August, moved to **Camp Meade** during August and early September. On 2 November 1898, Gen. Graham was relieved by Maj. Gen. **Samuel B. M. Young**, and the soldiers were moved to **camps** in the South with their headquarters at Augusta, Georgia. The corps, numbering 49 officers and 795 enlisted in April 1899, was discontinued on 3 May 1899.

SECOND MASSACHUSETTS INFANTRY (USV). Commanded by Col. Embury P. Clark, the regiment was organized and mustered into service on 8–10 May 1898, with 47 officers and 896 enlisted men. After arriving at **Tampa, Florida**, on 17 May, it was assigned to the First Brigade, Second Division, of the **Fifth Corps**. While at Tampa, Pvt. "Dido" Hunt of Company G became famous for foraging beer on the docks, which he, members of his squad, and others consumed the night before boarding their transport. Transported to **Daiquirí, Cuba**, on the *Knickerbocker*, *Manteo*, and *Seneca*, the regiment arrived on 22 June. Consisting of 44 officers and 863 enlisted men, it fought in the **Battle of El Caney** on 1 July, sustaining casualties of five killed and 40 wounded. It left **Santiago, Cuba**, on 21 August on the transport *Mobile* and arrived at **Camp Wikoff, Montauk Point,**

Long Island, New York on 25 August. Upon being welcomed home at a public reception at Springfield, Massachusetts, on 27 September, the men were still in poor condition because of the effects of **disease**. The regiment was mustered out on 3 November with 44 officers and 797 enlisted men. Frederick E. Pierce later chronicled part of the regiment's wartime experience in his *Reminiscences of the Experiences of Company L, Second Regiment, Massachusetts Infantry USV in the Spanish-American War* (1900). Casualties sustained while in service included nine killed, 44 wounded, and 88 died from disease.

SECOND NORTH ATLANTIC SQUADRON, U.S. NAVY. Under the command of Com. **Winfield S. Schley**, it was part of the **North Atlantic Fleet**, which was organized on 21 June 1898. According to Adm. **William T. Sampson**'s orders of 11 July, it included the flagship *Brooklyn*; the **battleships** *Iowa*, *Indiana*, and *Texas*; the **cruisers** *Detroit*, *Marblehead*, and *New Orleans*; the **gunboats** *Eagle*, *Helena*, and *Wilmington*; the armed tugs *Osceola* and *Wompatuck*; the lighthouse tender *Mangrove*; the armed **yachts** *Hist*, *Hornet*, *Scorpion*, *Suwanne*, and *Yankton*; and the armed revenue cutter *Manning*.

SECOND OREGON INFANTRY (USV). Commanded by Col. O. Summers, the regiment was organized and mustered into service on 7–15 May 1898 at Eugene and Portland, Oregon, with 50 officers and 970 enlisted men. It left San Francisco on the transports *Australia* and *City of Sydney* on 25 May, as part of the first expedition of the **Eighth Corps** to **Manila, Philippines**. Two companies landed and took official possession of **Guam** on 21 June, and the regiment arrived at Manila on 30 June. After the **Battle of Manila** on 13 August, six companies went ashore as a provost guard to police the city. Its exploits were praised by the regiment's songwriter McNail Howell in "The Oregon Volunteer." After fighting in the **Philippine Insurrection**, it left Manila on 14 June 1899. Arriving in United States on 12 July 1899, the regiment was mustered out of service on 7 August with 44 officers and 1,024 enlisted men. Casualties sustained while in service included 16 killed, 74 wounded, 38 died from **disease**, one was killed by accident, and three deserted. The regiment's history was chronicled by W. D. B. Dodson in his *Official History of the Operations of the 2nd Oregon Infantry United States Volunteers in the Campaign in the Philippines* (1899).

SECOND U.S. ARTILLERY, U.S. ARMY. Under the overall command of Maj. John H. Dillenback, two light artillery batteries of four guns each of the Second U.S. Artillery were assigned to the artillery battalion of the **Fifth Corps**. Battery A was under the command of Capt. **George S. Grimes** and consisted of three officers and 79 enlisted men. During the **Santiago, Cuba, campaign** it sustained combat casualties of two killed and eight wounded. Battery F was under the command of Capt. C. D. Parkhurst and consisted of two officers and 77 enlisted men. During the Santiago, Cuba campaign it sustained combat casualties of three wounded.

SECOND U.S. CAVALRY, U.S. ARMY. Commanded by Lt. Col. William A. Rafferty, troops A, C, D, and F, consisting of nine officers and 257 enlisted men, were assigned to the **Fifth Corps**. The only mounted cavalry in the Fifth Corps during the **Santiago, Cuba, campaign**, the troops were transported to **Daiquirí, Cuba**, on the *Matteawan*, *Morgan*, and *Stillwater* and sustained combat casualties of one wounded during the war.

SECOND U.S. INFANTRY, U.S. ARMY. Commanded by Lt. Col. W. M. Wherry, the regiment left Montana and North Dakota and arrived at **Camp Thomas**, Georgia. Upon arriving at **Tampa, Florida**, it was assigned to the Second Brigade, First Division of the **Fifth Corps**. After being transported to **Daiquirí, Cuba**, on the **transports** *Clinton, San Marcos*, and *Yucatan*, the regiment consisted of 20 officers and 618 enlisted men. During the **Battle of San Juan Hill** on 1 July 1898, it sustained casualties of one killed and 20 wounded. After sustaining total combat casualties of eight killed and 57 wounded, the regiment left on the *St. Paul* on 11 August for **Camp Wikoff, Montauk Point, Long Island, New York**.

SECOND WISCONSIN INFANTRY (USV). Under the command of Col. Born, the regiment was organized and mustered into service at Milwaukee, Wisconsin, on 12 May 1898, with 49 officers and 972 enlisted men. After arriving at **Camp Thomas**, Georgia, on 17 May, it was assigned to the Third Brigade, First Division, in the **First Corps**. The regiment left Camp Thomas on 5 July and landed at **Ponce, Puerto Rico**, on 27 July. It fought in the **Battle of Coamo** on 9 August and left Puerto Rico on the *Obdam* and *Alamo* on 1 and 8 September. After arriving in Milwaukee, Wisconsin, in mid-September, the regiment was mustered out of service on 9–21 November with 48 officers and 1,248 enlisted men. Casualties sustained while in service included 39 died from **disease** and one deserted.

SECRET SERVICE, U.S. TREASURY DEPARTMENT. Directed by **John E. Wilkie**, the Secret Service, which had a staff smaller than that of a local newspaper, assumed responsibility during the war for

U.S. domestic surveillance. Serving as the government's counterespionage agency, it investigated several hundred suspected foreign agents, captured a few spies, and, assisted by the U.S. Post Office, intercepted suspicious correspondence, particularly Spanish consular mail from Jamaica and the Bahamas, which it intercepted without their respective governments' permission. Most of its resources went into breaking up the Spanish-run **Montreal Spy Ring**. Assisted by Western Union, telegrams were intercepted and agents were sent into **Canada**.

SEGURANÇA. A **transport** with a displacement of 4,033 tons, it initially served on the U.S. and Brazil Mail Line and then was purchased by the Ward Line. Chartered by the **U.S. Army** in April 1898, it transported the **Twelfth U.S. Infantry**, the **Balloon** Signal detachment, seven reporters, foreign military attaches, and 26 private horses and forage to **Daiquirí**, **Cuba**, at a rate of $600 per day. During the **Santiago**, **Cuba**, **campaign** it served as Maj. Gen. **William R. Shafter**'s headquarters ship. It was broken up in 1921.

SENECA. As a 1,911-ton **transport** for the **Fifth Corps**, it carried the **Eighth U.S. Infantry**, two companies of the **Second Massachusetts Infantry**, Headquarters First Infantry Brigade, Second Division, and one light artillery battery to **Daiquirí**, **Cuba**, at a rate of $450 per day. Later, without adequate medical supplies and personnel, it was the first transport sent north with sick and wounded from **Siboney**, **Cuba**. Upon arriving at Old Point Comfort, Virginia, on 18 July with three people suffering from **yellow fever**, it was ordered to proceed immediately to the quarantine station at New York City, where it arrived on 20 July. The *New York Times* immediately reported "Yellow Fever on Seneca," and the **press** labeled such ships **"Horror Ships."** In early August it carried part of Maj. Gen. **John R. Brooke**'s forces to **Arroyo**, **Puerto Rico**.

SEVENTEENTH U.S. INFANTRY, U.S. ARMY. Commanded by Lt. Col. J. T. Haskell, the regiment left Ohio and, upon arriving at **Tampa**, **Florida**, was assigned to the Third Brigade, Second Division in the **Fifth Corps**. After being transported to **Daiquirí**, **Cuba**, on the *Cherokee*, *Iroquois*, and *Manteo*, it consisted of 24 officers and 482 enlisted men. During the **Battle of El Caney** on 1 July, the regiment sustained casualties of four killed and 27 wounded. Subsequently, **Congressional Medals of Honor** were awarded to nine of its men for actions during the battle. After sustaining total combat casualties of eight killed and 40 wounded, the regiment left on the

City of Macon on 14 August for **Camp Wikoff, Montauk Point, Long Island, New York**.

SEVENTH CORPS, U.S. ARMY. Organized at **Tampa, Florida**, the Corps was placed under the command of Maj. Gen. **Fitzhugh Lee** on 16 May 1898. With the exception of the First Division under the command of Brig. Gen. **Guy V. Henry**, on 21 May the corps moved to **Camp Cuba Libre** at Jacksonville, Florida, and consisted of 501 officers and 8,904 enlisted men. During June the First Division was transferred to the **Fourth Corps**, and the First Division of the Fourth Corps, under the command of Brig. Gen. **Theodore Schwan**, joined the Seventh Corps.

Although the corps had been organized to attack **Havana, Cuba**, in the fall of 1898, it never saw combat. While remaining in camp in the United States, it sustained 246 fatalities. After attaining its maximum strength of 1,226 officers and 29,940 enlisted in August, it moved to Savannah, Georgia, in October and was reorganized. Beginning in December, it was assigned to occupation duty in Havana Province and was discontinued on 3 May 1899.

SEVENTH U.S. INFANTRY, U.S. ARMY. Commanded by Col. D. W. Benham, the regiment left Denver, Colorado, and after arriving at **Tampa, Florida**, it was assigned to the Third Brigade, Second Division of the **Fifth Corps**. Transported on the *Comal*, *D. H. Miller*, and *Iroquois*, nine companies arrived at **Daiquirí, Cuba**, on 22 June 1898. Consisting of 25 officers and 891 enlisted men, the regiment fought in the **Battle of El Caney** on 1 July, sustaining casualties of 33 killed and 99 wounded. The companies left on 20 and 21 August on the *Yucatan* and *Prairie* for **Camp Wikoff, Montauk Point, Long Island, New York**. Total combat casualties during the war were 132.

SEVENTY-FIRST NEW YORK INFANTRY (USV). Commanded by Lt. Col. W. A. Downs, the regiment was organized and mustered in on the Hempstead Plains of Long Island, New York, on 10–12 May 1898, with 45 officers and 977 enlisted. After arriving at **Tampa, Florida**, the regiment was assigned to the First Brigade, First Division, of the **Fifth Corps**. In the scramble to board the **transports**, the regiment commandeered a train at bayonet point and went to the docks, where it found its assigned transport, the *Yucatan*, had already been taken by the **Rough Riders**. The regiment then commandeered the transport *Vigilancia* and landed at **Siboney, Cuba**, on 22–23 June. Consisting of 47 officers and 922 enlisted men, the regiment fought in the **Battle of San Juan Hill** on 1 July, when, as the lead battalion, it recoiled under Spanish fire and was ordered aside by Brig. Gen. **Jacob F. Kent**. Subsequently during the battle the regiment sustained casualties of 14 killed, 48 wounded, and 43 missing.

On 16 July, the *New York World* published the article "Conduct of 71st New York at Charge of San Juan." While the article exonerated the enlisted men, it referred to the cowardice of the regiment's officers under fire, resulting in a firestorm of criticism directed at the *World*. The *New York Journal* accused the *World* of slurring the bravery of the troops, and **Stephen Crane**, even though he did not write the article, was blamed as its supposed author. **Joseph Pulitzer**, the owner-editor of the *World*, sought to escape criticism by starting a fund for a battlefield memorial to the Seventy-First and to the New York men of the **Rough Riders**. To which **Theodore Roosevelt** replied that no Rough Rider could sleep in the same grave with the craven dead of the Seventy-First. In the end Pulitzer was forced to return the money he had collected.

After sustaining casualties totaling 12 killed and 68 wounded during the **Santiago, Cuba, campaign**, the regiment left on 10–11 August on the *Grand Duchess*, *St. Louis*, and *St. Paul* for **Camp Wikoff, Montauk Point, Long Island, New York**. On 15 November, the regiment was mustered out of service with 50 officers and 1,114 enlisted men. Casualties sustained while in service included 15 killed, 68 wounded, 79 died from **disease**, three killed by accident, one committed suicide, and five deserted.

SHAFTER, WILLIAM RUFUS (1835–1906). Major general (USV), commanded the **Fifth Corps**. A Civil War veteran and **Congressional Medal of Honor** recipient, Shafter served on the frontier, where he acquired the nickname "Pecos Bill." In command of the Department of California, he was appointed a major general (USV) and assigned to command the Fifth Corps. A man of laconic speech and crude manners, Shafter, who weighed 300 pounds, had no political ambitions and chronically suffered from gout.

After attending the **Aserraderos Conference** on 20 June, Shafter, who hated the **press**, refused to let the **correspondents** accompanying the Fifth Corps go ashore initially as the troops landed at **Daiquirí, Cuba**, on 22 June; consequently, he incurred the wrath of **Richard H. Davis** and most of the correspondents. Suffering from malarial fever and gout during the **Santiago, Cuba, campaign**, Shafter, who was unable to go to the front, had his orders transmitted by messenger and telephone. He never assigned the Cuban insurgents an important role in battle since he believed they would be better used as common laborers. He was also in constant conflict over tactics with Adm. **William T. Sampson**, demanding the navy force the entrance to Santiago's harbor without the army's assistance. Horrified by the number of casualties resulting from the **Battles of El Caney**, **Kettle Hill**, and **San Juan Hill** on 1 July, Shafter proposed on 2 July that the army withdraw; however, his proposal was voted down by his commanders.

At the **capitulation** ceremony of Santiago on 17 July, Shafter ordered **Harry Sylvester Scovel** arrested for trying to hit him and apologized to a Spanish naval officer for not dismounting. He explained that if he were to dismount he would not be able to get back on his horse. With **disease** incapacitating the Fifth Corps, he requested on 3 August that his army be transported back to the United States as soon as possible. After arriving at **Camp Wikoff, Montauk Point, Long Island, New York** on 1 September, Shafter was named commander of the Department of the East, and then transferred to the Department of California. He retired in 1899 and was promoted to major general on the reserve list in 1901. When asked about Cuban independence, he remarked that the Cubans were not more fit for self-government than "gunpowder was fit for hell." With respect to the **Philippine Insurrection**, he remarked that his plan would be to disarm the natives, "even if we have to kill half of them to do it."

SHAFTER'S STRATEGY. Although Maj. Gen. **William R. Shafter** intended to land his **Fifth Corps** and hold it near the coast until it was well supplied and organized, Maj. Gen. **Joseph Wheeler**'s decision to push inland and fight the **Battle of Las Guásimas** on 24 June 1898, and what turned out to be incorrect information that an 8,000-man Spanish relief force was on its way to **Santiago, Cuba**, forced Shafter to move inland and advance directly on the city of Santiago. Hoping to take the city before the relief force arrived, he ordered a two-pronged frontal assault on the **San Juan Heights** and **El Caney** on 1 July before his corps was prepared and before **disease** could seriously affect his army.

SHERMAN, JOHN (1823–1900). Secretary of state until 25 April 1898. A former secretary of the treasury, Sherman, a Republican senator from Ohio, was the chairman of the Senate Foreign Relations Committee. He branded the Spanish as "barbarous robbers" and believed the Cubans favored being annexed by the United States. Appointed secretary of state in 1897 by President **William McKinley**, Sherman, who was becoming increasingly senile, favored the acquisition of **Hawaii** and on 26 July 1897 issued a formal diplomatic note to the Spanish government, which was the **McKinley administration**'s first direct expression of its official view of the Cuban situation. In the note the United States offered to mediate the situation.

On 25 April 1898, he resigned his position and was replaced by **William R. Day**.

SHERMAN'S NOTE TO SPAIN (26 JUNE 1897). From Secretary of State **John Sherman**, the note, which was the **McKinley administration**'s first official statement of its Cuban policy, was delivered to Spain's Minister **Enrique Dupuy de Lôme**. It demanded the revocation of **reconcentration** in **Cuba**, an early end to the **Cuban Revolt**, and a change in Spain's relationship with Cuba. On 4 August 1897, Spain's Minister of State **Carlos O'Donnell Abreú**, citing the American Civil War and the Union's treatment of the South, rejected both U.S. interference in internal Spanish politics and Sherman's accusations, stating there was no real foundation for accusing Spain's army of excessive cruelty in Cuba and blaming the insurgents for causing the suffering of the civilian population.

SIBONEY, CUBA. Located on the southern Cuban coast five miles west of **Daiquirí**, nine miles east of **Santiago**, and 11 miles from the Santiago harbor entrance, Siboney, which had no pier, consisted of a little cove around which were the buildings of a railroad company. Approximately 600 Spanish soldiers were stationed here before the landing of the **Fifth Corps** at Daiquirí on 22 June 1898. As part of that landing, Siboney was bombarded by the *Bancroft*, *Helena*, and *Hornet* as a feint. After the Fifth Corps had landed, Brig. Gen. **Henry W. Lawton**'s forces left Daiquirí and occupied Siboney at 9:00 a.m. on 23 June; however, the Spanish had already withdrawn during the night, leaving behind 30 barrels of liquor, wine, and whisky and a locomotive.

Beginning on 23 June, 600 soldiers an hour landed using small boats, 50 out of 415 mules perished swimming ashore, and the *St. Louis* illuminated the beach with its **searchlights** so round-the-clock landings, which included 2,978 Cuban insurgents, continued until 26 June. Subsequently, **engineers** constructed a small pier, which was later replaced by a larger one built by the **Thirty-Third Michigan Infantry**. Along with Daiquirí, Siboney served as a principal depot in supplying the Fifth Corps during its **Santiago, Cuba, campaign**. Most commissary supplies and reinforcements were unloaded here, and it served as a pickup point for the wounded and sick. On 11 July, Maj. Gen. **Nelson A. Miles** ordered the village burned because it was a possible source of the **disease** that was ravaging the Fifth Corps.

SICARD, MONTGOMERY (1836–1900). Rear admiral (USN) and chair of the **Naval War Board**. A U.S. Naval Academy graduate and Civil War veteran, Sicard commanded the **North Atlantic Squadron**

until 26 March 1898, when because of bad health, he was replaced by Capt. **William T. Sampson**. As chair of the Naval War Board during the Spanish-American War, Sicard was Secretary of the Navy **John D. Long**'s principal advisor. He opposed Maj. Gen. **William R. Shafter**'s demand that the navy force an entrance to the harbor of **Santiago, Cuba**, because he did not want to risk losing the main fighting ships under Adm. Sampson's command. He retired in 1899.

SIGNAL CORPS, U.S. ARMY. One of ten agencies in the **War Department**, the corps was commanded by Brig. Gen. **Adolphus W. Greely**. With meager funding, its eight officers and 50 enlisted-man-staff was expanded by acts of **Congress** on 18 May and 7 July 1898, which formed a volunteer signal corps. Under these acts 115 officers and about 1,000 men were mustered into service.

During the war the corps operated and maintained the **U.S. Army**'s communications network of telegraph lines, built and equipped 250 miles of telephone and telegraph lines between the **camps** within the United States and their headquarters, assisted the **Military Intelligence Division** in gathering intelligence, and established a coastal signal service. Lt Col. Benjamin F. Montgomery directed the White House's **Operating Room**, and the corps maintained the **Hellings-Villaverde Network** based in **Havana, Cuba**, and **Key West, Florida**. Responding to an executive order by President **William McKinley** on 25 April, the corps put censors in the **cable** offices in major U.S. cities. Lt. Col. Grant Squires, who was in charge of the cable officers in New York City, later wrote about his efforts in his article "Experiences of a War Censor" *Atlantic Monthly* (March 1899).

Overseas, the corps was involved in **cable-cutting operations**, landed with the soldiers, laid telegraph lines, mapped the areas, and was put in charge of **censorship**. In the **Santiago, Cuba, campaign**, Major Frank Greene commanded the corps's detachment of seven officers and 81 enlisted men in the **Fifth Corps**, and Capt. E. A. McKenna commanded Company A of the corps, which consisted of five officers and 55 enlisted men, in the **Eighth Corps**'s campaign at **Manila, Philippines**.

SIGNAL 250. The signal raised to alert U.S. ships that Adm. **Pascual Cervera's Squadron** was coming out of the harbor of **Santiago, Cuba**, on 3 July 1898. It consisted of three flags: a yellow flag with a blue ball in the center, beneath it a half-yellow and half-red flag, and last of all a yellow swallow tail pennant with a blue cross. The flags symbolized the numbers "2", "5", and "0".

SIGSBEE, CHARLES DWIGHT (1845–1923). Captain (USN), commanded the *Maine* and after its destruction the *St. Paul*. A U.S. Naval

Academy graduate and Civil War veteran, Sigsbee had been an instructor at the U.S. Naval Academy and served as chief of the navy's Hydrographic Office from 1893 to 1897. Assuming command of the *Maine* on 10 April 1897, Sigsbee was in his cabin writing a letter when the *Maine* exploded on 15 February 1898. He promptly **cable**d Washington urging caution. However, he later testified to the board of inquiry investigating the *Maine*'s destruction and then in front of the Senate Foreign Relations Committee that he believed it had been caused by a mine detonated electrically from some position ashore. Until his death he remained convinced that a mine had caused the disaster, and supported his viewpoint in his book *The "Maine": An Account of Her Destruction in Havana Harbor* (1899). During the war he commanded the cruiser *St. Paul* and defeated the Spanish ships *Terror* and *Isabella II* off **San Juan**, **Puerto Rico** on 22 June 1898. After the war Sigsbee served as the navy's chief intelligence officer, was promoted to rear admiral in 1903, and retired in 1907.

SIGSBEE'S CABLE (15 FEBRUARY 1898). After the *Maine* blew up at 9:40 p.m. on 15 February 1898, Capt. **Charles D. Sigsbee** quickly scribbled a note to Secretary of the Navy **John D. Long** on the disaster. He then asked **George B. Rea**, a correspondent, to take the note to the **cable** office. After briefly detailing the disaster and the current situation, the note urged that "Public opinion should be suspended until further report." At 2:00 a.m. on 16 February, Long was aroused and handed Sigsbee's telegram. He promptly sent a messenger to the White House. The note was the principal source of information for the late editions of the morning newspapers across the United States, and because Rea had also sent the original message to his newspaper, the *New York Herald*, the *Herald* published a facsimile of the note. The original note was later returned to Sigsbee for a keepsake.

SILVELA Y DE LA VIELLENZE, FRANCISCO (1843–1905). Leader of the Spanish **Liberal-Conservative Party**. A lawyer who had broken with **Antonio Cánovas y Castillo**, Silvela, who controlled the newspaper *El Tiempo*, demanded in the **Cortes** that the **Cuban Revolt** be repressed and opposed **autonomy**, arguing that reforms would not work. However, during a governmental crisis in June 1897, he joined a few Conservatives and attacked the Conservative Party's Cuban policy and demanded that Lt. Gen. **Valeriano Weyler** be recalled and the war ended. After the assassination of Cánovas in August 1897, Silvela became the leading conservative politician, and by early April 1898, he favored autonomy, arbitration of the *Maine*, opposed U.S. intervention in Cuban affairs, and called for a political truce by all political parties in order to strengthen Spain.

Upon the outbreak of the war, Silvela favored the continuation of the government of **Práxedes M. Sagasta** and opposed sending Adm. **Pascual Cervera's Squadron** to the West Indies. After the disastrous defeat at the **Battle of Manila Bay** on 1 May, he criticized the government and openly stated that **Cuba** was lost. Consulted by Sagasta in early August as the government moved to sign the **Armistice Protocol**, Silvela supported the decision as long as it only involved Cuba and **Puerto Rico**. The publication of his article "Sin Pulso" in *El Tiempo* on 16 August inaugurated a painful self-examination of Spain's defeat. He argued that Spain was without a pulse and only a massive effort to reconstruct and dignify the state could restore the country. Subsequently Silvela refused to serve on Spain's **Peace Commission** to negotiate the **Treaty of Paris**, and after the treaty was formalized, he replaced Sagasta as Prime Minister in March 1899. He retired from politics in 1903.

SILVER REPUBLICANS. Republican supporters of free silver, they were frustrated over the defeat of **William J. Bryan** in the 1896 presidential election and looked to "free **Cuba**" as a new issue to use against the **McKinley administration**. Fearful that a financial conspiracy, which came to be known as the **Cuban Bond Conspiracy**, would attempt to forestall Cuban freedom and shackle the United States with a heavy debt transferred from the holders of Cuban bonds, Republican Senator William M. Stewart of Nevada charged that the McKinley administration was blocking attempts at intervention because of the influence of "the money power." Other silverite Republican senators included **Henry M. Teller** of Colorado, Richard F. Pettigrew of South Dakota, Lee Mantle of Montana, Frank J. Cannon of Utah, and John P. Jones of Nevada. Late in 1898, when they feared a similar conspiracy involving the Philippine debt, Stewart argued that there was no danger because Adm. **George W. Dewey** had conquered the islands and thereby extinguished Spain's title.

SIMS, WILLIAM SOWDEN (1858–1936). Lieutenant (USN), naval attaché in Paris, France. A U.S. Naval Academy graduate, he had close to 17 years of almost continuous sea duty before he became the U.S. naval attaché in Paris in March 1897. Sims, an officer for the **Office of Naval Intelligence**, established an intelligence network of agents, which included an impoverished French baron, a doctor among the Spanish aristocracy in Madrid, the mayor of a French town near Paris, "an Italian citizen" in the Canary Islands, and a former Swedish army officer in Port Said, Egypt. His network produced some useful reports on Spanish strategic plans, monitored the voyage of Adm. **Manuel de la Cámara's Squadron**, and in an effort to get Adm. Cámara's Squadron recalled to Spain, disseminated **disinformation** that the **U.S. Navy** would attack the Spanish coast. Upon orders from the navy, his network was dismantled after the war, and Sims resumed sea duty at the China station in 1900. He later served as a naval aid to the president of the United States, was president of the **Naval War College**, commanded U.S. naval forces in European waters during World War I, and won the Pulitzer Prize for history. He retired as a rear admiral in 1922.

SIXTEENTH PENNSYLVANIA INFANTRY (USV). Commanded by Col. **Willis J. Hullings**, the regiment was organized and mustered into service on 10 May and 18–20 July 1898, with 47 officers and 1,028 enlisted men. After arriving at **Camp Thomas**, Georgia, it was assigned to the **First Corps**. On 22 July, eight companies left Charleston, South Carolina, on the *Mobile* and arrived at **Ponce, Puerto Rico**, on 26 July. It bore the brunt of the fighting in the **Battle of Coamo** on 9 August after executing a night march that flanked the Spanish positions. Four companies arrived from the United States and joined the regiment after the end of hostilities. After leaving Ponce on the *Minnewaska* on 10 October, the regiment was mustered out on 22–29 December with 48 officers and 1,238 enlisted men. Casualties sustained while in service included one killed, six wounded, 38 died from **disease**, and three deserted.

SIXTEENTH U.S. INFANTRY, U.S. ARMY. Commanded by Col. H. A. Theaker, the regiment left Idaho and Washington and, upon arriving at **Tampa, Florida**, was assigned to the First Brigade, First Division in the **Fifth Corps**. After being transported to **Daiquirí, Cuba**, on the *San Marcos*, the regiment consisted of 24 officers and 655 enlisted men. During the **Battle of San Juan Hill** on 1 July 1898, the regiment sustained casualties of 14 killed and 87 wounded. After sustaining total combat casualties of 14 killed and 115 wounded in the **Santiago, Cuba, campaign**, the regiment left on the *Grand Duchess* on 10 August for **Camp Wikoff, Montauk Point, Long Island, New York**.

SIXTH CORPS, U.S. ARMY. Under orders of 7 May 1898, it was to be organized at **Camp Thomas**, Georgia, and was placed under the command of Maj. Gen. **James H. Wilson** on 16 May. However, it was never organized.

SIXTH ILLINOIS INFANTRY (USV). Commanded by Major D. E. Clarke, the regiment was organized and mustered into service on 11

May 1898 at Springfield, Illinois, with 50 officers and 973 enlisted men. Among the enlisted men was Carl Sandburg. After arriving at **Camp Alger** on 20 May, it was assigned to the **Second Corps**. On 10 July, the regiment left Charleston, South Carolina, arrived at **Santiago, Cuba**, on 15 July, was quickly sent to **Puerto Rico**, arriving at **Guánica** on 25 July, and participated in a brief engagement the next day. As part of Brig. Gen. **Guy V. Henry**'s division, the regiment left **Ponce** on 6 August and participated in a seven-day campaign without firing a shot, owing to the signing of the **Armistice Protocol** on 12 August. On 7 September, the regiment left Ponce and arrived at New York City on 13 September. Furloughed for 60 days, the regiment was mustered out at Springfield, Illinois, on 25 November with 49 officers and 1,224 enlisted men. Casualties sustained while in service included 24 died from **disease** and one deserted. R. S. Bunzey later chronicled part of the regiment's experience in his *History of Companies I and E, Sixth Regiment, Illinois Volunteer Infantry from Whiteside County* (1901).

SIXTH MASSACHUSETTS INFANTRY (USV). Organized and mustered into service at South Framingham, Massachusetts, on 12 May 1898, with 47 officers and 896 enlisted men, the regiment arrived at **Camp Alger** on 22 May and was assigned to the **Second Corps**. After leaving Charleston, South Carolina, on the *Yale* on 8 July, it arrived at **Santiago, Cuba**, on 11 July and did not disembark. As part of Maj. Gen. **Nelson A. Miles**'s force, the regiment landed at **Guánica, Puerto Rico**, on 25 July, where it fought in a brief engagement the next day. As part of Brig. Gen. **Guy V. Henry**'s division, the regiment, which included Company L (the only **black American volunteer** unit that saw combat during the war), the regiment left **Ponce** on 6 August and participated in a seven-day campaign without firing a shot because of the signing of the **Armistice Protocol** on 12 August. After leaving on the steamship *Mississippi* on 21 October, the regiment was mustered out of service at Boston, Massachusetts, on 21 January 1899 with 46 officers and 1,172 enlisted men. Casualties sustained while in service included four wounded and 25 died from **disease**. The regiment's exploits were later chronicled by Lt. Frank E. Edwards in his book *The '98 Campaign of the 6th Massachusetts, U.S.V.* (1899).

SIXTH U.S. CAVALRY, U.S. ARMY. Commanded by Lt. Col. Henry Carroll, it was in the First Brigade, Dismounted Cavalry Division, of the **Fifth Corps**. Eight troops were transported to **Daiquirí, Cuba**, on the *Rio Grande*, and with a strength of 16 officers and 435 enlisted men, the troops fought in the **Battle of San Juan Hill** on 1 July 1898, sustaining casualties of two killed and 55 wounded. The troops left **Santiago, Cuba**, on 7 and 8 August on the *Gate City* and *Matteawan* for **Camp Wikoff, Montauk Point, Long Island, New York**. Total combat casualties sustained included two dead and 57 wounded.

SIXTH U.S. INFANTRY, U.S. ARMY. Commanded by Lt. Col. H. C. Egbert, the regiment left Kentucky, and upon arriving at **Tampa, Florida**, it was assigned to the First Brigade, First Division, of the **Fifth Corps**. After being transported to **Daiquirí, Cuba**, on the *Miami*, the regiment consisted of 31 officers and 461 enlisted men. During the **Battle of San Juan Hill** on 1 July 1898, the regiment sustained casualties of 12 killed and 99 wounded. After sustaining total combat casualties during the **Santiago, Cuba, campaign** of 12 killed and 115 wounded, the regiment returned to **Camp Wikoff, Montauk Point, Long Island, New York** in August.

SIXTH VIRGINIA INFANTRY (USV). Commanded by Lt. Col. Richard C. Croxton, this **black American** regiment was organized and mustered into service from 9 July to 11 August 1898, with 29 officers and 824 enlisted men, because Virginia's Democratic governor, James H. Tyler, was unable to ignore President **William McKinley**'s request for the mobilization of **black American volunteers** owing to the general state of disintegration that characterized Virginia's national guard and the apathetic response of white **volunteers**. With a full slate of black officers at secondary command positions, the regiment arrived at Camp Poland at Knoxville, Tennessee, on 13 September and was assigned to the **First Corps**. When Lt. Col. Croxton, who had come to the conclusion that the officers of the second battalion were incompetent, ordered them to stand for examination before a review board, the officers resigned en masse rather than be subjected to what they considered a maneuver to discredit them. A letter signed by the regiment's officers was sent to the **War Department** stating that if blacks were not to be placed in command positions then the regiment preferred to be mustered out. When white officers arrived on 2 November to replace the black officers, not a man responded. Croxton immediately pronounced it a mutiny and relieved the regiment of its arms.

After leaving Knoxville on 18 November, the regiment arrived at Camp Haskell at Macon, Georgia, on 19 November. Because of incidents arising from the soldiers' conflicts with local segregation laws and the murder of a soldier by a streetcar conductor after he had refused to move out of a seat reserved for whites only, the regiment was disarmed and placed under arrest for 20 days. On 26–28 January 1899, the regiment was mustered out at Macon with 28 officers and

804 enlisted men. Casualties sustained while in service included two died from **disease**, two murdered, and three deserted. A member of the regiment known as "Ham" chronicled the regiment's experiences in his frequent letters to the *Richmond Planet* newspaper from November to January 1899.

"SMOKED YANKEES." Term used by Cubans referring to **black American** soldiers.

SMOKELESS POWDER. Both sides used the newly invented powder during the war. Spanish forces used it in their **Mauser rifles** and in much of their artillery. With only three U.S. contractors producing it upon the outbreak of the war, initially it was of limited supply for U.S. forces. Therefore, the **U.S. Army** and **Navy** worked out a priority system in which smokeless powder was allotted to **battleships**, **Krag-Jörgensen rifles**, and a variety of artillery pieces. By war's end, there was a surplus in the U.S. arsenal.

SOCAPA, SANTIAGO, CUBA. A 150-foot-high bluff on the west side of **Santiago**'s harbor entrance, Socapa was defended by a seaward facing battery of three eight-inch muzzle-loading howitzers and two 6.4-inch Hontoria guns taken from the *Reina Mercedes*. East of the battery, and lower down the hill, was another battery, intended for the defense of the channel's submarine **mines**. It was composed of one 57 mm. gun, four 37 mm. Hotchkiss guns, and one 11 mm. machine gun.

SOCIALISTS—UNITED STATES. Although a fractured movement, which held a variety of positions on specific issues, they were generally opposed to expansionism and against the war. *The People*, the Socialist Labor Party's newspaper, edited by Daniel DeLeon, opined that a war for Cuban freedom was but a pretext for U.S. expansion. The party led an antiwar parade on 1 May 1898, which was squelched by New York City authorities.

SOLACE. (USN) A 3,800-ton hospital steamer, commanded by Comdr. A. Dunlap. Formerly the *Creole*, it was purchased by the **U.S. Navy** on 7 April 1898 from the Cromwell Line and prepared for duty in 16 days. It could accommodate 200 patients and had the latest instruments for antiseptic surgery, a steam laundry plant, an ice machine, and cold-storage rooms. Most of the equipment was donated by the **American Red Cross**. It was the first vessel in the U.S. Navy to fly the Geneva Red Cross flag. Assigned to the North Atlantic Station on 11 May, it was in continuous duty between **Cuba** and the eastern coast of the United States as it transported sick and wounded sailors to naval hospitals at Norfolk, Virginia, New York City, and Boston. Included among those transported to Norfolk were Capt. **Víctor Concas y Palau** and 48 Spanish sailors who had been wounded in the **Naval Battle of Santiago** on 3 July.

SOMMERS N. SMITH. Ex-**filibuster** boat, converted into a **press boat** and jointly chartered by the *New York World* and *New York Herald* during the war. In May 1898, with **Stephen Crane, Harry Sylvester Scovel**, and **Jim Hare** on board, it circumnavigated **Cuba** while conducting a seven-day, 1,586-mile search in torrential storms for Adm. **Pascual Cervera's Squadron**. Not only did they fail to find the squadron, but they were fired on by the **St. Paul** before reaching **Key West, Florida**, on 1 June. Later it was used off **Guantánamo, Cuba**, where reporters from various newspapers described the landing of the **First Marine Battalion** on 10 June.

SPANISH ARMY. See ARMY, SPAIN

SPANISH NAVY. See NAVY, SPAIN

SPANISH SOCIALIST WORKERS PARTY (*PARTIDO SOCIALISTA OBRERO ESPAÑOL*—PSOE). Founded in 1874 and led by **Pablo Iglesias**, it was a small but growing party, which rejected the monarchy, opposed obligatory military service, protested the disgraceful conditions in which Spanish soldiers returned from **Cuba** and the **Philippines**, and maintained a consistent antiwar policy. After the outbreak of the Spanish-American War, the party proclaimed solidarity between U.S. and Spanish socialists on 10 June 1898 and on 9 July demanded an immediate end to the war in its newspapers *El Socialista* and *Lucha de Clases*. After the **capitulation of Santiago, Cuba**, it proposed abandoning the Philippines.

SPRINGFIELD RIFLE. Manufactured at the Springfield Arsenal in Springfield, Massachusetts, it was a .45 caliber, single-shot, breech-loading rifle that fired **black powder** shells. The lack of a magazine limited its ability to firing only 15 rounds per minute. Initially it was issued to all **volunteer** units of the **U.S. Army**, with the exception of the **Rough Riders**.

"THE STAR SPANGLED BANNER." Although not yet the national anthem, it was a highly popular song during the war. It was played as the soldiers of the **Fifth Corps** landed at **Daiquirí, Cuba**, on 22 June 1898, when Lt. **Richmond P. Hobson** was released on 6 July, and when **Manila, Philippines,** capitulated on 13 August, and was sung by U.S. soldiers upon learning of the complete destruction of Adm. **Pascual Cervera's Squadron** in the **Naval Battle of Santiago** on 3 July.

STATE DEPARTMENT. Directed by Secretary of State **William R. Day** during the war, it was run on a daily basis by Assistant Secretary of State and veteran diplomat Alvery (Alvee) A. Adee. It did not decide much policy because President **William McKinley** acted as his own secretary of state. However, its diplomats, particularly U.S. Minister to Spain **Stewart L. Woodford,** kept the government informed of overseas developments. Upon the request of **Horace Porter,** U.S. ambassador to **France,** it authorized, on 22 June 1898, the spending of $2,500 to bring about a more favorable French opinion of the United States in the French press. Although it authorized, on 18 July, the spending of $2,000 to improve German-U.S. press relations, U.S. Ambassador Andrew D. White, fearful that it might leak, declined to use the money. During the war, Philip C. Hanna, former U.S. consul at **San Juan, Puerto Rico,** consistently encouraged the **McKinley administration** to invade **Puerto Rico** as soon as possible. After Day resigned to head the U.S. **Peace Commission** to negotiate the **Treaty of Paris, John Hay,** U.S. Ambassador to **Great Britain,** became secretary of state.

STATE OF TEXAS. Steamer from the Mallory Line, it was chartered by the **American Red Cross** to carry food and medical supplies to **Cuba.** However, it was held in port in the United States for two months because Rear Adm. **William T. Sampson** refused **Clara Barton**'s request to let it pass through the **blockade** for fear its supplies would fall into Spanish hands. Finally, on 20 June 1898, the *State of Texas* left **Key West, Florida,** with Barton, **George Kennan,** and 23 Red Cross workers aboard, and arrived off **Santiago, Cuba,** where upon Sampson's request, it steamed to **Guantánamo.** After receiving word of the **Battle of Las Guásimas** on 24 June, it steamed to **Siboney,** where it arrived on 26 June and landed a team of medical officers and **nurses.** After the capitulation of Santiago on 17 July, it was the first ship to enter the harbor and the Red Cross workers distributed food and clothing, feeding approximately 50,000 people in five days from the ship's stores.

STAUNTON, SYDNEY AUGUSTUS (1850–1939). Lieutenant (USN), Adm. **William T. Sampson**'s assistant chief of staff during the war. A U.S. Naval Academy graduate who was promoted through the grades to rear admiral in 1910, Staunton drafted Adm. Sampson's instructions for the **blockade of Cuba**, which were issued on 27 April 1898, and was present at the **Aserraderos Conference**. After the **Naval Battle of Santiago** on 3 July, Staunton wrote **Sampson's victory message** and delivered it to the **cable** station at **Siboney**, where he prohibited Com. **Winfield S. Schley**'s aide from sending Schley's dispatch and then sent Sampson's. After the war he served on numerous ships, wrote "The Naval Campaign of 1898 in the West Indies" *Harper's Monthly Magazine* (January 1899), and retired in 1912.

STERNBERG, GEORGE MILLER (1838–1915). Brigadier general, U.S. surgeon general. One of the world's leading experts on **yellow fever**, Sternberg, a graduate of Columbia Medical School and an eloquent speaker and prolific writer, founded the Army Medical School and introduced X-ray machines and programs for the rehabilitation of disabled veterans. Prior to the war, he advised President **William McKinley** against invading **Cuba** during the wet months for fear of **disease**. Although Sternberg issued strict regulations on sanitary measures on 25 April 1898, his orders were not followed in the **camps** within the United States. He initially resisted the aid of **American Red Cross nurses** and after the war called for the **Reed/Vaughn/Shakespeare Commission** to investigate the origins of typhoid in the camps during the war.

Sternberg was severely criticized after the war because of the epidemics which ravaged camps within the United States. He pointed out in his article "Sanitary Lessons of the War" *Journal of the American Medical Association* (10 June 1899), that the epidemic could have been contained by prompt, accurate diagnosis, complete compliance with sanitary regulations, and a medical corps large enough to deal with the sudden influx of inexperienced soldiers. In his book *Sanitary Lessons of the War and Other Papers* (1912), he further argued that the shortage of trained army surgeons and the reliance upon inexperienced volunteer doctors had caused most of the problems, and that the mortality rate from disease during the war had been comparatively low compared with previous American wars, particularly the Civil War.

STICKNEY, JOSEPH L. (1848–1907). Correspondent for the *New York Herald*. A graduate of the U.S. Naval Academy and Civil War veteran, he resigned to become a reporter in 1873. An experienced war correspondent, from 1887–1898 Stickney was the foreign editor and an editorial writer for the *Herald*. Having wired Com. **George W. Dewey** on 9 April promising to send out no news except that approved by Dewey, he boarded the **cruiser *Baltimore*** at Yokohama,

Japan, and joined the **Asiatic Squadron** at **Hong Kong** on 21 April 1898.

During the **Battle of Manila Bay** on 1 May, Stickney acted as Dewey's aide on the bridge of the *Olympia* and wrote a dispatch that gave rise to the **"Breakfast Myth."** He accompanied Comdr. **Benjamin P. Lamberton** ashore on 2 May to take possession of the arsenal at **Cavite** and later wrote that Dewey had warned German Adm. **Otto von Diederichs** that a continuation of unfriendly German actions in **Manila Bay** would be construed as open hostility. After the war, Stickney wrote "With Dewey at Manila" *Harper's Magazine* (February 1899), served as a correspondent in the Philippines and South Africa, and wrote a laudatory biography of Dewey, *War in the Philippines and Glorious Deeds of Admiral Dewey* (1899).

SUBIC BAY, PHILIPPINES. Located 35 miles north of the entrance to **Manila Bay**, Subic Bay was potentially a strong point. On 15 March 1898, a conference of military commanders accepted the recommendation of Adm. **Patricio Montojo** to fortify the bay and fight any attacking U.S. squadron here rather than in Manila Bay. Six hundred tons of coal were sent, two merchant ships and an old transport were sunk to block the bay's eastern entrance, and the western channel was to be fortified by mounting guns on the coast and at **Isla Grande** and placing **mines** at the entrance.

On 25 April 1898, Adm. **Patricio Montojo's Squadron** left **Manila** at 11:00 p.m. and arrived at the bay the next day only to find that little progress had been made in preparing the bay's defenses. None of the four 5.9-inch guns that were to have been mounted on the little island of Isla Grande were in place, and only five of the 14 available Mathieson mines were in place at the bay's entrance. After being informed on 28 April that Com. **George W. Dewey's Asiatic Squadron** had left **Mirs Bay, China**, Montojo called a council of captains. The captains decided to return to Manila; consequently, at 10:30 a.m. on 29 April Montojo's Squadron left for Manila. The afternoon of the next day Dewey's squadron arrived, and the *Boston* and *Concord* reconnoitered the bay. At 6:24 p.m. Dewey's squadron left for Manila Bay.

SUBSISTENCE DEPARTMENT, U.S. ARMY. Directed by Brig. Gen. **Charles P. Eagan**, the commissary general of the **U.S. Army**, it consisted of 22 officers and was responsible for purchasing goods and then issuing them to the army. One of its jobs was to feed the army, and although there was no shortage of food, administrative incompetence and field conditions sometimes created shortages. However, it was the most successful department in supplying U.S. forces, because Brig. Gen. Eagan scrapped the requisition system and employed camp commissary depots that were much more responsive to the needs of the military units.

SUMNER, SAMUEL STORROW (1842–1937). Brigadier general (USV), commanded the First Brigade, Dismounted Cavalry Division of the **Fifth Corps**. A veteran of the Civil War and frontier, Sumner commanded the Dismounted Cavalry Division during the battles for the **San Juan Heights** on 1 July 1898, because of the illness of Maj. Gen. **Joseph Wheeler**, and was awarded the Silver Star. He signed the **Round Robin Letter** of 3 August and was promoted to major general (USV) on 7 September. After the war, Sumner served as a military attache in London, England, commanded a brigade in the Boxer Rebellion, fought in the **Philippine Insurrection**, and retired as a major general in 1906.

SUWANEE. (USN) Armed **yacht**, commanded by Lt. Comdr. D. Delehanty. Attached to the North Atlantic Station on 15 May 1898, it bombarded **Santiago, Cuba**, on 6 June, participated in the seizure of **Guantánamo Bay**, and, after shelling the **Daiquirí** landing site of the **Fifth Corps**, it towed launches full of soldiers from ships to shore. On 1 July, the *Suwanee* shelled **Aguadores** as part of a feint attack and on 17 July assisted in removing the **mines** from the Santiago channel. On 12 August, it fought in a naval engagement at **Manzanillo**.

SYLVIA. A steamship chartered by **William Randolph Hearst** from the Baltimore Fruit Company. It was fitted with offices, a printing press, and a darkroom. Hearst and companions, such as **John C. Hemment** and William Britz, a "biograph" expert who hoped to do something utterly new—take moving pictures of war action, arrived off **Santiago, Cuba**, on 18 June 1898. Hearst used the *Sylvia* as a base of operations in reporting the war until returning to Baltimore, Maryland, on 18 July 1898.

—T—

TALAVERA REGIMENT. Spanish regiment located at Baracoa, **Cuba**. Six companies totaling 822 men were ordered by Lt. Gen. **Arsenio Linares y Pombo** to **Santiago, Cuba**. Two of these companies fought in the **Battle of Las Guásimas** on 24 June 1898. On 1 July, one company fought in the **Battle of Aguadores**, one company totaling 137 men fought in the **Battles of Kettle** and **San Juan Hill**, and three companies formed a second line of defense behind the **San Juan Heights**. During the battles of 1 July, the regiment sustained casualties of 22 killed and 85 wounded. On 3 July, Maj. Gen. **William R. Shafter**'s first surrender demand was presented under a flag of truce to their commander, Lt. Col. Pedro Rodríguez. Later, on 15 July, Rodríguez agreed with all the other military commanders that Santiago should capitulate.

TAMPA, FLORIDA. A city of 26,000, Tampa, which was on a deep 40-mile-long bay, was closer to **Havana**, **Cuba**, than any other viable port. Therefore, in 1895 a **Naval War College** plan assigned it the role as a point of embarkation for troops to invade **Cuba**. On 14 April 1898, Franklin Q. Brown, a deputy of Henry B. Plant, owner of the Plant railroad and steamship lines, which serviced the city, met with President **William McKinley** to extol the use of Port Tampa, which was located several miles south of Tampa, as a point of embarkation in the event of war with Spain.

After the outbreak of war, McKinley, on 2 May, ordered that Tampa be used as an embarkation point for an invasion of Cuba. In May, the **Fifth** and **Seventh Corps** were organized here. Soon afterward, the Seventh Corps moved to Jacksonville, Florida. The city soon had almost as many soldiers as citizens as Tampa and nearby Lakeland became the base for the Fifth Corps, which numbered over 16,000 by the end of May.

Although Tampa was a terminus of the Plant railroad system, only two railroad lines reached the city proper and only a single track connected Tampa with Port Tampa. Almost all supplies for the Fifth Corps arrived over this system, which proved to be inadequate as trains were backed up as far north as Columbia, South Carolina. Moreover, owing to inadequate storage facilities, the unloading of supplies was slow at best. Further hampering logistics, Port Tampa's wharf facilities could only accommodate from 15 to 20 vessels at a time.

As officers, **foreign military observers**, **correspondents**, and sightseers congregated at the Tampa Bay Hotel, the Fifth Corps settled into what **Richard H. Davis** called the "rocking chair period of the war" because of the myriad rocking chairs on the hotel's huge porches. On 14 June, the Fifth Corps finally left Tampa and steamed to **Daiquirí, Cuba**. During the war, 48,072 soldiers, which included 20,470 **volunteers** and 27,602 regulars, encamped near Tampa, and 56 men encamped here died from **disease** and accidents. In early August, the remaining forces were transferred to **Camp Wikoff, Montauk Point, Long Island, New York**.

TAMPA, FLORIDA, RACE RIOT (6 JUNE 1898). Upon arriving at **Tampa**, **black American soldiers** were angered over local segregation laws and frequently attempted to break the segregation barriers. On 5 May 1898, the Tampa *Morning Tribune* wrote, "The colored troops are splendid horsemen and show off to great advantage. The colored infantrymen stationed in Tampa and vicinity have made themselves very offensive to the people of the city. The men insist upon being treated as white men are treated and the citizens will not make any distinction between the colored troops and the colored civilians." An altercation occurred in nearby Lakeland in mid-May, and the local press complained of "black ruffians in uniform." A black infantryman wrote to the *Baltimore Ledger* on 4 June 1898, complaining that in Tampa "prejudice reigns supreme," and when black soldiers, unwilling to put up with local segregation laws, closed up a saloon that had refused to serve them, it was written down as a "riot."

When drunken white **volunteer** soldiers from an Ohio regiment used a black child as a target to show their marksmanship, black soldiers of the **Twenty-Fourth U.S. Infantry** and **Twenty-Fifth U.S. Infantry** stormed into the streets firing their pistols, wrecked saloons and cafes that had refused to serve them, and forced their way into white brothels on 6 June 1898. After the local police failed, the Second Georgia Infantry, a white regiment, was ordered to restore order. By morning, 27 black soldiers and three white soldiers had been severely wounded. Even though the **War Department** censored reports of the story, it quickly reached the **press**. According to local press reports, the streets "ran red with Negro blood," and on 8 June the *Tampa Morning Tribune* complained that black soldiers had outraged white prostitutes. The *Atlanta Constitution* on 12 June editorialized that in view of "the wild and demoniac conduct of the negro regiments at Tampa" they should be "ordered back to the Indian reservations" lest they "assault white Cubans."

TAYABACOA, CUBA (30 JUNE 1898). After a detachment of the **Tenth U.S. Cavalry** landed at Jucaro, **Cuba**, it made contact with Cuban insurgents, and under the command of Lt. Carter P. Johnson, it was isolated from other U.S. forces for about three months and fought several small engagements against Spanish forces. One of these engagements, which was a daring rescue operation at Tayabacoa, Cuba, on 30 June 1898, resulted in four of the detachment's privates—Dennis Bell, Fitz Lee, William Thompkins, and George Wanton—receiving the **Congressional Medal of Honor** for voluntarily going ashore in the face of the enemy and aiding in the rescue of wounded comrades after several previous attempts had failed. The detachment rejoined its regiment in September 1898.

TAYLOR, HANNIS (1851–1922). Author, lawyer, and U.S. minister to Spain (1893–1897). An Alabama lawyer and well-respected Democrat, Taylor was appointed because of patronage by President **Grover Cleveland** as U.S. minister to Spain, even though he did not speak Spanish and had no diplomatic experience. During his service he pressed for Cuban and Puerto Rican **autonomy** and thwarted the **O'Donnell Memorandum**, which attempted to enlist European support against U.S. Cuban policy, by telling Spain's Foreign Minister the duke of Tetuán that such an effort would end President Cleveland's cooperation. He correctly summed up the European position, pointing out that Europe's diverse interests precluded any coalition against U.S. policy.

Replaced by **Stewart L. Woodford** after the election of **William McKinley**, Taylor launched a private effort to educate Americans about Spanish iniquities and to promote U.S. intervention in **Cuba**. An article that he published upon his return to the United States, "A Review of the Cuban Question" *North American Review* (November 1897), created a sensation in Madrid, because many diplomats considered it an unofficial statement by the **McKinley administration**. A blistering attack on Spain, it declared Spanish sovereignty in Cuba extinct, claimed Spain's colonial government was responsible for the **Cuban Revolt**, advocated against self-government by the Cubans, and advised **Congress** to pass a resolution authorizing intervention. After the war he served as a special counsel before the Spanish Treaty Claims Commission.

TAYLOR, HENRY CLAY (1845–1904). Captain (USN), commanded the first-class **battleship** *Indiana*. As president of the **Naval War College** from 1893 to 1896, Taylor, unhappy with the **Kimball Plan**, summarized new planning in "Synopsis of the War College Plan for Cuban Campaign in a War with Spain," which advocated a supporting demonstration against the **Philippines**; moreover, the Cuban campaign would have to be ended before any operation took place in Spanish waters. The Cuban coast would be **blockade**d and points seized as bases for land operations against **Havana** by a force to number 60,000. It was all to be accomplished in 30 days in order to prepare for the arrival of a Spanish expedition. Taylor was the senior naval officer of the convoy that escorted the **Fifth Corps** to **Daiquirí, Cuba**, and commanded the *Indiana* during the **Naval Battle of Santiago** on 3 July. After the war he urged the need for a general staff for the navy in order to increase its efficiency, served as chief of the Bureau of Navigation, and attained the rank of rear admiral.

TELLER, HENRY MOORE (1830–1914). Republican senator from Colorado (1876–1882, 1885–1909). A lawyer and former secretary of the interior, Teller bolted his party over the issue of silver and was reelected as a **Silver Republican** in 1896. An erstwhile expansionist and supporter of the Cuban insurgents, Teller had long advocated the annexation of **Cuba** and **Hawaii**; however, he opposed any forceful annexation, believing eventually the Cubans would willingly join the United States. When he introduced what came to be known as the **Teller Amendment** in April 1898, Teller, who believed in a **Cuban Bond Conspiracy**, wanted to recognize future Cuban independence because it would prevent the United States from becoming a guarantor of Cuban bonds or an originator of new bonds. However, **Congress** accepted only his language disclaiming any U.S. intent to exercise sovereignty over Cuba. Favoring the acquisition of the **Philippines**, he supported the ratification of the **Treaty of Paris**, only to turn critic of U.S. policy during the **Philippine Insurrection**.

TELLER AMENDMENT. Introduced by Independent Republican Senator **Henry M. Teller** of Colorado, it was initially a substitute for the Senate resolution that recognized the **Cuban Republic** and intended to prevent the United States from exercising legal authority over **Cuba**. Although rejected during passage of the **Turpie-Foraker Amendment**, at the last minute it was attached to a Senate resolution. Disclaiming any "disposition or intention to exercise sovereignty, jurisdiction, or control" over Cuba, "except for the pacification" of the island, the amendment was approved by the Senate without debate or a roll-call vote on 16 April 1898. It was not thought to be important at the time when it became the fourth part of the congressional resolution of 19 April, which authorized the use of force to eject Spain from Cuba.

The Cuban **Junta** later claimed credit for its introduction and passage. Moreover, although publicly denied, except for Spain's Minister to the U.S. **Luis Polo de Bernabé**, who claimed to have proof, there were possible behind-the-scenes efforts by John J. McCook and Samuel Janney, New York bankers, in distributing $2 million in Cuban bonds to various senators in order to get the amendment passed. There is no evidence that Teller ever received any money.

TENTH PENNSYLVANIA INFANTRY (USV). Commanded by Col. A. L. Hawkins, the regiment was organized and mustered into service at Mount Gretna, Pennsylvania, on 11–12 May 1898 with 36 officers and 604 enlisted men. After arriving at San Francisco, California, on 24 May, it was assigned to the **Eighth Corps** and left on the *Zealandia* on 15 June as part of the second expedition to **Manila, Philippines**. After arriving at Manila on 17 July, it was assigned to the **Second Brigade** and fought in the trench engagements of 31 July, sustaining casualties of six dead and 29 wounded. The engagement was chronicled by the regiment's poet J. A. Harshman in "Battle of Malate." Subsequently, the regiment, with an effective strength of 32 officers and 524 enlisted men, fought in the **Battle of Manila** on 13 August. Total combat casualties sustained during the Spanish-American War included six dead and 29 wounded. After fighting in the **Philippine Insurrection**, the regiment left Manila on 1 July 1899 and, after arriving in the United States on 1 August, was mustered out at San Francisco on 22 August, with 33 officers and 736 enlisted men. Casualties sustained while in service included 15 killed, 68 wounded, and seven died from **disease**.

The regiment's "mascot" was "Boots" McDermott, a 13-year old Pittsburgh shoeshine boy who slipped aboard the railroad cars bound for San Francisco. He went with the regiment to Manila, and during the battle of Manila, he served on the front lines as an ammunition bearer and carried water to the wounded. Adm. **George W. Dewey** had a sailor's suit made for him. Upon returning to Pittsburgh, "Boots" was welcomed as a hero.

TENTH U.S. CAVALRY (COLORED), U.S. ARMY. Commanded by Lt. Col. T. A. Baldwin, the regiment left Montana on 19 April 1898 and went to **Camp Thomas**, Georgia. After arriving at Lakeland, Florida, it was assigned to the Second Brigade, Dismounted Cavalry Division of the **Fifth Corps**. The regiment left **Tampa, Florida**, with three Hotchkiss guns on the transport *Leona* and landed at **Daiquirí, Cuba**, on 22 June. With Lt. **John J. Pershing** serving as quartermaster, the regiment, consisting of 27 officers and 453 enlisted men, fought in the **Battle of Las Guásimas** on 24 June, sustaining one killed and ten wounded. On 1 July, during the battles for the **San Juan Heights**, the regiment advanced along the slope of **Kettle Hill** and took the northern part of the heights, sustaining casualties of five killed and 26 wounded. During the **Santiago, Cuba, campaign**, the regiment sustained 45 total combat casualties.

During the war, the regiment was awarded 11 certificates of merit and five **Congressional Medals of Honor**, four of which were from the action at **Tayabacoa, Cuba**, on 30 June and one by Sgt. Maj. **Edward L. Baker Jr.** during the taking of the San Juan Heights on 1 July. After sustaining a total of 92 casualties during the war, the regiment left **Santiago** on the *Río Grande* on 13 August for **Camp Wikoff, Montauk Point, Long Island, New York**. After arriving, it moved to Huntsville, Alabama, where it confronted serious racial problems. By mid-May 1899, it was back in **Cuba** as part of the U.S. occupation forces and later fought in the **Philippine Insurrection**. Its actions during the war were commemorated in the poems "The Fighting Tenth" and B. M. Channing's "The Negro Soldier." The Tenth's record was compiled by Herschel V. Cashin in *Under Fire with the 10th U.S. Cavalry* (1899).

TENTH U.S. INFANTRY, U.S. ARMY. Commanded by Lt. Col. Edgar Romeyo Kellogg, the regiment left Oklahoma and went to **Tampa, Florida**, where it was assigned to the Second Brigade, First Division, in the **Fifth Corps**. After leaving Tampa on the transport *Alamo*, the regiment landed at **Daiquirí, Cuba**, on 22 June, and consisting of 23 officers and 432 enlisted men, fought in the **Battle of San Juan Hill** on 1 July 1898, sustaining five dead and 26 wounded. As a result of their actions in the battle Sgt. Andrew J. Cummings and Pvts. Charles P. Cantrell, William Keller, James J. Nash, and Alfred Polond were later awarded the **Congressional Medal of Honor**. After sustaining 45 total combat casualties, the regiment left **Santiago, Cuba**, on the *St. Louis* on 10 August for **Camp Wikoff, Montauk Point, Long Island, New York**.

TERROR. (SPN) **Torpedo-boat destroyer**, commanded by Lt. Comdr. Juan de la Rocha. A three-funneled sister ship to the *Furor*, the *Terror* was part of Adm. **Pascual Cervera's Squadron**. On 10 May 1898, Adm. Cervera detached it and the *Furor* to **Martinique** to try to obtain coal and news. A few hours later its boilers became unserviceable; therefore, it was left at Martinique. After being repaired, it left on 25 May and arrived in **San Juan, Puerto Rico**, the next day. On 22 June, along with the *Isabella II*, it briefly engaged the *St. Paul* off San Juan. As the population of San Juan looked on, a shell struck it about 12 inches above the waterline, wrecking the starboard engine, and exited below the waterline on the port side. Sustaining two dead and five wounded, it returned to port, and because it was in danger of capsizing, Lt. Comdr. Rocha beached it on Puntilla shoals. After being floated two days later, the *Terror* took a month to be repaired. On 14 September, it left San Juan for Spain.

La. 1896, dis. 380, hp. 6,000, sp. 28
Armament: 2–14pdr., 2–6pdr., 2–1pdr. M., 2–14″ tt.
Cc. 100, comp. 67

TERROR. (USN) Double-turreted **monitor**, commanded by Capt. Nicoll Ludlow. A sister ship to the *Amphitrite*, *Miantonomoh*, and *Monadnock*, it, however, had pneumatic systems for operating its guns, turrets, and steering. Assigned to the North Atlantic Station, it served on the **blockade of Cuba**, capturing the schooner *Tres Hermanas* on 24 April, the steamer *Ambrosia Bolivar* on 26 April, and the steamer *Guido* on 27 April 1898, near **Cárdenas, Cuba**. It participated in the bombardment of **San Juan, Puerto Rico**, on 12 May, but had to be frequently towed by the *New York* since its steering gears had broken down. It was stricken in 1915, and used as a gunnery target until the hulk was sold in 1923.

La. 1883, com. 1896, dis. 3,990, hp. 1,660, sp. 12
Armor: s. 7″, d. 1.75″, t. 11.5″, ct. 7.5″
Armament: 4–10″, 2–6pdr., 2–3pdr., 2–1pdr., 2–37 mm.
Cc. 270, comp. 151

TETUÁN, DUKE OF. See O'DONNELL Y ABREÚ, CARLOS

TEXAS. (USN) Second-class **battleship** commanded by Capt. **John W. Philip**. The first battleship of the New Steel Navy, it was the sister ship to the *Maine*. Attached to the **Flying Squadron**, it served on the **blockade of Cuba**, participated in the seizure of **Guantánamo Bay**, bombarded **Cabañas Bay** as part of a feint landing in support of the landing of the **Fifth Corps** at **Daiquirí** on 22 June, and was hit by a shell from the **Socapa** battery that killed one and wounded eight on 22 June. During the **Naval Battle of Santiago** on 3 July, the *Texas* fired 835 shots and destroyed the *Almirante Oquendo*. Although it was hit several times, it sustained no significant damage. Because the firing of its 12-inch guns had warped the main deck, it was sent to Guantánamo Bay for repairs on 25 July and then to the United States before the war ended. Decommissioned on 11 February 1911, it was sunk as a gunnery target on 20 March 1911.

La. 1892, com. 1895, dis. 6,315, hp. 8,600, sp. 17
Armor: s. 12–6″, d. 2–3″, r. 12″, t. 12″, ct. 12″
Armament: 2–12″, 6–6″, 12–6pdr., 6–1pdr., 4–1pdr. H. rev., 2 C. mgs.,
   2–14″ tt. (aw.)
Cc. 850, comp. 392

"THERE'LL BE A HOT TIME IN THE OLD TOWN TONIGHT."

The most popular American song of the war, it was sung so often by U.S. soldiers in the **Philippines** that many Filipinos thought it was the national anthem. It was sung by the men of the **Asiatic Squadron** en route to **Manila**, and the **First Colorado Infantry** sang it going into battle during the **Battle of Manila** on 13 August 1898. In **Cuba** it became the unofficial anthem of the campaign. It was sung by soldiers while landing at **Daiquirí** and by soldiers upon receiving news of the defeat of Adm. **Pascual Cervera's Squadron** in the **Naval Battle of Santiago** on 3 July. It became the unofficial theme song of the **Rough Riders**.

THIRD ALABAMA INFANTRY (USV). After Governor Joseph F. Johnston raised **black American volunteer** forces to regimental strength, Capt. **Robert E. L. Bullard** was appointed to command, and the regiment was organized and mustered in 4 June–5 August 1898, at Mobile, Alabama, with 46 officers and 1,185 enlisted men. It left Mobile on 7 September and arrived at Camp Shipp at Anniston, Alabama, on 9 September. Whereas the local papers excoriated the black soldiers, Col. Bullard defended them. Initially assigned to the **Third Corps**, the regiment was transferred to the **Fourth Corps** on 7 October. While at Anniston it was involved in the "**Battle of Anniston**" on 24 November. When reports arrived that the unit was to be mustered out, Col. Bullard and 456 enlisted men signed petitions requesting that they be allowed to remain in the volunteer army; nevertheless, the regiment was mustered out of service on 20 March 1899, with 46 officers and 992 enlisted. Casualties sustained while in service included seven died from **disease**, one was killed by accident, three were murdered, and 88 deserted.

THIRD CORPS, U.S. ARMY. Organized at **Camp Thomas**, Georgia, it was placed under the command of Maj. Gen. **James F. Wade** on 16 May 1898. Consisting of 811 officers and 16,223 enlisted men in May, the First and Second Brigades of the First Division and Second Brigade of the Second Division disintegrated with the departure on 1 June 1898 of most of their troops to **Tampa, Florida**, to join the campaign at **Santiago, Cuba**. On 31 July, Gen. Wade relinquished command to Brig. Gen. **Royal T. Frank**. On 28 August the corps, which had been diminished by mustering out to 530 officers and 11,007 enlisted men, was ordered to move to Camp Shipp at Anniston, Alabama. The remaining troops were consolidated into a first division, and the corps was discontinued on 7 October 1898. Its remaining regiments were transferred to the **Fourth Corps**.

THIRD ILLINOIS INFANTRY (USV). Commanded by Col. F. Bennitt, the regiment was organized and mustered into service at Springfield on 7–10 May 1898 with 47 officers and 983 enlisted men. After the regiment arrived at **Camp Thomas**, Georgia, on 16 May, it was assigned to the **First Corps**. On 24 July, it left Newport News, Virginia, on the *St. Louis* and landed at **Arroyo, Puerto Rico**, on 2 August. As part of Maj. Gen. **John R. Brooke**'s force, it fought in the **skirmish at Guayama** on 5 August. Frequent complaints about food by its soldiers gave rise to fallacious articles in the *Chicago Daily News* such as "Blundering in Porto Rico" (17 September 1898), and "Starvation Prevails in 3rd Illinois at Guayama, Porto Rico" (26 September 1898). After leaving Puerto Rico on the *Roumania* on 4 November, the regiment was mustered out on 13–14 January

1899, with 50 officers and 1,223 enlisted men. Casualties sustained while in service included 43 dead from **disease** and one deserted.

THIRD NEBRASKA INFANTRY (USV). Also known as the "Silver Regiment," it was organized and mustered into service on 1–17 July 1898, with 40 officers and 1,274 enlisted men. Commanded by Col. **William Jennings Bryan**, who left most military matters to Lt. Col. Victor Vifquain, a longtime Nebraska Democrat, the regiment arrived at Jacksonville, Florida, on 22 July and was assigned to the **Seventh Corps**. The regiment never left the United States but was hit hard by typhoid while encamped in Florida. In late September, Bryan appealed to President **William McKinley** to muster out the regiment, arguing that the men had not enlisted to support imperialistic aims. McKinley refused, specifying that the request had to go through channels. After Bryan resigned his command in December, three battalions served as occupation forces in **Cuba** from January to April 1899. The regiment was mustered out at Augusta, Georgia, on 14 May 1899, with 46 officers and 859 enlisted men. Casualties sustained while in service included 32 dead from **disease** and three deserted.

THIRD NORTH CAROLINA INFANTRY (USV). Upon the first call for **volunteers**, Daniel L. Russell, Republican governor, formed a **black American** battalion under the command of Maj. James H. Young, a leading black Republican and editor of the *Raleigh Gazette*. Organized and mustered in at Fort Macon on 12 May–19 July, with 43 officers and 978 enlisted men, it had a complete roster of black officers. After leaving Fort Macon on 14 September, the regiment arrived at Camp Poland at Knoxville, Tennessee, the next day and was assigned to the **First Corps**. While encamped, the regiment was fired on by a Georgia unit when it appeared on the drill field on 18 September. The Georgians were arrested and held until mustered out. On 5 October, members of all companies sent a letter to Secretary of War **Russell A. Alger**, demanding to be discharged because they were not going overseas to fight. Subsequently, the Third left Knoxville on 22 November and arrived at Camp Haskell at Macon, Georgia, the next day. The white **press** excoriated their presence, and although officially inspected and found to be well trained and well commanded, Brig. Gen. **John C. Bates**, the divisional commander, reported on 22 November that most of the officers were incompetent and that the unit was unfit to go to **Cuba** as an occupation force. It was mustered out of service at Macon on 31 January–8 February 1899, with 40 officers and 1,022 enlisted men. Casualties sustained while in service included 13 dead from **disease**, two murdered, one killed by accident, and 14 deserted.

THIRD U.S. ARTILLERY, U.S. ARMY. Commanded by Capt. William E. Birkhimer, a battalion of heavy artillery, composed of batteries G, H, K, and L and consisting of nine officers and 722 enlisted men, left San Francisco, California, on 27 June 1898 as part of the third expedition of the **Eighth Corps** to **Manila, Philippines**. After arriving on 25 July, the battalion was assigned to the **Second Brigade**, and with an effective strength of eight officers and 666 enlisted men, fought in the trench engagements on the night of 31 July, sustaining casualties of two dead and five wounded. Subsequently, it fought in the **Battle of Manila** on 13 August. Total combat casualties sustained during the war were two dead and five wounded.

THIRD U.S. CAVALRY, U.S. ARMY. Commanded by Major Henry W. Wessels, it left its stations in Vermont and Missouri and went to **Camp Thomas**, Georgia. After arriving at **Tampa, Florida**, it was assigned to the First Brigade, Dismounted Cavalry Division of the **Fifth Corps**. Eight troops went to **Daiquirí, Cuba**, on the transport *Río Grande*. Consisting of 23 officers and 433 enlisted men, the troops fought in the **Battle of San Juan Hill** on 1 July, sustaining casualties of three killed and 45 wounded. After sustaining 55 total casualties, the troops left **Santiago, Cuba**, on the **transports** *Gate City* and *Matteawan* on 8 August for **Camp Wikoff, Montauk Point, Long Island, New York**.

THIRD U.S. INFANTRY, U.S. ARMY. Commanded by Col. John H. Page, the regiment left Fort Snelling in Minnesota, went to Mobile, Alabama, and arrived at **Tampa, Florida**, where it was assigned to the Independent Brigade, under command of Brig. Gen. **John C. Bates**, in the Second Division of the **Fifth Corps**. It went to **Daiquirí, Cuba**, on the transport *Breakwater*. Consisting of 21 officers and 464 enlisted men, the regiment fought in the **Battle of El Caney** on 1 July 1898, sustaining casualties of two dead and three wounded. After sustaining 18 total casualties, the regiment left on the *Yale* on 19 August, for **Camp Wikoff, Montauk Point, Long Island, New York**.

THIRD U.S. VOLUNTEER CAVALRY. See GRIGSBY'S COWBOYS

THIRD WISCONSIN INFANTRY (USV). Organized and mustered into service at Milwaukee on 11 May 1898 with 50 officers and 975 enlisted men, the regiment arrived at **Camp Thomas**, Georgia, on 16 May. After leaving Charleston, South Carolina, on the *Obdam* on 20 July, the regiment landed at **Ponce, Puerto Rico**, on 28 July and, as part of a brigade under the command of Brig. Gen. **Oswald H. Ernst**, it fought in the **Battle of Coamo** on 9 August and in the skirmish at the **Asomante Hills** on 12 August. After leaving **Puerto Rico** on the *Manitoba* on 22 October, the regiment returned to Milwaukee on 30 October, was furloughed for 60 days, and was mustered out of service on 4–17 January 1899, with 49 officers and 1,196 enlisted men. Casualties sustained while in service included two killed in action, four wounded, 31 dead from **disease**, and one deserted.

THIRTEENTH MINNESOTA INFANTRY (USV). Commanded by Col. Charles McReeve, it was organized and mustered in on 7 May with 50 officers and 979 enlisted men. After leaving San Francisco on the *City of Para* on 27 June 1898, as part of the third expedition of the **Eighth Corps** to **Manila, Philippines**, it arrived at Manila on 31 July and disembarked on 7 August. After fighting as part of the **First Brigade** in the **Battle of Manila** on 13 August, the regiment served as a provost guard of Manila. The regiment's songwriter, Burt D. Carrier, wrote "A Hot Time for Minnesota," which covered the regiment's experience in the **Philippines** during the Spanish-American War. Col. McReeve was promoted to brigadier general and served as the deputy provost marshal and chief of police in Manila. His wife, who had been denied permission to travel with the regiment, hid on a transport and reached Honolulu, **Hawaii**, where she was taken off. She soon secured passage to **Hong Kong** and from there traveled to Manila to be with her husband. Subsequently, the regiment fought in the **Philippine Insurrection** and left Manila on 11 August 1899. After arriving in the United States on 7 September, it was mustered out on 3 October 1899, with 51 officers and 956 enlisted. Casualties sustained while in service included seven killed, 74 wounded, 34 dead from **disease**, two killed by accident, one drowned, and two deserted.

THIRTEENTH U.S. INFANTRY, U.S. ARMY. Commanded by Lt. Col. W. S. Worth, the regiment left Buffalo, New York, and arrived in **Tampa, Florida**, where it was assigned to the Third Brigade of the **Fifth Corps**. While trying to embark, its train was stolen by the **Seventy-First New York Infantry**. Therefore, the regiment found an empty train, hauled a sleeping engineer out of bed, and went to Port Tampa, where it boarded the transport *Saratoga* and went to **Daiquirí, Cuba**. After landing, the regiment, consisting of 24 officers and 441 enlisted men, fought in the **Battle of San Juan Hill** on 1 July, sustaining casualties of 18 killed and 86 wounded. For his actions during the battle, Sgt. Alexander M. Quinn was later awarded the **Congressional Medal of Honor**. After sustaining 109 total combat casualties, the regiment left **Santiago, Cuba**, and went to **Camp**

Wikoff, Montauk Point, Long Island, New York. U. G. McAlexander chronicled the regiment's exploits in his *History of the Thirteenth Regiment United States Infantry* (1905).

THIRTY-FOURTH MICHIGAN INFANTRY (USV). Organized and mustered into service at Island Lake, Michigan, on 17 May–2 June 1898, with 50 officers and 980 enlisted men, the regiment arrived at **Camp Alger** on 9 June and went to **Siboney, Cuba**, on the **transports** *Yale* and *Harvard*, arriving there on 27 June and 1 July. It was assigned to Brig. Gen. **Henry M. Duffield**'s brigade. The regiment participated in the **Santiago, Cuba, campaign** by building a road from Siboney to the front lines and arrived at the **San Juan Heights** on 2 July after they had been taken the previous day. After sustaining no combat casualties, the regiment left **Santiago, Cuba**, on the *Badger* and the *Leona* on 17 and 20 August, for **Camp Wikoff, Montauk Point, Long Island, New York**. After arriving at Detroit, Michigan, on 4 September, the regiment was furloughed for 60 days, and mustered out of service from 24 November 1898 to 2 January 1899, with 45 officers and 1,153 enlisted men. Casualties sustained while in service included 80 dead from **disease**, one killed by accident, and one drowned.

THIRTY-THIRD MICHIGAN INFANTRY (USV). Organized and mustered in service at Island Lake on 13–20 May 1898, with 44 officers and 978 enlisted men, the regiment arrived at **Camp Alger** on 31 May and was assigned to the **Second Corps**. After leaving Camp Alger on 22 June, it arrived at **Siboney, Cuba**, on 27 June. Assigned to Brig. Gen. **Henry M. Duffield**'s brigade in the **Fifth Corps**, the regiment, consisting of 43 officers and 958 enlisted men, constructed a larger pier at Siboney and worked on the road from Siboney to the front lines at **Santiago**. It fought in the engagement at **Aguadores** on 1 July, sustaining casualties of two dead and ten wounded. After sustaining 12 total combat casualties, the regiment left Santiago on the *Harvard* and the *Minnewaske* on 21 and 23 August for **Camp Wikoff, Montauk Point, Long Island, New York**. After arriving at Detroit, Michigan, on 1 September, the regiment was furloughed for 60 days and mustered out of service from 9 November to 6 January 1899, with 47 officers and 1,159 enlisted men. Casualties sustained while in service included three killed in action, ten wounded, 58 dead from **disease**, and one deserted.

THREE FRIENDS. A former **filibuster** boat piloted by **Johnny "Dynamite" O'Brien**, it served as a *New York World* **press boat** during the war. While **correspondents Stephen Crane, Ralph D. Paine**,

Harry Brown, and Ernest W. McCready were on board off the Cuban coast in early May 1898, it was almost rammed by the U.S. **gunboat** *Machias*. It later served off **Santiago, Cuba**, where it toured the wreckage of Adm. **Pascual Cervera's Squadron** after the **Naval Battle of Santiago** on 3 July.

TODD, CHAPMAN COLEMAN (1848–1929). Commander (USN), commanded the *Wilmington* May 1897–August 1899. On 17 January 1898, Todd was ordered to stop his cruise to the South Atlantic and soon joined the North Atlantic Station. He commanded the *Wilmington* during the naval **Battle of Cárdenas Bay, Cuba**, on 11 May 1898, and was in overall command of U.S. naval forces during the naval battle at **Manzanillo** on 18 July. He was advanced for his "eminent and conspicuous conduct" in battle and was promoted to captain in 1901. After 41 years of service, he retired as a rear admiral in 1902.

TODD Y WELLS, ROBERTO H. (1862–1955). A member of the Puerto Rican section of the **Cuban Revolutionary Party** in New York City. Born in St. Thomas, Todd was an advocate of Puerto Rican independence and eventual American annexation after a period of tutelage. Together with **José J. Henna**, he began lobbying in Washington, D.C., in March 1898 for the inclusion of **Puerto Rico** in U.S. war plans. In addition to meeting with **Theodore Roosevelt**, Todd and Henna provided the **Navy Department** with maps and information prior to the U.S. invasion. He later claimed in his book *La invasión americana: como surgió la idea de traer la guerra a Puerto Rico* (1938) that their actions were decisive in promoting the invasion of Puerto Rico by the United States during the war.

TORAL Y VELÁZQUEZ, JOSÉ (1834–1904). Spanish general of division, commanded one of the two brigades in the division at **Santiago, Cuba**. Toral served on the commission to strengthen the defenses of Santiago and became commander in chief of the **Fourth Corps** after Lt. Gen. **Arsenio Linares y Pombo** was wounded on 1 July 1898. He ordered Brig. Gen. Félix Pareja Mesa at **Guantánamo, Cuba**, to send reinforcements to Santiago, but the order never reached Pareja.

On 3 July, Toral refused Maj. Gen. **William R. Shafter**'s first surrender demand. However, because of deteriorating conditions in the city and the impossibility of reinforcements, Toral and his military commanders unanimously capitulated the military district of Santiago on 17 July 1898. Repatriated to Spain as part of the **Armistice Proto-**

col of 12 August, Toral was met with hostile demonstrations when he disembarked on 15 September.

He was jailed in cell no. 2 in the San Francisco prison in Madrid and court-martialed. His defense was conducted and written by Julián Suárez Inclán in his *Defensa del General Toral ante el Consejo Supremo de Guerra y Marina reunido y constituido en Sala de Justicia* (1899). Citing Toral's defense that continuing to fight would only have prolonged a vain sacrifice and that the honor of Spanish arms had been saved by his men's valiant fight, the court pointed out that Toral had exhausted every resource and had capitulated in compliance with instructions received from higher authorities; consequently, Toral was acquitted on 9 August 1899. However, the war and its aftermath proved too much for Toral, who mentally collapsed and died in a mental institution on 10 July 1904.

TORPEDO BOAT. Light, fast, darting craft with a limited range whose method of attack was to approach under cover of darkness or the smoke or confusion of battle within 500–600 yards before releasing its **torpedoes**, these boats also carried small rapid-fire guns and were believed to present a major threat to **armored cruisers** and **battleships**. However, they had never been tested in combat before the Spanish-American War. Spain had 19 but did not send any of them to **Cuba**, the **Philippines**, or **Puerto Rico** for fear of leaving its home shores and harbors unprotected. The United States had 15, but only five saw action in the war: *Cushing*, *Ericsson*, *Foote*, *Gwin*, and *Winslow*.

TORPEDO-BOAT DESTROYER. Larger sized **torpedo boats**, usually between 300 to 400 tons' displacement, with a speed of from 30 to 33 knots, they had an armament of rapid-fire guns and were intended to destroy the smaller torpedo boats while at the same time carrying a full complement of **torpedoes**, which enabled them to sink larger warships. They were later called destroyers. Spain had six. The *Furor*, *Plutón*, and *Terror* were part of Adm. **Pascual Cervera's Squadron**, and the *Audaz*, *Osado*, and *Proserpina* were part of Adm. **Manuel de la Cámara's Squadron**. The United States had none at the time of the war because it had just begun to build them upon the outbreak of the war.

TORPEDOES. During the Spanish-American War torpedoes were ineffectively used against ships and as converted submarine **mines**. The main types were **Whitehead torpedoes**, which were the most widely used by both the United States and Spain, **Howell torpedoes**, Bustamante, and Mathieson torpedoes. On both Spanish and U.S. ships, torpedoes were fixed fore, aft, and on the beam. They were fired above and below the waterline. In defending **Santiago**, **Cuba**, **Manila**, and **Subic Bay**, **Philippines**, the Spanish converted Bustamante, Mathieson, and Whitehead torpedoes into mines to defend the harbor entrances.

TORREY'S ROCKY MOUNTAIN RIDERS (RANGERS). Formerly known as the Second U.S. Volunteer Cavalry, the regiment, under the command of Jay L. Torrey, a judge and politician from Cheyenne, Wyoming, was organized and mustered into service at Denver, Colorado, and Cheyenne, Wyoming on 1–30 May 1898, with 41 officers and 968 enlisted men. It left Cheyenne on 25 June, and upon arriving at Jacksonville, Florida, on 28 June, it was assigned to the Third Division in the **Seventh Corps**. The regiment sat out the war encamped in Florida. It was mustered out of service at Jacksonville, Florida, on 24 October 1898, with 47 officers and 565 enlisted men. Casualties sustained while in service included 16 dead from **disease**, six killed by accident, and four deserted.

TRAIN, CHARLES J. (d. 1906). Lieutenant commander (USN), commanded the unprotected **cruiser** *Prairie* from March to November 1898. A Massachusetts graduate of the U.S. Naval Academy, Train produced a war plan at the **Naval War College** in 1894. Assuming a war between the United States and Spain, Train maintained that the belligerent who established command of the sea would prevail. Believing Spain would send a naval expedition from Cádiz, Train recommended seizing **Nipe Bay** on the northeastern Cuban coast as a rendezvous point, coaling station, and anchorage. Then the navy would **blockade** the principal Cuban ports of **Cienfuegos**, **Havana**, **Matanzas**, and Sagua la Grande. Subsequently, the navy would engage the approaching Spanish expedition. Train considered it unlikely that the expedition would go to **Santiago**, **Cuba**. Furthermore, in order for the navy to later attack Havana, he suggested the seizure of Mariel. During the war he commanded the *Prairie*, which was in the **Northern Patrol Squadron**. Later he commanded the *Puritan* and *Massachusetts* and was promoted to captain on 22 November 1898 and rear admiral in 1904.

TRANSATLANTIC COMPANY *(COMPAÑÍA TRANSATLANTICA).* Founded in 1881 in Barcelona, Spain, it quickly became the largest Spanish shipping corporation, and its primary stockholder was the Marqués de Comillas (Claudio López Bru), who ardently supported Spain's war efforts to crush the **Cuban** and **Philippine Revolts**. The company, which had a virtual monopoly over Spanish-

West Indies commerce, profited by transporting 241,000 Spanish troops and supplies to **Cuba** and **Puerto Rico**; yet, it refused to deliver Krupp artillery to Puerto Rico because of lack of payment. A patriotic supporter of the war against the United States, the company converted 14 of its steamers to serve as **cruisers** during the war. Included among them were the *Alfonso XII*, *Alfonso XIII*, *Alicante*, and *Montserrat*. On 20 July, even before the **Armistice Protocol** of 12 August 1898 ended hostilities, the company won the contract from the U.S. government to repatriate Spanish forces from the Caribbean; consequently, it transported 22,864 soldiers at a cost to the U.S. government of $513,000 between 9 August and 17 September 1898.

TRANSPORTS, U.S. MILITARY. Because the **Fifty Million Dollar Bill** of 9 March 1898 had stipulated that none of the money allotted to the **U.S. Army** could be used for the purchase or hire of troop transports until war was declared, the U.S. Army was relegated to obtaining what was left as the **U.S. Navy** had already taken the best ships available and converted them into auxiliary **cruisers**. In spite of the fact that shipowners had succeeded in blocking congressional attempts to facilitate transfers of registry, Secretary of War **Russell A. Alger** finally obtained the services of 32 old coastal steamers at two to three times the normal freight rates to transport soldiers. The navy helped by offering the army three of its leased ocean liners—the *Harvard*, *Yale*, and *Columbia*—and another vessel, the *Rita*. Alger later obtained the services of Frank J. Hecker, a Detroit businessman, who between 20 June and 25 July located and purchased 14 vessels for $16 million. These vessels were put into service in the Caribbean toward the end of the war. In most cases, the civilian captain and crew remained with their ship throughout the war.

In the **Santiago, Cuba, campaign**, 29 transports carried the **Fifth Corps** to **Daiquirí, Cuba**, at a rate of $450 to $625 a day. When traveling on the transports, **black American soldiers** were segregated and usually assigned the lowest decks. Upon arriving at Daiquirí on 22 June, transport captains refused to take their ships close to shore; therefore, a makeshift collection of navy boats was used to land soldiers and supplies. Most of these transports never made a second voyage because they could not be unloaded fast enough. After the **capitulation of Santiago** on 17 July, they transported soldiers of the Fifth Corps to **Camp Wikoff, Montauk Point, Long Island, New York**, and most were returned to their owners.

Seventeen ships were chartered and two purchased for service on the Pacific Ocean. Among them were the *City of Pekin* and *City of Sydney*, which carried the **Eighth Corps** to **Manila, Philippines**, at a cost of $1,500 a day. From 25 July to 26 August, 40 transports went to **Puerto Rico**. Thirty-six of them arrived without invoices showing their contents, thereby causing extreme confusion and delay; moreover, Maj. Gen. **James H. Wilson**'s forces were delayed in arriving in Puerto Rico because of the tardiness of the transports. The *City of Macon*, in addition to transporting soldiers, served as the headquarters of Maj. Gen. **Nelson A. Miles** when his forces landed at **Guánica** on 25 July. With the cessation of hostilities, transports such as the *City of Rome* were used to transport Spanish **prisoners of war** to the United States and later to repatriate Spanish prisoners of war back to Spain.

TREATY OF PARIS (10 DECEMBER 1898). In compliance with the **Armistice Protocol** of 12 August 1898, **Peace Commissions** from Spain and the United States opened negotiations for a final peace treaty in Paris on 1 October 1898. For nearly a month discussion centered on **Cuba**, with the main problem being the **Cuban Debt Issue**. The issue of the **Philippines** proved the most contentious, because Spain contended that the conquest of **Manila** had been illegal because it had occurred the day after the signing of the Armistice Protocol. On 26 October, President **William McKinley** ordered the U.S. Peace Commission to demand the entire Philippines, and in mid-November the United States offered an indemnity of $20 million in lieu of the Philippines. After a U.S. ultimatum on 21 November, Spain relented on 28 November.

For two more weeks the commissions discussed additions to the treaty, but few were made. Spain sought commercial concessions in the West Indies in exchange for **Kusaie**, but nothing came of this. The United States offered to repatriate the Spanish soldiers in the Philippines, and Spain accepted this gesture. Arrangements were made to recover Spanish **prisoners of war**, including those held by the Filipinos, all in return for the release by Spain of political prisoners. Spain's request for an international commission to investigate the sinking of the *Maine* was rejected because the American commissioners said the case was closed. The U.S. commissioners also rejected the proposition that in the future the United States should pay the pension paid since the time of Columbus to his descendants, $3,400 of which had been chargeable to the treasury of **Puerto Rico** and $4,000 to that of the Philippines.

On 10 December 1898, the treaty was signed by **William R. Day**, **Cushman K. Davis**, **William P. Frye**, **George Gray**, and **Whitelaw Reid** for the United States, and by **Eugenio Montero Ríos**, Buenaventura de Abarzuza, José de Garnica y Díaz, **Wenceslao Ramírez de Villaurrutia**, and **Rafael Cerero y Sáenz** for Spain. A note of protest by the Spanish delegation was praised in Spain as the last attempt to save national honor. The 17 articles of the treaty reflected a one-sided outcome.

The terms of the treaty included Spanish withdrawal from Cuba; the cession of Puerto Rico, the Philippines, and **Guam** to the United States; the United States paying $20 million to Spain and granting Spain temporary ten year commercial rights in the Philippines; the political status of the inhabitants of the new U.S. possessions was to be determined by the new governments; the United States paid for and sent back Spanish prisoners of war in the Philippines; Spain released all prisoners of war and political prisoners; a mutual relinquishment of all claims of indemnity, national and individual; and Spanish subjects remaining in the former colonies could preserve their allegiance to the crown of Spain or could elect U.S. citizenship. However, the treaty left open the question of the future status of Cuba and left out certain of the Sulu Islands in the Philippines, which was rectified by another treaty on 7 November 1900.

After the treaty was signed, it had to be ratified by both Spain and the United States. In each country the ratification process was met with opposition. When the treaty came before Spain's **Cortes**, it was approved by a vote of 120 to 118, a margin too narrow for legislative approval. Therefore, Queen Regent **María Cristina**, invoking her constitutional powers, overrode the Cortes and signed the treaty on 19 March 1899.

After the treaty was presented to the U.S. Senate on 4 January 1899, a heated and lengthy debate opened on 6 January with Democratic Senator Donelson Caffrey of Louisiana speaking against ratification and Republican Senator Orville H. Platt of Connecticut speaking in favor. In a debate that lasted a month, Senators **George F. Hoar**, Republican of Massachusetts, and most of the Democrats were in opposition. Senator George G. Vest, Democrat from Missouri, took a constitutional stand arguing that the U.S. Constitution did not provide the authority to govern colonies, and Senator Arthur P. Gorman, Democrat from Maryland, attempted to link his opposition to his presidential ambitions for 1900. A full-scale lobbying campaign against ratification was conducted by the **Anti-Imperialist League** and several labor and farm organizations.

Those in favor of ratification were led by Senators Nelson W. Aldrich, Republican from Rhode Island, and **Henry Cabot Lodge**, Republican from Massachusetts, and by **William Jennings Bryan**, the Democratic presidential candidate in 1896 and 1900. Significantly, on the eve of final balloting, the **Philippine Insurrection** erupted on 5 February 1899. Several senators who had been opposed to the treaty changed their opinions because of the fighting and promises of patronage and eventual Philippine independence. On 6 February, the

Senate ratified the treaty by a vote of 57–27. The one-vote victory had been achieved with 41 Republicans, ten Democrats and six Populists voting in favor whereas three Republicans, 22 Democrats, and two Populists voted against. Subsequently, the Senate defeated the **Bacon Amendment** for Philippine independence and passed the **McEnery Resolution** on 14 February. With the exchange of ratifications in Washington, D.C. on 11 April 1899, the treaty became official.

TROCHA. A line of trenches that were the backbone of Spanish strategy to defeat the Cuban insurgents. An old *trocha* from Morón to Júcaro had been built during a prior revolt, the Ten Years' War, to contain the insurgents in the two most eastern provinces. It was 200 yards wide, 50 miles long, and consisted of blockhouses supplied by railroad lines. After the arrival of Capt. Gen. **Valeriano Weyler y Nicolau** in February 1896, a new line was constructed from Mariel to Majana in order to contain the insurgents in western Cuba. Running along the border of the province of Pinar del Río, it was equipped with electric lights and artillery and manned by 14,000 soldiers. After it was completed it proved to be effective.

TURNO PACÍFICO. Arrangement begun in the 1870s whereby the Spanish electoral system took place through negotiations between the **Liberal-Conservative Party** and the **Liberal Party** before elections in order to alternate turns in power. The opposition was given a number of seats in the **Cortes** in order to maintain the peace. It brought over two decades of peace to Spain as conservative leader **Antonio Cánovas del Castillo** and liberal leader **Práxedes Mateo Sagasta** alternated as prime minister of Spain.

TURPIE-FORAKER AMENDMENT. On 16 April 1898, David M. Turpie, Democratic senator from Indiana, and **Joseph B. Foraker**, Republican senator from Ohio, offered an amendment to a resolution that recognized the independence of **Cuba**. The amendment recognized the **Cuban Republic** "as the true and lawful government" of Cuba. It was opposed by the **McKinley administration** because it infringed on the executive's prerogative in conducting foreign policy and recognized the Cuban Republic. Nevertheless, after an intense battle, it passed the Senate 51–37, with 29 Democrats, 11 Republicans, and 11 Populists and **Silver Republicans** voting in favor. After the House struck out the amendment on 18 April, the Senate did likewise the next day, and it was removed in a conference committee as **Congress** quickly moved to approve its resolution authorizing the use of force to evict Spain from Cuba.

TWELFTH U.S. INFANTRY, U.S. ARMY. Commanded by Lt. Col. R. Comba, the regiment left Fort Sam Houston in Nebraska and went to **Camp Thomas**, Georgia. After arriving at **Tampa, Florida**, it was assigned to the Third Brigade, Second Division of the **Fifth Corps** and went to **Daiquirí, Cuba**, on the transport *Cherokee*. Consisting of 20 officers and 564 enlisted men, it fought in the **Battle of El Caney** on 1 July 1898, sustaining casualties of eight dead and 31 wounded. After sustaining 45 total combat casualties, the regiment left **Santiago, Cuba**, on 14 and 16 August on the *Breakwater* and *Leona* for **Camp Wikoff, Montauk Point, Long Island, New York**.

TWENTIETH U.S. INFANTRY, U.S. ARMY. Commanded by Major **William S. McCaskey**, the regiment left Fort Crook at Leavenworth, Kansas, went to Mobile, Alabama, and arrived at **Tampa, Florida**, where it was assigned to the Independent Brigade commanded by Brig. Gen. **John C. Bates** in the Second Division of the **Fifth Corps**. It went to **Daiquirí, Cuba**, on the transport *Matteawan*. Consisting of 23 officers and 573 enlisted men, it fought in the **Battle of El Caney** on 1 July 1898, sustaining casualties of one dead and eight wounded. After sustaining 16 total combat casualties, it left **Santiago, Cuba**, on the *Yale* on 19 August, for **Camp Wikoff, Montauk Point, Long Island, New York**.

TWENTY-FIFTH U.S. INFANTRY (COLORED), U.S. ARMY. Commanded by Lt. Col. **Aaron S. Daggett**, the regiment left Montana and went to **Camp Thomas**, Georgia, and then to **Tampa, Florida**, where it was assigned to the Second Brigade, Second Division in the **Fifth Corps**. It went to **Daiquirí, Cuba**, on the transport *Concho*. Consisting of 18 officers and 509 enlisted men, the regiment fought in the **Battle of El Caney** on 1 July 1898, sustaining casualties of eight dead and 25 wounded. After sustaining 38 total combat casualties, the regiment left **Santiago, Cuba**, on the *Comanche* on 13 August, and went to **Camp Wikoff, Montauk Point, Long Island, New York**. After the war it briefly returned to duty in the Far West and then fought in the **Philippine Insurrection**. The regiment's wartime exploits, along with those of other **black American regular soldiers**, were chronicled by Theophilus G. Steward, its chaplain, in his book *The Colored Regulars in the United States Army* (1904).

TWENTY-FIRST U.S. INFANTRY, U.S. ARMY. Commanded by Lt. Col. **Chambers McKibben**, the regiment left the Plattsburg Barracks in New York and went to **Tampa, Florida**, where it was assigned to the Second Brigade, First Division of the **Fifth Corps**. It went to **Daiquirí, Cuba**, on the **transports** *Saratoga* and the *City of*

Washington. Consisting of 26 officers and 441 enlisted men, it fought in the **Battle of San Juan Hill** on 1 July 1898, sustaining five killed and 26 wounded. As a result of their actions during the battle, Cpl. Thomas M. Doherty, Musician Herman Pfisterer, and Pvts. John F. De Swan, Frank O. Fournia, Thomas Kelly, and George H. Nee were awarded the **Congressional Medal of Honor**. After sustaining 38 total combat casualties, the regiment left **Santiago, Cuba**, on the *Mortera* on 12 August for **Camp Wikoff, Montauk Point, Long Island, New York**.

TWENTY-FOURTH U.S. INFANTRY (COLORED), U.S. ARMY. Commanded by Lt. Col. **Emerson H. Liscum**, the regiment left Fort Douglas, Utah, went to New Orleans, and then to **Camp Thomas**, Georgia. After arriving there on 25 April 1898, it was ordered to **Tampa, Florida**, and upon arriving there on 2 May, it was assigned to the Third Brigade, First Division of the **Fifth Corps**. It went to **Daiquirí, Cuba**, on the *City of Washington*. Consisting of 23 officers and 516 enlisted men, it fought in the **Battle of San Juan Hill** on 1 July, sustaining casualties of 12 dead and 77 wounded. The regiment sustained 90 total combat casualties during the campaign. After eight other regiments had refused, the regiment worked in the fever hospitals at **Siboney, Cuba**. By the end of its 40 days of hospital service, 36 men had died, 40 had been discharged because of **disease**, and only three officers and 24 enlisted were healthy. The last regiment ordered to leave **Santiago, Cuba**, the Twenty-Fourth marched out of camp with only nine officers and 198 enlisted men remaining. It left on the transport *Nueces* on 26 August and went to **Camp Wikoff, Montauk Point, Long Island, New York**. It remained encamped there to recuperate until 25 September, when it was ordered back to Fort Douglas, Utah. Eight members were awarded certificates of merit, and later part of the regiment fought in the **Philippine Insurrection**.

TWENTY-SECOND U.S. INFANTRY, U.S. ARMY. Commanded by Col. **Charles A. Wikoff**, the regiment left Nebraska and went to **Tampa, Florida**, where it was assigned to the First Brigade, Second Division of the **Fifth Corps**. It went to **Daiquirí, Cuba**, on the transport *Orizaba*. Consisting of 29 officers and 467 enlisted men, the regiment was commanded by Lt. Col. J. H. Patterson after Col. Wikoff was promoted to command the First Brigade. It fought in the **Battle of El Caney** on 1 July 1898, sustaining casualties of seven killed and 42 wounded. After sustaining 54 total combat casualties, the regiment left **Santiago, Cuba**, on the transport *Mobile* on 12 August for **Camp Wikoff, Montauk Point, Long Island, New York**.

TWENTY-THIRD KANSAS INFANTRY (USV). By the time of the second call for **volunteers**, **black Americans** had organized a sufficient number of companies to constitute a two-battalion regiment. Through the efforts of Populist Governor John W. Leedy the regiment was organized as part of the state's quota and had a full slate of black commissioned officers. Commanded by Lt. Col. James Beck, a black Populist, it was mustered into service at Topeka from 2–19 July 1898, with 29 officers and 850 enlisted. After arriving in New York City on 25 August, it sailed on the *Vigilancia* and did occupation duty at **San Luis, Cuba.** Soldiers soon wrote home reporting the color line was quickly being drawn in postwar Cuba. After leaving **Santiago, Cuba**, on 28 February 1899, the regiment returned to Fort Leavenworth, Kansas, on 10 March, and was mustered out of service on 10 April, with 28 officers and 828 enlisted men. Casualties sustained while in service included 12 dead from **disease**, one killed by accident, and one murdered. Capt. John L. Waller bought into local real estate while stationed in Cuba and remained there championing the cause of black American emigration to **Cuba**.

TWENTY-THIRD U.S. INFANTRY, U.S. ARMY. Commanded by Col. Samuel Ovenshine, the regiment left San Antonio, Texas, went to New Orleans, Louisiana, and then to San Francisco, California, where it became part of the **Eighth Corps**. One battalion left San Francisco on 15 June 1898, as part of the second expedition to **Manila, Philippines**, and arrived there on 17 July. A second battalion left on 27 June, as part of the third expedition to Manila, and arrived there on 25 July. Assigned to the **First Brigade**, the two battalions, consisting of 18 officers and 714 enlisted men, fought in the **Battle of Manila** on 13 August. Total combat casualties during the war included one dead and two wounded. After another battalion joined the regiment, it fought in the **Philippine Insurrection**. The battalions returned to the United States in 1900 and 1901.

—U—

UNAMUNO, MIGUEL DE (1864–1936). Basque dramatist, essayist, novelist, philosopher, and poet. Before the war against the United States, Unamuno, a professor at the University of Salamanca, who became one of the most famous members of the **Generation of 98**, had helped publish the socialist weekly *La Lucha de las clases*. He also published *En torno al casticismo* (1895) and *Paz en la guerra* (1897), in which he viewed Spain as passing through a period of crisis and called for an awakening of the Spanish people. He criticized the regime of Capt. Gen. **Valeriano Weyler y Nicolau** in **Cuba**, and labeled the Spanish popular **press** as "criminal." Opposed to the war against the United States, Unamuno castigated the indifference of the Spanish people and the irresponsibility of the politicians in an article "Renovación," *Vida Nueva* (31 July 1898), and criticized the use of the **Quijote Motif** by writers such as Juan Valera y Alcalá and Benito Pérez Galdós as a consolation for Spain's defeats and the eventual loss of its colonies in his article "Muera don Quijote!" *Vide Nueva* (26 June 1898). In 1901 he became the rector of the University of Salamanca.

UNCAS. (USN) Armed tugboat, commanded by Lt. F. R. Brainard. Formerly the *Walter A. Luckenback*, it was purchased by the **U.S. Navy** on 4 April 1898, and while serving with the **North Atlantic Squadron** on the **blockade of Cuba**, it captured the schooners *Antonio Sanvez* on 30 April and *Antonio* on 5 May.

Com. 6 April 1898, dis. 441, hp. 750, sp. 12
Armament: 1–37 mm. rev. cannon, 1 G. mg.
Cc. 120, comp. 28

UNCLE SAM. The figure, which came of age during the Spanish-American War, was used consistently in cartoons, poems, and songs during the war. One song, "Our Uncle Sam," was sung to the tune of "Yankee Doodle," and George F. Taylor's poem "Colorado's Advance on Manila," which depicted the **First Colorado Infantry**'s actions during the **Battle of Manila** on 13 August 1898, ended with lines directed at Spain: "Uncle Sam" you must remember/ And don't forget the Maine."

UNIFORMS, U.S. ARMY. Prior to the war no provision had been made for a hot-weather uniform; therefore, the army generally fought the war in the standard blue woolen uniform. In April 1898, Maj. Gen. **Nelson A. Miles** had recommended to the **Quartermaster Corps** that it contract for the manufacture of 10,000 experimental khaki uniforms. Until the new uniforms were issued, various measures were tried. The weight in the blue uniforms was reduced and large quantities of a light cotton underwear were purchased and issued. Only 5,000 new uniforms reached Maj. Gen. **William R. Shafter**'s **Fifth Corps** before it left for **Santiago**, **Cuba**, in mid-June 1898, and although a shipload of the tropical uniforms arrived off the coast of **Siboney** in early July, transportation problems delayed their being delivered to the men in the trenches. Many of the soldiers who went to the **Philippines** and **Puerto Rico** were issued the heavy khaki uniform; however, it was not until the end of the war that the **War**

Department issued a true cotton khaki uniform. While the **marines** fared better throughout the war in their brown linen campaign suits, **volunteers** in camps frequently wore civilian clothes and some received old cast-off army uniforms.

UNITED STATES ARMY. See ARMY, UNITED STATES

UNITED STATES AUXILIARY NAVAL FORCES. Nicknamed the "Mosquito Squadron," it was one of five operational squadrons at the beginning of the war. Headquartered in New York City under the command of Rear Admiral Henry Erben, it was constituted mainly for **coastal defense**. Manned mostly by the **naval militia**, it was involved in protecting **minefields** and in quarantine patrol. It consisted of the single-turret **monitors** *Catskill, Jason, Lehigh, Montauk, Nahant, Nantucket, Passaic,* and *Wyandotte*; the **yachts** *Aileen, Elfrida, Enquirer, Free Lance, Huntress, Inca,* and *Restless*; the tugboat *Choctaw*; and the *Arctic*, which was leased from the city of Philadelphia.

UNITED STATES MERCHANT MARINE. See MERCHANT MARINE, UNITED STATES

UNITED STATES NAVY. See NAVY, UNITED STATES

UNITED STATES REVENUE CUTTER SERVICE. See REVENUE CUTTER SERVICE, UNITED STATES

UNITED STATES VOLUNTEER CAVALRY. Upon learning the Governor of Arizona intended to form a regiment of mounted riflemen, Francis E. Warren, Republican senator from Wyoming and chairman of the Senate Committee on Military Affairs, proceeded to arrange for the recruitment of three **volunteer** cavalry regiments. When **Congress** organized the **U.S. Army** for war on 22 April 1898, it authorized these three regiments. Although officially known as the First, Second, and Third U.S. Volunteer Cavalry regiments, they became known respectively as the **Rough Riders, Torrey's Rocky Mountain Riders**, and **Grigsby's Cowboys**. Of the three regiments, only the Rough Riders saw action, fighting in the **Santiago, Cuba, campaign**.

UNITED STATES VOLUNTEER INFANTRY. See "IMMUNES"

UPHAM, FRANK BROOKS (1872–1939). Ensign (USN). A recent U.S. Naval Academy graduate, Upham, an aide to Com. **George W.**

Dewey, posed as a civilian trader while the **Asiatic Squadron** was in **Hong Kong** and interviewed crews of steamers arriving from **Manila, Philippines,** gathering intelligence on Spanish military dispositions at Manila. Serving with Dewey's squadron throughout the war, he was later awarded the Navy Cross. After he commanded the U.S. Asiatic Fleet during the early 1930s, he retired with the rank of rear admiral.

UTAH LIGHT ARTILLERY. Organized at Salt Lake City, Utah, and mustered in on 9 May 1898, with nine officers and 242 enlisted men, batteries A and B left San Francisco on 15 June in the second expedition of the **Eighth Corps** to **Manila, Philippines,** and arrived at Manila on 17 July. Assigned to the **Second Brigade,** the batteries fought in the **Battle of Manila** on 13 August 1898. Their experiences were extolled by songwriter Frank T. Hines in "Battle Song of Utah" and lamented by poet/songwriter Fred Blake in "The Old Army Hard-Tack," which complained about the food. After fighting in the **Philippine Insurrection,** the batteries left Manila on 1 July 1899. After arriving in San Francisco on 31 July 1899, the batteries were mustered out of service on 16 August 1899, with ten officers and 263 enlisted men. Casualties sustained while in service included eight killed, 17 wounded, five died from **disease,** and one deserted.

—V—

VARA DEL REY Y RUBIÓ, JOAQUÍN (1840–1898). Spanish brigadier general, commanded the **San Luis Brigade** at **Santiago, Cuba.** Entering the army at 15, Vara del Rey fought against the **Carlists,** was promoted to lieutenant colonel while serving in the **Philippines** from 1884 to 1890, and governed the Marianas. After returning to Spain, he was ordered to **Cuba** in 1895, and commanded troops at Bayamo. Promoted to brigadier general, he was stationed at Santiago, Cuba, during the Spanish-American War. After forcing Cuban insurgents to withdraw from attacking Palma Soriano at the end of May 1898, he was in command of Spanish forces at the **Battle of El Caney** on 1 July 1898, where he and his two sons were killed and his brother, a lieutenant colonel, was taken prisoner. His sword and spurs were presented by Maj. Gen. **William R. Shafter** to General of Division **José Toral y Velázquez** at the **capitulation of Santiago,** Cuba, on 17 July 1898.

VATICAN. A strong supporter of Spain during the **Cuban** and **Philippine Revolts,** the Vatican was concerned by late March 1898 that a disastrous conflict against the United States would threaten the stability of Catholic, monarchical Spain. Therefore, under the direction of Pope **Leo XIII** and Foreign Minister Cardinal Mariano Rampolla, the Vatican attempted to mediate Spanish-American differences over **Cuba**. The effort failed because it was based on two mistaken impressions: 1) as a result of the diplomatic efforts of Prince **Bernhard von Bülow, Germany**'s foreign minister, the Vatican believed that Spain was ready to accept Cuban independence; and 2) as a result of Archbishop **John H. Ireland**'s meeting with President **William McKinley**, the Vatican presumed that McKinley wanted assistance to obtain peace.

Although unwilling to grant Cuban independence, Spain nevertheless accepted papal mediation and agreed to a suspension of hostilities in Cuba provided the United States withdrew its naval forces from Cuban waters. McKinley vigorously denied he had sought papal assistance, and on 3 April, Secretary of State **William R. Day** cabled **Stewart L. Woodford**, U.S. ambassador to Spain, that the president had "made no suggestions to Spain except through you . . . The disposition of our fleet must be left to us." Although diplomatic activity continued through the **Great Powers Note**, the Vatican's effort had failed by mid-April.

VELASCO. (SPN) **Gunboat**. Designated by the Spanish as an unprotected **cruiser**, it was an iron-hulled, bark-rigged ship with one funnel. Stationed at **Manila, Philippines**, the *Velasco* was part of Adm. **Patricio Montojo's Squadron**. Its main guns had been removed to strengthen the batteries at the entrance to **Manila Bay**, and its crew had been assigned to strengthen other ships. Anchored in **Bacoor Bay** while undergoing repairs, it was not engaged in the **Battle of Manila Bay** on 1 May 1898. Although it was fired by the *Petrel* after the battle, it was not seriously damaged.

La. 1881, dis. 1,152, hp. 1,500, sp. 14
Armament: 3–5.9″, 2–2.7″, 2 mgs.
Cc. 220, comp. 175

VESUVIUS. (USN) **Dynamite-gun cruiser**, commanded by Lt. Commander John E. Pillsbury. It was the only dynamite-gun cruiser in the **U.S. Navy**. Built strictly as a floating siege weapon, it handled poorly and rolled prodigiously. Its armament consisted of three 55-feet-long, 15-inch Zalinsky pneumatic dynamite guns that were mounted forward side by side. Because they were immovable at a fixed elevation of 18 degrees, they had to be sighted by aiming the ship itself. Using compressed air, the guns fired a 980-pound shell with a 500-pound dynamite warhead at a rate of about one a minute. Their range was between 1,700 to 1,750 yards, but this could be tripled by using a subcaliber shell.

Initially attached to the **North Atlantic Squadron**, the *Vesuvius* served on the **blockade of Cuba** and bombarded **Santiago, Cuba,** after it arrived there on 13 June 1898. Its bombardment was inaccurate and caused little damage. In late July it supervised the raising of the *Infanta María Teresa* and the *Reina Mercedes*. After the war it was ordered to Boston and taken out of active service on 16 September 1898. Recommissioned in 1905, it was used as a torpedo-testing vessel and sold for scrap in 1922.

La. 1888, com. 1890, dis. 929, hp. 3,200, sp. 21
Armor: d. 3/16″, sl. 3/16″, ct. 1″
Armament: 3–15″, 3–3pdr.
Cc. 152, comp. 70

VILLAAMIL Y FERNÁNDEZ CUETO, FERNANDO (1845– 1898). Captain, overall commander of the three **torpedo-boat destroyers**—*Furor*, *Plutón*, and *Terror*—in Adm. **Pascual Cervera's Squadron**. After entering the navy in 1861, Villaamil served on various ships, commanded the *Nautilus* in its around-the-world voyage and wrote about it in his book *Viaje de circumnavigación de la corbeta Nautilus* (1893). He was promoted and supervised the construction of Spain's first torpedo-boat destroyer, *Destructor*. A liberal deputy in the **Cortes**, Villaamil wrote articles in *El Globo* stating that Spain could not fight and win a war against the United States; consequently, he opposed the 23 April 1898 decision to send Adm. Cervera's Squadron to the West Indies by writing directly to Prime Minister **Práxedes M. Sagasta**.

After the squadron arrived at **Santiago, Cuba,** Villaamil opposed any thought of a sortie and argued that all the guns and men should be taken off the ships and used to defend the city. In overall command of the *Furor* and *Plutón* during the **Naval Battle of Santiago** on 3 July, Villaamil was on board the *Furor* when it was destroyed within 20 minutes after leaving the harbor entrance. He died on the beach. Rather than abandon his body, some of his men tied it in a wicker chair that had been washed up by the waves and hid it in the rocks before they made off for Santiago. Six years later his remains were found and returned to Spain, where they were buried with full military honors.

VILLAURRUTIA, WENCESLAO RAMÍREZ DE. See RAMÍREZ DE VILLAURRUTIA, WENCESLAO

VIXEN. (USN) Armed **yacht**, commanded by Lt. Alexander Sharp Jr. Formerly the yacht *Josephine*, it was purchased by the **U.S. Navy** on

9 April 1898 and assigned to the North Atlantic Station. During the war it served in Cuban waters. On 28 May an explosion in the lower front manhole gasket of boiler A endangered the ship until Firemen Peter Johnson and George Mahoney entered the fireroom and saved the ship. They received the **Congressional Medal of Honor** for their actions. While part of the blockading fleet at **Santiago, Cuba**, the *Vixen* transported Cuban troops on 21 June to Sigua and bombarded **Cabañas Bay** on 22 June as part of a feint attack during the landing of the **Fifth Corps** at **Daiquirí**. Although present, it did not take an active part in the **Naval Battle of Santiago** on 3 July. After the war it continued to serve in the North Atlantic Squadron and was sold in 1923.

La. 1896, com. 11 April 1898, dis. 806, hp. 1,250, sp. 16
Armament: 4–6pdr., 4–1pdr.
Cc. 190, comp. 82

VIZCAYA. (SPN) **Armored cruiser**, commanded by Capt. **Juan Antonio Eulate**. Spanish-built and patterned on the British *Aurora* class, it was a sister ship to the *Almirante Oquendo* and *Infanta María Teresa*. It had an armored belt that extended two-thirds of its length and a protective deck that was flat over the belt and curved at the extremities, leaving a high unprotected freeboard. Its 11-inch guns were mounted fore and aft in single barbettes with lightly armored shields, and its 5.5-inch guns were without any armored protection except shields.

Ordered to New York City as a counterpart to the *Maine*'s arrival in **Havana, Cuba**, the *Vizcaya* arrived on 19 February and was immediately surrounded by a flotilla of ships. When informed of the *Maine* disaster, Eulate had the colors half-masted and instituted strenuous protection measures. The *New York Journal* and the *New York World* headlined its presence as a direct threat to New York City. On 24 February, it left for Havana, Cuba, arriving there on 1 March. With a badly fouled bottom and two defective 5.5-inch guns, it left **San Juan, Puerto Rico**, with the *Almirante Oquendo* for the Cape Verde Islands on 9 April. Upon its arrival at Cape Verde on 19 April, Adm. **Pascual Cervera y Topete cable**d the minister of the marine that the Vizcaya was in such bad condition that it was "only a boil in the body of the fleet."

It returned to the Caribbean as part of Adm. **Pascual Cervera's Squadron**. After arriving at **Santiago, Cuba**, its sailors disembarked and were stationed ashore at El Cobre. During the **Naval Battle of Santiago** on 3 July, it was hit by almost every U.S. ship as it left the harbor entrance and at 11:15 a.m. struck its flag and turned toward shore. It was beached on a reef just east of Aserraderos about 15 miles from Santiago around 11:30 a.m. Burning fiercely, it exploded, and the survivors were rescued by the *Ericsson* and *Hist*.

La. 1891, dis. 6,890, hp. 13,700, sp. 20.2
Armor: s. 12–10″, d. 2–3″, b. 9″, ct. 12″
Armament: 2–11″, 10–5.5″, 2–2.7″, 8–2.2″, 8–1.4″, 2 M. mgs., 8 tt. (2 sub.)
Cc. 1,050, comp. 484

VOLUNTARIOS (VOLUNTEERS). Spanish sympathizing home guards in Spain's colonies. Although they rejected any compromise with Cuban and Filipino insurgents, they were often unreliable and played a marginal role in the Spanish-American War. Within the city of **Santiago, Cuba**, there were two battalions of 1,115 *voluntarios*. The first battalion of 630 men was commanded by Col. Manuel Barrueco, and the second battalion of 485 men was commanded by Lt. Col. José Marimón. During the battles of 1 July 1898, they sustained casualties of 25 killed and wounded. In **Puerto Rico**, they resisted an order to directly incorporate into the regular army and began to defect even before U.S. forces landed at **Guánica** on 25 July 1898. By early August virtually all these units were disintegrating.

VOLUNTEERS, UNITED STATES. After an intense debate and pressure from the **National Guard, Congress**, on 22 April 1898, organized the **U.S. Army** into two armies. One was composed of regulars and the other was composed of volunteers. President **William McKinley**, who preferred to entrust command of the volunteer troops to regular army officers, appointed 19 out of 26 major generals and 66 out of 102 brigadier generals from the regular army to command these troops. The governors of the various states retained their powers to appoint lesser officers.

On 23 April 1898, McKinley issued the first call for 125,000 volunteers to serve for a maximum of two years. Instead of calling for 60,000 men as the **War Department** had planned, McKinley yielded to National Guard pressure and asked for 125,000, the approximate strength of all the existing militia units. Thus, the call-up was mainly confined to members of the National Guard and quotas were assigned to each state according to population. One month later, on 25 May, McKinley issued a second call for 75,000 volunteers in order to bring the regiments up to strength.

In May, Congress authorized the enlistment of a volunteer brigade of **engineers**, three regiments of volunteer cavalry, and McKinley was empowered to raise up to 10,000 federal volunteers, which became the **"Immune"** regiments. Moreover, private citizens, for the last time in American history, were allowed to recruit and equip military units at their own expense. The resulting sudden expansion of the army beyond the bounds of any prewar planning caused numerous logistical, medical, and organizational problems.

Even though over one million men tried to enlist, 77 percent were rejected, mainly because of physical problems. By the end of July, only seven states—Indiana, Minnesota, Missouri, New Jersey, Rhode Island, West Virginia, and Wisconsin—had met or exceeded their quotas. All told, some 216,500 volunteers were authorized during the war. Of this group only 35,000 had been sent overseas or were even included in units assigned to overseas duty by the time the **Armistice Protocol** was signed on 12 August 1898. Consequently, most volunteers had sat out the war in **camps** in the United States.

Those volunteers who saw combat during the war were poorly equipped with single-shot **Springfield rifles**. Units that fought in the **Santiago, Cuba, campaign** included the **Rough Riders, Second Massachusetts Infantry, Ninth Massachusetts Infantry, Seventy-First New York Infantry, Thirty-Third Michigan Infantry**, and **Thirty-Fourth Michigan Infantry**. The expeditions of the **Eighth Corps** to the **Philippines** included 15 state regiments. Intense political pressure resulted in a number of volunteer units participating in the **Puerto Rican campaign**. After the signing of the **Armistice Protocol** on 12 August 1898, volunteer regiments were used to garrison **Cuba** and **Puerto Rico** and subsequently fought in the **Philippine Insurrection**.

When McKinley ordered the discharge of almost half of the volunteers shortly after the signing of the Armistice Protocol, he set off a widespread demand for the discharge of all volunteers. Desertions increased; regiments mutinied; hundreds brawled en masse at San Francisco; drunken soldiers rioted in the streets of Jacksonville, Florida; and petitions abounded demanding their immediate discharge. The **Third North Carolina Infantry** sent a letter to Secretary of War **Russell A. Alger** on 5 October 1898 stating, "We the undersigned did not join the service for garrison duty." Consequently, the United States rapidly demobilized its volunteer forces. Significantly, even though most volunteer troops had not fought in the war, the American public believed the overwhelming victories during the war had validated the nation's continued reliance on its volunteer system.

VULCAN. (USN) Mobile repair ship, commanded by Lt. Comdr. I. Harris. Formerly the *Chatham*, it was purchased by the **U.S. Navy** on 2 May 1898 from the Merchants and Miners' Line. The first mobile repair ship in the navy, it had a water distiller and was attached to the North Atlantic Station on 1 July. While stationed at **Guantánamo, Cuba**, after the bay was secured by the **marines** in June, the *Vulcan* accomplished 63 repairs on ships and supplied others with parts. It later participated in the raising of the *Infanta María Teresa* and did the greater part of the temporary repair work on it.

—W—

WADE, JAMES FRANKLIN (1843–1921). Major general (USV), commanded the **Third Corps**. A Civil War veteran who rose through the ranks to brigadier general commanding the Department of Dakota, Wade served as the chief organizer of the U.S. troops that initially arrived at **Tampa, Florida**. Appointed to major general (USV), on 26 May 1898, Wade assumed command of the Third Corps at **Camp Thomas**, Georgia, and commanded the camp from 23 July to 2 August. He relinquished command of the Third Corps to Brig. Gen. **Royal T. Frank** on 31 July. After the **Armistice Protocol** of 12 August, he headed the Cuban **evacuation commission** and was honorably discharged from volunteer service on 12 June 1899. After serving in the **Philippine Insurrection**, he was promoted to major general in 1903 and retired in 1907.

WAGNER, ARTHUR LOCKWOOD (1853–1905). Lieutenant colonel, on the staff of Brig. Gen. **Henry W. Lawton**, Second Division, of the **Fifth Corps**. A West Point graduate, Wagner, a veteran of Indian campaigns on the frontier, directed the **Military Information Division** from April 1897 to May 1898. Assigned to Lawton's staff, he fought in the **Santiago, Cuba, campaign**. During the campaign Wagner attended the **Aserraderos Conference** and supervised reconnaissance of Spanish positions before the battles of 1 July. After the capitulation of Santiago, he served with Maj. Gen. **Nelson A. Miles** in the **Puerto Rican campaign**. Although initially impressed by the Cuban insurgents, Wagner, the author of various works, wrote in his *Report on the Santiago Campaign* that they were "practically useless in battle" and recommended logistical and command changes for future overseas expeditions. After the war he served as adjutant general for the Department of Dakota, fought in the **Philippine Insurrection**, and was promoted to brigadier general.

WAINWRIGHT, RICHARD (1849–1926). Lieutenant commander (USN), commanded the *Gloucester*. A U.S. Naval Academy graduate, Wainwright, as chief of the **Office of Naval Intelligence** from 1896 to 1897, collaborated closely with **Theodore Roosevelt** in secret purchases of armaments and warships overseas and in the development of overseas spy networks. He ordered **William W. Kimball** to help draw up what became known as the **Kimball Plan**. After serving as the executive officer of the *Maine*, Wainwright survived the explosion of 15 February 1898 and subsequently directed the recovery of the bodies. While in command of the *Gloucester* during the war, he fought in the **Naval Battle of Santiago** on 3 July and accompanied U.S. forces under the command of Maj. Gen. **Nelson A. Miles**, which landed at **Guánica, Puerto Rico**, on 25 July. For his conduct during the war, he was advanced ten numbers in rank and presented with a silver loving cup by the citizens of Gloucester. After being promoted to commander in March 1899, he served as superintendent of the U.S. Naval Academy (1900–1902), was promoted to rear admiral in 1908, and retired in 1911.

WAKE ISLAND. A deserted Pacific island in a coral atoll composed of three small islands 2,000 miles west of **Hawaii** and 1,333 miles northeast of **Guam**, Wake Island was claimed by the United States on 17 January 1899, when the **gunboat** *Bennington*, under the command of Comdr. Edward D. Taussig, stopped en route from Hawaii to the **Philippines**. To compensate for its failure to obtain **Kusaie** in the Caroline Islands during the negotiations of the **Treaty of Paris**, the United States took it as a trans-Pacific **cable** landing.

WALKER, ASA S. (1845–1916). Commander (USN), commanded the *Concord*. A New Hampshire graduate of the U.S. Naval Academy, Walker had been at the U.S. Naval Academy before taking command of the *Concord* on 23 May 1897. He was advanced nine numbers for "eminent and conspicuous conduct in battle" during the naval **Battle of Manila** on 1 May 1898. After the war Walker served at the **Naval War College** and was promoted to rear admiral in 1906.

WANDA. A boat chartered by the **Associated Press** during the war. Flying the British flag, it picked up the survivors from the **torpedo boats** in Adm. **Pascual Cervera's Squadron** after the **Naval Battle of Santiago** on 3 July 1898. Upon delivering them to the *Gloucester*, a sticky problem of international protocol involving a ship flying the British flag delivering **prisoners of war** was resolved when Spanish Capt. Diego Carlier of the *Furor* signed a paper ordering his men to "report" to the *Gloucester*.

WANDERER **EXPEDITIONS.** Named after the steamer *Wanderer*, the first expedition, under the command of First Lt. John W. Heard (**Third U.S. Cavalry**), landed 11 soldiers, a small body of Cuban insurgents, arms, ammunition, and dynamite 75 miles west of **Havana, Cuba**, on 22 July 1898. After an engagement with Spanish forces the next day, the *Wanderer* returned to **Key West, Florida**. Under the command of Lt. Heard, it returned on 26 July and landed 25 miles west of its former landing place. Another engagement with Spanish forces soon followed, and the crew of the *Wanderer* mutinied, refusing to serve on the Cuban coast. Heard suppressed the mutiny, landed his remaining cargo on 1 and 2 August at two sites 360 miles east of Havana, and returned to Key West. After the war, Heard was awarded the **Congressional Medal of Honor** for his actions.

WAR DEPARTMENT. Directed by Secretary of War **Russell A. Alger**. Without an organizational plan to coordinate operations and no clear lines of command between Alger and Maj. Gen. **Nelson A. Miles**, it was a collection of disconnected agencies run by career officers. Included among them were the **Adjutant General's Department, Ordnance Department, Pay Department, Military Information Division, Quartermaster Corps, Subsistence Department**, and **Signal Corps**.

The War Department spent most of its $20 million from the **Fifty Million Dollar Bill** of 9 March 1898 on **coastal defense**: $10 million through its Ordnance Department and $5.5 million through the Engineer Department. Assuming that the army would play a minor role subordinate to the navy in a war with Spain, the War Department initially visualized a limited mobilization and expected the **National Guard** to staff the coastal defenses. Therefore, it was overwhelmed by a rapidly increasing army and hampered by the many shifts in the **McKinley administration's war strategy**.

Other problems faced by the War Department during the war included the appointment of **black Americans** to officer positions and the obtaining of **transports**. Initially the department believed that black Americans should be commanded by white officers; however, after a serious protest from the black community, it eventually decided that blacks could hold commissions as lieutenants in the four **"Immune"** regiments. When it proved difficult to obtain transports for the army, Alger brought in Frank J. Hecker, a Detroit business associate. Hecker, who was given a colonelcy, spent $16.5 million in purchasing 14 large steamers for Atlantic operations, two for Pacific operations, and secured a variety of tugs, barges, and lighters.

After the war it established the Division of Customs and Insular Affairs to run the newly won overseas lands, supervised the discharge of one-half of 200,000 volunteers from September to December 1898, established an occupation garrison of 50,000 troops in **Cuba**, and sent reinforcements to the **Philippines**. Accused of poor management, Alger requested a formal investigation of his department; accordingly the **Dodge Commission** investigated the department's efforts during the war with Spain.

WAR DEPARTMENT INVESTIGATING COMMISSION. See DODGE COMMISSION

WAR REVENUE BILL. Introduced into the House of Representatives at the end of April 1898, the bill was amended in the Senate and signed by President **William McKinley** on 13 June. Its war taxes went into effect on 1 July and yielded an estimated $150 million per year. Among the taxes levied, it doubled the tax rate on beer and tobacco, imposed license taxes on bankers and brokers, and levied amusement taxes on admissions to theaters, circuses, bowling alleys, and billiard rooms. It also placed stamp taxes on legal documents, cosmetics, drugs, chewing gum, and playing cards; imposed a transfer tax on stocks and bonds; and levied an inheritance tax on estates over $10,000 (with some exceptions).

WAR STRATEGY, SPAIN. Believing that diplomatic efforts would forestall war against the United States, the government of **Práxedes M. Sagasta** did not extensively prepare for war. The colonial army, which was tied down by the **Cuban** and **Philippine Revolts**, could not be resupplied or reinforced throughout the war because of U.S. control of the seas. Moreover, it remained scattered in its various garrisons throughout **Cuba**, the **Philippines**, and **Puerto Rico** and was never concentrated to meet the invading U.S. forces.

On 13 March 1898, the **Spanish Navy** began to deploy according to a plan by Minister of the Marine **Segismundo Bermejo**, which established two centers of resistance to protect Spain and Cuba. Accordingly, upon the outbreak of war, a 23 April meeting of high-ranking naval officers made the fateful decision to send Adm. **Pascual Cervera's Squadron** to the West Indies. In mid-May, Bermejo was replaced by Capt. **Ramón Auñón y Villalón**. Auñón issued detailed orders on 27 May that divided the Spanish home fleet into three groups. One group, under the command of Rear Adm. **Manuel de la Cámara**, was assigned to attack the American Atlantic Coast and then go to either **San Juan**, **Puerto Rico**, or **Santiago** or **Havana**, **Cuba**, to force the United States to divide its naval forces. The second group was assigned to defend Spanish waters, and the third, which consisted of three auxiliary **cruisers**, was to go to the West Indies to take U.S. **prizes of war** and then possibly to link up with Adm. Cervera's Squadron at Santiago, Cuba.

Events soon forced a change of plans as Auñón ordered Adm. **Manuel de la Cámara's Squadron** to the Philippines in mid-June, only to rescind this order with one that sent the squadron to protect Spain. After the overwhelming defeat of Adm. Cervera's Squadron at the **Naval Battle of Santiago** on 3 July, Spain moved quickly toward a negotiated solution.

WAR STRATEGY, UNITED STATES. Prior to the *Maine* explosion, neither the **U.S. Army** nor the **U.S. Navy** made comprehensive plans or preparations for a war against Spain. However, the navy, unlike the army, had undertaken prewar planning. This was done through the **Naval War College**, the **Navy Department**, and the **Office of Naval Intelligence**. Beginning in 1895, these plans, which centered around **Cuba**, frequently contained a **blockade of Cuba** and **Puerto Rico**, land operations against **Havana**, **Cuba**, the occupation of Puerto Rico, a **blockade** and direct assault on **Manila, Philippines**, and an attack in Spanish waters by the navy. With the army assigned to a limited role in offensive overseas war, the navy assumed most of the operational burden. Although no plan envisioned the conquest of extensive overseas territories, they did hope to achieve the independence of Cuba.

Prior to the war, the navy began to concentrate its ships at **Key West, Florida**, in January 1898, and on 25 February, **Theodore Roosevelt**, assistant secretary of the navy, ordered Com. **George W. Dewey** to prepare his **Asiatic Squadron** for a possible descent upon **Manila, Philippines**. On 4 April, a final prewar plan was approved, which included establishing command of the sea, a naval blockade of Cuba, a small army expedition to seize a port in eastern Cuba to supply the Cuban insurgents, an attack by the Asiatic Squadron on Manila, a proposed attack on Puerto Rico, and, if necessary, a 50,000-man force to attack and seize Havana. Accordingly, on 15 April, regular army regiments were ordered to concentrate at **Camp Thomas**, Georgia; Mobile, Alabama; New Orleans, Louisiana; and **Tampa, Florida**.

Upon the outbreak of war, President **William McKinley** adopted an overall strategy of victory by the quickest and least costly means and focused on Spain's forces in and around Cuba as the prime objective. A blockade was initiated at certain Cuban ports, and Dewey's squadron attacked and won an overwhelming victory at the naval **Battle of Manila Bay** on 1 May.

On 2 May, the **McKinley administration** reviewed the entire situation and changed its approach. An immediate attack on Havana by the army was endorsed based on Secretary of War **Russell A. Alger**'s claim that he had 75,000 men available, however, it was quickly discarded when it was determined no such force existed. Significantly, the meeting endorsed sending a 5,000-man expeditionary force to the

Philippines. Any thought of landing a small expeditionary force in Cuba was canceled by the arrival of Adm. **Pascual Cervera's Squadron** at **Santiago, Cuba** on 19 May. Accordingly, on 26 May, a new strategy emerged that would determine the course of the war. The army would send the **Fifth Corps** to attack Santiago, and a later expedition would attack Puerto Rico.

WARD, HENRY HEBER (1871–1916). Ensign (USN). A U.S. Naval Academy graduate, Ward had served as a decoder in the cipher room of the *Maine*. Along with **William H. Buck**, he volunteered to be a covert agent and was sent to Europe by the **Office of Naval Intelligence**. After leaving the United States on 30 April 1898, they arrived in Liverpool, England, on 8 May and assumed their disguises as British subjects. Leaving England on 13 May, they arrived at Lisbon, Portugal, and soon went to Gibraltar on chartered yachts to observe Adm. **Manuel de la Cámara's Squadron**, which was being fitted out at Cádiz, Spain. Buck and Ward then separated, and Ward went to Tangiers, then the Madeiras, and finally to the Caribbean, arriving at St. Thomas on 11 June. In late June, he was stopped by Spanish officials off the coast of **Puerto Rico** and was arrested and brought to **San Juan**. With the help of local authorities and British officials, he succeeded in convincing the Spanish he was not an American and so continued his intelligence-gathering activities until mid-July when he returned to the United States.

WASHINGTON, BOOKER T. (1856–1915). Black American educational leader. In March 1898, Washington, the founder of the Tuskegee Institute, offered to Secretary of the Navy **John D. Long** to recruit 10,000 men in the event of war; however, his offer was not accepted. Although initially supportive of the war effort because he believed it offered **black Americans** the opportunity to serve, Washington soon opposed the annexation of **Hawaii** and the conquest of the **Philippines**, because he believed they should be independent. On 16 October 1898, he spoke at the Chicago Peace Jubilee, and with President **William McKinley** in attendance, he praised the efforts of **black American soldiers** and pointed out that such service deserved to be rewarded by an effort to conquer racial prejudice. After the war he suggested that the U.S. government bring Afro-Cuban students to the United States for industrial education at the Tuskegee Institute, and in his book *A New Negro for a New Century* (1900), he wrote that the war had been precipitated by a desire for revenge and retaliation more than by a desire for justice for the Cubans. He praised the heroism of black soldiers at **Santiago, Cuba**, in helping to free **Cuba**

and thanked McKinley for his recognition of blacks in his appointments during the war.

WASP. (USN) Armed **yacht**, commanded by Lt. Aaron Ward. Formerly the *Columbia*, it was purchased by the **U.S. Navy** on 26 March 1898 and assigned to the North Atlantic Station. On 22 May it provided protective fire, along with the *Manning* and the ***Dolphin***, in a failed attempt to land two companies of infantry near Cabañas to make contact with insurgents, and on 27 May it carried Adm. **William T. Sampson**'s instructions to Com. **Winfield S. Schley**, ordering him to **Santiago**, **Cuba**, to **blockade** the port. After convoying the **Fifth Corps** to **Daiquirí**, the *Wasp* shelled the Daiquirí area before the Fifth Corps landed on 22 June. After participating in the seizure of **Nipe Bay** on 21 July, it was ordered to Puerto Rican waters and assisted in the capture of **Ponce**, **Puerto Rico**, on 27–28 July. It was sold in 1920.

Com. 11 April 1898, dis. 630, hp. 1,800, sp. 16.5
Armament: 4–6pdr., 2 C. mgs.
Cc. 108, comp. 78

WATSON, JOHN CRITTENDEN (1842–1923). Commodore (USN), commanded the **First North Atlantic Squadron** and the **Eastern Squadron**. A U.S. Naval Academy graduate and career naval officer, Watson served at the side of Adm. David Farragut during the Civil War. In late April 1898, he served as an assistant to Com. **George C. Remey**, who commanded the naval base at **Key West**, **Florida**. Commanding the First North Atlantic Squadron from 6 May to 1 July, Watson's force **blockade**d the northern Cuban coast. On 7 July he was assigned to command the Eastern Squadron and hoisted his flag on the *Oregon*. Promoted to rear admiral after the war, he commanded the Asiatic Fleet.

"WE PILFER THE NEWS." Incensed over the *New York World*'s mendacious reporting about the donation of his **yacht *Buccaneer*** to the **U.S. Navy**, **William R. Hearst** published a story on 8 June 1898 in the *New York Evening Journal* on the death of "an Austrian Colonel Reflipe W. Thenuz" from wounds suffered against American soldiers in battle in **Cuba**. The next day the *New York World* printed a story that contained an almost verbatim account of the valor of Col. Reflipe W. Thenuz. On 10 June, the *Journal* revealed that the name "Reflipe W. Thenuz" was an anagram of "we pilfer the news." Although pilfering the news did not really bother Hearst because it was a common practice of many newspapers, including Hearst's own, the *Journal* rubbed it in for a month with cartoons, letters to the editor, a poem in honor of the colonel, and a request for money for a fund for the colonel's memorial. Repudiated bonds and Confederate and Chinese money came in from around the country.

WEYLER Y NICOLAU, VALERIANO (1839–1930). Lieutenant general, captain general, and governor-general of **Cuba** (February 1896–October 1897). A stern career Spanish military officer, Weyler, the Marqués de Tenerife, was a military attaché in Washington, D.C., during the Civil War, fought against the **Carlists**, and served as captain general of the Canary Islands and the Balearic Islands, governor-general of the **Philippines** (1888–1891) and captain general of Barcelona.

Weyler arrived in Cuba in February 1896 and instituted a policy that attempted to isolate the insurgents through **reconcentration** of their supporters in the countryside and by establishing *trochas*, or fortified lines, across Cuba. Such methods, together with his ordering the arrest and expulsion of U.S. journalists, earned him the nickname "The Butcher" and aroused public opinion in the United States against Spanish policies in Cuba.

Recalled in October 1897 by the liberal government of **Práxedes M. Sagasta**, Weyler was replaced by **Ramón Blanco y Erenas**. Upon his return to Spain, he was mobbed by supporters, rejected joining the Carlists, and declined to participate in a military conspiracy to overthrow the government because he believed such an effort would divide the army and possibly cause a civil war. Upon the outbreak of the Spanish-American War, he joined in the initial braggadocio, describing how a Spanish army of 50,000 might invade the United States. As a senator in the **Cortes**, Weyler blamed the politicians for losing the war and defended the army and his methods in Cuba in his book *Mi mando en Cuba: história militar y política de la última guerra separtista* (1906). He frequently served as minister of war in conservative governments and as army commander in chief (1921–1923).

WHEELER, JOSEPH (1836–1906). Major general (USV), commanded the Dismounted Cavalry Division, in the **Fifth Corps**. A West Point graduate and former Confederate lieutenant general of cavalry, Wheeler, who was known as "Fighting Joe," was a pro-war Democratic congressman from Alabama. Upon the outbreak of war, he honored President **William McKinley**'s request that he enlist to help reunite the North and South. He left his seat in **Congress** and was appointed major general of **volunteers**. In command of the 2,737-man Dismounted Cavalry Division of the Fifth Corps, Wheeler went to **Daiquirí**, **Cuba**, on the transport *Allegheny*.

Wheeler became a national hero during the **Santiago, Cuba, campaign**. Supposedly during the **Battle of Las Guásimas** on 24 June, Wheeler, upon seeing the Spanish retreat, yelled "We got the damn Yankees on the run!" Because of illness, he was not in command during the battles for the **San Juan Heights** on 1 July; however, upon hearing the sound of battle, he had an ambulance carry him to the front where he remained the rest of the day. As a commissioner who negotiated the **Capitulation of Santiago Agreement** of 16 July, Wheeler favored allowing Spanish soldiers to return to their country carrying their arms.

Returning to the United States on 15 August, Wheeler commanded **Camp Wikoff, Montauk Point, Long Island, New York**, until the end of September and then commanded the **Fourth Corps** at Huntsville, Alabama, until December. Later, he commanded a brigade in the **Philippine Insurrection** and wrote *The Santiago Campaign, 1898* (1898).

WHITEHEAD TORPEDO. Originally called the "locomotive" **torpedo**, it was developed by an Austrian navy captain and Robert Whitehead, a Scottish engineer. Used by both the **Spanish Navy** and **U.S. Navy**, it was discharged from a torpedo tube either by compressed air or by a small powder charge. Usually fired from above the water level, it emerged through the side of the ship and was propelled by a small piston engine, although a later version was gyro-controlled. The torpedo had a diameter of 17.7 inches, weighed between 845 and 1,160 pounds, carried warheads of 118 to 220 pounds of guncotton, and had a range of 800 yards. A better depth-keeper than the **Howell torpedo**, it was relatively inaccurate in keeping course.

WHITNEY, CASPAR (1861–1929). Correspondent for *Harper's Weekly*. On a world tour writing on sports when the war began, Whitney returned to the United States and covered the embarkation of the **Fifth Corps** at **Tampa, Florida**, and the **Santiago, Cuba, campaign**. He was present at the **Aserraderos Conference**, accompanied Brig. Gen. **Henry W. Lawton**'s division during the Santiago campaign, and wrote "The Santiago Campaign," *Harper's Monthly Magazine* (October 1898). In his articles he praised U.S. soldiers as better than any in Europe, did not report the army's incompetence, and protested wartime **censorship** regulations. After the war he edited *Outline* magazine.

WHITNEY, HENRY HOWARD (1866–1949). Lieutenant in the **Military Intelligence Division**. A West Point graduate in 1892, Whitney was assigned to the Military Information Division in 1896. During the war he went on intelligence-gathering missions in **Cuba** and **Puerto Rico**. He carried out a courier mission to Cuban insurgent leader Maj. Gen. **Máximo Gómez**, a mission that nearly escaped published record; however, his other mission was front-page news. On 5 May 1898, he was ordered to southern Puerto Rico. Although disguised as an English seaman, U.S. newspapers published news of his trip beforehand, and when he landed on 15 May, he was nearly caught. Nevertheless, he carried out a two-week survey of Spanish military strength and defenses. After returning to Washington, D.C., on 9 June, his information was of great value to Maj. Gen. **Nelson A. Miles** and convinced Miles to land at **Guánica** on the southern coast. Whitney, promoted to captain, joined Miles's staff, helped to select the **Puerto Rican Commissioners**, and participated in the **Puerto Rican campaign**.

WIKOFF, CHARLES A. (d. 1898). Colonel, commanded Third Brigade, First Division, in the **Fifth Corps**. Wikoff, who had commanded the **Twenty-Second U.S. Infantry**, was in command of a brigade that included the **Ninth U.S. Infantry**, **Thirteenth U.S. Infantry**, and **Twenty-Fourth U.S. Infantry** during the **Battle of San Juan Hill** on 1 July 1898. While putting his brigade into position for the assault on San Juan Hill, he was mortally wounded and replaced by Lt. Col. W. S. Worth, of the Thirteenth U.S. Infantry. **Camp Wikoff, Montauk Point, Long Island, New York** was named after him.

WILDES, FRANK (1843–1903). Captain (USN), commanded the *Boston* in the **Asiatic Squadron**. A U.S. Naval Academy graduate and Civil War veteran, Wildes served at the navy's **torpedo** school and was a special ordnance officer. He commanded the *Boston* during the naval **Battle of Manila Bay** on 1 May 1898 and during the **Battle of Manila** on 13 August. After the war he was captain of the Navy Yard at New York City and was promoted to rear admiral.

WILDMAN, ROUNSEVELLE (1864–1901). U.S. consul in **Hong Kong** (1898–1900). In 1897, Wildman met with **Felipe Agoncillo**, a representative of **Emilio Aguinaldo**'s Filipino insurgent forces. Wildman was highly receptive to Agoncillo's proposal for an alliance between the insurgents and the United States. Promising to pay for U.S. arms when the insurgent government took power, Agoncillo had offered as collateral security "two provinces and the custom-house at **Manila**." Wildman, who expected a commission on the arms deliveries, **cabled** Washington on 3 November 1897, only to be rebuffed by the **State Department** on 15 December.

In May 1898, Wildman met with Emilio Aguinaldo in Hong Kong.

He encouraged Aguinaldo to return to the **Philippines** as soon as possible and, according to Aguinaldo, promised U.S. support for Philippine independence. Wildman contracted with Aguinaldo to purchase rifles and ammunition for a down payment of 117,000 pesos, with Wildman receiving a percentage for his services. After Aguinaldo returned to the Philippines on 19 May, the first arms shipment arrived on 27 May, the second shipment was never delivered, and Wildman never accounted for the money. By June, Wildman was informing the U.S. government that most Filipinos were in favor of becoming an American colony; however, on 25 July, he once again told Aguinaldo that the United States did not want colonies, and on 6 August he informed the State Department that he had never made any commitments or promises to the insurgents. Wildman disappeared in a shipwreck on his way back to the United States in 1901.

WILHELM II (1859–1941). German kaiser (1888–1918). Outspokenly pro-Spanish and friendly to the Queen Regent **María Cristina**, Wilhelm, in September 1897, scribbled in the margin of dispatch instructions to Foreign Minister **Bernhard von Bülow** that **Germany** should help Spain if the U.S.-British "Society for International Theft and Warmongering" seriously intended to take **Cuba** from Spain. However, his attitude was consistently moderated by von Bülow.

In early May 1898, while speaking at the closing session of the Reichstag, Wilhelm affirmed Germany's neutral policy regarding the war and later was amused by the lack of an effective American **censorship** as **press boats** accompanied U.S. naval forces. When he learned of a possible Great Powers peace effort to stop the war in early June 1898, he stated his opposition, believing that until one or the other of the belligerents had had its fill of fighting, mediation was folly. Wilhelm, who favored dividing up the **Philippines**, instructed his ambassador in Washington, D.C., to not let any opportunity slip by for the acquisition of maritime footholds in eastern Asia.

WILKIE, JOHN ELBERT (1860–1934). Secret Service director (February 1898–1912). A businessman and former city editor of the *Chicago Tribune*, Wilkie, as Secret Service chief, sent agents to **Canada** in an attempt to break up Spain's **Montreal Spy Ring**. He gave Lt. Ramón Carranza's letter to **Julian Pauncefote**, British ambassador to the United States, and probably released a copy of it to the **press**, because it showed up in the *New York Herald* on 5 June 1898. He subsequently wrote "The Secret Service in the War," which appeared in *The American-Spanish War: A History by the War Leaders* (1899).

WILLIAMS, OSCAR FITZALAN (1843–1909). U.S. consul in **Manila, Philippines** (January 1898–April 1898). An author, business college instructor for 20 years, and former consul to Le Havre, France, Williams, a Republican, was appointed consul to Manila because he was a friend of Republican Senator **Joseph Foraker** of Ohio. Sympathetic to the Filipino insurgent cause, he gathered intelligence information for Com. **George W. Dewey** before the war. Upon the outbreak of war, Williams left Manila on 23 April and arrived at **Mirs Bay, China,** on 27 April. He immediately informed Dewey that Adm. **Patricio Montojo's Squadron** had gone to **Subic Bay** and that the entrance to **Manila Bay** had been **mine**d. His report confirmed Dewey's assumption that the fortifications of Manila did not pose a serious threat. Williams went with the **Asiatic Squadron** to Manila, observed the naval **Battle of Manila Bay** on 1 May, and openly favored the American acquisition of the **Philippines**. After the war he served as consul general in Singapore.

WILMINGTON. (USN) **Gunboat,** commanded by Comdr. **Chapman C. Todd.** A single-masted boat designed with a very shallow draft, twin screws, and an oversize rudder for river operations, it was assigned to the **North Atlantic Squadron.** It participated in the **blockade of Cuba** and captured the schooner *Candidia* on 24 April 1898. On 11 May, the *Wilmington* fought in the **Battle of Cárdenas Bay** and in the naval attack on **Manzanillo, Cuba,** on 18 July. After the war it served in China on the Yangtze River and was sold in 1946.

La. 1895, com. 1897, dis. 1,397, hp. 1,900, sp. 16
Armor: d. 5/16″, sl. 3/8″
Armament: 8–4″, 4–6pdr., 4–1pdr., 4 mgs.
Cc. 277, comp. 199

WILSON, JAMES HARRISON (1837–1925). Major general (USV), commanded the First Division in the **First Corps.** A West Point graduate and major general in the Civil War, Wilson worked to build, promote, and manage railways, to reorganize public utilities companies, and as a stock market trader. Upon the outbreak of war, he volunteered his services and was assigned to command the **Sixth Corps.** Because the corps was never organized, he believed he was a victim of a plot to deprive him of a command; however, he was soon assigned to command the First Division in the First Corps.

Subsequently, his 3,571-man force left Charleston, South Carolina, on 20 July and arrived at **Ponce, Puerto Rico,** on 28 July. However, their complete disembarkation took ten days owing to a lack of launches. With the objective of advancing from Ponce to **San Juan,** part of his force, under the command of Brig. Gen. **Oswald H. Ernst,** won the **Battle of Coamo** on 9 August. Three days later Wilson's command briefly fought a skirmish at the **Asomante Hills** before news of the **Armistice Protocol** arrived.

After the war, Wilson, who favored the annexation of **Cuba** and **Puerto Rico**, briefly served as the military governor of the Ponce district, returned to the United States to command the First Corps at Lexington, Kentucky, and then served as the military governor of Matanzas and Santa Clara Provinces in Cuba. He later served as second in command of the China Relief Expedition between 1900 and 1901. He retired in 1901 and later wrote *Under the Old Flag: Recollections of Military Operations in the War for the Union, the Spanish War, and Boxer Rebellion* (1912).

WINSLOW. (USN) **Torpedo boat**, commanded by Lt. **John Baptiste Bernadou**. Assigned to the **North Atlantic Squadron**, the *Winslow* participated in the **cable-cutting operation** and naval **Battle of Cárdenas Bay**, **Cuba**, on 11 May. During the engagement, its steering gear was shot out, and it had to be towed out of the bay by the ***Hudson***; moreover, five of its men were killed, including Ensign **Worth Bagley**, and three were wounded, including its commander Lt. Bernadou. For their heroism under fire, four of its sailors were awarded the **Congressional Medal of Honor**. It was then sent to Mobile, Alabama, for repairs. It was sold in 1911.

La. 1897, com. 1897, dis. 142, hp. 2,000, sp. 25
Armament: 3–1pdr., 3–18″ tt.
Cc. 44, comp. 20

WINSLOW, CAMERON McRAE (1854–1932). Lieutenant (USN), navigating officer of the *Nashville*. He led a **cable-cutting operation** of 54 **marines** and sailors off **Cienfuegos**, **Cuba**, on 11 May 1898. Although two **cables** were cut, the operation, which came under heavy fire, failed to cut a third cable, and Winslow was wounded. He later described the operation in his article "Cable-Cutting at Cienfuegos," *The Century Magazine* (March 1899). Advanced five numbers for "extraordinary heroism," Winslow later served on the staff of Adm. **William T. Sampson** and as a naval aide to President **Theodore Roosevelt**. In 1911, he was promoted to rear admiral.

WOMPATUCK. (USN) Armed tug, commanded by Lt. Carl W. Jungen, a survivor of the *Maine* disaster. Formerly the *Atlas*, it was purchased by the **U.S. Navy** on 4 April 1898 and assigned to the North Atlantic Station. During the war it participated in the 12 May bombardment of **San Juan**, **Puerto Rico**, and engaged in **cable-cutting operations**. During the landing of the **Fifth Corps** at **Daiquirí, Cuba**, on 22 June, the *Wompatuck* bombarded the area before the landing and then towed launches full of troops near to shore. It was later involved in naval engagements at **Manzanillo, Cuba**, on 30 June and 18 July. For his heroism during the 30 June action, Mate Frederick Muller was awarded the **Congressional Medal of Honor**.

La. 1896, com. 6 April 1898, dis. 462, hp. 650, sp. 13
Armament: 1–3pdr., 1 G. mg.
Cc. 130, comp. 32

WOOD, LEONARD (1860–1927). Colonel (USV), commanded the **Rough Riders**. A doctor of medicine, Wood won the **Congressional Medal of Honor** for service during the Indian wars on the frontier and in 1895 became the White House physician. A close friend of **Theodore Roosevelt**, he and Roosevelt organized the Rough Riders at San Antonio, Texas. The regiment, as part of the **Fifth Corps**, landed at **Daiquirí, Cuba**, on 22 June 1898.

After the **Battle of Las Guásimas** on 24 June, Wood assumed command of the Second Brigade in the Dismounted Cavalry Division because of the illness of Brig. Gen. **Samuel B. M. Young**, and Roosevelt assumed command of the Rough Riders. Promoted to brigadier general, Wood signed the **Round Robin Letter** of 3 August. After the war, Wood, who favored the annexation of **Cuba**, commanded the Department of Santiago, was promoted to major general (USV), and served as military governor of Cuba from 13 December 1899 to 20 May 1902, when he relinquished power to **Tomás Estrada Palma**, the newly elected president of Cuba.

WOODFORD, STEWART LYNDON (1835–1913). U.S. minister to Spain (September 1897–21 April 1898). A lawyer and Civil War general, Woodford was a former congressman and lieutenant governor of New York. He favored the Cuban insurgents and made a financial contribution to their cause. With no diplomatic experience, he accepted the appointment as U.S. minister to Spain and received formal instructions on 16 July 1897, which told him to offer U.S. good offices for solving the Cuban situation on a basis that would be both honorable to Spain and just to the Cubans. When he provided the **press** with part of the instructions, he was reprimanded by the **McKinley administration**.

After arriving in Spain, Woodford moved within a narrow circle of diplomats, maintained an office with three assistants, and wrote 68 personal letters to President **William McKinley**. During his mission, Woodford, who was optimistic about a diplomatic solution almost until the outbreak of war, reported that Spain's government would choose war with the United States rather than face the overthrow of the government, cautioned McKinley to go slow, and became a convert to U.S. ownership of **Cuba**. He even proposed on 17 March 1898 that the United States purchase the island, a proposal that Spain rejected. Upon the outbreak of war, he left Spain on 21 April, turning over the American legation to the British embassy in Madrid. Although he later stated that he was never seriously consulted by McKinley, he believed that if **Congress** had provided more time, McKinley would have achieved Cuban independence without a war.

—X—

XIQUENA, CONDE DE, JOSÉ ÁLVAREZ DE TOLEDO Y ACUÑA (1838–1898). Spanish minister of production (October 1897–May 1898). A former deputy of the Moderate Party, Xiquena joined the **Liberal Party** and served as a minister in various cabinets, governor of Madrid, and president of the Council of State. In October 1897, he became the minister of production in the administration of **Práxedes M. Sagasta**. He opposed **Vatican** mediation between the United States and Spain over **Cuba**, harshly criticized **Segismundo Moret**, and rashly spoke of fighting the Americans in Cuba and on the Spanish peninsula. He warned that if Spain's government failed to uphold the nation's honor and rights, it would face civil war at home. Because of illness, he was replaced by **Germán Gamazo** in mid-May 1898.

—Y—

YACHTS. During the war the **U.S. Navy** acquired 28 yachts, mostly by purchase, to serve as tenders to the ships stationed on the **blockade of Cuba**, and as shoal-draft reconnaissance craft, picket boats, and harbor patrol boats. They were converted through the installation of small-caliber guns, a reduction of rigging, and rearrangements of cabins and stowage to increase bunker capacity. In addition to serving in the **Auxiliary Naval Forces**, many served in combat roles in the Caribbean. Among these were the *Eagle*, *Gloucester*, *Hawk*, *Hist*, *Mayflower*, *Scorpion*, *Suwanee*, *Vixen*, and *Wasp*. With the war over, many were returned to their owners; however, others remained in commission.

YALE. (USN) Auxiliary **cruiser**, commanded by Capt. William C. Wise. Built in Scotland, it was the ocean liner *Paris* when it was leased by the **U.S. Navy** from the American Line. Not fitted for fighting, the *Yale* was equipped with cable-cutting apparatus and used as a scout ship searching for Adm. **Cervera's Squadron** in Puerto Rican waters where it captured the Spanish cargo ship *Rita* on 8 May 1898. When it landed a small party near **San Juan, Puerto Rico**, on 14 May 1898, to pick up white sand for use in cleaning the ship's floors, a false alarm swept through San Juan that the Yankees had landed.

In late June the *Yale* transported units of the **Thirty-Third** and **Thirty-Fourth Michigan Infantry** to **Siboney, Cuba**. Later, serving as a transport carrying U.S. forces under the command of Maj. Gen. **Nelson A. Miles** to **Puerto Rico**, it arrived at **Guánica, Puerto Rico**, on 25 July 1898 and subsequently served as the flagship of the Puerto Rican expedition when the **battleship** *Massachusetts* was no longer required. In August the *Yale* transported soldiers of the **Fifth Corps** from **Santiago, Cuba**, to **Camp Wikoff, Montauk Point, Long Island, New York**. It was returned to its owners on 2 September 1898, only to be used again as a transport in World War I, after which it was again returned to its owners and eventually scrapped in 1923.

La. 1888, com. 2 May 1898, dis. 13,000, hp. 20,600, sp. 21.8
Armament: 8–5″, 4–6pdr., 4–3pdr.
Cc. 2,656, comp. 406

YANKEE. (USN) Auxiliary **cruiser** commanded by Comdr. Willard H. Brownson. Formerly the passenger steamer *El Norte*, it was purchased by the **U.S. Navy** on 6 April 1898 from the Morgan Line and staffed in part by eight officers and 274 men from the New York **naval militia**. Initially assigned to the **Northern Patrol Squadron** until 29 May, the *Yankee* then served on the **blockade of Cuba**, fought in a brief naval engagement at **Guantánamo** on 7 June, and suffered one wounded in a 13 June engagement off **Cienfuegos** against the Spanish torpedo gunboat *Galicia* and land batteries. On 7 July it was assigned to the **Eastern Squadron**. After the war it served as a training ship, transport, and supply ship and sank in 1908.

La. 1892, com. 14 April 1898, dis. 6,888, hp. 3,800, sp. 14.5
Armament: 10–5″, 6–6pdr., 2 C. mgs.
Cc. 1,000, comp. 282

YAUCO, PUERTO RICO. Located in southwestern **Puerto Rico**, less than 20 miles west of **Ponce** and six miles northwest of **Guánica**, Yauco, a town of around 22,000, was initially defended by one company of the **Alfonso XIII Battalion**.

YAUCO, PUERTO RICO, SKIRMISH AT (26 JULY 1898). After U.S. forces landed at **Guánica** on 25 July, 1898, six companies of the

Sixth Massachusetts Infantry and one company of the **Sixth Illinois Infantry** under the command of Brig. Gen. **George A. Garretson** immediately moved on **Yauco** on 26 July. Before reaching Yauco they briefly skirmished with Spanish forces, which included two companies of the **Patria Battalion** under the command of Lt. Col. **Francisco Puig**. Puig, whose orders were to merely ascertain American strength, quickly withdrew. This was the first land fighting of the war in Puerto Rico.

On 27–28 July, Yauco was occupied without opposition, and on 29 July the U.S. flag was raised and acting mayor Francisco Mejía y Rodríguez read a welcoming proclamation, hailing the U.S. invasion as the miraculous intervention of a just God. Company L (colored) of the Sixth Massachusetts Infantry remained to garrison the town.

YELLOW FEVER. Called "Yellow Jack," it was the **disease** most feared by the **Fifth Corps** during the **Santiago, Cuba, campaign**, especially after 6 July 1898, when the first cases were reported. However, because medical science did not know its cause or how it was spread, yellow fever was frequently confused with other fevers, particularly malaria, which in fact did devastate the Fifth Corps. In 1899 the Yellow Fever Commission investigations identified the mosquito as yellow fever's transmitter.

"YELLOW PRESS." Named after a popular cartoon character, "the Yellow Kid," this type of American journalism engaged in sensationalism, fabricated incidents and battles, used splashy headlines and lavish illustrations, and conducted dubious polls of members of **Congress**, governors, and other public officials and used them to support their **jingo**istic editorial viewpoints. Most yellow presses consistently blamed Spain for the ***Maine*** explosion and for causing untold human suffering during the **Cuban Revolt** through its **reconcentration** policy. Although the "yellow press" represented a minority of the **U.S. press**, its most famous practitioners—the *New York Journal* and *New York World*—frequently overstated their own importance. The *Journal* even claimed the Spanish-American War as the "*Journal*'s War."

However, there were few "yellow" journals in the Midwest and West, the two areas of the United States that were the most overwhelmingly in favor of going to war against Spain, and a significant number of newspapers, including the *New York Tribune* and the *Wall Street Journal*, condemned their methods, particularly after the *Maine* disaster on 15 February 1898, which brought forth the first nationwide outburst of indignation directed at the "yellow press." On 19 February 1898, the *Detroit Evening News* labeled both the *Journal* and *World* as "two insane papers," and on 26 February, the *Los*

Angeles Times complimented the public for not being "inflamed by the shrieking brotherhood of Hearst and Pulitzer." **Edwin L. Godkin**, editor of *The Nation*, referred to the "yellow press" as "venal and unspeakable sheets" and "public evils."

YOSEMITE. (USN) Auxiliary **cruiser**, commanded by Comdr. William H. Emory. Formerly the *El Sud*, it was purchased by the **U.S. Navy** from the Morgan Line on 6 April 1898 and staffed in part by 11 officers and 270 men from the Michigan **naval militia**. Initially assigned to the **Northern Patrol Squadron** until 30 May, the *Yosemite* then convoyed the *Panther*, which was carrying the **First Marine Battalion** to **Guantánamo**, **Cuba**, in early June. After replacing the *St. Paul* as the sole blockading vessel off **San Juan**, **Puerto Rico**, the *Yosemite* chased the Spanish transport *Antonio López* ashore on 28 June. It continued on **blockade** duty until it was relieved by the *New Orleans* on 14 July and was assigned to the **Eastern Squadron**. After the war it served as a station ship at **Guam** in the Pacific Ocean until it was destroyed by a typhoon off Guam in 1900.

La. 1892, com. 13 April 1898, dis. 6,179, hp. 3,800, sp. 16
Armament: 10–5″, 6–6pdr., 2 C. mgs.
Cc. 1,371, comp. 285

YOUNG, CHARLES (1864–1922). Major (USV), commanded the **Ninth Ohio Infantry Battalion**. A **black American** graduate of West Point, Young was a professor of military science at Wilberforce University at the beginning of war. Assigned to train and command the Ninth Ohio Infantry Battalion (colored), Young was one of a handful of black officers at the outbreak of the war. His unit never left the United States during the war. In late December 1898, upon hearing of plans to muster it out, he enlisted the support of Senator Jeter C. Pritchard and Congressman George H. White to delay the order until April 1899. He later fought in the **Philippine Insurrection** and was promoted to captain in 1901.

YOUNG, LUCIEN (1852–1912). Lieutenant (USN), commanded the armed **yacht** *Hist* during the war. A U.S. Naval Academy graduate, Young played a prominent part in protecting American interests during the Hawaiian revolt. He was advanced three numbers for his meritorious wartime conduct during the naval engagements at **Manzanillo**, **Cuba**. After the war Young served as captain of the port of **Havana** (1899–1900), and attained the rank of rear admiral in 1910.

YOUNG, SAMUEL BALDWIN MARKS (1840–1924). Brigadier general (USV), commanded the Second Brigade, Dismounted Cavalry Division, **Fifth Corps**. A hot-tempered, outspoken Civil War veteran, Young called the Cuban insurgents a lot of degenerates who were no more capable of self-government than the savages. After commanding U.S. forces during the **Battle of Las Guásimas** on 24 June 1898, Young was replaced because of illness by **Leonard Wood** before the **Battle of Kettle Hill** on 1 July. He soon returned to the United States, was promoted to major general (USV), supervised the establishment of **Camp Wikoff**, and on 2 November 1898 took command of the **Second Corps** at **Camp Meade**. Later Young served in the **Philippine Insurrection**, and became chief of staff of the **U.S. Army**, reaching the rank of lieutenant general.

YUCATAN. (USN) Transport. A 2,383-ton converted freighter, it served as a transport at a rate of $500 per day for the **Fifth Corps** to **Daiquirí**, **Cuba**, carrying headquarters, band, and Companies B, C, D, and G of the **Second U.S. Infantry** and eight troops of the **Rough Riders**.

Prior to leaving **Tampa**, **Florida**, for Daiquirí, Cuba, the *Yucatan* had been assigned to the **Seventy-First New York Infantry** and Second U.S. Infantry until it was commandeered by the Rough Riders during the mad scramble by units of the Fifth Corps to board their transports. **Theodore Roosevelt**, in defense of the Rough Riders' newly won transport, turned away two regiments after securing the boat but allowed four companies of the Second Infantry and two newsreel cameramen to board.

During the voyage to Daiquirí, travel rations quickly gave out, so the men ate their field rations and bought food from the ship's cook. Moreover, because the civilian contractor had used the cheapest and greenest lumber in installing bunks, many of the bunks gave way the first night out. Nevertheless, alcohol was available. Whiskey cost $20 a gallon, and beer retailed at 25 cents a pint.

After the capitulation of **Santiago, Cuba**, the *Yucatan* left Santiago for Tampa, Florida, on 28 July with civilian employees and sick and discharged soldiers. It returned to Santiago on 17 August, carrying **nurses** and surgeons, and left on 20 August, carrying the **Seventh U.S. Infantry** to **Camp Wikoff, Montauk Point, Long Island, New York**.

—Z—

ZAFIRO. A 1,062-ton British steamer, it was purchased by Com. **George W. Dewey** on 9 April 1898, for $18,000, while the **Asiatic Squadron** was anchored at **Hong Kong**. Its British captain and Chinese crew were retained when placed under the command of Lt. W. McLean (USN), and it served as a supply ship.

Dewey avoided British neutrality regulations by anchoring the *Zafiro* just outside Hong Kong's territorial waters and having Chinese merchants deliver goods to it under the cover of night. After steaming with the Asiatic Squadron to **Manila, Philippines**, its crew cut the **cable** connecting Manila with Hong Kong on 2 May 1898. It later served as Maj. Gen. **Wesley Merritt**'s headquarters during the **Battle of Manila** on 13 August 1898. Later it carried dispatches between Hong Kong and Manila, served during the **Philippine Insurrection**, and was decommissioned on 15 January 1906.

ZOGBAUM, RUFUS F. (1849–1925). An illustrator who, next to **Frederic S. Remington**, was the illustrator most closely associated with the war. Prior to the war, Zogbaum had published illustrations in *Harper's Weekly*, specializing in cowboys, Indians, and the military on the frontier. Upon the outbreak of the war, his Western work virtually disappeared as he depicted the heroic scenes of the battles at **Santiago, Cuba**, and naval subjects.

Bibliography

During and immediately following the war numerous accounts were rushed into print in the United States. Almost all were patriotic and highly critical of Spain; however, their factual information was often unreliable. The best contemporary account is French E. Chadwick's two-volume work, *The Relations of the United States and Spain: The Spanish American War* (1909, 1911). Compared with the United States, there was little writing about the war by Spanish authors, aside from a few military figures and politicians who were looking for an explanation for Spain's overwhelming defeat. The best of these accounts was Severo Gómez Núñez's five-volume work, *La Guerra Hispano-Americana* (1900–1902).

Within a few years interest in the war waned. As Spanish literary figures used the era in their works, Spanish historical scholarship almost disappeared. Although recently Spanish scholarship on the war has revived, it has been hampered by the lack of multi-archival work and good biographies on many of the politicians and military figures of the time; moreover, its main efforts have focused on the domestic history of the period. Similarly, American scholarship on the war waned until after World War II.

Presently a plethora of manuscript sources exists. However, the collections are frequently uneven, and there are far more in the United States than in Spain, Cuba, the Philippines, and Puerto Rico, especially concerning the private papers of key governmental and military officials. Because of the relatively liberal press laws in both Spain and the United States at the time, the press is a key resource. Key archival sources in the United States include the National Archives in Washington, D.C., the Archives of the Naval War College at Newport, Rhode Island, and the Archives of the U.S. Military Institute at the Carlisle Barracks, with its Spanish-American War Survey Collection. Spanish archives in Madrid include the National Historical Archives and the Ministry of Foreign Affairs Archives. Although the diplomatic archives are well ordered, the colonial records are incomplete, particularly those concerning the end of Spain's rule in Cuba. Other important archival resources include the National Archives in Havana, Cuba; the General Archives in San Juan, Puerto Rico; the Public Record Office, London;

the French Foreign Ministry Archives in Paris; and the German Foreign
Office Archives, which are available from University Microfilms in Ann
Arbor, Michigan.

Because of the abundance of material presently available on the Spanish-American War, any bibliography must by necessity be selective,
even more so in this case. Titles in this bibliography are listed under the
headings General Histories—Cuba—Europe—Guam, Hawaii, Japan,
and Latin America—Philippines—Puerto Rico—Spain—United States—
Biographies and Personal Accounts—Espionage—Imperialism and Anti-
Imperialism—Media—Medical—Treaty of Paris—Reference—Journals—Magazines—and Newspapers.

General Histories

Allendesalazar, José Manuel. *El 98 de los americanos*. Madrid: EDI-
CUSA, 1974.
Azcárate, Pablo de. *La guerra del 98*. Madrid: Alianza Editorial, 1968.
Chadwick, French Ensor. *The Relations of the United States and Spain:
The Spanish-American War*. 2 vols. New York: Scribner's, 1909–
1911.
Ferrara, Orestes. *The Last Spanish War: Revelations in "Diplomacy"*.
Trans. William E. Shea. New York: The Paisley Press, 1937.
Feuer, A. B. *The Spanish-American War at Sea: Naval Action in the
Atlantic*. Westport, CT: Praeger, 1995.
Freidel, Frank B. *The Splendid Little War*. Boston: Little, Brown and
Co., 1958.
Gómez Núñez, Severo. *La Guerra Hispano-Americana*. 5 vols. Madrid:
Imprimería del Cuerpo de Artillería, 1900–1902.
Harper's Pictorial History of the War with Spain. New York and Lon-
don: Harper & Brothers, 1899.
Leuchtenberg, William E. "The Needless War with Spain," *American
Heritage*, vol. 8, no. 2 (1957):32–41, 95.
Millis, Walter. *The Martial Spirit: A Study of Our War with Spain*. Cam-
bridge, MA: Houghton Mifflin, 1931.
Morgan, H. Wayne. *America's Road to Empire: The War with Spain
and Overseas Expansion*. New York: John Wiley & Sons, 1965.
O'Toole, George J. A. *The Spanish War: An American Epic, 1898*. New
York: Norton, 1984.
Pabón y Suárez de Urbina, Jesús. *El 98, acontecimiento internacional*.
Madrid: Ministerio de Asuntos Exteriores, 1952.
Pratt, Julius W. *The Expansionists of 1898: The Acquisition of Hawaii
and the Spanish Islands*. Baltimore, MD: Johns Hopkins Press, 1936.

Trask, David F. *The War with Spain in 1898.* New York: Macmillan Publishing Company, 1981.

Wilson, Herbert W. *The Downfall of Spain: Naval History of the Spanish-American War.* Boston: Little, Brown and Co., 1900.

Cuba

Archibald, James F. J. "The Day of the Surrender of Santiago," *Scribner's,* 24 (October 1898):413–416.

Blow, Michael. *A Ship to Remember: The Maine and the Spanish-American War.* New York: William Morrow and Company, 1992.

Bonsal, Stephen. *The Fight for Santiago: The Story of the Soldier in the Cuban Campaign, from Tampa to the Surrender.* New York: Doubleday and McClure Company, 1899.

Cervera y Topete, Pascual. *Guerra hispano-americana. Colección de documentos referentes á la escuadra de operaciones de las Antillas.* Madrid: El Ferrol, 1898. Translated as *The Spanish American War. A Collection of Documents Relative to the Squadron Operations in the West Indies.* U.S. Navy Department. Office of Naval Intelligence, War Notes No. 7, Washington, DC: Government Printing Office, 1899.

Cherpak, Evelyn M. "Cable Cutting at Cienfuegos," *Proceedings of the United States Naval Institute,* 113 (February 1987):119–122.

Chidsey, Donald Barr. *The Spanish-American War: A Behind the Scenes Account of the War in Cuba.* New York: Crown Publishers, 1971.

Concas y Palau, Víctor María. *La escuadra del Almirante Cervera.* 2d ed., corr. and enl. Madrid: San Martin, 1899. Translated as *The Squadron of Admiral Cervera.* Office of Naval Intelligence, War Notes No. 8, Washington, DC: Government Printing Office, 1900.

Dierks, Jack Cameron. *A Leap to Arms: The Cuban Campaign of 1898.* Philadelphia, PA: Lippincott, 1970.

Feuer, A. B. *The Santiago Campaign of 1898: A Soldier's View of the Spanish-American War.* Westport, CT: Praeger, 1993.

Foner, Philip S. *The Spanish-Cuban-American War and the Birth of American Imperialism 1895–1902.* 2 vols. New York: Monthly Review Press, 1972.

Gulliver, Louis J. "Sampson and Shafter at Santiago," *Proceedings of the United States Naval Institute,* 65 (June 1939):799–806.

———. "Gloucester at Santiago," *Proceedings of the United States Naval Institute,* 54 (August 1928):658–662.

Hanks, Carlos C. "Marines at Playa del Este," *Proceedings of the United States Naval Institute,* 67 (November 1941):1591–1593.

Healy, David F. *The United States in Cuba, 1898–1902: Generals, Poli-*

ticians and the Search for Policy. Madison: University of Wisconsin Press, 1963.

Heinl, Robert D. Jr. "How We Got Guantánamo," *American Heritage*, vol. 13, no. 2 (February 1962):18–21, 94–97.

Ibañez Marín, José. *Capitulación de Santiago de Cuba: Escrito leído ante el Consejo Supremo de Guerra y Marina en defensa del comandante militar que fue del Cristo: D. Clemente Calva Peiro, y algunos apendices y notas*. Madrid: Est. Tipografía El Trabajo, 1899.

Keller, Peter. "The Rescue of Admiral Cervera. The Narrative of the American Bluejacket Who, After the Destruction of the Spanish Fleet, Brought the Spanish Admiral and Certain of His Officers through the Surf to the American Boats," *Harper's Magazine*, 98 (April 1899):783–787.

Kennan, George. *Campaigning in Cuba*. New York: The Century Company, 1899.

————. "The Santiago Campaign: The Wrecking of the Army by Sickness," *Outlook* (22 October 1898):471–476.

Kennon, John W. "USS Vesuvius," *Proceedings of the United States Naval Institute*, 80 (February 1954):182–190.

Legrand, John. "The Landing at Daiquiri," *Proceedings of the United States Naval Institute*, 26 (March 1900):117–126.

McCawley, Charles L. "The Guantánamo Campaign of 1898," *Marine Corps Gazette* (September 1916):221–242.

Meriwether, Walter Scott. "Remembering the Maine," *Proceedings of the United States Naval Institute*, 74 (May 1948):549–561.

Müller y Tejeiro, José. *Combates y capitulación de Santiago de Cuba*. Madrid, 1898. Translated as *Battles and Capitulation of Santiago de Cuba*. Office of Naval Intelligence, War Notes No. 1, Washington, DC: Government Printing Office, 1899.

Offner, John L. *An Unwanted War: The Diplomacy of the United States and Spain over Cuba, 1895–1898*. Chapel Hill: University of North Carolina Press, 1992.

Parker, James. *Rear Admirals Schley, Sampson and Cervera: A Review of the Naval Campaign of 1898, in Pursuit and Destruction of the Spanish Fleet Commanded by Rear-Admiral Cervera*. New York: Neale Publishing Company, 1910.

Parker, John. H. *History of the Gatling Gun Detachment, Fifth Army Corps, at Santiago*. Kansas City, MO: Hudson Kimberly Publishing Company, 1898.

Parkinson, Russell J. "United States Signal Corps Balloons, 1871–1902," *Military Affairs*, 24 (Winter 1960–61):189–202.

Partido Revolucionario Cubano. *Correspondencia diplomática de la delegación cubana en Nueva York durante la guerra de independencia de 1895 á 1898*, 5 vols. Havana: Los Talleres del Archivo Nacional, 1943–1946.

Pérez, Louis A. Jr. *Cuba between Empires, 1878–1902*. Pittsburgh: University of Pittsburgh Press, 1983.

Pittman, Walter E. Jr. "Richard P. Hobson and the Sinking of the *Merrimac*," *Alabama Historical Quarterly*, 38 (1976):101–111.

Robles Muñoz, Cristóbal. "La lucha de los independentistas cubanos y las relaciones de España con Estados Unidos," *Hispania*, vol. 50, no. 174 (January–April, 1992):159–202.

Rodríguez González, Augustín. "Operaciones menores en Cuba, 1898," *Revista de Historia Naval*, 3, no. 9 (1985):125–146.

Roig de Leuchsenring, Emilio. *La guerra hispano-cubanoamericana fue ganada por el lugarteniente general del ejercito libertador Calixto García Iñíguez*. Havana, 1955.

Sargent, Herbert Howland. *The Campaign of Santiago de Cuba*. 3 vols. Chicago: A. C. McClurg, 1907.

Shaffer, Ralph E. "The Race of the *Oregon*," *Oregon Historical Quarterly*, 76 (September 1975):269–298.

Spector, Ronald H. "The Battle of Santiago," *American History Illustrated*, vol. 9, no. 4 (July 1974):12–24.

"The Story of the Captains," *The Century Magazine*, 58 (May 1899).

Torriente y Peraza, Cosme de la. *Calixto García cooperó con las fuerzas armadas de los EE.UU. en 1898, cumpliendo órdenes del gobierno cubano*. Havana, 1952.

True, Marshall M. "Revolutions in Exile: The Cuban Revolutionary Party 1891–1898," Ph.D. dissertation, University of Virginia, 1965.

U.S. Senate. *Report of the Naval Court of Inquiry upon the Destruction of the United States Battleship Maine in Havana Harbor, February 15, 1898, together with the Testimony Taken before the Court*. Senate Document No. 207, 55th Cong. 2nd Sess., Washington, DC: Government Printing Office, 1898.

U.S. Senate. Committee on Foreign Relations. *Report Relative to Affairs in Cuba (13 April 1898)* Senate Document No. 885, 55th Cong. 2nd Sess., Washington, DC: Government Printing Office, 1898.

Van Pelt, Charles B. "Fiasco at San Juan," *American History Illustrated*, vol. 3, no. 1 (April 1968):34–43.

Wexler, Alice. "Pain and Prejudice in the Santiago Campaign of 1898," *Journal of Inter-American Studies and World Affairs*, 18 (February 1976):59–73.

Europe

Bertram, Marshall. *The Birth of Anglo-American Friendship*. New York: University Press of America, 1992.

Campbell, Alexander E. *Great Britain and the United States, 1895–1903*. London: Longmans, Green and Company, 1960.

Campbell, Charles S. *Anglo-American Understanding, 1898–1903*. Baltimore, MD: Johns Hopkins University Press, 1957.

Einstein, Lewis. "British Diplomacy in the Spanish-American War," *Proceedings of the Massachusetts Historical Society*, 76 (1964):30–54.

Eyre, James K. "Russia and the American Acquisition of the Philippines," *Mississippi Valley Historical Review* (March 1942):539–562.

García Sáenz, Fernando. "El contexto internacional de la guerra de Cuba: la percepción italiana del '98' español," *Estudios de Historia Social*, 1–4 (1988):295–310.

Heindel, Richard H. *The American Impact on Great Britain, 1898-1914: A Study of the United States in World History*. Philadelphia: University of Pennsylvania Press, 1940.

Neale, Robert G. "British-American Relations During the Spanish-American War: Some Problems," *Historical Studies: Australia and New Zealand*, 6 (1953):72–89.

Offner, John Layser. "The United States and France: Ending the Spanish-American War," *Diplomatic History*, vol. 7, no. 1 (Winter 1983):1–21.

Perkins, Bradford. *The Great Rapprochement: England and the United States, 1895–1914*. New York: Atheneum, 1968.

Reuter, Bertha. *Anglo-American Relations during the Spanish-American War*. New York: The Macmillan Company, 1924.

Rippy, J. Fred. "The European Powers and the Spanish-American War," *James Sprunt Historical Studies*, 19, no. 2, Chapel Hill, NC, (1927):22–52.

Sears, Louis Martin. "French Opinion of the Spanish-American War," *Hispanic American Historical Review*, 7 (February 1927):25–44.

Shippe, Lester B. "Germany and the Spanish American War," *American Historical Review*, 30 (July 1925):754–777.

Guam, Hawaii, Japan and Latin America

Bailey, Thomas A. "The United States and Hawaii During the Spanish-American War," *American Historical Review*, 36 (April 1931):552–560.

———. "Japan's Protest Against the Annexation of Hawaii," *Journal of Modern History*, 3 (March 1931):46–61.

Beers, Henry. "American Naval Occupation and Government of Guam, 1898–1902," *Administrative Reference Service Report No. 6*. Washington, DC: Department of the Navy, March 1944.

Eyre, James K. Jr. "Japan and the American Annexation of the Philippines," *Pacific Historical Review*, 11 (March 1942): 55–71.

Farenholt, A. "Incidents of the Voyage of the U.S.S. *Charleston* to Manila in 1898," *Proceedings of the United States Naval Institute*, 50 (May 1924):753–779.

Gilmore, N. Roy. "Mexico and the Spanish-American War," *Hispanic American Historical Review*, 43 (November 1963):511–525.

Hanks, Carlos C. "When a Cruiser Captured an Island," *Proceedings of the United States Naval Institute*, 58 (July 1932):1011–1012.

Iriye, Akira. *Pacific Estrangement: Japanese and American Expansionism, 1897–1911*. Cambridge, MA: Harvard University Press, 1972.

Portusach, Frank. "History of the Capture of Guam by the United States Man-of-War *Charleston* and Its Transports," *Proceedings of the United States Naval Institute*, 43 (April 1917):707–718.

Quinn, P. E. "The Diplomatic Struggle for the Carolines in 1898," *Pacific Historical Review*, 14 (September 1945):290–302.

Shelby, Charmion C. "Mexico and the Spanish-American War: Some Contemporary Expressions of Opinion," in Thomas E. Cotner and Carlos E. Castaneda, eds. *Essays in Mexican History*. Westport, CT: Greenwood Press, 1958, pp. 209–228.

Tate, Merze. *Hawaii: Reciprocity or Annexation*. East Lansing: Michigan State University Press, 1968.

Treat, Payson J. *Diplomatic Relations between the United States and Japan 1895–1905*. Gloucester, MA: P. Smith, 1963.

Walker, L. W. "Guam's Seizure by the United States in 1898," *Pacific Historical Review*, 14 (March 1945):1–12.

Philippines

Agoncillo, Teodoro A. *Malolos: The Crisis of the Republic*. Quezon City: University of the Philippines Press, 1960.

Alfonso, Oscar M. *Theodore Roosevelt and the Philippines, 1897–1909*. Quezon City: University of the Philippines Press, 1970.

Bailey, Thomas A. "Dewey and the Germans at Manila," *American Historical Review*, 45 (October 1939):59–81.

"The Battle of Manila Bay. The Destruction of the Spanish Fleet Described by Eye-Witnesses," *The Century Magazine*, 56 (August 1898):611–627.

Braisted, William R. *The United States Navy in the Pacific, 1897–1909*. Austin: University of Texas Press, 1958.

Calkins, Carlos G. "Historical and Professional Notes on the Naval Campaign of Manila Bay in 1898," *Proceedings of the United States Naval Institute*, 25 (June 1899):267–231.

Concas y Palau, Víctor M. *Causa instruida por la destrucción de la escuadra de Filipinas y entrega del arsenal de Cavite: escrito y rectificación oral ante el consejo reunido en defensa del comandante general apostadero y escuadra de Filipinas Don Patricio Montojo y Pasarón.* Madrid: Sucesores de Rivadeneyra, 1899.

Conde de Torre Vélez. *Defensa del Excmo. Señor Don Enrique Sostoa y Ordóñez, ex-comandante general del arsenal de Cavite, ante el Consejo Superior de Guerra y Marina.* Madrid, 1899.

Diederichs, Otto von. "A Statement of Events in Manila Bay, May–October, 1898," *Journal of the Royal United Service Institution,* 59 (November 1914):421–446.

"The Diplomatic Correspondence (1898–1899) of Hon. Felipe Agoncillo," *Philippine Social Science Review,* 2 (1930):140–150.

Ellicott, John M. "Under a Gallant Captain at Manila in '98," *Proceedings of the United States Naval Institute,* 69 (January 1943):33–44.

———. "Corregidor in 1898," *Proceedings of the United States Naval Institute,* 68 (May 1942):639–641.

———. "The Defenses of Manila Bay," *Proceedings of the United States Naval Institute,* 26 (June 1900):279–285.

———. "Effect of Gunfire in Battle of Manila Bay," *Proceedings of the United States Naval Institute,* 90 (1899): 323–334.

Erye, James K. Jr. "The Philippines, the Powers and the Spanish American War: A Study of Foreign Policies," Ph.D. dissertation, University of Michigan, 1942.

Gates, John Morgan. *Schoolbooks and Krags: The United States Army in the Philippines, 1898–1902.* Westport, CT: Greenwood Press, 1973.

Harper, Frank. "Fighting Far from Home: The First Colorado Regiment in the Spanish-American War," *Colorado Heritage* (Spring 1988):2–11.

Johnson, John R. "The Saga of the First Nebraska in the Philippines," *Nebraska History,* 30 (June 1949):139–162.

Johnson, Robert E. *Far China Station: The U.S. Navy in Asian Waters, 1890–1898.* Annapolis, MD: U.S. Naval Institute Press, 1979.

Kalaw, Teodoro M. *The Philippine Revolution.* Manila: Manila Book Company, 1925.

Kalaw, Teodoro M., ed. and comp. *La Revolución Filipina Con Otros Documents de la Epoca.* 2 vols. Manila: Bureau of Printing, 1931.

McCutcheon, John T., and Thomas A. Bailey "The Battle of Manila Bay," *Proceedings of the United States Naval Institute,* 66 (June 1940):843–853.

Salgado Alba, Jesús. "El crucero *Castilla*: Heroe y holocausto en Cavite," *Revista General de Marina,* 191 (December 1976): 637–645.

Salinas y Ángulo, Ignacio. *Defensa del General Jáudenes hecha por el General de Brigada Don Ignacio Salinas y Angulo. Leida el 29 de septiembre de 1899 ante el Consejo Supremo de Guerra y Marina, reunida en Sala de Justicia.* Madrid: Impreso y Litografía del Depósito de la Guerra, 1899.

Saniel, Josefa M. "Japan and the Philippines, 1868–1898," Ph.D. dissertation, University of Michigan, 1962.

Spector, Ronald H. "Who Planned the Attack on Manila Bay?" *Mid-America*, 53 (April 1971):94–102.

Stokesbury, James L. "Manila Bay—Battle or Execution," *American History Illustrated*, vol. 14, no. 5 (August 1979):4–7,40–47.

Taylor, John R. M. *The Philippine Insurrection against the United States: A Compilation of Documents with Notes and Introduction.* 5 vols. Pasay City: Eugenio López Foundation, 1971.

U.S. Senate. *Report of the Philippine Commission to the President, January 31, 1900.* 56th Cong., 1st sess., Senate Document No. 138, Washington, DC: Government Printing Office, 1900.

Villanueva, Honesto A. "Diplomacy of the Spanish-American War," *Philippine Social Sciences and Humanities Review*, 14 (March 1949):135–182, 303–306, 429–468; 15 (1950):3–44, 103–162, 305–331.

Vivian, Thomas Jondrie, ed. *With Dewey at Manila; being the plain story of the glorious victory of the United States squadron over the Spanish fleet, Sunday morning, May 1st, 1898, as related in the notes and correspondence of an officer on board the flagship Olympia.* New York: R. F. Fenno & Company, 1898.

White, Douglas. *On to Manila: A True and Concise History of the Philippine Campaign, Secured while Afloat with Admiral Dewey's Fleet and in the Field with the 8th U.S. Army Corps.*

Wilcox, Marrion, ed. *Harper's History of the War in the Philippines.* New York: Harper and Brothers Publishers, 1900.

Wildman, Edwin. "What Dewey Feared in Manila Bay," *The Forum*, 59 (May 1918):513–535.

Williams, Vernon L. "The U.S. Navy in the Philippine Insurrection and Subsequent Native Unrest 1898–1906," Ph.D. dissertation, Texas A & M University, 1985.

Wolff, Leon. *Little Brown Brothers: How the United States Purchased and Pacified the Philippine Islands at the Century's Turn.* Garden City, NY: Doubleday, 1961.

Yutaka, Kondo. "La adquisición de las islas Filipinas por los EE.UU. en la guerra hispano-americana de 1898," *Revista de la Universidad de Madrid*, 9 (1960):925–926.

Puerto Rico

Berbusse, Edward J. *The United States in Puerto Rico 1898–1900.* Chapel Hill: University of North Carolina Press, 1966.

Carroll, Henry K. "How Shall Puerto Rico Be Governed?" *The Forum,* 28 (November 1899):257–267.

Church, John A. "The Occupation of Porto Rico," *Review of Reviews,* 18 (September 1898):281–289.

Cruz Monclova, Lidio. *Historia de Puerto Rico (Siglo XIX)* vol. 3, part 3: *1885–1898.* Río Piedras, Puerto Rico: University of Puerto Rico, 1964.

Davis, Richard Harding. "The Taking of Coamo," in *The Notes of a War Correspondent* by Richard Harding Davis. New York: Charles Scribner's Sons, 1912, pp. 101–112.

————. "How Stephen Crane Took Juana Dias" in *Many Wars by Many War Correspondents.* Edited by George Lynch and Frederick Palmer. Tokyo: Tokyo Printing Company, 1904.

Delgado Pasapera, Germán. *Puerto Rico: Sus luchas emancipadoras (1850–1898).* Río Piedras, Puerto Rico: University of Puerto Rico, 1984.

Fiala, Anthony. *Troop "C" in Service: An Account of the Part Played by Troop "C" of the New York Volunteer Cavalry in the Spanish-American War of 1898.* Brooklyn, 1899.

Munden, Kenneth, and Milton Greenbaum, eds. *Records of the Bureau of Insular Affairs Relating to Puerto Rico, 1898–1934: A list of selected files.* Washington, DC: U.S. National Archives, 1943.

Natal, Carmelo Rosario. *Puerto Rico y la crisis de la guerra hispanoamericana (1895–1898).* Hato Rey, Puerto Rico: Ramallo Brothers, 1975.

Negrón Portillo, Mariano. "El liderato anexionista antes y despues del cambio de soberania," *Revista del Colegio de Abogados,* 33 (1972):369–391.

Nieves, Juan B. *La anexión de Puerto Rico a los Estados Unidos de America.* Ponce, 1898.

Partido Revolucionario Cubano. *Memoria de los trabajos realizados por la Sección Puerto Rico del Partido Revolucionario Cubano, 1895–1898.* New York: Imprenta de A. W. Howes, 1898.

Perez y Soto, Juan B. *Causas y consecuencias antecedentes diplomáticos y efectos de la guerra hispano-americana.* San Juan, Puerto Rico, 1922.

Picó, Fernando. *1898: La guerra despues de la guerra.* Río Piedras, Puerto Rico: Ediciones Huracán, 1987.

Rivero Mendez, Angel. *Crónica de la Guerra Hispanoamericana en*

Puerto Rico. Madrid: Sucesores de Rivadeneyra, Artes Gráficas, 1922.

Todd, Roberto H. *La invasión americana: como surgió la idea de traer la guerra Puerto Rico*. San Jose: Cantero Fernández & Co., 1938.

Spain

Amador y Carrandi, Ernesto. *La guerra hispano-americana ante el derecho internacional*. Madrid: Imprenta de la Viuda de M. Minuesa de los Ríos, 1900.

Andrés-Gallego, José "Los grupos politicos del 98," *Hispania*, 38, no. 138 (January–April 1978):121–146.

Auñón y Villalón, Ramón. *Discursos pronunciados en el parlamento por el ministro de marina D. Ramón Auñón y Villalón durante la guerra con los Estados Unidos*. Madrid, 1912.

Baker, Thomas Hart Jr. "Imperial Finale: Crisis, Decolonization, and War in Spain, 1890–1898," Ph.D. dissertation, Princeton University, 1976.

Balfour, Sebastian. "Riot, Regeneration and Reaction: Spain in the Aftermath of the 1898 Disaster," *The Historical Journal*, 38, no. 2 (June 1995):405–423.

Baquer, Miguel Alonso. "The Spanish American War of 1898 and Its Effects on Spanish Military Institutions," *Proceedings of the 1982 International Military History Symposium*, Washington, DC: U.S. Army Center of Military History, 1984.

Bécker, Jerónimo. *Historia de las relaciones exteriores de España durante el siglo XIX (Apuntes para una historia diplomática)* vol. 3 *1868–1900*. Madrid: Editorial Voluntad, 1926.

Blanco Aguinaga, Carlos. *Juventud del 98*. Barcelona: Crítica, 1978.

Casellas, Salvador E. "Causes y antecedentes diplomáticos de la guerra hispanoamericana," *Revista de Ciencias Sociales*, 4, no. 1 (1965):55–75.

Clarke, Jack A. "Spanish Socialists and the Spanish-American War: A Note," *Mid-America*, 40 (October 1958):229–231.

Fernández Almagro, Melchor. *Historia política de la España contemporánea*, vol. 2: *1885–1897*, vol. 3: *1897–1902*. Madrid: Alianza Editorial, 1959, 1968.

———. *La reacción popular ante el desastre*. Madrid: Arbor, 1948.

———. *En torno al 98. Política y literatura*. Madrid: Ediciones Jordán, 1948.

Galindo Herrero, Santiago. *El 98 de los que fueron a la guerra*. Madrid: Editora Nacional, 1955.

García Barrón, Carlos. *Cancionero del '98*. Madrid: Cuadernos para el Diálogo, 1974.

García Escudero, José María. *De Cánovas á la república*. Madrid: Ediciones Rialp, 1951.

Granjel, Luis S. *La Generación literaria del noventa y ocho*. Salamanca: Ediciones Anaya, 1966.

Harrison, Joseph. "The Regenerationist Movement in Spain after the Disaster of 1898," *European Studies Review*. 9, no. 1 (January 1979):1–27.

Headrick, Daniel R. *Ejercito y política en España (1866–1898)*. Madrid: Editorial Tecnos, 1981.

Jover Zamora, Jose María. *1898: Teoría y práctica de la redistribución colonial*. Madrid: Fundación Universitaria Española, 1979.

———. *Política, diplomacia y humanismo popular: Estudios sobre la vida Española en el siglo XIX*. Madrid: Turner, 1976.

Laín Entralgo, Pedro. *La generación del Noventa y ocho*. Madrid: Espasa-Calpe, 1979.

López Morillas, Juan. *Hacia el 98. Literatura, sociedad, ideología*. Barcelona: Ediciones Ariel, 1972.

Marinas Otero, Luis. *La herencia del 98*. Madrid: Editora Nacional, 1967.

Maura Gamazo, Gabriel. *História crítica del reinado de don Alfonso XIII durante su menoridad bajo la regencia de su madre doña María Cristina de Austria*. 2 vols. Barcelona: Montaner y Simón, 1919, 1925.

Meléndez y Meléndez, Leonor. *Cánovas y la política exterior española*. Madrid: Instituto de Estudios Políticos, 1944.

Moradiellos, Enrique. "1898: A Colonial Disaster Foretold," *Journal of the Association for Contemporary Iberian Studies*, 6, no. 2 (1993):33–38.

Nido y Segalerva, Juan del. *Historia política y parlamentaria del Excmo. Sr. Práxedes Mateo Sagasta*. Madrid: Congreso de los Diputados, 1915.

Ortega y Rubio, Juan. *Historia de la regencia de María Cristina Hapsbourg-Lorena*. 5 vols. Madrid: Felipe González Rojas, 1905–1906.

Pérez Delgado, Rafael. *1898: El año del desastre*. Madrid: Tebas, 1976.

Pilapil, Vicente R. "Spain in the European State System 1898–1913," Ph.D. dissertation, Catholic University of America, 1964.

Piñeyro, Enrique. *Como acabó la dominación de España en America*. Paris: Garnier Hermanos, 1908.

Ramsden, Herbert. *The 1898 Movement in Spain: Towards a Reinterpretation*. Manchester, England: Manchester University Press, 1974.

Rodríguez González, Agustín Ramón. *Política naval de la Restauración (1875–1898)*. Madrid: Editorial San Martín, 1988.

Saint Hubert, Christian de, and Carlos Alfaro Zaforteza. "The Spanish Navy of 1898," *Warship International*, 7 (1980):39–59, 110–119.

Sales, Nuria. *Sobre esclavos, reclutas y mercaderes de quintos*. Barcelona: Ariel, 1974.

Serrano, Carlos. *Final del Imperio: España, 1895–1898*. Madrid: Siglo XXI de España Editores, 1984.

―――. "Guerra y crisis social: los motines de mayo de 1898," *Estudios de Historia de España*, vol. 1. Madrid: Universidad Menéndez Pelayo, 1981, pp. 439–450.

Sevilla Soler, Rosario. "La Intervención Norteamericana en Cuba y la Opinión Pública Andaluza," *Anuario de Estudios Americanos*, 43. Seville: Escuela de estudios hispanoamericanos de Sevilla, 1986, pp. 469–516.

Spain. Minister of State. *Spanish Diplomatic Correspondence and Documents, 1896–1900, Presented to the Cortes by the Minister of State*. Washington, DC: Government Printing Office, 1905.

Spain. Ministry of the Marine. *Correspondencia oficial referente á las operaciones navales durante la guerra con los Estados Unidos en 1898*. Madrid, 1899.

Varela Ortega, José. "Aftermath of Splendid Disaster: Spanish Politics before and after the Spanish American War of 1898," *Journal of Contemporary History* 15, no. 2 (April 1980):317–344.

―――. *Los amigos políticos, partidos, elecciones y caciquismo en la restauración, 1875–1900*. Madrid: Alianza Editorial, 1977.

United States

Ballard, Larry A. "Camp Russell A. Alger, Virginia: 1898," *Northern Virginia Heritage*, 5 (June 1983):3–6, 19–20.

Benton, Elbert J. *International Law and Diplomacy of the Spanish-American War*. Baltimore, MD: Johns Hopkins Press, 1908.

Bermeosolo, Francisco. "La opinión pública norteamericana y la guerra de los Estados Unidos contra España," *Revista de Estudios Políticos*, 123 (1962):219–233.

Bradford, James C., ed. *Crucible of Empire: The Spanish-American War & Its Aftermath*. Annapolis, MD: Naval Institute Press, 1993.

Brownlee, James Henry, ed. *War-Time Echoes: Patriotic Poems Heroic and Pathetic, Humorous and Dialect of the Spanish-American War*. Akron, OH: The Werner Company, 1898.

Challener, Richard D. *Admirals, Generals and American Foreign Policy, 1898–1914*. Princeton, NJ: Princeton University Press, 1973.

Chapman, Gregory D. "Army Life at Camp Thomas, Georgia during the Spanish-American War," *Georgia Historical Quarterly*, 70 (Winter 1970):634–56.

Coletta, Paolo E., ed. *Threshold to American Imperialism: Essays on the Foreign Policies of William McKinley.* New York: Exposition Press, 1970.

Cosmas, Graham A. *An Army for Empire: The United States Army and the Spanish-American War.* Columbia: University of Missouri Press, 1971.

———. "From Order to Chaos: The War Department, the National Guard, and Military Policy, 1898," *Military Affairs,* 29 (Fall 1965):105–121.

Coston, William Hilary. *The Spanish-American War Volunteer: Ninth United States Volunteer Infantry, Roster, Muster, Biographies, Cuban Sketches.* Middleton, PA: Mount Pleasant Printery, 1899.

Dobson, John M. *Reticient Expansionism: The Foreign Policy of William McKinley.* Pittsburgh, PA: Duquesne University Press, 1988.

Frye, Joseph A. "William McKinley and the Coming of the Spanish-American War: A Study of the Besmirching and Redemption of an Historical Image," *Diplomatic History,* 3 (Winter 1979): 77–98.

Gatewood, Willard B. Jr. *Black Americans and the White Man's Burden 1898–1903.* Urbana: University of Illinois Press, 1975.

———. "Black Americans and the Quest for Empire, 1898–1903," *Journal of Southern History,* 38 (November 1972):545–566.

———. "Negro Troops in Florida, 1898," *Florida Historical Quarterly,* 49 (July 1970):1–15.

Gianakos, Perry E. "The Spanish-American War and the Double Paradox of the Negro American," *Phylon,* 26 (Spring 1965):34–49.

Gould, Lewis L. *The Spanish-American War and President McKinley.* Lawrence: Regents Press of Kansas, 1982.

Grenville, John A. S. "American Naval Preparations for War with Spain, 1896–1898," *Journal of American Studies,* 2, no. 1 (April 1968):33–47.

———. "Diplomacy and War Plans in the United States, 1890–1917," *Transactions of the Royal Historical Society,* series 5, vol. 2, London, 1961, pp. 1–21.

Grenville, John A. S., and George Berkeley Young. *Politics, Strategy and American Diplomacy: Studies in Foreign Policy, 1873–1917.* New Haven, CT: Yale University Press, 1966.

Hofstadter, Richard. "Cuba, the Philippines, and Manifest Destiny," *The Paranoid Style in American Politics and Other Essays.* New York: A. Knopf, 1965, pp. 147–187.

Holbo, Paul S. "The Convergence of Moods and the Cuban Bond 'Conspiracy' of 1898," *Journal of American History,* 55 (June 1968):54–72.

Hyde, Frederic G. "American Literature and the Spanish-American War: A Study of the Work of Crane, Norris, Fox, and R. H. Davis," Ph.D. dissertation, University of Pennsylvania, 1963.

Johnson, Edward Austin. *History of Negro Soldiers in the Spanish-American War; and other items of interest.* Raleigh, NC: Capital Printing Company, 1899.

Jones, Virgil Carrington. *Roosevelt's Rough Riders.* Garden City, NY: Doubleday & Company, 1971.

Karracker, William A. "The American Churches and the Spanish American War," Ph.D. dissertation, University of Chicago, 1940.

Kennedy, Philip W. "Race and American Expansionism in Cuba and Puerto Rico, 1895–1905," *Journal of Black Studies*, 1 (March 1971):306–316.

Lees, Jeannie C. *Men in Militia, 1898: Spanish American War.* Hopkinton, RI: The Compilor, 1986.

May, Ernest R. *Imperial Democracy: The Emergence of America as a Great Power.* New York: Harcourt, Brace and World, 1961.

Morales Lezcano, Víctor. "Ideología y estrategia estadounidense: 1898," *Hispania*, 29, no. 113 (September–October 1969):610–626.

Morgan, H. Wayne. "The De Lôme Letter: A New Appraisal," *The Historian*, 26 (November 1963):36–49.

Nalty, Bernard C. *The United States Marines in the War with Spain.* rev. ed., Washington, DC: U.S. Marine Corps, 1967.

Offner, John. "President McKinley's Final Attempt to Avoid War with Spain," *Ohio History*, 94 (Summer–Autumn 1985):125–138.

Ranson, Edward "The Investigation of the War Department, 1898–1899," *Historian*, 34 (1971):78–99

Schellings, William J. "Key West and the Spanish-American War," *Tequesta*, 20 (1960):19–29.

Steward, Theophilous G. *The Colored Regulars in the United States Army.* Philadelphia, PA: A.M.E. Book Concern, 1904.

Thompson, Woodruff C. "The Spanish-American War in American Literature," Ph.D. dissertation, University of Utah, 1962.

Traverso, Edmund. *The Spanish-American War: A study in policy change.* Lexington, MA: D.C. Heath, 1968.

U.S. Army. *Annual Report of the Major-General Commanding the Army, 1899.* Washington, DC: Government Printing Office, 1899.

U.S. Navy Department. *Record of Proceedings of a Court of Inquiry in the Case of Rear-Admiral Winfield S. Schley, U.S. Navy: Convened at the Navy Yard, Washington, D.C., September 12, 1901.* 2 vols., H.R. Document No. 485, 57th Cong., 1st sess. Washington, DC: Government Printing Office, 1902.

———. *Annual Reports of the Navy Department for the Year 1898.* 2 vols. Volume 1: *Report of the Secretary of the Navy, Miscellaneous Reports.* Volume 2: *Appendix to the Report of the Chief of the Bureau of Navigation.* Washington, DC: Government Printing Office, 1898.

U.S. Revenue Cutter Service. *The United States Revenue Cutter Service in the War with Spain, 1898.* Washington, DC: Government Printing Office, 1899.

U.S. Senate. *Report of the Commission Appointed by the President to Investigate the Conduct of the War Department in the War With Spain.* 8 vols., Senate Document No. 221, 56th Cong., 1st sess. Washington, DC: Government Printing Office, 1900.

U.S. State Department. *Papers Relating to the Foreign Relations of the United States, with the Annual Message of the President: Transmitted to Congress December 5, 1898.* Washington, DC: Government Printing Office, 1901.

U.S. War Department. *Annual Reports of the War Department.* 1898 and 1899, Washington, DC: Government Printing Office, 1898 and 1899.

U.S. War Department. Adjutant-General's Office. *Correspondence Relating to the War With Spain and Conditions Growing Out of the Same, Including the Insurrection in the Philippine Islands and the China Relief Expedition, between the Adjutant-General of the Army and Military Commanders in the United States, Cuba, Porto Rico, China, and the Philippine Islands, from April 15, 1898, to July 30, 1902.* 2 vols. Washington, DC, Government Printing Office, 1902.

Westermeier, Clifford Peter. *Who Rush to Glory: The Cowboy Volunteers of 1898: Grigsby's Cowboys, Roosevelt's Rough Riders, Torrey's Mountain Riders.* Caldwell, ID: The Caxton Printers, 1958.

Witherbee, Sidney A., comp. and ed. *Spanish-American War Songs: A Complete Collection of Newspaper Verse During the Recent War with Spain.* Detroit, MI: John F. Eby & Co., 1898.

Wood, Richard E. "The South and Reunion, 1898," *Historian,* 21 (May 1969):415–430.

Biographies and Personal Accounts

Alberts, Don E. *Brandy Station to Manila: A Biography of General Wesley Merritt.* San Francisco: Presidio Press, 1980.

Álvarez Angulo, Tomás. *Memorias de un hombre sin importancia, 1878–1961.* Madrid: Aguilar, 1962.

Arderius, Francisco. *La escuadra española en Santiago de Cuba: Diario de un testigo.* Barcelona: Maucci, 1903.

Atkins, John Black. *The War in Cuba: The Experiences of an Englishman with the U.S. Army.* London: Smith, Elder and Co., 1899.

Beach, Edward L. Sr. "Manila Bay in 1898," *Proceedings of the United States Naval Institute,* 46 (April 1920):587–602.

Benítez, Frances Tomás. *El 3 de julio desde el "Viscaya": El manuscrito de un combate.* Madrid: El Ferrol, 1898.

Bigelow, John Jr. *Reminiscences of the Santiago Campaign*. New York: Harper and Brothers, 1899.

Bradford, James C., ed. *Admirals of the New Steel Navy: Makers of the American Naval Traditions, 1880–1930*. Annapolis, MD: U.S. Naval Institute Press, 1990.

Carlson, Paul H. *"Pecos Bill": A Military Biography of William R. Shafter*. College Station: Texas A & M University Press, 1989.

Coletta, Paolo E. *French Ensor Chadwick: Scholarly Warrior*. Lanham, MD: University Press of America, 1980.

———. *Bowman Hendry McCalla: A Fighting Sailor*. Lanham, MD: University Press of America, 1979.

Concas y Palau, Víctor María. *Sobre las enseñanzas de la guerra hispano-americana*. Bilbao: Imprenta y Litografía de Ezequiel Rodriguez, Sucesor de J.E. Delmas, 1900.

Conde de Romanones (Alvaro Figueroa y Torres). *Sagasta o el político*. Bilbao: Espasa-Calpe, 1930.

Corral, Manuel. *El desastre! Memorias de un voluntario en la campaña de Cuba*. Barcelona: A. Martínez, 1899.

Cortés-Cavanillas, Julián. *María Cristina de Austria: Reina regente de España de 1885 a 1902*. 2d ed. Barcelona: Juventud, 1980.

Davis, Richard Harding. *The Cuban and Porto Rican Campaigns*. New York: Charles Scribner's Sons, 1898.

Dewey, George W. *Autobiography of George Dewey, Admiral of the Navy*. New York: Charles Scribner's Sons, 1913.

Efeele. *El desastre nacional y los vicios de nuestras institución es militares*. Madrid: Imprenta del Cuerpo de Artilleria, 1901.

Faust, Karl Irving. *Campaigning in the Philippines*. San Francisco: The Hicks Judd Company, 1899.

Fiske, Bradley Allen. *From Midshipman to Rear Admiral*. New York: Century, 1919.

Funston, Frederick. *Memories of Two Wars: Cuban and Philippine Experiences*. New York: Charles Scribner's, 1911.

Gatewood, Willard B. Jr. *"Smoked Yankees" and the Struggle for Empire: Letters from Negro Soldiers, 1898–1902*. Urbana: University of Illinois Press, 1971.

Goode, Wiliiam A. M. *With Sampson Through the War: Being an Account of the Naval Operations of the North Atlantic Squadron During the Spanish American War of 1898*. New York: Doubleday and Mc-Clure, 1899.

Hagedorn, Hermann. *Leonard Wood: A Biography*. 2 vols. New York: Harper and Brothers, 1931.

Harper, Frank, ed. *Just Outside Manila: Letters from Members of the First Colorado Regiment in the Spanish-American and Philippine-*

American Wars. Essays and monographs in Colorado History, no. 7, Denver: Colorado Historical Society, 1991.

Jeffers, Harry Paul. *Colonel Roosevelt: Theodore Roosevelt Goes to War, 1897–1898.* New York: J. Wiley & Sons, 1996.

Johnson, Virginia W. *The Unregimented General: A Biography of Nelson A. Miles.* Boston, MA: Houghton Mifflin Co., 1962.

Leech, Margaret. *In the Days of McKinley.* New York: Harper & Row, 1959.

Lema, Salvador Bermúdez de Castro and O'Lawlor, Marques de. *Mis recuerdos (1880–1901).* Madrid: Compania Ibero-Americana de Publicaciones, 1930.

Lodge, Henry Cabot, and Charles F. Redmond, eds. *Selections from the Correspondence of Theodore Roosevelt and Henry Cabot Lodge, 1884–1918.* 2 vols. New York: Charles Scribner's Sons, 1925.

Mahan, Alfred Thayer. *Lessons of the War With Spain and Other Articles.* Boston: Little, Brown and Co., 1899.

Martín Cerezo, Saturnino. *El sitio de Baler (notas y recuerdos).* Guadalajara, 1904. Translated by F. L. Dodds as *Under the Red and Gold: Being Notes and Recollections of the Siege of Baler.* Kansas City, MO: Franklin Hudson Publishing Co., 1909.

Mayo, Lawrence Shaw, ed. *America of Yesterday: As Reflected in the Journal of John Davis Long.* Boston, MA: Atlantic Monthly Press, 1923.

McClernand, Edward J., comp. *The Santiago Campaign: Reminiscences of the Operations for the Capture of Santiago de Cuba in the Spanish-American War, June and July 1898.* Society of Santiago, Richmond, VA: Williams Printing Company, 1927.

Miles, Nelson A. *Serving the Republic: Memoirs of the Civil and Military Life of Nelson A. Miles, Lieutenant-General United States Army.* New York: Harper and Brothers, 1911.

Morales Lezcano, Víctor. *León y Castillo, embajador (1887–1918): Un estudio sobre la política exterior de España.* Las Palmas: Cabildo insular de Gran Canaria, 1975.

Morgan, Howard Wayne, ed. *Making Peace with Spain: The Diary of Whitelaw Reid September–December 1898.* Austin: University of Texas Press, 1965.

———. *William McKinley and His America.* Syracuse, NY: Syracuse University Press, 1963.

Newell, George L. "Manila to Peking: Letters Home, 1898–1901," *Oregon Historical Quarterly*, 80 (Summer 1979):170–196.

Post, Charles Johnson. *The Little War of Private Post.* Boston, MA: Little, Brown and Company, 1960.

Pritchett, Henry S. "Some Recollections of McKinley and the Cuban Intervention," *North American Review*, 189 (March 1909):397–403.

Ría-Baja, Carlos. *El desastre filipino. Memorias de un prisonero.* Barcelona: Pipografía la Academica de Serra Hermanos y Russell, 1899.

Risco, Alberto. *Apuntes biográficos del Excmo. Sr. Almirante D. Pascual Cervera y Topete.* Toledo: S. Rodríguez, 1920.

Roca de Togores y Saravia, Jose. *Bloqueo y sitio de Manila en 1898.* Huesca, Spain: Tipografía de L. Pérez, 1908.

Sastrón, Manuel. *La insurrección en Filipinas y la guerra hispanoamericana en el archipelago.* Madrid: Imprenta de la Sucesora de M. Minuesa de los Ríos, 1901.

Sexton, William Thaddeus. *Soldiers in the Sun: An Adventure in Imperialism.* Harrisburg, PA: The Military Service Publishing Company, 1939.

The Spanish-American War: The Events Described by Eye Witnesses. Chicago: Herbert S. Stone & Company, 1899.

Spector, Ronald H. *Admiral of the New Empire: The Life and Career of George Dewey.* Baton Rouge: Louisiana State University Press, 1974.

Thompson, H. C. "War without Medals," *Oregon Historical Quarterly,* 59 (December 1958):292–325.

Toral, Juan. *El sitio de Manila (1898). Memorias de un voluntario.* Manila: Imprenta Litografía Partier, 1898.

West, Richard Sedgwick Jr. *Admirals of American Empire: The Combined Story of George Dewey, Alfred Thayer Mahan, Winfield Scott Schley, and William Thomas Sampson.* Indianapolis and New York: Bobbs-Merrill Company, 1948.

Weyler y Nicolau, Valeriano. *Mi Mando en Cuba: Historia militar y política de la última guerra separtista.* 5 vols. Madrid: Imprenta de Felipe González Rojas, 1910–1911.

Young, James Rankin, and Joseph Hamilton Moore. *Reminiscences and Thrilling Stories of the War by Returned Heroes: Containing Vivid Accounts of Personal Experiences by Officers and Men: Admiral Dewey's Report of the Battle at Manila, Graphic Account by Admiral Schley of the Naval Battle at Santiago to Which is Added Admiral Cervera's Story of His Attempt to Escape from the Harbor of Santiago, Hobson's Vivid Account of the Sinking of the Merrimac. Poems and Songs of the War.* Denver, CO: Western Book Company, 1899.

Espionage

Dorwart, Jeffrey M. *The Office of Naval Intelligence: The Birth of America's First Intelligence Agency, 1881–1918.* Annapolis, MD: U.S. Naval Institute Press, 1979.

Giddings, Howard A. *Exploits of the Signal Corps in the War with Spain.* Kansas City, MO: Hudson-Kimberly Publishing Company, 1900.

Jeffreys-Jones, Rhodri. "The Montreal Spy Ring of 1898 and the Origins of 'Domestic' Surveillance in the United States," *Canadian Review of American Studies*, 2 (Fall 1974):125–127.

Mount, Graeme S. "The secret operations of Spanish consular officials within Canada during the Spanish-American War," in *North American Spies: New Revisionist Essays*. Edited by Rhodri Jeffreys-Jones and Andrew Lownie. Laurence: University of Kansas Press, 1991, pp. 31–48.

———. "Friendly liberator or predatory aggressor? Some Canadian impressions of the United States during the Spanish-American War," *North/South: Canadian Journal of Caribbean and Latin American Studies*, 11, 22 (1986):59–76.

Sherrin, P. M. "Spanish spies in Victoria," *BC Studies*, 36 (Winter 1977–1978):23–33.

Trask, David F. "American Intelligence During the Spanish-American War," *Crucible of Empire: The Spanish-American War & Its Aftermath*. Edited by James C. Bradford, Annapolis, MD: Naval Institute Press, 1993, pp. 23–46.

Imperialism and Anti-Imperialism

Adams, Brooks. "The Spanish War and the Equilibrium of the World," *The Forum*, (August 1898):641–651.

Becker, William H. "American Manufacturers and Foreign Markets, 1870–1900: Business Historians and the New Economic Determinists," *Business History Review*, 47 (Winter 1973):466–481.

Beisner, Robert L. *Twelve against Empire: The Anti-Imperialists, 1898–1900*. New York: McGraw Hill Book Co., 1968.

Carnegie, Andrew. "Distant Possessions—the Parting of the Ways," *North American Review*, 167 (August 1898):239–246.

Collin, Richard H. *Theodore Roosevelt, Culture, Diplomacy and Expansion: A New View of American Imperialism*. Baton Rouge: Louisiana State University Press, 1985.

Field, James A. Jr. "American Imperialism: The 'Worst Chapter' in Almost Any Book," *American Historical Review*, 83, no. 4 (June 1978):644–683.

Freidel, Frank B. "Dissent in the Spanish-American War and the Philippine Insurrection," in *Dissent in Three American Wars*, by Samuel Eliot Morison, Frederick Merk, and Frank Freidel. Cambridge, MA: Harvard University Press, 1970, pp. 65–95.

Harrington, Fred H. "The Anti-Imperialist Movement in the United States, 1898–1900," *Mississippi Valley Historical Review*, 22 (September 1935):211–230.

Healy, David F. *U.S. Expansionism: The Imperialist Urge in the 1890s.* Madison: University of Wisconsin Press, 1963.

Hernández Sandoica, Elena. "La expansión imperialista y su repercusión en las doctrinas de derecho internacional, 1890–1905," Ph.D. dissertation, University of Madrid, 1976.

Kennedy, Philip W. "Race and American Expansionism in Cuba and Puerto Rico, 1895–1905," *Journal of Black Studies*, I (March 1971):306–316.

LaFeber, Walter. *The New Empire: An Interpretation of American Expansionism, 1860–1898.* Ithaca, NY: Cornell University Press, 1963.

Lasch, Christopher. "The Anti-Imperialists, the Philippines and the Inequality of Man," *Journal of Southern History*, 24 (August 1958): 319–331.

McCormick, Thomas J. "Insular Imperialism and the Open Door: The China Market and the Spanish-American War," *Pacific Historical Review*, 32, no. 2 (May 1963):155–169.

Miller, Richard H. "The Peace of Paris, 1898: A Case Study of the Dilemmas of Imperialism," Ph.D. dissertation, Georgetown University, 1969.

Paterson, Thomas G., ed. *American Imperialism and Anti-Imperialism.* New York: Thomas Y. Crowell Co., 1973.

Pratt, Julius W. "American Business and the Spanish-American War," *Hispanic American Historical Review*, 14 (May 1934): 163–201.

———. "The 'Large Policy' of 1898," *Mississippi Valley Historical Review* 19 (September 1932):219–242.

Schurz, Carl. "Thoughts on American Imperialism," *The Century Magazine*, 16 (September 1898):781–788.

Sumner, William Graham. "The Fallacy of Territorial Expansion," *The Forum*, 21 (June 1896):414–419.

Tompkins, E. Berkeley. *Anti-Imperialism in the United States: The Great Debate, 1890–1920.* Philadelphia: University of Pennsylvania Press, 1970.

United States. Department of War. *Report on the Legal Status of Islands Acquired during the War with Spain.* Washington, DC, 1900.

Varg, Paul. "The Myth of the China Market, 1890–1914," *American Historical Review*, 73 (February 1968):742–758.

Welch, Richard E. Jr. "Motives and Policy Objectives of the Anti-Imperialists, 1898," *Mid-America*, 51 (April 1969):119–129.

Weston, Rubin F. *Racism in U.S. Imperialism: The Influence of Racial Assumptions on American Foreign Policy, 1893–1946.* Columbia: University of South Carolina Press, 1972.

Young, Marilyn Blatt. *The Rhetoric of Empire: America's China Policy 1895–1901.* Cambridge, MA: Harvard University Press, 1968.

Media

Army War College. Library. *Newspaper History of the Spanish-American War, April 21, 1898–January 1, 1899.* 20 vols., Carlisle Barracks, Carlisle, PA: U.S. Military History Institute.

Auxier, George W. "Middle Western Newspapers and the Spanish-American War, 1895–1898," *Mississippi Valley Historical Review*, 26 (March 1940):523–534.

———. "The Propaganda Activities of the Cuban Junta in Precipitating the Spanish-American War, 1895–1898," *Hispanic American Historical Review*, 19, 3 (August 1939):286–305.

Baker, Ray Stannard. "How the News of War is Reported," *McClure's Magazine*, 11 (September 1898):491–495.

Brown, Charles H. *The Correspondents' War: Journalists in the Spanish-American War.* New York: Charles Scribner's Sons, 1967.

Cartoons of the War of 1898 with Spain from Leading Foreign and American Papers. Chicago: Belford, Middlebrook and Company, 1898.

Chicago Record. The Chicago Record's War Stories, 1898.

Crane, Stephen. *The War Dispatches of Stephen Crane.* New York: New York University Press, 1964.

Donahue, William J. "The United States Newspaper Press Reaction to the Maine Incident—1898," Ph.D. dissertation, University of Colorado, 1970.

Mander, Mary S. "Pen and Sword: Problems in Reporting the Spanish American War," *Journalism History*, 9 (1982):2–9, 28.

Méndez Saavedra, Manuel, comp. *1898: La Guerra Hispanoamericana en Caricaturas (The Spanish-American War in Cartoons).* San Juan, Puerto Rico: Gráfica Metropolitana, 1992.

Milton, Joyce. *The Yellow Kids: Foreign Correspondents in the Heyday of Yellow Journalism.* New York: Harper & Row, 1989.

Noreña, María Teresa. "La prensa madrileña ante la crisis del 98," in Jose María Jover Zamora y aa. vv. *El siglo XIX en España: doce estudios.* Barcelona: Planeta, 1974, pp. 571–611.

Ponder, Stephen. "The President Makes News: William McKinley and the First Presidential Press Corps, 1897–1901," *Presidential Studies Quarterly*, vol. 24, issue 4 (Fall 1994):823–836.

Serrano Anguita, Francisco. "Los escritores del 98 y los periódicos," *Gaceta de la Prensa Española*, no. 166, April 1965.

Wilkerson, Marcus M. *Public Opinion and the Spanish-American War: A Study in War Propaganda.* New York: Russell & Russell, 1932.

Wisan, Joseph E. *The Cuban Crisis As Reflected In the New York Press, 1895–1898.* New York: Columbia University Press, 1934.

Medical

American National Red Cross. Relief Committee. *Relief Committee Reports. May 1898, March 1899*. New York: The Knickerbocker Press, 1899.

Dunham, Dr. Carroll. "Medical and Sanitary Aspects of the War," *Review of Reviews*, 18 (October 1898):415–427.

Girard, A. C. "The Management of Camp Alger and Camp Meade," *New York Medical Journal* (24 September 1898):1–12.

Hofker-Lesser, Bettina. *Work of the Red Cross Sisters in Cuba before and during the Spanish-American War*. New York: Strauss & Scheib, 1898.

Monaelesser, Adolph. *Report of the Red Cross Hospital Training School and Home for Red Cross Sisters: Work in Cuba before and during the Spanish-American War*. New York: Strauss & Schieb, 1899.

Senn, Nicholas. *Medical-Surgical Aspects of the Spanish-American War*. Chicago: American Medical Assoc. Press, 1900.

Sternberg, George H. "The Work of the Medical Department during the Spanish War," *Journal of the American Medical Association*, 31 (December 1898):1356.

Sutton, R. Stansbury. "A Story of Chickamauga," *Journal of the American Medical Association*, 31 (8 October 1898):854–855.

Thomas, Donna. " 'Camp Hell': Miami During the Spanish-American War," *Florida Historical Quarterly*, 57 (October 1978):141–156.

Turnbull, Wilfrid. "Reminiscences of an Army Surgeon in Cuba and the Philippines," *Bulletin of the American Historical Collection*, 2 (April 1974):31–49.

U.S. Senate. *Food Furnished by Subsistence Department to Troops in the Field; Letter From the Secretary of War, Transmitting, in Response to Resolution of the Senate of March 30, 1900, the Original Record of the Court of Inquiry Relative to the Unfitness for Issue of Certain Articles of Food Furnished by the Subsistence Department to Troops in the Field During the Recent Operations in Cuba and Porto Rico*. 3 vols. 56th Cong. 1st sess., Senate Doc. No. 270, Washington, DC, 1900.

U.S. Surgeon-General's Office. *Report on the Origin and Spread of Typhoid Fever in U.S. Military Camps During the Spanish War of 1898*. 2 vols., Washington, DC: Government Printing Office, 1904.

Vaughn, Victor C. "Typhoid Fever Among American Soldiers in the Spanish-American War," *Journal of the Military Service Institute*, 25 (1898):85–88.

Wright, Scheffel H. "Medicine in the Florida Camps during the Spanish-American War—Great Controversies," *Journal of the Florida Medical Association*, 62 (August 1975):19–26.

Treaty of Paris

Coletta, Paolo E. "McKinley, the Peace Negotiations, and the Acquisition of the Philippines," *Pacific Historical Review*, 30 (November 1961):341–350.

———. "Bryan, McKinley, and the Treaty of Paris," *Pacific Historical Review*, 26 (May 1957):131–146.

González Bernard, J. M. *Proceso histórico del tratado de Paris de 10 diciembre de 1898, con algunas ideas de derecho internacional público.* Valencia, 1903.

Murphy, James Thomas Jr. "A History of American Diplomacy at the Paris Peace Conference of 1898," Ph.D. dissertation, American University, 1965.

National Archives Microfilm Publications. *Records of the Department of State Relating to the Paris Peace Commission, 1898.* Washington, DC, 1965.

Smith, Ephraim K. " 'A Question from Which We Could Not Escape': William McKinley and the Decision to Acquire the Philippine Islands," *Diplomatic History*, 9 (Fall 1985):363–375.

U.S. Department of State. *Papers Relating to the Treaty with Spain.* Senate Document No. 208 (five parts), 55th Cong., 2nd sess. Washington, DC: Government Printing Office, 1899.

U.S. Senate. *A Treaty of Peace between the United States and Spain.* 55th Cong., 3rd sess., Senate Document No. 62, Washington, DC, 1899, pp. 404–440.

Reference

Aguilera, Alfredo. *Buques de guerra españoles, 1885–1971.* Madrid: Librería Editorial San Martín, 1972.

Armstrong, Le Roy. *Pictorial Atlas Illustrating the Spanish-American War; Comprising a History of the Great Conflict of the United States with Spain.* New York: George F. Cram, 1900.

Beede, Benjamin R., ed. *The War of 1898 and U.S. Interventions, 1898–1934: An Encyclopedia.* New York: Garland Publishing, 1994.

Bleiberg, Germán. *Diccionario de historia de España.* 3 vols., 2nd ed., Madrid: Ediciones de la *Revista de Occidente*, 1969.

Conway's All the World's Fighting Ships, 1868–1905. New York: Mayflower Books, 1979.

Dyal, Donald. *Historical Dictionary of the Spanish-American War.* Westport, CT: Greenwood Press, 1996.

Hannaford, Ebenezer. *The handy war book: a new book of important and authentic information and statistics, with accurate war maps and photographic pictures of U.S. war vessels.* Springfield, OH: Mast, Crowell & Kirkpatrick, 1898.

Jane, Fred T., ed. *Jane's Fighting Ships—1898.* London: Low Marston, 1898–1899.

Martínez Arango, Felipe. *Cronología crítica de la guerra hispano-americana.* 2d ed., Santiago, Cuba: Universidad de Oriente, 1966.

Neeser, Robert Wilden. *Statistical and Chronological History of the United States Navy 1775–1907.* New York, 1909.

Pamphlets in American History, Spanish-American War. microfiche series nos. 1–394. Glen Rock, N.J.: Microfilming Corporation of America, 1978.

Sánchez Alonso, Benito. *Fuentes de la historia española e hispanoamericana; ensayo de bibliografía sistemática de impresos y manuscritos que ilustran la historia política de España y sus antiguas provincias de ultramar.* 2d ed. rev. and expanded, Madrid, 1927.

Soldevilla, Fernando. *El año político, 1896–1898.* Madrid: Enrique Fernández-de-Rojas, 1897–1899.

Spanish-American War Cyclopedia: a complete compendium of facts and statistics. Chicago: A. N. Marquis & Co., 1898.

Spiller, Roger, Joseph G. Dawson III, and T. Harry Williams, eds. *Dictionary of American Military Biography.* 3 vols. Westport, CT: Greenwood Press, 1984.

Venzon, Anne Cipriano. *The Spanish-American War: An Annotated Bibliography.* New York: Garland Publishing, 1990.

Journals

American Historical Review
Anuario de Estudios Americanos
Army-Navy Journal
Diplomatic History
Estudios de Historia Social
Hispania: Revista Española de Historia
Hispanic American Historical Review
Historian
Journal of the Military Service Institution of the United States
Journal of Modern History
Journal of Negro History
Mid-America
Mississippi Valley Historical Review
Pacific Historical Review
Philippine Social Sciences and Humanities Review
Philippine Studies

Magazines

American Banker
The Atlantic Monthly
The Century Magazine
The Forum
Harper's Monthly Magazine
Harper's Weekly
The Independent Journal of Commerce
Leslie's Illustrated Weekly
The Literary Digest
McClure's Magazine
Munsey's Magazine
The Nation
North American Review
Public Opinion
Review of Reviews
Scribner's Magazine

Newspapers

Atlanta Constitution
La Bomba (Ponce, Puerto Rico)
Boston Herald
La Bruja (Mayagüez, Puerto Rico)
Chicago Record
Chicago Times-Herald
Chicago Tribune
Chronicle (San Francisco, CA)
Colored American (Washington, DC)
El Correo (Madrid)
El Correo Militar (Madrid)
La Correspondencia (San Juan, Puerto Rico)
La Correspondencia de España (Madrid)
La Correspondencia Militar (Madrid)
Courier-Journal (Louisville, KY)
La Democracia (Ponce, Puerto Rico)
Detroit Free Press (Detroit, MI)
El Diario de Barcelona
La Epoca (Madrid)
Evening Post (New York City)
Freeman (Indianapolis, IN)
Gaceta de Madrid

Gaceta de Puerto Rico (San Juan)
El Heraldo de Madrid
El Imparcial (Madrid)
Minneapolis Journal
Minneapolis Tribune
Morning Tribune (Tampa, FL)
El Nacional (Madrid)
New York Age (New York City)
New York Herald
New York Journal
New York Sun
New York Times
New York Tribune
New York World
El País (Madrid)
Patria (New York City)
Richmond Planet (Richmond, VA)
St. Louis Globe-Democrat
St. Louis Post-Dispatch El Tiempo (Madrid)
Washington Bee (Washington, DC)
Washington Post

About the Author

Brad K. Berner (B.A. St. Olaf College; M.A. University of Arkansas) has taught history in private secondary schools and is an adjunct assistant professor of history at Western International University in Phoenix, Arizona. Having traveled widely in Mexico and Central America, his specialization is U.S. and Latin American history.